Eubie Blake

Eubie Blake

Rags, Rhythm, and Race

RICHARD CARLIN AND KEN BLOOM

OXFORD
UNIVERSITY PRESS

OXFORD
UNIVERSITY PRESS

Oxford University Press is a department of the University of Oxford. It furthers the University's objective of excellence in research, scholarship, and education by publishing worldwide. Oxford is a registered trade mark of Oxford University Press in the UK and certain other countries.

Published in the United States of America by Oxford University Press
198 Madison Avenue, New York, NY 10016, United States of America.

Library of Congress Cataloging-in-Publication Data
Names: Carlin, Richard, 1956– author. | Bloom, Ken, 1949– author.
Title: Eubie Blake : rags, rhythm, and race / Richard Carlin and Ken Bloom.
Description: New York : Oxford University Press, 2020. |
Includes bibliographical references and index.
Identifiers: LCCN 2019055822 (print) | LCCN 2019055823 (ebook) |
ISBN 9780190635930 (hardback) | ISBN 9780190635954 (epub)
Subjects: LCSH: Blake, Eubie, 1887-1983. | African American composers—Biography. |
Composers—United States—Biography. | Jazz musicians—United States—Biography.
Classification: LCC ML410.B6247 C37 2020 (print) | LCC ML410.B6247 (ebook) |
DDC 782.1/4092 [B]—dc23
LC record available at https://lccn.loc.gov/2019055822
LC ebook record available at https://lccn.loc.gov/2019055823

1 3 5 7 9 8 6 4 2

Printed by Sheridan Books, Inc., United States of America

Contents

Prelude

"It's Getting Dark on Old Broadway"

"It's been more than a decade since a colored musical attraction figured in a long run in New York . . . Now comes "Shuffle Along" faithfully functioning as a stream-roller. It has knocked over and crushed to earth many of the barriers that have stood in the path of the colored show's progress. Precedents have been established."

—Lester A. Walton, *The New York Age*

"Shuffle Along *is a darky show that has lost most of its darkness. The men 'black up' just as though they were tintless; the women rouge up, very much as they do in non-colored performances. One expects to see an essentially colored aggregation, but it isn't that by any means. It is a semi-darky show that emulate the 'white' performance."*

—Alan Dale, *New York Journal American*

When *Shuffle Along* opened in an ex–lecture hall located at the upper reaches of Broadway on Monday, May 23, 1921, the all African American team who wrote, composed, and acted in the show were nervous. No one had successfully mounted an all-black show on Broadway since the days of Bert Williams and George Walker at the turn of the 20th century; there had never been a show completely staged, written, and performed by an all-black ensemble. After a period of tryouts on the road, the show limped into New York, carrying a considerable debt; its producers—also its writers and composers—would either face total ruin or incredible success, depending on whether an all-white audience would accept a revue that featured black characters who went well beyond the well-worn stereotypes of minstrelsy. Why, the lead male and female characters even shared an onstage kiss, something that was unheard of in the days when romantic love was the purview of only the lily white.

In many ways, *Shuffle Along* was an oddity: an all-black show that emulated white models; a show that insisted that black characters could be politicians, business owners, and even romantic lovers as well as blackface comedians; a show that touted jazzy new rhythms but still maintained hummable melodies. If it was a success, it could open the doors of "legitimate" theater to a pool of great actors, singers, dancers, musicians, songwriters, and playwrights—so a lot was hanging on the reaction of its white audience on opening night. For the show's producers lingering in the wings, the outcome was anything but assured. Just in case the audience's mood turned ugly, they had placed themselves strategically at the theater's exits; only Eubie Blake, the composer, was trapped in the orchestra pit and would be unable to flee if mayhem broke out. And yet, despite these long odds, the show was an immediate smash hit, running for nearly two years in over 500 performances. For Blake and his partners, it was an unexpected validation of their belief that they could challenge Broadway's best and succeed. But it was not the first or last time Blake would struggle with the racism inherent in American culture.

Shuffle Along's success did open the door for black performers, inspiring dozens of imitators both on Broadway and in New York's toney nightclubs. But most of these shows were still produced, staged, and written by whites and promulgated the basest stereotypes in their dialogue and characterizations. Even more ominously, white composers who had previously dominated the Broadway scene viewed the newfound success of black writers as a threat to their very existence. In the wake of *Shuffle Along*'s popularity and the production of countless imitators, leading Broadway lyricist Gene Buck (later the head of the powerful ASCAP [American Society of Composers, Authors and Publishers] union that represented Tin Pan Alley's most successful composers) penned the song "It's Getting Dark on Old Broadway" for *Ziegfeld's Follies of 1922*. It's hard not to read Buck's lyrics as reflecting the anxiety felt by the white audience to the new ascendance of black performers:

> It's getting very dark on old Broadway
> You see the change in ev-ry cab-a-ret,
> Just like an eclipse on the moon,
> Ev'ry café now has the danc-ing coon. . . .
> Yes the great white way is white no more
> It's just like a street on the Swan-ee shore

Ironically, such was the deeply embedded atmosphere of racism in society that Eubie Blake took Gene Buck's song as a compliment, not as a knock: Buck "was boosting us—we were putting Negroes *back* on Broadway [he was saying]," Blake told an interviewer many decades later. At the same time, Eubie would also strongly object to be treated as a second-class citizen, feeling that his success spoke for itself. In the same interview in which he praised Gene Buck for writing this song, he told of an experience he had when the black doorman at the Cotton Club refused to let him in to see the show, Blake quipped, "I don't like no one 'letting' me in anyplace. My money lets me in—you don't." Blake knew his value as a man and as an artist and he didn't suffer treatment that he felt was unworthy of his stature.

Blake's acceptance of the racist sentiments behind Buck's song is a mystery—until you consider his entire life story and the time in which he was born. Blake had grown up in a world of often bitter racial relations, but one filled with contradictions. His boyhood home—Baltimore's tenement district—was economically segregated but not racially so; he often commented that among his family's neighbors were many working-class whites facing similar struggles to make a living. But of course Blake encountered racism on a nearly daily basis; when he was walking to school, white children would throw rocks at him, and there were clearly parts of Baltimore where blacks were unwelcome.

Blake's attitude toward race is one of the many fascinating aspects of his character. His father—whose job was unloading freight on Baltimore's docks—often advised him that not all white men were evil and that his own prospects were dependent on the goodwill of his white employers. "Our house is owned by white people," his father told young Eubie. "Every morsel of food I bring in the food I get the money from the white man. Don't me never let me hear you say, never bite the hand that feeds you, no matter how small it is, it's keeping you alive, feeding you. That's why I'm not prejudiced."

Although he faced considerable prejudice, Blake was not bitter, and could turn potentially difficult racial stereotypes on their heads by refusing to accept common cultural norms. He never wore blackface when he was performing on the vaudeville stage; along with his partner, Noble Sissle, he donned a tuxedo when he played to white audiences to indicate his pride in the music that they performed. The sheet music for his most popular songs did not feature the racist graphics that were part and parcel of how most black music was marketed in his day. Yet Blake did not fault those performers, like the lead comedians in *Shuffle Along*, who wore burnt cork and laced their jokes with "dems, dese, and dose"; he knew that behind the mask they were canny entertainers, who were able to earn unheard-of money for blacks on stage. Working prejudice to your own ends was no sin to Blake, who realized that his first responsibility was to entertain his paying customers.

Shuffle Along overcame the prevailing racial prejudice of its day in a similar way, taking advantage of the limitations faced by an all-black production. The best theater available to them was hardly adequate for a musical revue, since the theater had previously hosted lectures and debates. Because its stage was long and narrow, only a single line of dancers could be accommodated; rather than abandoning big dance numbers, the show's choreographers came up with the ingenious idea of a moving line that would progress across the stage. New costumes were too expensive for this fledgling production to afford; instead, they recycled costumes available from older productions. Given a pile of sweat-stained gypsy outfits, the show's creators wrote a "gypsy" number into the production.

And *Shuffle Along* and Blake's life story were far from unique. They are very much reflected in both the challenges and successes faced by countless other black performers and composers active in the early 20th century. Blake's life story is particularly compelling because it lasted nearly 100 years, through countless changes in America's music and culture. Few figures have made their marks as innovative performers, composers, and musical mentors over such a long period of time. Blake's fame stretches from the original ragtime era through the ragtime revival; from vaudeville to Broadway to television to films; and from piano rolls and 78 rpm recordings to streaming audio. He was already performing in his preteen years, dancing on Baltimore's street corners and singing in youth quartets; by his early teens, he was a working pianist, employed at some of the city's rowdiest saloons and lowliest bawdy houses. Along with Sissle, he was among the first African American musicians to perform on the white vaudeville stage. The duo joined forces with comedians Flournoy Miller and Aubrey Lyles to create the first all-black-written, performed, and produced show on Broadway, 1921's *Shuffle Along*—the show that launched the Roaring Twenties.

While his career faded for a while in the mid-century, Eubie's life and musical influence was far from over. In a strange twist of fate, it was Eubie Blake who helped bring about the historic ragtime music revival in the 1970s. In 1969, John Hammond produced a new recording of Blake playing piano, titled *The Eighty Six Years of Eubie Blake*. It was followed in 1973 by Robert Kimball and William Bolcom's landmark book, *Reminiscing with Sissle and*

Blake. Eubie Blake became the living, breathing symbol of ragtime's vitality, an art form that had previously been relegated to nostalgia. He literally saved the ragtime era from obscurity. For nearly two decades following, he wowed audiences around the world with his incredible showmanship and magnetic stage personality.

Eubie was best known for finger-busting, virtuosic piano solos like "Charleston Rag" and "Troublesome Ivories," along with classic songs like "I'm Just Wild about Harry" and "Memories of You"; his music ranged from the groundbreaking syncopated ragtime of his youth through the creation of some of the greatest show tunes to ever grace the Broadway stage. Plus, he was one of the finest natural performers, whose stage presence was undiminished even as his health declined in his later 90s. While Blake achieved significant fame in his later life, the true breadth of his achievements has not been adequately documented before. Spanning nearly a century of creativity, Blake's work taken as a whole makes him one of the most important American musicians, black or white, of the 20th century.

Blake was blessed with an incredible musical ear from an early age. Trained to accompany barroom singers who rarely performed a hit song in its original key, Blake could effortlessly transpose a song on the spot to suit his partner's vocal range. He had a great musical memory, absorbing the tricks of the various piano "professors" whom he encountered along the way. However, he did more than emulate the tricks; he used them as raw material to create his own style, adding subtle variations and assembling an entire repertory of piano mannerisms that he could use as the basis for everything from informal improvisation to serious composition.

Blake's incredible ear and prodigious memory also made him a master storyteller. Well into his 90s, he could recall with clarity and amazing detail events that occurred decades earlier. Like many older people, he occasionally conflated events or placed some anecdotes in the wrong time period, but remarkably he was more often correct than not when recalling the genesis of his music. He also was a wonderful vocal mimic; anyone who has listened to the many recorded interviews he gave later in life would be amazed to hear him reproduce everything from the rumbling bass voice of Bert Williams to the singing style of long-forgotten performers.

Blake would often end a story by stating, "Now, I'm not lying to you." Indeed, he felt a unique responsibility to accurately portray his own personal history along with the broader struggles of African Americans in the entertainment world. He could be remarkably blunt and steel eyed in assessing his own motives, admitting to carrying on a multitude of sexual affairs throughout his life. Blake famously quipped that even at age 95 he couldn't say when his sexual drive might decline, and his two loyal wives long suffered from his serial philandering

Eubie Blake was also highly unusual in another way: he saved just about every contract, financial ledger, and royalty statement that he received from the earliest days in his musical career. Thus we were able to review his 1917 agreement to record 78s for the long-defunct Pathé label, along with several royalty statements. Reading his account books from several Broadway shows reveals the sad truth that major composers—particularly African American composers—were often paid far less than what was called for in their contracts. Plus, when a show collapsed, it was difficult if not impossible to collect any remaining wages or moneys owed for performance rights. The (white) producer could just reincorporate under a new name—easily raising money for yet another venture—while the black actors, musicians, and writers could not draw from the empty shell left behind. While white composers were often put on a standing advance against future royalties by music publishers, blacks rarely had that privilege, instead having to accept nothing or as little as $1.00 as an advance on a song. Thanks to the success of *Shuffle Along*, Eubie was made a member of ASCAP in 1921—highly unusual for a black composer in that time—but his composer rate was at the bottom of the scale for popular songwriters. It remained unchanged until the late 1940s, when his second wife prodded the organization to increase it in light of the success of "I'm Just Wild about Harry" as a campaign song for Harry Truman.

Like many others, we were first introduced to Eubie's personality and music through the landmark 1969 album, *The Eighty Six Years of Eubie Blake*, produced by John Hammond. Hammond had the clout with Columbia Records to issue a two-record set of the then barely known artist. Hammond also had the good sense to record part of the album with a small audience of admirers of Eubie and his music; in this way, Eubie could introduce each number as if he were giving a live show. Although he was long retired from performing on stage, Eubie's obvious rapport with his audience comes shining through in not only the spoken introductions but also in the many vocal asides that punctuate his performances. And, true to the pride he took in his music, Eubie insisted that Hammond allow him to record by playing a special Steinway piano that Columbia otherwise reserved for just one artist, Vladimir Horowitz.

Eubie's remarkable second career continued unabated from 1969 through his death in 1983. Awards and accolades were showered upon him, and a new Broadway revue helped revive interest in his musical theater career. He was always aware of the importance of honoring those long-forgotten performers who influenced him in his youth, along with the many talented collaborators—some as well-known as Andy Razaf and others virtually forgotten, like Milton Reddie—to make sure an accurate picture was given of how African Americans shaped American music. We hope that in a small way we have helped build on that tradition by documenting as fully as possible a key figure in American cultural life.

Acknowledgments

We would like to acknowledge the many researchers who have worked in the field of African American music and theatrical history, both in the past and those who continue to do this important work. While we've attempted to list every person's work consulted in creating this book, we apologize if we inadvertently failed to include other materials that we have consulted over the years.

We have relied on the archivists and librarians who host the major collections who have freely advised us and pointed us to materials that we might not otherwise find. Most important has been the staff of the Maryland Historical Society, where Eubie Blake's personal papers, sheet music collection, and photos reside. Without their assistance, we would not have been able to complete this book. Similarly, Lynn Abbott provided helpful guidance and insights at Tulane University's Hogan Jazz Archives, including access to cassette interviews by Al Rose with Eubie conducted when Rose was preparing Eubie's biography. At New York Public Library's Billy Rose Theater Archive, Curator Doug Reside, Jonathan Hiam of the Dance Collection, and the staff directed us through Carl Seltzer's papers and recordings, including copies of many unpublished interviews with Eubie along with outtakes from his record label, Eubie Blake Music. Also extremely helpful was the staff at Emory University's Rose Library, the Library of Congress, and the Schomburg Center for Research in Black Culture.

We also were privileged to interview many people who knew Eubie or had previously studied his music. Again, we've listed the key people we interviewed as part of the bibliography for this text, but we also had less formal conversations with dozens more, to whom we offer our thanks.

Among individuals who were especially helpful in our research, first and foremost, we'd like to thank David A. Jasen and Susan Jasen, long-time friends and advisors. Dave is one of the leading scholars of ragtime music with a prodigious amount of knowledge, based on years of research. He was also a close friend of Eubie's during the last decades of his life. Both Dave and Susan freely shared their memories of Eubie, along with many documents and other important insights. We cannot thank them enough.

For sharing their personal archives and memories, we'd like to thank (in alphabetical order) the following: Bill Bolcom and Joan Morris; Robert Kimball; Barry Singer; and Terry Waldo. Jon Mizan kindly provided items from Charlie Rouse's personal collection. Rachman Vaughn Reddie sent materials related to her father, Milton Reddie, along with sharing memories of both her father and Eubie.

Great thanks to everyone at Oxford University Press who helped support this book, beginning most importantly with Norm Hirschy, who accepted our proposal and encouraged us as we worked through writing the manuscript. We'd also like to thank Suganya Elango, Project Manager, at Newgen KnowledgeWorks, who oversaw the copy editing and typesetting of the manuscript; Norm's associate, Lauralee Yeary, for her behind-the-scenes assistance; and Brady McNamara for his wonderful cover design.

Richard Carlin's Acknowledgments

As always, Jessica Myers was invaluable as a research assistant, all-around-critic, and supporter of this project from day one. She has been the inspiration to me for my writing for over 30 years. For listening to my endless discussions about the book as it was developed, I'd like to thank (in alphabetical order): Malcolm Lynn Baker; Ben Bierman; Bob Carlin; Dale Cockrell; John Edward Hasse; Dick Hiserodt; Thom Holmes; Tom Laskey; Richard Norton; Chris Smith; Ed Solecki; Atesh Sonneborn; David Szatmary; Peter Szego; Perry Werner; Amy Whitmer. All supplied important encouragement and support as Ken and I worked through the large volume of information consulted to create this book.

Ken Bloom's Acknowledgments

Thanks to Harry Bagdasian, Bari Biern, Noah Griffin, Dan Levinson, Richard Norton, Pat Plowman, Caesar Rodriguez, and Scott Sedar. They all provided encouragement and sometimes hospitality or historical resources.

1

Family and Early Life

1887–1903

James Hubert Blake was born on February 7, 1887, in Baltimore, Maryland. Although Eubie in later life consistently said he was born in 1883, records indicate that his actual birthdate was four years later.[1] Eubie also said he was born on the exact date of his father's 50th birthday, which—while maybe family lore—was not accurate, as his father was born on July 7, and the year of his birth is not exactly known. Eubie said he was the youngest (of 11 children) and the only one to survive infancy. He later recalled that his mother would often question why the Lord had let him survive when all her other children had perished either at birth or shortly after:

> It's so vivid in my mind, she'd say to me, "I don't know what God left you to live"; I'm the only one who survived. That's why she said . . . "I don't know why God left you . . . [but she'd also add] I'm not questioning God, I'm not questioning God." I had 10 brothers and sisters, but I never saw anything [of] them.[2]

As with many African American families, it is difficult to trace the exact history of Eubie Blake's lineage beyond his immediate parents. Blake said his father and mother told him little about their family histories, perhaps because of their roots in slavery. Blake thought that perhaps both of his parents were either orphaned or sold as infants, thus explaining the lack of information about their forebears. His mother does appear to have been orphaned, but his father (Figure 1.1) had a rich family history. While Eubie did not know his full lineage, he was aware that his father had several siblings.

Blake's father, John Sumner Blake, was born into slavery on July 7, c. 1838, in Middlesex County, Virginia.[3] Throughout his life, Blake idolized his father, whom he viewed as a "man's man." His charcoal-dark skin color stood out to the younger Blake, who noted that "my father was as black as that piano":[4]

Eubie Blake. Richard Carlin and Ken Bloom, Oxford University Press (2020). © Richard Carlin and Ken Bloom 2020.
DOI: 10.1093/oso/9780190635930.001.0001

Figure 1.1 Eubie's father, John Sumner Blake, in an undated photograph.

> My father was a big man, masculine . . . My father had . . . 11 brothers and
> 1 sister, and during slavery, all of my father's brothers were big strappin'
> men, so they put them into stud. This was in Virginia; see, that's why I don't
> like Virginia . . . [The men] only got fresh meat, and they only got sugar,
> preserves, when they were going into stud. . . . They had everything just like
> the white people had.[5]

Eubie's implication, of course, was that the slaves were treated to such good
food only when their masters hoped to boost their fertility; otherwise, they
were provided just the minimal food for survival. Eubie was impressed by his
father's physical strength and stamina, particularly because as a youth Eubie
had little taste for athletics.

Blake's father made no bones about his having been a slave, and
proudly showed his son the whip marks on his back, much to his
mother's chagrin:

My father would show me the stripes on his back. And my mother would say . . . "John, don't tell that boy about slavery." And he'd say, "Yes, he has to know about slavery." Then he'd turn to me and say to me, "Don't you hate people," because he could see the scowl on my face. "The people in the South were almost as ignorant as we were. They thought they was right, and they were told that we were nothing. And a man can only go by his convictions."[6]

"Everybody, especially colored children, needs to know," his father would say when Blake's mother protested his sharing stories of his days in slavery.[7] John Sumner's acceptance of white people—despite his poor treatment during slavery—and understanding that their prejudice against blacks was based on ignorance had a great influence on the young Blake.

Sometime in the 1840s, John Sumner's family had relocated to Somerset County, Maryland, on the Eastern Shore, in a town called Potato Neck. The town was populated by free blacks, perhaps suggesting that the Blakes had either purchased their freedom or been freed by their master.[8] In 1847, John Sumner's younger brother James Henry Blake was born there. By 1860, Blake's 44-year-old widowed mother Henrietta was listed as holding $200 of real estate there and having a personal estate of $100. John Sumner Blake and his brother were living with her on the property; next door lived William Blake, presumably a close relative, age 25, and his wife and child, also owning $200 of property.[9] Many of the same names are given in the 1870 Census at this location, although mysteriously the family is now listed as "white"; nonetheless, it appears that these are the same people. By this time, John Sumner's mother (now listed as age 61) had real estate holdings of $400 (perhaps just reflecting inflation over the ten-year period) and he is listed as having personal holdings of $400. These would have been significant amounts at the time for blacks in the area, so that the Blake family may have been better off (at least during this period) than Eubie believed. In this census, the occupations of both John Sumner and his brother James are given as "sailors," a designation that may reflect the fact that most people living in the area made their living by oystering on the bay.[10]

During the Civil War, Eubie's father enlisted, working as a "landsman" for the Union Navy in Baltimore. He served a little less than a year, from November 1863 to September 1864, supporting vessels sailing out of the Baltimore harbor.[11] He may have already been working on the harbors, as this would be his profession throughout most of the rest of his working life. Presumably he was living in Baltimore during this period, although as late as

1877 he was listed on a county map along with his mother as still farming in Potato Neck.[12]

Blake's mother (Figure 1.2)—who, he variously said, was 13 to 20 years younger than his father—was born Emma or Emily Johnstone in Matthews County, Virginia, c. 1856. (Blake claimed his mother originally had a different first name, although he said he didn't know what it was.) Although his mother denied being born a slave, Eubie said his father often reminded her that, in fact, she was a slave in everything but perhaps name:

> During slavery she was a young girl, and she was very proud. She was a *"Johnstone,"* that was her maiden name. [She'd say] "I never was a slave in my life." My father would be back of her, he'd say, "Did you pick cotton?" "Sure I picked cotton!" "Did the master pay you?" "No." He called me Bully. "You see Bully what I'm talking about?" She never did admit that she was a slave, but she was. She picked cotton and never got paid for it.[13]

Figure 1.2 Eubie's mother, Emma Blake, probably around the time of his birth.

John Sumner nicknamed his son "Bully," perhaps after Teddy Roosevelt, in hopes that Eubie would emulate Roosevelt's hyper-masculinity and not kow-tow to anyone.

Eubie knew less of his mother's early life than his father's. Emma Blake was much fairer skinned than her dark-hued husband, suggesting perhaps that in her recent past she had white or mixed-race relatives. And, unlike Eubie's father who rarely attended church, she was an intensely religious person. The 1870 Baltimore city census notes an "Emma Johnstone," age 14, who was a "scholar" boarding at the St. Frances Convent and Orphan Asylum in Baltimore. Assuming this was Eubie's mother, it suggests that she may have been orphaned or at least separated from her parents. The school/orphanage was founded by a French priest who came to the United States in 1825 after overseeing a similar facility in San Domingo. Unusually for the time, it was dedicated to providing "colored students" with a broad education, according to the *Baltimore Sun*:

> The objection [*sic*] of the institution is to give instruction to girls in useful branches, suitable to their wants and convenience, adding the still more ex-alted acquisition of habits of solid virtue, and the exact observance of piety and correct principles of morality. In addition to their religious instruc-tion, the pupils are taught the English and French languages, arithmetic, geography, history, English grammar, orthography, writing, sewing in all its branches, embroidery in cotton, silk, chenille or gold, tapestry, tufted work, bead work, lace embroidery, wax-flowers and fruits, music and painting also, if desired.[14]

The newspaper reported that the academy had about 25 boarding students ("including two students from Cuba, Spanish children") and 27 orphans living on site. When Emma was a boarder, the Academy was located in a building on Forrest Street, in the same neighborhood where the Blake family would later live. Living conditions were far better than most black children would have enjoyed at the time, with "light and airy" bedrooms "and a large playground and flower garden surround the institution." Along with their studies, the girls sang in the school's chapel choir, gave musical performances, and, on occasion, presented what sound like religious (or at least moral) plays, including *The Youthful Martyrs of Rome*.[15]

By 1880, Census records indicate that Emma and John Sumner were mar-ried and living in Philadelphia, along with her brother George who was four years her elder. Both John Sumner and George's occupations are listed as "stevedore," or dock workers, an occupation that John Sumner would follow until ill health caused him to retire sometime around the turn of the 20th century. Emma's occupation was given as "wash-woman," labor that she also would continue to practice throughout Eubie's youth. Eubie recalled his religious mother singing, "Lord, how long do have I got to do this? How long?" as she bent over a washtub, caked with soap, cleaning the "white folk's clothes."[16]

Blake was proud of his parents, whom he viewed as religious, educated, and "respectable" members of society, despite their lack of personal wealth. He was particularly proud of their both being literate, saying his father had beautiful penmanship: "the master's daughter used to take him down in the woods and teach him to read and write . . . he could have written calling cards, he had beautiful handwriting."[17] Blake's father also was a voracious reader, telling his son, "Everything I ever knew I learned from reading." He insisted that Eubie learn to read, encouraging him to page through the *Baltimore Sun* to get the latest news. When he would come home in the evening, the first thing he would ask his son was "Bully, tell me what the white folks are doin' today."[18] In several later interviews, Blake emphasized that his parents were legally married, in church, and they hadn't just "jumped the broom," as in the common folk practice. (Many African and Caribbean people conducted folk ceremonies to celebrate and formalize a marriage. One such ceremony involved the bride and groom jumping over a broom, indicating their change in status.)

When Eubie was a child, his father kept a US flag proudly displayed in the front room of their home as a reminder of his Civil War service and his appreciation of being a US citizen. Sometimes, when someone would open the front door of the house, the draft would knock down the flag. When that happened, his father would bark at his son, "Bully! Go pick up Old Glory!"[19]

Eubie could recall his father hitting him only three times during his childhood, and that was because he told him he was afraid of ghosts. "He didn't want me to be afraid of nothing," Blake recalled, admiring his father's toughness in the face of all obstacles. On the other hand, Eubie said he was often beaten by his mother, even well into his teens when he was still living at home.[20] However, Eubie emphasized that his mother never beat him on a Sunday: "If [he was] caught dancing on a Sunday, or committed any other misdemeanor, on a Sunday, a whipping would have to be put off."[21]

While Eubie took pride in both his parents, he found his mother control-ling and overly religious.[22] Eubie recalled spending endless hours on Sundays in church throughout his childhood:

> My mother was too religious. On Sunday the other kids are in the streets enjoying themselves, and I'm singing "Jesus knows all about my troubles." All day Sunday. Nine o'clock, Sunday School. Eleven-thirty preacher. Two-thirty, Sunday School again. Four o'clock, T.Y.P.U. (Baptist Young People's Union). Seven o'clock, preacher. You couldn't open the church unless my mother was there.[23]

Eubie noted that his mother was a prominent member of the church, and she "sang *on* the church choir"—noting, with a chuckle, that "sang on" was the expression used back in the day when she was a member of the church.[24]

By the time of Eubie's birth, the Blakes were living in Baltimore's predom-inantly African American neighborhood located adjacent to the teeming harbor where John Sumner worked on the docks, loading and unloading ships. Eubie's father was in charge of a group of stevedores, and thus was paid more, earning $9.00 a week (about $250 in today's money)—when he was working. He was not paid a fixed wage, but rather by the task, so that $9.00 was presumably the highest amount that he brought home.[25] In bad weather or when things were slow, he was laid off and earned nothing. Blake must have been a leader among his coworkers, because in 1897 he was one of the cofounders of the Longshoremen's Christian Association, a group

> formed for the purpose of protecting stevedores and lumber-handlers, for the mutual assistance of its members and for "the promotion of Christian spirit of brotherly love and charity."[26]

Stevedores were often injured at work, unloading heavy cargo off of ships in poor working conditions. A premium was placed on getting ships unloaded quickly so that they wouldn't spend too long in port (and thus generate extra costs for their owners/operators). A survey of accidents among stevedores re-ported in the local press during this period included many injuries resulting from falling into a ship's hold (including broken arms, hips, and legs); head injuries, primarily concussions and broken collar bones from falling objects, including steel bars and barrels; accidental drownings; and general illness and diseases such as smallpox that could easily spread among the dockworkers.[27]

Eubie's father apparently developed "carbuncles," or boils that can be extremely painful, which eventually ended his career as a stevedore.

The Blakes' neighborhood consisted of a grid of streets fronting many smaller alleyways, with row upon row of poorly maintained two-story row homes filled with poor families. (Although the neighborhood was predominantly black, there were working-class white families living in the area as well; Eubie recalled that "[c]olored people and white people used to live in the same block and nobody thought anything about it."[28]) Behind the row houses that fronted the narrow streets were inner yards filled with ramshackle shanties and improvised structures that housed even more people. Baltimore historian Hamilton Owens described the living conditions as grim:

> Nearly every one of the fair blocks of row houses was the outer wall behind which were hidden labyrinths of hovels, each swarming with from two to half a dozen proliferating family groups . . . Most of the children had rickets and sore eyes, while tuberculosis was as common as measles.[29]

When Eubie was two years old, he himself had rickets, due to malnutrition, leading him to limp for the rest of his life.[30] He recalled that their home was often invaded by rats, until one day his father purchased a trap and, upon catching a large rodent, doused it with kerosene and set it on fire. The rat, in flames, ran down the block. Eubie mused, "He must have told all the other rats, 'Don't bother around that Blake house,' 'cause we were never bothered anymore!"[31]

Eubie claimed that his family never had to live in the less desirable inner yards, but they did move frequently within a radius of a few blocks, either seeking less expensive or more roomy lodgings. Nonetheless, the lodgings were small in these two-story structures, featuring just two rooms on each floor. Cooking was done in a shed that was attached to the back of the building. There was no running water, so Eubie's mother had to rinse their clothes at the fire hydrant. The outhouse was about 20 yards behind the kitchen door, located in the back alley. On cold winter days, Eubie's father would go out while wearing only his bathrobe: "He'd sit out there and read the *whole* paper. Then he'd come in frozen and sit by the fire. And of course in my mother's house there was no such thing as taking a drink to warm yourself up. You just sat by the stove."[32] Rent was $3.00 a week, a third of his father's paycheck.[33] Eubie described one of their homes as "lopsided, not perpendicular," attesting to its poor overall condition.[34]

Despite their humble living situation, Eubie claimed that the family always had the best of everything, although mostly these were hand-me-downs from his mother's white employers. He told interviewers Ian Whitcomb and Neil Conan, "We had the finest silver, the finest cut glass, the finest rugs that anybody could have. And we lived in a rat trap. You know how we got those things? The white people that [my mother] worked for, go to Paris and get that stuff."[35]

Although Eubie mentions only himself, his father, and his mother in his childhood stories, census records show that other relatives were living in their tiny homes with them at different times. It was not unusual for large, extended families to live together, despite the fact that these small row houses had only two bedrooms. In 1900, the family was joined by two nieces and two nephews. John Sumner's occupation was listed as "day laborer," as was that of the two nephews. Both Eubie and his cousin Lucy Blake were listed as being "at school."[36] By 1910, the household was equally overcrowded with Eubie (now listed as working as a pianist at a hotel); his father (working at a lumberyard); his mother (a seamstress); an adopted daughter, Viola Morgan, age 14, who was also working as a seamstress; and a niece and nephew. Strangely, though, with the exception of his adopted sister, none of these people were mentioned by Eubie in the many interviews he gave later in life or in his official biography.[37]

Although Eubie described his neighborhood as being racially mixed with few people making any fuss about it, this claim didn't mean that black children were treated well by their white peers. Eubie was a small child, earning him the nickname of "Mouse" from the neighborhood kids.[38] Despite his small size, he described himself as "scrappy." When larger kids attacked him, he learned to successfully ward them off by stepping back and throwing a well-timed blow to the solar plexus. Eubie recalled being regularly beaten by white kids while he was walking to attend the neighborhood black school. Eubie also remembered the white children taunting him and his friends as they walked past on their way to school: " 'Here comes the Niggers! Let's get the Niggers!' . . . And I going to get beat all right, and so they get clubs. I never hit them in the face, bam!, I hit 'em in the stomach, and they would fall."[39] Coming home crying, he told his father that he hated these white boys. His father's response taught Eubie a lesson that he would never forget:

When I had to go to school, I was around 12–13 years old, I was a pretty good scrapper. You had to fight, back then, in the ghetto. And I came home and I had to pass two white schools to get to my school. And I fight every day, I was so tired of fighting. I'd fight two or three boys; I didn't win 'em, black my eye. So one time I walked in the house, my father say "Hi Bully, what's the matter with you?" [tearfully] "Honestly papa, I don't care what you say, I don't like white people." And he looked at me about 5 seconds, "Don't you ever let me hear you say that again. I'm the one who should not like them. But all the people weren't against us in the South. I could go to Mr. Sharsky (that's the man he worked for) . . . for $10 or $15 (that's a lot of money those days), anytime I wanted, he'd give it to me. The house is owned by white people. The ground, Lord Baltimore gave the ground, he could have said, "I don't want no Negroes to live on this ground," and they wouldn't have let us. Every morsel of food I bring in the food I get the money from the white man. Don't me never let me hear you say, never bite the hand that feeds you, no matter how small it is, it's keeping you alive, feeding you. That's why I'm not prejudiced.[40]

Eubie's father's ability to overlook his own personal suffering at the hands of his white masters (and later employers) made a huge impression on his son.

Having the name of "James Hubert Blake" caused Eubie endless trouble as a child. The other children in the neighborhood and at school relentlessly teased him, mangling his name. Finally, he had enough and insisted on them calling him "Eubie":

My mother named me after a concert pianist; his last name was Hubert, see. He was a Frenchman. I can't think of his first name. She just liked the sound of "Hubert." . . . When I was a kid in Baltimore, [of] course, we all lived in a pretty tough neighborhood. Those guys, they couldn't say "Hubert," nobody could say that. My mother called me "You-Burt"; she couldn't [pronounce] "Hubert." So these guys would call me "Eubie, Doobie, Zoobie," everything but "Hubert." I got around the third grade, see, then I could spell pretty fair . . . Well, anyhow, I coined my own name.[41]

When interviewer Rudi Blesh asked Eubie how he got the neighborhood kids to stop making fun of his name, he replied if they didn't call him Eubie, he "batted them in the jaw." Through sheer brute force he made sure that he was respected.

Eubie showed unusual musical talent from an early age. In an oft-repeated story, he noted how, at the age of three, he was walking with his parents while they were going to the market and heard music coming from a local store:

My mother and father were very poor, well all Negroes were poor. They'd go to the market late at night, they'd get the food cheaper because the farmers don't want to take it back to the farm. . . . Get the bread the next day, see it come out today, 3 cents Irish loaf of bread for 2 cents; two loaves together. So, my mother and father were going down Broadway 'cause at the end of Broadway is the wharf, to get food. My mother said I wasn't quite 3 years old. I'm behind them. . . . So, anyhow, there's a man had a store named Isenberg, he had a music store. I'm going down Broadway to the wharf, they had big markets . . . Anyhow my mother and father are talking and I'm behind them, and all at once my ma looked around and she didn't see me. In those days, there weren't automobiles, just a whole lot of wagons, and this was late at night. And I heard this organ, see, according to my mother, I just heard this organ. It was one you pump with your feet. I went across the street and there was a white man behind my mother and father and me. And my mother screamed, and they can't find me. And he said, "What's the matter?" I started to say "lady" but he wouldn't have called her "lady" in Baltimore . . . she said, "My son, I lost my son." "I saw him go across the street" [the man told her] . . .

And I'm in there putting my hand on there . . . , and there's a man in there demonstrating an organ to someone who's thinking of buying an organ. And I'm trying . . . but it won't work because you got to pump it, see. And my mother ran in and grabbed me up, and this fellow, this salesman [says], "He's a genius," he wants to sell the organ, you know. How the heck could he tell I'm a genius, I can't even talk good yet, see . . . The organ costs $75.00, you pay $1.00 and 25 cents a week, that makes you pay for it the rest of your life, you know what I mean. . . . The man says, "Oh this boy is a genius, he'll grow up to be the greatest . . . ," you know what they say when they're hustling you. She says, "I don't want my boy to be no musicianer." Yeah, "musicianer." . . . that's the way my mother talked. . . .

So anyhow, somehow they got the address, now this was on a Saturday night. Set the organ up in my house on his own. . . . And listen this is what I played when I got to be about 4 years old . . . [Eubie plays melody of "Marching through Georgia" with his right hand] I'm standing [to pump the pedals]. I can remember that, see. I'm about 4 years old. That's the first tune I played. And if my mother and father had *known* the name of that tune . . . you know what it's called, don't you? "Marching through Georgia." But she didn't like nothing down that way, see.[42]

Eubie said he didn't remember any of this happening, but that his parents often related it and he believed it to be true. He may also have been exaggerating how young he was at the time, but nonetheless his ear for music must have developed early on. He claimed he could remember that the first melody he picked out at age four was "Marching through Georgia," a choice that he found amusing, because his parents had little love for the "Old South." When interviewer Rudi Blesh asked Eubie how he learned this tune, he said that he had heard bands playing it in the streets to advertise local picnics. Of course, the lyrics celebrated the Union's triumphant subjugation of the Confederacy, perhaps one of the reasons it was popular among African American bands and audiences at the time.

Most black families could not afford a piano, so it was not unusual that the first keyboard instrument that came into their homes was a much less expensive pump organ or harmonium. Even that would be purchased "on time," because few could afford to pay for an instrument all at once. The organ's association with the church (while pianos were associated with saloons and houses of ill repute) made it more acceptable to religious people like Eubie's mother, who at one point hoped her son would become a minister.

When learning his first tunes, Eubie began by picking the melody out with just one finger. He told interviewer Jim Standifer that, even when he was first beginning, he could hear the "missing parts" that needed to be added to the melody:

I [first] played with one finger. Well, all my lifetime I could hear other parts . . . I could always play ahead something else in the music. So I tried two fingers, then applied three fingers. I'm about four or five years old now. I got so . . . I could hear four part harmony. Musicians don't believe this, but I always could hear something else added to the melody, so I kept on tinkering and tinkering and I got the bass. Then I got so that I would play that one tune, but I can't play but only that one tune.[43]

The daughter of a neighbor and friend of his mother's named Margaret Mitchell heard Eubie playing and recognized his talent. Mitchell played organ at one of the black churches in the neighborhood. Her talent attracted the attention of the white family for whom her mother worked. After moving to Paris, the family gave the Mitchells their piano for Margaret to play at home. Mitchell was attending high school at the time Eubie was about five or six years old. Eubie said she talked his mother into letting her give him piano lessons:

> She would [say], "Miss Blake, you ought to get that boy a music lesson." Now I'm speaking in the vernacular of my mother, now, "I don't want my boy to be a pie-ano player," that's the way she spoke, she didn't have an education. But Margaret says, "But try anyhow," 25 cents a lesson.[44]

Eubie recalls working through the standard piano exercise books of the day. When playing at home, he would run through the pop songs, marches, and hymns that he had heard in church or on the streets, "ragging" the melodies to make them more interesting. His mother, predictably, was angered any time she heard him stray from the straightforward church rhythms. "Take that ragtime out of my house," she'd yell. Eubie took to playing whenever his mother was doing her laundry work outside the home so she couldn't hear him.

Even as a youngster, Eubie had unusually long and thin fingers, eventually enabling him to play octaves, 10ths, and even 11ths and 12ths with ease. His unusually large hands, though, were also somewhat of a problem for him. His ever-vigilant mother feared that he'd be accused of being a pickpocket by whites who saw him out on the streets. "Double those fingers up," she'd scold him when they were out of their home, "don't let your fingers hang down." Although this "made [him] feel bad," whenever outside of the safety of his own neighborhood, Eubie learned to keep his hands in his pockets.[45]

Eubie's father had fewer qualms about exposing his boy to "sinful" entertainment beyond the world of the church. Eubie said that when he was around the age of 10 his father would sneak him out of the house to take him to the local burlesque house on Saturdays. ("If my mother ever knew, she'd throw us both out of the house," he quipped.[46]) The youngster was particularly impressed by the performance of an "all-Negro" drill team at one of the shows; this experience inspired him to gather a group of his friends from his family's Methodist church to form their own drill team. Entering a contest held during the Christmas season when Eubie was about 11 years old, his team won the prize—a $2.00 medal! Shortly thereafter, Blake formed a quartet with three local friends to sing outside of bars for tips. They performed all the popular hits of the days, songs like "Two Little Girls in Blue" and "Daisy," he said, emphasizing that they didn't sing anything syncopated like ragtime.[47] Eubie ran the quartet with an iron fist; when a member didn't measure up to his standards, he wasn't shy about letting him go, as he recalled in a later interview:

> I guess I was about 12, 13 years old. . . . Cooch Jones, Ned Jones, Stump Stamfer, and myself, I had a quartet, sing. Go to the bars, swinging doors, we go out there and sing . . . And Ned had a natural bass voice, see. [Imitates bass voice] And we rehearsin', and I says, "No, Ned you're singing wrong." And he could fight like hell. I could too, see. But Ned was older than me. "What's wrong about it?" Now he had me. He's singing melody instead of singing the bass part. He's singing the same thing I was singing, I was the lead, but he's singing an octave lower. But I don't know [how to explain this to him] . . . all right "Mouse, you think you're so smart." I couldn't tell him. "If you can't tell me, keep your mouth shut." I hauled off and hit him and that's all I remember. So, [I] put him out of the quartet.[48]

Eubie also took up buck dancing, practicing his art on neighborhood street corners. Open sewers ran along the side of every street, with a piece of slate placed at each intersection so you could cross over them. "You take a handful of sand, see, and you sprinkle it on the slate, and then you dance and it makes that little sound—but you know what it sounds like," Eubie told biographer Al Rose.[49] Blake danced for tips outside of bars.

Another family was lodging with the Mitchell family next door to the Blakes. Their young son, Howard "Hop" Johns, became a lifelong friend of Eubie's (Figure 1.3). Hop owned a cornet, and they began to take lessons with "a white boy across the street, he played in the white band, and he was older than we were."[50] When the two boys were about 12 years old, they auditioned to play in a local brass band, the Monumental City Guards Band, led by "Captain Harris." The band played for church outings and excursions, performing on Friday nights around town to advertise the upcoming event scheduled for the following Monday:

> They had picnics and excursions, the church would give these picnics and excursions, [they called them] excursions when you'd go on the train, and they called it picnics when you went on a furniture wagon. And you'd go off to the beach or parks or something. . . . [T]he excursion going to be

Figure 1.3 Hop Johns and Eubie Blake on the front stoop of the Blakes' house, when Eubie was about eight years old.

Monday, you play Friday night, torchlight parade. And you gotta go around the colored neighborhood with banners. Now you parade down to the station or the boat, now that's Monday morning, that's twice we played. And then you played on the boat or on the train . . . You don't play going up, but you play until 5 o'clock in the evening, from whatever time they get there. That's three times. So when it was over, the guy come [and] hand[ed] me 50 cents.

Now I get paid 50 cents, three times I'd played. [And] Hop got a dollar. But the other men in the band, they got 2 dollars. And we took up just as much time, so I said to Cap, "Listen Cap, you gonna pay. . . ." [He said,] "You oughta be glad you're getting 50 cents. You have no business being in the band. You don't play the notes, you play what you want to. You think I don't hear you; I hear you. You're putting a whole lot of rotgut music in it. First thing, I don't want you in the band anyhow." And I says, "Don't worry, you ain't going to get me in the band . . . I played once. One day, three settings to do one day." It swelled my neck up, anyhow.[51]

Not happy playing straight from the score, apparently Eubie was adding his own embellishments to his part:

I played third [cornet]. . . . And when the chord held, I'd play [sings rag-time melody] and they'd look back at me. You see, they didn't fill out the arrangements; if the chord held, they didn't fill it out. They [didn't] fill up those places. So I put in my own stuff in there. And Cap Harris says "Hey Mouse! Take that ragtime out, I don't want it in my band."[52]

Angered that he was being paid less than his friend, Eubie apparently quit the band after playing just one day with them. That, and the fact that blowing on the horn caused his neck to swell, led Eubie to abandon his career as a band musician.

As in many of his childhood memories, Eubie gave different accounts of how extensive his own education was. While he attended school through about the age of 12, he sometimes said that he failed to complete several grades but was nevertheless advanced to the next level. While he was fully lit-erate, he never completely mastered spelling and grammar, as reflected in his correspondence. Nonetheless, he was highly educated, particularly in music composition, and he studied formally and informally throughout his life with several mentors. Eubie gave various reasons for why he left school. In some tellings, he said he was thrown out of the eighth grade for bad behavior—insisting that in fact it was not his bad behavior but other boys' mischief that was blamed on him. This was probably around 1899 or 1900, when Eubie was 12 or 13 years old. Eubie resented the all-white teaching staff; he felt that they purposely denied him a chance at bettering himself through education. However, it was not unusual for young boys to leave school after the eighth grade at this time, particularly those who came from the working classes. What was unusual was that, once Eubie had left school, he never did manual labor. Eubie lucked into his first job as a piano player at a local "house of ill repute"—and thus the beginning of his long career as a musician.

Blake's school years were also significant because it was there that he first spotted his future wife Avis Lee. Precocious in music, Eubie apparently was also precocious in his interest in the female sex. Eubie gave different versions of how he first met Avis, although he did say she was ahead of him in school.

The school house was divided into four rooms, Eubie said, so that several grades were placed in the same classroom, and thus the two came to be educated together. Eubie never could master mathematics in school; sitting in front of him in class, Avis would slip him answers so he could pass the exams.[53] Eubie says that when his school friend Hop Johns told Avis that Blake planned to marry her someday, she hit him on the head with her music book so hard that it knocked him out. Nonetheless, when Hop and Eubie would sit together on the stoop in front of Blake's home, Eubie claims they would watch Avis walk by and Eubie would say, "Here comes that young girl—I'm going to marry her."[54] After Eubie left school, he didn't see Avis again until several years later, when he renewed his courtship of her.

Sometime shortly after his formal education ended around 1900, Eubie began playing piano at a local "house of ill repute" run by a white German madam named Agnes "Aggie" Shelton.[55] Shelton operated her house in the black neighborhood but it was patronized by whites; Baltimore historian William Hyder surmises that the location was chosen so the white patrons could visit there without being spotted by their neighbors or family members. Eubie said the house was located on a narrow alley where several other houses were in operation.

Eubie says he got the job after the house piano player, Basil Chase, inherited a large sum of money. Chase both was the house pianist and managed several of the girls; it was not unusual for piano players to work as pimps, as they were always on hand to keep an eye on the customers and make sure everything was on the up-and-up. Previously, Chase had taken Eubie around with other pianists and pimps to visit the various "hook shops" (slang for whore houses) "because they never had to pay me, I could play the organ and I knew all the tunes. Now these are colored houses now we're going to, you couldn't go into no white house, and I'd play piano for these guys." Chase was sufficiently impressed with Blake's playing to recommend him as his replacement after Chase came into a "large inheritance" (according to Blake) and decided to retire from working:

> [Basil Chase] called, "Hey mouse, I'm not going to work tonight. And I'll call Miss Shelton, let her know, and you go up there and play." Now, I don't know where Miss Shelton's house is, I don't know nothing about it, I never been on that street before. So I went up there in the daytime to get the job, and I had on short pants. I didn't know I had to have on long pants or nothing. And she say—she's German, great big woman, "You play huh,

right?" Oh boy she was big, woman must have weighed near 300 pound, not fat, just a big woman. They had a piano and I played. She said, "You get [a] pair of long pants and you come at 9 o'clock." She had white girls, this is a five dollar house, man.[56]

A "five dollar" house was considerably more classy than the many one or two dollar places that blacks patronized. Blake described Shelton's establishment as a "big time house" where "nothing vulgar" occurred in the parlor where he played his piano; the men and women engaged in polite conversation, and maybe would exchange a kiss, but any further action occurred in a more discreet part of the establishment. Only champagne was served in Shelton's establishment.[57] Eubie claimed that he "never knew all the time I worked at Aggie's that champagne had alcohol in it. I never knew you could get drunk from it, and I used to drink at least a couple of bottles a night."[58] Eubie's high tolerance for alcohol served him well, as many other working musicians became alcoholics, thanks to the ready availability of free drinks in hook shops and night spots.

When Eubie first took the job, he had to sneak out of his home to play it. He was particularly concerned that his mother would object to his working in such a place:

I lived on Jefferson Street and Caroline, and there's an alley in back, and there's a shed . . . My mother and father slept in the front room, and I slept in the backroom. So 9 o'clock I'd go to bed, see. And I know . . . they die when they go to sleep. And I go out the window, go across the street to the poolroom, I'd cross the streets, and get my long pants, 25 cents. I give this guy 25 cents . . . I put these pants on, and roll them up on the bottom, and they'd come way up to my chest. And I could play like hell then, no kidding, I could play the piano.[59]

Shelton was to pay Eubie $3.00 a week, but he said she never paid his salary; instead, he relied on patrons' tips, collecting sometimes as much as $8.00 to $12.00 a night, much more than he would have by working as a laborer. His repertory typically included popular songs of the day, particularly "real sentimental songs like 'You Made Me What I Am Today, I Hope You're Satisfied,'" Blake said. He never played "dirty songs" at Shelton's or anything suggestive. Light classics like the "Blue Danube Waltz" and other popular numbers were often requested, as were hit ragtime-flavored songs like "Hello, Ma Ragtime Gal" and "Any Rags?"[60]

Work was tough for many of the ragtime players. W. C. Handy told the following story:

As I was walking down Beale Street one night, my attention was caught by the sound of a piano. The insistent Negro rhythms were broken first by a tinkle in the treble, then by a rumble in the bass; then they came together again. I entered the cheap café and found a colored man at the piano, dog tired. He told me he had to play from seven at night until seven in the morning, and rested himself by playing with alternate hands.[61]

Eubie's mother wasn't too pleased when one of her church friends told her that she had heard Eubie playing at Shelton's house. Eubie said it was his unique piano-playing style that gave it away that he was working at a sporting house. His mother's friends "hear me, I played wobble bass, because that was the way Jesse Pickett [an early mentor] played: wub-wub-wub-wub. 'Nobody wobbles the bass like little Hubie, that's how I knowed it was him,' [they said]."[62] That distinctive wobble—a slightly off-beat syncopation that Eubie would vary as the feeling of the music demanded—is one of the elements that sets off his piano playing from many others and gives it its unique drive and swing.

Eubie related how his mother learned the news:

Some lady come, "Sister Blake, I heard a man up there sound just like little Eubie." "Where?" "Aggie Shelton's." But she don't know no Aggie Shelton, see. "Aggie Shelton? Where's that?" She told her the name to it. "What time was it?" "Five to one o'clock, two o'clock." "Oh, no, he go to bed at 9 o'clock," see. Now that's one sister [fellow church member]. And then comes another sister, "Sister Blake, is Little Eubie playing at Aggie Shelton's?" "What is this Aggie Shelton's?" "It's a sporting house up in So-and-So-Street; I don't say it was him, but somebody playing just like him." Now when a third woman came, she was somebody. . . .

So she said to me, "Sister Johns tells me and Sister Smith and Sister Brown, three different friends of mine they heard you play the piano in a bawdy house." She says, "Don't lie to me." This is in the summertime, see. And I says, "Well, mama, I go up there sometimes and play." . . . So, she's getting mad now, she could pick up this piano and knock you in the head with it, sit down and cry about it after. . . . Miss Johns, Hoppy Johns' mother out in the yard, she's stringing beans or something. And [my mother] says, "I'm going to kill you. How can I meet the people in the church and you playing in a sporting house, see. Now I'm going to kill you."

So Miss Johns came over, look over the fence, "Sister Blake?" "Yeah." "Now, I heard you and that boy arguin'. Now that boy's talented. He's got to play somewhere, where's he gonna play. He's got to make a livin'." And she talked her out of whipping me. "All the fellows play, but nobody plays like him."[63]

When Eubie's father returned home from work, his mother told him what she had discovered. Eubie showed his father how he had taken his earnings and hidden them under a mat in his room (the family had straw mats in their bedrooms, not being able to afford carpeting). "I have almost a hundred dollars stashed, because I'm too young to spend it, see. My father doesn't say anything for a moment. 'Well, son,' finally he says, 'I'll have to talk to your mother.'"[64] Eubie's father had to admit that Eubie's work was a boon to the family, telling his mother: "Now Em', this boy is doing nothing wrong. He's gonna have to work, and this is good work with good pay. You just better leave him alone."[65]

Although his mother objected to his piano playing, Eubie knew the family needed the extra income and thought her deep faith made little sense:

My mother said I don't want him to be no "pie-ano plunker." . . . I used to worry about her after I got to be around 13, 14. 1 said she's nuts. I used to think she was crazy because everything was "the Lord this" and "the Lord that," and I used to look and say we ain't got nothing. Half the time we didn't have nothing to eat in the house. My father had carbuncles and he can't work. My mother would go out and wash white people's clothes and all . . . [she'd make] $1.25 for the two baskets.[66]

Eubie liked the relaxed atmosphere at Shelton's house and the other houses where he performed. He was usually done by midnight so he had ample time to hear other pianists playing informally in the bars that catered to a late-night crowd:

I got out of the houses . . . at 12 o'clock. I got a chance to play poker, go around hook shop hopping, where I'd go around. . . . Well you see, the sporting houses they call them "hook shop houses." You get hooked all right, you get everything there. You could go to different places, you could go to speak easies, houses rents, and everything, because you only worked until 12 o'clock. You had the rest of the night to yourself. When you're playing in a sporting house, you play what the company please. All night, every night.[67]

Eubie worked about three months for Shelton, and then around 1901 to 1902 briefly joined two traveling troupes. Although the exact chronology and dates are not clear, Eubie first joined a traveling medicine show, playing the organ on the back of the wagon to attract customers. Again, Eubie gave different versions of how this occupation came about, including this one to interviewers Rudi Blesh and Mike Lipskin:

I went away with a Medicine show. Dr. Frisbee[68] . . . Now, this guy came in, and he heard me play. I don't think . . . This man [came into the place where I was working and] said, "Listen, I give you $3 a week, room and board, you get me four boys." Knotty Bakeman [a comedian], Slewfoot Nelson, Yellow Nelson, Preston Jackson [all singers and dancers], that's my pal, and myself. And this man was a real doctor, he wasn't no phony, and had a great big furniture wagon and you pulled the tailgate down, had a melodeon on it, and you'd play on the tailgate. And gasoline light, great big gasoline lights. And they'd take a big dishpan, "Bing bing bing bing bing!," they'd hit on that, and the people they'd come and stand, then we come out [and sing a song]. That's the open[ing], then. It was no band, it was a show. I got $5 a week, that's right, and the other guys got $3. No tips. But you get room and board. No uniforms, just street clothes, no makeup or nothing.

Apparently, "Doctor" Frisbee was a real horse doctor, who had developed his own special ointment for curing horses of their ailments:

This guy was a surgeon, a veterinarian. He had a liniment, and he'd take Vaseline rub on the horse's hip, and rub it in good. We'd ballyhooed already. Now he's spieling. His sales talk, they call it "spiel" in those days. Now, two or three guys come up with horses. He'd only take one horse, and let the audience pick the horse, cause if he picked it, it would be phony. He wasn't phony, honest to God. And he'd rub it this Vaseline on, and while he's spieling, he'd tell him "Walk him around." And the guy would walk him around the horse like that and after a while he'd be walking just as straight, honest to God. They had phony doctors, they sell you medicine for this or that, but this guy was [honest].

The show made its way across Maryland into southern Pennsylvania. Despite "Doctor" Frisbee's promise to provide room and board, the provisions were fairly minimal and the doctor did not provide meals on Sundays. When the troupe arrived in Fairfield, Pennsylvania—about 63 miles northwest of Baltimore, just across the Maryland line—Eubie's friend Preston Jackson revolted, and pressed Eubie to quit the company. Eubie was loathe to go back on his commitment, but went and spoke to the doctor, collecting their remaining salary. With just $2.50 in their pockets, the boys decided to walk back to Baltimore, encountering trouble along the way:

> Now, so we start to walk . . . and this is Sunday. When we get to Silver Spring, Maryland [about 70 miles] . . . we see some people sitting on the porch, and we go and ask, "Which way do we go to get to Baltimore?" And the man says "I'll give you 5 minutes to get off my land," and reached down and had a shotgun. He was going to shoot us. You know what he called us [i.e., the "n-word"]. Knotty Bakeman, another wise guy, [says] "I know a short cut. . . . See those mountains there, right over those mountains, come right down in Baltimore." Now Preston says, "Don't follow that guy, he don't know where he's going." And he went on. . . . [Knotty] goes in the woods, and I never seen him, I don't know if he's dead or what.

Meanwhile, Preston and Eubie walked on, running out of food and money. At around seven in the morning, they found a bar open that catered to working men who were having drinks before they loaded up their hay wagons. Preston talked the owner into letting Eubie and him perform and pass the hat. When the boys finally made it back to Baltimore, Eubie discovered that Preston had been cheating him all the time, hiding a "roll" of dollar bills that he didn't share with Eubie when he claimed to be broke. Nonetheless, the two apparently continued together for a while, working excursions to popular local parks south of the city, including Brown's Grove, the only seaside resort catering to Baltimore's inner-city black population.[69]

In this same period, around 1902, the duo signed on as dancers with a troupe traveling to New York to perform in the popular play *In Old Kentucky*. Different versions of the play had been on the road since 1893, produced and directed by Jacob Litt, who was said to have earned a million dollars touring this one production. He later owned New York's Broadway Theatre on 42nd Street, as well as a chain of venues in the West. The sentimental story focused on at life on the fictional old Southern plantation "Woodlawn," nestled in the Kentucky mountains. As expected, plantation life for the black slaves was portrayed as an idyllic and happy one, where their benevolent overseers ensured that they were treated fairly and with kindness. Unlike other plantation-life plays, the added novelty to this production was the addition of a dramatic horse race that concluded the third act, including "real" Kentucky thoroughbreds. (It is interesting to note that Sissle and Blake's later production of *The Chocolate Dandies* also revolved around a race featuring real horses.) The romantic subplot focused on the young master of the estate falling in love with a "simple mountain maiden." Other clichés of Kentucky mountain life—including moonshiners and a character described as a "real Kentucky Colonel"—added to the play's allure for Northern audiences.

The play's main attraction was its "celebrated pickaninny band," "The Woodland Wangdoodles," who performed between the acts. The band was described in a 1903 announcement:

> The famous and original brass band is made up of Pickaninnies gathered from different parts of the South by "the management," and was organized and is conducted by Master John Powell. Robert Bibbs and James Roberts, champion drum majors of the colored race, will be seen with the Wangdoodles, as well as Swinton and Emery, buck and soft shoe dancers.[70]

"Pickaninnies," or "picks" (as they were commonly called in the theater world), were black children between the ages of about 5 and 12 years old, who portrayed the happy children of plantation slaves in plays like *In Old Kentucky*. They also were called on to sing and dance and, in this case, to perform in a brass band. Apparently, the performance of this "band of darkeys" also included a "typical plantation performance," which would have included minstrel-show–like elements like comedic sketches and singing and dancing.[71] Eubie said he performed as a buck dancer in the production, while Preston sang and danced.

The *In Old Kentucky* company regularly played Brooklyn, and sometimes also New York City, in late January/early February of each year during this period.[72] The company then moved on to upstate New York to play Rochester and Buffalo. Eubie mentions only one engagement when he was with the company, which he said played at the Academy of Music on 14th Street. (The

1902 version played New York's Grand Theater at 28th Street for two weeks from February 17 to February 28; perhaps Eubie mistakenly confused this location for the Academy of Music.) Excited by the chance to see the big city—and particularly Broadway—Eubie had a rude awakening when they arrived in the city, where he was lodged far from Broadway's bright lights:

> The way they did, they backed the truck up to the stage door and we went into the theater and did the show. Then we got back in the truck and they took us to this little boarding house on Bleecker Street . . . Then we go to bed, and the next day the same thing.[73]

Unhappy with the arrangement, Blake soon quit the show after its New York City run to return to his native Baltimore. (He rather sheepishly admitted to Rudi Blesh that his mother had insisted on his return.) Back living at home, Eubie returned to playing whorehouses and bars, some less savory than others, catering to a lower-class clientele. He told black music historian Eileen Southern that he worked the entire gamut of places in Baltimore during the period of about 1900 to 1904:

> I played at a place called Greenfield's. When I would come into the house, my mother would say, "Take your shoes off and wipe the saw dust all off of you; don't bring it in my house." There were no chairs in the bar; you sat on beer kegs. The "ladies of the evening" all had green moles . . . tattooed on their faces. The "gentlemen of leisure" wore tight pants, full-back coats, and great big diamonds. I played in the dumps. I played one place down in Mash Market Place, called the White House. . . . Nobody living today . . . has played in a place lower than that. And I have played for the lowest type of people. Now these weren't all colored people. In the White House, there were colored and white. Bums, nothing but bums and derelicts! I only played for one week, because I couldn't make it myself down there. It was too tough for me.[74]

Greenfield's was a hotel/saloon where "Big-Head Wilbur" was the main pianist. He offered Eubie a job as his "relief" man; Wilbur would quit playing around four in the afternoon, and Eubie would take over on the piano, playing until midnight. The bar had no chairs, but only large beer kegs and boxes to sit on; the rough crowd would slow-dance across the floor, shuffling through the sawdust that was piled higher than the soles of their shoes.

However, Eubie didn't like Greenfield's as much as Shelton's place, where he had a less formal arrangement and sometimes could leave early.

After leaving Greenfields, Eubie was hired to play at Annie Gilley's, a dancehall and saloon where you could have a girl for $1.00 an hour. The girls who worked there were tough, Eubie said, noting, "I thought the customers needed to be protected from *them* more than the other way [around]. . . . The men had to watch their wallets, too." Consisting of a single large room, the place was packed with people dancing, with customers attracted by the music, sex, excitement—and the occasional brawl. "Customers came in with brass knuckles and knives and sharp razors," Eubie said, "Just lookin' for a fight."[75] Despite the noise, Eubie developed a following by working at Gilley's, with patrons gathered around the piano to hear him play. He claimed that the patrons would sing along on the big hits of the day, lustily roaring on the choruses of songs like "Down Where the Wurzburger Flows."

Eubie would have liked to work only in classier places, but noted that the less reputable ones were the only venues available to a black musician to work. Like all sporting-house pianists, he played requests ranging from light classics to ragtime numbers to popular songs like "After the Ball" and "Down Went McGinty." Good working pianists had to be able to play all requests (like a human jukebox). They also had to be able to accompany singers, so the ability to play any song in all keys was highly prized. Amateur and self-taught pianists—like Irving Berlin—would learn to play by using primarily the black keys on the piano. Eubie quipped to interviewer Jim Standifer: "I have people ask me 'Why do all the colored play on the black keys all the time?' I say, 'Well, I'll tell you, one reason is because they are mostly from the south. You can't hit no white keys down south, I'll tell you that!'"[76] Great pianists also were quick to develop their own personal signature—including "tricks" such as distinctive melodic embellishments, basslines, and chords. Eubie soaked up the sounds he heard from many popular Baltimore pianists of the day. Most had colorful nicknames and played primarily for their own amusement and in informal "cutting contests," each trying to outdo the other:

When I was a kid, they had pianos in the back of the bars. In the summer time the bars had swinging doors . . . and I would sit and listen to Jesse Pickett, Big-Head Wilt, Shout Blake (no relation to me), Big-Head Wilbur, Slew-Foot Nelson (funny, eh?), Knotty Bakeman, Yellow Nelson, and Big Jimmy Green. These men were what they used to call "piano sharks." These guys could play! And only one of that group (that I know of), Shout Blake,

could read music. The rest of them couldn't read, but they could play in any
key. You very seldom meet pianists today, readers, that can play the music
in any key. If you say "Home, Sweet Home" in E major, they can't do it; they
have to have the music. But we had to play in every key because we had to
play for so many different singers, and no one sang songs in the keys in
which they were originally written.[77]

Blake explained that one hallmark of all of these pianist's style was the
creative use of the left hand. He described one of these semiprofessionals
as having a "left hand like God." He meant that they developed unique bass
patterns and runs that were set in opposition to the main melodic part. He
believed these pianists developed this approach because they were playing
as soloists, without assistance from a drummer, so they had to emphasize the
rhythm part.

Among all the pianists Eubie encountered in the mid-1890s through the
turn of the 20th century, he was particularly impressed by Jesse Pickett, an
itinerant gambler and "man of leisure" (pimp) who, Blake believed, was originally from Philadelphia but was active in Baltimore in this period. ("Craps
put a lot of money in his pocket," Eubie said, "work didn't mean nothing
to him."[78]) Pickett would hang out in bars and brothels and play when the
spirit moved him. Pickett's signature piece was known as "The [Bull Dyke's]
Dream," and featured a tango-like rhythm. Tangos had swept the country,
thanks to touring bands from the Caribbean; W. C. Handy picked up on this
trend and inserted a tango section as the third part of his major hit, "St. Louis
Blues." Eubie said he heard the rhythm throughout this period but didn't
actually hear the term "tango" used to describe it until he was working in
New York with James Reese Europe, about 15 years later. "The Dream" was
written in two tricky keys (Eubie said "it was written in six flats, and its goes
from six flats to six sharps"[79]), giving Pickett an edge in the informal contests
held to establish superiority among the "plunkers" who'd take turns working
the barroom pianos. Eubie recalled that Pickett was sufficiently impressed
by his playing to teach him his signature piece. Pickett was said to have wandered as far as Chicago before returning sometime in the middle of the first
decade of the 20th century to his hometown of Philadelphia, where he died.
Through his signature showpiece, his impact on East Coast pianists was considerable. In the 1940s, James P. Johnson recorded the piece, as did Eubie in
1969. Eubie's recording features the exciting tango rhythm in the opening

section, as well as unusual syncopations and dramatic rhythmic shifts between the later sections of the piece.

Eubie emphasized that many of the working pianists in Baltimore had classical training. One talented player whom Eubie admired was Freddie Bryant. Eubie nicknamed him "Chopin" because Bryant had been trained by a classical musician who venerated the Polish pianist. While he played everything from tangos to sentimental songs, Blake said Bryant always played them in Chopin's style![80] There was little opportunity for a black to perform as a classical pianist at the time, so most had to make a living playing in the hook shops or bars.

Still living at home in 1903, Eubie was doing well by working as a pianist. It is likely he would have continued pursuing this career, never leaving his home town, if it weren't for two events, about a decade apart, that brought major changes to his life.

2

Becoming an Established Musician

1904–1915

On Sunday, February 7, 1904, a major fire broke out on the edge of downtown Baltimore and quickly spread to devastate a large section of the city center, all the way to the docks. While the official count listed no fatalities—although the city admitted that there were blacks who died in the fire who weren't included in these "official" numbers—many businesses, large and small, were affected by the fire. Among the ruins were many bars and bawdy houses that were burned among the more distinguished edifices. The remaining venues catering to the city's night life saw a decline in business, with manpower and capital being diverted to the rebuilding of the city. Early that Sunday morning, Blake was returning from a long night of piano playing when he heard something "like a bomb going off." Luckily, the fire did not reach his parents' home, but it undoubtedly affected his main livelihood.[1]

While Eubie does not give the fire as a reason for his leaving, in 1905 he made his first extended trip to work in New York City. Perhaps he felt he was outgrowing the limits of the venues that he was playing in the local area. Perhaps he heard from others that New York offered a chance for greater pay and more visibility. He certainly was interested in being exposed to the varied theatrical offerings available in New York, having already heard touring companies perform the popular operettas of American composer Victor Herbert and British composer Leslie Stuart. Stuart's big hit—*Floradora*, first produced in London in 1899 and premiering on Broadway a year later—made a big impact on the young composer. Traveling companies continued to perform the work through the early years of the 20th century. The show featured an attractive chorus of, for the time, scantily clad young girls—who drew a large audience. Its biggest hit was "Tell Me Pretty Maiden," sung by a sextet of the lovely girls as they're questioned by six would-be male partners. One could easily imagine the four-square song, set as a moderate-tempo march,

Eubie Blake. Richard Carlin and Ken Bloom, Oxford University Press (2020). © Richard Carlin and Ken Bloom 2020.
DOI: 10.1093/oso/9780190635930.001.0001

being syncopated under Blake's fingers. Besides being performed on stage, the song was available on recordings in the first years of the 20th century. On hearing this hit number, Eubie believed he could write songs that were every bit as pretty—and popular—as Stuart's hits.

Eubie had come to New York previously while he was appearing in *In Old Kentucky*. He was impressed with what he thought was the sophistication of the black ragtime musicians. "I'd look at all of these fine people and I'd know that somewhere some day [I could] be like that. I'm not saying I wanted to be a pimp or nothin' like that, but I wanted to be somebody who could *live* like that."[2] When Eubie returned to New York City in 1905, the black population had not yet migrated uptown to Harlem. Instead, most blacks lived in the Tenderloin district between about 20th and 50th Streets, from 6th Avenue west in what today is Herald Square, the Garment District, and parts of Chelsea. Bars, social clubs, and presumably whorehouses catering to the black population were also located there. While many bars and clubs employed house pianists, others became popular gathering places for musicians to shoot the breeze and share information on gigs, and even as informal booking offices where wealthy whites could come looking to find musicians to play for their parties and dress balls. Newcomers could get a chance to show off their talents, playing for tips. One of the most popular gathering places when Eubie reached the city was Baron Wilkins's club located on West 37th Street. (Wilkins would later move his operation uptown when Harlem became the dominant black neighborhood.)

In an interview with Hazel Bryant, Noble Sissle described Wilkins's bar and how black musicians came to gather there:

> Anybody who came into [Baron Wilkins's] saloon, he'd allow them to go on and sing a number and pass the hat. . . . The women in those days did not go to nightclubs . . . The men with their concubines they'd go to those places. But some of the young white fellows, like they do, they go where they want to. They went to Baron Wilkins' Place because the Negro fellows there were such marvelous singers and entertainers . . . So they wanted to get them up there among their people. And, as I say, the white women [were] kept away from the theater . . . Negroes too, our women didn't go there neither. So to get the fellows up to their place, just like you go to a dinner-dance now, and before your dinner you have some entertainment, [the white patrons] commenced to bring these Negroes up to stroll and entertain.[3]

Further, Baron's was a place where a newcomer could informally audition either to join a popular dance orchestra or to appear in a Broadway band or show. Sissle said,

> Every white and colored performer of reputation in those days would at some time drop down in Baron's place and sing or dance, or in some way display their talent. It was to such saloons that theatrical producers and managers would go to look for talent. Many a Broadway star today owes his or her success to his appearing in one of these underworld dives, and having been seen by a scout for some manager . . . [they] were given [their] chance and made good.[4]

The atmosphere for would-be performers in New York was certainly more cutthroat than what Eubie knew in Baltimore. Pianists vied for paying jobs, and amateurs were not afraid to challenge house pianists in order to gain employment, impress their friends, or win over women. Eubie's younger contemporary, James P. Johnson, vividly described how piano players in the New York area would battle one another, asserting their supremacy through their flashy clothing and keyboard prowess. Even their entry into a room was choreographed for maximum impact; Johnson said:

> When a real smart tickler would enter a place, say in winter, he'd leave his overcoat on and keep his hat on, too. We used to wear military overcoats . . . We'd wear a light pearl-gray Fulton or Homburg hat . . . set in a rakish angle over on the side of the head. Then a white silk muffler and a white silk handkerchief in the overcoat's breast pocket . . .
>
> Many fellows had their overcoats lined with the same material as the outside—they even had their suits made that way. Pawnbrokers . . . would give you twenty or twenty-five dollars on such a suit or overcoat. They knew what it was made of. A fellow belittling another would be able to say, "G'wan, the inside of my coat would make you a suit."
>
> . . . When you came into a place you had a three-way play. You never took your overcoat or hat off until you were at the piano. First, you laid your cane on the music rack. Then you took off your overcoat, folded it and put it on the piano, with the lining showing.
>
> You then took off your hat before the audience. Each tickler had his own gesture for removing his hat with a little flourish; that was part of the

attitude, too. You took out your silk handkerchief, shook it out and dusted off the piano stool.

Now, with your coat off, the audience could admire your full-back or box-back suit, cut with very square shoulders. . . . Full-back coats were always single-breasted, to show your gold watch fob and chain.[5]

Johnson noted that Jelly Roll Morton—one of the proudest and most flamboyant of all the piano players—would lay his overcoat on the side of the piano, inside out, so all could admire the quality of its lining. "He would do this very slowly, very carefully and very solemnly," Johnson related, "as if the coat was worth a fortune and had to be handled very tenderly."[6] It must have been intimidating, to say the least, for Eubie to encounter these sharks when he first arrived in the city.

Eubie said that he first came to New York to work for "a man named Edmund . . . bad guy" who operated a bar on 27th Street. However, Eubie disliked the bar and its clientele. According to him, the police regularly harassed him at the club, particularly if they caught him playing after 1 a.m., the legal closing time. One policeman even threatened him with his nightstick until the manager assured the cop that Eubie was new to town and didn't know the curfew rules.[7] He also didn't like living in what was then a rough section of town, dominated by Irish street gangs. Valuing his privacy, he didn't appreciate New Yorkers' habits of dropping by unannounced in his small room:

> I didn't like everybody coming into my house, where I live, and I don't know these guys, see they coming in and out all the time. I don't like it here. . . . Everybody's Negro, so in order to get something you either got to go to 8th Avenue or 9th Avenue. 9th Avenue was where they sold things cheaper than they did on 8th Avenue. And then a Big Irishman would kill you over a peach . . . Irish neighborhood; tough, tough. . . . I lived up over top of a store, it was a private house. A rooming house, on 37th Street, downtown, between 8th and 9th Avenue. You couldn't go right around the corner unless you get into some argument. I never liked the damn town. So I wouldn't stay in New York.[8]

Most of the piano "thumpers" in New York dressed up in fine clothes and sported large diamonds (mostly purchased from pawn shops). Eubie tried to measure up to their style but could afford only three "diamond" accessories made of paste. A local huckster whom Eubie knew only as "Crow" asked him where he got his "diamonds," and Eubie tried to pass them off as real. Pretending to be concerned about Eubie's safety, Crow then asked what route he took to walk home each night after playing at Edmund's, and the naive pianist dutifully told him how he had to step over bums on the way back to his rooming house. Of course, Crow arranged to have the pianist ambushed on his next trip home. Eubie laughed that at least they weren't real diamonds, and his total investment had been only three dollars.[9]

While it's not entirely clear, it appears that after his initial experience in 1905, Eubie continued to work New York for a few weeks each year, but didn't want to move there permanently. One reason might have been the divisions between blacks and whites outside the Tenderloin. More than 50 years later he was still wary of Manhattan's higher-class restaurants. A white friend of Eubie's wanted to have a meal in a Times Square restaurant. Eubie demurred, telling the friend, "If we go in there, they'll piss in my soup."[10] He preferred to be a big fish in the small pond of Baltimore's music scene to acclimating to the strange social and musical worlds of New York. Also in 1905, "Hubert J. Blake" made his first appearance in the Baltimore phone directory as a "pianist," indicating his rising status as a professional player; a year later, he listed himself with the even grander title of "musician."[11] (Eubie would alternate between using the names "Hubert J." and "James H." through about the mid-1910s, according to the city directories.)

Back in Baltimore, Eubie found higher-paying and better work at the Middle Section Club than he had previously had. This venue was a private club catering to African Americans. The Club was founded sometime around 1892 and was located in the heart of Baltimore's black neighborhood on East Lexington Street. "There was a craps game on the first floor and a poker game upstairs on the third floor," Blake said.[12] The second floor featured a bar and dining area. Catering to Baltimore's middle-class black population, the Club would be visited even by the better class of black women, the churchgoing ladies like Eubie's mother and upward-aspiring younger people like his first wife, Avis Lee. Eubie took the job when his friend and fellow pianist Hughie Wolford left for a better-paying gig at a white establishment. Eubie's first date was on a Sunday evening, and—raised to think that playing popular music on the Sabbath was sinful—Eubie took it as an ominous sign when, out of nowhere on a perfectly clear night, a violent thunderstorm broke out as he sat down at the piano bench.[13]

Eubie viewed Wolford as one of his strongest competitors on the Baltimore scene. According to Eubie, Wolford would enter a bar where another player was working and sneer, "Get up, get up! You're ruining the people's music. You don't know what you're doing." His superior attitude did not endear him to the other local pianists.[14] Blake claimed he composed "Tricky Fingers" at this time to impress Wolford with his own keyboard prowess.[15] Wolford would rag any piece, even playing the church ladies' requested hymns in syncopation, much to their annoyance. Eubie, on the other hand, was happy to play their requests as written, because he knew that was the quickest way to get a tip. He thought it was foolish to be so strong headed, although Eubie's disapproval inspired Wolford to create a unique new composition:

> "Why do you play everything in ragtime?" [I asked. Wolford said,] "She say play 'Hosannah,' [a hymn tune] "I plays 'Hosannah.'" I said "But you played it in ragtime." It's a church number, you know. "I bet you if somebody asked you to play the scales, you'd play them in ragtime." . . . So he goes on home, he practices all day long. And he comes back in with "Ragging the Scale." I played until 6, 7 o'clock in the morning, he's playing the bawdy house, and he comes in and said, "You remember how you said if I play the scales I'd have it all in ragtime?" And he had it all in one key, he didn't change the key. I listened to him. He says, "How do you like that, Eubie?" And I says, "That's crazy, man." . . .
>
> "Well, now I want to play a joke on him. I go home and put the scale in five keys, and the next day I come in where Hughie is shootin' pool. They got a piano in there. So I go and sit at the piano and rag the scale in five keys. He says, "Hey, you copped that from me!"
>
> I say, "I copped it from *you*? I didn't have to cop that from nobody. Don't you understand? That's the scale. Nobody owns the scale."[16]

Wolford went on to play at a local bar where two white musicians were also in residence. One of them, Ed Claypoole, copyrighted "Ragging the Scale" about a decade later—in five keys, as Eubie had arranged it. Eubie lamented, "[I] never thought to copyright it or anything . . . I'd have felt foolish tryin' to copyright the scale."[17]

The Middle Section Club—like similar white organizations of the era—was formed as a way of having a semiprivate gathering place, beyond the eyes and ears of the local authorities. This arrangement allowed for gambling and the serving off-hours of liquor. However, the Club and its members were not free of harassment by the police. In 1912—a few years after Eubie played there—a group of Baltimore's finest approached the Club's door at 2 a.m. on a Sunday morning with the intent of raiding the place. The doorman refused to allow them to enter, and subsequently was badly beaten with their "blackjacks and fists." When the incident was brought before the Police Board, the question that they were asked to address was "whether members of the police force have authority to beat a negro because he refuses to open the door of a place where they believe the law is being violated,"[18] rather than their culpability in beating him. The Club had repeatedly applied for a liquor license, only to be denied one. Police often cased saloons and clubs to try to catch them in violations. Even those with a liquor license could be fined for serving alcohol on a Sunday (the cutoff time for alcohol sales was originally midnight on Saturday, but raised to 1 a.m. on Sunday in 1912). The hope of finding the Middle Section Club in breach of the law may be why the policemen decided to raid the Club at 2 a.m. that Sunday.

Eubie became close with the club's manager, Edward Myers, and in turn mentored Myers's son James ("Buster") after the elder Myers passed away. Buster described his father as a "local kingpin" who was a key player in the African American community, as well as co-owner of the club. Buster recalled that early on Eubie emulated the well-dressed and affluent pimps who frequented the club, until his father set him straight:

> Eubie wanted to be a pimp then. They wore diamonds in their ties, carried big rolls of money, wore fine clothes and had girls. Eubie was a young man, but he liked the girls and fine clothes. But my father told him to keep straight or he'd send him home to Uncle John [Eubie's father]. Eubie called my father his "street father" [protector].[19]

Eubie's job at the Middle Section Club was also important because it introduced him to many major celebrities in Baltimore's black society. One of the most important was the well-known prize fighter Joe Gans, who was a hero to black America, thanks to winning the World Lightweight Title in boxing in 1902 when he defeated white pugilist Frank Erne, the first African American to do so. Eubie told various stories of how he first became acquainted with Gans; in some tellings, he claimed to have met Gans when the future boxer was working as a fishmonger in a local market, stating that Eubie and his childhood buddy Hop Johns ran errands for the future fighter.[20] In another telling, Eubie said he played marbles with Gans when they were both children (although Gans was a good 12½ years older than he was). They reconnected, according to Blake, when he and Preston Jackson returned to Baltimore from their ill-fated engagement with Dr. Frisbee's Medicine Show, and the three became inseparable friends.[21] However, it is most probable that Eubie didn't meet Gans until around 1905, when Gans was known to be a "member" of the Middle Section Club.

Gans proved to be an important figure in Eubie's career. In 1906, Gans had won a well-publicized bout against the "Durable Dane," Oscar "Battling" Nelson, a fight that was held in Goldfield, Nevada. Flush with his winnings, he returned to his native Baltimore to open a lavish hotel and saloon on October 19, 1907, to cater to the better class of black society.[22] The *Baltimore Sun* noted that the hotel was "the resort of all the colored sports" in town, describing its barroom as being painted "a light mulatto" in color—as if its color reflected the lighter skin tones of its patrons.[23] "The very highest class of people came to the Goldfield," Eubie said, "Every race, every color. Nothing but the finest food, liquor, and champagne."[24] Gans operated the hotel until his death from tuberculosis in August 1910; afterward, his wife continued to operate it. In 1912 she married the African American composer/performer Ford Dabney,[25] who had been producing revues in Washington, DC. At least in 1913 he staged similar shows at the Goldfield.

Gans hired Eubie to be his house pianist, paying him $55 a week for his services—good pay for those days.[26] The original Goldfield house "band" consisted of just Blake's piano and a drummer, but eventually grew to an ensemble of 19 men, including saxophonist Mike "Prince" Venable, according to Blake.[27] Originally, Eubie alternated with pianist "Boots" Butler, but Butler suddenly died a few weeks after the hotel opened. Gans then hired One-Leg Willie Joseph, who was a powerful, classically trained pianist. Eubie says Willie's playing was so strong that he would regularly break the hammers and keys on the house piano.[28]

Willie told Eubie that, when he was younger, he had competed in a contest held at the Boston Conservatory. Willie took top honors, only to be denied his prize when the judges realized he was black:

His mother worked for some millionaires in Boston, you know. And millionaires years ago used to go to Paris. Summertime, wintertime, Paris, yeah. And Willie would play the piano. And his mother says . . . "Willie, come away from that piano, the white folks come home, and you're playing that piano." In the house there, that's where they lived. And . . . something happened in Paris, [their white employers] had to come home. And [Willie] sat there playing the piano and he heard the key going in the door. And he got up, and the man came in, and he said, "Wait a minute, don't run. Keep on playing." . . . And, whatever the man's name was, he says, "This boy should be in the Conservatory of Music."

So, they [took] him [to] the Boston Conservatory . . . of Music . . . Now he was the only Negro that was in it. They don't say Negro anymore but I'm going to say it because I'm used to saying it. They had a cubicle, nobody knows who's in the cubicle. And Willie played one of Liszt's numbers, he told me what it was, I think it was the 12th, the hardest . . . And when One-Leg Willie played, they can't tell who it is. They don't go by the audience, you could have the plants in the audience. They go by the 7 men: 4 pianists and 3 composers, judges. And Willie won it. I told you, he's the same color as this piano. My father was the same color. And [the judge] says "Mr. Joseph, you won, but I can't give it you. I'm sorry." Willie says, "Why?" He says, "I['ll] let you judge that," and he never did tell him why, but everybody knew.[29]

This kind of unspoken racism was something Eubie confronted throughout his life. Joseph wanted to play classical music, but Blake said that even when he played for "high-class Negroes," they asked him to play ragtime. Blake said that Joseph turned to drink and became addicted to cocaine; he believed he died around his 30th birthday in 1908.[30]

In addition to offering food and libations, the Goldfield was home to illegal gambling, in which Gans himself participated. Thinking of winning some money himself, Eubie began wagering his tips in these games. Unfortunately, he was no match for the sharpies who made their living as gamblers. One particular gambler, known as "Jew Abie," convinced him of the folly of his ways: "I'm a gambler. A professional gambler. I win. You're a professional musician. You don't know how to gamble. It's dopes like you that put my two daughters through college."[31]

Another trick that pianists did to augment their income was to play "lemon pool." Basically, this was a form of hustling in which the player challenged other patrons in the bar to a "friendly match," and then purposely lost, pretending to be a raw novice. After losing a round or two, the lemon player would then suggest they "make it interesting" by placing a wager on the next game's outcome. Of course, the supposed novice would then show his true colors, suddenly becoming an ace player and raking in the cash. Eubie was a talented pool player himself, a skill he honed through his years working in barrooms, but he refused to play a "lemon" game. One of the worst offenders was fellow pianist and composer "Luckey" Roberts. Unlike Eubie, Roberts prided himself on scamming unsuspecting players, and even pulled off his scheme in bars that catered to whites. Eubie warned him to back off, saying "If they ever catch you, they'll kill you."[32] It was one thing to trick drunken black patrons, another and far more dangerous thing to try to pull a scam on white hustlers.

Just as in his earlier jobs, Eubie had to accompany singers at the Goldfield, playing the songs that patrons requested. These were usually the sentimental hits of the day; a few titles Eubie mentioned include "Heart of My Heart," "I've Got Rings on My Fingers," "Put on Your Old Gray Bonnet," and the popular railroad ballad "Casey Jones."[33] While he might have played tricky rags to impress other pianists, Eubie's working repertory was designed to please his audience.

Eubie met several other influential musicians who would shape his career during this period. One was his contemporary Llewellyn Wilson. Wilson would become a famous music teacher in Baltimore's "colored" high school, training a range of musicians, including Cab Calloway and his sister Blanche; Ellis Larkins; and many others. Wilson also became the music critic for the Baltimore *Afro-American* and played cello for and eventually led the Baltimore City Colored Orchestra and chorus. (Baltimore was one of the few cities to form a separate classical orchestra to accommodate black musicians, who weren't welcome into the city's primary orchestra.) Wilson is said to have worked on Baltimore's docks to earn enough money to take lessons from the Peabody Conservatory's faculty—who would take on African American students for private lessons, even though they could not be admitted to the school.[34] He had considerable music education, and Blake sought out his help in learning how to write music and to compose without sitting at the piano:

> Llewellyn Wilson asked me what kind of music did I want to write. Did I want to the write the "longhair" [classical music], and I told him I really want to write popular music. I went to his home, and the room where he played piano was totally soundproof. It was where he taught all his students . . . He told me to go to another room and to sit down and write a 16 and a 32 bar chorus. He said, "Eubie, you're going to go places where there is no piano and all of a sudden you're going to get an idea. What are you going to do? By the time you get to a piano you'll have forgotten what it was you

wanted to write. So you've got to learn, pianistically, in your mind, what you want it to sound like."[35]

Eubie made a distinction between composing melodies and accompaniments with developing "tricks" as a barroom pianist. True composing meant he had to think beyond the confines of what was possible on the piano and focus on creating attractive melodies that would appeal to singers and listeners. From Wilson, he learned that writing while sitting at the keyboard would limit his success as a songwriter:

> I don't go to the piano to write melodies. I don't have to go the piano to write piano scores either. When I want some tricks that I use in music, then I go to piano, so I won't use the tricks I used in [a previous performance]. For me, to write a melody or a piano score, I don't go near the piano. Because, if you do, you write pianistic.[36]

Blake's informal lessons with Wilson would prove vital to his success as a songwriter in the coming years.

By this time, Eubie was the primary breadwinner in the family. His father was suffering from a variety of disabilities developed over his decades of working as a longshoreman; his mother made only a small income from doing laundry for "white folks." Eubie provided support to both his parents, as well as his adopted sister, whom his mother had convinced his father to add to the household. Despite his mother's disapproval, Eubie also helped his father keep a supply of high-strength whiskey outside the house:

> When you pour it out, it look like beer, because of the foam on top. 100 proof whiskey—it was dog whiskey. And the man said, "Eubie, you're going to kill the old man with that." I'm a man now, I'm bringing the whiskey. . . . And he'd take one swallow, all day long he's doing it. Couldn't bring no whiskey in the house, but I used to bring him whiskey.[37]

Blake's position at the Goldfield raised his stature in Baltimore's music community substantially, among white listeners as well as blacks. He began to get pickup jobs in local theaters while also continuing to perform for outings and picnics at the various parks catering to black patrons. Blake told several interviewers a story that he claimed took place around the period of 1905 to 1907 but that in fact probably occurred toward the end of his residency in

Baltimore in 1915. Blake said that Chicago-based Billy King was performing in Baltimore with his traveling company. King was an African American comedian who led various companies through his career. In 1915, he settled in Chicago, where he had his greatest success.[38] His company appeared at Baltimore's Orpheum Theater in the spring of 1915, presenting the musical plays *Two Bills from Alaska* and *My Old Kentucky Home*.[39] Both featured a female chorus line that included an end-woman who clowned around to please the audience—something that Josephine Baker would later do when she joined Sissle and Blake's *Shuffle Along*.

Although primarily catering to white audiences, the Orpheum—like other Baltimore theaters—often hosted touring black theater companies. Black Patti (aka Sissieretta Jones, the celebrated black vocalist who specialized in performing opera selections) and her company appeared at the theater in 1914, presenting the musical revue *Lucky Sam from Alabam*.[40] The show was written by and featured black comedian Harrison Stewart. In both 1914 and 1915, Salem Tutt Whitney's Smart Set company performed at the Orpheum, presenting the comic drama *His Excellency the President* there the week before King's company took the stage.[41] The theater didn't just present African American novelties; the same month that King appeared there, Sholem Aleichem—"the Jewish Mark Twain," as the *Sun* described him—did a one-night show.[42] The theater also featured speakers like Presidential candidate William Jennings Bryan in 1913[43], and vaudeville-type bills including magicians, animal acts, singers, and dancers. Silent movies ("photoplays," as they were advertised) were also part of the fare.

According to Blake, King's company didn't tour with a full band. Instead, he employed a local contractor to hire musicians to accompany the show, but used his own pianist-conductor to make sure the score was performed properly. The musicians who were available were white players who worked Baltimore's theaters. Apparently, King's regular conductor was taken ill, so— in a jam—King asked the contractor for help. The contractor suggested Eubie for the job.

Blake initially was unwilling to even enter the orchestra pit, knowing of the prejudice of the white musicians who were playing there. The local musicians made it clear in no uncertain terms that they wouldn't follow the lead of a black conductor (they used a less polite term in describing their aversion to Blake). The contractor and King, however, were insistent, and with the threat of losing future gigs, the musicians finally relented. The score for the show apparently featured arrangements of some of Scott Joplin's recent rags.

Being mostly conservatory-trained theater musicians, the players were not able to master the syncopations. Blake assured them that they could master the tricky new rhythms, demonstrating the entire score on the keyboard for them—and in the process, he claimed, winning their trust and admiration.[44]

In 1910, Eubie had reached a secure enough position as a working pianist to take a wife. Blake had first met Avis Lee (Figure 2.1) when he was in grade school. Lee was born c. 1884 and thus was about two to three years older than Eubie (although, as we have seen, Blake later adjusted his birth year to 1883, perhaps to make up for this difference). Eubie said that the Lee family was considerably better off than his own, belonging to Baltimore's black middle class. Avis was raised in a household led by her grandfather, Draper Lee (born c. 1846), who was born in rural Dorchester county, Maryland, the same region where Blake's father and grandmother owned land. Lee moved to Baltimore sometimes around 1870; he had married his wife Elizabeth

Figure 2.1 Avis Blake, probably photographed in the mid-1920s. She is wearing a mink coat that Eubie was able to purchase for her after his success with *Shuffle Along*.

around 1868. Street directories show that Lawrence Lee, Avis's father, was living in the same home around the turn of the century; Lawrence was said to be a member of the Black Patti minstrel company, a popular traveling show headed by the famous black operatic singer.[45] Draper was listed as a "laborer" in the 1870 and 1880 censuses, but by 1900 was in the hardware business; like Eubie's father, he could read and write. Lawrence is listed as a "laborer" and "can maker" in city directories from 1885 to 1895. The Lees lived in the same neighborhood as the Blakes, and also rented their home.[46] Unlike Eubie, Avis attended high school, entering in the fall of 1900 at age 15.[47] Eubie said that she was trained as a pianist by Fanny Hurst, an older pianist/singer in the neighborhood who had classical training; later in life, he noted that Hurst had attended Baltimore's prestigious Peabody Conservatory by passing for white. Avis was an excellent classical piano player, another thing that impressed Eubie about her.[48]

Eubie hadn't seen Avis since he left elementary school when he met her again around 1909 or 1910 while they were attending a picnic at Round Bay, about 20 miles south of Baltimore. Eubie was hanging out with a friend, Eddie "Eggie" Nealy (so nicknamed for his egg-shaped head), who was a waiter at the Goldfield Hotel. Nealy's girlfriend was a friend of Avis's, so the four ended up spending the day together. Eubie said he continued to date Avis over the next several months. One time, to impress her, he borrowed a car from the Goldfield's manager, Eddie Myers, hiring a chauffeur because he hadn't yet learned to drive, to take her out for the day. At the end of the day, on the way back to Avis's home, Eubie says he "pop[ped] the scagmo question"—in other words, he asked her to have sex with him. Eubie says that Avis replied, "I know all about you, Eubie Blake, and I know all about all your women. You better understand right now that that's not what I want out of life."[49] Faced with this ultimatum, Eubie says, he had "no choice" but to marry Avis a month later. Before the marriage, he had to pass muster with Avis's grandmother, who was skeptical about his ability to support Avis. "I make fifty-five dollars a week," Eubie assured her, "I can take care of her. She ain't going to spend more than fifty-five dollars a week."[50] (This was before tips; in 1910, the average worker was making 22 cents an hour, or about $10 to $11 a week.) Avis was skeptical about Eubie's intentions, so Eubie approached Joe Gans's wife Martha, who had attended high school with Avis, to put in a good word for him. Apparently that did the trick, and Avis agreed to travel with Eubie to Atlantic City in the summer of 1910. Although Avis was two years older than Eubie, she looked considerably younger, leading one of his employers to express concern that Eubie might be charged with transporting a minor across state lines. Perhaps for this reason, the couple quickly married, and Eubie carried their marriage certificate with him wherever he performed, to show that their marriage was legitimate.[51] As she was also light skinned, Eubie may have been concerned that he needed to be able to prove that they both were the same race, in case this issue came into question.

The well-educated Avis felt her family was definitely "higher class" than Blake's. Blake said that she called him "Dummy" throughout their marriage, because he had been thrown out of grade school while she was high-school educated. Blake contended that his mother's neighbors were surprised that he was able to land such a desirable woman. He said that—even after the marriage—his mother's Baltimore friends referred to her as "Avis Lee," not as "Avis Blake."[52] (Throughout his life, Eubie was attracted to better-educated people, both in his sex life and his business dealings. Both of his wives were well educated and savvy about business; and, as we shall see, his performing and composing partner Noble Sissle was college educated and handled all of the duo's business affairs.)

Atlantic City was a hopping summer resort during this time. "High society" from as far south as Washington and north to New York City and its environs would escape the heat there. The vibrant nightlife scene there attracted major pianists from the same area, including younger players like James P. Johnson and Fats Waller, and legends like Luckey Roberts. The clubs catering to blacks (and slumming whites interested in black culture) were all centered in a district about 20 blocks from the ocean. Eubie worked at several spots, notably Kelly's, which was typical of many small clubs in the area. Willie "The Lion" Smith recalled it as having a bar in the front room and a back room with tables seating about 70 or so customers.[53] In this club and others like it, Eubie was exposed to a higher caliber of competitor. He developed his own set of "tricks" in order to keep his rivals at bay, a habit that led to his first original compositions. While it's impossible to date specifically these pieces, it's likely that Eubie was already performing "Charleston Rag" (which, although he claimed he "composed" in 1899, more probably was developed around a decade later) and showstoppers like "Tricky Fingers" and "Troublesome Ivories." Eubie says he created other pieces during this period, including "Kitchen Tom," in honor of his favorite Atlantic City chef, who also played folk-style piano, and "Baltimore Todolo," based on the popular dance fad of the period. (A "todolo" or "toodle-oo" was a strutting dance step similar to the cakewalk; Duke Ellington later immortalized it in his "East St.

Louis Toodle-oo"). While primarily hired to accompany the house vocalists, Blake would play these pieces when they took a break.

Among the pianists who carefully studied Eubie's pianistic tricks was young James. P. Johnson. "Still in short pants," according to Blake, Johnson would sit next to Blake and "cop" his better tricks. At the time, Eubie ranked Johnson as a good working pianist, a "good house-rent player," but not of the first rank. However, Eubie came to regret teaching his better pieces like "Troublesome Ivories" to Johnson: "I'm sorry today that I used to play it for him, because he'd play it twice as fast as I could . . ."[54] While he had a longer reach than James P. Johnson, the latter "could speed faster [with his smaller hands], you don't have so far to go."

Johnson was suitably impressed with Eubie's skills when he first encountered him in the summer of 1914:

> I went for a visit to Atlantic City and heard Eubie Blake . . . one of the foremost pianists of all time . . . Eubie was a marvelous song player. He also had a couple of rags. One, "Troublesome Ivories," was very good. I caught it.
>
> I saw how Eubie . . . could play songs in all keys, so as to be ready for any singer—or if one of them started on a wrong note. So, I practiced that, too.[55]

Also on the Atlantic City scene was Charles "Luckey" Roberts. Born in Philadelphia approximately the same year as Eubie (like Eubie, Roberts gave different stories at different times as to his actual birthdate), Roberts was one of the most accomplished of the East Coast pianists. His first hit came in May 1913 with the publication of "Junk Man Rag."[56] The piece was advertised as a "one-step," as a means of promoting it with dancers. The song's publisher, Joseph Stern, placed a photo of the popular husband-and-wife dance duo Maurice and Florence Walton on the sheet's cover, claiming they "introduced" the piece to society; the Waltons were equal in popularity in their day to Vernon and Irene Castle, who were central—as we shall see—in establishing the career of James Reese Europe. Luckey said in one interview that he originally composed the piece in 1901—perhaps, like Eubie, pushing back the composition date to make the feat seem even more remarkable.[57] Unlike Eubie's "Charleston Rag," if we judge from an early recording by Roberts, Luckey's piece depends far more on "tricks" in the right hand, such as rapid sweeps up the keyboard, and borrows more heavily from standard figures heard in other early ragtime and jazz compositions. The actual publication was "arranged" by Artie Matthews, the well-known ragtime composer from St. Louis, who favored a politer, more toned-down style—like his mentor's Scott Joplin's—than the East Coasters performed. Not surprisingly, the published score is much barer than Robert's own recording, to accommodate amateur pianists.

"Junk Man" became a hit when its publisher, Joseph Stern, had lyrics added to it. Eubie noted that he began to hear it performed on Baltimore's streets by local organ grinders, a sure sign of its popularity.[58] Following its success, Roberts arranged for Eubie to have his first two published rags with Stern, "The Chevy Chase" (promoted as "a fox trot") and "Fizz Water" (labeled by the publisher as a "trot and one-step").

Ragtime scholars David A. Jasen and Trebor Tichenor note that "both of these early tunes . . . are in the mold of the popular one-step and foxtrot dance tunes of the teens." They incorporate the typical syncopated fox-trot rhythm found in many other dance numbers of the time.[59] Eubie was disappointed when Stern had arranger Stephen O. Jones "simplify" his pieces to make them easier for the amateur pianist to play. (Jones was a Broadway orchestrator of the 1910s and 1920s who worked for a number of Tin Pan Alley publishers.) Eubie complained to Stern, "I don't tell you people how to write *your* music . . . I think I ought to know my own style. . . ."[60] Eubie felt offended that a white arranger would have to "adapt" his music for a different audience. Nonetheless, the piece was published in this simplified arrangement. On his first published compositions, he was credited as "J. Hubert Blake ("Eubie")."

It's impossible to know how Eubie played these pieces himself, as they were "arranged" for publication and he didn't record either rag at the time. On the basis of the published scores, "Chevy Chase" is the more interesting of the two works, with a dramatic minor opening theme set against a contrasting major B section and jaunty trio. The piano effects—including dramatic stop time, unaccompanied right-hand riffs (in the opening), and Eubie's characteristic bass—all make this a memorable rag. "Fizz Water" is altogether more conventional, at least as it exists in score, sounding like a typical novelty piece of the era.

Eubie's contract with Stern was none too generous; he was paid $1.00 out of hand, along with a royalty of one cent per copy sold, for all rights to two piano solos. In the account statements that Eubie saved, in their first year "Chevy Chase" sold 1617 copies, earning him $16.17 in royalties, while the less popular "Fizz Water" managed to sell only 388 copies, earning him a meager $3.88.[61] In all likelihood, Stern trashed all copies after the first year's sales were so poor. (In comparison, Irving Berlin's 1909 hit "Alexander's Ragtime

Band" reportedly sold half a million copies in its first month of sale.[62]) Eubie quickly learned that writing virtuosic piano pieces was not a path to easy riches; even Roberts's "Junk Man Rag" became a hit only after it was wed with lyrics. Eubie's desire to write songs clearly was motivated partially by the fact that they could become major hits through their performance by vaudeville and Broadway stars. A tricky finger-buster was too good to capture the hearts and fingers of amateurs.

Eubie claimed that he also played for Stern another piece that he had adapted from pianist Hughie Woolford—a piece that would later become the major hit "Ragging the Scale."[63] As we already noted, Woolford was inspired to write the tune by Eubie's quip that he'd rag anything—including the scale. However, when Eubie played it for Stern, the publisher said, "Great, but who the hell can play it? You can't sell that," so passed on it. When "Ragging the Scale" became a major hit for white composer Edward Claypoole later in 1915, Eubie was justifiably irritated that someone else had scored on his idea, so he started to think about another simple theme he could "rag." The result was a collaboration with popular white composer Carey Morgan on a piece called "Bugle Call Rag," which Stern published to cash in on Claypoole's hit. Morgan is best-known today for composing pop ditties like "Sippin' Cider through a Straw." Although called a "rag" and published as a "fox trot," the piece's opening section is actually a march playing off the well-known short bugle melody used by the army to rouse the troops. Written in four parts— like most marches (and rags)—there are touches of syncopation in some parts and a few of Eubie's characteristic "trick" embellishments. Although it far outsold Eubie's own rags, it didn't match the success of Claypoole's number. "The novelty had worn off," Eubie said ruefully.

Atlantic City attracted many musicians and performers, including some old-timers who were hitmakers in their day but more or less forgotten by most people at this time. Eubie recalls meeting the African American composer James A. Bland—famous for composing the minstrel-style songs "Carry Me Back to Old Virginny" and "Oh, Dem Golden Slippers" some 20 years earlier—one night on the Boardwalk. Bland offered to take his younger peer out for a drink, and Eubie was surprised when he took him "past all the places the colored people could go safely, to this real high-class place. Now there's no colored people in here. Even the bartender is white, see." Bland and Eubie sat at the bar and had a few drinks, and then the older composer excused himself to go the men's room. Eubie waited a while, and then realized that the older man had skipped out on the bill. Lacking enough money to pay for them both, Eubie talked the bartender into letting him pay just his tab. Bland was undoubtedly down on his luck and took advantage of Eubie in order to get a few free drinks at his expense.[64]

Throughout this period, Eubie often worked with a partner, a comedian/singer/songwriter named Madison Reed.[65] Reed was born to a farming family in Boykins, Virginia (on the North Carolina border) around 1875; his first notice as a professional singer occurred in Washington, DC, in 1900.[66] By mid-decade, Reed was working in Baltimore as a member of the Dixie Serenaders, then a vocal quartet, and also performing as a soloist. Blake recalled that Reed's act included cross-dressing (he worked as a "wench" comic in Blake's words, "but he was a real man"[67]). Blake said that Reed's big number was a song about a local celebrity named Hannah Elias, a black woman who took up with a prominent white politician. Blake partnered with Reed for work in both Baltimore and during the summers in Atlantic City. Reed was an ideal frontman for Eubie, who was just learning how to be an entertainer; Eubie recalled, "He was a great floor man.... A floor man ... stands on the floor while the pianist plays and he sings and tells jokes, they call them MCs now."[68] Willie "The Lion" Smith recalled hearing them work, noting that Reed carried a song list "almost as long as the piano keyboard," with all the songs he knew, including the keys in which he sang them. The Lion was particularly impressed that Eubie could accompany any one that Reed sang, in the key of his choice.[69] Blake also recalled accompanying singers Mary Stafford, Mabel Richardson, Mary Strange, Lottie Dempsey, and "Big Lizzie." Stafford was perhaps the best known of the group, generally credited as the first female blues singer to record for the major label Columbia in 1921. Although she recorded blues, Stafford sounds more like a big-lunged cabaret singer on these records, probably reflecting her career of singing in barrooms and nightspots like those in Atlantic City; Blake compared her voice to Kate Smith's, saying she had a similar brassy delivery.

Patrons would throw change at the singers while they were performing, and Eubie made it his business to keep a careful count of the coins as they landed, to be certain he got his cut of the tips. He had the front of his piano "glazed" (shined like a mirror) so he could keep an eye on the money flowing in:

I could look right at my piano and see where the money was going. So, when they'd throw the money on the floor ... I used to count the money—pip-pip-pip—I'm playing and I'm listening.... I counted as fast as that thing hit the floor. Now what used to jam [confuse] me was when the gamblers come in with the money bags, see, in Atlantic City. They take a handful of quarters throw a handful of quarters, and they'd jam me . . . I couldn't count that many.[70]

Blake also met the younger white songwriters from New York during his time performing in Atlantic City, including Irving Berlin. Berlin's "Alexander's Ragtime Band" was a major hit in this era, and patrons requested the song so often that Blake said that he and partner Madison Reed would perform it between 10 and 20 times a night. The two were popular enough that New York's Tin Pan Alley publishers made sure they had access to their latest songs:

The publishers used to send around professional copies of new tunes, and I always had a stack this thick [indicates two inches] of bran' new music. Madison goes through the stack and picks out the ones he wants to sing, and one of 'em is "Alexander's Ragtime Band." Now I already knew Izzy [Irving Berlin] because he used to hang around the Boathouse [one of the Atlantic City clubs where Eubie played] asking me to play his songs, and I always did because they were very good. . . . He used to come by the place wearing his little derby hat and his yellow . . . pointed shoes, and he'd say in his raggedy voice, "Hey Eubie, play my tune, play my tune!"[71]

"He was the saddest looking fellow I've ever seen. He looked so thin and hungry that I felt sorry for him," Blake said of the young composer.[72]

Another Broadway star who hung out summers in Atlantic City was George M. Cohan, then just at the start of his career. Eubie claimed that Cohan would often stop by the club where he was playing, and would perform his songs to Eubie's accompaniments. Eubie said that Cohan gave him a particularly valuable piece of advice: He should never write to impress his fellow composers, but instead "write simply so that little working girl can carry your tune."[73] Cohan also told him that, if he was lucky enough to form a successful partnership with a singer, "you'll *hate* him, but if you're a success, stick with [him] until the day you die . . . Take anything he puts on you, but never walk away from success."[74]

Eubie also hobnobbed with other celebrities in Atlantic City, black and white. He said he first met fighter Jack Johnson there, who was celebrated in the black community for both his pugilistic prowess and the fact that he openly traveled with his white mistress—at a time of strong racial prejudice. Eubie claimed that Johnson's flaunting of the color line was one factor that led to the drying up of performing opportunities for blacks on Broadway at the time.[75]

Eubie's status as a working musician in Baltimore continued to grow through the mid-1910s. He appeared at several major concerts, making his first appearance in the press (albeit the reporter misspelled his name as "Rubie Blake"). The performance that drew press notice was produced by Ford Dabney. It was a benefit concert for Baltimore's Provident Hospital—the "only place in Maryland where colored physicians can treat their patients"[76]—staged in July 1913, an event that included Eubie accompanying Madison Reed, among other performers, including Baltimore's Dixie Serenaders (with whom Eubie would perform in the summer of 1915), Will Marion Cook, Abbie Mitchell, and future *Shuffle Along* star—and Blake mistress—Lottie Gee, then working with a partner, Effie King.[77] *The New York Age* reported that the benefit drew "Baltimore's [African American] elite," adding "Society was out in force and the boxes were occupied by Baltimore's most beautiful women, whose gowns, flowers and jewels added but little to their own natural charms."[78] The sold-out benefit raised $600 for the hospital.

Early in 1915, Blake formed a small dance band of his own to play for dance classes at a Baltimore fraternity hall.[79] In addition to Blake on the piano, the group included trumpeter Clifton "Pike" Davis (who later recorded with Ellington and Leroy Smith, and appeared with the Plantation Orchestra along with Florence Mills in London in the 1920s[80]); clarinetist Clifton "Hawk" Dorsey (who previously played with the minstrel company Woodbury's Black American Troubadours[81]); banjo player Herbert Faulkner; drummer Ike Dixon (who would lead a band working local Baltimore clubs and dance halls from 1920 to 1934 before opening his own nightclub[82]); and vocalist Theodore Upshur. Eubie told jazz historian John S. Wilson that he often had to work without a drummer when playing at local dance halls, having only "a fellow playing a triangle tied to the back of a chair." This was another reason he said that he had to develop a powerful left hand, to keep a steady rhythm for the dancers.[83]

Elmer Snowden later replaced Faulkner on banjo; Snowden and Faulkner were both native Baltimoreans and had been taught to play banjo and mandolin by Faulkner's father. As preteens, they had played and sang popular songs outside of bars and clubs for tips. Snowden was about 15 years old when he was introduced to Blake:

> "Bring him up here," [Blake] said, "And let me hear him." He was playing at the Pythian Castle, a fraternity place, where they had a dance floor and a man teaching dancing. . . . Eubie [led] the band, about five pieces. So he got me to come in on banjo. I . . . couldn't read, but I had a very quick ear and could play anything.[84]

After moving to New York in 1916, Eubie left the band and pianist Joe Rochester replaced him as its leader. Snowden said that Rochester's day job was working as an undertaker and—unlike Eubie—he was a fairly primitive pianist, playing only on the black keys.[85] The Rochester-led band got gigs in Washington, DC, where a young Duke Ellington heard them play. Snowden admired Ellington and would later hire him as the pianist for his own band in the early 1920s.

Besides leading this band, Eubie joined one of the more successful locals, Joe Porter's Dixie Serenaders (Figure 2.2), as their pianist, also around 1914 to 1915. The group had between four and seven members, depending on the date and availability of musicians, playing a variety of banjos (tenors, banjo-mandolins, and banjo-ukes), guitars, and piano and bass, with a vocalist and drummer. Some of the players must have doubled as singers because contemporary reviews mention that besides playing dance music the group also performed vocal quartets. A photo of the group appears on a contemporary piece of sheet music, "Won't You Let Me Call You Honey?," composed and self-published by Lester Charles Reimer of Atlantic City. On the sheet, they are credited as having been members of the *Red Moon* company, Cole and Johnson's last touring show, presumably as members of the show's orchestra (no known members are listed among the featured players in the show itself). However, it is interesting to note that the *Red Moon*'s music director was James Reese Europe, who later would be a mentor to Blake.[86] Europe also co-composed several songs for the second edition of the show in 1909.

With other national touring groups having similar names, it is difficult to exactly track the group's history, but it appears that as early as 1910 the Dixie Serenaders were appearing in the basement bar of the Hotel Kernan in Baltimore. In 1911, they had a summer residency at a seaside resort in Neptune, New Jersey, appearing from the park's opening day "until the last run of crabs and complete exhau[s]tion of river sea food requires the annual

Figure 2.2 Porter's Dixie Serenaders on the cover of a locally published sheet, c. 1916. Porter may be the man standing in rear center behind the banjo-mandolin player; the other musicians are unknown.

fall closing" of the resort.[87] Besides their regular work at the Kernan hotel, the group was hired to entertain private parties and dances, performing at a dinner attended by "Diamond" Jim Brady when he visited town.[88] The group even entertained at Baltimore's prison and for a Christmas concert for "local cripples." The Serenaders announced a planned European tour scheduled for six weeks in the spring of 1913; among its members at that time was vocalist "J. Madison Reed," Blake's partner, but not Eubie.[89]

Between 1912 and 1916, Porter's band performed regularly during the summer season at the popular Riverview Park, which city dwellers could easily visit, thanks to a regular streetcar line that served it. The trip took 20 minutes from downtown Baltimore. The 50-acre park did not charge an admission fee, advertising that the nickel street car fare was all that was required to attend. In 1915, the Park was totally refurbished, including the installation of a Ferris wheel that was 100 feet tall and featured 3500 electric lights.[90] Other attractions included pony rides, novelty animal acts (including dancing bears from time to time), a miniature train that ran through the park, and nightly firework displays, along with opportunities for swimming, boating, and even bowling.

The park featured a band shell where military band concerts and singers performed; a separate "Vienna garden" featured a string quartet. Porter's "popular group of Negro singers and musicians" performed both in the garden-restaurant area and in the band shell, when the featured act, the "Royal Artillery Band, led by the world's greatest Trombone Soloist, Sig. Salvatore Orriunno" took its breaks.[91] Advertisements noted that "the man who sings with the [military] band,"[92] Eddie Nelson, was a featured performer; as we will see, Nelson would play a key role in helping to author Blake's first published song. The white singer Nelson lived in Baltimore and was "well known to the patrons of the dancing pavilions of many summer resorts" in Maryland.[93]

It's not entirely clear when Blake first joined Porter's outfit, or even if he was a permanent member or simply was added on an as-needed basis from time to time. However, he definitely was working with the group in the summer of 1915 at the park when Porter invited a newcomer to the Baltimore area to join the band: vocalist Noble Sissle. Their meeting launched one of the key partnerships in American popular music.

3

Blake Meets Sissle

1915–1919

In mid-May of 1915, a new vocalist arrived at Joe Porter's office to join the Dixie Serenaders: Noble Sissle. As Sissle was walking up the stairs, Porter and Eubie Blake were coming down, getting ready to travel to Riverview Park to play an engagement. Porter quickly introduced the two men; on hearing the name Noble Sissle, Eubie recalled that he had seen Sissle's name before on a piece of sheet music: "I said, 'Didn't I see your name on a song?' He says, 'Yeah.' And I says, 'Well, I'm looking for a lyricist.' And we shook hands."[1] With that handshake, a musical partnership was born.

Sissle was born in Indianapolis on July 10, 1889, the son of George A. Sissle, a minister and organist at the African Methodist Episcopal (AME) Chapel. His mother, Martha, worked in the Indianapolis school system as a teacher and juvenile probation officer. His parents were solidly middle class, and instilled in their children the ideals of Booker T. Washington and other African American leaders that they should aspire to acquire the diction, manners, and general deportment of white America. When Noble joined the choir of his father's church, Sissle discovered he had a good voice.

In 1910,[2] Noble moved with his family to Cleveland, Ohio, where he was one of the six black students to attend the Central High School. While there, Sissle established the school's glee club and was active on its baseball and football teams. Sissle mixed easily with his white schoolmates and claimed to not encounter any prejudice either in high school or later in college. Eubie often commented on the ease with which Sissle fit in with white society, enjoying a level of comfort with whites that Blake himself could not quite achieve. Sissle attended college, first at DePauw University in Greencastle, Indiana, and then at Indianapolis's Butler University in 1914 and 1915, where he studied to become a minister.

In order to make money for tuition, during summer breaks Sissle toured the Midwest evangelical Chautauqua circuit with the Edward Thomas Male Quartet, and then, around 1911 or 1912, he joined Hann's Jubilee

Eubie Blake. Richard Carlin and Ken Bloom, Oxford University Press (2020). © Richard Carlin and Ken Bloom 2020.
DOI: 10.1093/oso/9780190635930.001.0001

Singers under the direction of William A. Hann. Sissle traveled as far east as New York and west to Denver with this group.[3] Hann later formed the group The Four Harmony Kings to perform on the vaudeville circuit, with Hann as its bass singer, and Ivan Harold Browning as the group's tenor. They would later be featured performers in Sissle and Blake's major Broadway hit, *Shuffle Along*.[4]

As early as 1912, Sissle was beginning to make a name for himself. The Indianapolis *Freeman* featured a photo of Sissle with the caption "Cleveland's Famous Tenor Boy."[5] Two years later, the paper published a review of Sissle's New Year's Eve recital. Sissle sang a selection of popular and semiclassical numbers—none drawing on his African American roots—including "Ave Maria," a revised version of Reginald De Koven's "Oh Promise Me," "Rose in the Bud," "I Know Two Bright Eyes," and a "Spanish"-flavored song, "Nita Gitana."[6]

In early 1915, while in Indianapolis, Sissle was asked to make up a society dance orchestra to perform at the Severin Hotel. According to an interview with Sissle from 1942, he "had heard several colored bands in the big spots of the big cities. These bands were playing a new kind of music that had four beats to the bar. And, most amazing of all was the fact that people were crazy about it. He had to have such a band."[7] These dance orchestras marked the first evolution from the world of traditional dance bands and the emergence of syncopation. Sissle's Hoosier Society Orchestra offered "regular New York style entertainment."[8] The band consisted of a violin, mandolin, piano, and saxophone with Sissle, who could not actually play an instrument, doing his best to play the trap drums.

Sometime during the late spring and summer of 1915, Sissle travelled to Baltimore, where he was hired as a vocalist by Joe Porter's Serenaders to replace another singer, Frank Brown, as Eubie recalled:

[Brown] used to be with [the Broadway composing/acting duo] Cole and Johnson, and he had a very jealous wife. And they worked in cabarets. [They] work[ed] in white face. And when Frank would walk out on that floor, the white women would go, "Ooooohhh." And the white men didn't like it. . . . So [his wife] wouldn't let her husband come to Baltimore. So Sissle came in his place.

Besides being the vocalist, Sissle played bandolin (a hybrid of a mandolin with a banjo head) with Porter's group, handling the rhythm part. Blake commented, "He was a real musician, but he couldn't play [melody on] the banjo. [He played chords:] plunk, plunk, plunk, just like that."[9]

Sissle and Blake worked together through the summer and early fall in Porter's group. During this period, the duo wrote their first song, "It's All Your Fault," with some help from white singer Eddie Nelson on the lyrics.[10] (Nelson was singing at River View Park at the same time Sissle and Blake were performing there with Porter's band.) Sissle successfully pitched the song to vaudeville singer Sophie Tucker when she was appearing in town at the Maryland Theater that August. Blake admitted that he lacked Sissle's gumption to approach this major star with their song:

> Sissle says, "Let's take the song up to Miss Tucker." I said, "Oh, man, you can't go to Sophie Tucker, the big star. What are you talking about?" He says, "She can't kill us; let's try." Sissle was more aggressive than I was. He was a fighter, he's a go-getter. I never was that way. If you didn't like my music, I just took it and walked away, but he argued with you and sell it to you. He was a good salesman. So we went up to see Miss Tucker. . . .
>
> So Sissle says, "Will you listen to a song?" [Tucker said,] "Yes, yes, yes, go ahead, go ahead." She's a big star, you know. We weren't nothing. . . . So we sang it. She said, "I like that song, I like it, I like it. I'll get orchestrations made this week and do it." This was on a Monday. On a Wednesday or Thursday, she had [the] orchestrations ready. We didn't pay for it. I couldn't make no orchestrations then. You are supposed to make orchestrations and give it to her if people are going to sing the stuff for you. . . . [but] she said "I'll have some boys in the band make an orchestration and we'll put it on."[11]

Tucker performed the song on stage on August 21, 1915, which the sheet's publisher, the Maryland Music Co., proudly announced in an advertisement in the *Baltimore Sun*. The ad described it as "[a] triumph of the country in Songland, an unprecedented success, such as has never been."[12] This appears to have been pure puffery, as the song didn't catch on much beyond Baltimore, according to Blake:

> I'll bet you there wasn't 10 people in Washington, that's only 44 miles away, ever heard that song. But everybody in [Baltimore] sang it. We got a hit on our hands! We think it's a hit. Nobody heard it but in Baltimore. They bought it. I guess it sold about 30,000 copies.[13]

It must have been sufficiently popular to warrant several printings, as it appeared with at least three different covers, the most common featuring Tucker's photo (Figure 3.1). A fancier illustrated cover featured an inset photo of Nelson. It was available in both a piano-vocal arrangement and a four-part harmony setting for vocal groups. Unlike many other songs composed by black lyricists in this period, it is not written in dialect, nor is the

Figure 3.1 Sophie Tucker on the cover of one of Sissle and Blake's first published songs, "It's All Your Fault." The sheet was issued by a small Baltimore-based music publisher and gained local success.

topic stereotypically "black." It is a fairly conventional love song, which could easily have been written by a white composer. Sissle and Blake's aim was to write popular songs that would appeal to a broad audience; and while some of their early songs reflect black stereotypes, most are conventional in structure and subject matter.

Of course, Tucker was known as a "coon shouter," a reputation that undoubtedly influenced how the song was received. In 1912, a reporter from the Baltimore *Evening Sun* asked her how she became an expert at singing "coon songs," surmising that she must have been born in the South. Tucker quickly corrected his misconception: "Don't you know I am a Jewess and that I was born in Hartford, Conn.? . . . I know no more about the negroes than an Eskimo, but I guess I am just a natural-born singer of coon songs."[14] In her appearances in Baltimore over the next few years, critics universally applauded her ability to make such "vulgar" material attractive to a white audience. Tucker also performed a second song composed by the duo, "Have a Good Time, Everybody," and their fortunes slowly improved.

Another song from this period—just credited to Sissle and Blake—is "My Loving Baby," published in 1916 just after "It's All Your Fault." The cover touts it as "a tremendous song success" that was performed by Irene and Bobby Smith, a sister act billed as "two girls and a piano."[15] The sisters' photo also appear on some printings of "It's All Your Fault," so perhaps they had an arrangement with the publisher to use their photo as a means to promote their act. Or perhaps, because they had local success, the publisher hoped their picture would help sell these songs. In any case, "My Loving Baby" sold few copies, and the sheet itself is very rare. However, it is important in the history of the songwriters. Ragtime scholar David A. Jasen found a copy in the 1970s, and upon playing it discovered that the chorus's lyrics were lifted nearly intact for the duo's later hit, "I'm Just Wild about Harry." When he asked Eubie about it, the composer had no memory of the song or this later recycling.[16] However, it is not unusual for composers to recycle earlier lyrics or even melodic ideas (particularly from songs that failed to attract notice) as source material for later works.

Sissle's success in Baltimore did not go unnoticed back in his home state of Ohio. The *Xenia Daily Gazette* noted that he was

making it nicely in Baltimore. He is entertaining at the Hotel Kernan [where Porter's group regularly played] and also writing lyrics as a side issue. His songs are meeting with success. The well known Sophie Tucker is at present using two of his compositions, which is very complimentary to Sissle. The music of the two songs are by Edward [actually Edgar] Dowell and Eubie Blake, young men of Baltimore, and of whom Sissle has a good opinion of their ability.[17]

This short notice sounds suspiciously as if it were written by Sissle himself, as his fame was fairly limited at this point in his career. Edgar Dowell was also an African American composer, later known for his jazz-flavored songs and instrumentals; among his later collaborators was Andy Razaf, who also wrote lyrics for Blake.

Blake's initial songwriting success and his continuing career on the local scene must have made him feel secure enough to purchase a house for his mother and adopted sister. The family had previously only rented lodgings, so this was a considerable move up in the world. Emma Blake would remain in the house at 915 Rutland Avenue, on the east side of town, until her death. Eubie continued to pay the mortgage, repairs, and local taxes—although he sometimes waited until receiving a final notice to scrape together the money needed to keep the town from putting the house up for auction.[18]

The October 9, 1915, edition of the Indianapolis *Freeman* reported that Sissle and Blake were playing in DC at the Howard Theatre's Sunday supper show and the "two very talented young men . . . gave a knockout piano and singing act." The *Freeman* also informed their readers that the duo sang "It's All Your Fault" and "Have a Good Time, Everybody," and Eubie played his "famous fox-trot Chevy Chase." Just one week earlier, Will Marion Cook's musical *Darkydom* opened in the same theater, featuring Flournoy Miller and Aubrey Lyles in the cast. Toward the end of its run, James Reese Europe replaced Cook in the orchestra pit. Whether Sissle and Blake met Miller and Lyles, or Cook and Europe at this time is unknown.

In December 1915, Bob Young—Porter's drummer—landed a job playing at the Royal Poinciana Hotel in Palm Beach, Florida, and took Sissle with him as vocalist.[19] If we can judge from a photo taken at the hotel, Young's group was a string band led by tenor banjo and banjo-mandolin on melody, with accompaniment on piano, second banjo (played by Sissle), and drums. Young's band kept up a classy appearance, always appearing in formal dress. For whatever reason, Eubie elected to remain in Baltimore, continuing to work with his own band and as a solo pianist.[20]

The highlight of the season at the Royal Poinciana was its Washington Birthday ball; this elaborate event was attended by the crème de la crème of high society wintering in Palm Beach. Over 3000 people attended in February 1916; a contemporary report focused on the lavish decorations, including floral displays on the theme of "a Hawaiian garden," decorated thus:

> in the center of the ceiling . . . [hung] a large medallion, symbolizing a tropical moon, the ever-changing lights shifting from sunset to moonlight effects. At either side of this moon were a series of canopies of lattice covered with southern smilax and large pink roses. Beneath these canopies hung large Hawaiian lanterns of mogi wood, illuminated with electric lights.

Although there is no description of the band accompanying this dinner dance, it obviously was the focal point of the evening:

> The seated supper was served at midnight and there were innovation [*sic*] favors from Paris—gay head-dresses of every description, butterflies, parasols and noise-makers galore. During the midnight dance preceding the supper there was a battle of confetti and thousands of yards of streamers were thrown upon the dancers from above.[21]

Sissle later said that that he met several leaders of New York society (the Wanamakers, Astors, Warburtons, and Harrimans) while he was performing at the hotel. Afterward at another society event for the benefit of the Red Cross, Young's ensemble along with Sissle accompanied Broadway star Nora Bayes. In attendance was theater magnate E. F. Albee of the Keith-Albee vaudeville circuit. He booked them into the pinnacle of vaudeville, New York's Palace Theatre, for a "Palm Beach Week." They were the first African Americans to perform at the Palace without the use of blackface. After appearing at another Palm Beach society event, the Washington Birthday Ball, Mary Brown Warburton gave Sissle a letter of introduction to bandleader James Reese Europe. Sissle travelled to New York after the winter season ended and soon was within Europe's orbit.

James Reese Europe was a key figure in the development of African American popular music on the New York scene. He was born in Mobile, Alabama, on February 22, 1880, to a middle-class black family. The family moved to Washington when Europe was ten, and as a young teen he established himself as an up-and-coming classical violinist. His teacher was Joseph Douglass, the son of noted African American author Frederick Douglass and himself a well-known performer in the black community. Coming to New York to pursue his career in 1899, Europe found the classical-music world closed to him because of his color. Instead, he started to work in local cafes and barrooms, but found it hard to compete as a solo violinist. In an unpublished memoir of Europe written later by Sissle, he described how Europe struggled in his early New York days as he tried to establish himself as a musician:

> In those days the Negroes who worked for the wealthy white people were mostly singers and dancers, and the instruments they played were mandolins and guitars. It was this fact that kept [Jim] out of work . . . It was weeks before he woke up to the fact that it was the instrument he played [the violin] that was keeping him from the "Big Money" he had dreamed of . . . He was at the point when he must either give up the fiddle or face starvation, so . . . [he laid] down his favorite instrument and [took] up the mandolin. . . . Having also been accomplished in piano playing, between the two, he easily got work, and with his organizing ability, it was not longer before he had organized a quartette of players and singers. Before many months had rolled around, we find him . . . the official musician in the famous Wanamaker Family, which, as Jim often declared was the beginning of his becoming the society favorite of Music producers in the drawing-rooms of New York's Four Hundred.[22]

Europe's quartet often performed in the bar at the Marshall Hotel on 53rd Street, then the major spot for black musicians seeking work to be heard by members of society. As Sissle recalled,

> It was a famous Black and Tan resort that the Elite of New York usually patronized on slumming expeditions. . . . [T]here were very seldom any colored patrons there except musicians. Mainly because the prices charged for wine and food were prohibitive for most colored people. It was, however, a place frequented by musicians and entertainers . . . It was well worth while to come in and give their services because Marshall (who was a Negro) would feed them and the money given them by the wealthy patrons [as tips] was a good amount. In most instances, the [white] guests engaged them for future entertainment . . . There were suites of rooms above the café and these were occupied by such famous stars as Williams and Walker, also Cole and Johnson. And Paul Lawrence Dunbar. It was quite often they

would be brought down to the different parties that frequented the place. It was in this way that the great stars met and knew so many of the people whose names stand high in the list of "Who's Who."[23]

John Love, working as secretary to the mighty Wanamaker family, first heard Europe's group performing at the Marshall in 1903, and soon hired him to play for the family's many social affairs, from weddings to farewell parties before the family embarked on its annual jaunts to Europe. Love noted that "Mr. Rodman Wanamaker was a man of marked tolerance," a veiled allusion to his willingness to hire black musicians, "but he cannot tolerate mediocrity," showing that his regular employment of Europe's band was a reflection of "the excellence of [Europe's] work."[24] Europe probably met the major theatrical stars of the day at the Marshall, and was soon working as a bandleader for Bert Williams and George Walker and for Bob Cole and J. Rosamond Johnson. He served as musical director for Cole and Johnson's successful productions of *The Shoo-Fly Regiment* (1906) and its follow-up *The Red Moon* (1908). In 1908, Ernest Hogan, one of the most popular comedians of his day, suffered a nervous breakdown. Europe arranged for a benefit performance to help the ailing performer. The event was so successful the musicians joined together and created a fraternal club, The Frogs, to benefit African American performers. Europe became a leading member of the organization, appearing at their annual "frolick" in 1910. He also collaborated with other leading black songwriters of the day.

Recognizing the poor conditions faced by blacks seeking employment in New York, Europe established a kind of musician's union/booking agency/ concert promotion and performing organization called the Clef Club in 1910. The purpose was to offer white patrons a central office where they could book the highest-quality black musicians who, they would know, were vetted for both their talent and reliability. Europe felt it was demeaning to have to rely on chance encounters in noisy clubs like the Marshall Café to find work; plus, he found it embarrassing when asked by his patrons for his contact information only to have to tell them he could be reached only at some lowly barroom. As Sissle recalled, "It was galling for him . . . to have to give the address of some café or saloon, because there were many people of that set that would not like to be calling up those kind of places. . . . "[25] In order to raise money for a permanent home office for the club, Europe determined the best thing to do was to put on a concert that would showcase its members' talents: "He felt sure that from his experience with the [white society] people he had been entertaining," Sissle said,

> that a big male chorus and stringed orchestra, with instrumentations such as his fellow musicians had been using, on a small scale ought to prove a big drawing-power for the elite. That is providing the concert was given in a place that those people were used to attending. . . . Jim [en]visioned a crowd and an income of finance that would enable the Club to get its own Club room, and Headquarters, thus putting their entertaining on a more dignified plane.[26]

Europe bought a house at 136 West 53rd Street to serve as the club's head-quarters, which was incorporated on June 21, 1910. The club soon had 200 members (women were not allowed to join or come into the clubhouse). James Weldon Johnson described the Club:

> [James Reese Europe] gathered all the coloured professional instrumental musicians into a chartered organization and systematized the whole busi-ness of "entertaining." The organization purchased a house . . . and fitted it up as a club and also as booking-offices. Bands from three to thirty men could be furnished any time, day or night. The Clef Club for quite a while held a monopoly of the business of "entertaining" private parties and fur-nishing music for the dance craze, which was just then beginning to seep the country. One year the amount of business done amounted to $120,000.[27]

In fact, the Clef Club was able to organize several grand concerts, with an orchestra numbering as many as 75 to 200 pieces, primarily made up of banjos, mandolins, and guitars, the instruments most in use by black performers of the day. These stringed instruments were portable and able to take the place of a piano when some white households wouldn't let the musicians use their pianos. Europe recalled his frustration trying to get the band together for rehearsal; without offering any pay, he couldn't be sure that the same musicians would show up each time, and he often had to show the players how to finger the notes of each passage, as many did not read music.[28] Europe described how he solved this problem: "I always put a man who can read notes in the middle where the others can pick him up."[29] In 1910, an en-semble of 100 pieces appeared at the uptown Manhattan Casino, located at 155th Street and 8th Avenue, in a concert advertised as a "musical mélange and dance fest."[30] Their follow-up show in 1911 at the same venue was highly praised by well-known black critic/dramatist Lester A. Walton, who regularly reviewed and encouraged black performers for the African American newspaper *The New York Age* during this period. Walton praised Europe's judgment for not only including "classical" works but also devoting a portion of the program to a minstrel-show revue. Walton scolded those who shunned popular entertainment in their efforts to "uplift" black performers:

> The success of the Clef Club should serve as a lesson to those musicians who have been wont to give musical entertainments which have savored only of the classics, grand operas and the like. My argument always has been that while the public appreciates dramatic compositions, etc., it is unwise to present a musical program containing classical numbers only. The Clef Club fell into instant popularity for two reasons—because of the praiseworthy manner in which the numbers were rendered and by reason of the good judgment in selecting the numbers. So there should be no argument as to what the public wants. The success of the Clef Club is the answer.[31]

To underscore his point, Walton reproduced the evening's entire program in his column, showing that they performed a range of works primarily by African American composers, including Harry T. Burleigh, William H. Tyers, Will Marion Cook, and Europe himself in the "classical" style of the day, along with more popular numbers by Ford Dabney and minstrel-style and "jubilee" (spirituals) numbers.

Europe's crowning achievement with the Club came when he was able to book a show for them at New York's prestigious Carnegie Hall in May 1912. The concert was to benefit the Music School Settlement for Colored People, a proposed new conservatory for black musicians being promoted by David Mannes, a white violinist. The band that Europe put together for this concert featured, in his words, "20 pianos, 60 guitars, 14 cel[l]i, and 20 basses, and I had one man on the pipe organ, and all he was to play was the deepest bass tones. Among the two hundred pieces, was every kind of instruments you ever heard of, but all balanced according to my idea of instrumentation for effective interpretation of the kind of music we were to play."[32] The primary lead instruments remained banjos and mandolins, probably in similar numbers as the guitarists providing accompaniment.

Walton again lavished the group with praise, and was particularly pleased that they had appeared before a racially mixed audience without any separation of the races: "Some of the leading white citizens sat in evening dress in seats next to some of our highly respectable colored citizens, who were also in evening clothes. No color line was drawn in any part of the house, both white and colored occupying boxes. . . ." To underscore his point, Walton added ironically, "No calamity occurred because the colored citizens were not segregated in certain parts of the house."[33] Walton noted that the white audience listened respectfully but without passion to the music being performed, until the band played William Tyers's "Panama," a syncopated dance tune:

> White men and women then looked at each and other and smiled, while one lady seated in a prominent box began to beat time industriously with her right hand, which was covered with many costly gems. It was then that after a brief soliloquy I was forced to conclude that despite the adverse criticism of many who are unable to play it that syncopation is truly a native product—a style of music of which the Negro is originator, but which is generally popular with all Americans.[34]

Here again Walton was implicitly scolding critics—both white and black—who believed that black musicians should emulate the best "European" models in order to prove their worthiness to white audiences. Recognizing the popularity of syncopated dance music, Walton saw in it the true path for blacks to win acceptance as the equals—if not superior to—white composers and performers. Walton noted that Will Marion Cook's "Swing Along!" was performed three times due to the great audience response and was "the hit of the program." The song became an anthem for African Americans seeking equality in the highly segregated society of the day. According to Sissle, Cook had been a reluctant participant in the Club's concerts. Having a strong ego and being known for his hot temper, Cook may have resented Europe's role as a leader in the black musical community that he felt rightfully belonged to himself.

New York's mainstream (white) press greeted the concert with some amount of wonder and skepticism. The *Brooklyn Daily Eagle* gave a generally favorable review to the performance, although its critic seemed surprised that the music had "little of the minor feeling, which might have been expected, judging from the weird slave songs of the South." He praised Europe and William H. Tyers as conductors, although he found the orchestra had "a superabundance of shading" (an unfortunate use of this musical term), "yet a glory of tone makes up for it, in part."[35] This critic seemed unwilling to give unqualified praise to the concert, although he did single out Will Marion Cook's "Swing Along!" and Cook's handling of the choir that performed it.

Similarly, *The New York Times* lamented the lack of "the real Negro spirit" in the performers or the music. Seemingly uncomfortable with the notion of black musicians playing and singing classical styled music, the *Times'* critic described the entire event as featuring "as odd a collection of instruments as were ever gathered together . . . Where the violinists of the Philharmonic Society usually sit were gathered a formidable army of banjoist[s]. . . ." The critic enjoyed most the performance of "traditional negro melodies" on the program, primarily well-known spirituals sung by members of the chorus, although he faulted them for failing to make "much attempt to interpret the songs in the traditional negro manner." [36]

The Victor Talking Machine Company was one of the first labels to sign black performers. Among them were the Fisk University Jubilee Quartet, the Tuskegee Institute Singers, and comic Charley Case. In 1913, Victor signed Europe's Society Orchestra, the first African American band to record for a top company. Victor advertised the records as containing, "The Tango, Maxixe, Turkey Trot, Hesitation, Boston, One-Step, Two-Step—all . . . selections [that] are . . . now most in demand in dancing circles."[37] Because Europe wasn't known farther west than the Hudson River, Victor touted Europe's resume: "During the past three seasons Europe's Society Orchestra of Negro musicians has become very popular in society circles in New York and vicinity, and has played for social affairs in the homes of wealthy New Yorkers and at functions at the Tuxedo Club, Hotel Biltmore, Plaza, Sherry's, Delmonico's, the Astor and others. Mrs. R.W. Hawksworth, the famous purveyor of amusements for society, used the Europe players regularly, and they have recently been engaged to play for Mr. Vernon Castle, the popular teacher and exponent of modern dances."[38]

Around 1914, Europe along with his assistant, musician Ford T. Dabney, left the Clef Club due to infighting among its members. Dabney came from a prestigious musical family and was best known for writing the 1910 song "That's Why They Call Me Shine," along with lyricist Cecil Mack. He had met Europe in 1909 and they shared conducting jobs for the team of Bert Williams and George Walker. After leaving the Clef Club, they established the Tempo Club with Dabney as vice president and formed the New National Negro Orchestra, of which Europe was the conductor. Dabney went on to distinguish himself as the leader of Florenz Ziegfeld's New Amsterdam Roof nightclub, becoming the first black orchestra to have a regular "gig" in a white production.[39]

But Europe's most important association of the period was with the popular dancers Vernon and Irene Castle. In 1914, Europe and the Castles played the Manhattan Casino in a Midnight Frolic and were an immediate sensation. They followed the engagement with a tour of the country, visiting 35 cities in 28 days.[40] Later that year, Europe and the Castles were contracted to tour Europe with a 40-piece band, but war broke out and the tour was canceled. The Castles helped introduce new dance styles to New York's white elite. And, by employing James Reese Europe and his band for many of their demonstration-concerts, they helped legitimize black music for a white audience. They also helped popularize his music, employing him as a composer for many of their most famous dance numbers (many cowritten with Dabney).

According to Noble Sissle, when he first worked with Europe to accompany the Castles' dance classes, he was amused by the fact that all the dances were performed at the same fast tempo. Sissle said the Castles focused on the fast one-step because

> it's very easy, because all Europeans, especially the Irish, had that same fast tempo . . . So Mr. Castle, he realized, these people do the One-Step 'cause their dance numbers are "Roll Out the Barrel," all those things, and it's easy to just keep on doing that. They used to teach them some fancy steps at that tempo. The One-Steps were fast; the whole country was doing the One-Steps. They were runnin' wild; they was flyin', see.[41]

Sissle was worried that the energetic one-step would eventually exhaust its popularity, so he said he suggested to Europe that they try a different approach:

> I told Mr. Europe, "This ain't gonna last long. These people going to be dancing all full of sweat and perspiration." . . . I kept watching those women all they had their evening gowns, and all the perspiration. So I says to Mr. Europe, "We ain't going to be playing for these people very long." And he says, "What's the matter?" And I says, "These people with all their money and everything are ruining their costumes and everything," running around, but they was having fun. But I said, "How long it's going to last?" He says, "What do you suggest?" I says, "I suggest that you play a slow number,

but you have it with a beat so they can dance. Not they'd be walking around so that they have a rhythm to it." "All right I'll try it," he said. So what he tried was the blues, any blues. And of course for the blues he was able to slow the tempo down. That drag, the first beat is on the beat, the second kind of drags it, and the third is on it [again]. . . . So, as soon as those white people heard that beat, you should have seen them, boy, grab one another going down the hall rockin', boy. [Laughter] That was the outlet for us, and it started with the "St. Louis Blues." Now every song you got, every romantic song that you have, they call it the "Freedom Beat." The Negroes really the ones that started it. It's restful. It's not driving you. . . . It wasn't fast like the One-Step. It's a tempo that Jim discovered that today the world has accepted.[42]

Sissle credits Europe with introducing the Castles to a new dance that came to be known as the foxtrot that could be performed to this new, blues-inflected rhythm. Europe used W. C. Handy's "Memphis Blues" as the basis for the new dance.[43] Vernon Castle told the *New York Herald* that the steps "had been danced by negroes, to his personal knowledge, for fifteen years."[44] Europe told the *New York Tribune*, "Mr. Castle has generously give me credit for the fox-trot yet the credit, as I have said, really belongs to Mr. Handy. You see, then, that both the tango and the fox-trot are really negro dances, as is the one-step."[45]

The Castles helped introduce this new black rhythm to a white audience, in turn paving the way for the popularity of new black musical and dance styles. The importance of the foxtrot can't be overestimated. It was the dance of choice for over three decades until the 1940s gave birth to many other dance crazes. Even into the 1950s early rock-and-roll songs like "Rock around the Clock" were promoted as foxtrots. It was also the pathway for the blues to enter the musical mainstream. It was six years later that the first blues were recorded.

Gypsy music was all the rage in society, and Europe's band was often featured following a performance by a gypsy-style group. Europe and the Castles wanted to bring their audiences into the rhythms of black music and had a plan on how to do it without shocking their upper-class audience. Sissle recalled that the Clef Club band "used to go on after the gypsy band finished playing, and whatever waltz the gypsy band played, the Clef Club would start off by playing it in ragtime. All of a sudden, people commenced getting up and trying to dance to it."[46]

By early 1916, Sissle had become one of the key figures in Europe's oper-
ations. Smart, well-organized, energetic, and enthusiastic, the young singer
became an indispensable aid to the older conductor. He also urged Europe to
bring Eubie up from Baltimore to join his organization. According to Sissle,
Europe knew of Blake's talents but was convinced Blake would never leave
Baltimore. However, the combination of events in Baltimore and Eubie's desire to work further with Sissle led him finally to leave his native city.

There may have been another reason Blake finally was convinced that he
needed to leave Baltimore. The years 1912 to 1915 brought a crackdown on
Baltimore's nightlife from the authorities, particularly the bars, saloons, and
bawdy houses that catered to the "less desirable" instincts of its citizens. As in
many major cities, an anti-vice commission had been formed specifically to
address the problem of prostitution, gambling, and drinking. Fire-breathing
anti-vice crusaders like New York's Anthony Comstock inspired the movement, leading to the establishment of Baltimore's own anti-vice commission
in 1888. This action combined with similar movements to improve working
conditions for women and general sanitation and health in the city. In 1912,
a Maryland Vice Commission was established to investigate and report on
these urban problems. The report inspired a crackdown on bawdy houses,
with the police reporting that the last house of prostitution was shut down by
September 15, 1915.[47] While the direct impact on musicians cannot be fully
known, undoubtedly work in the city's sporting houses, bars, and social clubs
was affected by these efforts. Blake could see the writing on the wall; his days
of gainful employment as a barroom pianist were numbered.

After playing Atlantic City in the summer of 1915, Blake came up to
New York to join Europe's organization. Eubie settled in Harlem, living in
a series of apartments over the next few years, along with his wife Avis and
one of Ford Dabney's sons, who, Eubie said, the couple raised as their own.[48]
By this time, Europe's band was in such demand that he would send out various different units in order to cover as many parties and events as possible;
Europe himself would show up only for a few minutes to make sure everything was proceeding correctly. It was Sissle's job to visit some of the fancy
events and make excuses for why Europe could not be there to conduct. "I
would have to visit some of the places, and try to make excuses for his non-
appearance, a duty I dreaded because it was never satisfactory—everyone
wanted Jim."[49] Perhaps thanks to his association with the Castles, Europe's
band and other black musicians were in high demand among the city's
elite. It reached a point where they were commanding higher salaries than

their white brethren, and even the all-white union began recruiting black members.[50]

When he was first hired, Blake worked as a second conductor, overseeing the bands that Europe himself could not lead and even conducting while Europe schmoozed with the rich patrons. As Blake told Vivian Perlis, Europe would take the stage, bow to the audience, and instruct the drummer, "All right, all right, Buddy—Buddy was the drummer—all right, let's go—all right. He'd take the stick—bing—downbeat—and hand the stick to me and he'd go out and sit with the millionaire's guests." Blake said that the prickly Will Marion Cook gave him lessons in conducting. Blake also managed Europe's office, overseeing the many booking requests and lining up musicians for performances as needed. He even had a secretary![51]

Blake was impressed by Europe's skills as a musician, an organizer of bands, and an envoy to the white world. He later compared Europe to Martin Luther King Jr., as equal in importance to convincing the white world that blacks were every bit their equals, and that black musicians deserved to be treated with dignity and respect.[52] Europe told Sissle, "I would never come before the public with a musical organization that I was not positive would be a revelation and a credit to the race. Because it would hurt the race, and set it back in the minds of the world more than anything else inasmuch as any race's progress is rated by its artistic attainments."[53]

Blake was particularly amused by the charade that Europe and his band members enacted for their white audiences. Whites were convinced that blacks were "natural" musicians and doubted their ability to read conventional notation. Of course, Europe was highly trained, as were members of his bands, and was quite capable of handling any score. Eubie bragged that the band's cornet player was so talented that "if a fly landed on the music, he'd *play* it, see, like *that!*"[54] Nonetheless, the band members hid this fact from their white patrons. Blake told interviewer Max Morath,

All the musicians were told [by Europe] never to let a white man think you can read music. That lessens the money he's going to give you. Take the Astoria Hotel on Broadway—the music never stopped. White band at that end [of the room] . . . and we'd play at the other end. They'd play [Blake hums a waltz-like tune]. Then we'd play [hums the same tune in a syncopated version]. And the people'd come around [saying]: "Isn't it marvelous? *Those boys!*" . . . But we never let the white people know we could read music.[55]

"The white bands all had their music stands," Eubie noted ironically, "but the people wanted to believe that Negroes couldn't learn to read music but had a natural talent for it."[56]

Although Europe's bands were popular with the well-to-do white New Yorkers, this popularity didn't mean that the whites were without racial prejudice. Eubie recounted to biographer Lawrence T. Carter an incident involving the band's drummer/singer Wilbur White when the band was playing for private parties. While the band was playing at a millionaire's mansion one evening, White spotted a large classical harp sitting on the landing above the ballroom. He darted from the bandstand and dared to sit and try it out—much to Eubie's dismay. When the hostess heard the noise, she ran up to White and scolded him, "Keep your goddamn black hands off my harp!" She was ready to throw the entire band out of her house, but the other guests—who had been enjoying their music—talked her into letting them stay.

A second incident occurred on a private yacht where the band was hired to entertain. Comedian/singer Carl Cook was performing with them, and he had the audacity to grab a panama hat off of one of the audience members and to place it on his head during his routine. When he returned the hat to its owner, the angry white man threw it into the water—refusing to wear it after it had been on a black man's head.[57]

Eubie recalled that though they were welcomed into the upper set's homes, "we didn't use the Steinway either. It was locked up and covered with velvet and flowers that said, 'Keep off the grass!' There would always be a rented piano."[58] And the houses' staffs also kept a close eye on the musicians. At one soirée given by a wealthy man for his granddaughter the guests were told to bring a present "wrapped in a five cent red handkerchief." One of the musicians wandered over to the table to try to peek under the cloths. A Pinkerton guard hired for the occasion caught him and put him in handcuffs. The miscreant was brought over to Eubie, and the Pinkerton man warned him, "I've seen you warn this fellow to stay away from the table. I could take him downtown right now for attempted theft, but I won't if you keep him away from there. And you better pray to god nothing's missing!"[59]

Blacks were equally wary of allowing whites into their world. Eubie related how one night he and Jim Europe took Vernon and Irene Castle on a tour of Harlem nightclubs. The performers wanted to see "real" black dancers. However, when they arrived at Leroy Watkins's nightclub, Watkins turned them away, refusing to allow any whites into his club. According to Eubie, Europe argued with Leroy, saying,

"You know me Leroy. You know I wouldn't bring anybody in your place that wasn't all right. Why, this is the famous, the great Mr. and Mrs. Vernon Castle." Jim was probably the best-known man in Harlem and his feelings were hurt. "Jim," said Leroy, "I know you, all right, and I respect you. But I don't care who they are. They're white, and they can't come in here. That's my policy, and I'm sticking to it."[60]

And some blacks treated other blacks as if they were beneath them. Blake told how the Wanamaker's butler refused to feed Europe and the band the leftovers after the guests were done:

Now, the butler, he thinks he ain't like other Negroes. He don't like it when Jim complains [about the lack of food for his musicians]. But anyway, in a little while, they tell us to sit down at a table in this big room, and a [black] waiter brings in this big china thing they use for soup, and he serves us all. I can't wait now, see—we're all dyin' from hunger. Now we grab our spoons and as soon as I tasted this stuff, I had to spit it out. And I see everybody else is doin' the same thing. This stuff, I'm sure, is the water they washed the dishes in—soap, everything. And it's because the butler is mad, see. He don't like no colored people to complain. But Europe—I see Europe is eatin' the stuff just like it's soup, he don't pay it no mind, just keeps eatin'! My God, I thought, that Europe will eat anything. Now everybody else is watchin' him too, see. It ain't just me. I realize Jim Europe didn't get where he is with the white folks by complainin'. At home or in the White House, it was all the same to him. You couldn't make him mad.[61]

Europe's band didn't play only for the upper set. They were also hired to play for college dances. Occasionally, Europe would allow some of the students to sit in with the band. During a fraternity party at Yale, a student joined the band on piano. It was the young Cole Porter. Porter would remain a fan of Blake's talents, and would later play a role in finding Sissle work after the lyricist had settled in Europe.

In late September 1916, Europe and Sissle enlisted in the 15th New York National Guards, a regiment being organized by Colonel William H. Hayward, to enlist African Americans in the war effort. Although they could not be members of the US Army because of their race, their unit would eventually see action when it was assigned to the French army. (They didn't actually sail to France until December 1917, arriving on January 1, 1918.)

Hayward encouraged Europe to form a band as a means of encouraging en-listment and building morale. With funding from Hayward, Europe trav-eled to Puerto Rico, which was known to be the home of many talented brass performers "of color" (most actually of Spanish or mixed Spanish and African descent), while Sissle (as drum major for the band) remained in New York to recruit local players. Many of the Puerto Rican musicians had served in military bands during the Spanish American War, so they were well trained in technique and the band repertoire.

While both Sissle and Europe were enthusiastically preparing for the war, Blake showed little interest in serving abroad. Claiming in some later interviews that he was too old to serve—which wasn't in fact true—Blake more honestly said that he simply had no interest in putting himself at risk for his country. Eventually, Eubie had to register for the draft, but Armistice was declared before he was called up to serve. He later recalled how his very religious mother believed that God had spared him the danger of serving; ever the skeptic, Eubie replied that God didn't seem too concerned for the others who had died in battle:

> Yeah, [Jim Europe and Noble Sissle] went to war, and they tried to make me to go to war, and I said, "No I ain't going to war." . . . But I registered. They sent [the paperwork to] my mother to sign it and my mother signed it and she sent it . . . She was endowed with religion. She said the mailbox lit up, God showing her son ain't going to war. She came up the street, shouting and all, and the lady next door took her in the house and humored her. You know the mailbox didn't blaze up in fire. She said that was God answering her prayers. I said, "Well, what about those other guys? Their mothers prayed and they had to go to war."[62]

Sissle and Europe didn't hesitate to tease Blake about his unwillingness to fight, despite the fact that, in Eubie's words, "everybody [knew] they're goin' to the war, but they're just gonna be musicians. Ain't none of us was a fighter, you know. But they'd introduce me to girls and they'd say, 'This is Eubie Blake, the slacker.' "[63]

In the summer of 1917, Eubie made his first recordings for the Pathé label.[64] Sissle had already recorded as a vocalist for the label that spring in between attending training camp with Europe's regiment. Among the num-bers he recorded was the song "Good Night Angeline," written with Blake and Europe (Figure 3.2); a sentimental ballad, the song remained in the

Figure 3.2 Sheet music cover for "Good Night Angeline," issued in the wake of World War I. James Reese Europe is featured in the middle of the sheet, with a cameo photo of Noble Sissle on the lower left in his military dress.

Sissle and Blake repertoire for decades. It is possible that Sissle's success with Pathé led the label to consider recording Blake. Three 78s were issued in 1918 under the name of The Eubie Blake Trio, featuring Blake and an unknown second pianist (possibly pianist Elliott Carpenter, who had also worked with Jim Europe's band and would remain a lifelong friend of Eubie's) as well as a barely heard percussionist (perhaps Buddy Gilmore, the percussionist from

Europe's band).[65] Another possibility is that the drummer was the come-
dian/vocalist Broadway Jones, with whom Blake said he was performing in
New York during the war years. (Jones became Blake's performing partner in
the later 1920s and early 1930s.) The description in Pathé's catalog makes it
sound as though they were a regular performing unit:

> The Eubie Blake Trio comprises an organization of three extremely clever
> colored musicians whose talents in entertaining the "400" and ultra-
> fashionables of N.Y.C,. are extremely in favor and much sought after. As
> exponents of "jazz" and "ragtime" piano, two of its members are "King
> Pins." . . . The two selections. . . afford fine opportunity for display of real
> "down south" ragging both on the piano and in the drummer.[66]

In all, three selections made that day can be definitively attributed to Blake
and his trio, the novelty song "Sarah from Sahara" (composed by Hugo Frey
and published in 1918) and two novelty rags, "American Jubilee" (written
by Tin Pan Alley composer Edward B. Claypoole in 1916, with snippets of
bugle calls and patriotic melodies like "Yankee Doodle" thrown in for good
measure) and "Hungarian Rag." All were marketed by Pathé as foxtrots for
dancing.

On "Hungarian Rag," a novelty written by Julius Lenzberg in 1913,
one pianist plays the steady bass part while the second pianist handles a
highly ornamented part in the upper keyboard, including many fast scale
flourishes. If we judge from Blake's recordings made a few years later, it is
likely that Eubie was playing the upper part, which is more prominent than
the lower accompaniment. Just as when he cut piano rolls a few years later,
Eubie may not have selected this piece to record, but rather was responding
to the producer's needs for a popular item. For this reason, there's not
much distinctive about the playing here beyond what would have been
heard from other novelty pianists of the period, such as Zez Confrey. It is
interesting to note, however, that the piece features a descending, harmonized progression in its first part; Blake used a similar figure in his own
compositions of the period.

Besides recording for Pathé, Eubie also made his first piano rolls in 1917
through early 1918, including the first recording of his "Charleston Rag," issued by Ampico.[67] Although Eubie claimed to have written this piece in 1899,
it is likely that it did not reach its final form until this time; this probability
is further supported by the fact that Blake copyrighted the work in 1917.[68]

The tune was named after a well-heeled Baltimore gambler who requested it when Eubie was working in the city's sporting houses:

> There was a fellow known as Charleston, a gambler, who used to say to me, "Play that rag that you wobble your bass all the time." He'd pay me money and one time he asked me what was the name of the piece. I'd actually been calling it "Strawberry Rag" or something. But I said, "Oh, that's the Charleston Rag."[69]

Eubie told his biographer Al Rose that he didn't write down the piece himself, but asked a member of Europe's band, Nelson Kinkaid, who played the saxophone and clarinet and was a talented arranger, to notate it for him—which would again support the fact that it wasn't composed at least in its final form until Eubie was working for Europe after 1915.[70] The piece opens with a dramatic bass run punctuated by a series of off-kilter treble chords; it is an extremely forceful and ear-catching opening. "Charleston Rag" would remain Blake's masterpiece in the ragtime style, combining fancy fingerwork, dramatic stop time, orchestral-like voicings, and a nearly unstoppable forward momentum.

The piano-roll version is not the best introduction to the piece, perhaps because of the limitations of the technology used to record Blake's playing. Hearing the roll decades later, he commented, "I do more tricks on it now than I did in those days. The arrangement is almost the same."[71] Actually, the piece is played at a slightly faster tempo than in his later recordings, and the subtleties of the interplay of Blake's left and right hands are lost. Also, in most later recordings Eubie doesn't repeat the opening A section after playing the B, as was a convention of the earlier classic ragtime style. However, unlike some of his later rolls, this one doesn't appear to have been doctored, as the performance pretty much could all be accomplished by one (talented) pianist. (It was common at the time to add ornamental runs and extra harmony notes by hand after a roll was cut, creating a performance that could never be duplicated by a single pianist.)

Blake's next series of rolls was issued in late 1917 through early 1918; these were on the Rythmodik division of Ampico and probably were cut at the same session as "Charleston Rag." One of the few originals that Blake cut for this company was "Good Night Angeline." Sissle had recorded it for Pathé in 1917, and it had gained some popularity, which was probably why Blake was asked to make the roll. Unlike his other rolls, this performance is credited to Blake along with "assistance" from pianist/arranger Edgar Fairchild (real name, Milton Suskind), who was a regular Ampico artist. Fairchild would go on to become a bandleader and a featured pianist in Broadway pit orchestras. In 1972, Blake commented that the recording was "the right tempo for someone to sing" and also admired the countermelody he played in the left hand in the second chorus. The second pianist (if indeed there is one) is hard to pick out. The roll leader features a picture of Blake at the piano, and also describes the song as "a typical Southern number with a touch of 'blues.'" The term "blues" is used rather loosely (perhaps thanks to the popularity of blues numbers by other artists). Another Sissle-Blake-Europe number, "Mirandy (That Gal o' Mine)" a foxtrot, was also recorded.

Also among these rolls was Blake's version of "Rain Song" by Will Marion Cook. Blake was a major fan of Cook's music, and the elder composer—as we shall see—took a strong interest in his career. "Rain Song" was a semiclassical number in the manner of the popular "Negro Spirituals" performed at the time. Unfortunately, no copies of this roll have been found, so we can't hear if Blake followed faithfully Cook's score.[72]

Also in 1917, Eubie's father passed away suddenly, dying of an apparent heart attack while riding a streetcar in Baltimore. Eubie says that, after examining him, the coroner said that the cause of death was "parts worn out."[73] Eubie idolized his father, and his passing must have made a huge impact on him. Eubie's mother—who was considerably younger—lived on, and Eubie provided both a home for her and regularly sent her money to support both her and his adopted sister. His mother also received a pension based on John Sumner's service in the Civil War.

After the fighting ended, Europe's band remained in France, serving as both entertainment for the remaining troops and as cultural ambassadors. They found an excited audience for their music in France who treated them with respect and dignity, the kind that was rarely extended to black musicians in the United States. The French were enthusiastic for this new, lightly syncopated music that was described as "jazz," even though it was closer to orchestrated ragtime in its style. Of course, jazz had not yet matured into its classic style; the word itself was less than a decade in circulation, and was applied rather indiscriminately to many different forms of dance music.

Members of the "Hell Fighters" band—as Europe's black regiment became known, thanks to their bravery in battle—were entranced by Paris, where they could move freely, be seated in any restaurant or bar with other patrons, and find work at the same or better pay than their white counterparts. They offered something the French musicians could not equal: "authentic" African American music performed by "real" African Americans. One such musician was drummer Louis Mitchell, who had previously worked with various Clef Club ensembles in New York (after Europe had formed his own rival organization) with the club's leader, pianist Dan Kildare.[74] Kildare formed a band to travel to London in 1915, taking Mitchell with him as his drummer.[75] Mitchell soon went out on his own, touring Britain's music halls initially with pianist/composer Joe Jordan.[76] Sometime in 1917, he enlisted most of the members of Kildare's band to form his own group, "The Seven Spades; The Greatest Combination of Rag-Time Instrumentalists, Singers, and Dancers."[77] The group enjoyed success playing around Britain.

Ironically, opportunities opened up for black musicians in England during the war because the previously employed German players who had provided music for dancing and parties were now unavailable. Lester Walton noted,

Before the present war in Europe, German musicians had the call in most of the [London] cafes, but as friendly relations no longer exist between England and Germany, it is impossible for Germans to secure employment . . . This new state of affairs should make it possible for colored entertainers to ultimately corner the cabaret work in London.[78]

However, Walton feared that the black musicians who were in such demand in Europe

might make a mess of things. . . . With such alluring prospects in sight for colored entertainers abroad, we respectfully beg of those who go to England to use good judgment and to remember that while it is important that their work be of high order, it is equally important that their CONDUCT be above reproach. For no matter how highly their work is regarded, if they become obnoxious, because of their CONDUCT their stay abroad will be painfully short. [Capitals in original][79]

Walton's fears reflected many of the black elite who knew that the race itself was being judged by the behavior of its cultural ambassadors, including musicians. To "uplift the race," one had to be careful to project the proper image of class and dignity, particularly when working abroad. Mitchell worked hard to project a respectable image, not only for himself but also for the musicians he hired to work with him.

Sometime either in late 1917 or early 1918, Mitchell moved on to working in France. He found his greatest success in Paris, and formed at least one band using local white players. Then, with the end of World War I in sight, there was an increased demand for the "real thing" in Parisian night spots. The management of one popular club—the Casino de Paris—asked Mitchell to enlist a group of black musicians to play there. He sailed to New York to recruit musicians, and returned with a group of seven performers who were eventually called the Jazz Kings (Figure 3.3). The ensemble worked from written scores and played the same style of lightly syncopated dance music that the Clef Club orchestras had offered to socialites before the war back in New York.[80]

With so much demand for musicians in Paris, however, Mitchell had trouble holding on to his men, who could easily find higher-paying jobs on their own. On August 21, 1918, Mitchell wrote to Eubie about the opportunities black musicians had in France. He met Blake while performing in Baltimore around 1913, and then reached out to him five years later to try to convince him to join him in Paris:

Figure 3.3 Mitchell's Jazz Band on the cover of a sheet issued in France at the end of World War I. Drummer Louis Mitchell (at far left) wrote to Eubie in the hopes of enticing him to come to France to join his band.

Dear Friend Eubie:

I suppose you will be surprised to hear from me, as I have not seen you since the last time that I was in Baltimore over five years ago. I have been over her for nearly five years, that is between London and Paris.

I suppose that you have heard of the success that I have had with my bands over here, I have just formed another band of Frenchman and I am teaching them to play rags and they are getting along fine better than I thought they would. I have them at one of the best Theatres in Paris, but I am now looking for a band of coulard boys to put in there place as soon as I can get them over here, and I will shift the white band to another Theatre in Paris.

Now I shoud like very much to get you over here with me, Jim Europe told me that you wanted to come so that is why I am writeing to find out if you would like to come as there is a great field over here for me but I am handycaped by not having enough men to put to work.

Now if you care to come I can offer you 75 dollars a week and give you a Contract for six Months or one year which ever you prefer to have. If you know of a good bandoline player that you could get to come with you let me know who he is and what he can do, wether he can sing or play another Instrument, as the more Versatile a fellow is over here the more work he can get. . . .

Eubie this is the finest Country in the world and if you once get over here you will never want to go back to N.Y. again, I intend to stay here the rest of my life, as you can go where you want too and have the time of your life just like Mr. Eddy and no one to bother you.

I have seen all the fellows of Jim's band and they all want to stay here after the war if possible, I have all ready signed some of them up for after the war, I am in right here which any one over here will tell you, all that I need is the men to fill the places that I have open. . . .

The work that we do over here now is different than the work in the States and not half so hard, we never work over two hours a day at most, where I am now and want you and the fellows to come, we only work fifteen minutes a day and thirty minutes on the days that we have Matenees, so you see it is like stealing money, and you are treated white wherever you go as they like spades here and these Yanks can't teach these French people any different, and I intend to stay here for ever, and I am sure you will feel the same way if you come over. [Grammar and spelling as in the original][81]

Mitchell's pitch was based on the good money, short working hours, and lack of racial prejudice found in Paris. Seventy-five dollars a week was unheard of for a black musician working in New York at the time, and to have steady employment guaranteed for as much as six months, rather than having to constantly scuffle for one-nighters, was also highly attractive. As we have seen, when working in the brothels and sporting houses of Baltimore, Blake had to work long hours—often from 10 p.m. to sunrise—for little pay—starting as a teen at just $3.00 a week[82] (although tips from patrons often helped make up for the lack of salary).

However, what is most noteworthy about this letter is that, as early as 1918, Mitchell recognized the lack of racial prejudice in Paris, noting that even the presence of the bigoted American soldiers could not change the French enthusiasm for black culture. Even working for Europe by playing in New York in the finest society homes, black musicians faced prejudice, entering through the back door, staying with the servants until being called on to perform, and not daring to eat or drink the food that was being served to the guests.

One white French musician who was close with Mitchell was Leo Vauchant, who became one of the elder musician's closest disciples. His memory of learning from and playing with Mitchell's group shows how much the French admired and accepted the new musical style and the musicians who created it:

> I loved these black guys. I used to stay up all night because I enjoyed their company, and playing with them . . . Mitchell formed a Tempo Club above Joe Zelli's club and I was the only white guy in the outfit . . . They accepted me because I played their way . . . They enjoyed that.

Vauchant noted that Mitchell and his musicians were sophisticated players, with a better sense of rhythm than their French imitators, as well as an equal knowledge of melody and harmony:

> It was a challenge—learning their way of playing. . . . I liked the way they approached dance music. It was rhythmical, and the tempo never varied within the tune. Whereas, when the French would play, there was no sense of beat . . . It didn't swing. It didn't move. The blacks, on the other hand, seemed to be skilled musicians. They knew about chords. At least that trombone player did—Frank Withers. And Cricket Smith [the cornet player]

certainly did. If he didn't know the name of a chord, he certainly didn't miss any of the notes. When he improvised, it was right on the nose.[83]

Thus, despite the prejudice that spread the notion that black musicians were "unschooled" and "primitive" when it came to their knowledge of music, it was clear to Vauchant that these performers were sophisticated interpreters of the new musical style.

Like Reese Europe—and later Sissle and Blake—Mitchell maintained a high level of decorum in the presentation of his bands. Belgium-born critic Robert Goffin wrote about the impression Mitchell made on the bandstand in a review published in 1920 in a French jazz journal:

Mitchell, his handsome Creole face mobile smiling, always meticulously dressed in the latest style, as are all Negroes in Europe, a marvelous jazz drummer with a world of imagination, irradiating nervous tics which he delicately transmitted to his instruments to the amazement of the women who adored him.[84]

Goddard's note that "all Negroes" then performing in Parisian night spots maintained a level of sophisticated dress and happy expression acknowledges that in some ways the mask of minstrelsy still overshadowed black performers. Despite the notable difference in their treatment by their white French admirers, black musicians had to work against the prejudice that they were poorly clothed, illiterate, and uneducated, night after night as they worked on stage.

Trumpeter and bandleader Arthur Briggs noted that a colony of black musicians formed in Paris who provided support for one another. Mitchell even opened his own club, which attracted these expatriate musicians.[85] Briggs commented that both the good money and friendly community were attractive to black musicians like himself:

At the time in Paris there was a nice little colony of blacks. We had artists and musicians and boxers. We had certain bars where we met and we all got along nicely. Most of us behaved ourselves pretty well. Others took advantage. . . .

We didn't just come her for the lifestyle. We had wonderful contracts. It was a question of business and pleasure both. There was very little prejudice among the musicians. Most of my orchestras were French [white] musicians. It wasn't a question of color. It was a question of talent. Most of the work was cabarets and tea and supper dancers. . . . You always had two orchestras, one for tangos and one for jazz.[86]

Pianist Elliott Carpenter—who also came to work in Paris around this time, subsequently moving to London—also noted the opportunities that black musicians had in the European clubs. With these opportunities, however, also came problems, as few were used to dealing with their newfound wealth and success:

These boys were making money like they'd never seen before you see we were doing nightclub work. Anyway, you know that money will tell on you. I called rehearsals. I said we're going to rehearse Mondays. And someone said, "I can't make it Mondays because I've got to go to my tailor's on Monday." So I said Tuesday. "Oh, I can't make that because Tuesdays is the day I go to the masseur." So I says, "Anybody got anything on on Wednesday?" And [Roscoe] Burnett says, "That's my day for going to the race track. And you know I ain't going to lay that one down." Thursday? So [vocalist Opal] Cooper says, "That when I meet my chicks. I like to meet the chicks on Thursday. I can't put that off." So I says, "What in the hell do you want with them tramps anyway? Let's do it Friday." "Oh, that's a bad day because I've got this that and the other." So we don't learn new songs. No new music.[87]

Although Carpenter noted that black musicians "had a freedom you didn't get here [in the United States]. Over there you didn't have to hide away," many just

wasted themselves. . . . They all had wives back in the States so they just went for the whores. And the whores took 'em for everything they could get when they saw they were in demand . . . I thought maybe I'd go the same way. I said, "I'm going to get out of here."[88]

Although Blake had not traveled to France to play with Europe and Sissle, he must have been at least tempted by the rosy picture painted by Mitchell of an easy life of gainful employment. That temptation was understandable, since by early 1918 the opportunities for black musicians had dried up. The Tempo Club, the booking agency for Blake and other black musicians, had for all intents folded, because of the lack of demand during the war. Working with singer Broadway Jones, Blake went on the road to play in vaudeville to make ends meet.[89] Even before corresponding with Mitchell, he must have expressed concerns to his employer, Jim Europe, about his ability to succeed financially by working as his factotum in New York. Europe wrote to Blake on April 14, 1918, to reassure him that, once the war was over, there would be good, lucrative work to be had with his organization:

> I know business must be dull for I see and hear it from everybody I know over here.
>
> Just stay on the job and take your medicine. If you think of the comforts you are having over there and think of the hardships we are having over here you'd be happy I am sure to go on "suffering" . . . I have some wonderful opportunities for you to make all the money you need. Eubie, the thing to do is to build for the future, and build securely and that is what I am doing. When I go up I will take you with me. You can be sure of that.[90]

Mitchell's letter must have renewed Blake's sense that he might be better off leaving Europe's employ. This reaction is probably why Sissle wrote to Eubie on October 14, to reassure him that he should stay in New York and manage the Tempo Club because there would be good opportunities for them both after the war:

> I saw Mitchell. He said you wrote to him. Well, old boy, hang on and we'll be able to knock them cold after the war. It will be over soon. Jim [Europe] and I have P[aris] by the balls in a bigger way than anyone you know.[91]

It's obvious that Sissle had low regard for Mitchell as either a band-leader or prospective employer. Mitchell's poor spelling in his letter to Blake reveals his lack of education—certainly compared to the college-educated lyricist, who prided himself on his fine elocution and penmanship. The letter also is slightly condescending to Blake himself, as if he were not capable of knowing any one as talented as Sissle or Europe. Sissle would be the more business minded of the pair, and treated Blake as a lesser-educated partner who needed careful guidance in order to succeed. Blake must have resented this treatment on some level, even though he relied on figures like Sissle throughout his life to tend to his interests.

After the war, the "Hell Fighters" had a triumphant homecoming, including a grand parade through Harlem. Rather than playing military marches, Europe had the enlightened idea to have the band begin by striking up a popular song, "Who's Been There While I've Been Gone?," which, in Sissle's words,

> was a master stroke of diplomacy on Jim's part . . . for the tune . . . had always been a source of amusement to the men while abroad, the song brought a spirit of revelry over the gathered multitude and turned the home-coming into one of happiness, at the same time not losing any of the patriotic spirit.[92]

The song rather humorously tells the story of a husband accusing his wife of seeing other men while he was out working; she disingenuously replies to each accusation, assuring him that the man was a preacher or other harmless character, and certainly not her lover.[93] During the war, the soldiers, being separated from their own wives and girlfriends, enjoyed hearing this comic song. Thanks to its association with the acclaimed regiment, the band was in demand for performances around the country, and embarked on a ten-week multi-state tour of opera houses and vaudeville theaters in the spring of 1919. The band was joined by a vocal quartet called the Four Harmony Kings, who had been part of Europe's Tempo Club orbit before the war. Sissle was the featured artist throughout the tour, with his presence noted on advertisements and flyers. According to a Philadelphia critic, "no sweeter voiced tenor has been heard . . . in years."[94] His most popular song, "On Patrol in No Man's Land," was cowritten with Europe and Blake; featuring dramatic effects played by band members The Percussion Twins (including the sound of bombs flying overhead and exploding on the ground), it was one of several items recorded for Pathé in the spring of 1919 by Sissle and Europe's 22-piece band prior to the tour. It emphasized Sissle and the band's connection with the just-ended war and the bravery they displayed in battle:

CHORUS
There's a Minenwerfer [a German mortar] coming—look out! (boom!)
Hear that roar (bang!)
There's one more (bang!)
Stand fast—there's a Very light (sound of flare)
Don't gasp, or they'll find you all right

Don't start to bombin' with those hand grenades (sound of machine gun)
There's a machine gun, holy spades!
Alert! Gas! Put on your mask!
Adjust it correctly and hurry up fast
Drop! There's a rocket form the Boche barrage!
Down, hug the ground
Close as you can, don't stand
Creep and crawl, follow me, that's all
What do you hear? Nothing near?
Don't fear, all's clear
That's the life of a stroll
When you take a patrol
Out in No Man's Land
Ain't it grand?
Out in No Man's Land

The song would form the backbone of Sissle and Blake's vaudeville act for years.

On the evening of May 10, after playing the first half of a concert in Boston's Mechanic's Hall, Europe—who had suffered from a gas attack in June of 1918 while commandeering a machine-gun company and had been in declining health through this period—met backstage with one of the band's two drummers, Herbert Wright. Sissle noted that Wright had long complained that Europe made him work too hard and never praised his playing. After complaining to Europe, Wright left the room, only to reappear, brandishing a pocket knife. In the confusion that followed, Europe was stabbed in the neck. He was carried out of the theater, and his assistant conductor had to carry on for the second half of the show. Although the wound appeared to be superficial at the time, Europe subsequently died of a severed artery, and was buried with full military honors in Arlington Cemetery on March 14, 1919. Europe's death effectively ended the band and booking agency. Sissle was asked to take a 15-piece band on a tour, but he turned the work down, preferring to cast his lot with Blake.

Now unemployed, Sissle and Blake had to determine the best path forward to further their careers. Sissle wanted to continue to perform; Blake wanted to continue to compose. Sissle's performances with Europe had attracted attention to him as a vocalist, so it seemed there might be work to be had continuing to tour the vaudeville circuit. Thus was born the new touring duo of Sissle and Blake.

4

Vaudeville

1919–1921

After the death of Jim Europe, Eubie was left somewhat at loose ends. There was some effort to keep the booking agency and band dates going, but without Europe's leadership work started to dry up. It's possible that Eubie would have moved back to Baltimore, where he had an established career, as he had no great love for New York. However, the ever-resourceful Sissle recognized a new opportunity with the band's decline. He had been the star vocalist on Europe's tour, particularly shining on the dramatic song "On Patrol in No Man's Land." It made sense to continue touring, but there was no need to hire a full band; Sissle figured that with his vocalizing and stage presence coupled with Blake's talents on the keys, they would be a surefire hit.

Sissle approached Pat Casey, the agent who had set up Europe's tour, with the idea of booking the new duo. After his start selling peanuts at ball games during his teen years, Casey had risen to managing a traveling circus and progressed to having his own vaudeville booking agency by the end of the first decade of the 20th century. Over the next 20 years or so, he represented diverse performers like monologist/fancy rope twirler Will Rogers and crooner/bandleader Ted Lewis. Casey was a big man, known for his infectious laugh and large appetite; he built his agency through advertisements announcing that, for him "No Act Too Big; No Act Too Small. I Shall Make the Pat Casey Agency the Biggest in the World."[1] Eubie quipped that Casey's language was so profane that he was surprised that the phone company let him keep his line.

Sissle recalled that, following Europe's death, Casey initially wanted him to continue touring with the Europe band as its leader:

> [Casey] wanted me to go on vaudeville and probably take 12 or 15 of the band. I said, "No, no, this band's too great. We ain't going to bring nothing with that name on it. Let it die like it is." But I says, "Eubie Blake—he's the fellow I've been writing music with—and I, we'll go on vaudeville."[2]

Eubie Blake. Richard Carlin and Ken Bloom, Oxford University Press (2020). © Richard Carlin and Ken Bloom 2020.
DOI: 10.1093/oso/9780190635930.001.0001

Casey recognized Sissle's talent as a vocalist and saw the potential in the duo's act. And, in an unusual move, he also supported their desire to appear in white vaudeville without blackface makeup or adapting demeaning characterizations. By this time, Casey was working for the powerful Keith Orpheum organization—a major owner of vaudeville houses across the country—so he had the clout to insist that the act be presented in a dignified way. However, Casey wisely did not book them in the South. Judging from newspaper notices and advertisements, the duo were primarily booked in the Northeast, including a few weeks in Canada; the farthest South they seem to have appeared is Eubie's hometown of Baltimore and nearby Washington, DC.

Casey had some initial trouble convincing bookers to take on the duo as a "serious act." Blake said that when Casey approached Newark's Palace Theater to book the act, the owners suggested that they appear in blackface, dressed in overalls, and speak in typical stuttering "darkie" dialect. The owners suggested that the piano be placed on stage and the two would enter and approach it gingerly, and then Sissle would say, "Hey, hey, hey Eubie, wh-wha-wha-what is that over there?" Blake was to respond, "I don't know, I ain't never seen one of them things," and then approach the instrument carefully before touching its keys. You can imagine the rolling of the eyes, exaggerated expressions of fear and humility, and general clownishness that would have been expected as they carried out this dialogue. Casey, however, would not accept this request. As Eubie later recalled, Casey yelled at the Palace's operators,

> "Do you know these fellows? Do you know who there are? They were with Jim Europe's band . . . The big Negro band. They worked for all the millionaires in the world. You can't put no overalls on them, you might can, but I'm not going to put them on them. They're going to work in tuxedos, like they always work, and play the piano and sing. And if you don't want 'em, just say you don't want them." And he was a big guy. Course, I can't say the language THAT HE SAID. Boy he cussed the heck out of them. And we went on, in tuxedos.[3]

As Eubie frequently said, Sissle and Blake were not a "black" act, in the sense that their repertory, presentation, and dialogue were all geared to appeal to a white audience. It is true that Blake sometimes spoke in dialect—much to the annoyance of Sissle—but he recognized that to do so was necessary to appeal to the audience. However, their dress and demeanor were equivalent to the white vaudevillians of the day, like the very popular Van and Schenck. And, unlike Bessie Smith or Ma Rainey, Sissle and Blake played exclusively in white vaudeville houses and theaters, not in theaters catering to black audiences. In later interviews, Blake insisted that they shouldn't be categorized as a "black act":

> They'd say "We drew Negroes." We *didn't* draw Negroes, because we didn't have a Negro act. I'm the only one did light comedy, Negro comedy. I said, "Is you a fool? What you think I is?" That's all, once or twice. Sissle didn't like that, but it got laughs. [When he protested] I said, "Got a laugh didn't it? I *know* how to talk different." But he never liked that.[4]

Blake accepted the expediency of using comic dialect to please the audience; the college-educated Sissle didn't like it, and always pitched the duo as a "class act." And Eubie took pride in the fact that he knew how to speak like a proper gentleman, so the only people being fooled were the customers in the audience.

Although they didn't wear dark makeup themselves, Sissle and Blake often appeared on bills featuring "burnt-cork" comedians (white comics in blackface). The convention of blackface performance remained in place for comedians (black and white), and for some white singers (like Al Jolson and Eddie Cantor). However, Sissle and Blake skirted the issue of race in both their appearance and selection of material. In reviews that appeared in both the white and black press, while the duo's race is usually mentioned, there is no discussion of the white audience rejecting them because of their skin color.

Nonetheless, Blake was not embarrassed by the blackface tradition, and had great respect for earlier comic performers like Bert Williams and Ernest Hogan. Asked by pop-music historian Ian Whitcomb whether he felt that minstrelsy was demeaning, Blake replied that both minstrelsy and burlesque were important training grounds for black singers, actors, and dancers. Specifically asked about Ernest Hogan's 1896 song "All Coons Look Alike to Me," Blake defended the singer/songwriter:

> I knew Ernest Hogan, personally. . . He was a fine gentleman. But, [he wrote] that [song] to sell it . . . because they called us "coons." No matter what they did to us, in those days, it was all right. . . . I hear a lot of colored

people knock Ernest Hogan because he wrote that tune. [But] it was the vogue in those days.[5]

Hogan defended his song by saying it was a major reason for the broad acceptance of ragtime, and several historians do credit him with popularizing the form. It was white performer May Irwin who first introduced the song in the musical, *Courted into Court*. Hogan was simply catering to the market; the fact that he could make a good living—substantially better than the average black worker—was more than enough justification for catering to the day's racial stereotypes. Hogan's song was a tremendous success, selling 40,000 copies per month a year after its publication. Hogan was bringing in $400 per month in royalties, a fortune in 1898. However, the song's popularity led to a spate of other coon songs written by whites as well as blacks, including the most famous of black acts, Williams and Walker. Hogan was also revered by fellow stage personalities. Younger comedian Flournoy Miller proclaimed Hogan "the greatest of all colored showmen." And Luckey Roberts thought he was "the greatest performer I ever saw." Hogan was billed as the "Unbleached American" and despite his use of the word "coon" had great pride in being black.

Although Sissle said he was unwilling to don blackface, his aversion to playing to racist stereotypes did not stop him from writing and performing the duo's song "Pickaninny Shoes"—a song that Blake noted was a real show-stopper. So-called pick acts—young colored children who would sing and dance, usually in the company of an older white performer—were tremendously popular on vaudeville, a holdover from minstrel shows. Sissle and Blake's song played on this stereotype, celebrating the "idyllic" childhood recalled by the song's narrator. While the song plays on a racist stereotype, typically of Sissle's lyrics there is no use of dialect, and the sentiments expressed about the fond memories of childhood are totally generic—with very little alteration, one could image the narrator being a white man who was raised in Connecticut reflecting on his own pair of baby booties. One vaudevillian suggested that Sissle find an actual pair of baby shoes to use in the act. Both Sissle and Blake, however, agreed that it was far more effective for the audience to imagine the presence of these symbolic items, so Sissle held his hands open to indicate their presence.[6] According to Blake, there wasn't a dry eye in the house when Sissle finished. Even worse, Eubie had to follow Sissle's act with his featured piano solo. Blake always felt slightly upstaged by his partner.

The act took the name "The Dixie Duo," despite the fact that neither had direct Southern roots. This generic name could have equally been applied to a white act of the day, although some may have picked up the hint that their "Dixie" identity referred to their skin color. In fact, there were several other white acts performing at this time under the same name. Two Southern-born women toured under this name, promoted as "The Southland's Sunshine Girls."[7] Two white banjo players who performed songs and sketches also toured under this name. These two acts probably drew more on stereotypes of Southern living than did Sissle and Blake.

Sissle and Blake composed the peppy "Gee! I'm Glad I'm from Dixie" as an intro for the act, which Sissle recorded in 1920 for Pathé. The song's home-sick hero—longing to catch a train for "old Dixie land"—name-checks all the familiar landmarks (the "Swanee River" and "old Virginia")—but there is no mention of plantations or an idealized slave life, as was common in typical minstrel-style and coon songs of the era. If we judge from its 1920 recording, Sissle's peppy performance is no different from that any other white vaudevillian would have given the song.[8]

After making their first appearance in early July 1919 in Baltimore[9], the duo opened at Newark's Palace Theater on July 4, 1919. Besides his power as an agent, Casey was friendly with *Variety*'s owner/editor, Sime Silverman. It is probably through Casey's pull that the act earned a brief notice in the important industry journal, which described them as

> the new colored team of Noble Sissle and "Eubie" Blake, who were over-seas with Europe's band. They proceeded without event with their song and piano routine, getting little in the way of returns until the finale number, descriptive of the action in No Man's Land. This took the team off to a strong round of applause.[10]

Sissle and Blake appeared second on the bill, a common place for lesser-known acts. (Audiences would often arrive late to shows and critics usually didn't turn up until later in the program, so the second spot was not considered very desirable.) The main attraction of the evening was Fanny Brice appearing in a condensed version of the show *Toot Sweet*, followed by eight "turns," or acts. The other big attraction was Jack Norworth, whose hit number was "Pickaninny Paradise," featuring Norworth performing with a young black child in the tradition of pickaninny acts. The other acts drew only tepid response, according to the *Variety* critic, so the fact that Sissle and

Blake scored with their signature "No Man's Land" song was something of a coup. That they "proceeded without event" was the critic's shorthand way of saying that no one in the audience reacted negatively to their skin color.

In the early days of touring, life was tough on the road and the young act did not get much notice. Blake's name was often misspelled as "Ubie" in newspaper announcements. Still, by January 1920, they were starting to get recognition—primarily through their association with Jim Europe and the hit song "On Patrol in No Man's Land"—and getting brief reviews like one that appeared in the Scranton, Pennsylvania, newspapers, praising their "highly effective" presentation.[11] When the duo appeared at Eubie's hometown Maryland Theater in early July 1919, prominent mention was given to Sissle's military rank and assignment; similar mention was given to the military service of two white vocalists on the bill, as a sign of their patriotism and service. Clearly, the theater owners were hoping to draw customers on the basis of these associations.[12]

It made sense that in the direct aftermath of World War I the duo would play on their association with the well-known "Hell Fighters" band. Notices like this one in a Norwich, Connecticut, newspaper emphasized their patriotism and wartime service (although Blake had never gone overseas):

> The fourth act is . . .The Dixie Duo, a couple of colored lads who went "over there" with Uncle Sam's other nephews—and who distinguished themselves in the fighting. When that was over they distinguished themselves as entertainers and since their return to America . . . both press and public have acclaimed their act.[13]

Grouping the two black performers with "Uncle Sam's other nephews" may have been a backhanded compliment (as the US military was closed to black men)—or perhaps a comment on the race's second-tier status as merely "nephews" of their white peers.

The duo used "On Patrol in No Man's Land" as their big closer, and it got a huge audience response, according to Blake:

> Nobody could follow that over the top thing ["On Patrol in No Man's Land"]. We [were] right out of the war. It's all about the war, what happened, down in the trenches . . . It was dramatic, [Sissle's] doing all that stuff . . . That guy was an actor; nobody wanted to follow us.[14]

Sissle would hover under the piano, react with fear to the simulated explosions, and gingerly tiptoe across the stage, avoiding imaginary landmines. On Europe's Pathé recording of the song—sung by Sissle—you can hear how he dramatizes the story while the band provides sound effects of exploding bombs landing all around the hapless soldiers. While this re-enactment would appear overly melodramatic today, for many in the audience this interpretation resonated with their own experiences or those of their loved ones fighting abroad or who had perished in the trenches. The duo also performed well-known World War I hits, including "Over There," as part of the act.[15]

While they sought to appeal to white audiences, the duo certainly faced prejudice while on the road. Sissle noted that—despite being a top draw and working their way up to a featured spot on the program—their pay remained at the bottom of the pay scale:

You had to stop the show to get in the Keith circuit. Nobody could follow you on the goddamn stage. The next act might be a white act headliner and [the audience would] run 'em off the stage because they want what they want. And we were the only colored persons on the bill. . . . Now the unfair part about it was . . . they put us on the old #2—and the #2 salary, about $250. Now then, the third act couldn't get on, so they wouldn't follow us, so they pushed us down to the fifth act, [and] pretty soon we'd be down to [the] act next to closing. Now, there was no complaining from that act, because they were the animals, the dog acts, something like that. But they didn't change our salary; #4 should be $450–500 if you could hold that spot.[16]

Recall that when they appeared in Norwich, Connecticut, in May 1920—less than a year after they first hit the road—the duo were placed in the number four slot, a far more desirable position than their original slot. According to Sissle, though, their salary was not adjusted to reflect the act's popularity with the audience.

Decades later, Blake continued to complain that—at their height after the success of *Shuffle Along*—Sissle and Blake made only $3000 a week in vaudeville, while the white Van and Schenck got $5000 for essentially the same amount of work. Of course, $3000 a week was considerably more than other black acts earned at that time, but still it irked Blake that the duo were not paid as much as their white counterparts.[17]

Prejudice also extended to the owners and management of the theaters where they performed. As Blake noted, because of their race they were never booked into the so-called deluxe houses, playing mostly second-tier theaters on the Keith circuit. Even the stagehands could be surly towards them. Blake recalled one incident that occurred at the Maryland Theater in his hometown of Baltimore[18]:

> I'm standing in the wings, listening to [the act on stage] . . . And the stage manager, he keeps looking at me.
>
> He says, "Hey you Sissle and Blake? Do you know you follow that act?"
>
> "Yeah, I know I follow that, yeah I'm up on the board."
>
> And he says, "Well, when are you going to makeup?"
>
> Now, he's talking about cork, but I don't know what he's talking about. I says, "I just put a little powder on my face, take the shine off, I'm already made up."
>
> He says, "No, when you going to put the cork on? You ain't going on my stage with the . . ." and dah-dah-dah, and I walked right out on stage. [The first act] was off, this guy says I ain't going, but Sissle's on that side of the stage, he don't know, and so we go out, do the act, and stopped the show cold. . . .
>
> When we got off stage, I told Sissle. Now Sissle knows [the theater's owner], because he worked there with Bob Young. And [the owner] come back and says to this guy, "[Why] are you meddling with [their] act?"
>
> He says, "I'm the stage manager. They're colored, ain't they." He didn't say that; you know what he said.
>
> But the owner said, "I raised those boys. Don't you be so smart. They don't put on no cork."[19]

Blake noted ironically that it was only because this owner had known Sissle previously that he was willing to push back on the (usual) demand that they wear blackface. Blake believed that whites who "raised" black artists were like plantation owners who "raised" slaves; they recognized the humanity of those they knew, but did not necessarily apply the same open-minded attitude toward others.

Humiliations on the circuit extended to the act being provided with the shabbiest dressing facilities, usually located either in the basement or the uppermost floors, as far from the stage as possible. Eubie recalled an exchange he had with one manager while he was on the road:

Stage manager says to me "Are you going to your dressing room?"

"Yeah."

He says, "Did you look at the board?"

"No, I know where my dressing room is?"

"How do you know? Ever play this theater before?"

"No, but I know where my dressing room is. It's on the last floor, next to the toilet."[20]

Another aspect of the vaudeville grind was constant traveling, which Eubie never enjoyed. Travel plans could change as dates were added or canceled; the performers had little time to sightsee or enjoy local food; and conditions in each theater—from dressing room space to how the act was treated by management—could vary greatly. Writing from Toronto, Canada in late September 1920, Eubie lamented to his wife Avis, "We have no route . . . as yet but I think we will go west as all the acts are going west but we are trying to keep from going. I'm very tired." About a week later, he wrote again, ironically describing the conditions in Hamilton, Ontario, where the duo were then appearing: "Just a line to let you know what kind of a Burg this is. A good place to come & die when you feel like dying alone."[21]

The duo's success on the road gave them an entrée into the world of music publishing. In 1919, several of their songs that were cowritten with Jim Europe appeared, including "Good Night Angeline" and "Mirandy (That Gal o' Mine)." Both songs are in typical sentimental style, with a descriptive verse leading into a snappier, upbeat chorus. "Angeline" is mostly written without dialect—save for the substitution of "dat" for "that"—and the style and subject matter is very much in the mainstream of white pop songs of the day. The song's protagonist could easily be white, expressing his love in the language and terms of sentimental verse. The sheet's cover did not feature the degrading art found on coon songs, but rather a genteel-looking Victorian (white) lady. On the other hand, the lover in "Mirandy" is clearly labeled as "the darkest dude of Jacksonville," with his lover "a long, tall sealskin brown," yet the lyrics are free of demeaning dialect and the song again is very much in the style of a sentimental ballad of the day. Sissle had recorded it with the Europe orchestra for Pathé earlier that year, as is prominently advertised on the sheet's cover.

Also in 1919, Sissle and Blake contracted with the major white Tin Pan Alley publishing firm headed by Julius Witmark, which would remain their publisher through 1923. (Witmark had also published "Good Night

Angeline," so perhaps the duo made the connection through Europe.) According to researchers Dave Jasen and Gene Jones, they signed a contract to publish approximately a dozen songs, being paid a retainer of $25.00 a week and 2 cents a sheet on sales of their titles.[22] From the list of titles, it's clear that they were experimenting with a variety of popular styles, including black-themed dialect songs ("Mammy's Lit'l Choc'late Cullud Chile"), sentimental love songs ("Ain't You Comin' Back Mary Ann, to Maryland," later recycled in *Shuffle Along* [Figure 4.1]), a "blues," at least in title ("Baltimore Blues"), and even an "Asian" genre song ("Michi Mori San"). Despite his aversion to using dialect himself, Sissle must have been comfortable writing the stereotypical lyrics for "Mammy's Lit'l Choc'late Cullud Chile," which expressed classic sentiments of a black Mammy for her "kinky headed" baby. Unlike other "coon" songs, it was published with a plain type cover, an odd choice, as this treatment was usually used for light classical or operatic selections. (Usually covers of popular minstrel or coon songs featured grotesque illustrations to indicate to the target audience—white amateur pianists—that they were being offered something in this genre.)

"Baltimore Blues" features an illustrated cover showing a ragtime-style pianist pictured from behind; from the small areas of his face and hands that are visible, the pianist appears to be white. The cover art is suspiciously similar to an earlier sheet by W. C. Handy, 1913's "Jogo Blues." On its cover, a pianist is also seen from behind, in a similar pose—but this pianist is clearly black. Why the racial identity of the pianist was altered is a matter of conjecture—although the Sissle-Blake number was clearly aimed at a white audience. While its subject—a ragtime piano player named "Piano Joe"—might be black, the lyrics lack any cues that would indicate this is a "coon" or dialect song. And although Piano Joe's "specialty" is the blues, the song is not a blues in either structure or content, but rather a jaunty-paced verse-chorus pop song. While the chorus does end with an echo of a blues-like couplet ("I got those blues, those weary blues / I've got those dog-gone Baltimore blues"), the music does not follow a blues progression and the melody is upbeat. It's clear that this lyric is meant to represent a quotation of the kind of song Joe played. The intended audience would be white listeners who were interested in black music, not black performers themselves. Like the duo's other works of this period, a similar song could easily have been written by white lyricist/composers. In performance, Sissle apparently drew out the word "bloo-hoos" in an exaggerated semi-yodel—a typical affectation of white pop vocalists as well.[23]

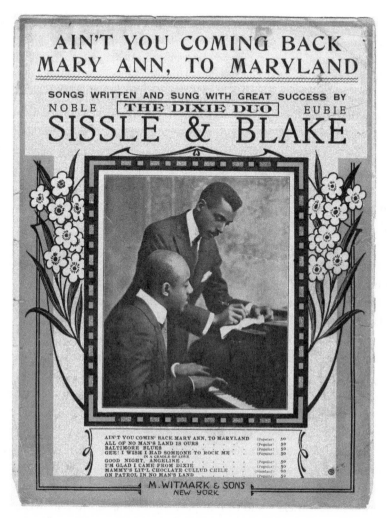

Figure 4.1 "Ain't You Comin' Back Mary Ann, to Maryland," by Sissle and Blake, 1919. This sheet was issued during their touring days as "The Dixie Duo."

The duo's stage show is best preserved in an early sound film made by engineer Lee de Forest, who made a few shorts to promote his "Phono-film" recording method in April 1923. The six-minute short—titled *Sissle and Blake Sing Snappy Songs*—includes four numbers, three composed by Sissle and Blake—"Sons of Old Black Joe," "My Swanee Home," "Affectionate Dan"—and an upbeat reworking of the spiritual "All God's Children Got Shoes." During the first two numbers, Sissle sits on one end of the piano bench, turned at 90 degrees to the piano, with Blake at the other end at the keyboard. Sissle's exaggerated gestures—particularly his eye rolls, upheld hands, and facial expressions—clearly show he was used to "projecting" to the auditorium. What is most surprising about the performance is how much Blake is involved vocally, singing harmony parts and occasionally interjecting a comment or two. In later interviews, Blake claimed he rarely sang as part of the act, but this is clearly not the case at least in this film. While Sissle is the more emotive and the focus of attention, Blake holds his own as the second banana. The duo appear in full tuxedos, which was their normal stage attire, and the songs—while referring obliquely to the South and minstrel stereotypes like "Old Black Joe"—are performed straight, with no dialect.

Of their original songs, "Sons of Old Black Joe" is a song they used to introduce the act (replacing the earlier "Gee! I'm Glad I'm from Dixie"). While acknowledging their racial heritage—or at least their heritage as represented on the minstrel stage through the stereotype of "Old Black Joe"—the lyric makes clear, in a non-threatening and peppy way, that Sissle and Blake represent a more advanced black act. They are not reviving Old Black Joe, but rather are more advanced descendants of the original black performer. The song both reassures the listeners that they will get the same kind of pep and good feeling they got from listening to minstrel and coon songs but also advances the idea that they will get the refinement they enjoy from white popular singers. "My Swanee Home" illustrates how they updated the minstrel format, taking the familiar trope of the old South but eliminating any mention of slavery or life on a plantation. While some might view this approach as erasing history, for Sissle and Blake it was asserting that black acts could equal their white counterparts by writing up-to-date lyrics and employing jazzy syncopations.

"Affectionate Dan" might be the hardest of the songs to swallow, particularly because of Sissle's eye-rolling performance.[24] Again, the lyrics are somewhat ambiguous as to Dan's racial background, and there is no offensive dialect or are there any indirect references to sex or lovemaking, as were sometimes found in blues lyrics. But the performance is way over the top and does recall minstrelsy—even without blackface makeup. On the other hand, contemporary white performers like Al Jolson used similar exaggerated gestures and eye movements, so Sissle may simply have been following the style of the day. Playing large vaudeville houses without amplification meant that performers had to be able to project both their voices and facial expressions out to the uppermost seats. It's said that that with this short Sissle and Blake were the first black performers to appear in a sound film.[25]

De Forest also filmed Eubie playing his set of variations on "Swanee River," although this film was apparently not released at the time. Two versions of the performance survive, each similarly set in the light classical form of the day. Eubie's variations include a bravura introduction in the grand style of 19th century classical piano virtuosis; a statement of the familiar melody in the left hand accompanying by harp-like glissandos in the right; and several other variations ranging from a frenzied minor variation and a staccato block-chord setting that imitates the strumming of a banjo. There is no syncopation and barely a hint of the kind of advanced harmonies that Blake brought to his popular rags and songs. This was Eubie's big solo number on the vaudeville stage, designed to please the crowd.

Meanwhile, the demand for black performers in England and Europe was growing during this period. As we have noted, several musicians associated with Jim Europe had remained abroad after World War I to work in Paris and London. English producers were eager to find other "authentic" black acts to bring over. Sissle had particularly enjoyed his time in France, and may have taken the initiative in locating an agent who could get the duo work abroad. In 1919, they signed an agreement for a six-week tour with a London-based promoter named Maxim P. Lowe, guaranteeing them 60 pounds a week less 10% agent's fee, with their fee increasing if they remained longer. (Lowe had previously worked in New York City as a theatrical booker/promoter and perhaps had met Sissle and Blake while he was working there.) Whether Lowe was unsuccessful in finding them work at the time, or whether Sissle and Blake's stateside commitments made it impossible for them to travel, is unknown; the duo would not travel abroad together until 1925.[26]

The duo's success on the road—and the popularity of the songs they had written with Jim Europe and newer numbers they composed on their own— may have led to invitations to Blake to make more piano-roll recordings in 1919. As with other piano-roll artists of the day, most of Blake's recordings were probably made at the request of the roll producers and were not part of his normal repertory. In some cases, when listening to these rolls replayed in the early 1970s, Blake either disputed his participation in making them or did not recall playing the tunes. This reaction was true of a medley of pop tunes that he apparently made for the company Artrio-Angelus in Meriden, Connecticut. The roll—released as "Shubert Gaieties of 1919" to cash in on the recent successful show—is played rather stiffly, as if the pianist were sight-reading from a score. In fact, this is probably what happened. After hearing the roll played in 1972, Blake insisted that it was not his performance: "That don't sound like me—no, I never play hardly anything straight. Whoever did that must have been reading. That's a bootleg. I never played that way."[27] The evidence, however, is strong that Blake did make the roll, as its serial number falls logically within the progression of the other rolls he cut for this firm.

Eubie said he was invited to make rolls for this company, thanks to a chance meeting with one of its producers on a train from Boston to New York:

> I'm coming down from Boston . . . and a guy keeps sittin', lookin' at me, and lookin' at me, and he made me nervous—an ofay [white] guy. So he came over to me and says, "Don't you conduct an orchestra?" . . . It's 1919. I was conducting for Jim Europe then. Jim was dead, but I had charge of his work. And he said, "You like to make some piano rolls?" I got off the train with him and I think he said, "Play anything you want to play but just tell me the names of them," and I played, played, played. I think I made about $250 or $300 for the whole session. He paid me in cash; I didn't get any royalty.[28]

This recollection would indicate that these rolls were made before the Dixie Duo began touring in the fall of 1919, although Eubie may have had the chronology off. The fact that he was returning from Boston would seem to indicate that he had been on the road, performing. In any case, his vaudeville work undoubtedly added to his fame, attracting the company to have him record his numbers along with the pop songs of the day. Among other rolls cut at this time include medleys from the 1919 *Ziegfeld Follies* and *Greenwich Village Follies*; and two Sissle and Blake originals, "Good Night Angeline" (previously cut by Eubie in 1917) and "Gee! I Wish I Had Someone to Rock Me in the Cradle of Love," later published by Witmark. Eubie says the session lasted about an hour-and-a-half.[29]

Eubie's final piano rolls were made for the Mel-o-Dee and Duo Art divisions of the Aeolian company, among the era's biggest producers of rolls. Again, a chance encounter led to this session; Eubie was walking down Broadway when he ran into Jack Bliss, who was employed by Aeolian. Bliss was a big fan of Eubie's playing and asked him to come in and make some rolls. As Bliss joined the firm in April 1919, the timing of this encounter was probably sometime in late summer or early fall. Mel-o-Dee rolls were promoted as "song rolls," and were intended to be used to provide accompaniments for amateur singers. For this reason, artists were encouraged to record the pop-song hits of the day. Many of these rolls suffer from additional flourishes added after the initial performance, probably to give a fuller sound to the rolls. Inevitably, though, these touches obscure Eubie's unique approach, and many would be impossible for a single player to execute. Only one number was a Sissle and Blake composition, "The Good Fellow Blues." In advertisements and on the rolls themselves, the pianist was credited sometimes as "Ubie" and others as "Eubie" Blake.

For Duo Art, Eubie made an unusual recording, a medley of Negro spirituals. Again, it sounds as if Blake were sight-reading from a formal arrangement; Duo Art credited it to Blake, although it was not part of his performing repertory as far as can be told. This "serious" performance reflects both the interest in spirituals among African American composers of the day and their (often white) audiences. None of Blake's characteristic ragtime effects are heard here, although the playing is more nuanced than anything heard on the other rolls. Duo Art marketed this roll in its "Popular Salon Music" category, emphasizing that the intended audience was white fans of spiritual numbers, not blacks.[30]

By 1920, Sissle and Blake were recognized as leading songwriters as well as performers. They had the opportunity to compose two songs for white revues produced by J. J. Shubert and Lee Shubert: "My Vision Girl" for the *Midnight Rounders of 1920*, presented after the main production at the Century Promenade theater; and "Floradora Girls" featured in one of the Shuberts' 1920 productions at the Winter Garden (perhaps *Broadway Brevities,* which opened that fall, and featured Bert Williams in its cast). According to Eubie, they were paid $400 for each song, a considerable sum. Writing to order while traveling on the road, Eubie had no compunctions about borrowing what he thought was an old folk melody for another one of these songs. It turned out, however, that the melody came from an earlier song by the African American composer William Tyers, who wasn't particularly pleased when he discovered that it was being performed nightly at the Shubert Theater. Eubie recounted that a friend of Tyers's accosted him on the street, accusing him of stealing the song:

I'm coming downtown 7th Avenue between 38th and 39th Street, and the guy says, "What the hell you want to steal 'Filipino Dance' from Bill?" I says, "I didn't steal no song. That's an old folksong." And this is a bad guy too ... So I meet [Tyers] a couple of days [later] ... And I says, "Hey

Bill, what's the idea of everybody telling me about you going to give me hell about I stealing your 'Filipino Dance'?" I says, "You didn't write no 'Filipino Dance.' That's a folksong." And he says, "I just happen to have a ragged piece of paper. Can you read? Who's name is that there?" I says, "Oh Bill, honest to God I didn't . . ." I says, "I'll tell you what I'll do. I can't give you half of Sissle's money, he wrote the lyric to it. But I says we got 400 dollars to place this song in the show. I'll give you 100 dollars of my dollars." And he says, "You got some goddamn nerve." . . . It was wrong. But to me it was a folksong.[31]

Apparently, Tyers had the original sheet music with him, which convinced Blake that he had indeed pilfered the melody. It is unclear which song by Tyers that Eubie inadvertently plagiarized, although it possibly was his 1908 hit, "Maori: A Samoan Dance," which was widely recorded, particularly after lyrics were added to it in 1913. Tyers was associated with the Clef Club and Eubie knew him and his work from the time he arrived in New York. Eubie told biographer Lawrence T. Carter that he unsuccessfully tried to have the song pulled from the show once he realized he had unintentionally taken the melody from Tyers's earlier hit.[32]

Later in 1920, Sissle and Blake would make an important connection with another black duo working the Orpheum Circuit: the popular comic duo of Flournoy Miller and Aubrey Lyles (Figure 4.2). As Blake told it, they did not meet—despite working the same circuit—until performing at a benefit for the NAACP at Philadelphia's Dunbar Theater sometime in mid-1920, and then didn't see them again until the two acts ran into each other on Broadway that summer. Subsequently, the duos may have appeared on the same vaudeville bill at least once, in August 1920 in Brooklyn, as part of *The Chameleon Revue*, led by singer, dancer, and comic monologist Corinne Tilton. In notices dated a week apart, cast members Sissle and Blake were listed as performing their hit "No Man's Land," while Miller and Lyles were appearing as "two colored men who are thrown into a snowstorm without the protection of their overcoats"—a typical comic premise for their act, which could build humor out of the slightest predicaments.[33] It is possible that they did not appear together in the same performance, as the revue seemed to have a floating list of acts; Blake commented that, on white vaudeville, they'd never book more than one black act per performance, because of prejudice. However, they were probably at least aware of each other's participation in this revue and may have met backstage.

Figure 4.2 Flournoy Miller (left) as Steve Jenkins and Aubrey Lyles (right) as Sam Peck in a scene from *Shuffle Along*. The duo had first introduced these two characters in their vaudeville act. Note that the third actor does not appear in blackface; only the comic leads wore this makeup in *Shuffle Along*.

By the time Sissle and Blake met Flournoy Miller and Aubrey Lyles, the two men had extensive careers in musical theater. As with many of his contemporaries, it is difficult to pinpoint Miller's year of birth. The most probable date is the one on his draft registration card, April 14, 1885, but in two articles Miller also claimed to have been born three years earlier, while some sources date his birth to five years earlier. He was born in Columbia, Tennessee, to a middle-class family. Miller's grandmother, Elizabeth Miller, was a house slave. During the Civil War, when the Union soldiers occupied the town, Elizabeth sold the soldiers her fried chicken, cakes, and pies. When the war ended, she bought herself several properties and built a house all with money she earned by selling food to the troops. His grandfather, Alexander Miller, would go out into the country and set off dynamite in order to loosen up the earth. He'd then break up the rocks and sell them to the city of Columbia for use in paving their dirt roads.

In 1882, Flournoy's father, William Lee Miller, graduated from Roger Williams University in Nashville and, on graduation, married Mary Irvin.[34] He went on to work as a principal in public schools in both South Pittsburg[35] and Columbia, Tennessee. While living in Columbia, Miller joined an amateur quintet, singing the (white popular) songs of the day, including "Silver Threads among the Gold," as well as popular "coon" and minstrel songs like "Golden Slippers."[36]

Remarkably for the time, William Miller began writing editorials for two white papers, the *Chattanooga Times* and the *Nashville Banner*. After serving briefly in the advertising department, he became editor of the newly established *Nashville Globe*, an African American weekly newspaper, in 1906, holding the position for 12 years.[37] The *Globe* was established by Richard Henry Boyd, who was born in slavery in Texas. Boyd moved to Nashville in 1896, becoming a prominent figure in the black community, establishing a bank for blacks in 1904. When the city decided to segregate all of its streetcars, Boyd led a boycott that inspired him to begin the *Globe* as a means of fighting prejudice.[38] William Miller knew firsthand about prejudice among the city's white population. In 1907, he was beaten on the head by a white police officer. (The offense he committed—if any—is unrecorded.) The case was brought before the city council, but was dismissed with the statement "the officer was justified in maliciously assaulting" Miller. The *Globe* ran a brief statement about the incident, demanding of the city's white council members, "Where were [you] when men were needed to help fight against race oppression?"[39]

The Miller family was solidly middle class and William and Mary aspired for their five children, three boys and two girls, to have good educations. For the boys, they hoped they'd pursue careers in the "respected" occupations of teacher, doctor, pharmacist, or the priesthood, all of which would "almost ensure success." However, all three boys grew up to have notable careers in theater—which, at the time, as they noted, "was not too respected as a profession. It was uncertain. It had its risks. But it had its thrills. . . ." Flournoy's older brother, Irvin C. (born c. 1883), performed in vaudeville and then began producing shows. And his younger brother, Quintard (born c. 1896), also appeared as an actor, writer, and producer. The three brothers' careers sometimes merged with one or another acting in another brother's production or touring with the same vaudeville and stock companies. By the 1910 census, Irvin's occupation was given as "acrobat (theater)" and Flournoy's as "playwright."[40]

Miller's first brush with the theater was in an amateur performance with his father and his two uncles. When his father became a newspaper editor, Flournoy and his brother Irvin met many performers, mainly those touring the South in minstrel shows. The stories these men related made a deep impression on the two youngsters. They were regaled not only with the romance of the theater but also with the perils of black minstrels performing in the South: Rocks were thrown at the performers on their way to the theater, and melees were common in which the blacks were rounded up and sent to the local jail while the whites were exonerated—and in some cases lynching. When Flournoy and Irvin heard these tales of horror they asked their father why the black performers continued despite all the dangers. "How could they do it? How could they continue on, following this call to make people happy and receive so much unhappiness themselves? What motivated them?"

Their father responded, "Some day you may understand, these men have a divine gift. You will meet others with the same gift, the same drive that makes them perform, sing, dance, bring happiness to the world no matter what the odds."[41] Their father's explanation struck a chord and inspired them both to pursue theatrical careers. Like other African American performers, they would find themselves in similar situations but they would go forward undaunted.

Flournoy and his brothers had seen black minstrel shows but not what were called "colored musicals." That changed when they saw a bill posted on a wall that announced, "Coming, Mme. Sissieretta Jones." Flournoy recalled their excitement:

> We could scarcely contain ourselves. She was known as Black Patti. She was a legendary figure adhering to the mystery, glamour and exclusiveness that are integrally the want of a star. She was never seen in a public restaurant, always traveled in a closed carriage and her reputation was above reproach.

A beautiful brown woman, with the sweetest voice I have ever heard. She sang spirituals but always included opera in her performance.

By the time he entered Fisk University, Flournoy was well and truly bitten by the stage bug. And it was there that he met Aubrey Lyles.[42] Lyles was born in Jackson, Tennessee, on January 8, 1884.[43] His father was Robert Lyles and his mother Lena Bishop; the couple had three children, the eldest being Aubrey, and two younger girls. By 1900, Lyles's mother had married a man named Boon, who was working as a locomotive foreman, and the family was living with him.

Miller later wrote about the importance of Aubrey Lyles in his life:

There was an immediate affinity, an understanding between us that remained unchanging from the day we met, until the day of his death some thirty years later. To say that we shared the same enthusiasm for the theatre, is an understatement. To say that the Fisk Faculty was not kindly disposed toward students with theatrical aspirations is also an understatement, but our minds were made up and their warnings and dire prophesies only served to strengthen our resolves.

As he wrote, "In spite of Fisk's apathy to Show Business as such, it had a fine music department." And that department was known worldwide because of the Fisk Jubilee Singers, whose success earned the money for the construction of the University's Jubilee Hall.

While still at Fisk, Miller and Lyles decided to write a play. The administration frowned on their idea but Miller's brother Irvin was editor of the *Fisk Herald,* and his cousin Clifford Miller and friend George Haynes were both honor students. The three of them convinced the faculty to let the show go on, and with *Down in Eagles Nest,* the team of Miller and Lyles was born. The show did so well that its proceeds helped build Fisk's Theological Hall building.

Upon graduation, both Miller and Lyles set out for careers in the theater. For a short while after leaving Fisk, Lyles joined the John Robinson circus, in which he was assigned the unenviable role of riding a bucking mule. As a newspaper man commented decades later, "He didn't mind the mule, but when it became part of his job to pack up the tents, he left the 'big top.'"[44]

In 1905, Miller and Lyles traveled to Chicago, then the leading theatrical town for black performers. The most successful venue for blacks in Chicago was the Pekin Theatre, known as the "Temple of Music," at the corner of 27th and State Street. It was more of a cabaret than a theater, with seating for 325 people at tables on the main floor and a small balcony; later seats were added to bring the capacity to 400. The theater/cabaret had already presented black musicals that were in the "European style of entertainment" adjusted for the "darktown" patrons. In 1905, it planned to present "A Beautiful Spectacular Musical Comedy from the pen of Mr. Charles S. Sager, dealing with the Negro of the 50th Century."[45]

The original building burned down in March 1906, a disaster that turned out to be bad for the owner and its clientele but good for Miller and Lyles. In its place, owner Bob Motts built the first American theater devoted solely to black shows; its company would be known as the Pekin Stock Company. Motts wrote a letter to the *Indianapolis Freeman* on March 17, 1906, stating that the theater "shall be a playhouse worthy of the name and a credit to the Negro race." The new theater seated 1200 patrons.

Miller and Lyles wrote their second play, *The Man from 'Bam*[46] as a way of introduction to Bob Motts. To their surprise, after some adjustments to the script, Motts agreed to produce it and hired theatrical veteran Joe Jordan to write the score along with lyricist Will Vodery. The show opened in 1906, and the consensus was that it could have been better. While Miller and Lyles thought their script was to blame, Bob Motts blamed it on the director and cast, noting that they had come from the previous theater's cabaret. He assured them that henceforth he would use only people with theatrical experience.[47]

The following year, Miller wrote another show, *The Mayor of Dixie*, while Lyles, newly married, worked as a dining-car porter for trains in and out of Chicago between engagements. With Motts's new company of experienced performers, *The Mayor of Dixie* was a huge hit, with Miller and Lyles playing small roles. Other future notables in the cast were Will Marion Cook, a composer who later studied with Dvořák, and songwriter James T. Brymn, who later wrote special material for Fanny Brice and Broadway shows. When it closed after a sold-out three week run, Lyles returned to working for the railroad.

But word of mouth about the show built among the black community and even among white patrons of the theater, and the show was brought back by popular demand. No less a luminary than Mrs. Potter Palmer, doyenne of Chicago society—a businesswoman in her own right and a noted philanthropist, along with Mrs. Armour of the meatpacking company—bought out a house. White society thrilled to the performance on stage. *The Mayor of Dixie*'s book would later loosely serve as the basis for *Shuffle Along*.

In April 1907, Miller and Lyles's *The Husband* opened with songs by Joe Jordan and interpolations by James T. Brymn, Bob Cole, and J. Rosamond Johnson. The show was an immediate success. At the urging of Will Marion Cook and famous manager/comic actor/playwright Ernest Hogan, Motts brought the production to New York. It opened on August 12, 1907, at Hurtig & Seamon's Music Hall Theatre, playing a two-week run. After it closed, Miller and Lyles stayed in New York. Hogan—a well-established comedian—asked Miller to write a starring vehicle for him. *The Oyster Man* opened on November 25, 1907 at the Yorkville Theatre in New York City and was an immediate success.

The team returned to Chicago and Miller then undertook a stab at vaudeville, along with a partner, Do Do Green. They played a series of one-night stands in small towns. The act was a flop and the manager skipped town, but it gave Miller the idea that he and Lyles should try their luck in vaudeville. They started in 15-a-day nickelodeons. Though Miller and Lyles stuck to their comic routines, they hired three black girls to provide singing, dancing, and sex appeal. They were billed as The Ebony Five but the girls soon decamped. When the comic team tried to replace them, the theater's manager suggested that they didn't need any support; their comedy act was even stronger on its own.

After a brief stint leading a black company in Montgomery, Georgia, in April 1908, Miller rejoined Lyles and the Pekin Stock Company for a new show, *Dr. Knight*, which they wrote and starred in. The music was again by James T. Brymn. It was followed by *The Colored Aristocrats*, with music by Sidney Perrin. It opened in 1908 at the Pekin and began touring in 1909. Flournoy, his brother Irvin (who also produced the show), and Aubrey were the show's stars. Apparently, the trio made sure the play's opening preview for the press would be well attended and received, according to noted African American drama critic Sylvester Russell:

> When the trio of stars . . . entered . . . there was a deafening thunder of applause, which must have proved to these three youngest of stars and playwrights in the history of the colored race, that friends galore had made good their promise to give them the swellest audience of the season[,] "Goat cheers," and a handsome send-off.[48]

In this play, Flournoy Miller and Aubrey Lyles introduced their stage characters, Steve Jenkins and Sam Peck. Jenkins was played by Miller as the cosmopolitan brains of the duo and Lyles portrayed Peck, a smart-ass whose bravado got them in an endless variety of scrapes. While both Miller and Lyles were credited with this script, it was mainly Miller who did the writing. But a team was a team and so both took credit for what was largely Miller's work throughout their partnership.

Then it was back to vaudeville, with Miller and Lyles working their way up from small-time theaters to larger circuits, including the Keith Orpheum two-a-day theaters in major cities. Their first appearance at a white vaudeville theater in Chicago in 1910 attracted a positive notice from the *Chicago Defender*, despite the act's rough edges. The duo were still experimenting with the content of their act, even performing an opening comic song. Not surprisingly, given their race and their unproven appeal to a white audience, the act appeared near the start of the bill, when critics and a majority of the audience were often not yet in attendance. The *Defender*'s critic wrote,

> Miller and Lyles had a chance to shine even at half past 7. . . . Although the stage seemed large to them at first and the environment somewhat different from what they had been accustomed to, it put them to their wits' end to find a winning spot in their dialogue . . . which brought the house down. . . . a burlesque fight was all that could be desired in the finish of an act that will successfully entertain anywhere. Miller and Lyles are the young face [of] comedy playwrights, and in view of their future work and the good and recent criticisms have done for them, their every movement will hence be looked upon with growing interest.[49]

Their acrobatic boxing match—in which the much taller Miller held the scrappy Lyles at bay merely by extending his arms—went over so well with audiences that the duo continued to perform it for many years, incorporating it into other shows, including *Shuffle Along*.

In February 1911, Miller and Lyles opened on Broadway at Hammerstein's Victoria Theatre, a rival of the Palace Theatre, located farther down Broadway. Unlike other acts that combined music, dance, and dialogue (and sometimes acrobatics and other novelties), Miller and Lyles relied primarily on their verbal interplay. Ironically, though they portrayed Southern characters, the duo never performed south of Indianapolis, because of racial prejudice. Flournoy's father—"a typical southerner [who] seldom leaves southern territory"—had to travel to the Northern city in order to get his first experience of the act.[50]

In 1914, the team took a break from vaudeville to star in the musical revue *Darkydom*. It was their first appearance in a show that they did not write, although they played their characters Steve Jenkins and Sam Peck. It tried out at the Howard Theatre in Washington and then moved to the Lafayette Theatre in Harlem in October 1915. The show attracted both black and white audiences. It is considered to have been the last major success for black actors with white audiences before *Shuffle Along* opened six years later.

Later in 1915, Miller and Lyles traveled to London and starred in *Andre Charlot's Revue* on the West End Stage. They were the second black act to play in London. The first was McIntyre and Heath, who were an enormous flop. Miller and Lyles ascribed McIntyre and Heath's failure to their Southern accents. To avoid a similar fate, Miller and Lyles performed their act with English Cockney accents (despite portraying Southern black characters). Their tour took them throughout the British Isles and then Europe, attracting favorable press for Miller back in his hometown of Nashville. The local white newspaper took note of their "high-class" act and took some credit for molding the young star's character[51]

After returning from Europe later in 1916, the duo remained in high demand on the US vaudeville circuit, appearing with and having equal appeal to the biggest white acts. Along with Sissle and Blake, they became perhaps the most successful black performers in mainstream vaudeville.

When the two duos met in 1920, Sissle and Blake were anxious to escape the vaudeville grind and Miller and Lyles hoped to have a show premiere on Broadway. On meeting Sissle and Blake at the NAACP benefit, Miller immediately saw the opportunity that combining their talents would bring to both acts. According to Eubie, Miller approached them, saying,

> "You boys is the missin' link of Negro show business. Why can't we put on a colored show for Broadway?" That was the same as saying, "Why can't we get a colored man for president of the United States?"
>
> So we looked at him, see. So Sissle has always been more commercial than I, he could see further than I. I didn't respond to Miller, because I never saw the act, I didn't know what they could do. Sissle says "Alright, we try it." "Alright, we try it" (he's a college guy now) "Me and Lyles . . ." that's the way they talked, see. Now they wouldn't talk that way in front of [white people], see. [They'd speak in] perfect English. [Miller's] getting down with

me. "Yeah, I'll write the meat . . . me and Lyles will write the book"—Lyles never wrote nothing in his life . . . "And you'all write the music."[52]

In an interview conducted by the black press after the show's success, Sissle recalled, "Blake and I always wanted to take out a show, but needed a book. Miller and Lyles had taken out several [shows], but had little success because they lacked original music."[53] They made an ideal match.

A pact was made that they would join forces to try to mount a Broadway show. Eubie says the show was originally to be called *Who's Stealin'?*, "because there's a drugstore and everybody was stealin' in the drugstore." With their touring company, Miller and Lyles had previously produced a play called *Who's Stealin'* in 1920 that had the duo portraying co-owners of a small department store; elements of this script were probably used as the basis for *Shuffle Along*.[54] The duo were constantly recycling their signature characters, placing them in different situations but drawing on similar verbal and physical humor. Sissle objected to the title, perhaps because of its focus on minstrel stereotypes of thieving blacks, and—as the show developed—it became *Shuffle Along* (Figure 4.3).

Figure 4.3 Clockwise from top: Flournoy Miller, Noble Sissle, Aubrey Lyles, and Eubie Blake at the time they joined forces to create *Shuffle Along*.

Another early title that appeared in the press was *The Mayor of Jimtown*—reflecting the fact that the story centered on a political campaign in a small Southern black community. The first announcement of the forthcoming show appeared at the end of February 1921, with a projected opening date that April; the comic duo canceled a planned European tour, while Sissle and Blake were released from their contract with Keith Orpheum to work on the show.[55]

5

Shuffle Along

1921

As the decade turned from the years of the Great War to the Roaring Twenties, America was set to be the most powerful and most influential country in the world. While Europe was still suffering from the devastation of the war, America enjoyed the greatest economic boom in its history. The stock market was on its way to the stratosphere and industry grew at a previously unknown rate. Social change—including the passage of the 18th Amendment banning the sale of alcohol, a ban that launched the growth of speakeasies; and the 19th Amendment giving women the right to vote—was leading to transformations in the entertainment world. The sounds and slang of New York and Broadway began its reach into the hinterlands in November 1920 with the establishment of the first radio-broadcast station. This rising economic tide also lifted the plight of blacks, at least in New York, which found itself the financial and entertainment capitol of the world. The stage was now set literally and figuratively for the remarkable success of *Shuffle Along*.

Another key ingredient *in Shuffle Along's* success was the growing impact of African American culture on New York's life. The 1910s saw the black population of Harlem explode by over 66%.[1] It had previously been a mostly white enclave, but with blacks coming to New York from the South and Midwest for both the new jobs and the slowly changing attitudes toward race, the black population of Harlem grew to 200,000 by the end of the 1920s. White New York became fascinated with this growing population, with cultural leaders particularly fascinated by the new art forms that were developing in Harlem.

Another reason for the great success of *Shuffle Along* is that in the early 1920s Broadway's roots were still firmly in the operetta tradition. Only Irving Berlin was slowly incorporating the new influences of syncopation and jazz into his music. As early as the 1910s, Berlin was paying homage to jazz and black culture. Though not from a musical comedy, his first great song success, 1911's "Alexander's Ragtime Band," was a radical departure from the

Eubie Blake. Richard Carlin and Ken Bloom, Oxford University Press (2020). © Richard Carlin and Ken Bloom 2020.
DOI: 10.1093/oso/9780190635930.001.0001

waltz rhythms of Broadway and popular song. And it should be noted that "Alexander" was Tin Pan Alley's code word for a black man. (Similarly, "baby" was descriptive of an African American woman.) Berlin took black musical elements—adding light syncopation to a jaunty march rhythm—in this song and others like it to make them palatable for white audiences. Similarly, *Shuffle Along* would wrap black musical elements and comedy in a package that white audiences could accept and enjoy.

As a vaudeville duo, Sissle and Blake shared a common goal: to make it to Broadway. For Sissle, it would be a chance to prove his skills as an actor and vocalist; for Blake, it would mean graduating to the highest tier of popular-songwriters and orchestra leaders. Success on Broadway meant entering the world of the entertainment elite. Beyond these personal goals, they shared a common belief that if they could prove that black songwriters and performers could produce music that equaled (if not bettered) the work of their white peers, they would not only open the doors to other composers/performers but also promote the broader idea that blacks were just as capable of artistic expression as anyone else.

Sissle's and Blake's personal struggle was wrapped in a belief in racial progress and equality, showing the influence of black social philosophers such as W. E. B. DuBois and other prominent black intellectuals of the day. These individuals promoted what was known as the "New Negro." Highly educated and interested in the arts, the younger generations celebrated their race and even whites became infatuated with these young black writers, artists, and performers and their works.[2] In the words of theater historian Peter Woods, the time was ripe for blacks to present their music, dance, and song to a mainstream audience:

> The factors for a significant cultural development in the American popular theatre were all present: a white audience fascinated by the Negro, though in many ways obviously misinformed[;] critics and writers interested in the possibilities of seeing Negro themes and actors on the stage; and a great pool of Negro talent, trained in cabarets, vaudeville houses, and Negro theatres.[3]

Black performers had to overcome a legacy of theatrical stereotypes that dated back to the early 19th century. This was the era of blackface minstrelsy, when the common characters of "Old Black Joe" (the rural bumpkin) and "Zip Coon" (the urban hipster/conman) were developed. A repertoire of dance music and song also developed, mostly written by white composers like Stephen Foster, but with a few blacks in the mix as well. (African American songwriter James Bland wrote the popular "Carry Me Back to Old Virginny," among other hits.)

In the original minstrel companies, white performers appeared in black-face. However, a thirst to see the "real thing" led to black companies being formed, most of which picked up the same stereotypes of the white shows, with black performers themselves forced to don blackface. Soon after the end of the Civil War, a new middle class emerged in the black population and began to strive for equality, both in society and in the theater. Many of these blacks were educated in the new African American universities, and yearned for the same opportunities as whites. For them, the minstrel stereo-types were degrading. They hoped to forge a new role for blacks in popular entertainment.[4]

The best-known performers to emerge from blackface minstrelsy were the comic duo Bert Williams and George Walker. They formed a touring company that featured Walker's wife, dancer/ingénue Aida Overton Walker (sometimes referred to as "Ada"). The group presented *The Gold Bug* (1896) at New York's Casino Theatre, a show that helped popularize the cakewalk. But the first full-length, all-black Broadway musical, written by and star-ring African Americans, was *A Trip to Coontown* (1898), by lyricist Bob Cole along with composer Billy Johnson. The show had both dramatic moments and vaudeville specialties in its plot and dealt mainly in stereotypes. However, in his later shows, Cole and composer J. Rosamond Johnson eschewed black stereotypes. They were more interested in the rise of blacks into the middle class, consciously attempting to elevate the status of blacks in the entertain-ment field while changing white audiences' perceptions at the same time.

Like Eubie and Noble Sissle after *Shuffle Along*, Cole and Johnson were asked to write material for white audiences by the most preeminent produc-ers of their time, Marcus Klaw and Abe Erlanger. Cole and Johnson wrote songs for white shows and the team's work became known to a white audi-ence. In 1902, Cole and J. Rosamund Johnson's *Sally in Our Alley* opened but was not a success—although Cole and Johnson's song "Under the Bamboo Tree" became the first song from a black musical to become a Tin Pan Alley hit.

The second black show on Broadway was *Clorindy*, also in 1898, with songs by Will Marion Cook and Paul Laurence Dunbar and starring come-dian Ernest Hogan. When it arrived, Cook exclaimed, "Negroes are at last on

Broadway and here to stay!"⁵ Cook believed that African Americans should make their own style of theater and not emulate what "the white artist could always do as well, generally better." Cook also wrote the first black musical to play London's West End, *In Dahomey* (1903), and the first interracial musical to play Broadway, *The Southerners* (1904). Cook took one of *In Dahomey*'s hit songs, "Swing Along!," and wrote a choral version in 1912 that became a standard expression of racial pride. Its success could have inspired the decision for Sissle and Blake to title both the song and show "Shuffle Along."

The Southerners' interracial cast was cause for alarm and nervousness. The critic for *The New York Times* wrote about the opening night,

> When the chorus of real live coons walked in for the cake . . . mingling with the white members of the cast, there were those in the audience who trembled in their seats, as if expecting an . . . explosion. It was only a year ago that the entire cast of a farce at Madison Square struck because a single gentleman of color was engaged to play the part of a Negro porter, and held out until the gentleman was entirely cast out. And here were scores of blacks and whites mingling. But it presently became evident that the spirit of harmony reigned. Marion Cook. . . all alone had succeeded in harmonizing the racial broth as skillfully as he had harmonized the accompanying score.⁶

Cook's dream of a respected black theater was echoed beyond the borders of Broadway. Chicago's Pekin Stock Company was founded by producer Robert T. Motts. His Pekin Theater would be according to Motts "a playhouse worthy of the name and a credit to the Negro race."⁷ We have seen how Flournoy Miller and Aubrey Lyles's careers were launched by a series of successful shows that they wrote and starred in at the Pekin—an important incubator for *Shuffle Along.*

Meanwhile, black Broadway shows continued to emerge sporadically, including *Mr. Lode of Coal* and *The Red Moon*, both produced in 1909. The last all-black Broadway show of this period was 1911's *His Honor, the Barber* with music by James T. Brymn. By 1909, the number of black shows had diminished because of the deaths of Ernest Hogan and George Walker and, in 1911, Bob Cole. In addition to their skills as performers or songwriters, these men also managed their own companies—which were on consistently shaky financial ground. Still, troupes like Williams and Walker (without Walker), the Black Patti Troubadours, the Smart Set, and the Negro Players all produced shows throughout the United States, some surviving into the 1920s.

Although there was black vaudeville as well as black musicals touring the country, between 1910 and the opening of *Shuffle Along* in 1921 there was no black musical on Broadway save for the failed *Darktown Follies* in 1913. And there were no black stars of any consequence except Bert Williams, who was a featured performer in the *Ziegfeld Follies* through 1919; he died in 1922. Broadway audiences had grown tired of the black stereotypes and lightweight plots of black musicals. For almost a decade, there was little or no interest in black musical theater, although black vaudeville continued to be successful, mainly for black audiences.

Following the limited integration of World War I, the country was gripped with race riots. Black soldiers returning from Europe received a hostile reception from the white majority. Lynchings and rioting followed. Returning from the war, black fighters expected to be hailed as heroes. The backlash of whites against them and their music made producing black shows, even touring black shows meant for black audiences, problematic. Productions were discouraged for reasons of racism and the safety of the casts. In several later-life interviews, Eubie also claimed that interest in black acts in vaudeville and Broadway ended when Jack Johnson—the famous black boxer—wed a white woman in 1912, scandalizing white America.

Nonetheless, around the mid-1910s in New York City there was a growing interest in black artists by white society folk and the intelligentsia. As we have seen, James Reese Europe and his orchestra were able to establish themselves among the white elite as a popular provider of music. The time was ripe for a new generation of black songwriters to try their hand on Broadway. Europe was involved with an important theatrical production in late autumn of 1915, *Darkydom*. Europe worked with lyricists Henry Creamer and Lester Walton to supply some songs, although the main portion of the music was by Will Marion Cook. Theater critic Lester Walton was the director of this revue-like show that the principals hoped would be staged on Broadway. Sadly, they were unable to raise the funds to have it appear downtown. However, the show did introduce Miller and Lyles to the New York legitimate stage. They performed in their well-known characters as Steve Jenkins (Miller) and Sam Peck (Lyles), whom they had introduced in earlier productions at Chicago's Pekin Theater and in vaudeville; these comic personae would also be revived in *Shuffle Along*.

After previewing at Washington's Howard Theater, the show did strong business at Harlem's Lafayette Theatre, and *The New York Age* noted that the premiere performance attracted the very best of Harlem society.[8] Black musical shows usually had a difficult time finding theaters and an even more difficult time keeping them. These shows were usually inexpensive to produce and had a low running cost. So, even at half or three-quarters full they could make a profit. But producers didn't want only half a house; they wanted full houses and few black shows could draw enough of an audience to sell out its performances.

After its engagement at the Lafayette Theatre, *Darkydom* subsequently played in Asbury Park, New Jersey, and then was taken on tour by producer John Cort—the same producer who would later provide the theater and old sets and costumes for *Shuffle Along*.[9] Although Blake claimed that neither he nor Sissle met Miller and Lyles at this time, it's at least likely that both were aware of the show's production through their association with Europe. Europe's dream for a hit show on Broadway scripted, composed, and performed by blacks was an inspiration, Sissle later said, for *Shuffle Along*.

Whereas their black predecessors leaned toward operetta forms for their musicals, Noble Sissle and Eubie Blake straddled the line between ragtime and Tin Pan Alley. Blake was also influenced by the popular English composers of the day, particularly Leslie Stuart, who composed the songs for the hit show *Floradora* (1900). While many black musicians would find it hard to relate to the refined sentiments of Stuart's music, Blake heard an echo of his own musical personality in it. It inspired him to believe that he could write for the musical theater: "I heard [Stuart's] music and said I could write like that."[10]

Blake acknowledged other influences on his composing. He had first heard classical composer Edward MacDowell's "To a Wild Rose" in the 1890s and it later inspired Blake's "Memories of You." Blake's "Gypsy Blues" was influenced by Victor Herbert's Broadway song "Gypsy Love Call." And Irving Berlin's use of syncopation also made an impact on Blake. Berlin's "Alexander's Ragtime Band" was a favorite of Blake's and he often played it during gigs in Atlantic City.[11]

Eubie was also a fan of Bob Cole and James Rosamond Johnson's 1909 show *The Red Moon*; the show also featured some songs with melodies by Eubie's future employer, James Reese Europe. Elements of the melody of *Red Moon*'s "I Ain't Had No Lovin' in a Long Time" are echoed by *Shuffle Along*'s "If You've Never Been Vamped by a Brownskin," showing the unconscious influence Cole and Europe's song had on Blake.

Not all of Broadway accepted black songwriters and librettists writing shows without stereotypes. The Shubert Brothers' publicist told Lester

Walton, drama critic for *The New York Age* newspaper, that critics weren't invited to *The Red Moon* because it "did not contain enough 'niggerism.'"[12] A week after Walton's declaration, the old *Life* magazine and *The Sun* wrote that Shubert was wrong—which only made Walton sure he was correct.[13]

Shuffle Along owed another debt to *The Red Moon*. The earlier show featured a couple in a serious romance. But *Red Moon* wasn't the first show to portray love between two African Americans without comic overtones. An early black musical opened in October 1913 at Harlem's Lafayette Theatre. The show was an amalgam of earlier shows and was billed as *The Darktown Follies in "My Friend from Kentucky."* Author James Weldon Johnson said that the show "drew space, headlines, and cartoons in New York papers; and consequently it became the vogue to go to Harlem to see it. That was the beginning of the nightly migration to Harlem [by whites] in search of entertainment."[14] The show took romance between blacks seriously. J. Leubrie Hill, "dubbed the black George M. Cohan," wrote the love song "'Rock Me in the Cradle of Love." James Weldon Johnson reported that the song "had been sung by the Negro tenor to the bronze soubrette in a most impassioned manner, demonstrating that the love-making taboo had been absolutely kicked out of the Negro theatre."[15]

Like many other show creators, the team behind *Shuffle Along* (Figure 5.1) were not afraid to recycle their earlier efforts to create the new show. The show's book was based on Miller and Lyles's earlier success, *The Mayor of Dixie*, which was chock full of racial stereotypes, as befitted most of the black musicals produced during the first decade of the century. However, it was a big success in Chicago and the comic duo were well suited to the lead parts. As we shall see, Sissle and Blake would recycle many of the songs they had performed in their vaudeville act in order to create the show's score.

As Eubie tells it, Sissle and he wrote the songs independently of the work Miller and Lyles did to create the show's "script":

[Sissle and I worked together in my apartment] on 138th Street. We don't know what Miller, Lyles gonna write. They would say, "We gotta say—. . . 'The cow jumped over the moon'—Sissle, what do you think would fit there?" He'd say, "So-and-so," and write the title down. And I'd write that. We hadn't seen no book.

Indeed, a "book" wasn't written down for the show until several years later, after its successful New York run, in order to copyright it.[16]

Figure 5.1 The opening number of act 2 of *Shuffle Along*, which introduced the show's title song and featured the full chorus line.

Initially the two duos approached a well-known black banker, E. C. Brown, to finance a tour of black theaters with the hopes of eventually reaching Broadway. Brown's bank provided funding to three major East Coast black theaters, Harlem's Lafayette, Philadelphia's Dunbar, and Washington's Howard.[17] They proposed co-producing the show with the bank and splitting potential profits; the creators would draw salaries of $75.00 a week. Sissle assured the banker that they intended to produce a show that would appeal to "White and Colored lovers of good clean wholesome entertainment."[18] Unfortunately, Brown's bank was facing its own financial difficulties at the time and was unable to bankroll the performers.

They next approached Al Mayer, a white booker for the Keith vaudeville circuit and friend of Miller and Lyles. Mayer was impressed by what he saw; he told a contemporary interviewer, "I had always believed there was room for a good Negro show, but I had never found the show. I had taken out seven Negro productions and all were flops. But I saw the possibilities as outlined by Miller and Lyles, and Sissle and Blake, and got busy."[19]

Mayer took his friend Harry Cort to lunch (with $2.50 to pay the tab lent by Sissle and Blake[20]). Harry, the son of theater owner and producer John Cort[21], liked the idea of a black show, and an audition was set up with his father. As Blake told Robert Kimball and William Bolcom,

We ran down a few songs and Old Man Cort—well, he just sat there with a glum look on his face. When we did our theme song, "Love Will Find a

Way," the old man didn't say anything. Nothing. He just got up and walked out, saying, "Thank you, boys. Thank you very much." I thought we were dead for sure, but it turned out the old man liked the song so much he said he'd help us and give us a theatre, sets, [and] some old costumes, if we would just give his son Harry an interest in the show.[22]

Sissle and Blake were already familiar with John Cort, having played a series of Sunday shows at his uptown Cort Standard theater (located at Broadway and 96th Street). Cort arranged for them to use the space for auditions for the show. Sissle, fearing that would-be performers would be put off by its location, somehow convinced Cort to let them use his downtown house situated on the Great White Way. As Sissle recalled, Cort was shocked when 80 auditioners showed up on his doorstep.[23]

Once the show had been cast, Cort also agreed to provide the company with a place to stage the show. Located a half-mile from the northernmost point of Times Square, Daly's 63rd Street Music Hall stood on the corner of Broadway. It was hardly a well-known space; a critic for *The New York Age* described it as being "sandwiched between garages and other establishments representative of the automobile industry, [which] was little known to the average Broadway theatregoer."[24] The space had a small stage and hardly a backstage at all. It didn't even have an orchestra pit, so the first three rows were removed and the boxes demolished to accommodate the musicians. Being used primarily as a lecture hall, the venue had very little depth to its stage. Even though the stage was extended a few feet, most of the dance numbers were limited to being choreographed horizontally across the width of the stage. A makeshift curtain was added and soon the space was a passable theater. Blake commented that the theater "violated every city ordinance in the book," adding ironically, "It wasn't Broadway but we made it Broadway."[25]

To produce the show, Mayer and Cort agreed to an unusual arrangement for the time: a 50-50 co-ownership deal with the actors Miller and Lyles and songwriters Sissle and Blake. Rarely if ever did black performers have a stake in their own productions; this arrangement would prove to be a financial boon to all involved once the show became a hit. In May 1921, they established the "Nikko Producing Corporation" with "Cort and Mayer providing the capital, and the others the production."[26] Profits were to be split among the principals.

Many in the business were skeptical of the prospects for a "colored show" to succeed on Broadway. Blake recalled when the foursome ran into Sime Silverman, the powerful editor of *Variety*, on the streets of New York, he advised them that a black musical revue would never fly:

It was at 59th street and Broadway, [near] the statue [of Christopher Columbus; i.e., Columbus Circle]. He says, "What are you doing . . . cooking up a show?" So Sissle says, "Yes." He says, "What, a minstrel show?" [Sissle] says, "A book show, like a revue, but it has a book, but a very thin book." And Sime says to the four of us, "You have to have colored girls in the show." "Yeah, we have some of the most beautiful colored girls in the world." He says, "The white women aren't going to stand for you having colored girls in the show. You're crazy. You're throwing away your time." Now by this time we're right under Columbus' statue. And Lyles says this, after [Sime] had gone (you had to be careful what you['d] say in front of a white man derogatory in those days). . . . Lyles says, "Hey," now we're standing right under the statue, Lyles reach[es] up and says, "You see that guy right there? They say he was crazy, too. But he discovered America, didn't he?"[27]

Silverman believed that the reason a black show could never play Broadway was because the wives of the white businessmen wouldn't stand for their husbands leering at the pretty black chorines. (It was well-known that wealthy white men haunted the theaters in the hopes of picking up showgirls.)

Despite their partial ownership of the show, Sissle and Blake still had to bow to the will of their white partners. While the show was initially directed by Laurence Deas—an actor and choreographer in New York's African American theater—the producers insisted on bringing in a white director named Walter Brooks, who had previously staged popular musical comedy hits, to polish it up. Blake claimed that Sissle bowed to their pressure and hired Brooks to "put the Broadway touch on [the show]. Now the way we had the show set, it was right. All this guy did was cut the dancing." And, to add insult to injury, Blake fumed, "he got 2% of the show." Deas went uncompensated, according to Blake.[28] However, Deas did receive credit for staging the dances along with Charles Davis. And he appeared in the show as the detective, Jack Penrose.

Casting the show was difficult, but not because of scarcity of talent. Word got out to black performers that a new black musical was finally getting ready to open on Broadway. Even extremely talents actors were rejected. Ethel Waters was among those who auditioned but she was deemed to be too "black" to appear on stage. Word got out that people with a darker complexion weren't wanted. Future star Adelaide Hall, one of the best blues/jazz singers of her day, couldn't get an audition. She blamed Noble Sissle for having a "color complex," considering her "too dark to be in his show . . . I lived to tell him what I thought about him." As we shall see, Josephine Baker got a similar impression when she auditioned for Sissle, saying he thought she was "too dark." While it was acceptable and expected for the lead comedians to be "dark" (even if that meant sporting blackface makeup), the show's dancing chorus girls were expected to be light-skinned—indeed, some could have easily passed for white.

The show was produced on the cheap. After all, no one except the authors were convinced that it would be a success. Savings were realized by stripping down the staging to only the most necessary pieces of scenery. One anonymous critic wrote that the show had "no more scenery than you could pack into a taxicab."

Variety's correspondent wrote that the show's scenery was terrible and opined that the costumes looked as if they had come from another Cort show.[29] Indeed, Cort came up with the costumes from his earlier productions. Most originally appeared on stage in the Eddie Leonard show *Roly Boly Eyes,* which had premiered in 1919. Added to those were costumes from *Frank Fay's Fables.* Dusty and mildewed, with sweat stains under the arms, out from storage they came. The chorus girls would cry every time they had to put them on. Although the style of the clothes from *Roly Boly Eyes* didn't exactly complement the backwater locale of *Shuffle Along,* they were free.

Recycling the backdrops was not ideal, as Blake recalled:

I'll show you how inconsistent it was. [In the set,] the grocery store was on this side, and the hotel was over there. . . . [In] the scenery, they had it wrong [i.e., the hotel appeared on the opposite side from where it was placed on the set]. But we had to take it because that was the way they had it from this other show, where they got the drop from.[30]

Just as they had to adapt to the ill-matching set, the authors were not above writing material as needed to fit the costumes. A bunch of cotton-picker costumes from an earlier play inspired Sissle and Blake to write a song that gave a nostalgic look at the rural South, entitled "Bandana Days." As Blake later recalled, it was the rhythm of the title that influenced its jaunty melody:

Sissle is in Boston and I'm in New York [talking by telephone] and Sissle said, "I have a title for the song, "Bandana Days." I said, "Say Bandana." . . . and I wrote down the rhythm of it. You write the rhythm on the melody: "Bum-dum-dum." So, I did that and got the rhythm. Now the title has to come in two or three times. Then he talked the rhythm of it to me."[31]

Blake's rhythmic sensitivity to language was one of the hallmarks of the duo's songs, and one way that ragtime's vitality and syncopation was worked into their hits.

The "vaguely Oriental" costumes from *Fables* were used for the song "Oriental Blues" (which Blake quipped was "neither Oriental nor a blues"). The song came from the duo's trunk. Its origin was especially interesting and illustrated the close relationship of Sissle and Blake. As he recalled,

> W.W. Watson's father bought him a seat on Wall Street, [for] $250,000. And each time we'd go to his home to entertain. Sissle's over here and you know I don't write melodies at the piano. And Watson said, "Write me an Oriental number." I'm writing down the rhythm and I don't know what Sissle is writing over there. When [Watson] came out and asked us, "You got my song ready?," Sissle says, "Yes, we do." Sissle writes under pressure and he's over there writing the lyric. Sissle don't hear no melody. And the thing fit together. I don't know what he's got over there and he don't know what I've got. We were tuned into each other. I had to change about five notes from the verse and chorus. That actually happened. Twice it happened.[32]

Sissle and Blake had a rich back catalog of other songs that were stage proven during their years in vaudeville. As Blake explained to interviewer Bobbi King, "We'd been hustling our songs for some time without much luck [to publishers and Broadway producers]. Well, when we hit on *Shuffle Along*, what we actually did was to take those same songs that no one had wanted to publish and that we had really originally written for vaudeville and fit them into [the show]."[33] In fact, the second act stopped to allow for a brief show-case of their vaudeville act with Blake leaving the conductor's stand to join Sissle onstage to perform a medley of their earlier songs.

They also borrowed from their back catalog to rework songs that hadn't been hits. As we previously noted, Sissle borrowed the chorus lyrics from the duo's forgotten 1916 song, "My Loving Baby," for one of the show's biggest numbers, "I'm Just Wild about Harry."[34] "Harry" was originally written in a waltz tempo. Lead actress Lottie Gee, who was going to sing the song in the show, asked, "How can you have a waltz in a colored show?"

Blake responded,

I reminded her of a waltz "When the Pale Moon Shines,"[35] which had been
in a colored show. Lottie answered, yes, she had been in that show, and the
song wasn't a hit. Well, she had me there. "Make it a one-step," said Lottie.
A one-step! That cut me to the quick—she was going to destroy my beautiful melody! I loved that waltz! Then Sissle went along with her. He was always more commercial than I was. "All right, I said, I'll make it a one-step."[36]

Despite the new up-tempo arrangement, the song just wasn't working.
Sissle explained,

Something seemed to just miss in its presentation, and we were about to
throw the song out of the show in Philadelphia, where we were playing
prior to taking it into New York.

One night one of the chorus boys was sick, and Bob Lee, a member of the
singing ensemble, was drafted to replace him in the number. Bob couldn't
dance very well, so we sent him on stage leading the [chorus] line so that
he would be the last off and not in the way of the others when they made
their exit.

Miller and Lyles and myself were making a change and Blake was in the
pit, conducting, when all of a sudden we heard a roar of laughter from the
audience. Lyles said, "I bet Bob Lee fell down." Then there was terrific applause and we all three ran to the wings to see what happened. Blake flew
up out of the pit, wild-eyed: "Keep him in! Keep him in!" he yelled, and
disappeared. We thought he had gone nuts, but by then the encore was on.
Then we saw. Bob Lee could not do the steps the other fellows were doing
and couldn't get off the stage, so he dropped out of line and with a jive smile
and a high-stepping routine of his own stopped the show cold.

"I'm Just Wild about Harry" was the hit of the show and Bob Lee took ten
encores every night.[37]

The show's title song, "Shuffle Along," was performed as a gala march by
the entire cast to open the second act. Its title was undoubtedly inspired by
Will Marion Cook's major hit, "Swing Along!" Besides being featured in *In
Dahomey*, the song was conducted by Cook at the famous Carnegie Hall
Concert that was held by James Reese Europe and the Clef Club in 1911, and
was greeted by thunderous applause. It also appeared in a four-part choral

version arranged by Cook that was published by the prestigious white classical firm, G. Schirmer, a year later. The song's lyrics transcended their original use in the show to become an important expression of racial pride, underscoring the idea of African American achievement as ever moving forward.

Both the music of "Swing Along!" and "Shuffle Along" are lightly syncopated marches. As we have seen, Blake was friendly with Cook and undoubtedly at least subconsciously he borrowed much of the spirit of Cook's original. Not surprisingly, Sissle was more circumspect in his lyrics; rather than expressing a bold vision of a new day for the African American race, "Shuffle Along" takes the more mundane view that it's better to keep a sunny disposition—no matter what struggles life presents to us. While not overtly responding to Cook's message, Sissle's lyric could be interpreted as urging blacks to accommodate to a racist society. And, of course, the image of "shuffling" along is borrowed from the footsteps of minstrelsy—a kind of sideways progress at best—rather than the strident exhortation by Cook to "swing along!"

After the show opened and the score was celebrated as one of the best of the season, Blake was asked for his opinion on why it was so successful:

The successful song writer of today must be something more than a mere juggler of harmonious sounds. He must be a student of what the public wants—a sort of a psychologist. The mushy, sobby, sentimental love songs of twenty or more years ago would not be at all popular today. Nor would the semi-martial music of songs popular during the United States' participation in the war make a hit now. What the public wants today are lively, jazzy songs, not too jazzy, with love interest, but without the sickly sentimentality in vogue a generation ago.

Blake made a similar point in another contemporary interview. To be a hit, a song had to combine both a danceable rhythm and a memorable tune: "A modern song, to make any kind of a hit at all, must have 'pep' to it, and also must have a 'catchy' tune that unconsciously sticks to the mind of the listener."[38] The balancing of "hot" rhythm with singable melody was one of the great achievements that Blake brought to the Broadway musical. Blake's analysis of the contemporary song scene reflected America's fascination with black music and its danceable syncopations at the same time it revealed the audience's hesitancy to fully embrace it. A successful song should be "jazzy" but "not too jazzy," as Blake stated. The trick was to give the audience a taste of the "exotic" new sounds without alienating them.

While *Shuffle Along* would eventually prove to be a transformational and hugely successful show, the producers faced a rocky road getting it to Broadway. The out-of-town tryouts were not uniformly successful, while the company struggled to keep going with its limited backing. The first stop on the tryout tour was Trenton, New Jersey, but the company couldn't afford the train fare for the short voyage across the Hudson River. Blake recalled, "We got down to Penn Station and I was ready to turn around and go straight home but Sissle wouldn't let me. He said we'd get there somehow, and we did. I think Sissle still felt Jim Europe's hand guiding us."[39]

Earlier the team had noticed an unshaven, poorly dressed man hanging around rehearsals. They assumed he was there to leer at the showgirls. Blake continued the story, "But Al Mayer knew him and said we should get him to stay with us on tour. When we were at the station, Al went to him and sold him one-half of his share in the show to get us on the way to Trenton."[40]

The show opened in Trenton with a cast of 78. The local critic singled out for praise the song "Love Will Find A Way" along with Sissle's performance of James Reese Europe's "On Patrol in No Man's Land" during the second act interlude that he performed with Blake. The reviewer concluded, "With additional rehearsing and a few superfluous parts combined . . . 'Shuffle Along' should be a musical comedy much above the average by the time it arrives on Broadway."[41] Critic "Billboard" Jackson, writing in the African American newspaper the *Chicago Defender*, praised the production, which he said was presented under its old name, *The Mayor of Jimtown*. He praised the show's comedy for presenting a natural picture of black music and comedy, particularly noting that the music spanned a wide variety of influences:

> [its authors] succeeded in constructing a vehicle that carries all of the unctuous humor and the piquant melody of their race without for one moment getting away from its natural atmosphere . . . the harmonies of camp meeting, Spirituelles [*sic*], other day minstrelsy, crooning, longing love and the effervescent happiness of the Race have all been utilized to good effect.[42]

Though well received, the show's opening was not profitable. Mayer reported that after all the receipts were in, he was $20 short of enough cash to take the troop to its next stop, Washington, DC. He had to borrow the money from "an usher who was saving for a new suit . . .upon my promise to send him $30 from Washington" when they arrived.

Blake recalled a slightly different chain of events that enabled them to proceed to Washington:

[We had] no money for train fare. Al Mayer is down at the station, walking up and down the platform wondering what to do. Up walks this man and says:

"Say, did you see that nigger show here in town last night?"

"Yah," said Al.

"That was the best thing I ever saw, that nigger show. Yes, sir!"

"'Yeah," said Al. "It's my show. I'm the manager."

"Well, you've got a gold mine there."

"Yeah," said Al. "Well, sir, that's nice to hear, but we don't even have enough money to get to the next town." So the man said he'd be right back, walked into the ticket office, and talked to the station master.

It turns out that man was one of the owners of the railroad, for when he came back he had tickets for the whole company.[43]

Mayer noted that the company was able to "breathe easy" once they reached the nation's capitol, because they had a guaranteed income there for two weeks, before moving on to Philadelphia.[44] But in Washington, they discovered that the person manning the box office had used the show's receipts to gamble on the horses. Once again, they were stuck without cash. Although the cast often didn't get paid, they stuck with the show, hoping that if and when they finally opened in New York it would be a hit. Sissle recalled, "The players knew they had little future in vaudeville because of their race and when we told them we had no money but would not take them farther than walking distance from New York, they agreed to gamble with us."[45]

Blake explained how the company managed during its pre-Broadway days:

We'd play one-night—if we were lucky, two-night—stands. No one knew us, so they'd only book us for a short time. We'd get good reviews in one town, but before they could do us any good we'd be on to another town—that is, if we had the money. One night Sissle and I were sitting on the steps of a building, and Sissle was writing out checks. They weren't any good until we could wire the box office receipts into the New York bank—we were always one day behind at the very least. I looked up. "Sissle" I say, "Do you know where you're sitting?" "No," he said, and looked around. We were sitting on the steps of the jailhouse, writing bum checks! We broke up in a fit of laughing and couldn't stop.[46]

Life on the road was hard and not only because they had no money. There was the problem of being allowed to stay only in black hotels and most of them were not too nice. Instead, they booked rooms in boarding houses and private homes in exchange for tickets for the show. On one occasion they had no money so Lyles talked a cab driver into lending them some cash to pay for their lodging with the promise that the New York office would repay him later. As Blake told it, "There were five of us. Miller and Lyles slept in one bed, Sissle in another; Paul Floyd, who was in the show, was in the bed with me. All night long the chinches [bedbugs] had a picnic, and Paul kept waking me up, slapping the chinches."[47]

The next morning, they tried to sneak out of the rooming house but the large proprietor blocked the steps and demanded his money. They couldn't get past him no matter what. He berated them, "I didn't trust you minstrel niggers! You're all no good!" Lyles replied, "Sir, the boy will be here with the money very soon."[48] Astoundingly, the cabbie actually came and paid the bill.

But the show's creators did not starve. As Flournoy Miller said, "You learn a lot of tricks on the road. Sissle and I would visit people who were boarding some members of the cast—always at mealtime—and I would take a bite of everything on the table and insist that Sissle taste it too, because it was so delicious. Then we'd go to another house and do the same thing—we usually had plenty to eat."[49]

Their engagement at Philadelphia's Dunbar Theatre, a black venue, was a hit. According to Sissle, however, producer John Cort and the theater owner Abe Erlanger were worried that the show's audience was entirely black and therefore it was not certain that it would appeal to a white audience—despite, in Sissle's words, "laugh[ing] themselves sick."[50] To hedge their bet, producer Harry Cort booked the show into a series of one-night stands in white theaters around Philadelphia, including two nights in late April 1921 in Reading, Pennsylvania, at the Rajah Theater. The show garnered positive reviews in the local paper, which raved that "*Shuffle Along* [is] the best colored musical comedy since the days of Williams and Walker . . . [It] contain[s] many catchy tunes and many cleverly written comedy scenes."[51] The show's success even at white theaters convinced Cort that the show might just succeed on Broadway. However, by the time the show landed on Broadway, it was $18,000 in the hole.[52]

Sissle and Blake and the producers were nervous about the chances for the show. Would white audiences accept two black characters falling in love and singing a serious, non-stereotypical love song, "Love Will Find a Way"—just like white characters? Flournoy Miller learned that "a newspaper man told Mr. Cort that the public would not stand for Negroes acting romantic on a stage and suggested that the entire love plot be excised." The idea of blacks being capable of having romantic feelings—as opposed to the "animal" sexuality associated with jazz music—was controversial for white audiences. It implied an equality of the races that few were ready to accept.

An African American critic writing for *The New York Age* commented on this prejudice among white audiences:

> White audiences . . . do not want colored people to indulge in too much love-making. They will applaud if a colored man serenades his girl at the window, but if, while telling of his great love in song he becomes somewhat demonstrative . . . then exceptions are taken. It may be the general impression prevails that Negroes are only slightly acquainted with Don Cupid; or maybe it is thought they have no business being ardent lovers.[53]

Actually there had been earlier black shows that honestly portrayed love between a black man and woman. Cole and Johnson's *The Red Moon* (1909) was perhaps the first. The most notable example was James Weldon Johnson's *My Friend from Kentucky* (1913), which was produced at the Lafayette Theatre in Harlem. As its composer stated, "'Rock Me in the Cradle of Love'. . . [was] sung by the Negro tenor to the bronze soubrette in a most impassioned manner, demonstrating that the lovemaking taboo had been absolutely kicked out of the Negro theatre."[54] But *My Friend from Kentucky* was an aberration. Although white audiences came up to Harlem to see it, it was primarily aimed at a black audience. And that show was not as successful as *Shuffle Along* and influenced far fewer people.

And it wasn't just the producers and writers who were nervous about the show's prospects. Noble Sissle wrote that "very few people of the Broadway theatrical managerial staffs believed in us and there were few among our own group who felt we had a chance. However, we felt we had a message—we felt that the gloom and depression as an aftermath of the war had left the country hungry for laughter . . . that was so expressed in our music and rhythms."[55]

Blake agreed with Sissle's assessment:

We were afraid people would think it was a freak show and it wouldn't appeal to white people. Others thought that if it was a colored show it might be dirty. One man bought a front row seat for himself every night for a week. I'd notice him—down in the pit you notice things in the audience—and finally, after the whole week was past, he came and told me that now he could bring his wife and children because there was no foul language and not one double-entendre.[56]

Finally, after months of hard work, on Monday, May 23, 1921, *Shuffle Along* opened. However, Sissle and the company were still concerned about the depiction of the love affair and especially the love song "Love Will Find a Way." Sissle recalled,

On opening night in New York, this song had us more worried than anything else in the show. We were afraid that when Lottie Gee and Roger Matthews sang it, we'd be run out of town. Miller, Lyles, and I were standing near the exit door with one foot inside the theatre and the other pointed north toward Harlem. We thought Blake stuck out there in front, leading the orchestra—his bald head would get the brunt of the tomatoes and rotten eggs. Imagine our amazement when the song was not only beautifully received, but encored.[57]

While the show's producers' fears of a backlash against its love story proved unfounded, it was the more upbeat singing and dancing—flavored with just the right amount of jazz rhythm—that made it a big success. As Sissle recalled of its opening night,

The biggest moment of all came near the end of the show, with a number called, "The Baltimore Buzz." I sang it while Blake and the orchestra played like fury and the girls danced up a storm. People cheered. I almost fell of[f] the stage when I looked out into the auditorium—there was old John Cort dancing in the aisles! His faith in us had been borne out. That night it looked like we were home.[58]

While its music and dance were new and exciting, *Shuffle Along*'s plot, such as it was, was a creaky combination of age-old stereotypes. It was primarily contrived to allow Miller and Lyles to show off their well-beloved characters that they had been playing for years on vaudeville. They portrayed a pair of comic grifters who shared a mutual distrust that occasionally flared into playful dust-ups. One of their favorite bits, a mock boxing match, was recycled in the show, moving one critic to note that the routine "invariably goes big" with audiences.[59] Meanwhile, the young leads—Lottie Gee playing the soubrette and Roger Matthews her lover—have to overcome the objections of Gee's stage father to finally find true bliss together. The backdrop was a three-way race for mayor in the backwater burg, Jimtown, with Matthews playing the true-blue candidate and Lyles and Miller the conniving blackguards. The plot would occasionally come to a halt for set pieces by the two comedians and—in the second act—it was entirely suspended so Sissle and Blake could give a taste of their popular numbers.

The most surprising thing to the creators and critics was the show's great success from the get-go. Where most shows opened and closed quickly, *Shuffle Along* just kept on going. The African American press was quick to notice; at the end of its first week, the *Brooklyn Life* newspaper reported, "This all-negro show has proved one of the biggest drawing attractions New York has had in some time. With its exceedingly funny comedy . . . and its scintillating melodies, 'Shuffle Along' has amused hundreds of people with in the past week."[60] As a confirmation of its staying power, the critic noted that for the second week's performances "the same cast remains intact," which was also unusual for the time.

Much of the success of *Shuffle Along* was due to the excellence of the show's orchestra. Several of its members—Felix Weir, Leonard Jeter, Hall Johnson, Edgar Campbell, William Grant Still, and Russell Smith— had played in James Reese Europe's ensembles. Felix Weir founded the American String Quartet, which was renamed the Negro String Quartet, perhaps the earliest black classical ensemble. Among the quartet's members was Hall Johnson. Johnson achieved fame in 1928 as the leader of his eponymous choir, which toured the country and appeared in many motion pictures. William Grant Still was the most accomplished of black composers of his time, arranging, conducting, and composing everything from songs to symphonies. In 1926 his suite of songs *Levee Land* featured Florence Mills as a soloist.

After everything that Sissle, Blake, Miller, Lyles, and the rest of the company went through to get to Broadway, the show was triumphant. It validated their belief that black artists could be treated as the equals to whites, judged by the quality of their work, not the color of their skin. Blake later recalled, "The proudest day of my life was when *Shuffle Along* opened. At the intermission of the show, all those white people kept saying: 'I would like to touch him, the man who wrote the music.' . . . It made me feel like, well, at last, I'm a human being."[61]

While successful from the start, the show was slow to be mentioned by the white press. *The New York Times* was most impressed with the music, calling Blake's score "swinging and infectious," noting that it drew on both qualities "inherent to the Negro" while being "frankly Remickniscent [*sic*]" of standard Broadway songs. However, the critic found little to like in the show's book or acting:

> It has here and there a broad comedy scene that is effective, but little or none of it is conspicuously native and all of it extremely crude—in writing, playing and direction . . . The authors have the leading roles but except in a burlesque boxing bout . . . they revealed no marked comic talents. There is a good male quartet, and now and then some entertaining dancing.[62]

While praising Sissle and Blake's songs, industry paper *Variety* generally faulted the cheap production, the weak script, and—surprisingly—the lack of dancing (the show would become famous for its dancing chorus line). "The musical numbers are worthy of a real production, which 'Shuffle Along' lacks entirely," the reviewer huffed, noting that "dancing [did not start until] the second act, [and] there was comparatively little of it," spending more time describing the "bobbed hair effect" sported by the troupe's "high brown" chorus than their feet. Gertrude Saunders, Lottie Gee, and particularly Roger Matthews were all praised for their singing, and Miller and Lyles's boxing routine, which they had perfected during their vaudeville years, was noted as "the hit of the show." "Love Will Find a Way" was singled out as "a peach," and considerable coverage was given to the specialty interlude performed by Sissle and Blake in the second act. The *Variety* critic believed that the show would mostly appeal to a black audience, noting,

> The 63rd Street Theater is . . . a few blocks to the westward . . . [of] a negro section known as "San Juan Hill." The Lennox [*sic*] avenue colored section is but 20 minutes away on the subway, so that "Shuffle Along" ought to get all the colored support there is, along with the white patrons who like that sort of entertainment.[63]

Despite the $2.00 ticket price for the front half of the auditorium, "colored patrons were noticed as far front as the fifth row." (Allowing blacks to be seated in the main part of an auditorium was noteworthy for the day; usually they were relegated to the upper balcony.) Ironically, it turned out that it would be the "white patrons who liked that sort of entertainment" who would propel the show to great success—despite this initial reaction from the entertainment industry.

The New York Age's Lester A. Walton, the best-known African American critic of the period, was saddened by the white critics' expectations for both the types of characters, songs, and dances that were appropriately "African" that were the acceptable limits for black performers. "Unless you are in overalls and wearing a perpetual grin you are apt to create the impression of assuming too much dignity," Walton believed was the typical attitude of white critics and theatergoers. Ironically, though, the dances and routines created in *Shuffle Along* "have already been confiscated by white performers for their personal use," he noted.[64] In a later piece, Walton thought a show that depicted blacks as "nice-looking young men and women, well dressed and using plain United States language"[65] couldn't succeed with white audiences.

Another early review in the white press appeared on May 29, oddly enough in the *Chicago Daily Tribune*. It began on a sour note, before admitting the many virtues of the show:

Negro humor is better in print or in the synthetic face of Frank Tinney[66] than coming from the mouths of its originators. Fifty Negroes have banded together into a musical comedy company which is playing to white audiences . . . "Shuffle Along" . . . makes brave attempts to entertain the white folks in the intervals between its gorgeous songs. It subscribes to the musical comedy formula that, when you are singing a song, you must be acting a joke.

But racial genius grips the cast and you when the songs begin. At a grand piano in the orchestra pit sits Mr. Eubie Blake, composer of all of the music. He is surrounded by fifteen helpful harmonists. Miss Lottie Gee or Roger Matthews . . . sets a metronomic foot to beating a rhythm. . . . In two semi-quavers you are quivering to the same magic that has set all these spontaneous musicians to reeling melodiously. You may resist Beethoven or Jerome Kern, but you surrender completely to this.[67]

The anonymous reviewer gives Blake his biggest compliment by comparing him to white musical theater greats like Jerome Kern. The "racial genius" of Blake's melodies was slow to make it to Broadway, this critic opines, but he believed they would quickly make it 20 blocks farther down to the heart of the theater district: his melodies "will be carried right down . . . by the audience's memories."[68]

Notably, some white critics found the show lacking in sufficient echoes from the "deeper jungles," as well-known critic Heywood Broun stated in the *New York Tribune*. His review didn't appear until July, when the show itself was already the hit of the season. While he admired the show's energetic troupe and the "frenzy and rigor" of their dancing, he found that

> [o]n the whole, "Shuffle Along" follows Broadway models. The African contribution is not large. Most [of] the music is lively and agreeable, but not much of it is new. The book could be rewritten for any pair of German dialect comedians.

The expectation was for more stereotypical depictions of blacks, particularly in the show's non-comedic moments. Not surprisingly, Broun singled out for praise "the choral work [and] . . . the singing of a male quartet" for their "primitive power," reflecting the white belief that all of the best black music was spirituals sung in harmony. However, he also noted that Blake was "a performer of unusual merit."[69]

According to Blake, one white critic helped really put the show over the top: "It was Alan Dale's review that really made people want to see the show."[70] Writing in the *New York Journal American*, Dale recognized that this show "with no ostentation of scenic effects and no portentous 'names' and no emphasized 'sensations'" put most mainstream musicals to shame. Also uniquely among the early white critics, Dale celebrated the power of the show's dancing, noting that the cast's energy and enjoyment of the material was one of the highlights of the show:

> How they enjoyed themselves! How they jigged and pranced and cavorted, and wriggled, and laughed. It was an infection of amusement. It was impossible to resist a jollity that the company itself appeared to experience down to the very marrow. Talk of pep! These people made pep seem something different to the tame thing we know further downtown. Every sinew in their frames responded to their extreme energy.[71]

Nonetheless, like the critic Heywood Broun, Dale thought the show lacked a certain "darkness." However, unlike Broun, Dale doesn't believe that black actors were unable to match white performers; in fact, he singled out singers Lottie Gee and Roger Matthews as being every bit as talented—if not more so—than the day's white stars:

> "Shuffle Along" is a darky show that has lost most of its darkness. The men "black up" just as though they were tintless; the women rouge up, very much as they do in non-colored performances. One expects to see an essentially colored aggregation, but it isn't that by any mean. It is a semi-darky show that emulate[s] the "white" performance and—goes it one better.[72]

Describing Sissle and Blake's songs, Dale again lamented their lack of "molassesian" style and "primitiveness," while praising their "simplicity and charm."

The African American critics were much more sympathetic to the production, but no less surprised by the show's success with white audiences than the show's producers. Lester A. Walton reported his own pleasure that the show was such a success:

> Some weeks ago I had the pleasure of seeing "Shuffle Along" at the Dunbar Theater, Philadelphia, where it broke all previous records held by the house for attendance. I attended a performance last week [in New York] for the express purpose of paying particular attention to the manner in which the white patrons received the show. . . . Knowing the strange workings of the Caucasian mind at times on matters in which the Negro is directly involved, I was curious to learn if "Shuffle Along" would find its way into the category of what is known in the language of the performer as "a white folk's show."[73]

Walton was most concerned that the white preference for stereotype images would prevail. White audiences, he believed, were accepting of either the rural "Uncle Joe" or strutting "dandy darkey" characters, but not open to representations of blacks as solidly middle-class people. Walton was pleasantly surprised not only by the show's warm reception but also the quality of the music: "The musical numbers in 'Shuffle Along' are original, tuneful and worthy of a place in a Broadway musical show. If 'Love Will Find A Way' were featured in a white production it would be proclaimed one of the season's hits." He also praised Lottie Gee—who appeared "to better advantage than at any time during her career"—as well as Roger Matthews and Gertrude Saunders. His review concluded, "Speaking as a colored American, I think 'Shuffle Along' should continue to shuffle along . . . for a long time."[74]

Surprisingly, the *Chicago Defender*—perhaps the most prominent of all national African American papers—ran only a short note acknowledging the opening of the show. The anonymous writer was lukewarm about it, saying that it was "not up to the standard of the old Williams & Walker shows," although admitting "this new show is quite a departure from similar offerings. On the whole, it was well received and generally voted a good show."[75]

After the show was a success, white critics like Gilbert Seldes—who wrote for the influential magazine *Vanity Fair*—reflected on why it had such strong appeal. Seldes felt the show was "without art, but with tremendous vitality." Nonetheless, he thought the comportment of the dancers "a little too piercing at times, the postures and the pettings and the leapings all a little beyond the necessary measure. It remains simple; but simplicity, even if it isn't usually vulgar, can be a bit rough." Writing later in his influential book *The 7 Lively Arts,* he reflected on his original criticism:

> It was fairly obvious that *Shuffle Along* had been conceived as an entertainment for negroes; that is why it remained solid when it took Broadway, to the intense surprise of its producers. It was, in short, an exotic for us, but it wasn't an exotic for themselves. Its honesty was its success, and its honesty put a certain stamp upon its successors. In all of them there is a regrettable tendency to imitate, at moments, the worst features of our usual musical comedy. But the major portion of each show is native, and so good.[76]

John McMullin gave another reason for the success of black shows starting with *Shuffle Along*: the lure of the "exotic" among white intellectuals and fellow artists. He noted that "[i]f by chance you have not seen [one of the new all-black revues], you are not 'in it.' All the modernists and musicians you know, are mad about this new phase of the development of coloured talent."[77] Irving Berlin musicalized the same idea when he wrote the song, "Let's Go Slumming on Park Avenue."

This fascination with black culture was noted by author Langston Hughes:

> Thousands of whites came to Harlem night after night, thinking the Negroes loved to have them there, and firmly believing that all Harlemites

left their houses at sundown to sing and dance in cabarets, because most of the whites saw nothing but the cabarets, not the houses.[78]

Shuffle Along was an important transitional piece. It had the humor of the old blackface tradition counterbalanced by the modernity of its jazzy score and choreography and modern depiction of the young black couple. And in that it satisfied whites, gently nudging them into a new way of seeing blacks on Broadway and thus blacks in general. And it's important to note that the show satisfied white and black audiences alike.

That curiosity and acceptance of blacks in New York was also occurring in Europe. Classical composers like Anton Dvořák and Darius Milhaud both professed the influence that black music had on their works. Black American singer Roland Hayes arrived on the Continent in April 1920 and proved that black singers could match the Europeans in their musical skills and interpretations of the classical repertoire. European artists had discovered African art and were incorporating their style into their own artwork. And most importantly, jazz was continuing its inroads into popular song. The ragtime rhythms of Scott Joplin and his brethren were the opening salvo. When players and composers like Eubie Blake came along, they built upon the ragtime foundation to create real jazz.

In the history of Broadway, some of the biggest hits have been outliers, those shows that are different to anything else on the boards. And the success of *Shuffle Along* must also be attributed to just how different it was from the usual Broadway fare. Just five days before the opening of *Shuffle Along* an operetta version of *The Three Musketeers* opened at the Manhattan Opera House. It lasted only 5 performances. Just a week before that the show *Two Little Girls in Blue* opened with a fine Broadway pedigree. The music was by Vincent Youmans and the lyrics by Ira Gershwin (writing under the pseudonym Arthur Francis). There were 40 people in the cast and the action took place on an ocean liner and in India. Over the three acts of the show there was extensive scenery and costumes all meant to dazzle the eyes of the audience. The score was lively and had a few songs that were minor successes. But it played only 135 performances.

Many people today think that *Shuffle Along* was a small show but it employed 42 singers, dancers, and actors, a number just about equal to the typical Broadway musical of its time. However, the similarity ended there. The show was presented at a lecture hall turned theater off the beaten track. It had an all-black company of performers. And its music was unlike any other heard on Broadway. The dancing was unique compared to other shows. It had blacks in leading roles, who were not just glimpsed as maids and butlers. It had energy in abundance without the trappings of Ruritanian romances of the typical operetta. Most notable was that it opened under the radar of most Broadway audiences and critics. There was no hype and no buzz. It opened to an audience that had no idea what to expect when the curtain went up. Frankly, it was like no other show on Broadway: a true sleeper hit.

Business was so good that three weeks into the run the company canceled the Wednesday matinees and added Wednesday midnight performances that were heavily attended by theatrical folk. A few weeks later, all the matinees were canceled. *Shuffle Along* soon grew into the most successful show playing on Broadway, with a weekly gross averaging $13,000 a week (almost $180,000 in today's dollars) against $7500 (a little over $100,000) in weekly expenses. Once the show had become a verified smash, the top ticket price was raised to $3.00, or about $40 in today's dollars.

By the time *Shuffle Along* reached its half-year anniversary, the African American press was celebrating its success. *The New York Age* noted that it was a "record run for a colored attraction," drawing "capacity audiences at every performance [with] present business point[ing] to a long and pros-perous run." By this time, the show's producers could add "new costumes" (presumably made for the show), including the "latest fashions" for the chorus girls.[79]

Lester A. Walton wrote a longer article celebrating the show's six-month run, noting the importance of the milestone, which he found to be "pregnant with historical significance":

> It's been more than a decade since a colored musical attraction figured in a long run in New York . . . To parallel this record was the burning ambition of many a colored performer . . . [However] it has been a herculean task to secure a suitable downtown theatre for a colored musical show. Archaic ideas, predicated on the futility of such a step, have invariably prevailed.
>
> Now comes "Shuffle Along" faithfully functioning as a stream-roller. It has knocked over and crushed to earth many of the barriers that have stood in the path of the colored show's progress. Precedents have been established.[80]

Not only did *Shuffle Along* mark a highpoint for blacks on stage, but it broke the color barrier for the audience as well. *Variety* noted that blacks were seated in the orchestra section of the house and not forced to sit in the balcony, as in most other theaters. True, the paper noted that "the two races rarely intermingled"[81]—a situation that made its white readers less nervous at the possibility of being seated next to a black patron. In fact, the orchestra section had a line of demarcation between the three-quarters of the downstairs reserved for whites and the rest offered to blacks. But even that small step proved to be historic. *Shuffle Along*'s desegregation policy, as tentative as it might have been, was the first step in an eventual true opening of theater seats to all races. In its tours and subsequent productions, the producers insisted that the theaters become fully integrated with seating reserved for blacks on all levels. By 1930, critic, social activist, and songwriter James Weldon Johnson proudly wrote, "At the present time the sight of colored people in the orchestras of Broadway theatres is not regarded a cause for immediate action or utter astonishment."[82]

But not all of the black population were as amused with the proceedings. Leaders of the black community decried the show for its blackface musical comedy tropes. They felt that black theater should be refinements of the black experience and not exploit the usual black clichés. Miller and Lyles's blackface, exaggerated black dialect, and old-fashioned stereotyping did disservice to the black cause, they believed. And the light-skinned black chorus also riled the critics. Nonetheless, the highlight of the show was the chorus numbers, featuring light-skinned dancers hoofing to the jazzy score. Its "selection of bronze beauties made . . . 'Shuffle Along' the talk of the world. Only perfect 36's were chosen and [the production's] idea of perfection in feminine beauty was marvelous."[83] Indeed, like the Cotton Club revues, *Shuffle Along*'s dancers fit a European model of beauty, from their fair skin to long limbs. This model made the show more acceptable to white audiences.

The big chorus number came in the opening number of the second act. A policeman is shown directing traffic, urging both automobiles and pedestrians to keep moving—to "shuffle along." The title song is then performed by the chorines who perform the cakewalk-like shuffle. Several young performers got their first taste of any stage by dancing in the chorus line, among them blues singer Adelaide Hall. (A reviewer gave Hall special note for "her work [that] is unusual enough to be singled out" on the song "Bandana Days."[84]) Fredi Washington—later a singer associated with Duke Ellington—also appeared as a chorine.

The two female leads, Lottie Gee and Gertrude Saunders, saw their careers boosted, thanks to the show. They were given different types of tunes to perform to suit their different characters. Good-girl Gee performed "Love Will Find a Way" and "I'm Just Wild about Harry." "Modern Woman" Saunders's songs were the jazzier ones, "I'm Just Simply Full of Jazz," "I'm Craving for That Kind of Love," and "Daddy Won't You Please Come Home." *The New York Age* praised Saunders's lusty vocals, saying "for the first time white theatregoers . . . are having such numbers . . . as they really should be sung."[85] And *Billboard* praised her singing: "She is one of the very few sopranos with a voice of such timbre as to qualify for the successful production of records. This is in itself an unusual distinction."

Unlike others in the show, Saunders was already well established on the stage and records. Even before the show opened, OKeh Records invited her to record two of her featured numbers—"I'm Craving for That Kind of Love" and "Daddy Won't You Please Come Home." She was accompanied by African American bandleader James T. Brymn's group. Listening to these recordings today, we find it hard to understand how revolutionary they must have sounded in 1921. It is clear that Saunders was used to projecting her voice in the days before amplification, as her powerful voice nearly leaps off the wax. However, her wide vibrato and stage-like diction seem hopelessly antique to modern ears, hardly exuding raw sexuality as they did for listeners in her day. And despite critics raving that she performed "real" African American music, she sounds not that much different from similar white belters of the day—and nothing at all like the blues singers like Bessie Smith and her contemporaries. Nonetheless, Saunders's success was such that she was soon lured away by vaudeville promoters Hurtig and Seamon's promising her a $50 raise from her $125 weekly salary (about $1720 in today's dollars) if she would open at their Reisenweber's Cabaret.

After Saunders left the show in August 1921, the hunt was on for a suitable replacement, a tall order, given her great success. Eventually, Florence Mills (Figure 5.2) was hired, although the creators were initially unsure that she could take over from the great Saunders. Mills had begun her professional career at age four in 1899. As a toddler she had a walk-on part in a revival of the Cole and Johnson show *A Trip to Coontown*. But in the early 1920s she was best known for her work in vaudeville partnering with her husband, U. S. ("Slow Kid") Thompson, a comic dancer. Sissle recalled,

They were both in the Keith circuit in an act called "The Tennessee Ten." I only knew her slightly as the singer in a little gingham dress who made a sensation in *Swanee River* with her birdlike voice. The four of us ate

Figure 5.2 Florence Mills shortly after she left *Shuffle Along* to appear in Lew Leslie's *Blackbirds* in London. Eubie was surprised when the petite Mills turned into a magnetic firecracker on stage.

together . . . at our boarding house, and when Florence and Kid left the dining room, my wife Harriet said, "Why don't you give Florence a chance to replace Gertrude?" I smiled and said, "Why, she's a ballad singer. Gertrude's part calls for dancing and singing blues." Harriet told me Florence was singing "I'm Craving for That Kind of Love" at Baron Wilkins' nightclub, and at her insistence I went to see her without saying anything to my partners. The next night I told them we were saved, but Lyles, in his dry way, said, "She ought to sing—she has legs like a canary."

She was Dresden china, and she turned into a stick of dynamite.[86]

Singer Ada Smith—known by her stage name of "Bricktop"—tells a slightly different story. Bricktop was performing in Chicago in the Panama club in 1915 when she convinced the club owner to hire Mills, who was looking for a steady club job after touring on the vaudeville circuit. Soon, along with singer Mattie Hight, they formed the Panama Trio, singing and dancing at the club.[87] They performed together for a few years before breaking up, and Bricktop moved on to New York. There, she got a job at Barron Wilkins's club, home to Duke Ellington's Washingtonians, in the early 1920s, and soon was joined in the cast by her old singing partner, Florence Mills. Bricktop recalled that she recommended Mills to Harriet Sissle when she heard that Saunders was leaving *Shuffle Along*. Mills had to audition multiple times before Sissle and his partners were convinced to hire her, according to Bricktop.[88]

Mills signed a contract on August 4, 1921. Originally the contract stated she was to receive $100 a week, but Sissle wrote in an amendment giving her $125. Another part of the deal was that Kid Thompson would also have a role in the show. So, a new part was conceived, that of a dancing porter in the Jimtown mayor's office. Thompson's dancing drew praise from contemporary reviewers, showing that the producers were wise to add him to the cast.[89]

The cast had the same misgivings about Mills as did Sissle. They couldn't believe that such a small, demure girl could fill Saunders's role. Cast member Bee Freeman remembered, "The first time I saw Florence Mills she was walking onstage . . . wearing a black, rusty looking dress. It seemed like she had no glamour at all. She looked like one of those little girls you would see working in a store. . . . We thought, 'How dare they inflict this thing on us.'"[90] Blake confirmed that, off-stage, Mills was not much to look at, but she "lit up" when she hit the boards:

She had a little figure; she had nothing in the world to help her. When the woman's on the stage, you gotta have a woman that men can say "Oh God, I'd like to [go] out with that girl." I never heard *anybody* in my life say they'd like to be out with *her*. But, brother, when she walked on the stage, she lit the stage up. . . . One time, I was going down Broadway, and there were two women, white women, behind me. And Florence was coming up Broadway. The woman behind me says, "Look, look, look, there's Florence Mills." And the other woman says, "Where?" And she's looking right at her, see. . . . She looked like nothing, scrawny little thing.[91]

On Mills's opening night, Thompson did his part to make sure she would have a successful opening; he recalled,

The first night I had about 20 fellows . . . in the theatre what they call a clique. . . . I had three or four fellows on this side, three or four fellows on that. I bought tickets for them, put them in, see. So when she came on by herself, that's when I had the clique all rehearsed. So Florence was singing "Kiss me, kiss me, kiss me with your tempting lips," and she could flaunt, you know, a lot of things, and make her eyes look so good. When she got through and finished . . . I gave the signal.[92]

But Mills's success in the show was assured well before Thompson's friends did their job. By the middle of "I'm Craving for That Kind of Love," as she inched her way slowly downstage to the very edge of the footlights, the audience was spellbound. Bricktop, the noted cabaret owner, claimed Mills had 17 curtain calls. Eubie Blake echoed the approbations for Mills's performance; as he put it so succinctly, "She killed the song."[93]

Mills soon erased the memories of Gertrude Saunders. Part of her success was exactly based on the audience's surprise that such a delicate-seeming gamin could belt out the jazziest, sexiest numbers. Maude Russell, herself a singer to be reckoned with, told author Bill Egan, "Lottie Gee was more like the prima donna and Florence Mills was more like the jazz singer. Florence Mills was an all-round singer; she could sing a sweet song would make you cry, and then she could sing a jazz song and jazz it." [94] Eubie compared Lottie Gee to Kate Smith, whereas Florence Mills was more like Barbra Streisand.[95] Critic Gilbert Seldes, one of the most adventurous critics of the time, described Mills's magnetic stage presence in *Vanity Fair*: "Merely to watch her walk out upon the stage, with her long free stride and her superb, shameless swing, is an aesthetic pleasure; she is a school and exemplar of carriage and deportment."[96]

And it wasn't only the professional critics who came under the spell of Mills's talents. Future poet Langston Hughes had the choice of studying at Columbia University or following his father's wishes to escape the prejudice of America life and study in Switzerland. It was a very tough decision for a young man whose future might hang on his choice. This is how he made up his mind: "*Shuffle Along* had just burst into being, and I wanted to hear Florence Mills sing. So I told my father I'd rather go to Columbia than to Switzerland." And so he "sat up in the gallery night after night at *Shuffle Along*, ador[ing] Florence Mills."[97] Noël Coward was equally smitten by Mills's talents: "There darted the swift vivid genius of Florence Mills, at one moment moving like a streak of quicksilver, the next still against some gaudily painted backdrop. Nothing animated about her at all, except her wide smile and the little pulse in her throat, throbbing like a bird."[98]

Mills's success was so great that she was quickly lured away by producer Lew Leslie, who had come to see *Shuffle Along* and was immediately smitten with Mills's performance.[99] During the last few months of *Shuffle Along*'s run, she also appeared in Leslie's *Plantation Revue* on Times Square. The *Plantation Revue* was a cabaret show that played late shows in the rooftop theater above the Winter Garden Theatre at 51st Street and Broadway. After shows at the Winter Garden, audiences could retire to the rooftop theater for a Southern-inspired dinner and a 45-minute show.

Seeing the success of his show, Leslie decided to expand it into a full-fledged revue, albeit still in a cabaret space. More importantly, to Mills at least, was the salary of $500 per week he offered to her to appear in the revised show. So, in March 1922, Mills gave her notice to the producers of *Shuffle Along*. They tried to stop her leaving their show, accusing her of breach of contract. But she had a two-weeks notice clause in her agreement and so they could not stop her. She also took along her husband, "Slow Kid" Thompson, although there was no fight to keep him. Will Vodery was also hired for the *Plantation Revue* as an arranger and bandleader.

Another future star joined the company at about the same time as Mills did. In the summer of 1921, a close-harmony group, the Four Harmony Kings, were added to the production (Figure 5.3). The Kings had been touring vaudeville successfully since the mid-1910s, billing themselves as "A Symphony of Color." The group not only sang but also played instruments and even did some comic routines. The group's leader, Ivan Harold Browning, was also hired to play the male lead in the show. In a special spot during the second act, the group sang favorites like Stephen Foster's "Old Black Joe," "Ain't It a Shame," and "Snowball." But they also undertook sophisticated vocal works, including William Horace Berry's poem "Invictus" as arranged for orchestra by Bruno Hahn.

We can get a sense of the Kings' vocal style through a record they made while appearing in *Shuffle Along*: "Good Night Angeline," which was one of

FOUR HARMONY KINGS.

Figure 5.3 The Four Harmony Kings, the successful vocal group who were featured in *Shuffle Along*. This image appeared on a song by Noble Sissle in the later 1920s, issued in London after Sissle and Blake had broken up.

Sissle and Blake's first hits (co-written with James Reese Europe). Recorded for the black-owned label, Black Swan, the disc opens with a brief piano introduction that might have been played by Blake—it's impossible to know, although it is similar in style to Blake's accompaniments for Noble Sissle from the era. The Kings then perform the song a cappella, in a complex arrangement that reflects standard vocal-harmony style of the era. Indeed, if you didn't know their race, you probably couldn't identify this performance as being by an African American group. Not surprisingly, the attraction of acts like the Kings was their "sophistication"; white audiences marveled at the ability of African American vocalists to perform in a "refined" style.

Blake was elated by the impact of the quartet, again emphasizing their education and the class they brought to the show:

> They were sensations. All college men, not only could they sing, but they were very polished and stylish. They came out on the stage dressed in gray evening clothes. The suits were cutaway, and their top hats, ties, and shoes were also matching gray. They had everything. After their performance, Flo

Mills had to be behind to top them. No one else could follow—that's how great they were.[100]

At one point, Hann took a brief leave of absence from the show. The search was on for a replacement who could, if not exactly equal Hann, at least be close to his talents. Browning described how he found the perfect substitute. He and his wife were out walking with another young couple. His friend was a recent graduate of Rutgers University, an athlete named Paul Robeson:

> When I mentioned to Paul that our bass singer was leaving the show for a short time and that we had to find a bass to replace him, Paul looked at me and said, "You're looking at a bass singer!" Paul was quite emphatic about it, and when I told him to stop kidding, he said, "I am not kidding; I am your bass." So I told him to come to the show and see Eubie and me . . . After Paul sang about seven or eight bars, Eubie jumped up and exclaimed, "That's the man!"[101]

However, Blake and his partners were concerned about Robeson's ability to act. The young singer had never been on the stage before. "Both Browning and I agreed about Paul's voice," Blake explained. "He was able to learn the songs and small speaking parts in a matter of hours, but moving his massive body around the stage was a challenge. Paul stood out like a sore thumb." In fact, Sissle commented, "That guy's too big!" Sissle was proven right on Robeson's opening performance. Blake took Robeson to the back of the curtain and the two men looked through the peephole at the audience filing into the theater:

> We looked at the audience filling up and I pointed to the spotlight in the back of the hall. I cautioned Paul that when he came out onto the stage, above all, he was not to look at the spotlight, because it would blind him. But, sure enough, when they came out onto the stage, Paul looked straight into the spotlight and was blinded. . . .He fell right into the footlights, which sloped down into the stage gutter, and pop, pop, pop went the broken lights. Down he went like a ton of bricks, but you know, it never fazed him; he got right up and went into the songs. It takes guts to do what that guy did. I've known people who had been on the stage for years and they couldn't have pulled that off.[102]

Robeson won audiences over and stood out from his partners in the quartet as well as the other cast members. Blake explained,

> The white audiences—they were all white then—liked him. Paul sang some of Hann's solos, including "Invictus," "Mammy" (we sang a lot of mammy songs in those days), Will Marion Cook's classic "Rain," and a favorite of Paul's, "Old Black Joe." "Old Black Joe" was our last number and Paul just loved it. Paul was still huge on the stage; he was so big that we had him sit down while we sat around him on the stage. But you could see that Paul, awkwardness and all, was going to be a hit, even then.[103]

Early in 1922, Robeson left the company to join the cast of Mary Hoyt Wilborg's play, *Taboo,* and Hann resumed his role with the quartet.

The show also featured a talented all-black orchestra, another first for Broadway. Blake took conducting lessons to polish up his skills from William Grant Still (who also played oboe in the ensemble) and led the band from the pit. The group landed a recording deal with Victor and also played for private parties and events on evenings when the show was dark. Many of its musicians went on to gain great fame. The arrangements for the show were by Will Vodery, who arranged for Bert Williams during his vaudeville days, was Florenz Ziegfeld's music supervisor for the *Follies* for over 20 years, and would later work with George Gershwin (whom he hired for his first job in the theater as rehearsal pianist for a Ziegfeld show), Jerome Kern, and Duke Ellington. The critic in *The New York Age* called Vodery "one of the most talented and efficient musicians of the race."[104] Sissle gave Vodery much of the credit for the show's success, writing that Vodery "solved the problem of getting theatre orchestras to play with African American rhythmic inflections." Sissle went on to call Vodery "the rhythm life of legitimate Broadway."[105]

Of course, Blake himself was a great talent. His own piano playing helped propel the 16-piece orchestra. Blake's keyboard virtuosity was a highlight of each performance. The *New York Age*'s critic noted that "one of the highlights [of the show is] 'A Few Minutes with Sissle and Blake.' Mr. Blake as a piano virtuoso, uses the theme [of 'Love Will Find a Way'] as a basis for a series of pianist . . . variations, which bring unstinted applause."[106]

With expert musicians as these along with a heartfelt storyline, a hugely talented cast, and a jazzy sound new to Broadway, *Shuffle Along* was the first great step forward in black musical entertainment. It brought the art form from the minstrel and vaudeville traditions into the jazz age with a show that was the equal of any white show of the period. And the white audiences came in droves. In fact, the traffic was so congested that the city made 63rd Street one way.[107] White audiences might have thought themselves to be slumming by attending the show, but they came out of the theater with a newfound respect for black artists. In the wake of the success of the New York production, a second (and eventually even a third) company was formed to tour smaller towns.

Neither the profits, important as they were to the investors and artists, nor the excellent score nor its eminent alumni were the most important legacies of *Shuffle Along*. The show's subliminal message that blacks actually thought and felt and acted the same as whites was brought home to white and black audiences alike. And though today much of *Shuffle Along* appears stereotypical, at the time it was a huge breakthrough in its depiction of blacks. The show brought a new respect and regard for black performers, opening the door for shows like Lew Leslie's *Blackbirds* series and *Porgy and Bess*, among others, and allowing black performers to become true Broadway stars. Still, even after the success of *Shuffle Along*, almost all black shows were produced by whites in white-owned theaters and catered to audiences that were a majority white.

With *Shuffle Along*'s success, soon blacks had their own professional theatrical social club much like whites-only Lambs Club. The Dressing Room Club was established in 1921 by Jesse Shipp, following in the steps of the first black theatrical social club, The Frogs (1908–1920s). Blacks realized that their hopes for equality with whites needed an organization around which they could realize their goals. The Dressing Room Club's credo was "to impress the world with the dignity and economic value of the Negro element of the profession" and "to preserve to posterity the history of the Negro in theatricals." There were over 250 members of the club coming from backgrounds in minstrel shows, vaudeville, musicals, and straight plays. Naturally, Sissle and Blake were esteemed members of the organization.

On the anniversary of the show's year on Broadway, members of the touring company, then playing Brooklyn, joined the cast at the 63rd Street Theatre for a gala midnight performance. There were 140 performers on the stage and the reaction was tumultuous.[108] The Broadway production of *Shuffle Along* closed on July 15, 1922 after 504 performances. At the time of its closing *Shuffle Along* could boast it had the 11th longest run of any Broadway musical up to that time, including *Show Boat*, which ran 572 performances.

And the show had two numbers in the top 50 songs of the year, "Bandana Days" and "I'm Just Wild about Harry."

"I'm Just Wild about Harry" would prove to be a godsend for the songwriters. The song became a true standard even before Harry S. Truman gave it a boost. More than forty shorts, cartoons, and features used the songs on their soundtracks before 1950. That doesn't count innumerable radio and live performances and recorded covers as well as sheet music sales. With the advent of television, the song continued to provide royalties to the songwriters.

While not the only reason for the emergence of the Harlem Renaissance, *Shuffle Along* certainly contributed to the remarkable blossoming of black entertainment's inroads to popular song and theater. In 1923, the Cotton Club opened its doors. Though it catered to white audiences and its songs were written by the likes of white songwriters Harold Arlen and Ted Koehler and the team of Jimmy McHugh and Dorothy Fields, the casts were all black and featured such future stars as Lena Horne. The Shuffle Inn opened in 1921 and soon had its name changed to Connie's Inn. That nightspot sported black songwriters Thomas "Fats" Waller and Andy Razaf in a series of all black revues, including *Hot Chocolates* and *Keep Shufflin'*. Razaf would soon become one of Blake's major collaborators. And although Small's Paradise at 229¼ 7th Avenue mainly hosted white audiences, blacks were also welcomed. There were other venues around Harlem, particularly on "Jungle Alley," 133rd Street between Lenox and 7th Avenues. And it was *Shuffle Along* that helped jump-start it all, making black entertainers safe for white audiences and giving a leg up to hundreds of African American singers, dancers, choreographers, writers, and songwriters.

The closing of *Shuffle Along* on Broadway was just the beginning for Sissle and Blake as the show hit the road, spreading the popularity of this innovative show. The show's success would have a deep impact on Blake personally and professionally, putting strains on his marriage and his partnership with Sissle. Although the show should have opened doors for its creators, it still was not easy for African Americans to succeed in the cutthroat entertainment world—as Blake would quickly discover.

6

Shuffling On

1922–1923

Shuffle Along made its four creators wealthy men. It also made Sissle and Blake the best-known African American songwriters in the country. Blake bought a fancy Paige car, tooling around town with an eye on impressing his fellow musicians—and for attracting women. He didn't stint on his wife, though, providing Avis with furs, jewels, and a nicely furnished apartment. Sissle bought himself a Paige Daytona roadster, an even more expensive vehicle, known for its high-powered six-cylinder engine. He also opened up "Noble Sissle's Song Shop" on the corner of 138th Street and 7th Avenue.

Blake saw the show as an opportunity to pick up women, both among the pretty chorines and the show's stars. He was in constant competition with the other men in the company, including his partner Noble Sissle and oboist/composer William Grant Still. Eubie couldn't get either one to be his wingman:

> Grant Still was a real ladies man. He and Noble Sissle knocked me out of more pretty women. See, [Still] was a handsome guy. I'd say, "Still, Suzie Jackson and Lizzie Brown, let's take them out." Now, he'd never go out with *me*. Some of the most beautiful women, now they be sittin' in the audience. Maybe one of the girls had a crush on me before. They come backstage . . . [and say to me], "Can we go out together and have a nice time. You know that guy who played the oboe [William Grant Still], can he come out with us?" And I'd go to him, "Still, you want to go out. . ." Now he says, "Now, Eubie, I got to make an arrangement . . ." Sissle was the same way. He'd go out and he'd *never* tell me about it.[1]

Eubie apparently felt no qualms about his many romantic liaisons, telling his biographer Al Rose,

Eubie Blake. Richard Carlin and Ken Bloom, Oxford University Press (2020). © Richard Carlin and Ken Bloom 2020.
DOI: 10.1093/oso/9780190635930.001.0001

I wasn't foolin' with jail bait. These were all grown-up women. They were in the theatrical world, and a woman in the theatrical world needs to know it ain't the same as the rest of the world. Show people think a certain way. They act a certain way—and what I did was what show people did. Maybe I did it more than most of the others—but it wasn't the kind of thing you just decide you're gonna do! It just comes up on you and there you are.[2]

Although Eubie liked to act the innocent, who was relentlessly pursued by beautiful women he couldn't turn down, he sheepishly admitted to Rose that this was something of a ruse. "I've been gettin' away with that act for sixty years," he admitted.[3] According to a close associate of Blake's, "Eubie would pore over pictures of *Shuffle Along*, recalling the chorus girls he'd slept with. He would just point with his finger—'This one, this one, this one.'"[4] When David Jasen asked blues singer Eva Taylor—then in her mid-80s—whether she "knew" Eubie Blake while working as a chorus girl in *Shuffle Along*, she replied, "Certainly not! I had just gotten married to Clarence Williams," the well-known music publisher and songwriter. "I was *acquainted* with Mr. Blake," she said, making the distinction clear between "knowing" someone (in the biblical sense) and "knowing" that person.[5]

Blake may also have been exaggerating his sexual prowess somewhat. In later life, he gave conflicting accounts of whether he had a sexual relationship with Josephine Baker. He told one close associate that he had slept with her only once, while telling Baker biographer Lynn Haney that he had an affair with the singer that lasted until she left for Paris.[6] The later seems unlikely, because Eubie was maintaining a relationship with both his wife and Lottie Gee (Figure 6.1)throughout this period, and even he probably didn't have the stamina to deal with three women simultaneously.

Besides his two wives, the longest relationship Eubie formed with a woman was with *Shuffle Along*'s leading lady, Lottie Gee. Gee's life story would turn out to be quite tragic, despite its hopeful beginnings and the considerable acclaim she gained for her role as the love interest in *Shuffle Along*. It's not clear exactly when Blake first met Gee, although it may have predated their working together on *Shuffle Along*; he was certainly aware of her previous performing career. They had possibly met when Blake and Gee were on the same bill to benefit Baltimore's Provident Hospital on July 2, 1913, although in later interviews Blake never mentioned meeting her at this performance. In any case, it wouldn't be until they worked together in *Shuffle Along* that their relationship changed.

Figure 6.1 Lottie Gee (on right) with Bob Lee (holding cane) in a scene from *Shuffle Along*. Gee was an exceptional beauty who was Blake's lover for over a decade.

Born Charlotte M. Gee in Millboro, Virginia, on August 17, 1886, Gee worked her way up from chorus girl to leading lady.[7] She made one of her first appearances as a chorine in the 1909 touring cast of Cole and Johnson's *The Red Moon*. Her light complexion allowed her to appear as a "Gibson girl" in the show's chorus, a role not usually associated with black actresses. In 1911, she partnered with singer/dancer Effie King, first touring with Ford Dabney's company as "Ford Dabney's Ginger Girls," and then as a vaudeville duo. A reviewer writing in the African American press praised them for weathering the difficult conditions faced by black performers and succeeding on the stage:

> In no other field have colored Americans with artistic aspirations found the road to success so hard as that leading to prominence upon the stage. As a rule, those who have selected the stage for their professional career have been given very little consideration by our writers and critics. . . . [While] the profession has in the past merited severe criticism . . . it has improved with time . . .

Conspicuous on the rol[1] of those who are endeavoring daily to raise
the standard . . . [are] Misses Effie King and Lottie Gee . . . as a refined
singing and dancing act.

These talented young women . . . have excellent voices and know how
to use them. The act is beautifully costumed and staged with artistic taste.[8]

The reviewer used code words like "refined" and "artistic taste" to indicate
that the performers were a notch above black-faced minstrels, representing
an advance beyond earlier stereotypes. The reviewer also proudly noted that
both women came from educated families and had sung in their church
choirs in their younger years, subtly countering the stereotypes that female performers were lower class and lacked moral direction. The review
concludes with the solidly middle-class endorsement that "both [performers]
own property, thus showing that their efforts have not been in vain."

In 1913, Gee married pianist Wilson Harrison "Peaches" Kyer (c. 1888–
1982).[9] Originally from Charleston, South Carolina, Kyer was musical director for the well-known black touring company The Smart Set for their
1911–1912 season. After his marriage to Gee, the pair entertained for a period in 1914 at Hayne's restaurant in New York City.[10] In the 1915 New York
Census, they are listed as living in Harlem, with Lottie's occupation given as
"housewife" and Kyer listed as a musician; it is possible that she retired from
performing for a while after her marriage. Kyer apparently left her in 1919,
but the couple were not formally divorced until 1924.[11]

Gee was back to performing by the late 1910s, and appeared at least occasionally as a vocalist with Will Marion Cook's Syncopated Orchestra. In
late 1919, she secured work in England, where she performed for much of
the next year. She then toured France, Italy, and Asia with Cook's orchestra.
Gee reported to Josephine Baker that playing in Europe was a joy and that
she encountered very little racial prejudice. In fact, newspapers in France
reported that the government would deport any Americans who made a
scene in French nightclubs where "management permits Negroes to dance
with white girls."[12] Her popularity was so great that she returned briefly to
New York for an appearance at the Lafayette Theatre[13] that August, winning
rave reviews in the African American press:

Miss Lottie Gee is appearing this week in one of the most pleasing single
turns that has been put on by a colored member of the gentler sex. Miss Gee
has an act that can bear rigid inspection and severe criticism from every

angle. This young lady is attractive in appearance and her costumes, particularly that creation of black which she dons toward the close of her skit, make her doubly pleasing to gaze upon. She sings and dances well, showing ability to render both ragtime songs and high class ballads. . . .

Miss Gee has made wonderful improvement since the days of Cole & Johnson, when she was a chorus girl, and she is the most promising young colored woman who has flashed across the vaudeville horizon in years. Anyone who can do as strong a single as Miss Gee can hold their own in fast company—musical comedy especially.[14]

The reviewer compared Gee's performance to Abbie Mitchell, one of the great stars of the turn-of-the-century black theater (and Will Marion Cook's wife). Gee returned permanently to the states that December, resuming work on vaudeville.[15]

At the end of the 1910s, Gee was managed by Lew Leslie, who would later achieve Broadway fame as the producer of all-black musical revues, most famously *Blackbirds of 1928*. One of Gee's closest friends was Elizabeth Hall. Elizabeth's daughter Adelaide was going to appear in her school's concert marking the end of the semester. Gee convinced Leslie to escort her to the concert and Leslie was immediately struck with Adelaide's talents. He befriended the family and a few years later would shepherd Adelaide through her audition for *Shuffle Along* with Gee watching over the 16-year-old during the rehearsals and run of the show.

In 1921, Gee was hired to play the love interest in *Shuffle Along*. Eubie told his biographer Al Rose that Sissle and he were so anxious to have Gee in the lead role that they paid her expenses and provided lodging for her throughout the rehearsal and tryout period for the show.[16] It's likely that her recent successes in London and New York added to her marquee value. Blake was immediately smitten with the young singer/actress, and she would live as his mistress for the next decade.

Gee was an ideal performer to play the controversial role of a romantic lead. Besides her great talents as an actress and singer, she was fair skinned with straight hair, which she wore in the popular style of the day. She could easily have passed for white. In this way, she fit into the standard for black chorines in general, who were expected to be light skinned and conventionally attractive. Drawing on her conventional good looks, Gee landed an endorsement deal with "Sophia's Triple Pomade," a hair-straightening treatment that promised to "make the most Stubborn, Harsh, or Unruly Hair

Lay Right." Gee's photo appeared in advertisements that ran in the African American press, along with a testimonial letter praising "the wonderful merit of [this] beauty system."[17]

Once the show had hit Broadway, Blake set Lottie up in her own apartment, while continuing to live with his wife. Eubie was impressed with her talent and theatrical experience, as well as her good looks:

> She was starring in London, playing the biggest clubs and theaters . . . She really knew her business and she could really sing! Beautiful!
>
> I guess I have to say I was smitten. When I was at a party and she was there, she acted like she barely knew me. Called me "Mr. Blake" because, of course, nobody is supposed to know I'm livin' with her, see. But she never came near me in public. Alone though, she called me "Daddy." Poor Lottie! I never bought her a *thing*! I put a *piano* in her house, but just so I could teach her the new songs. Ten years I spent with that girl.[18]

Eubie's wife Avis was, in his words, "no dummy," and soon realized that the pianist was maintaining a separate household with the young starlet. According to Eubie, when a friend asked Avis how she could put up with Eubie's philandering, his wife was more than able to stand up for herself:

> "Honey, you see that l'il ol' box on the vanity? Just go over there and open it."
>
> Filled with diamonds and emeralds, the visitor found.
>
> "My husband, that no-good nigger gave me those. Now, baby will you just slide open that closet door and count the fur coats?"
>
> Five.
>
> "Kitten," Avis pursued, "What are you going to do in the morning?"
>
> Well, since it was a week-day, she'd go to work.
>
> "Not me, kiddo!" Avis assured her guest smugly. "I'm stayin' right here in bed until I feel like gettin' up. That no-good nigger husband of mine bought me those jewels and those furs. He takes care of me so I don't have to lift a finger. I don't have a maid, because I don't want on[e] around the place, but I've got a car *and* a chauffeur. I can't drive, you know. And I'm gonna worry what the no-good nigger might be doin' behind my back? No, Gal, you need to get *you* a low-down cheater like my Eubie."[19]

According to Blake's biographer Al Rose, the two jealous women tried to control Blake's sex drive in an unusual manner; before he left home, Avis would force him to have sex with her until he ejaculated, and then Lottie would do the same every time Blake was about to leave her apartment.[20]

The relationship of Gee and Blake created friction not only in his marriage but also with his partner Noble Sissle, who took a much more traditional view of the sanctity of marriage—this despite his own affairs with chorus girls. In an undated letter, Sissle scolds Blake for his extramarital flings, advising him that he's risking the future of their partnership:

> Eubie I hope you have your family troubles straightened out. Don't let no other woman break up your home. The woman you took before Gods sacred shrine as your wife is the only woman in the sight of God and man beside your relatives you have any right to take care of. Now I have made for myself a name among the best of New York City and I don't intend to be disgraced by any of your affairs so I give you warning. Unless you are straight with your wife and decided to let that other woman alone for life as far as living with her is concern than its all off. I have never been mixed up in any mess like that and I don't intend to be bothered or worried. You are a man so choose for your self. But what every you do please refrain from drink and scandal. [Spelling and punctuation as in original] [21]

Of course, Blake wouldn't—or perhaps couldn't—change his behavior to please his persnickety partner. Sissle's upbringing as the son of a minister made him appear to Blake to be a humorless scold. The successful partnership was starting to show the first signs of friction, which would eventually lead to the duo splitting up.[22]

Blake's affair with Lottie Gee had little effect on the show itself, which continued its success following its Broadway run. The first stop of the touring company was Boston where, in late July 1922, producer and theatre owner Arch Selwyn booked the show into his theater initially for a two-week run. Blake was surprised to find the long line at the box office made up mostly of blacks. This was strange, because the New York audiences were primarily white. Upon questioning the queue, Blake discovered that the blacks were household help or chauffeurs who were sent by their white employers to buy tickets to the show.

The New York Age proudly reported the many positive reviews in the Boston press, including a "flattering half-column review and . . . a [separate] picture of Miss Edith Spencer [who had taken the role originated by

Gertrude Saunders] in the pictorial section" in the Boston *Herald*.[23] As a publicity stunt, the show's creators were invited to meet with Boston's mayor to be photographed and presented with keys to the city. Under the headline "Colored Pair Honored," *Variety* reported that this was "the first time that any member of the negro race, in the acting profession, has been thus honored by any American city."[24] The *New York Morning Telegraph* wryly noted, "The keys are guaranteed to open anything in town, including the klavern of the Ku Klux Klan."[25] *Shuffle Along* eventually played almost three months in Boston before closing in late November, and would have run longer but for a lawsuit from the classical theater company that had the following booking at the theater.

The *Boston American* praised the production, noting "from the moment Eubie Blake turns his Mona Lisa smile on his orchestra . . . until the last double shuffle of the finale, 'Shuffle Along' is concrete proof of what we have known—namely, that the Negro has a sense of harmony, rhythm and melody that no others can equal." Speaking of Miller and Lyles, he noted, "They have not tried to glorify their Race, as they might pardonably be expected to do, but . . . each twist of the dialogue is new." The review was so positive that it was proudly reprinted by the African American newspaper the *Chicago Defender*.[26]

This reviewer particularly praised a "chorus girl who literally 'walks off with the show' . . . not by mere beauty . . . but by her comedy dancing." Although she is not cited by name, this review clearly refers to the huge impression made by Josephine Baker, who first joined the main company in Boston. Baker would become the surprise hit of the show, despite having a nonspeaking role.

The show's creators were initially reluctant to hire Baker when she auditioned for the original company. Sissle remembered,

> We had turned her down when she tried out for us in Philadelphia because she was not yet sixteen. We had wanted to hire her but by law we couldn't.[27] She was heartbroken. We produced a number-two company to play one-nighters throughout New England while we were still in New York. Word got back to us that a comedy chorus girl had joined the company after we had rehearsed it and sent it out on the road—it was Josephine. She had slipped out on the road to join that company because she thought we didn't like her or want to hire her. How glad we were to get her back.[28]

Baker's memory of the audition was even more traumatic. She related,

> I found myself face to face with Mr. Sissle, a thin man with a full head of
> hair. Mr. Blake, plump and bald-headed, sat at the piano, his nose buried
> in his music. He never once opened his mouth. Nor did Mr. Sissle waste
> words. "Too young," he snapped. I began my usual routine. "But I'm seven-
> teen . . ." "Sorry. Too small, too thin, too dark." . . . Sissle wanted his chorus
> to look like Tillers, a highly successful white company.[29]

The Tiller Girls were a popular white chorus line of the day. Baker felt that
Sissle was "ashamed" of his race, but he would have argued he simply was
trying to break into the white theater world.

While the show was still in New York, Al Mayer hired Baker for the touring
(or second) company. She was finally given her chance on stage as one of the
chorus. After one of the chorus's numbers, she broke free and started dancing
wildly. The conductor tried to keep time but she was out of control. The stage
manager fired her on the spot. Blake called the theater to inquire about how
the show was doing and was told that Baker was fired. Blake asked, "How
did the audience react?" The stage manager told him that the out-of-town
audiences thought she was terrific. Blake immediately responded, "Put her
back in."[30] Baker's success on the road secured her a place in Boston. And
from the time she set foot on the stage, audiences adored her. Now a full
member of the company, Baker really started to shine, with many other
critics noting how her comedic dancing was making her a star of the show. In
a review titled "A Chorus Girl, But Can't Be Overlooked," one critic enthused,

> Where the best part of a capacity house singles out one little girl in the
> chorus and gives her attention every time she appears, it shows the recog-
> nition of qualities such as stars are made of. There is a little girl like this
> in the all colored musical success "Shuffle Along" . . . A sturdy youngster,
> with a comedy way that asserts itself in everything she does . . . her name
> is Josephine Baker. Jolly as she seems to be in her work, the stage romping
> is serious business with Josephine. She has to work to help support her
> mother and little brother at home in Washington, DC.[31]

Typically, this white critic emphasizes that Josephine took to the stage only
to help support her family, giving her an "honest" motive to pursuing what
many viewed as the scandalous life of a traveling actor.

Despite the show's success on Broadway and in Boston, other bookings were harder to come by. Blake recounted, "We had to jump all the way to Chicago—nobody else would take us. At the last minute we were let in by a lady who owned the Olympic, a rundown burlesque house. The audience was peeking around a lot of posts to see the show."[32] Nonetheless, the show was a smash success, running in Chicago from late November 1922 through mid-February 1923. A reviewer in the African American newspaper the *Dallas Express* reported on the show's success:

> Shuffle Along "shuffled" into the Olympic theater . . . with a verve and a swerve which has made all Chicago sit up and take notice. That this stellar organization has lived up to all advance notices . . . is the opinion to be heard not only in the places where the "brethren" hold forth but all over this little town and the daily paper critics who have spelled death for so many shows this fall have been unanimous in their approval.[33]

The newspaper noted that it was not surprising that "Colored Chicago" pronounced the show the "best ever" but it was the "downtown theatre" critics' response that was so surprising: "Ashton Stevens of the *Herald Examiner*, the ace of critics here [reported] . . . 'It is the real Colored thing: it is ETHIOPIA.'"

The arrival of the company in Chicago was itself an event:

> [T]he sensations from Broadway . . . disembarked from their special train with 18 motor cars and numerous [bags] full of the latest in togs. Not for the stage, no bless you, but for the "stroll." Sartorially the outfit has 35th and Indiana Avenue up on its tiptoes and gasping for breath and it's a toss up which are the best dressed, the lads or the slinkers. Class and prosperity are sticking out all over them.[34]

The *Chicago Defender* reported that Lyles made a splashy entrance into town, driving his brand-new $18,500 (a little over a quarter million dollars in today's dollars) custom Rolls Royce directly from Boston. The car was described as having an "ice box in the rear, four-wheel brakes, and a bed for reclining while touring."[35] The sight of a black man piloting such an expensive car was another sign of racial progress to the paper's reporter.

The Dallas writer was particularly enthusiastic about Blake's music and command of the show's band, saying,

But I am sure there is . . . more music than that you will hear in Mr. Berlin's most musical *Music Box Revue*. And it is very real music. It is a score that abounds in what . . . tin pan alley call "natural" melodies. . . . They make you say that the tunefulness of the Colored man is more than superstition.

Eubie Blake composed them, and he . . . is my idea of a star in the orchestra pit. He makes his fourteen bandsmen to play like forty when needs be . . . He sits at the concert grand juggling a cascade of ebony where it will do the least harm . . . Mr. Blake's black bandsmen . . . [are] the life of the show.[36]

Chicago's white critics also praised the show, assuring audiences that the production was "as clean as a hound's dentistry" and that "any Caucasian producer who achieves an ensemble of such spirit and abandon would regard it as a triumph."[37] Clearly, they wished to assure white Chicagoans that the show didn't feature any "low" moments that would be disturbing to their families. Nonetheless, Ashton Stevens initially seemed uncomfortable with the way the show's leads were flaunting their wealth:

Our colored brothers . . . who sing and dance in "Shuffle Along," have eleven limousines and their own chauffeurs. It is easy come, easy go with them. "What's money for but to spend?" is their slogan, and they live up to it in union suits that cost $40 . . . Just before they came to Chicago, Mr. Eubie Blake, the Paderewski of the production, bought himself a raccoon coat . . . Mr. Lyles is not a frugal person, either. His waist-coast is attached to a platinum watch trimmed with diamonds that cost a thousand dollars.[38]

Stevens concluded that the white producer Al Mayer carried "the only Ingersoll in the organization"—an inexpensive but reliable watch.

Apparently Mayer, Sissle, and Blake made a concerted effort to win over this important critic, inviting him backstage to meet the cast to show him that they were just hard-working actors—and not lording their wealth and success over others. In a follow-up column headlined "Colored Actors 'Good Winners' Says Stevens," the critic lavished praise on the company:

These very prosperous music comedians were about as modest and decent and stageworthy a company as I had ever seen. They respect their audiences, themselves and their show. Their dressing rooms and their toggery they keep as spotless as their libretto, than which there is no cleaner in all the literature of song and step.[39]

Like many other white critics, Stevens applauded the "clean" nature of the show, countering the common stereotype that African American entertainments were full of sexual innuendo and banter that was not appropriate for "family" audiences.

While some whites were made uncomfortable by the financial success of Sissle and Blake, Blake himself insisted that the duo were not motivated by money. In an interview with the *Cleveland News-Leader*, Blake said "It isn't the money that interests us," instead insisting that their main goal was "to do everything we can to convince the skeptical white people of this country that the Negro has a legitimate place on the stage as an entertainer, a logical and proper place, the same as anyone else."[40] Sissle went further, saying the pair were "evangelists" for blacks on stage, relating his success back to his father's role as a minister:

Here I was, the son of a Cleveland Colored preacher of the gospel. Now, father was liberal-minded . . . but he had not the slightest doubt that I would become a singing evangelist. That was in his mind during the years that I was getting my education. . . . That's in reality what I have become, or more correctly speaking, that's how I think of myself. . . .

I believe that my father would not be disappointed in me. I am in the theater and I am not singing in churches . . . Still, my partner and I want to be evangelists. We want to do something for the Negro race . . . And if we compel white audiences to listen to us; if we entertain them and . . . [they] think a little better of the Colored man than in the past, then we have done something that's better than salary. In fact, that's what we want to do, it is our biggest aim.[41]

Underscoring the sophistication of the show's creators, the African American press gave favorable coverage to them even when they were not on stage. The *Chicago Defender* was quick to take note when Blake and his wife Avis attended a concert by Russian concert pianist Mischa Levitski. The correspondent praised Blake's appreciation for classical traditions, as well as his skill as a composer:

His devotion to his art is apparent in his music which shows he has studied and absorbed it zealously and with success . . . in his "Love Will Find A Way," he uses an upward progression of ninth chords which would be disastrous in the hands of a novice, but under Mr. Blake's deft finger they give an exotic colour [sic] to the numbers.

Throughout all his music I find a faithful alliance to harmonic structure, melodic colours far in advance of the popular music trade and a rather chaste liaison between the voice and accompaniment, which serves to make his songs thoroughly appealing to both singer and player . . . both [Blake and Levitski] are great artists in their specific professions, contributing to the culture and joy of life.[42]

As was typical of the black press, the highest praise was reserved for those black musicians who emulated white, European models. To "uplift the race," it was believed that it was important to show that blacks were able to equal the white world.

One perhaps eccentric critique appeared in an African American newspaper, the *Chicago Star*, published and mostly written and edited by Sylvester Russell. Russell had been a well-known critic of black theatrical productions since the early 1900s, with his reviews regularly appearing in the major national African American papers, the *Indianapolis Freeman* and *Chicago Defender*. In his front-page review/editorial, Russell took to task the show's local producers by saying that they purposely blocked black audiences from attending during its opening week to reserve seats for whites:

"White People First" is the slogan clearly demonstrated by the new color line preferential method which the Olympic theater . . . has invented . . . a barrier to colored patronage to discourage them from attending . . . for the first week in order to accommodate the autocrats of the white race.[43]

Russell also claimed that the Olympic purposely did not advertise the show in Chicago's Jewish newspapers, hoping to keep out that audience as well. In a follow-up article, Russell interviewed Flournoy Miller, pointing out to him that several blacks had been denied seats at the theater. He did not record Miller's reaction to this statement. Nonetheless, Russell praised all four of the show's creators, urging his readers to "[g]o and see them. They are fine. And so is the show."[44]

The show left Chicago and moved on to Des Moines, Iowa, for a five-night run to similarly glowing reviews. Locals lined up to get tickets, and the critics hailed the show and its "Negro" creators. One critic offered a somewhat patronizing—if at least complimentary—assessment of the show:

> We thought, as we watched this whirlwind of song and dance and fun, how much the American Negro has contributed to American music and American humor. A leaf from every page of the Negro's life in America is there—from his plantation songs to his most delirious blues.[45]

After leaving Des Moines, the show moved to Sissle's hometown of Indianapolis. The critic there was particularly impressed by Eubie's musicianship as he conducted from the pit:

> This writer sat where he could watch the pianist, and listened to him so intently that part of the happenings on the stage were lost. Wicked bits of counter-harmony, of cadenzas, of jazz combinations of notes and what not were thrown off with nonchalance, no two alike, and all of them marvelous: an instance of jazz "as is" jazz. Others in the adjoining seats also found themselves watching Blake, whose exposition of ragtime, while he was in the pit, was far more interesting that his exposition of pyrotechnics in his solo on the stage.[46]

While the reviewer found the production "inferior" and the comedy "dull," the high energy of the dancing and quality of the music more than made up for it, in his estimation.

The show next opened in St. Louis, where the local paper was far more critical, faulting it for its lack of humor and "Negro" elements. The local critic seemed particularly annoyed that the production was in the style of conventional white musical comedies, rather than pandering to minstrel-era stereotypes:

> Shuffle Along is scarcely a negro show at all: it is a musical comedy which happens to be performed by negroes. It is merely an imitation of the conventional musical show.
>
> Although the scene is laid in Dixie the characters are of the Northern rather than Southern type. The plantation darky has virtually disappeared. Instead, we have negro merchants, whose children have attended high school, lost every trace of dialect, and learned to sing according to the Italian method. The gain in tone and decorum seems more than offset by

loss of humor, pungency and picturesqueness. . . . It was interesting to note that whenever a character was indicated as a full-blooded negro, it was necessary to use burnt cork.[47]

Particularly galling to this Midwestern critic was the fact that Sissle and Blake were writing songs that equaled the work of pop tunesmiths like Irving Berlin and the Gershwins. Managing to offend both blacks and Jews, he complained, "The negro invented jazz and 'blues,' but in this score we have a mimicry by negroes of the imitation of negroes practiced by the Levantines of Tin Pan Alley." The critic also noted that most of the applause came from the balcony—where blacks were forced to sit—rather than the main floor. Nonetheless, a society note from Union, Missouri, underscored that local nabobs were flocking to the big city to see the show, noting, "Mr. and Mrs. John C. Jacobs . . . report it the very best musical comedy they have ever seen. According to Mr. Jacobs, the 'niggers' were on dress parade throughout the entire show."[48]

Seeking to further cash in on the show, the producers licensed various offshoot versions to tour, including one under the direction of George Wintz, featuring John Vaughner and Edgar Connors as the comic leads. This version hit smaller cities in the Midwest and even ventured into the deep South, including a three-day run in Nashville toward the end of December 1922. The local producer noted that the show played to "absolute capacity" and that it was the "cleanest and fastest dancing musical comedy" ever to appear there.[49]

When the Wintz company hit Birmingham, the local critic was astounded by the lack of "negro humor—typical, traditional and fictional, as the South knows it" when he encountered instead "a smart, light stepping, wise cracking bunch of New York actors who, with clear enunciation and cream-like complexions, upset expectations. Indeed, the absence of dialect is marked even in . . . the principal comedians." Nonetheless, once the critic had realized that "the show is a straight musical comedy . . . in the hands of trained negro actors" he found it "rattlingly good, altogether diverting, and a piece of stage work regular theater goers will enjoy."[50]

In March 1923, a "third" company was announced as appearing at Harlem's Lafayette Theatre, this one led by the well-known black comedians Homer Tutt and Salem Whitney. It also was apparently sanctioned by the original producers, as it featured the original script and songs.[51]

Shuffle Along's success also inspired imitations and downright pirated productions. Lawrence Deas, who was replaced as director of the Broadway production, produced his own show, titled *Plantation Days*. According to Sissle and Blake, this new show was advertised as being from the "producer of *Shuffle Along*"—despite the fact that Deas did not produce the original show. Even worse, for his revue Deas lifted many of their songs from the original show—but thinly disguised the fact by changing the song's titles. Sissle and Blake sought a restraining order in Federal Court against his use of their copyright songs when Deas's production was playing in Chicago.[52] *Plantation Days* featured the stage debut of Ethel Waters, who was turned down in *Shuffle Along* supposedly because her skin was too dark. She received a rave review from Chicago's main critic, Ashton Stevens of the *Herald and Examiner*.[53]

For the lead company, the plan originally was to go to London that April under the auspices of British producer Charles Cochran. When Cochran saw *Shuffle Along*, he immediately fell in love with Florence Mills's talents. Cochran wrote of his admiration for Mills: "Florence Mills was one of the greatest artists that ever walked on to a stage. But for her color she would have been internationally accepted as one of the half dozen leading theatrical personalities of this century, and worth all the money in the world."[54] He signed a contract to bring *Shuffle Along* to London but when Mills exited the show, he lost interest in the property. Instead, he brought Mills to London to star in *Dover Street to Dixie*, which opened in May 1923.

With the London tour canceled, *Shuffle Along* continued to perform stateside, appearing in Brooklyn in early June, followed by a brief run in Atlantic City. However, trouble was brewing with author/actors Miller and Lyles. Sissle had served more or less as the foursome's voice with the show's white producers; the comedians suspected that he was taking advantage of the situation, and taking a bigger cut than he deserved.[55] Meanwhile, Sissle and Blake as songwriters were earning additional income from music publishing and recordings, revenue that Miller and Lyles did not share. After their Atlantic City appearance, Miller and Lyles quit the show, without giving any notice to Sissle, Blake, or the producers. As reported in *Variety* in June,

Miller and Lyles have been dissatisfied for some time and recently petitioned for a share in the song royalties coming to Sissle and Blake....

Their request was not granted and consequently wishing to sever their connections with the company, they made a contract with George White to appear in a new production, upon which ... White is to spend $75,000 of his own and his backers' money.

Harry Cort was not about to take their defection sitting down. Although their three-year contract with him was up, he argued that they had to remain with the show as long as it was still touring:

> Cort claims that he has the show booked for the next year and that he will apply for an injunction if the colored team tries to break their contract.
>
> Miller and Lyles counter this claim by saying that they have an interest in the show and, as part owners, are privileged to substitute someone in their place if they wish.[56]

In mid-July, George White announced a new edition of *Shuffle Along* would open in the fall, premiering in Washington, DC, before moving to Boston. It would feature Miller and Lyles, with music by James P. Johnson and lyrics by Cecil Mack. The lead duo were to be paid $2000 a week.[57] This was a clear slap in the face to Cort and his producing partners, who were planning to continue touring the original *Shuffle Along* that fall. Cort immediately sent lawyers to the theaters planning to present the alternate production, advising them that "Miller and Lyles . . . have no right to the title . . . [and] that two attractions of the same name though dissimilar would be running at the same time,"[58] which would not be tolerated. An injunction was issued against White and the comic duo by the original production company on July 30.[59] The court found in favor of Miller and Lyles, who went on with their plan for their own show, which would eventually open as *Runnin' Wild*.

Sissle and Blake meanwhile spent the summer of 1923 in heading a revue at the Café La Marne on Atlantic City's boardwalk, drawing on their songs from *Shuffle Along*.[60] They stole its title, *Plantation Days*, from rival Lawrence Deas, perhaps thinking it would be revenge for his attempt to cash in on their show. The revue featured a number of specialty acts, including dancer/mime Johnny Hudgins, who would later star in the duo's next show when it opened in New York. (Hudgins's wife, Mildred, had been a chorus girl in *Shuffle Along*.)[61] In addition to Hudgins and his wife, Lottie Gee and Josephine Baker appeared in the abbreviated production.

The recast *Shuffle Along* began its fall 1923 tour, opening in late August in Toronto, Canada. Miller and Lyles were replaced as the comic leads by tall Lew Payton and his diminutive partner Joe Simms. Payton had previously worked vaudeville with various partners, and even co-owned a music publishing firm in the late 1910s; he had also appeared in the first touring company of *Shuffle Along*. He was praised for adding "jollification" to the show, with this critic comparing him to Bert Williams, although he was "not so shuffle-footed, stoop-shouldered and hesitant of speech as the late leader of his race on the stage."[62] Lottie Gee remained as the romantic lead, with Sissle playing a political boss.

In September 1923, the show reached Pittsburgh's Pitt Theater and was well received by the press. The local critic praised the show, although mostly because in his eyes it supported his stereotypical view of what a black show should be:

> Ebony bell[e]s, whose every skip and step and arm movement were timed with rollicking tunes, give a Dixie dash to the Ethiopian company's frolic . . . styled "Shuffle Along" . . . These steppers personify the jazz jingle of motions, always going gleefully with the festive orchestra of all-colored musicians.[63]

Naturally, the local African American press gave the tour ample coverage, with a long article on the evolution of *Shuffle Along* and the difficulties faced by black artists. Conditions at the theaters were mostly deplorable and pay was low. Noble Sissle commented that "[m]ost towns [we] played to would not allow [us] to eat or sleep in the hotels or restaurants." Often it meant they would, "have to travel 25 or 30 miles to find a place." No white hotel would allow the company to stay in them.[64] In an interview with the *Pittsburgh Courier*, Sissle also reflected on the difficulties he faced by being a black song-writer. When the interviewer asked if he felt that his career had been hampered by his skin color, Sissle replied,

> Yes and no. Our race has been an asset in the success of "Shuffle Along," but a handicap in our song writing. Publishers looked to us for jazz music and would accept such, but when we offered something more serious they would not take it.
>
> For example, we wrote "Baby Bunting," the song hit of "Elsie," seven years ago, but could not sell it. "Two Hearts in Tune," another hit of "Elsie," also was written several years ago, as were "My Vision Girl," "Mary Ann of Maryland" [aka "Ain't You Comin' Back Mary Ann, to Maryland"], and several others. But the publishers could not see them until after our success with "Shuffle Along."
>
> Now that we have arrived, so to speak, the handicap of race has been forgotten.[65]

Following the Pittsburgh engagement, the show went on to St. Louis. The American Theatre announced, "Entire CENTER and LEFT section in the FIRST BALCONY Has Been Reserved For Colored Patrons"[66] –perhaps as a reassurance to white patrons that they would be safely separated from the black audience attracted to the show.

The show returned to Toronto in late September. Robert P. Edwards, who covered Canada for the Associated Negro Press, reported that the show was so successful there that "hundreds were turned away nightly, and various movements were inaugurated to persuade the management to lengthen their stay." He particularly noted the audience's enthusiastic response to Eubie, who

> despite his coolness and calmness[,] the audience becomes hilarious, as wielding his baton with one hand and tickling the ivories with the other, he brought forth such music . . . and from SOME ORCHESTRA.[67]

The tour continued through major Midwestern towns, reaching Cincinnati in November (where the initial two-week run was held over due to sell-out crowds)[68], and looping back to Buffalo, New York, by December. According to ledgers kept by the producers, the show netted almost \$33,000 (or about \$475,000 in today's dollars) from the box office for the entire tour.

A high point for Eubie of this tour was an appearance in his hometown of Baltimore, Maryland. It was particularly important to him to show the members of the elite of the city's black society how high he had risen in the world. Blake related how Sissle convinced the theater management there to allow blacks to be seated not only in the upper gallery but also in the second balcony—usually reserved for whites only:

> In those days, the high brown Negroes, coachman wifes, they were big-time Negroes. They ain't going into no gallery, see. So we're playing the Ford's theater, and so you gotta go in the gallery because we're colored. . . . So Sissle goes to the manager and says, "Now listen. You're here to make money, ain't you? The colored people, the better class of colored people, they won't sit up in that gallery. Why don't you open the second balcony?" And he opened the second balcony.

In order to let the local population know that the theater would be open to black audiences, Blake came up with an ingenuous plan:

You know how we had to do it? I know this from carnivals, see. You get a drum, a fife, or a bugle and put it in the wagon and go around in the colored section up town, and that draws Negroes. And you got a big sign on there, "Ford Theater open to Negroes—Balcony."

Blake also convinced his mother—who as a church-going woman felt music and theater were the "Devil's work"—to attend one of the performances, even arranging for her to be seated in the owner's box. It did take some extra per-suasion, however, on the part of his adoptive sister to convince her:

My adopted sister says, "He owns the show. And he had it fixed [for you to attend it]. If you let him down, it will break his heart." So [my mother] agreed and she told some of the Sisters of the Church, and they got their bonnets on, they all dressed up . . . And I had everything fixed at the time that my mother came into the lobby, and honest to God the white people and the colored people stood up, when she came and got a seat. . . . [W]hen the show was over, I held the curtain . . . and gave an introduction to my mother.

Eubie arranged to have flowers in his dressing room to host a little recep-tion after the performance for his mother and her friends, serving them all ginger ale, lemonade, and cake (replacing the usual whiskey he kept for his own libations). Although the sisters were greatly impressed, typically, Eubie's mother was dismissive of his success:

So the sisters come back in my [dressing room]. One of the sisters says, "Sister Blake, you certainly must be proud of that boy. Just to think he's playing the Ford's Theater." We couldn't even *come in* the Ford's Theater. . . . You couldn't go in the theater at all, they don't care where you sit. Now my mother says, "I ain't, I ain't, I ain't." "You're not proud? His name is up in the lights . . . "She says, "He could be doing that for Jesus!" And I came damn near telling her, "I would be working for Jesus but he don't pay you nothing," but I didn't want to be breaking her heart. I hadn't accomplished nothing with her. She wanted me to be Reverend Eubie Blake.[69]

Eubie's inability to win his mother's approval remained a thorn in his side for his entire life.

As Sissle indicated, the success of the *Shuffle Along* score led to many new opportunities, including a chance to provide songs for a "mainstream" (white) musical, *Elsie*. Produced by John Scholl, the show's numbers were split about equally between Sissle and Blake and Carlo and Sanders (whose previous show was *Tangerine*). Monte Carlo and Alma Sanders were a husband-and-wife songwriting team with several Broadway musicals to their name. Apparently, Sissle and Blake were brought in to spice up the score after the show previewed in Chicago to somewhat tepid response. An agreement with Scholl and coproducer Edgar J. MacGregor gave the duo a measly $1.00 upfront payment, but in return promised a royalty of 1½ percent of the show's weekly gross for the length of its run—wherever it played. The producers held the song rights as long as the play was performed at least 50 times in any theatrical season following its initial run. Even more generously, Sissle and Blake were to collect this percentage even if their songs were subsequently dropped from later productions. Clearly, the savvy songwriters were trading immediate profit for long-term income—although sadly the play had little success and the promised income failed to materialize.[70]

Elsie was a typical son-of-a-millionaire-courts-a-showgirl romance, with the family disapproving of the match until the charming soubrette wins them over. Several critics mentioned Sissle and Blake's song "Baby Bunting" as being the hit of the show without mentioning that its authors were black. Besides occasionally mentioning the hit *Shuffle Along*, both songwriting teams were treated more or less as equals; in fact, Sissle and Blake's contributions were more often called out as song hits than the others. Alan Dale noted that he particularly appreciated that the score wasn't "jiggy or jazzy," perhaps a backhanded compliment to the fact that Sissle and Blake's contribution was squarely in the mainstream Broadway style.[71] Despite solid reviews, *Elsie* was not a hit, but it did attract the attention of British producer Charles Cochran, who would hire Sissle and Blake to provide songs for a few shows that he produced.

Another benefit of *Shuffle Along*'s success was an invitation to Sissle and Blake from major label Victor to record for their popular music series. This was a decided step up from the smaller labels that previously had issued their recordings. Both the duo and the *Shuffle Along* orchestra were recorded by Victor. The label did not issue Sissle and Blake's recordings on their "race" series; according to Sissle, they approached the black market warily and signed the duo because they had a reputation as a "class" act that had succeeded on white vaudeville and Broadway. Nonetheless, Victor was aware of the tremendous success of blues recordings, beginning with Mamie Smith's "Crazy Blues" on OKeh. Sissle and Blake also noted the popularity of the recording, particularly after hearing it played by an enterprising Baltimore shopkeeper, as Sissle later recalled:

> I was in Baltimore; it was wintertime. And this record just came out [Mamie Smith's "Crazy Blues"]. And a fella in a cigar store put a phonograph [in the doorway of his store] and pointed the record out the door, so people could hear it, at about 5 o'clock in the evening. . . . And come the sound of that record, and people run right over and said, "Give me that." Because they'd been waiting for that sound so long. . . . And of course the South, where the blues started, all of them [knew] about it, . . .
>
> So [Victor] sent for Eubie and I to do the "Crazy Blues." Mr. King, the head of Victor . . . the move was on for race records. So, they sent for Blake & I because we were in vaudeville, we were more or less on the sophisticated side, so King had the idea that we would [clean] it up. So we did "The Crazy Blues." . . .
>
> I can hear right now old man King at Victor, "I'm not going to have that noise on my label. Now, Sissle and Blake, you come down and sing it, and that's enough for Victor. We don't want that 'bang bang' and all that stuff here." But one year after that they had all the "bang bang" they could get. It was on, see.[72]

Indeed, white record labels and music publishers quickly jumped on the blues bandwagon, with labels creating special numbered series for so-called race records. Both Sissle and Blake viewed the blues as a rather common type of music, and neither had much interest in performing it. In 1936, when Al Rose asked Sissle about the many ragtime and blues-flavored songs that he wrote and performed with Blake, Sissle snootily said, "I was and am a professional entertainer . . . Part of our art lies in being prepared to give the public what it wants. When they wanted ragtime, I sang ragtime—Not that I ever enjoyed it particularly."[73] Once blues recordings were a commercial success, Sissle and Blake realized the need to include this material at least in their recorded repertory.

The Victor deal was apparently not exclusive. Sissle continued to record for Emerson, which ran ads in the *Chicago Defender* touting his association with "the Negro Broadway jazz success 'Shuffle Along.'"[74] The duo also made records for OKeh and Edison. (Like many black artists, the duo had trouble getting promised payment from the labels; a check for $25 to Eubie issued by OKeh bounced.[75]) In July 1921, Blake made his first solo recordings of his own compositions, his rag "Sounds of Africa" (aka "The Charleston Rag") on one side and a medley of "Baltimore Buzz" and "In Honeysuckle Time," from *Shuffle Along*, on the other. Blake said that "Charleston Rag's" new name, "Sounds of Africa," was suggested by Will Marion Cook, perhaps as a way of linking the piece with the vogue for African-themed works among African American composers.

Blake's 1921 recording of "Charleston Rag" is remarkably close in spirit and execution to his many later recordings and performances (beginning with 1969's *The Eighty-Six Years of Eubie Blake*). There are a few variations that were dropped over the decades; in the final statement of the A theme, Blake plays the melody both in the normal register and then, in response, in the upper keyboard (something he didn't do in later recordings), showing off his considerable dexterity as a pianist. Pianist/ragtime historian Terry Waldo notes that the dramatic opening bassline—the "wobbly bass," as Blake described it—is played an octave higher, closer to middle C, then on later versions.[76] But mostly he sticks to the score, showing that Blake was not an "improviser" in the sense of later jazz pianists, but more of a classicist like his fellow ragtimers (and theatrical composers) who viewed a composition as a "finished work." His mature style can be heard in full flight here, including his dramatic use of bass runs, flights up the keyboard in the right hand, and use of unusual counter rhythms. As Blake quipped during a live performance in the early 1970s, what distinguished ragtime (at least the rags he wrote) was the independence of the two hands: "This hand has nothing to do with this hand," he chuckled.[77] He insisted on the equal importance of both hands, with the bass keeping time for dancers (who were the original audience for this music) and thus to be treated with the same respect as the melody. The dramatic staccato chord sequence that increases both in pitch and speed to introduce the final section of the work is one of the piece's most dramatic moments. Blake would use this effect in other showy rags that he composed, including "Tricky Fingers."

While Blake's ragtime style was meant to dazzle and perhaps intimidate other pianists, his playing on his show tunes was more subdued, particularly when he was accompanying vocalist Noble Sissle. His Broadway show style can be heard on the "flip side" of "Sounds of Africa" in Blake's solo renditions of two of the song hits from *Shuffle Along*, "Baltimore Buzz" and "In Honeysuckle Time." After a rather dramatic ascending chord introduction (seemingly taken from the concert hall), the upbeat singable melody of "Baltimore Buzz" is presented with fairly straightforward accompaniment, although Blake's bass work is more active and audible than was the case when he was working as an accompanist. He also can't resist adding a few of his characteristic decorative runs to the melody from time to time. As the performance continues, the playing becomes increasingly syncopated, and the two lines start to follow their own logic. This approach is particularly true in his freer interpretation of "In Honeysuckle Time," which is introduced by another dramatic chordal sequence. Then "Baltimore Buzz" returns, this time with more ornamentation and a more active bass, before a novelty ending concludes the performance with a brief chord figure transposed up in a series of repetitions.

This performance is interesting to compare with Blake's recording of the same medley made the same year for Victor with the "Shuffle Along Orchestra." Unlike his solo piano playing, the instrumentation and performance is typical of the kind of house military bands employed by the labels in the day. The syncopation is much more subdued, and while there are moments of stop time, it is not really a "jazz" performance, but rather a fairly straightforward rendition of each melody, carried by the horns. The piano is kept in the background throughout. A white band of similar makeup of the period could have produced an identical recording. Along with Blake's recording, popular bandleader Paul Whiteman cut "Gypsy Blues" from the show for Victor. (Blake related in several later-life interviews that the song was an homage to Victor Herbert's "Gypsy Love Song," using its chord progression to "weave a blues melody above it."[78]) The two discs were promoted together. Another band recording was made by "Noble Sissle and His Sizzling Syncopators," for Emerson, and featured a (barely audible) Blake on piano. Sissle's version features his typical exaggerated vocal style and a prominent banjo part (perhaps a banjo mandolin or tenor banjo). The instrumentation is less dense than on Blake's Shuffle Along Orchestra version, but otherwise the performances are similar.

Blake's leadership of the Shuffle Along Orchestra was recognized by both the white and black press as vital to the success of the show. Lucien White, writing in *The New York Age*, noted that the success of black shows on Broadway in the future would depend on the quality of the orchestras that were hired to accompany them. White praised Blake's professionalism and leadership of his band:

There are two principal reasons why the Shuffle Along Orchestra reached such heights of accomplishment. One was its leader, Eubie Blake, a man of forceful personality and tireless energy, to which was coupled an ample musical equipment. The other was that the group of musicians making up the orchestra were well prepared for the task. The majority of them were more than just ordinary players—they were students of music and masters of their instruments. The conductor, Mr. Blake, was able and competent, and the men behind him were loyal and efficient.[79]

As an African American, White was emphasizing the need for blacks to receive classical training as a means of showing that they were every bit the equals of their white colleagues. White also made a point of applauding the "loyalty" of Blake's band members to their work; he lamented that there was "too much division among the [black] purveyors of music"; only by banding together could blacks succeed in a white-dominated entertainment world. However, the coming of jazz bands led by Duke Ellington and others would render the work of groups like the Shuffle Along Orchestra as hopelessly old-fashioned.

Shuffle Along was also a boon to the duo's music publisher, M. Witmark & Sons. The company issued all of the songs from *Shuffle Along* on sheets, testifying to their popularity. A standard cover was used, showing the *Shuffle Along* logo along with an illustration of a line of chorines' legs—just barely identifying it as an all-black show. Royalty statements for the show's first year showed the immense popularity of the show's music. The bestsellers did incredibly well, notably "Gypsy Blues" (selling 81,355 copies), "I'm Just Wild about Harry" (Figure 6.2) (the only song from the show to get its own unique cover; 77,014 copies), and "Love Will Find a Way" (32,595 copies). "Gypsy Blues" may have garnered additional sales simply by having the word "blues" in its title, as 1922 was the year that the blues craze really took off. The worst seller was "I'm Craving for That Kind of Love," which managed to sell only 600 copies, despite being a major hit on stage when sung by Florence Mills. Eubie complained that the audience knew the song by its provocative chorus lyrics—leading it to be known as the "Kiss me" song—and didn't recognize the title on the sheet. All in, Eubie earned $5727.50 from his share of the songwriting royalties for 1922, a considerable sum. However, by the end of 1923, his position had changed considerably; with advances against royalties paid out and sales slowing considerably, Eubie ended up owing Witmark a little over $1300.[80]

As 1923 ended, it was clear that *Shuffle Along* was getting tired and needed updating if it was going to continue to be profitable. Plus, Miller and Lyles

Figure 6.2 The sheet music cover for "I'm Just Wild about Harry." Unlike the show's other songs that were issued with generic covers, this song was popular enough to merit its own illustration, showing a black dandy entertaining his sweetheart. It's one of the few Sissle and Blake songs to feature blacks depicted on its cover.

were already trying out their new show—now called *Runnin' Wild*—on the road, brazenly advertising "Ricks' Shuffle Along Orchestra" as providing the music.[81] At first Sissle and Blake announced plans to produce a show to be called *Shuffle Along of 1924* in partnership with producers B. C. Whitney and

Abe Erlanger.[82] However, this plan was complicated by the fact that Sissle and Blake were still partners in—and presumably under contract to—Shuffle Along Inc. (the new name of the Nikko Production Company). An agreement was hammered out whereby the duo's ownership was taken over by producer Milton Gosdorfer; in return, the corporation freed them from their performance contract so they could work with Whitney and Erlanger. The other stipulation was they could no longer use the *Shuffle Along* name; *Variety* announced the planned name for the new Sissle and Blake show would be either *Bandanna Days* or *Bandanna Land*. The Gosdorfer *Shuffle Along* started touring immediately, with Rufus "Rah-Rah" Greenlee and Thaddeus "Ga Ga" Drayton taking over the lead comic roles.[83] The duo were a well-known vaudeville dance act who pioneered the soft shoe (known then as the "Virginia Essence"), so presumably this dance was incorporated into the show.

The new producers represented a considerable step up in the theatrical world for Sissle and Blake. Bertram C. Whitney began his theatrical career in his native Detroit, where he was born around 1870. By around the turn of the century, he was operating the Detroit Opera House, booking touring productions as well as staging original shows. Over the coming years, he expanded his empire into parts of Canada and the Midwest. His theater was serviced by the Klaw & Erlanger theatrical syndicate, operated by A. L. (Abe) Erlanger and Marcus Klaw. The duo were ruthless in their business dealings. Their monopoly locked down contracts and bookings and could make or break careers. From 1896 through the first decade of the 20th century, Klaw & Erlanger ruled American theatre. Critic Brooks Atkinson called Erlanger "a fat, squat, greedy, crude egotist who had no interest in the theatre as an art or as social institution. He was a dangerous enemy." However, Erlanger did have a soft spot for some artists, especially George M. Cohan and his family, and they appreciated his support.

Erlanger did have an excellent track record in producing shows for Broadway. Among his great successes were *Ben-Hur*, with real teams of horses running on treadmills in the stage floor—an effect that was revived for Sissle and Blake's new show. Other hits included *Dracula*, George M. Cohan's *Forty-Five Minutes from Broadway*, John Phillip Sousa's *The Free Lance*, and Victor Herbert's musical comedy *Little Nemo*. Erlanger also was the producer of Edward Knoblauch's play *Kismet*, the play *The Jazz Singer*, and also Winchell Smith and Frank Bacon's comedy *Lightnin'*, which enjoyed one of the longest runs of any show in the first half of the 20th century.

By the 1920s, Whitney had partnered with Erlanger to produce plays in New York, including two starring vehicles for comedian Ed Wynn in 1924, the same year they signed Sissle and Blake. To produce what would become *Chocolate Dandies*, Whitney, Erlanger, Sissle, and Blake formed the Sislake Producing Corporation, including a six-year contract with the songwriters to create shows for the new organization.[84] While Whitney put up the lion's share of the funding, Sissle and Blake were also financially involved with the show, as they had been in *Shuffle Along*, and hoped to reap similar benefits from their share of its profits. Throughout the show's run, Whitney served as the official frontman for the production company, with Erlanger taking a more shadowy role.

While putting their new show together, Sissle and Blake and "the ORIGINAL SHUFFLE ALONG CAST" made an appearance at New York's New Star Casino for a "Monster Charity Benefit" on February 15, 1924. Much of the original cast was on hand, including the Four Harmony Kings, the Shuffle Along Orchestra, and star Lottie Gee—whose "gowns alone are worth the price of admission."[85] This was a nostalgic gathering and the last hurrah for the historic cast.

A major blow came to Sissle and Blake with the death of their long-time production partner, Al Mayer. Mayer had been the earliest believer in *Shuffle Along*'s potential, and provided the nascent show a foothold in the world of white theater. After a short battle with cancer, Mayer was hospitalized in early March and passed away three weeks later at the age of 45. "It is due to his sacrifices that 'Shuffle Along' . . . was put on the stage. We are sorry that Mr. Mayer did not live to see our present show, patterned after his first success and played by the original characters," Sissle commented to the press.[86] Sissle and Blake even took out a small notice in *Variety* "in memory of our pal."[87]

At the same time, the duo were hard at work polishing up their new show, now known as *In Bamville*.[88] Sissle took on authorship duties, working with Lew Payton, the comic lead, on the book. Besides Payton and Sissle, the production included other *Shuffle Along* alumni, including Ivan Browning and Lottie Gee in the "serious" lead roles, the Four Harmony Kings once again performing their specialty songs, and Sissle and Blake's vaudeville turn. Also returning from *Shuffle Along* was dancer Josephine Baker. Baker's success as the comic chorus girl in *Shuffle Along* earned her a large, featured part, and a salary of $125 a week. She had several dance numbers, including one performed in blackface, and one in which she parodied a sexy vamp.[89]

Payton's foil was initially played by George Cooper. Cooper had previously played white vaudeville as the straight man/vocalist for a young dancer named William Robinson, who would gain fame in the 1920s as Bill "Bojangles" Robinson. The duo performed comic skits featuring their vocals and dancing from about 1900 through 1918, with occasional breaks when they went out on their own. Cooper even improbably portrayed a stock Jewish character in some of their routines. Like other black acts, they were promoted as "real coons" to distinguish them from blackface delineators, but they did not appear to sport burnt cork in publicity photos.[90] More recently, Cooper had appeared as the straight man opposite comic singer Eddie Hunter in Hunter's production *How Come?*, which featured music by Ben Harris, Henry Creamer, and Will Vodery. The show played at Harlem's Lafayette Theatre and then briefly on Broadway before touring for a few months in 1923.

Also new to the company was singer/actress Valaida Snow, who received notice for both her singing and dancing when the show played Pittsburgh in March 1924. Describing her as "a brown nymph of captivating personality," the Pittsburgh critic compared her favorably to Ada Overton Walker, one of the major stars of the black theater at the turn of the 20th century.[91] Snow would later gain fame as a singer/trumpet player/bandleader in the 1930s. The total company numbered 125, perhaps in an effort to outdo Miller and Lyles, who were advertising a company of 110 in *Runnin' Wild*. The *Buffalo American* newspaper marveled that it "requires four extra length baggage cars and five sleepers to transport the company."[92]

A further attraction brought into the show was "eccentric" cornetist Johnny Dunn. Dunn had made a big splash in Lew Leslie's *Plantation Revue*, the after-hours show that made Florence Mills a major star after she left *Shuffle Along*. Originally from Memphis, Tennessee, Dunn was "discovered" by its most famous African American musician, W. C. Handy, who brought him to New York around 1916. Later Dunn toured as a member of Mamie Smith's backup band. The *Plantation Revue* made him a star both in New York and during its London run, and later he backed singer Edith Wilson—also in the show—leading her band, the Original Jazz Hounds, on tour and on record. Dunn's incorporation into *In Bamville* was an acknowledgment of the growing popularity of jazz music (still viewed as a novelty, hence his billing as an "eccentric" musician). Other jazz players who were briefly in the show included saxophonist Sidney Bechet.[93]

Sissle and Blake once again dipped into their trunk for songs for the new show, including "Sons of Old Black Joe" and "Pickaninny Shoes" (featured in the Sissle and Blake interlude in act 2) from their vaudeville act. However, they also composed several new numbers to fit the show's plot, including "A Jockey's Life for Me" and "Manda" (promoted as a "Fox-Trot Blues," perhaps in an attempt to cash in on both the dance craze and the new popularity of blues songs). Despite Sissle's assertion that the show avoided racial stereotypes, the song-and-dance number "Chocolate Dandies" drew on the age-old minstrel figure of Zip Coon (the nattily dressed urban dweller and con artist); on the other hand, "Land of Dancing Pickaninnies" drew on the imagery of happy-go-lucky rural black children, living in a kind of paradise on the "old plantation."

Like *Shuffle Along*, the plot was just a loose structure onto which a series of dance numbers, comic routines, and songs could be hung. It revolved around a horse race held in the black town of Bamville. Lew Payton portrayed the comic lead, Mose Washington, a ne'er-do-well who enters his horse, Dumb Luck, into the race. Dreaming that his horse wins the purse, Washington finds himself unexpectedly made the president of the local bank. Enjoying his new status for a while, Washington eventually loses everything in a bank run—and awakens from his dream to find his horse actually didn't win. In reality, his rival, Dan Jackson (Ivan Browning), has taken the prize, and wins the girl Angeline Brown (Lottie Gee) to boot. The first act concluded with a group of real horses running on a treadmill to simulate a race. As we've noted, the effect was borrowed from the evergreen production, *Ben Hur,* which had been touring for about a decade and featured a similar chariot-race scene. "Those horses were a lot of trouble," grumbled Eubie.[94]

In Bamville opened in Rochester, New York, where *Shuffle Along* had previously had a successful run, in early March 1924. The initial reviews were positive, despite the fact that the show "ran too long by about three quarters of an hour and was a little slow and unfinished in some comedy spots." The opening night critic found the comedy somewhat lacking, but praised other aspects of the production: "It was the dancing . . . and the excellent pictorial and vocal effects of the ensembles . . . that made the show go pretty strongly much of the time." He particularly praised the "attractive chorus girls and about the most clean-cut group of young chorus men seen . . . this season." He particularly singled out Josephine Baker, "the cross-eyed chorus girl . . . her remarkable ability in ludicrous strutting and unbelievable eye crossing made her a most amusing grotesque," and fellow dancer George Bagby for his "astonishing ease and agility and originality of style and steps."[95] Indeed, another critic enthused that "*In Bamville* is without question the 'dancingest' show that Rochester has had in many months."[96]

Later in March, the company moved to Detroit and then on to Pittsburgh, where Sissle was interviewed backstage by a reporter from the *Pittsburgh Courier*. Sissle commented on what the duo had learned from *Shuffle Along*'s success on the road:

> We learned what the white audience wants, and why. We learned that the whites without question will accept colored artists and production of merit. They do not demand that we be buffoons and clowns, either. Of course, there must be comedy for an audience comes to a musical comedy primarily to laugh, but the more art we can work into the different scenes and situations, the better the show takes with the public. The singing and dancing are big parts of our success. The jokes are clever, but not vulgar. And we portray Negro characters—not try to give an imitation of whites. Our love scenes are not as romantic as the whites, but they have the same universal touch and are applauded and appreciated.[97]

Sissle's downplaying of the value of humor in their new production may have been a thinly veiled knock of *Runnin' Wild*, which featured the blackface routines of Miller and Lyles. It's interesting that Sissle still was sensitive to the question of the portrayal of black romance on stage; for many, the idea of romantic attraction that went beyond the mere sexual among blacks was unimaginable.

In this interview, Sissle made a point of emphasizing the large investment made in the production by Whitney, said to total $75,000 (a little over a million dollars today). He noted the significant improvement in costumes, scenery, and overall production values over their earlier hit:

> If you saw 'Shuffle Along" . . . and noticed what a small place we had for scenery, you can appreciate what it means to us to be in a place like this. . . . For instance, in the Music Hall [where *Shuffle Along* originally played], the only place we could get . . . [the audience] saw at a glance that we didn't have room to spread out and do better. But after our astonishing success there the big houses opened up to us and we had the embarrassing experience of taking a play designed for a small house into theaters whose patrons were accustomed to lavish display. . . . The fact that [our show] was

"colored" wouldn't count large. So "Shuffle Along" . . . taught us we must build our next production on a mammoth scale, with the idea of going into the biggest houses from the start.[98]

From the earliest planning of the new show, Sissle aimed to create a more "sophisticated" production—not only in terms of production values, but also in contents. He clearly wanted to set their work apart from the "lower" comedy of Miller and Lyles. One of the chorus numbers featured the girls in hoop skirts and broad hats, in the kind of glamourous display associated with white revues like the *Ziegfeld Follies*. Blake thought this was going too far, telling producer B. C. Whitney, "That scene is too *beautiful* for a colored show," to which Whitney responded, "Eubie this is a *not* a colored show. This is Sissle and Blake's show for Broadway."[99] According to Blake, the white audience always gasped when they say this number, shocked by the idea of fashionable black women.

While emulating white musical comedies, Sissle still emphasized the unique "colored" flavor of the plot, music, and dancing. Josephine Baker had a featured dance appearing as "Topsy" (based on the popular stereotype of the little country "pick") in ragged clothes and blackface, and the lead comedians performed typical blackface routines. The *Courier* reporter noted that despite the fact that both Sissle and Blake were Northerners, "they portray Southern Negro life next to perfect." Trying to straddle the fine line between "colored" and "white" musicals would prove to be the key challenge and ultimate undoing of the duo's new work.

The show's next stop in April was Chicago, where *Shuffle Along* had previously played to capacity crowds. Whitney took a full-page ad in *Variety* to trumpet the Chicago production, celebrating the "all-around-the-world musical knockout." The *Chicago Daily News* critic noted that the new production opened just after D. W. Griffith's *Birth of a Nation* was shown at the same theater, comparing the two disparate pictures of black life:

"In Bamville" . . . arrived at the Illinois [Theater] . . . close upon the heels of Griffith's noble picture, "The Birth of a Nation," suspected and maligned by the same race so proudly acclaiming the Sissle and Blake products. Nothing could have been more effective in pointing out a good reason for objecting to [Griffith's portrayal of] their own nation . . . than the advantage of following the frowned-upon work of film art . . . by Mr. Griffith. Because not only was the Illinois stage blossoming with splendid talent entirely of the race who were slaves when the nation was in the throes of birth, but the delightful music and book, written by colored men, were both illuminative of their race and delivered by the colored actors in a way no white people could hope feebly to imitate.[100]

Although this critic admired Griffith's work, he at least admitted that there was a reason that black viewers might object to it and point to the work of Sissle and Blake as an answer to the racist stereotypes promoted in the film. The critic praised the production created by "100% black-and-tan American[s] and that means much to this country just after the glorious service the same race gave us in the big war." Nonetheless, while acknowledging its inherent quality, the critic underscored that the players did not try to encroach on white theatrical styles:

> They keep the comedy their own kind of comedy, they tune the jazz and balladry their own way and they dance . . . as only those whom we call Afro-Americans . . . There's a lot of "Africa's sunny clime" in Sissle's music and a lot of the orient in their dances but it is American. And nobody on earth can dance exactly as they do no matter what great white dancers try to imitate our blacks.[101]

Even worse than describing the cast as "our blacks," this critic also noted that most of the players were not truly dark skinned; instead they were "mostly mulattos or octoroons fairer than they need be . . . and were black only when made up with burnt court." While blacks viewed fair skin as a desirable trait, clearly whites were more comfortable with darker-skinned actors keeping to stereotypical roles on stage.

The *Daily News* critic also singled out the Four Harmony Kings for their contribution to the show, revealing how white viewers interpreted their work:

> The Four Harmony Kings . . . made an enormous hit and all of these smiling, happy relievers of the world's care took their honors easily, with no airs, no excitement, no affectation. Just blessed "darkies," like they always are when they amuse and appeal and win us over beguilingly because they are entirely different from less human "white folks," and always belong to the best of us.[102]

In trying to be complimentary, the reviewer reveals himself to be more than a little racist, or at least supports unfortunate stereotypes about this highly trained musical quartet. Many white critics praised the show's "eager to please" singers and dancers, another code phrase for "well-behaved Negroes" who wouldn't challenge white audiences.

While the *Daily News* critic compared *In Bamville* to *Birth of a Nation*, O. L. Hall writing in the *Chicago Journal* referenced Eugene O'Neill's latest controversial play:

> While Eugene O'Neill employs the title of an old spiritual to aver in his new and much debated multi-part drama that "all God's chillum got wings[,]" [t]he authors of "In Bamville" do not discuss matters of the soul, but their show decisively proves that all God's chillum got dancin' feet . . . While O'Neill, his brow furrowed with world-shaking thought, writes of misceg-enation, these chanting, crooning, caroling, humming negroes just throw back their heads and let their hearts sing.

Clearly, the questioning of laws against racial admixture that O'Neill portrayed made this critic uncomfortable, who preferred "humming negroes" who didn't push against social norms. The critic assures us that *In Bamville* is a show that won't offend delicate white sensibilities:

> You never saw a cleaner musical comedy in all your born days. There is never the slightest offense of speech or action; there always is a great out-pouring of negro humor and melody.[103]

When directly asked whether they approved of O'Neill's production, Sissle (speaking for the duo) typically took a conservative position, not questioning the artistry of the work but uncomfortable with confronting prejudice head on:

> Personally, we would prefer not to have any play on the stage that may tend to stir up racial prejudice, which we are endeavoring to avoid. There's too much prejudice as it is . . . Live and let live is our motto. But prejudice exists—that fact can not be doubted and we have reason to know. So why add fuel to the flames?[104]

Ashton Stevens—who previously praised *Shuffle Along* during its Chicago run—found *In Bamville* not sufficiently "African" to suit his tastes.[105] The

African American paper the *Buffalo American* responded to Stevens review by noting that the majority of Chicago's critics recognized that the show was the equal (if not better) of any white production. Going further, this writer noted that the white public was increasingly willing to attend black shows:

> The production shows that colored America has more than arrived in musical entertainment, this is the verdict of . . . all people attending, attested by applause and comment. The show is accept by the theatre going public strictly on its merit . . . A serious study of "In Bamville" discloses the untouched opportunities for racial development in music and theatrical possibilities. There is the spirit, the beauty and the intelligence[,] there is the desire to entertain the public, and the public has in recent years shown a splendid taste for Ethiopera.[106]

Tony Langston, the *Chicago Defender's* critic, also praised the show to the skies; he stated it was "the best show seen in Chicago during the entire . . . season and it ranks right along with the best ever seen here during any season."[107] This African American critic was impressed by the professionally staged production and how it reflected on blacks' status in the musical theater.

Despite the mixed reviews, *In Bamville* had a solid run in Chicago, continuing through April. The original plan was to move on to New York, but apparently Whitney felt the show needed some further improvement. Specifically, he sought to bring in a stronger second lead than George Cooper, whose performance had attracted almost no critical attention. To fill the role, he hired Johnny Hudgins, who had been winning rave reviews for his comic turn in the burlesque *Town Scandals* revue. Whitney bought out his contract from that show's producers and offered the performer a salary of $150 to increase to $200 after the show opened in New York.[108] Baltimore-born Hudgins had developed a unique routine in which he combined eccentric dancing with pantomime and so-called freak movement (including a form of moonwalking and a slow-motion spin). He joined the company when *In Bamville* opened in early June in Baltimore.

The production then moved onto Boston, where it played through mid-July. E. F. Larkins, writing in the *Boston Sunday Advertiser*, disputed the fact that the show was merely an imitation of "the average Great White Way carnival," stating,

> The comedy is essentially southern. So is much of the music. And, of course, all the performers with the exception of a few pale-faces in the chorus are

sure-enough representatives of the old plantation Race. They all belong to that Race . . . no matter how deceptive they may look. It's an all-Dixie show, and you can see for yourself that these shows are better today than they ever were before.[109]

This critic, of course, reveals his own prejudice in his critique that blacks were better off presenting an "all-Dixie show" than in emulating white Broadway. This tension between being a black show emulating white Broadway versus a "black show" as defined by the white audience would continue to plague the reception of the show.

After Boston, the show took a break to prepare for its New York premiere scheduled for Labor Day. It would open there under a new name: *The Chocolate Dandies*.

7

Chocolate Dandies and the End of Sissle and Blake

1924–1930

After touring the country, *In Bamville* had racked up considerable losses—over $22,000 (about $325,000 in today's dollars)—just as *Shuffle Along* had done during its tryout period. However, the much more lavish production with its associated costs meant that this deficit was considerably greater than the earlier show's. The shortfall would have been far greater if the cast had not accepted considerably less than their promised salary. Sissle and Blake were promised $500 a week for the run, but the actual account books showed salaries of $300—and these often went unpaid in the form of IOUs. The other cast members were similarly shorted. By the time the production made it to New York, Blake had been paid a little under $1000 for his six months on the road—but was owed close to $4000 more.

Typically, the show cost between $7000 and $12,000 a week simply to operate, while ticket sales accounted only for a low of $4500 to a high of about $9000. A look at the show's expenses from its one week in Rochester, New York, gives an idea of how much the lavish production costs were eating into the profits:

Salaries	$7,943.38
Carpenter's Bills	$243.61
Extra Musicians	$224.00
Extra Advertising	$601.54
Business Mgr. and Agent's Expenses	$17.53
R.R. Fare N.Y. to Rochester	$1,645.16
Baggage and Scenery Transfer and Expressage	$229.60
Electric Account, Operator, and Material	$135.94
Costume Account Dressers and Material, etc.	$100.46
Office Expenses	$50.00

Eubie Blake. Richard Carlin and Ken Bloom, Oxford University Press (2020). © Richard Carlin and Ken Bloom 2020.
DOI: 10.1093/oso/9780190635930.001.0001

Enquirer Job Printing Co.	$187.48
Producing Managers' Weekly Dues	$237.48
TOTAL	**$11.644.13**[1]

A lot was riding on a Broadway success to wipe out these losses.

But there was more than just money at stake. Sissle and Blake wanted to prove they could score a success without their *Shuffle Along* partners Miller and Lyles—one that would show that black musicals could be successful without relying on minstrel-style comedy. By the time *Chocolate Dandies* opened on Broadway on September 1, 1924, Miller and Lyles's *Runnin' Wild* already had opened in late October 1923, and racked up an impressive 228 performances when it closed in May 1924. It played at the New Colonial Theater, which was newly converted from a vaudeville house—the same theater where *Chocolate Dandies* was to open. Like *In Bamville*, the show sported a huge cast—advertised as 100 strong—and producer George White (of White's *Scandals* fame) promoted the accompanying band as "Rick's Shuffle Along Orchestra"—a clear slap in the face to Sissle and Blake. (Later on, the band was renamed the "Runnin' Wild Orchestra" after the show was established.)

Even as *Runnin' Wild* was reasonably successful, the white audience's appetite for "negro" productions was beginning to lag. *Shuffle Along*'s success had inspired several copycat productions—including *Strut, Miss Lizzie* and *Liza*—not to mention various revues staged at clubs. Many white reviewers expressed at best lukewarm enthusiasm for *Runnin' Wild* on its opening, complaining that the earlier shows had set the standard so high that the only option for new productions was to be even faster and funnier—which could overwhelm the audience. The critic in the *Brooklyn Eagle* wrote, "To arouse new attention, the negro show will be obliged to exhibit even more hysteria, better dancing, and worse singing and comedy than it now possessed." Even the fancy stepping of the chorus line could not impress this critic:

> The regular run of chorus ladies, who range from a high yellow to a higher yellow, strut and prance uncommonly well, but, for that matter, so did those in the other negro shows. The "*Runnin' Wild*" chorus might easily be distinguished, other than by sight, from that of any white company, but it couldn't be from any other negro company.

Miller and Lyles's verbal comedy is given a particularly harsh review:

They thunder their comedy with the same vehemence with which the chorus girls dance, and the ears tire faster than the eyes. As the evening wears on, such a steady bombardment of tone is likely to numb the nerves, and there becomes nothing so pleasurable about the show as an exit of the two comedians.

The critic warmed to only two moments in the show: The singing of "Old Fashioned Love" and the finale, in which

[s]ix or seven of the loveliest of the chorus participate. It is a frame, even as the whites have shown, of brownish girls, which the whites would never have shown, reclining in posture which, for want of a better term, might be called artistic. They are nearly, if it is necessary to say it . . nude. It is very, very beautiful.[2]

This reviewer made no mention of what would become the show's most famous dance number, "The Charleston." The dance was performed as part of a medley of fancy steps by the chorus girls and lead dancer Tommy Woods at the close of the first act. It became a rage in ballrooms, abetted by the quick release that November by Victor of "The Charleston Medley," described as a "fetching and timely fox trot."[3] The other major label, Columbia, issued its own version soon thereafter. Even Sissle and Blake recorded the show's hit song "Old Fashioned Love" for Victor, which was issued in February 1924.

Of course, Sissle wasn't about to let his old competitors take full credit for popularizing "The Charleston." To his hometown paper, he commented, "The 'Charleston' isn't as new as some folks might think. They were dancing the 'Charleston' fifty years ago at Savannah, Ga.; at least they were dancing it twenty years ago, because that's when I learned it."[4] Once the Charleston had become a fad among white dancers, many others took credit for originating the dance. Of course, it incorporated movements that were common in other African American dance forms, so it's not surprising that the dance had many claimants to be its creator.[5] Not surprisingly, Sissle and Blake added the Charleston to the *Chocolate Dandies* as part of the show.

Chocolate Dandies opened on an unusually hot and humid night— complicating its initial critical reception. The white critics in attendance had a decidedly mixed reaction to the production. Sissle and Blake's aspiration to produce a more serious and legitimate show was greeted with some befuddlement by those who expected more typical "negro" fare. Even the lavish sets and costumes were critiqued for being out of character for what a white audience might expect from an all-black production. Most focused on the dancing as the most successful aspect of the production. The critic for the *New York Sun* expressed a common reaction:

> The *Chocolate Dandies* . . . is a musical comedy of witty feet. There are songs which persist to a varying degree and jokes at which one might smile gently if so inclined, but if the Sissle and Blake production continues to light the uptown theater it will have kicked its way to success.
>
> Everybody, principals and chorus, is marked by a mad will to dance. These more or less black people can dance themselves quite out of Broadway sophistication . . . their feet vanish in a maze and flashing legs chuckle in the astonished air.

The critic's snide comment on the light-skinned dancers (describing them as "more or less black") was just a prelude to his real complaint about the production: There was not a touch of the expected "darkie dialect" in the comedy that was expected by the white viewer:

> For some odd reason—which we make no attempt whatever to explain, well realizing that dialect may be the native tongue of most of those on stage— the negro patter is flatly theatrical. It seems absurd to tell the negro cast of "The Chocolate Dandies" that negroes do not talk that way, but they really don't.[6]

The critic in the *New York Telegram* seconded these sentiments: "Negro humor as it exists off stage is hardly to be improved upon," he sniffed. "And, since the scene is set in Mississippi, why not let the accent conform?"[7] White audiences knew how blacks were supposed to talk and act; *Chocolate Dandies* upended these expectations, challenging the image of the "happy negro" on stage.

Of course, not all the white papers were this critical, but the subtext was there. For some, the black musical had become last week's news, so that any show based on black comedy and dancing would be tiresome. "Those who like this form of entertainment," sneered the critic from the *Evening World*, "probably will like" the production.[8] On the other hand, the critic from the *Brooklyn Eagle* seemed dismayed by the show's attempt to equal the quality of white shows in its staging and costumes. "The *Chocolate Dandies* is good entertainment—far better than the average Broadway musical show," the critic opined, "[b]ut is nothing but a Broadway musical show with colored performers."[9]

Racial issues were part and parcel of the show's reception. Even the black press was anxious to show that "colored artists don't seek much," as an interview with Sissle and Blake was headlined by the *Kansas City Advocate* when *Chocolate Dandies* hit the city. The interview quoted the duo as approving of white blackface artists: "If the white minstrel be a good actor, then he gives a characterization of the Negro which we recognized and admire." However, the duo were quick to reject the idea of "Negro actors [putting] on white make-up":

> We . . . never expect the time to come when it would be desirable. We believe we have something exactly as artistic to offer, mind you in characterizing our own people. No, Negro actors should offer only what they have.

The reporter concluded his article by acknowledging that "prejudice exists" but noted that, given that fact, Negro artists should not "add fuel to the flame."[10]

The *Chicago Defender* also was quick to point out that—by avoiding controversy—Sissle and Blake had made it possible for other black entertainers to be successful:

> It is not so many years ago the Racial entertainers were little better than a tolerated curiosity in the country's first-class [i.e., white] theaters. Today, our actors, singers, and dancers are among the leaders of the theatrical profession and such shows as Sissle and Blake produce, rank with the best in the land.
>
> Sissle and Blake have conquered prejudice by sheer artistic ability and it is claimed "The *Chocolate Dandies*" is the crowning triumph. It has established a standard of music and comic excellence native to the soil, that white composers, librettists and lyricists in the field will find difficulty in equaling.[11]

Some middle-class black critics and audience members found it objectionable that the show included an interlude featuring the Four Harmony

Kings singing "Negro spirituals." Writing in *The New York Age*, critic Lucien White—who praised the Kings for their unique talents and vocal blend—was dismayed that they chose to "debase" these songs by including them in such lowly surroundings as the popular stage. He wrote,

> These songs always poignant, touching, and appealing were so out of place under such conditions and amid such surroundings, that all the pleasure of the performance was tinged with regret that so unnecessary a sacrilege should have been committed by such talented singers.[12]

White claimed that he heard similar grumblings from female audience members, recalling Eubie's own mother's objection to his performing "secular" music. The critic concluded his critique by "meekly" requesting that they "omit from their renditions these sacred songs of the people."

There were some bright spots in the reviews, particularly in the reception of Johnny Hudgins. *Variety*'s critic reported, "Johnny really scored the individual hit . . . with his peculiar sliding and eccentric stepping and pantomimic warbling."[13] The *New York Times* critic also singled out Hudgins for his "pantomimic performance which was as funny as anything one could hope to witness. He was the regular old negro type in tattered attire, and his dancing was original and pleasing."[14] The fact that Hudgins's stage dress corresponded with the "regular old" stereotype undoubtedly aided in his positive reception by the white critics. Besides his dancing, Hudgins developed a unique mimed routine in which he imitated the sound of a solo jazz trumpet, silently mouthing along as cornetist Joe Smith played bluesy riffs offstage. This "Mwa Mwa" routine was a regular showstopper for the production. Smith's hot playing was also widely admired and regularly drew the attention of audiences and critics.[15]

Another eccentric dancer drew special praise, thanks to her prominent roles in this production: Josephine Baker. *Variety* described Baker as "a sort of colored Charlotte Greenwood . . . an eccentric dancing comedienne, affecting a regulation boy's hair cut, with her locks plastered so that she appears to have satin hair."[16] (Greenwood was a white dancer/performer known for her comic routines.) *The Times* also applauded Baker, describing her as a "freak Terpsichorean artist," and praising "her imitation of Ben Turpin's eyes."[17] Hudgins and Baker emerged as the production's biggest draws.

Most of the critics found the songs not to be as catchy as those in *Shuffle Along*. This reaction may have been exacerbated by Sissle and Blake's

second-act interlude—which on opening night came at 11 p.m. in the swel-
tering heat—during which they reprised the earlier show's hits. Further,
Eubie had asked the show's arranger, William Grant Still, to lift familiar
melodies from *Shuffle Along* for the incidental music between scenes.[18] The
perhaps unintentional outcome was to unfairly place their new songs in competition with their best-known and successful ones. Some critics thought the
new songs were "perhaps of a higher class" and "the harmony and the melody
is at all times beautiful."[19] But this again was a backhanded way of indicating they missed the more "negro" flavor of the duo's earlier songs, preferring them to write in the acceptable idioms of ragtime and jazz, rather than
emulating "straight" Broadway composers. The reviewer in *Variety* bluntly
summarized the general consensus of the white critics, saying that the show's
"pretensions toward white musical comedy [are] achieved at the expense of
a genuine Negro spirit." The critic noted "there is plenty" of "white folks entertainment," but that "good darky entertainment" was rare—and this is what
African American entertainers should stick to doing. This opinion would
become a common theme in reviews of black musical productions going
forward.[20]

Eubie commented that when the show previewed in Boston, one of the
new songs, "There's a Million Little Cupids in the Sky," was removed from
the production at the insistence of the local management, which felt the song
was "too high class" for a Negro show.[21] In later life, Eubie singled out "Dixie
Moon" from the show as one of his favorites of all of his songs; while Sissle's
lyrics flaunted all the typical imagery of minstrel-era songs, Blake's music
showed unusual sophistication in its melody and harmonic progressions.
Nonetheless, few seemed to appreciate his innovations, and the show produced no hit songs.

Another sticking point for the songwriters was the publishing arrangement for the songs. Working with their old publisher, Witmark, Eubie said
they were lucky to get a $1500 advance per song; Whitney convinced T. B.
Harms to pay an unheard of $5000 advance for the rights to the *Chocolate
Dandies*' numbers. However, the white producer pocketed all the money
himself, claiming that it was part of the show's proceeds.[22] This theft was particularly galling to Blake.

Perhaps disillusioned with commercial publishers, in 1924 Sissle and Blake
self-published a song that might have been originally intended for *Chocolate
Dandies*—the charming love ballad "You Ought to Know." The publisher was
listed as the "U.B. Noble Pub. Co." on the US edition of the sheet music—an

unmistakable indication that they published it themselves.[23] Eubie's unusually sophisticated melody and harmonies forecast his later hit "Memories of
You," and were far advanced for the period. When Sissle and Blake toured
England a year later, they recorded the song for the UK market, but it was
never issued on record at home. The sheet itself is fairly rare, indicating that it
sold poorly on its initial publication.

Notwithstanding the lukewarm response to the new songs in *Chocolate
Dandies*, many critics enthused about Eubie's talent as a pianist and orchestra
leader. Several went so far as to note that his presence alone was the reason
they were so happy to see the show. "Eubie Blake at the piano is all that this
writer needs to inspire a night of enjoyment," James P. Sinnott wrote in the
New York Telegraph:

> When Eubie Blake plays, the piano sings. He writes great popular music,
> too . . . Don't overlook Eubie. I never can, and never want to.
> Go to the Colonial and laugh with Lew Payton and Johnny Hudkins
> [*sic*]. There's a team of Negro comics for you! Listen to Joe Smith the jazz
> cornetist. He's there forty ways! And Eubie Blake is at the piano! Enough
> said![24]

The critic in the *New York Tribune* repeated the old saw that Blake's orchestra
"uses no sheet music, knowing every quirk of the score by heart."[25] Of course,
Blake was an old hand at fooling a white audience; he knew that they preferred to believe that blacks were natural musicians, so his band never played
from scores. He learned this trick from his old employer, James Reese Europe.

Despite leading the orchestra from the pit for much of the show, Blake
made sure that he would be a presence. The show's electrician rigged up a
conducting baton with a green light on the end of its tip. The light would
move in synchronization with Eubie's conducting, drawing attention to his
artistry:

> I had six [batons]. Before anybody had used them before. At the end of the
> stick was [a green light], and [it] had a battery in the back. You didn't know
> when they were going to burn out, I had 6 of them, see. When we had the
> dark scenes. There weren't no light. The lights was on the stage when the
> drops that come down, they were all amber. It was the most beautiful scene
> in your life. I could hear the people saying, "They're trying to outdo the
> *Follies*!"[26]

It wasn't long before Hudgins's success attracted the attention of rival producers Lee and J. J. Shubert, who offered the comic dancer double his salary to perform at their Winter Garden theater for Sunday vaudeville shows; the Shuberts coupled this arrangement with weeknight performances in a revue at the Club Alabam, produced by the club's manager Arthur Lyons.[27] By mid-September, Hudgins had left the *Dandies* company for these more lucrative offers. Producer B. C. Whitney brought an injunction against the Shuberts and Lyons, claiming that he had purchased Hudgins's services from his previous employer, the producers of the show *Town Scandals*, for the sum of $251; moreover, he increased Hudgins's salary from what he received in the *Scandals* from $125 to $150 a week during the show's pre-Broadway tour, and again to $200 when *Chocolate Dandies* opened on Broadway. In his complaint, Whitney explained why he had brought Hudgins into the production:

> It became apparent that it lacked a very essential quality in a colored production—the quality of humor and comedy, and I set out to remedy this want and to procure a colored artiste who would be of Broadway caliber . . . This was a very difficult thing to do. There are not many colored actors who have sufficient ability to create comedy sufficiently original, spontaneous and pleasing [*sic*] to a New York audience.[28]

In essence, Whitney was arguing that Hudgins was a unique talent who provided an act that could not be replaced by anyone else. *Variety* commented on this unheard of development, as no "Negro performer" had ever been judged "unique and extraordinary" before.[29] Whitney's lawyer went further, enumerating the many ways that Hudgins's performance was original to himself:

> The defendant Hudgins is an actor, dancer, mimic and pantomime comedian of novel, special, unique and extraordinary ability; that he has an original and unique manner of performing a shuffle dance; that he performs negro dances with rare grace and ease; that he goes through the pantomime of singing a song in a most comical manner . . . and the services rendered by said Hudgins are such that no other performer could be obtained who could perform in like manner.[30]

In order to battle this lawsuit, Hudgins was put into the ironic position of having to argue that he was in fact not "unique" in his performance and could be replaced by another actor. Meanwhile, the black press was celebrating the fact that the lawsuit could set a precedent establishing that a colored performer *could* be considered uniquely talented.[31] Hudgins's lawyers argued that he had never appeared on Broadway prior to his engagement with *Chocolate Dandies* and in no way had established a reputation among white audiences. (This argument was not entirely true; he had been touring for several years with various productions of *Town Scandals*, and had earned many positive notices in the white and black press.) Hudgins's name did not appear separately in the show's advertisements or in its on-site billing, nor was special mention made of him in the show's publicity. Further, Hudgins himself testified that "I am a dancer like hundreds of others among my people, and there is nothing unique or extraordinary in my steps."[32] It must have been humiliating for the dancer who indeed had established a unique and applauded routine to have to make this counterargument, but he obviously had no desire to take a pay cut and return to working for Whitney. In fact, during the summer months when Whitney reduced all of the cast's members by 25% before the show reached Broadway, Hudgins had refused to sign an amendment to his original contract accepting this pay cut. His lawyers argued that Whitney's ruse in effect voided the original agreement, and that Hudgins had the right to sign with another party at any time. The upshot was that Whitney lost his case, and *Chocolate Dandies* never recovered from the loss of its biggest box-office draw. Ironically, when Hudgins was performing in London in the later 1920s he actually published a book describing his routines, copyrighting them as his unique creations.

The loss of Hudgins spelled doom to the Broadway production. Jimmy Ferguson, another comic dancer, was brought in as a replacement, and even attempted to reproduce some of Hudgins's specialties. However, the loss of the show's biggest attraction couldn't be easily remedied. White audiences couldn't decide whether this was an old-fashioned "Negro" show or some kind of newfangled creation that emulated lavish productions like the *Ziegfeld Follies*. The enormous cast and high quality of the production demanded a large paying audience to support it. Despite cheery reports in the press of landmark business, *Chocolate Dandies* was hemorrhaging money, so much so that by the time the production closed in New York in December its total debt had nearly doubled from when it arrived in town to over $41,000 (nearly $600,000 today). The cost of operating the show—even with salary cuts and other fixes—were simply too high to be covered by ticket sales. Whitney's only recourse was to send the show back out on the road and hope to make his money back that way.[33]

The company hit the road for a grueling tour that took them through much of the eastern part of the country, through cities big and small, beginning in Philadelphia; next to smaller towns through Pennsylvania; then on to Toledo, Detroit, Indianapolis, and Louisville; back to Ohio to play Cincinnati, Columbus, and Dayton; through major Midwest towns, including St. Louis, Kansas City, Des Moines, Minneapolis, St. Paul, and Peoria; return trips to Sissle's hometown of Indianapolis and Cincinnati; up north to Buffalo, Toronto, Canada, and Rochester; and then to Newark, New Jersey, Baltimore, and finally Brooklyn, New York. Despite receiving generally favorable reviews wherever it went, the production remained in the red. Salaries were cut and general conditions on the road were difficult.

Whatever the show's attraction to white audiences, black theater owners were anxious to book the touring company. In Philadelphia, John Gibson, who owned the black Dunbar Theater, guaranteed $50,000 for a four-week run of the show, beating out the "uptown" (white) theaters according to local accounts.[34] However, it was telling that while *Shuffle Along* played white theaters when it toured, *Chocolate Dandies* was primarily limited to the more restricted TOBA (black vaudeville) circuit.

Eubie thought the tour was ill planned and had argued against trying to take the show on the road. Given his personal loss, he tried to convince Sissle that they should close the show, but Sissle wouldn't hear of it:

When I was $21,000 out of my pocket, I went to Sissle and I says, "Hey Sissle, let's close this thing." [Sissle] says, "You didn't want to go, when you got to the station, going to Trenton [to present *Shuffle Along*], you said 'Let's quit this thing and don't take these people,' because we don't have no money. We had a hit, didn't we?" He says, "You ain't got no heart." "But I'm $21,000 in the hole, paying the show." Costumes that did it, those beautiful girls. It broke my heart. He wouldn't close it. Then old man Erlanger [the producer] arranged for the road tour after the show closed in New York. I don't remember much after Chicago. Then he sent us into Minneapolis and everybody's Catholic and it was during Lent. I said to Sissle, Sissle's a college man, hell I only went to eighth grade, he must know what he's doing, "Why Old Man Erlanger give us the show?" He gave us the show. Minneapolis to Eau Claire, and everybody in Minnesota, people are Catholic, and this during Lent. It didn't break me, but I had about $8000 or $9000 left, with the girls, had my funds and all. But I lost $21,000. I said, "I was that much looser, but I ain't gonna lose no more money."[35]

By early April, Lottie Gee had dropped out of the show, perhaps seeing the handwriting on the wall. By early May, Arthur Lyons—who had previously helped encourage Hudgins to leave the show—announced he was arranging a new company to produce the suspiciously similarly named *Chocolate Kiddies* for a tour to Germany with Lottie Gee among the featured performers. A few nights before sailing, Gee ironically performed the song "For My Man" with Eubie Blake at the piano at a celebratory party held for the company, also attended by Miller and Lyles.[36] Gee's relationship with Blake was becoming increasingly strained, and her abandonment of *Chocolate Dandies* couldn't have helped. Her demands that Blake leave his wife and marry her were also beginning to wear on him. Meanwhile, Eubie's womanizing continued unabated; one of his targets, Valaida Snow, ironically inscribed a photo to Avis Blake with the line "[t]o a broadminded woman with a no good husband."[37]

The tour dragged on even after Gee left. When the show hit Toronto, Sissle and Blake were involved in a bizarre incident. They were hired to entertain at the after-party of another touring production, *Dream Girl*. The all-white cast threw a party after their 100th performance, with a lavish dinner for the cast, orchestra, and other local actors that began at 12 a.m. The United Press syndicate reported, "Liquor was a necessary accompaniment [to the dinner]. Hotel officials disclaim there were any unusual hilarity." The show's male lead, Carl W. Lynn, left the party with his agent around 4 a.m. to retire to his room; four hours later, he was found dead at the bottom of the hotel's stairs with a fractured skull. The leading lady, Fay Bainter, who paid for the party, initially claimed that she was unaware that alcohol was being served, which was illegal in Toronto at the time.

The police arrived just as Sissle and Blake were leaving the hotel around daybreak. They "noticed a suspicious bulge" under their clothes, finding three bottles of liquor on them. A day later, the duo appeared before a local magistrate. When asked why they were carrying the whiskey, Sissle gave a cheeky response:

"We can do it in New York," commented Sissle.
"Well, you can't do it here," retorted the magistrate.[38]

At the following inquest, Sissle and Blake testified to the presence of liquor at the party, which the white attendees had previously denied:

> Blake said he was invited to a room where Miss Bainter was entertaining friends, and helped himself from a bottle of whisky which he saw on the table.
>
> Liquor was found on Sissle and he was fined $50 for violation of the Ontario Temperance Act. Both said that this was given Sissle by a masked guest.[39]

Blake was freed of all charges, thanks to his testimony, but Sissle had to pay the fine. The shocking death of the well-known actor was widely covered by the news services, with many appending to the lurid headlines the detail that "two negroes" were in attendance. Sissle and Blake were put into a particularly awkward situation in the aftermath of Lynn's death. As blacks entertaining at an all-white party in a foreign country, they must have been keenly aware that they were in danger of being jailed if they were implicated in supplying illegal drinks at the party itself. On the other hand, they would be hesitant (to say the least) to identify any of the white actors in the inquiry. Paying the $50 fine was little cost to avoid any further involvement in the affair. They must have been greatly relieved when *Chocolate Dandies* moved on to Rochester, New York, for its next appearance. Given the fact that the production was clearly on its last legs, this incident must have only added to the stress felt by Sissle and Blake.

The show's last hurrah came in May 1925 at Werba's Theater in Brooklyn. Apparently, Sissle and Blake were hoping that by playing Brooklyn they could make up for the losses incurred since the show hit the road; unfortunately, though, these last performances only added to the debt. *Variety* reported that following its closing:

> the show was in arrears to the principals for considerable money . . .
>
> Stagehands received their pay, the crew getting first chance at the box-office returns . . . the Brooklyn receipts not being sufficient to square up all of the salaries . . .
>
> It is understood that the show was going along the past few weeks on the commonwealth plan, expecting to get a break in Brooklyn.

Several principals were in Broadway offices this week seeking new arrangements and telling of the disastrous closing of the Sissle and Blake outfit in Brooklyn.[40]

Not only was the show in arrears, but Sissle and Blake were also facing serious financial problems due to the loss of their investment in the production. Ultimately, Sissle declared bankruptcy in July, facing $3000 in judgments against him and having "no property or other assets, excepting $6000 in back salary due him from 'Chocolate Dandies.' Since this show has broken up, there is little likelyhood [sic] of his collecting his salary," The New York Age reported. Although Eubie Blake wasn't mentioned in Sissle's petition, the reporter noted that he also was in "desperate financial straits."[41] The heyday of the black musical that Shuffle Along launched in 1921 was already coming to a close just four short years later, at least for Sissle and Blake.

The duo spent the summer of 1925 in touring on the Gus Sun vaudeville circuit in the Midwest, earning $1000 for six to seven shows a week, undoubtedly to work off their debt. They followed with a six-week tour of motion picture houses, during which their agents announced, "PROFITS rolled in and crowds went wild at every theatre where these artists appeared."[42] Despite their continuing stateside success, Sissle had long hoped to take the act abroad, where the hunger for black entertainment was great and the lack of prejudice also a major attraction. Finally, they were offered the opportunity to go to London by the William Morris Agency, which booked an extended engagement for the duo at London's Piccadilly Club for the fall.[43] On September 25, Sissle, Blake, and their wives arrived by sea (Figure 7.1) in Southampton, England. Blake's old paramour, Lottie Gee, was also in London at this time, although as Blake was traveling with his wife Avis, it is unknown whether the pair resumed their affair.

On their arrival, Sissle and Blake opened for an eight-week run in a revue titled Playtime at the Piccadilly. The white American singer Jane Green and bandleader/saxophonist Isham Jones were also on the bill. Providing additional music for dancing while the acts took a break were several British light jazz orchestras, including Jack Hylton's orchestra. Eubie admired Hylton, calling him the equal of Paul Whiteman. Billed as "American Ambassadors of Syncopation," Sissle and Blake appeared while wearing their stage attire of full formal dress.

Each week, a poll was taken of the Piccadilly's audience to select the top three acts that they'd like to see appear at the club's sister location, the Kit Kat

Figure 7.1 Sissle and Blake on board ship on their way to England in 1925. Left to right: Eddie Gray (singer); unknown woman; Billie McKinney (singer and wife of Bill McKinney); Eubie Blake; Fanny Robinson (wife of Bill Robinson); Bill "Bojangles" Robinson (with life preserver around him); Bill McKinney; Avis Blake; and Noble Sissle.

Club. Sissle and Blake apparently won a spot there, appearing each night at both locations, starting in late October. The lead singer with Isham Jones's orchestra—who apparently was also Jones's girlfriend at the time—lost to the American duo. Eubie recalled how upset she was that the audience chose a black act over her, saying that the bandleader had to buy her an expensive mink coat to make up for the slight.[44] In addition to their work at the Piccadilly and Kit Kat, the duo were also appearing on the bill at the Victoria Palace.

Throughout their London performances and subsequent tour of other British towns, Sissle and Blake performed a mix of their own familiar numbers, such as "Pickaninny Shoes," along with presumably newly composed songs, including "Why Did You Make Me Care?" They also covered songs by white songwriters including lyricist Bud Green and composers Wright and Bessinger's "Oh! Boy, What a Girl!" (Figure 7.2), which was successfully performed by Eddie Cantor in *Kid Boots*. They also included in their act minstrel-era numbers, including a showstopping version of "Alabamy Bound." According to one critic who saw them perform the song,

Figure 7.2 During their London tour, Sissle and Blake performed their own songs and other popular numbers, including this one, "Oh! Boy, What a Girl!" They were so successful that their tuxedo-clad image was even placed on songs that they didn't write.

[t]hey can sing *Alabamy Bound* faster than any other music-hall performers imaginable. Sissle's lips alternately disclose and uncover his white teeth at an amazing rate and Blake shivers on the piano stool like an electrified jelly while he rattles the keys faster than one would previously have thought possible.[45]

The reference to "white teeth" and "electrified jelly" were, of course, minstrel stereotypes. While less openly racist then their American peers, the British were unembarrassed to express their admiration for African American performers on the basis of these ideas, which, at best, gave credit to these performers for their energy and excitement and, at worst, relegated them to a lower cultural status. Even less flattering was a brief description of the act as "darkies at the piano in the manner of Layton and Johnson [*sic*]" on their appearance at the Alhambra music hall.[46] Turner Layton and Clarence Johnstone were a popular African American duo who had been performing in London since 1924. The implication was that all black performers offered similar fare.

Nonetheless, by the time of their appearance at the Alhambra in late November, the British press recognized the duo's popularity. The critic in *The Stage* noted,

The new American Ambassadors of syncopation, Noble Sissle and Eubie Blake, appear to have established themselves very quickly as staunch favorites . . . The songs of these coloured performers have a flavor of their own, and the pianist . . . is one of the best of the kind we have heard for some time.[47]

As part of the act, Eubie always took a solo number, although the exact pieces he played were not recorded. His syncopated playing was an incredible novelty to British listeners. In an interview on his return to America, the pianist commented on how his music baffled English players:

My playing of Jazz seemed particularly astounding to the English musician. They tried to classify it according to musical form, but failed. Yet when each measure would come out even as the schoolboy says of his sums they were further nonplussed. However our audience . . . fell a victim to syncopation . . . and we were called upon to play many repeat dates.[48]

Sissle and Blake continued to work London through Christmas, where they ended the year with a two-week appearance at the London Coliseum. The Coliseum bill shows the typical eclectic offerings that were common in British music halls; besides the American duo, Diaghilev's Ballet Russes presented a short ballet; acrobats Christo and Ronald showed off their hand- and head-balancing talents; and the multi-instrumentalists of Elliott's Candies performed a "Mayday scena." A dance band and "bioscope pictures" (silent films) rounded out the program, giving "further pleasure to visitors," in the words of a reviewer.[49] On other dates, they shared the bill with jugglers, marionettes, and performing animals, to mention just a few. Also that fall, Sissle and Blake recorded for the British Edison Bell label, and published songs with several local music publishers. On Christmas Eve, they appeared at a charity event for British soldiers and their families at the Fulham Theater in south London.

In January 1926, the duo took to the road for the next month and a half, appearing at the Argyle Music Hall in Birkenhead, as well as in Leeds and Birmingham, before returning to London for engagements at the Alhambra and the Cosmo Club. In early March, they performed in Birmingham, and then appeared in Belfast, Ireland, for what was apparently their last appearance in the United Kingdom. The London-based producer Charles Cochran—who had previously brought Florence Mills to London—commissioned three songs from the duo. The first, "Lady of the Moon," was featured in the fall in his revue *Still Dancing*. The other two, written for his spring 1926 revue, were "Tahiti" and "Let's Get Married Right Away." These songs were performed by Basil Howes and Elizabeth Hines in the show and published that April.

Ever the homebody, by March Eubie was tiring of working in England. The food was unfamiliar to him, he missed steam heat and hot baths (neither of which were available in London), he couldn't adjust to the bustling traffic coming at him on the wrong side of the road, and the grind of running between as many as three engagements a day was wearing on him. Blake was also appalled by the poverty he observed on London's streets and advised other black performers not to visit:

My advice to all American Negroes is to stay away from Europe. Particularly is this so if you are poor. No matter what happens or what the conditions may be in America, they can be nothing like the deplorable conditions that exist in London. I have seen thousands sleeping in the streets, bread lines with human beings standing four abreast and other distress that I hate to remember.[50]

Little did Blake know that in a few short years, with the coming of the Great Depression, these sights would become common in his home country—and that he too would have to scramble to make ends meet.

While Eubie couldn't adjust to British culture, Sissle was a natural aristocrat, fitting in well with English high society. He would have loved to extend his time abroad, particularly after facing the stress of the failure of *Chocolate Dandies* and his personal bankruptcy back home. Some sources claim that Cochran wanted the team to remain in London to write the entire score for his next revue; others say that Sissle went ahead and made initial plans to extend their booking into 1927 without consulting Blake. Whichever the case, the duo had what Eubie said was their first major disagreement. As Eubie later recalled,

Now I got a dollar and 45 cents in my pocket, and I want to come home. Worked every theater in the United Kingdom. And when you get to Alhambra, you play 2 to 3 weeks at that time. So I'm sitting in front of the Piccadilly Circus. So he come, "I did it again, kid. I booked the circuit over again." I said, "Without telling me?" "Well, I take care of the business . . ." "Well, you're going to play it yourself!" And boy did he bawl me out for 15 minutes.[51]

Apparently, Eubie won the argument, at least temporarily, and the duo made plans to return home. The last week of March, they took a short side trip to Paris, where they visited with Josephine Baker, who was then at the height of her success. They then sailed back to America from there on March 31.

Returning to his native country was a relief to Eubie but it must have been a difficult adjustment for Noble. After enjoying seemingly limitless opportunities to perform and write for major producers, and being accepted as an equal by white upper-class society, the duo were returning to the familiar grind of touring smaller town theaters where racism was very much still in evidence. Sissle and Blake were not novelties at home the way they were in England; virtuosic jazz bands and soloist/performers like Louis Armstrong were grabbing the attention of white listeners, while the older-fashioned themes of Noble's lyrics—drenched in minstrel imagery—were no longer the rage. Their old comrades Miller and Lyles were struggling to equal their original success on Broadway, with each successive production pulling smaller audiences and less critical acclaim. The door that had briefly opened for black performers and creative voices on Broadway was slowly but surely slamming shut.

Vaudeville was also in the process of a major transformation. Most houses were now featuring motion pictures along with live acts, and increasingly it was the films that were attracting the audiences. When talking pictures debuted in 1927, the end was in sight for live entertainers, although many would struggle on through the early 1930s. Why pay for a live act when you could more economically have the biggest stars appear on screen? Sissle and Blake were among those whose livelihood would be transformed by this new technology.

Less than a month after their return to the states, the duo were beginning a long tour of Loew's movie houses that would run from the spring of 1926 through the following fall. Their agents, William Morris, took a full-page advertisement in *Variety* to promote it, noting that "[s]mart business judgment demands that managers everywhere arrange bookings for the greatest entertaining and profit-producing attraction on the American stage."[52] Beginning in Cleveland in mid-April, Sissle and Blake crisscrossed the country, in what must have been an endless series of railroad trips between dates. A typical appearance came in St. Louis toward the end of 1926 at Loew's State Theater. The major attraction was the live appearance of actress Claire Windsor, who was on hand to introduce her latest film, a World War I comedy titled *Tin Hats*. Sissle and Blake got second billing, along with soprano Della Samoloff and Creatore's Orchestra.[53] At least in some cases, their appearance on a bill could boost the box office; in Pittsburgh, where other theaters were suffering from ticket sales of about $3000 to $3500 during the week of their appearance, Sissle and Blake helped pull in a nearly $20,000 gross in support of the film *The Plastic Age*.[54] It undoubtedly helped that the film was a major hit for its star Clara Bow, and the other major release in town that week was a Hoot Gibson western.

After their session for Victor in the fall of 1924, featuring their *Chocolate Dandies* songs, Sissle and Blake's recording career Stateside had gone into decline. Blues records were now the big sellers for black acts, not Broadway-styled show tunes. Besides a single session for Edison in June 1925, and their recording activity during their visit to England, the duo would not return to the studio until February 5, 1927, now working for OKeh, a decidedly lower-rent operation than Victor. They would have difficulty collecting their fee for this session, turning to lawyers to try to pry loose their payment from the label. Once again, they recorded "Crazy Blues," but the performance went unissued; they also cut two popular songs of the day and their evergreen stage number, "Pickaninny Shoes." This would be the last Sissle and Blake session; when Sissle returned to OKeh in May, he was accompanied by white pianist/songwriter Rube Bloom, despite the fact that he was still on the road with Eubie. He would continue to record with Bloom, and various others, for OKeh through the fall of 1927.

Three days after their OKeh session, the duo went to the Manhattan Opera House to make a short for Vitaphone. Vitaphone shorts were produced by Warner Brothers with a system whereby a disc recording was synchronized with film to capture a live performance. Due to the limitations of length available on the disc, the films were necessarily short (between 7 and 11 minutes). These proved popular as shorts shown in conjunction with major silent films, and heralded the coming era of talking pictures. It was a major coup for Sissle to arrange for the act to be filmed. Their contract called for the duo to "sing, perform on the piano, act and pose scenes, arias, and other numbers and selections designated by Vitaphone."[55] Vitaphone further stipulated that the duo could not make a similar film for six months following the release of the short. They were paid $1000 for their services. The agreement was signed by Noble Sissle alone—not surprisingly, as Blake allowed Sissle to handle all of the duo's business matters.

The release of the short was big news in the African American community. As late as the winter of 1929, the short was still being featured in black theaters. Notably, it was shown following a performance of *Junior Blackbirds of Harlem*, a revue led by Ralph Cooper and his band at Harlem's Lafayette Theatre:

> As a special attraction, the producers sprang a surprise by presenting Nobel [sic] Sissle and Ubie [sic] Blake, the international stars of syncopation. This was, of course, accomplished on the marvelous Vitaphone. This wonderful pair of entertainers sing three songs. The reception which they received . . . could hardly have been greater had they appeared in person, so perfectly were they heard and seen over the wonderful Vitaphone system which has been installed in the Lafayette Theater.[56]

Sadly, this short has never been found, although Bolcom and Kimball report that copy of a recording featuring "My Dream Parade" (written by Al Dubin and Jimmy McHugh) and "All God's Chillun Got Shoes" on a Vitaphone disc survived at least until 1970. The first number featured Blake leading a full band along with a dramatic recitation by Sissle, while the second just features the duo on vocal and piano.[57]

The duo then hit the road once more, continuing to work the movie theater circuit. While in later-life interviews Blake denied there was any tension between him and Sissle at the time of their breakup, clearly Sissle was looking for a way out. The break came when the duo were appearing in Columbus, Ohio, sometime in the summer of 1927. To biographer Al Rose, Blake admitted that the situation was exacerbated by Sissle's first wife, Harriet, who was poisoning the water behind his back:

> Harriet says, "This guy don't do nothing, he just sits there and plays the piano. You're the one out there doing all the work. . . ." Now when a man loves a woman, you know what happens. I have no proof of this, but I've taken psychology for it. So we're playing at the Keith Theater in Columbus, Ohio. . . . so I says to Sissle, "I heard you're going to Paris." "Oh yeah, I'm going with the American Legion." And I says, "When you coming back?" We got 11 more weeks set, and we never got under $1500, we got $2000 in St. Louis on the books.
>
> "When you coming back?" "I don't know," he says. I says, "You don't know when you coming back? And we got 11 weeks work!" "Yeah, but I don't know when I'm coming back." And I says, "This is the end of Sissle and Blake." He never answered; to this day he never answered.[58]

Blake looked down on Harriet, whom he called a "juicehead," his term for a heavy drinker; as we shall see, Blake had little tolerance for women who drank. The last documented performance by the duo occurred in Port Chester, New York, at the Capitol Theater from August 18 to August 20; they were paid all of $300 for their three nights of work. In early September, Sissle sailed to Europe to attend an American Legion convention for World War I veterans; soon thereafter, he was hired to lead an orchestra at a Paris nightclub, Les Ambassadeurs.

Eubie must have seen the writing on the wall, because in early June he was already in correspondence with arranger Harold Tillotson, who apparently was helping Eubie place several compositions with publishers and performers. Eubie had written a semiclassical work, "Blues Classique," in the mode of the popular combination of jazz–light-classical styles that had been popularized by Gershwin's 1924 "Rhapsody in Blue," among others. Tillotson hoped to place the piece with Paul Whiteman—who had made Gershwin's piece a hit—along with finding a publisher for it. He also was trying to line up a session for Eubie as a solo artist in Chicago. Tilottson urged Eubie to take advantage of the opportunity to record popular songs along with his own numbers:

> You just get right to work and talk that fellow out there [in Chicago] into making plenty of records. Be sure and make a popular record too. I am anxious to see you on the records, as I know that you can play rings around Lee Sims, or any of these other fellows. Make as many of your own numbers as you possible can, by that I mean, popular numbers and numbers that you own the copyright on, so that you will collect all the royalties.[59]

Lee Sims was a popular white pianist who broadcast out of Chicago; his impressionistic playing deeply influenced later jazz keyboardist Art Tatum.

Tillotson also told Eubie to try to get "some accompanying work. You may as well do it and make that extra jack."[60] Tillotson also hoped to place two of Eubie's songs, "Cold Weather" and "You Ought to Know," on record. Apparently, Blake had reunited with singer Lottie Gee by this point, because Tillotson said he could arrange for Gee to record in Chicago if she was traveling with the pianist. There is no record of a Chicago recording session being held in 1927 or any further information about Tillotson's work on Eubie's behalf, although Eubie did wire him $40.00 at this time, perhaps in payment for his services.

Besides breaking up with Sissle, Eubie faced another loss that July with the death of his mother. Although she never really accepted his career in popular music, Eubie was extremely close to her. After the end of his UK tour in 1926, Eubie's first stop was to visit his mother in Baltimore, reconnecting with the country—and his home town—that he loved. Eubie arranged for her to be buried by the side of his father. Her house—which he had purchased for her and then transferred co-ownership to his wife and adopted sister—was sold in 1932 for $800.

Back in New York by the fall of 1927, Eubie was scrambling to find work and a new performing partner. That October, the press announced that he would begin touring with tenor Paul Bass, who had just finished an engagement in *Africana* on Broadway, a revue starring Ethel Waters.[61] Bass may have filled in for some remaining dates that were booked before Sissle left for Europe. To replace Sissle as a lyricist, Blake began working with Henry Creamer on a projected show to be called *Teddy*; it was never produced.[62] Eventually, Eubie found a permanent performing partner in an old friend, Henry "Broadway" Jones.

Jones was born in 1888 in Florida, in the coastal town of Fernandina, north of Jacksonville. The family owned a small farm, where Jones worked as a teenager; he had little education, and could neither read nor write. By 1915, Jones was in New York City, where he joined the Clef Club. He earned his nickname because he always dressed sharply in the finest suits. (Eubie jokingly referred to him as "the man with a million suits."[63]) From the mid-1910s, Broadway led a small dance band that worked around New York City and Long Island. In 1916, Jones began a regular annual gig at the Royal Poinciana Hotel in Palm Beach, Florida—the same hotel where Sissle had performed in 1915 with Bob Young's orchestra. Jones was a major hit among the society crowd there, and played for private parties as well as his hotel appearances through at least the late 1920s.

In 1923, Jones briefly operated a nightclub in Harlem, known variously as Broadway Jones' Rendezvous and The Bamville Club. A poor businessman at best, Jones struggled to keep the club open. Apparently one of the performers who worked there who went without pay was Eubie. In October 1923, Broadway sent him a telegram while the pianist was on the road with Sissle, begging him not to sue for back payment:

> terribly sorry you feel hurt about my action the truth is I am almost crazy trying to get enough money to pay my debts and still remain in the business which is very bad Hope you will consider all legal action could not help either one of us as man to man you will get every dollar I owe you if I can just get an even break[64]

By early 1924, Broadway declared bankruptcy. However, he continued to perform at the same location when it was taken over by new management and renamed the Club Tennessee later that year.

Eubie had first worked with Broadway while Sissle was serving abroad in World War I, appearing at a few local New York restaurants and accompanying the singer along with a drummer. He apparently began working with Jones again sometime in the fall of 1927, because Blake later claimed that he was with the singer when Jones tragically turned down a part in what would prove to be an epoch-making musical, *Show Boat*. According to Eubie, Oscar

Hammerstein had heard Jones sing in Palm Beach and thought he'd be the ideal candidate to sing "Old Man River." Hammerstein and Kern sent for the singer who—again according to Eubie—was not much of a businessman. At the time, Romaine Johns—a childhood friend of Eubie's—was handling Blake's business affairs, replacing Sissle as a kind of de facto business manager. Jones asked Johns to represent him in the negotiations for his appearance in *Show Boat*, saying, "You go down and represent me. The less [i.e., least he'd accept] is 500 a week, but ask for 6, or 7, and fight 'til it gets down. If it don't get down to 5, to hell with it. I can make that much money with Eubie, or anybody." The producers wouldn't meet his asking price, and so Broadway lost his chance to appear in the production. Ironically, in an early version of *Show Boat*, a dance number accompanied by the *Shuffle Along* hit "I'm Just Wild about Harry" was part of the production; it was pulled after the Washington, DC, tryouts, however.[65] Once "Old Man River" had become a major hit, Jones featured the song in his appearances with Eubie.

Eubie joined the singer in February 1928 for Jones's annual engagement in Florida, which must have been a godsend to Blake, who had been trying to line up work for the previous six months with little success. They worked in Florida through the "high season" in April. The following fall, the duo began working theaters primarily in the greater New York City area, averaging about $200 to $300 per engagement (although sometimes earning as little as $50). Clearly, Blake and Jones could not command the same fees as Sissle and Blake had done, but with little expense for travel, they were able to make do. Neither Jones nor Blake was a savvy businessman; and, unlike Sissle, Jones had even less education than Blake. For the first time in his professional career since he left Baltimore, Blake was going to have to manage his business affairs on his own. The results would be disastrous—and were exacerbated within the next two years by the general collapse of the economy.

While he admired Jones's "big voice," Eubie complained that—unlike Sissle—Jones was not a natural showman. "All he knows is to go out there and sing," Eubie lamented. If anything was changed on stage—the piano was moved to a different position, for example—Jones couldn't adjust. Eubie was also uncomfortable with how Jones handled their white audiences, particularly when they performed in a nightclub. While Eubie didn't kowtow to his audiences, he was smart enough to play any requests, to avoid any trouble. On the one hand, Jones knew how to properly "con" his audience into giving him tips, but sometimes he would seemingly ignore their requests to the detriment of the duo's success:

Talk about connin' ofays. I worked with him at a cabaret. Broadway ain't going no closer than this. "Mr. Rose, may I sing something for you, sir?" Well, white people like that. No Tomming, he ain't that kind of guy. But he'd bow over like that. He ain't going up too close to them, he's standing here. And the man would say, would hand Broadway 5 or 6 dollars that time. When that guy came off the floor, he'd have 5, 15, 20 dollars at the time. But you know what was wrong with [Jones]? The head waiter would say, "Mr. Abbadabba, say, sing 'Cow Jump Over the Moon.'" I play it, [Broadway] don't get up and sing. That was the way he was: Moody. After a while, the head waiter say "Mr. Abbadabba ask you to sing." He'd say, "All right." After a while, he'd go out and sing the song. But he didn't sing it when the man asked for it. How he made his money, I don't know.[66]

Sometime in mid-1928, Blake and Jones decided to put together a touring company to work the vaudeville circuit. Working with Blake's old vaudeville manager Pat Casey through the Keith Orpheum circuit, they put together a tab (30-minute long) show that they called *Shuffle Along Jr.* The show opened in Paterson, New Jersey, in early August before moving to Proctor's Theater on 86th Street in New York City, and then travelled on the Eastern leg of the Orpheum circuit through early 1929. More a revue than a true show, it had its closest ties to the original production through the presence of the female chorines known as the "Panama Pansies." (Blake himself described the show as a "girl act," meaning its major attraction was the scantily clad chorus girls.) The show's featured stars were eccentric dancer Dewey Brown and his sometimes vaudeville partner, singer Katie Crippen. Crippen had previously recorded for Black Swan Records under the nom de disc of Ella White, accompanied by Fletcher Henderson's band. Vocalists Hilda Perleno (who had previously appeared in the chorus of *Chocolate Dandies*) and Mae Diggs were also in the cast. Leonard Harper was credited with staging the dance numbers. Just as Blake was still riding *Shuffle Along's* coattails, Miller and Lyles were in rehearsal for their next Broadway production, *Keep Shufflin'.* The *Shuffle Along* name was still a strong attraction for audiences, even though neither production was derived from the original show. *Shuffle Along Jr.* played continuously throughout the day in between film showings so that the company was kept busy from 11 in the morning until midnight at each stop on the tour.

The show rarely was reviewed, and when it did attract notice it was not favorably compared with either the original *Shuffle Along* or even Sissle and

Blake's old vaudeville act. *Billboard* called the show "fairly entertaining" when it played Chicago but "not as good as the old Sissle and Blake act." The only performer singled out for praise was Dewey Brown. The reviewer noted that Brown "works under cork," emphasizing this hangover from minstrelsy days.[67]

Blake was appointed the road manager for the production, a title that meant he was in charge of collecting the box office receipts, paying the expenses and salaries, and giving accurate reports to the Keith Orpheum offices. Almost immediately, this job proved to be difficult for Eubie. He had problems following the office's rules for calculating expenses and was not keeping accurate books, at least according to the managers back home. In October, John Schultz of the Orpheum offices wrote to Eubie when the company reached Minneapolis to explain to him how to account for the travel expenses for the show, particularly focusing on the chorus girls' sleeping arrangements:

> With reference to our paying of sleepers with regard to the chorus. We will pay all over $3.00 sleepers. For example: If the sleepers would cost $12.00 a piece for the girls you would arrange in in the following manner.
> $12.00
> Less-$3.00 which the girls will have to pay
> $9.00 balance that the office is to pay.
> In the case of the chorus girls there is no reason why they cannot double and have two girls sleep in the lower berths. We do that with all our girls all over the circuit. This is what I mean by the doubling.[68]

More disturbing to Schultz was reports he was receiving from managers along the tour's route saying that—despite the quality of the lead actor's performances—the chorines were not up to par:

> I have wired you today stating that the Minneapolis report reads— "PRINCPALS VERY GOOD CHORUS VERY POOR." Cannot understand this myself as when you left here you had a very good chorus. Is it that the girls are laying down on the job or the constant changes confusing them. This must be remedied or I will have to close the act as the office is very much disturbed and insist that I remedy this at once.[69]

On October 18, Schultz wrote again to complain that several costumes were not returned to the rental company in Minneapolis by the chorines. Schultz

concluded his letter ominously: "You will have to check this up more carefully or I will have to pay for same personally, and I do not intend doing so."[70]

There was serious disagreement between the Orpheum offices and Eubie
over costs incurred on the road, with Blake apparently claiming higher
expenses than were acceptable. The accountings given by the various theaters
for weekly profits were not lining up with the money sent by Blake to the
home offices. Blake's various explanations for the shortfalls fell on deaf ears;
Schultz's assistant coldly replied to Eubie's most recent excuses in November,
stating, "I am positive of one thing, if there is very much more trouble I know
the office is going to close the act, so if you want to keep working see that
there is no trouble."[71]

Unable to get what they felt was an accurate accounting from Blake, by
mid-1929 the home office resorted to instructing their local theaters to pull
the shortfall from Blake's and Jones's salaries. Effective that May, they asked
their local managers to hold $608 of Eubie's weekly salary on the basis of their
estimate of what the show should be earning after expenses. "The only way
we will reduce [the amount withheld]," the company informed its agents, "is
to have BLAKE immediately make out a statement covering these two weeks
so that we can actually determine the exact amount."[72] The local promoter
asked Blake to "please advise" what action he should take in light of this letter
from the main office. The show was shut down soon after, and Blake reluc-
tantly agreed to pay off the balance of his debt of a little over $609 from future
weekly earnings. Keith's management wrote to him,

> Taking under consideration the circumstances set forth in your letter and
> the expression of your willingness to cooperate with us, we will agree to
> take $50.00 per week until the full amount due and owing by you is paid.
> As evidence of your good faith in the matter, we shall expect a check in that
> sum at the end of this week. Of course, in the event that you do not work in
> any particular week, we shall expect no payment.[73]

Keith's forgoing payment for weeks when Eubie was idle must have seemed
to them to be particularly generous, although one can image Eubie found the
entire situation galling. *Shuffle Along Jr.* ended up being an expensive folly
for him, neither building his marketability on the road nor leading to future
work for more legitimate shows.

Owing money to Keith Orpheum, Blake quickly grabbed the next opportunity that came along, to appear with Jones as an added attraction in the

latest version of Fanchon and Marco's *Oddities Idea*. Fanchon Simon and her brother Marco Wolff produced and directed elaborate stage shows that played in major movie palaces between pictures. Often the stage show was the draw, especially if the picture was weak. These were big productions with the Fanchonettes, 48 talented women who could sing, dance, and juggle. They also appeared as posing on top of giant beach balls and in other novel settings. Often a headliner would appear while sets and costumes were changed and that's where Blake and Jones came in. Their particular F&M production was titled *California Capers* and traveled across the country working the Keith Orpheum vaudeville circuit. The *Chicago Defender* proudly proclaimed that the duo were "the only Race members of the cast."[74] A reviewer in Great Falls, Montana—making note of the fact that the duo were "colored," unlike the other performers on the bill—noted that Jones's performance of "Old Man River" was "so enthusiastically received that they are forced to respond to several curtain calls." Blake was described as a "real pianist," who impressed the audience with his solo playing.[75] Blake may have also reconnected with Lottie Gee while the show was on the West Coast; Gee had traveled to Hollywood in April 1929, in expectation of being cast in a forthcoming film by Paramount.[76] Apparently, this casting never happened, but Gee remained in Los Angeles through the early 1930s, and Blake would visit with her when he passed through the town, particularly on his second Fanchon and Marco tour in 1931 into 1932.

Returning to New York by late 1929, Blake and Jones made a few appearances in revues at the Lafayette and on the road. They also made four recordings for Victor in December, none of which were issued at the time. The duo cut two songs by Eubie, including "House Rent Lizzie," with lyrics by Arthur Swanson, and "Dissatisfied Blues," written with Jack Scholl, along with Andy Razaf and Fats Waller's recent hit "My Fate Is in Your Hands."

In January 1930, the Blake-Jones duo appeared in a revue staged by Lawrence Deas at Harlem's Lafayette Theatre, titled *Birth of Syncopation*. A tab show, it featured a 15-minute slot for the duo, who probably performed a similar routine to their work on vaudeville. The show appeared between screenings of the "all-taking, singing, dancing, dramatic masterpiece," *Woman to Woman*.[77] The duo would appear in similar shows—which were basically a mix of sketch comedy, music, and scantily clad dancers—over the next years, with titles like *Shaky Feet*. These titles reflected the idea of a racy night's entertainment, and played on stereotypes that blacks were "natural" singers and dancers, even though they were presented for a primarily black audience in Harlem.

At the same time, Blake was hired by producer Will Morrissey to provide music for his *Folies Bergere Revue* that premiered in Greenwich Village's Gansevoort Theater in April. Morrissey himself appeared in his revues, often in the audience, greeting the attendees while portraying an old-style Irish comedian. This mixed-race revue opened with a monocle-wearing announcer, sporting a faux-English accent, who introduced Eubie and his "Uptown Gang": "whereupon Eubie treats the audience to a jazz soliloquy. A dozen or more mulattoes and octoroons, light of foot and gown flit in, do a congregational contortion, and flit out, to the delectation of the audience."[78] The *New York Times* critic was impressed with Eubie's score, calling it "tuneful and catchy, and syncopated to a high degree."[79]

John Scholl—one of the producers of *Elsie*—was an investor in the revue, and may have recommended that Morrissey hire Blake to be part of it. He also encouraged Blake to compose some songs for the show[80], suggesting to Blake that he work with his young son, Jack, who had just graduated from college. Eubie recalled,

[Scholl] says to me one day . . . "I got a son, bores me to death, Eubie. He thinks he can write lyrics. Now get him off my shoulder. Go up and doodle something down." And he wrote the lyric and I set it. And the song hit. . . . Universal hit.[81]

The song they crafted was titled "Loving You the Way I Do," and—of course—Morrissey added his name as lyricist along with Scholl's son Jack. Although the show was a flop, the song was a hit, leading to Jack Scholl's getting an offer to go to Hollywood, although he initially worked writing comedy plots, not song lyrics. Eubie ruefully noted, "Hollywood sent for him, [but] didn't send for me, and he left me and he went out there." Eubie's anger that Scholl—a greenhorn—got a Hollywood job on the basis of one song's success while Eubie lacked the same opportunity reflects the overall racism in the movie business. While a few black specialty pictures were being made, black composers had few—if any—opportunities to work for the major studios.

During this period, Eubie was also showing a growing interest in composing classical-flavored pieces. Blake may have been inspired by the success of Gershwin's "Rhapsody in Blue" and the work of African American composers like his old friend James P. Johnson, whose extended work "Yamekraw" was premiered in 1928 by W. C. Handy. ("Yamekraw" features a paraphrase of a melody from Eubie's "Charleston Rag."[82]) William Grant Still was working on his own major piece, the *Afro-American Symphony*, at this time, which may have also influenced Eubie's new direction. Pieces like his "Blues Classique," which wed jazz and blues elements with light classical touches, come from this period. Blake and Broadway Jones also sought out opportunities to perform in more "refined" settings than vaudeville. They appeared with Harlem's Monarch Symphonic Band[83] in mid-1930 in a concert setting featuring Blake playing the piano part of "Rhapsody in Blue" along with Jones singing "Old Man River" with Blake at the keyboard.[84] Blake would appear with this orchestra through the 1930s in various concert programs. Eubie's attempts to cross over to the more respectable semiclassical field as both composer and performer, however, were not very successful.

With a song success and good notices for their appearance in Morrissey's revue, Blake and Jones were establishing themselves as a popular act just as vaudeville-style revues were fading in the face of talking pictures. To make matters worse, Radio Keith Orpheum (RKO), the prime booker for vaudeville acts—which hired Blake and Jones among many others—indicated at the end of 1930 that it would no longer promote mixed-race bills, explaining that it would cut back on the number of black artists it would put on the boards. As reported in *Billboard* about the organization,

> Instead of putting itself on the record officially as being opposed to mixing colors—and thereby drawing the unwelcome support of anti-racial extremists—the major circuit is handling the matter along common-sense lines. Each booker is permitted to use his own discretion in doing business with mixed acts. What might evolve as a result . . . will be an undisguised coldness to acts mixing white and Negro races in ensembles. Acts carrying large companies of whites and using a dusky hoofer or two will not be affected, since this practice has been in vogue for many seasons and has not yet drawn the fire of carping critics . . . The circuit has had several unpleasant experiences this season with colored "names" and is thinking seriously of severing contractual relations with these. But the matter is strictly personal, and does not reflect discredit on other colored turns.[85]

Blake was listed as "among the colored acts" that had worked on the RKO circuit recently. Although RKO tried to deny it, the upshot would be less work for black artists. RKO's skittishness was reflected by other major vaudeville chains, who wanted to avoid "controversy" at all costs. With the Depression underway, racism was again raising its ugly head, particularly among unemployed white workers. With vaudeville becoming a less viable option for blacks, Blake was desperate to return to Broadway. As luck would have it, a major producer was under pressure to find a black composer for his latest revue. This producer—Lew Leslie—would pair Blake with his second great lyricist/partner: Andy Razaf. The show would be known as *Blackbirds of 1930*.

8

Hard Times

1930–1936

In the annals of theater history, there are many colorful characters among the actors, agents, producers, and critics who populate the Broadway scene. Lew Leslie was undoubtedly one of the most eccentric, with a meteoritic rise and fall worthy itself of a Broadway show. Leslie's place and date of birth are in dispute—as with many other figures of the period—but it is certain that he was of Russian-Jewish ancestry. He began his career as a vaudevillian in partnership with Belle Baker, who would become his first wife. Leslie quickly switched to being an agent/producer, representing a few up-and-coming white acts with limited success. His big break came when he was hired to produce a revue at Broadway's Plantation Club in 1922, and was able to lure away Florence Mills from the cast of *Shuffle Along* to be his star. Suddenly finding a mission in life, Leslie became a champion of African American performers, producing elaborate productions under the banner of "glorifying the American Negro," a takeoff of the *Ziegfeld Follies*' motto, "Glorifying the American Girl."

In 1923, Leslie took Mills to England, along with several other performers, including comic-dancer Johnny Hudgins (later in the ill-fated *Chocolate Dandies*). Titled *Dover Street to Dixie*, the show had as its highlight Mills's performance of the song "I'm a Little Blackbird," which she sang after emerging from a giant pie. It became Mills's best-known song and she quickly earned the nickname of the "little blackbird." Capitalizing on the song's success, Leslie next placed Mills in a revue titled *Blackbirds of 1926*, which played in Harlem and then Paris. However, just as she was achieving great success, Mills tragically died in 1927, so Leslie had to find a new star for his next production, *Blackbirds of 1928*. He hired Adelaide Hall to be the star of the show, which also featured dancers Bill "Bojangles" Robinson and "Peg Leg" Bates. Leslie hired the white songwriting team of Dorothy Fields and Jimmy McHugh to compose the songs, and several became major hits, including "I Can't Give You Anything but Love" and "Diga Diga Do." The show broke

Eubie Blake. Richard Carlin and Ken Bloom, Oxford University Press (2020). © Richard Carlin and Ken Bloom 2020.
DOI: 10.1093/oso/9780190635930.001.0001

records for an all-black revue on Broadway, with over 500 performances. However, Leslie worked his cast mercilessly, adding midnight shows to capitalize on the production's success. He also paid poorly and irregularly—not unusual for the time—so that eventually Hall left the production in disgust after it went out on the road.

Perhaps under pressure to live up to his image as a champion of black artists, Leslie decided to produce *Blackbirds of 1930* with all black-talent, even behind the scenes. He turned to Flournoy Miller, who had recently split with his stage partner Aubrey Lyles. Lyles had decided to move to Africa to escape American racism, leaving Miller high and dry. In Lyles's place, Miller partnered with Mantan Moreland, who would remain his sidekick for several decades. Miller was hired to write the show's book, which like most revues was fairly loosely constructed to accommodate the various acts. Ethel Waters—who had achieved great success in Harlem's nightclubs—was to be the leading lady for the production. Also included were the vocalist Minto Cato, the dance duos the Berry Brothers and Buck and Bubbles, and Blake's partner Broadway Jones.

Waters had already made a mark on Broadway in her previous revue, *Africana*. Tellingly, the critics compared her to Florence Mills. Richard Watts Jr. wrote, "Since Florence Mills first showed Broadway in 'Shuffle Along' what a gifted Negro comedienne could really do when she set her mind to it, no similar players has proved so ingratiating as did Miss Waters last night."[1] *The New York Times* critic Rowland Field agreed with the comparison to Mills, saying that Waters "must be ranked on an equal footing with Florence Mills and Josephine Baker as a colored chanteuse."[2]

Leslie came to Eubie with a rich offer to compose the score: a $3000 advance (about $45,000 in today's dollars) to write 28 songs from which several would be selected for the show.[3] Blake was also hired to conduct the orchestra at a promised salary of $250 a week ($3750 in current dollars). This was very good money for the period, considering that the Great Depression was just beginning. Blake's contract with music publishers Shapiro Bernstein for the songs was less generous, although typical for the period: Blake was to earn royalties of two-tenths of a cent on sheet music sales, and 17½% of moneys from license fees.[4] Leslie would earn a greater percentage for himself from sheet music sales as producer of the show.

On hearing about Eubie's good luck landing the assignment with Leslie, Jack Scholl wrote from Hollywood, asking the composer's help in getting him work with Leslie:

Glad . . . to hear that you are going to do the "Black-Birds"—Wish I were in on it. Who's going to do the lyrics? If I thought I could, I'd get right back to New York. . . . Could you interest Lew Leslie in signing me up to write material and lyrics with you?[5]

Scholl mentions several songs that he and Blake wrote together, saying that "[t]hey'd be perfect in the Blackbirds—I could write the continuity and blackout leading up to the numbers so that they would be appropriately spotted."[6] However, none of these songs appeared in the production.[7]

Another colleague looking for possible work in *Blackbirds* was pianist Earl Hines. Eubie first heard a young Hines playing in a small club in Pittsburgh when he was touring *Chocolate Dandies*, which featured trumpeter Joe Smith, a native of the city and friend of Hines's aunt. Hines described Eubie as being quite the swell at the time, sporting a raccoon coat and carrying a cane. Eubie recognized the younger musician's unique talents, and urged him to leave the city; Hines later recalled that Eubie told him, "You'll never get anywhere staying in Pittsburgh—it's off the beaten path," with the composer admonishing Hines that, if he saw him again hanging around town the next time he visited, he'd "wrap [his] cane around your head."[8] Hines took this advice and moved to Chicago in the mid-1920s.[9] Hines ran into Eubie again when the young pianist was leading a band in Chicago in the late 1920s. Hines wrote to Eubie in February 1930, asking him to consider using his band in the forthcoming revue:

I hear you are getting up a review [*sic*], and I certainly wish you much success. And, was wondering if you were going to use a band, and if so, have you already selected it?

I wish it was possible for you to give my band a trial. Remember when you were here last I was at the Grand Terrace on South Park Way and 39th and I am still there, but would like to get under something you handle or come East for a change if I could get something worth while.

If you have made all plans for your band, I would appreciate it if you could put me in touch with something or someone there that could handle it.

Wishing you much success again, hoping to hear from you,

Earl Hines (Pianist)[10]

Eubie wrote on the back of the letter "Don't know if I can bring band in will find out by Union." It turned out that Leslie would hire local musicians for the production.

For the lyricist, Leslie turned to Andy Razaf (Figure 8.1), who had scored several hits in partnership with the pianist/singer Fats Waller, among others. Andriamanantena Paul Razafinkarefo was born in 1895 in Washington, DC, to a father who was a member of the royal family of Madagascar. Razaf's mother was the American daughter of a former slave who rose to the position of United States Consul to Madagascar. Pregnant with her child, she left for America so she could give birth in the United States. After quitting school, Razaf joined a Negro League baseball team and then turned to songwriting. His first published song was "Baltimo'," which was placed in *The Passing Show of 1913*. Razaf subsequently wrote with J. C. Johnson, James P. Johnson, and then Fats Waller.

Razaf was among the most sophisticated lyricists of the period, bringing a unique combination of wit and a bit of a political edge to his work. When writing for Waller, Razaf said, "[Y]ou can almost hear how he's going to sing

Figure 8.1 Lyricist Andy Razaf, c. 1943. Razaf was one of Blake's most talented lyricist-partners; he appreciated Blake's sophisticated approach to composing melodies.

your words while you're still writing them down on paper." His job was to fashion lyrics that fit Waller's larger-than-life stage personality. But writing with Eubie would prove to be different:

> When you're writing to his music, you never know who's going to sing it . . . When I write for Eubie, I think of big sets, a chorus line, elaborate costumes. Of course, Eubie's melodies lend themselves so perfectly to sophisticated lyrics, and they're sort of a challenge, too, because musically he's so far ahead of most contemporary popular composers.[11]

For his part, Eubie was impressed by Razaf's lightning-fast lyrical mind. He not only wrote witty lyrics, but he also fit them perfectly to the melodic and rhythmic twist and turns of Eubie's songs. Blake commented, "You play a melody and he makes a whole new thing out of it . . . He never had to change anything. His meter was always *perfect* and he could write nearly as fast as I could whistle the tune."[12] And, unlike the somewhat stuffy Sissle, Razaf and Blake hit it off immediately, with Razaf's sense of humor strongly appealing to Eubie. The two spent the winter working together, holing up at Andy's mother's house in Asbury Park, New Jersey.

Eubie was less tolerant of Razaf and his pals James P. Johnson and Fats Waller drinking, gambling, and womanizing. He was particularly shocked because they chose to associate with "the lowest damn women." Eubie couldn't understand how Razaf—raised by a "high class" mother—could be attracted to these women, noting, "If they went with nice ladies, I could see it because, hell, I want one of them girls, too. But not the—snuff [prostitutes]! I never go nowhere near them."[13]

Blackbirds of 1930 was a hugely ambitious production. Typical of Leslie, he couldn't stop tinkering with its various components, adding new segments and dropping others, while also fussing over every detail—even leaping into the orchestra pit during rehearsals to show Eubie how to properly conduct. Eubie found Leslie difficult to work with throughout the rehearsal process and began to suspect that Leslie was slightly unbalanced—or perhaps even using drugs. "Somethin' went wrong with Leslie, somethin' went wrong with his head," Eubie told Razaf's biographer Barry Singer.[14] Leslie argued with Blake about the music and how he interpreted it, and worked the cast nearly to death in perfecting their routines. On its opening in New York, the show's playbill acknowledged its changeable nature, stating "Program subject to change due to magnitude of the production." In an interview with Barry

Singer, John Bubbles noted that throughout the production there was a lot of friction between Leslie and Blake: "Eubie wanted things to go the way *he* wanted to go, and Leslie wanted things the way *he* wanted to go."[15] Bubbles concluded, however, that ultimately it was Leslie's show and he could make any changes that he wanted whenever he wanted to do so.

Although created by blacks, the show played on the familiar stereotypes that white audiences expected. Its opening scene was set on a "Levee on the Mississippi," with Broadway Jones singing the traditional spiritual "Roll, Jordan, Roll" accompanied by Cecil Mack's "Blackbird Choir." The Razaf-Blake song "Memories of You" was introduced in this opening scene, although it didn't have much to do with "life on the levee." It was sung by Minto Cato, who was known for her amazingly high vocal range. In the words of the *Chicago Defender*, for Cato a "high C is low,"[16] and the song was custom tailored to show off her vocal chops. In the next scene, Miller and Moreland were introduced, Miller taking his familiar character as "Steve" [Jenkins] and Moreland taking Lyles's old character, now renamed "Caesar." Then, we travel to "An African Jungle" for the song "[Doin' the] Mozambique," again sung by Minto Cato. A few specialties and skits follow, with the song "You're Lucky to Me" introduced. It was initially sung by Neeka Shaw and John Bubbles (of Buck and Bubbles) in a song-and-dance skit, and then immediately reprised by Waters accompanied by the full orchestra. The song's theme reappeared throughout the balance of the show, and obviously it was selected to be the "hit" of the evening. The first act concluded with a takeoff on the then-popular play *Green Pastures*—a typical feature for this type of revue.

Act 2 basically offered more of the same, satires of *All Quiet on the Western Front* and *The Last Mile,* retitled *All Quiet on the Darkest Front* and *The Last Smile;* feature spots for the Berry Brothers, Buck and Bubbles, and Ethel Waters; and several comic skits, including the unfortunately titled "Aunt Jemima's Divorce Case" with Cato in the title role, Buck and Bubbles appearing as Cream of Wheat (her husband) and The Ham What Am (the judge), respectively, and Broadway Jones as Sambo the lawyer. Miller clearly was comfortable with these comic stereotypes, as was the white audience. As if all this material weren't enough, the show concluded with a medley of hits from the 1928 production. All in all, the show ran nearly four hours!

Blackbirds had an out-of-town tryout, opening on September 1, 1930, although it was just across the river in Brooklyn. At the time, shows would try out and even tour after Broadway on what was called the "Subway Circuit" (the outer boroughs of New York). The Brooklyn reviewer found the show enjoyable but—typical of Leslie's over-the-top approach—too long, advising him to cut at least an hour before moving it to Broadway:

> Like so many others, [Leslie] believes in . . . giving his first night audience all he can think of to give . . . [ellipsis in original] and finding after the first night that among his riches were really only a few jewels . . . Jewels had best have fine settings, not be buried at the bottom of a grab-bag.

The reviewer particularly praised the work of the Berry Brothers, focusing on 17-year-old Ananias, whom he described as a "lithe blackboy with muscles that move instinctively to music as a lily shivers in the wind and feet that leave the following eye behind." (Typically, Ananias was praised for his "instinctive" talents, as if he were born to dance and had not worked hard to hone his technique.) Waters was singled out as "one of those lucky singers who do not have to perspire to be meaningful." This appears to be a backhanded compliment to Waters for singing in a more demure, "white" manner, as opposed to the blues belters like Mamie Smith who forcibly delivered their songs.

The critic's sharpest barbs were reserved for the show's humorous sketches. In an almost unbelievably racist passage, he stated that black comedians needed

> the white man to snap [them] up and tell [them] when to stop. . . . [Black comedians] are at their worst when trying slavishly to reflect the humors of the whites. Lincoln freed the slaves but their dark descendants of Broadway do not yet know what to do with their freedom. And not having as yet hit upon an effective kind of revue humor of their own, they still need a white mind to guide them . . . What couldn't they do if they were content to be black? And knew how! They are colorful as their skins. They are "naturals."

In this critic's mind, whites knew best how blacks should appear on stage. If they'd only be content to stick to their "natural" roles they would succeed. Inherent in this critique is that Leslie—as the white "overseer" of the production, if you will—failed to rein in his actors: "He could have given birth to a Negro 'Follies,' or something blacker and deeper and more pungent . . . [ellipsis in original] if he had a finer imagination."[17] In a newspaper interview given at the time, Leslie echoed this racist sentiment that white men "understand the colored man better than he does himself."[18]

This was the toughest of all the reviews of the Brooklyn production; most agreed, however, that the show could use some trimming (it ran past midnight on its opening night) and that the satires of current Broadway hits could particularly benefit from being shortened. Given Leslie's constant need to "improve" the show, Eubie was not surprised when the producer immediately began reworking the show after its opening night:

The show opened in Brooklyn at the Majestic Theater. . . . The *Brooklyn Eagle*, the man says, "I feel sorry for the people that didn't see the show tonight. It's the most beautiful thing and put together perfectly. But it won't be that way tomorrow night. Because—as I know Leslie—he's going to tear it apart." And don't you know, when the curtain come down, "Nobody leave. Rehearsal at 12 o'clock." And [he] tore it apart.[19]

After Brooklyn, the show played Boston for further tryouts. The critic in the *Boston Post* was far more enthusiastic about the show and its reception, saying "number after number stopped the show." He was particularly impressed by Eubie's work in the orchestra pit:

Blake played one of the two grand pianos in the pit, with his own orchestra augmented to the number 30 by white players drawn from the local union forces. And it fell to Eubie Blake, performing from the piano, to sweep the house into a frenzy of applause when he and Miss Waters did the reprise "Lucky to Me" . . . Not since the memorable days of that famous first entrance of the chorus of "Shuffle Along" has a number in a colored show made as great a hit.[20]

It is interesting to note that the orchestra was integrated in Boston—perhaps out of necessity, but still an unusual decision for the period.

Leslie was already shorting the salaries of his principals during the tryouts. In his personal journal, Razaf complained about his difficulties collecting his weekly royalty payments, lamenting that, nonetheless, he also had to work overtime to fulfill Leslie's demands for new material. "Imagine, the writer of a show and a total stranger in Boston, worse off than any chorus girl," he privately lamented.[21] At the end of the Boston run, Leslie sent Eubie a royalty statement noting that the composer was owed $666.64 in back royalties (about $10,000 in today's dollars) to date for the production.[22] Ethel Waters wrote, "The show started off by almost being stranded in rehearsal. Leslie was splitting up quarters each day among the cast so they wouldn't have to walk home to Harlem."[23]

The show finally opened in New York at the Royale Theatre on October 22, more or less unchanged in length or format since it originally previewed. Not surprisingly, the New York critics were most impressed by the show's dancing and least by its comedic sketches. Brooks Atkinson, writing in *The New York Times*, saw little to recommend it beyond the dancing, faulting even the songs as being "tepid Tin Pan Alley tunes." As did most other critics, Atkinson wanted to like the blackface comedy, but was ultimately disappointed:

> Even when they have no material at their disposal Negro comedians promise well. Black as the ace of spades, with those enormous white circles around their lips, they have questioning eyes which flutter and roll with comedy eloquence. Flournoy Miller, tall and brutal, and Mantan Moreland, his frisky satellite . . . [are] suitably raffish. But the skits they have to perform have little racial humor to enliven them, nor humor of any color.[24]

Once again, Atkinson raised the question of whether black performers should "remain faithful to Negro characteristics or should abide by the white man's formula for stage diversion." He noted that "even the best Negro shows we have are predominantly white in their direction"—ignoring the fact that *Shuffle Along* was produced entirely by a black creative team.

The reviewer for the *New York Telegram* was even blunter in his appraisal of the show's appeal. Under the headline "Spirit of Jungle Drums Dominates New Revue," he opened his review with a long paean to the show's dancers and their "natural" sense of rhythm:

> Rhythm. Rhythm. All Gods chillun got rhythm. At the Royale, all Lew Leslie's Blackbirds got rhythm, too. Rhythm that's born, not made. He's got rhythm. She's got rhythm. They've all got rhythm there together . . . The intoxication of their rhythm fills the theater, fills the hearts of the spectators, fills a deep, dark hunger they will not acknowledge, even to themselves.[25]

Again faulting the show's book and music, the critic continues his theme, noting that "silly words and empty tunes cannot destroy [the allure of its rhythm]. A far too-ardent orchestra leaves it unharmed." Although he singled out for praise Waters, the Berry Brothers, and even Eubie Blake, it is only for their mastery of "rhythm," not for any other qualities.

Percy Hammond acknowledged the show's key attractions in his review that was aptly titled, "Glorifying the American Negro": "The dusky young women of the ensemble sing well and undress successfully; and the dancing is rhythmic and acrobatic."[26] Sexy outfits and happy feet were what drew the white businessmen who made up a large swathe of Broadway's audience.

One critic at least had a more progressive view of the black stereotypes in the show. Richard Lockridge, the critic for the *New York Sun,* wondered why

[y]ou take a Negro, apt to have naturally certain qualities which the white race cannot acquire, and Black him up. You lay on his dialect with a trowel— and with no closer relationship with the actual dialect of the Negro than may be found in the phonetic idiosyncrasies of the average white writer about him. You tell him it is funny to twist words, using, for example, "evict" in place of "convict," which ninety-nine times out of a hundred, it isn't. You make him, in short, a bad imitation of what was not a very good imitation in the first place, and you tell him to make the people laugh. He—and I shall never know why—believes you.[27]

One addition made in Boston would prove controversial—at least to the critics—in New York. Waters had enjoyed a hit in 1928 with the song "My Handy Man," a slightly ribald blues number written by Razaf in which she bragged about her lover's amorous capabilities; the song itself was a takeoff on an earlier double-entendre blues. Leslie may have requested a follow-up, which Razaf produced as the clever "My Handy Man Ain't Handy No More," in which Waters now complains that her lover has seemingly lost his previous pep when it comes to serving her needs. The *Brooklyn Daily Eagle* reviewer— noting that the show was little improved since its tryout there in September— lambasted the song on the show's return to New York, calling it "probably the dirtiest song Broadway has heard since the demise of burlesque."[28] While this type of song was acceptable on record or in nightclubs, it was not appropriate for the Broadway stage, at least in the minds of white critics. The same news- paper picked up the theme a few days later in a short article on Waters, under the lurid headline "She likes to sing something sinful":

Ethel Waters, who changed the torch song into a scorch song, could do quite readily without her handy man. Nor is this amenability to separation at all due to any of the failings that she ascribes to him these evenings in Lew Leslie's "Blackbirds" . . . She just doesn't care whether her songs have a double meaning or not. They are included in her repertoire only in obedience to what she believes is a popular demand.[29]

While noting that Waters herself "prefers the simpler, unblushing emotions of her own people's folk songs, particularly the abiding faith of the spirituals," she was forced to focus on "leering type of ballads" that the "American public wanted." With unhidden distaste, the author commented, "Colored entertainers everywhere found that the broadest sort of suggestive lines when put over with a straight face were the surest road to popularity and big time contracts." With both of Razaf's songs, Waters was building a reputation for singing suggestive numbers. But some critics were not as judgmental of Waters's racy numbers; *Dance* magazine's anonymous critic thought "her impish grimaces and her casual jollity slip over many a wisecrack that might be objectionable under less infectious guidance." Earlier black productions went out of their way to present themselves as suitable family entertainment, avoiding even the hint of sexual humor. It is clear that this rule was no longer applicable to producers like Lew Leslie.

Not surprisingly, the critic in the African American paper *The New York Age* was more positive about the show, its songs, and its humor. He even thought that Waters performed the "highly suggestive" "Handy Man" "with such artistry as to raise it up from its native mud and give it some semblance of decency." This reviewer praised Waters as "the outstanding delineator of uptodate [*sic*] jazz," and even had kind words for Flournoy Miller, finding his comedy "more striking than ever."[30]

While agreeing that the show lacked humor, the *Chicago Defender* countered the argument that it was a "carbon copy" (pun perhaps intended) of white shows:

> No white chorus could ever dance like the one in Blackbirds; no white singer could put the same expression in her songs like Ethel Waters and few of Ethel's own race can equal her; no score could be played with the same rhythm that Eubie Blake with his orchestra plays . . . Blackbirds cannot be called a copy of any white revue.

Surprisingly, though, this critic agreed that some of the humor was "too dirty for an average audience which would include children."[31] Solidly middle class, the black papers worked hard to promote a more refined image for the race.

Initially the show did well in New York, and Eubie received his weekly salary (more or less) on time. However, by late October his official salary was cut to $165 a week and he was collecting only $65 of that amount; in December his pay was again cut to $125 a week. Oddly, he was paid in full for the remaining dates in January, according to his own account books, perhaps as a means of keeping him with the show, as it was clear the production was floundering.[32]

The show produced two major hits for Razaf and Blake, "You're Lucky to Me" (Figure 8.2) and "Memories of You." Razaf's lyrics for "You're Lucky to Me" take many twists and turns, as he approaches the punchline/chorus that his superstitious need for voodoo and good-luck charms to bring him happiness in life are allayed by his newfound love. Eubie's melody similarly follows an unusual wandering shape as it works its way to the main theme, perfectly suiting the lyrics. The song's chorus's unusual chord progression was admired by Waters herself, who said she had never sung anything like it previously.[33] Her 1930 Columbia recording (with "Memories of You" on the flip side) is taken at a moderate pace, with Waters initially accompanied by a syrupy orchestra, before she offers a more jazzy take on the lyric accompanied by a piano, bass, and drums, with the full band rejoining for the finale. After her initial crooning style, Waters's voice becomes slightly more throaty, adding a few growling touches. Still, this is fairly tame compared with Louis Armstrong's version recorded the same year. Armstrong had a big hit with his recording in a full swing-band arrangement. His singing of the chorus emphasizes its offbeat charm, with slight delays and dramatic pauses underscoring the witty lyrics.

The song's publisher, Elliott Shapiro of Shapiro Bernstein, was concerned that the lyric's mention of the unlucky number thirteen might limit its appeal. In a typically witty response, Razaf wrote a letter defending his wording, while also offering to make changes if necessary:

Dear friend Elliott:
First of all, I want to make it clear that you are the boss if it will make you happy to change the line referring to "thirteens," I shall do so.

However, you've never known me to be a "yes-man" or one who would prostitute his art for the sake of gain, so I must say that, having more mentality than "the couple of chorus girls and boys" who, you allege, walked out on one line in question, I honestly feel the song should remain as written.

I'm sure you'll agree that few know how to evaluate the lyrics of a song better than Lew Leslie or Ethel Waters and, last but not least, the public.

Figure 8.2 Razaf and Blake's song "You're Lucky to Me" from *Blackbirds of 1930*. The song's publisher was originally concerned that the song's mention of the (unlucky) number 13 would limit its sales.

All three enjoyed and applauded LUCKY TO ME and the "THIRTEEN" line never failed to register! That "thirteen" is unlucky, is a national superstition, that's why you never see 13 on a door, but the compromises: 12½ or 12A etc. Now, when I tell my loved one that you are so "Lucky to Be Me" until I even defy the superstition and not only write one thirteen on my door but cover my door with them, no one needs a college degree to understand the meaning and vitality of the line!

Brown, Hammerstein or Porter would have used the line and rated a big Bravo! (Smile)

Well, enough of this (you know we must have our usual friendly exchange of words) and back to business:

Your "horseshoes" is a good suggestion so I would offer this line: "I'm painting horseshoes all over my door."

Here are a few more to ponder over:

I

"Nothing but rainbows and clover in store."

II

"Bluebirds are nesting up over my door."

III

"You've sent Good Fortune to Knock on my door."

Or

"Good Luck is written all over my door"

Since I have thrown you a line or two for some song you asked me to pass on, on several occasions, gladly and gratis, a similar favor can be done for me, should you not care for any of the lines I've submitted.

But I hope you will reconsider and pass "Lucky" as is!

Best wishes and

Cheerio

Andy Razaf[34]

Armstrong also covered the show's other major hit, "Memories of You." The song was originally sung by the show's second lead, Minto Cato. Cato was Razaf's girlfriend at the time, and the two apparently planned to get married, although that never happened. Eubie found her to be decidedly low class, noting "she wasn't a girl . . . that I would take to marry like that."[35] He also was dismayed by her heavy drinking. Oddly, Waters, not Cato, made the first recording of the song in August 1930. She says in her autobiography that she was imitating the popular warbling style of Rudy Vallee in her performance, and indeed her exaggerated enunciation and totally unsyncopated reading of the lyrics is much in the style of this popular crooner. Eubie would later regret crafting the song specifically for Cato, saying the song's wide range limited it to a select group of performers. Nonetheless, in the mid-1950s, it was revived as an instrumental by Benny

Goodman, becoming a major hit. Along with "I'm Just Wild about Harry," it became Eubie's most reliable royalty producer.

Although he did not write the lyric, Blake claimed "Memories of You" was inspired by one of his other short-lived love affairs, this time with a woman in Chicago who was two-timing her own man. Eubie told Al Rose,

> It was a girl I was going with, she gave me the title [of "Memories of You"]. . . . She told me she was going with a fellow, and said she was going to be back at 2 o'clock, and at 2 o'clock she didn't come back. And Broadway Jones come in and says, "Hey Blake, where's your old lady?" Damn, I hate that word. "It's half past two, Blake, where's your old lady," kidding you see. . . . And I know I was wrong. And I know she was going with the guy and I'm cutting in on the guy.[36]

The heartbroken Eubie noted to Rose, "I told you men can't take it; they can give it but they can't take it."

Despite the quality of its music, the show closed in December after only 57 performances. In her memoir *His Eye Is on the Sparrow*, Waters ironically noted "Blackbirds opened . . . right next to the flea circus. Our show was a flop, and the fleas outdrew us at every performance. The depression came in and made our business worse. But it didn't dent the take of the flea circus at all."[37] A short road tour to Philadelphia followed—where the show had a strong showing, at least according to the local press. Nonetheless, Leslie's shaky finances were catching up with him, and Flournoy Miller had to take the unusual step of putting an attachment on the box office in order to collect his royalties for the script. Leslie suffered the indignity of being arrested by a local judge, and had to raise enough money for his bail.

Scheduled to go on to Baltimore and then Washington, the show took a detour to Newark, New Jersey, where finally it all fell apart. Working behind the scenes to secure the sets and costumes, Leslie confidently told the cast that the tour would continue, although the *Amsterdam News* reported that "many [members of the cast] did wonder about the roundabout bookings." This reporter sadly noted that "Leslie simply found himself in the position of many white men backing colored shows before, and turning everywhere in a frenzy to extricate himself from the depths to which he was carried by the failure of the 1930s edition of his show, he is said to have made promises which he could not live up to." The cast realized that "as near as Washington as they would get this trip would be Washington Street on the way to Harlem."[38]

With the cast stranded and broke, there was little anyone could do but to make their way back home. Waters mused, "The back of my car almost broke down under the weight of all the entertainers I drove back to Harlem with me."[39] A revue titled *Lucky to Me* ran briefly at Harlem's Lafayette Theatre in mid-February 1931 with many of the same cast members and songs, although Eubie's orchestra was no longer associated with the show.

Blake also suffered from Leslie's financial woes. Working through the American Federation of Musicians (AFM), Blake tried to collect the salary and royalties he was owed on the songs from *Blackbirds*. He made his initial claim in June 1931, stating his other professional obligations had delayed his filing because he was working such long hours. In a follow-up letter, Eubie outlined his claim:

> I am sending you a salary list for the amount of money I have coming to me from Mr. Lew Leslie when I was with the *Blackbirds of 1930*. To which you can see from said list is $800.00.
>
> Now in addition to this I was to receive a royalty of my song writeing [*sic*], also to which has never been paid, now please let me know if I should send you a copy of that list also, for I have only recovered two payments on my royalty'es [*sic*] while working with the show, amounting to the sum of $145.80.[40]

By mid-1933, Eubie had received only $500 of the $800 that he said he was owed by Leslie. Eubie wrote again to the AFM, saying that Leslie had indicated that this was the last payment he was going to receive and asked them to investigate further. His union representative replied, "[T]he reason you were told no more money would be paid out on the Lew Leslie account, is that there is no more money left, and we cannot collect anything from Leslie until he again goes back into production."[41] Weeks later, the union reported that Leslie's 1933 production was apparently a bust, but that "we have by no means marked this claim as uncollectible and I assure you that as soon as the opportune time arrives we will enforce collection of the balance."[42] While Shapiro Bernstein paid their (small) royalty to Eubie, he doubtless never collected either the balance of his salary or the royalties owed by Leslie. This situation was not at all unusual for Eubie, who had to rely on a show's success—and the honesty of its producers—to be able to collect what was due to him. Invariably he was paid less than was promised, even at the height of his success.

Although the chronology is not entirely clear, it appears that Blake and Jones worked again on the West Coast with the Fanchon and Marco organization in late 1930 through early 1931. While in Los Angeles, Blake reconnected with Lottie Gee. By this point, Gee was drinking heavily, something that Blake could not accept. She also demanded that he be monogamous, something Blake was loathe to do. Blake could be remarkably cold hearted when he decided to end an affair, as he told his biographer Al Rose:

> Once you hurt me, I don't hurt you. I don't want no more to do with you. I'm not going to do nothing to harm you. I'm not going to help you either. You be overboard and you's drowning, I'm gonna hand you a lead pipe something to catch onto. I don't do nothing for you no more. My father was that way.

Eubie concluded ruefully, "I'm trying to break myself of that."

Gee was preparing for a tour of China with another ex–*Shuffle Along* star, Edith Spencer. Eubie wrote some material for them to perform. Apparently, while they were abroad, Gee suffered from a breakdown:

> She's singing in Shanghai. And you know how they've got two bars of music playing and there's no singing? Well, she starts right in to singing. . . . And Edith says to her, "What the hell's the matter with you? You crazy?" And bing!—She went right off. They took her off the stage.

Documents on her return to Los Angeles note that her permanent address was a "Psychopathic Ward," with the word "Insane" written next to her name.[43] Her hospitalization may have been to treat alcoholism or mental problems, or perhaps both.

Eubie's final encounter with Gee occurred shortly afterward in New York. Again, Gee suffered from a breakdown while singing on stage, inspired by Blake's presence in the audience:

> She [was] singing at the Nest at 33rd Street. And somebody told me to go down there. And I know she's going to break down, but I don't think she's going to break down on stage. She's singing "Lover Come Back to Me." And I come down the steps, and she's on the floor singing. . . . And she got to that line and she sing it, "I remember every little thing you used to do," and I looked at her, and a tear come in her eye. "I'm so lonely. . . ," and she sing

it once, and then she sings the melody again, and she fell out on the floor. Ain't nobody in there, and [she] hit her head on the table. . . . And she's laying out there, dead as a doornail. And I got some spirits of ammonia and brought her to.[44]

This was the end of their relationship; Blake expected his girlfriends and wives to support him, not vice versa. Gee worked sporadically through the 1930s in the Los Angeles area. She was employed by the local Federal Theater Project during the later 1930s, but by 1940—when the census gave her occupation as "singer"—she was unemployed.[45] There is no further record of her performing and eventually she remarried in 1967, and died in Los Angeles on January 13, 1973.[46]

The early 1930s was also the beginning of the so-called big band era, and many black composers/performers were beginning to achieve success leading bands, including Fletcher Henderson, Duke Ellington, and Cab Calloway. From his work in *Shuffle Along* and subsequent productions, Blake had established himself as a Broadway conductor, and also had played private dates for wealthy patrons. Hoping to ride the popularity of other African American bands, in April 1931 Eubie signed a one-year contract with agent Harry A. Romm. Romm was confident he could get Eubie's band dates and also arrange for a recording session with Victor and a spot on radio." In May, Romm booked Eubie and his band on a dance tour, guaranteeing him the first $1000 in receipts, with the remainder to be split 60-40 between Blake and the agent.[47] Romm also promoted the band to Eli Oberstein, head of Artists and Repertoire (A&R) at Victor, who attended one of Blake's shows in Philadelphia, as well as Jack Shiffman, the owner/booker for the Apollo Theater in New York. Before sending him out on the road, Romm warned Eubie to "get someone you know to stay in [the] box [office] to see that you do not get the worse of it"—as dance promoters were likely to underreport the attendance in order to pocket a bigger profit. Indeed, by late May, Romm was writing Eubie in desperation trying to collect his share of the proceeds, while also lamenting that the band was not drawing as well as he had hoped.

A few contracts survive in Blake's papers to suggest that his nightly guarantee was low (between $150 and $200) for the 12-piece ensemble, against either 50 to 60% of the box office earned. A handwritten note on one contract indicated that for that particular night Blake collected $500.[48] A typical date for Eubie and the orchestra occurred July 4 at Fernbrook Park, a small amusement park in Wilkes Barre, Pennsylvania. The Park's shows varied in content and quality; the night before Blake played there, a "novel evening" was presented, featuring "plainsmen engage[ing] in rustic dances." In announcing the dance, the park noted that "the reputation of the colored orchestra is nation-wide." In other words, white patrons were amply forewarned that the band was led and staffed by African Americans. Blake's band provided music for the Fourth of July festivities, along with Broadway Jones's "splendid vocal numbers and . . . eccentric dancing." [49]

Just as with the *Shuffle Along Jr.* tour, Eubie was a poor business manager, unable to navigate the shark-infested world of small-time promoters. Eubie couldn't keep track of the cash payments and complained to Romm about the problems he was having with collecting the fees. Blake also took little pleasure in trying to keep tabs on the orchestra's musicians, who were often late to gigs, were drunk, or failed to show up at all. Eubie shared his woes with bandleader Paul Whiteman, who told him that he too had trouble managing his band:

> Paul Whiteman was in my room, sitting there drinking my whiskey. . . . "I bet you I don't have 36 men in this band. I bet you I don't open without 18 or 20. The guys get drunk, miss trains and all." I said to him, "Do *white* bands do that?" He says, "Eubie, people are people. Same thing happens in my band that happens in your band."[50]

Eubie admitted to interviewer Al Rose that he didn't like leading a band because of all the problems of dealing with the individual musicians:

> I didn't like the band. I have nothing against the person that drink. The guys come on the show, I didn't want that. . . . I had a boy named George Richmond . . . everybody thought he was a white boy. He could play the piano. And I give him shots there to play. . . . The band would play a number, and I'd give him 32 bars, just the brushes goin', that guy could play. He was a tough man to follow. I'd go out and say, "Now ladies and gentlemen. This is the luckiest audience in the world to hear George Richmond to play the piano. This is the last week that he'll play with me." . . . I says, "George take a bow." Nothing, he didn't have nothing. The guy was dead. First thing he was drunk all the time.[51]

When Rose asked Eubie why he didn't feature himself on the piano with the band, he replied, "I'm a conductor, so I ain't goin' to play in the band. [When the band takes a break,] then I'd do my specialty." He saved himself for the solo spots.

Individual musicians could create problems for the band going beyond tardiness or being unprepared for a gig. Late one night, Eubie's trombonist, Calvin Jones, got into an argument with two other musicians and was stabbed; he subsequently passed away. The publicity reflected poorly on Eubie's band and furthered the notion that black musicians minimally consorted with—if not belonged among—society's lowest members. Eubie's concern was always to reflect well on his race, so this kind of incident was difficult for him.[52]

In 1929, Romm arranged for a session by Eubie and his band with Victor, resulting in a single side being released.[53] Romm next turned to the budget Crown label, which agreed to record the group. The initial agreement called for the band to report to Crown's studio 12 times over the next year to recorded four dance records on each date. Vocalist Broadway Jones was included in the agreement to record with the group, when available. However, he did not appear on any of the recordings; instead, white vocalist Dick Robertson was featured. Robertson had previously sung with society bands led by Roger Wolfe Kahn and others as well as recording under his own name, primarily for low-priced labels like Bluebird and Banner. Robertson was a plain vanilla tenor crooner, a poor man's Rudy Vallee, as opposed to the more spirited bass of Broadway Jones. It's possible that the label insisted on the substitution.

The band was to be paid $450 for the initial date (for Blake and 12 pieces), and $500 for those following; they would receive no royalties on sales. Blake was also forbidden to sign with "any other record [company] retailing for 75 [cents]."[54] (This would preclude recording for Columbia or Victor; so-called budget labels retailed their records at 35 cents each.) Blake recorded a total of 12 sides in two sessions in March and April of 1931 and a final session in September. The band included Eubie on piano along with favorites Calvin Jones on trombone and Leroy Vanderveer on banjo. They had all worked together, beginning with *Shuffle Along*. Other musicians included George Rickson, Ben Whittet, and Ralph Brown, who had played with orchestras led by Johnny Dunn, Charlie Johnson, and Fess Williams. The repertoire ranged from tepid hits like "Life Is Just a Bowl of Cherries" to standards like "St. Louis Blues" (with a cloying vocal by Robertson). The numbers were not written by Blake, and were played in the style of the "sweet" jazz of white bands like Whiteman's. Many of the arrangements sounded dated, such as a cute-as-pie version of "Two Little Eyes" that could have been recorded by a white band in the early 1920s. The piano solo on this recording doesn't sound much like Blake's other work, with the right hand playing a tinkling theme in the upper octaves against a muted left hand—which was nothing like Blake's normal powerful bass. It's unclear if Eubie is the pianist on the other numbers cut at this session. The piano is never featured, and there's little aural evidence of Eubie's personal "tricks" and touches that are the mark of his solo work. Whether these recordings represented the actual sound of Eubie's band at this time is not known, because presumably they were sight-reading stock arrangements on numbers chosen by the label. As Eubie's band was playing for theater audiences and at dances across the country, however, it's likely that they played a similar repertory in standard arrangements.[55] Typically for the time, the records were issued on other related labels to Crown under different names, including "Dick Robertson and His Orchestra."

Romm was less successful getting a radio job for Blake. The orchestra auditioned for NBC and CBS, with the African American press reporting that "big bank-rolled sponsors" were invited to the auditions. However, the majors apparently either couldn't find sponsorship for a black band, or were uncomfortable themselves with the idea—something that Eubie suggested in several later-life interviews. At year's end, however, an announcement appeared in the press that Blake was signed with "America's biggest radio distributors for a network series."[56] This "major distributor" was probably RCA, because an announcement appeared in the *Chicago Defender* that Eubie would start broadcasting nationally on NBC (the radio station owned by this major conglomerate). However, Blake himself claimed that NBC wouldn't use him on the air because he was black, although they did hire him occasionally to conduct for rehearsals.

While still on the road playing dance dates, Eubie was hired to conduct the band for a new Broadway production, *Singin' the Blues*, produced by Alex Aarons and Vinton Freedley. The producing duo had previously had success with white jazz-flavored shows like *Girl Crazy*, and were known for their lavish productions. While they wanted Blake to conduct the show, they hired the popular white duo of Jimmy McHugh and Dorothy Fields—who had written the songs for *Blackbirds of 1928*—to compose the music. Nonetheless, the producers included Blake's name in all of the promotions for the show, as if having him on hand added extra authenticity to their all-black production. This move must have been particularly frustrating to Eubie, who was shut out of an opportunity to compose for Broadway.

The show was to open mid-September in New York after a brief run out of town. In July, Freedley wrote Eubie to insist that he stop booking new band dates so he'd be ready to rehearse the show:

> In view of the fact that we shall have some new orchestrations and at least one new number it will be imperative for you to work on these prior to full rehearsals with the company . . . The engagements which you have already secured for the month of August will not interfere with your work in our production, but before accepting any further dates I wish that you would consult with me.[57]

Eubie, of course, had to keep working, as he had no other source of income. However, the offer from Freedley was good—$1200 a week, including the band—so he was willing to forgo some engagements to be available for the show.

Billed as a comedy-drama, *Singin' the Blues* followed in the wake of the success of *Show Boat* in dramatizing a story that was not usually the subject of musical comedy. The action was set behind the scenes at a "Negro night club" in Chicago, with the grim murder of its male protagonist bringing down the curtain on the performance. White critics were baffled by its blend of music and drama—particularly in a black show. The *Brooklyn Daily Eagle* critic repeated the racist trope that it was up to "skillful white producers" to capture the true spirit of African American life on stage:

> [The production] had the air of a thing in which skillful white producers had successfully harnessed the strange talents of the Negro actors, giving the Negro spirit a better setting than it has ever had in the Broadway drama before. . . . [Aarons and Freedley] were more likely than most to have the gifts needed for putting Negro entertainers over brilliantly. They have not quite succeeded, but "*Singin' the Blues*" is a good try.[58]

This critic found McHugh and Field's songs "not so fetching" as their previous more upbeat numbers, although he did note that "Eubie Blake and his orchestra play the[ir] tunes seductively."

Burns Mantle, writing in the *Daily News*, was equally baffled by the wedding of a lavishly produced "full-sized floor show" with its "man-sized melodrama." He saved most of his praise for the dancing, singing, and comedic elements that were common to most black shows, and least for the more serious drama.[59] It seemed that black shows, even under the hands of white producers, were best received when the plot was light and the feet were fast. The production lasted on Broadway only a little over a month.

Eubie's orchestra was also hired to provide the music for a revue led by dancer/comedian Bill "Bojangles" Robinson called *Hot from Harlem*. It played Atlantic City and Washington, DC, and perhaps other locations along the East Coast for a scattering of dates during August through December 1931. The orchestra's featured numbers were Blake's 1930 hit, "Memories of You," along with "Mississippi, Roll On." The show primarily showcased Robinson and his incredible tap skills, along with "a fast-stepping chorus of dusky damsels."[60]

Hot from Harlem served as the inspiration for a low-budget film, *Harlem Is Heaven*, that featured Blake and his band on the soundtrack. Robinson made his debut in a lead role in this feature that was produced in 1932 by Lincoln Film Company (a small black film company). It featured an all-black cast and was made for a black audience. The film included numbers from *Hot from Harlem* alternating with a rather stiff melodramatic subplot involving Harlem gangsters. The opening credits are accompanied by Blake's big hit "I'm Just Wild about Harry," but otherwise the music was not composed by him. Most famous is the sequence where Robinson performs his iconic stair dance, accompanied by Eubie playing solo piano variations on "Swanee River," his old show piece. Blake's sensitive and spare piano accompaniment leaves plenty of room for Robinson's virtuosic rhythms.[61]

Blake did get a chance to perform on film that same year in a short feature titled *Pie, Pie Blackbird* featuring singer/actress Nina Mae McKinney. She had been a chorine in Lew Leslie's *Blackbirds of 1928*, in which she was spotted by film director King Vidor. He hired her for his all-black feature, *Hallelujah*, which premiered in 1929. Because Vidor was a successful, mainstream director working for a major Hollywood studio, the film got a lot of attention, and seemed to forecast new opportunities for black performers in this primarily white medium. McKinney's performance was universally praised, leading to further opportunities for her in film. *Pie, Pie Blackbird* was released in early 1932 as a Vitaphone short. Eubie and his orchestra play a prominent role through this 11-minute film, which also featured the film debut of the then very young tapdancing siblings, the Nicholas Brothers. While Eubie's orchestra plays competently in a light, swinging style, they don't have a particularly distinctive repertory or sound.

The entire premise of the film is steeped in racist stereotypes; McKinney, dressed in full "kitchen Mammy" attire, opens the film while she is preparing to bake a "Blackbird pie" for her young charges, the Nicholas Brothers. McKinney's first number, "It Takes a Blackbird to Bake the Sweetest Kind of Pie," reinforces this stereotype. The "pie's" lid then pops open to reveal Eubie and his orchestra, dressed in full chef regalia, including baker's toques. After a grand introduction, including chord flourishes by the orchestra followed by a dramatic quotation from Liszt's Hungarian Rhapsody Number 2 played by Eubie, the band launches into his recent hit "Memories of You." This is the only Blake original featured in the film and the band takes it at two tempos: moderate dance tempo, with sweet trombone and muted-trumpet solos; and full swing time. The band then accompanies McKinney in the somewhat suggestive song "Everything I've Got Belongs to You," with McKinney adding a slight bluesy rasp to her voice from time to time and even doing some mild scat singing. The band returns with the hit " You Rascal You"—made famous by Louis Armstrong—with Eubie appearing to sing a verse (although the singer's voice was dubbed in later by an unknown performer). The film concludes with a tap number by the Nicholas Brothers with the band playing a muted version of "China Boy" behind them. Toward the end of the number, flames break out (perhaps the pie is burning in the oven?) and all of the performers are reduced to performing skeletons. This oddly disturbing image concludes the film.

With the Depression deepening in the early 1930s, opportunities for black performers and composers were quickly drying up. Sometime around 1932 or 1933, Broadway Jones told Eubie that even though he'd like to continue performing together, he could make more money working alone because he wouldn't have to split his fee with the pianist.[62] Through early 1932, Eubie continued touring with his band, but the guarantees were going down, the box office take were declining, and the costs of being on the road were eating up what little profits that he could earn. Costs also included buying arrangements, copies of scores, and of course agent's fees. Desperate to raise cash, Eubie had his wife Avis sell his mother's house (the title of which he had previously transferred to her and his adoptive sister); the house sold for $800, and the amount was presumably split between them. Soon thereafter, Eubie sold "all of my goods, chattels and house hold effects" to Avis for $500, perhaps as a means of transferring the money she earned from the house's sale to him.[63]

Times were getting tougher even in Europe—where in the late 1910s and 1920s black performers enjoyed better pay and working conditions than they could find anywhere else in the world. Noble Sissle, who had been working in Paris since the late 1920s, was not immune to the changing climate. Unable to find work in the off-season in Paris, Sissle brought his band back to the United States in early 1931 for a four-month tour of ballrooms and theaters. Speaking to a reporter from the newspaper *Negro World*, Sissle explained how he tried to straddle the line between the "noisy, slap-bang orchestra[s]" who rode the jazz trend and Paul Whiteman's "so-called symphonic jazz" that was just a more

> intricate interpretation by trained white orchestras of the simple Negro music which originated in the spiritual. The beautiful, haunting strains of the laments of a sorrowing, oppressed people run through this . . . music like a shining, silvery thread. When we move to the blare of the saxophone and the loud beating of the drums, we are delighting by the vibrant melody which lies beneath.[64]

Sissle was laying claim for his band to being the most appropriate interpreters of this music because—unlike Whiteman and his musicians—they come from African American roots. "If our orchestra is 'different,'" he told the reporter, "it is because we are different from the white man." The challenge for the "Negro orchestra" is to appropriately exploit their musical heritage. Sissle was naturally more attracted to the sweet dance music of his day, rather than the more raucous bands that emphasized bawdier songs and fast-paced dance music. For him, this approach would lead to greater acceptance and recognition for black musicians.

However, Sissle was facing the same economic realities that Eubie was on the road. Touring with an 11-piece band in Depression-era America was tough, and turnout (and therefore box office) was not always as good as expected—even when Sissle was able to collect from the sometimes fly-by-night promoters who sponsored their shows.

Meanwhile, Miller and Lyles had reunited, following Lyles's return to the United States from his year in Africa. Each of their follow-ups to 1923's *Runnin' Wild* were less successful, with their (white) audiences growing tired of their blackface routines. Ironically, their iconic characters and even entire routines formed the basis for a new hit radio program, *Amos 'n' Andy*, which featured two white actors portraying blacks. The show was a major hit, first regionally out of Chicago in 1928, and then nationally for NBC, beginning in the fall of 1929. It was so popular that in 1931, a rival network hired

Miller and Lyles to broadcast in the same time slot, hoping that "real" black performers could beat the imitators. Oddly, the white imitators won the battle of the ratings. Miller and Lyles even considered suing them for stealing their material.

Sometime in 1931 or early 1932, Eubie ran into his old partner, Noble Sissle, on the street. They were both desperate for cash and looking for a way back onto Broadway, so it was natural that their thoughts would turn to their past success with *Shuffle Along*. Meanwhile, Miller and Lyles were looking for a comeback vehicle, so as early as the winter of 1931 the four were in discussions about how to revive their hit for a new audience. Miller was soon at work on a new script, this time focusing on the iconic characters of Steve Jenkins and Sam Peck returning to their hometown of Jimtown, Mississippi, to open a molasses factory. Sissle would portray a local sharp (literally named "Tom Sharp") looking to take their money. Things were going along well until Lyles fell ill and unexpectedly died on July 28, 1932, of a perforated ulcer.

While Lyles's death put a damper on their plans, there were pressing reasons to get *Shuffle Along* back on the boards. Before the end of the year, both Sissle and Miller sought bankruptcy protection to deal with their creditors. Sissle's band tour had bled money, while Miller and Lyles's last Broadway production ended deeply in the red. Eubie was making do through band dates and the occasional job accompanying revues, including a short tour with white comedians Olsen and Johnson's show, *Atrocities of 1932*.

Their plight inspired comment in the black press, notably an article in the *Chicago Defender* by Edward W. Smith. Smith commented that "[s]trange as it may seem, the four [creators of *Shuffle Along*] tried their individual talent in the production of new shows, but they failed to click and the house was invariably dark after a short run." He noted that, following his death, Lyles's estate "had dwindled almost to nothing" and both Sissle and Miller "found solace in the bankruptcy court." Smith noted that some believed that the teams brought this tragedy on themselves by going their separate ways. He also wondered whether the largest share of the money generated by the original *Shuffle Along* went to "Nordic hands" and not to the creative team. Finally he noted that it was a mistake on the part of the show's creators to believe that " 'Shuffle Along' would pave their way for all future productions."[65]

Nonetheless, *Shuffle Along* remained their most famous show and Miller, Sissle, and Blake knew that it offered their best chance for a successful return to the stage. As in the past, to maximize their own profits, the remaining trio formed a new entity, Mawin Productions, to produce the show. Composer Will Vodery served as the secretary for the new organization, and also directed the choir and provided the orchestrations for the show.[66] While the principals provided the talent, producer George Wintz—who had licensed the original *Shuffle Along* for a series of tours in the Midwest—was the primary source of finances. Comedian Mantan Moreland was enlisted to take on Lyles's role and the script adjusted with "Sam Peck" now renamed "Caesar Jones." The action was now moved to "Jimtown, Mississippi," and the grocery store setting changed to the "U-EAT-'EM Molasses factory." Edith Wilson, Fay Canty, and Lavada Carter (Valaida Snow's sister) were hired to be the female leads and vocalists, and burnt-cork dancer-comedian George McClennon was prominently featured. Sissle and Blake composed an entirely new score, although some of these songs intentionally recalled their earlier *Shuffle Along* hits, including "Bandana Ways" (echoing the earlier "Bandana Days"), "Falling in Love" ("Love Will Find a Way"), and "Arabian Moon" ("Oriental Blues"). They also performed a second-act interlude of songs from the original production; other numbers, like the standard "St. Louis Blues," were interpolated into the show, as were specialty numbers by the various featured acts. Although not listed in the cast, Broadway Jones was featured on one number, "Waiting for the Whistle to Blow." Sissle's orchestra was employed to provide the music (perhaps to help him dig out of his bankruptcy) rather than Blake's, although Eubie served as its conductor and had a small speaking role. Blake was paid a salary of $250 a week to conduct Sissle's men.

The show previewed in Brooklyn in mid-November 1932. The reception was lukewarm, with one Brooklyn critic finding Sissle's acting uninspiring, although he praised the jazzy score, noting "the tempo of this new revue gets hotter than hot, until it crashes into a blazing finale."[67] The show toured for a few weeks, including stops in New Haven; Hartford; Wilkes Barre, Pennsylvania; and Albany, New York. The white critic in Albany revealed his bias in the headline for his review: " 'Shuffle Along' Shows You 'Why Darkies Were Born.'" Yet again, he focused on the "natural" talents of black performers and their eagerness to please their white patrons:

> Born to sing with a fervor that makes you tingle; born to dance like Mad Mullahs and with the fiery rhythm of a Congo rite; born to jest cheerily about themselves and to make play of work and give and give and give as if it was all great fun and they were glad you white folks liked it.[68]

After touring, the show—now titled *Shuffle Along of 1933*—opened on Broadway the day after Christmas, again to somewhat mixed responses. *The New York Times* gave it a tepid endorsement, noting "the book of this latest edition of *Shuffle Along* is no prize winner," and

> [t]here have been better colored shows . . . there has been more torrid music and wilder dancing flung against the vault of heaven by dark-skinned youths and maidens. But in times which can hardly be said to ring with gaiety and mirth, this show. . . will do to light—and heat—the theatre in which it resides. . . . All that a group of colored entertainers need is a wooden floor to tap on, a drum to beat and a liver-lipped boy with a trumpet to split the air at frequent intervals.[69]

Robert Garland in the *New York World Telegram* revived the age-old tropes that blacks should stick to hot music and dance, and avoid trying to emulate white Broadway shows:

> Like most dark-skinned entertainments, it is at its best when dancing, at its worst when trying to tell a story. The piece. . . is not all unworthy when it pulls itself . . . into the keen, clear air of blackface vaudeville. . . . To come upon it at its worst, you come upon it in an imitative mood, parroting the white folks with a "Falling in Love" or a "In the Land of Sunny Sun Flowers" . . . and a couple of other poor white trash numbers . . . For when "Shuffle Along of 1933" goes into whiteface it is pre-war musical comedy of a somewhat uninspired kind.[70]

While this complaint was common among white critics, Garland did hit on a fact that would dog the subsequent *Shuffle Along* revivals. Sissle and Blake were raised during the age of operetta, and the musical dramas that they admired most were created then; Miller's comedic roots were in the blackface era. Both styles were rapidly becoming outmoded and—particularly blackface comedy—slightly embarrassing. Their pre–World War I roots were limiting their ability to change with the times. As the critic in New York's *Daily News* noted, "After all is said and done, nobody wants Harry B. Smith back again,"[71] referring to the turn-of-the-century operetta librettist/lyricist. So the show was damned for being both imitative of earlier white shows and not up to the par of contemporary black revues.

Even the African American papers gave the show a lukewarm response. The *New York Age* found the book weak, describing the overall production as "credible [with] occasional comedy."[72] The *Chicago Defender* critic was more sympathetic, particularly focusing on George McClennon's show-stopping performance, incorporating movements that sound remarkably like those found in breakdance:

> McClennon . . . nonchalantly strolled out and laid into the hearts of the hearers, [with] the melancholies of the "Sore Foot Blues," playing a clarinet in a manner which, to say the least, was amazing. He also danced, spinning on his stomach and then to show his versatility, spun around while sitting down. All done with elaborate unconcern and yet with the suggestion he was having far, far more than unexpressed joy out of it than anyone watching him.[73]

The new production survived on Broadway only through January 7. It then moved on to Washington, where the *Pittsburgh Courier* reported it played to "large crowds" (perhaps exaggerating its success), and by mid-February opened in Philadelphia.[74] Critics there again focused on the music and dance, while finding the comedic scenes less compelling. The *Philadelphia Ledger's* critic commented, "As usual in most Negro shows the flying feet of the cast are called in when the story action lags." Like many other critics, the *Ledger's* writer found the songs less memorable than the original *Shuffle Along* score, although he did single out "Falling in Love" as the most likely hit. Critic J. H. Keen was perhaps the most outrageously racist in his response to the show. He dismissed the show's plot from the get-go, noting, "A story is about as useful to a sepia musical as a pants-pressing establishment in a nudist colony. . . . the story is the sort that is abundantly supplied with footnotes, if you know what I mean, and is, therefore, frequently laid aside for what is most descriptively labeled as hide-de-ho." He described singer Lavada Carter as "a torrid piece of baggage, who is far more inspiring when she is hide-hide-hoing, kicking her heels up around her ears and flipping her hips and tossing her torso in a mad rhythmic fashion than she is when she is enacting a part in a play."[75] While praising the music of Sissle and Blake, this critic obviously looked mostly for sex and shimmy as the key elements in any black production.

On the other hand, the critic in the *Philadelphia Bulletin* found the show *too* tame, focusing on the more old-fashioned numbers in its score:

> Those who like this brand of diversion and at the same time like to leave the theatre with their nerves intact will, no doubt, welcome the information that the current version of "Shuffle Along" is rather more subdued and disciplined than its predecessors. As a matter of fact, it occasionally seems almost too doggedly restrained.[76]

The prohibition against blacks emulating white musical styles continued unabated, while the desire for stereotype "ha-cha-cha" limited the possible palette for most shows. Sometime in the spring, the tour was temporarily stranded in Long Beach, California. Sissle left the production with his band, with Eubie's band brought in to fill the gap. It is likely that there was a falling out among the principals as the show struggled to make a profit. Sissle found work at New York's Park Central Hotel. He wasn't the only defector in California. The show's pianist was a young Nat Cole and he decided not to travel on to Chicago with the show.[77]

By the time the show reached Chicago in May, it had become more of a loose revue with the story pushed even further into the wings. However, it may have been too little, too late, as the critics remained lukewarm about the production. The white critic for the *Chicago Daily News* scolded producer "Ol' Massa Wintz" for packing the production with

> a bushel of extraneous skits, acts, ensembles, mobs . . . Ol' Massa Wintz . . . should take the book . . . and throw it out of the [theater's] back door . . . Then Ol' Massa ought to throw out about half of the play's supernumeraries after it . . . and go ahead on the plan of letting Miller and Mantan do their own chattering comedy, Eubie Blake play his head off in his own way, the chorus dance by itself, and above all, order the Boatner choir to quit showing off how swell it can sing German and make it instead, get down to Moses, the lonesome road and that sweet chariot which swings so low and so beautiful.[78]

The Chicago-based Edward Boatner Choir was known for its concert-style performances of spirituals and light classical selections. They were undoubtedly added to the production to help draw local audiences.

Even the critic in the *Chicago Defender* warned audiences that "you'll hardly rave over it as you did ten years ago."[79] He faulted the quality of the songs, the slim comedy of the plot, and even the singing of the principal players. Nonetheless, apparently the show did good business, so good that its original two-week run was extended to a full six weeks. While the show's white producers were finally able to make a profit, Miller and Blake felt they were being denied their fair share. They wanted to leave Chicago so they could tour the Midwest, where they could more closely monitor the box-office take. At the end of the sixth week, they took the company on the road against the wishes of their backers. Now reduced to a "tab" show—like the earlier *Shuffle Along Jr.*—the show played movie houses as an "added attraction" before the feature film was shown. The tour wended its way around mostly the Midwest through the summer and fall of 1933.

Apparently, Miller and Blake made an arrangement to pay Sissle $50 a week for his rights in the production for this tab tour. Meanwhile, there were still outstanding bills from the earlier performances, and Sissle was put in the position of having to settle with various creditors. In late September, the angry vocalist fired off a telegram to the duo, demanding payment at once:

> Per our agreement I expect fifty dollar for each week you play *Shuffle Along* this season . . . Remit same to my office immediately. Union just made me pay Shrimp Jones hundred twenty five of what our show owed him. That is about four hundred[.] You know I played more than fair with you both and you must pay or I[']ll use the same course that you know you will loose [*sic*] . . . Rights you know are respected by ligitimate [*sic*] circuits and courts. Answer my office immediately with payments. Hope you will save me taking action and continue successful.[80]

The tension between Miller and Sissle over the finances of this production would continue to color their relationship over the years to come. Typically, Blake didn't concern himself too much with the show's finances, and left it to these two more strong-willed men to work it out between themselves.

Miller faced criticism within the black theater community for failing to pay salaries to his actors. Of course, he faced the daunting task of overseeing the production, trying to collect receipts from white bookers, managing the shipping and set up of props and set pieces, and arranging for transportation for a large group of actors and musicians. Still, rumors flew among actors that Miller was profiting by shorting his actors' pay checks. *Pittsburgh Courier* columnist Floyd Snelson accused Miller of exploiting young women by promising them success on the stage without raising sufficient money to ensure its long-term success:

> [Miller rustles] girls into a show on a promise of pay, and after weeks of rehearsals and performances close[s] the show without giving them their salary or even carfare home . . . How can Mr. Miller expect these girls to live if they are not paid. What can he expect will be the end of a girl who is stranded 400 miles from home . . . no friends . . . but Mr. Miller's shining smile and EMPTY pocketbook? . . .
>
> Let Mr. Miller back up his wonderful stage dreams with money . . . sufficient to take care of the people he employs . . . and then when the show fails . . . send them home where he got them from . . . [Ellipses in the original][81]

In fairness to Miller, white producers—like Lew Leslie—also were known for stranding their companies miles from home when their funds ran out. The contemporary ethics of show business were certainly sketchy, but black producers faced additional obstacles; they were not able to raise much capital for their productions and had to rely ultimately on success on the road to make ends meet—let alone eke out a small profit.

By the time the show returned to Chicago in October 1933, Blake, Miller, and Moreland were among the last of the original cast still employed. Eubie served as master of ceremonies for what was essentially a series of vaudeville routines, dances, and songs, with Miller and Moreland performing short comedic sketches. Geneva Washington joined the show as the prime vocal attraction. Her features included "Chloe" (which she had sung in Lew Leslie's *Rhapsody in Black,* which was staged in 1931 and 1932) and "Tomorrow." The Sepia Song Birds (a Boswell-sisters style trio) and dancers The Three Brown Spots also performed their own established routines. The Chicago production was not presented in a legitimate theater, as was the case earlier in the year; instead, it was relegated to a vaudeville house on a bill that also featured "Pickard and his 'talking seal.' "[82] The company next played Sandusky, Ohio, and then reached Louisville, Kentucky, on Christmas.

Early in 1934, the show, renamed for the new year, but largely unchanged, opened in Pittsburgh. Under the headline "Piano Plinker Plunks at Pitt," the local reviewer praised Blake's work while finding the balance of the production uninspiring:

> A dusky fellow who makes a piano do everything but cook—and he gets it hot enough to do that—shuffles off with all the honors in [this] new show . . . Eubie Blake by name, he's orchestra leader and co-producer of the midget version of "*Shuffle Along*," and really good enough as a piano plinker to rave about. . . But he's alone in his glory. The rest of the show—well, its drawback, chiefly, is that while it[']s entertaining enough it's stale.
>
> About five years ago Negro orchestras with plenty of screechy cornets, tap dancers who bang instead of tap, and pell-mell syncopation was hot stuff. That was in the vo-do-de-do era, which followed the great ice age and melted the age.
>
> But now people who go to stage shows like hey-nonny-nonny. Vo-do-de-do is old stuff.[83]

New soubrette Delia Newson won special praise from the *Chicago Defender* critic, who noted, "This young lady, who is pep and verve personified behind the footlights has that 'something' which seems to reach into every corner of the theater and hold her audience spellbound." This critic faulted "our people" who were seated in "the far confines of the second-balcony" for failing to applaud the featured acts, while the whites in the crowd were vocal in their appreciation.[84]

The tour went on with more appearances opening for movie shows, bouncing between second-tier Eastern and Midwestern towns. It continued to lose money, so much so that even with salary cuts for the principals it was not breaking even. Harry Rogers, who had taken over as its producer, wanted to shut the show down in mid-April, despite bookings that extended through May. If they wanted to honor these dates, he wrote Miller and Blake, they should "wire me immediately that you release me from all obligations . . . and you have my permission to use wardrobe and scenery for month of May."[85] The show did go on, with Rogers presumably convinced to continue backing it.

The revue reached Harlem in September, and played Manhattan's famous Palace Theater in late November 1934. About this production, the *Billboard* critic asked,

> Can this be the once famous Palace or a tab house somewhere in the sticks? Looks more like the latter with the all-colored *Shuffle Along* unit

holding the stage. This unit has no Broadway standing. It is a cheap and very noisy affair . . . The music is just okeh [*sic*] under the baton of Eubie Blake. . . . Business was only fair at this viewing. Audience applauded the deserving spots, but in general kept quiet.[86]

The show continued through at least April 1935 (with the new year added to the title), but then Miller, Mantan, and Lavada Carter reunited with Sissle for an appearance in a different revue in Washington, DC.

In August 1934, Eubie wired Andy Razaf to let him know that the new Harlem nightclub, the Ubangi Club, had approached him about writing songs for their floor show. Blake noted, "They want you to write the lyrics with me," and urged the lyricist to come to New York as soon as possible. However, Razaf at the time was tied up working in a Chicago nightclub controlled by mobster Al Capone, so couldn't break his contract. The duo would eventually write a few songs for the nightclub, none of which were hits.[87] Meanwhile, Blake made another attempt to land a job on the radio. A show to be called "The Negro Hour" was pitched by NBC to feature "quality" black performers like the Hall Johnson Choir along with a major band. Initially, Listerine was to sponsor, but pulled out, perhaps fearing that a show featuring all-black performers might not play well in the South. NBC decided to stage a performance for potential sponsors to sell the show. Drummer Chick Webb and Eubie vied for the role of bandleader for the audition; ironically, NBC chose Webb's band but—untrained in conducting from a score—Webb could not successfully lead it to accompany the vocal acts that were planned as part of the entertainment. So Eubie was hired to conduct Webb's men. "Comment was loud and strong at the mysterious situation," reported the *New York Age*, "Eubie's men hollered, musicians on the street could not understand how Eubie could consent to lead a band that was in competition with his for a job, leaving his [Eubie's] own men in the street."[88] Apparently, NBC was unsuccessful in lining up a sponsor following the audition. Although he was pleased to receive a $75.00 fee for his half-day of work, Eubie blamed racism for their unwillingness to put him on the air. He said he overheard one technician muttering to another, "That's Eubie Blake. . . . Don't you know that's the guy that filled Broadway up with niggers before? Now you're going to bring him down here, see, and fill the radio up with niggers."[89]

The same month, Noble Sissle staged a mammoth pageant in Chicago called *O Sing a New Song* to celebrate African American musical achievements. Five thousand amateur and professional musicians participated in the performance, which was presented as part of the Chicago Century of Progress World's Fair. Sissle made sure to include his old partner Eubie Blake among the participants—who also included notable African American composers and performers Harry T. Burleigh, Will Marion Cook, W. C. Handy, Earl Hines, and Will Vodery—although exactly what part Blake played is unknown. This style of performance harked back to the 19th century, in productions that included parades, dance movement, song, and lofty sentiments expressed through a solemn narration to celebrate historic achievements in American life.

O Sing a New Song purported to trace black music from its African roots to its contemporary expression, although it traded on age-old stereotypes and corresponded with Sissle's own beliefs that blacks achieved their greatest success in emulating the "refined" music of Europe. Even black critics bought into this narrative. Writing in the *Chicago Defender*, Julius J. Adams praised the show for tracking

> the slow but certain transition of an ignorant, unorganized band of savages to a thrifty, intellectual group, coping with the highest cultural civilization of the West . . . Right before the eyes of thousands of spectators a veritable metamorphosis took place, transforming the jungle being, dancing happily to the weird, rhythmic sounds of the tom-tom to a gentleman dressed in the height of fashion tapping away to the most modern strains of music. The show was colossal![90]

According to Adams, the pageant's message to African Americans was that they should turn away from the "despair and discouragement" often expressed in the blues and spirituals and "sing a new song" celebrating "the stupendous progress the Race has made." While the pageant's overall worldview was old fashioned, to say the least, the performance drew 60,000 spectators to Soldier's Field and became a source of pride for Chicago's black citizens.

Around this time, Eubie took a job in the offices of music publisher W. C. Handy, working as an arranger as well as weeding through the submissions of would-be songwriters. He may have crossed paths there with Handy's secretary, Marion Tyler, who would later become Eubie's second wife, although Blake did not mention meeting her in the offices. In 1935, Handy published a new dance tune by Eubie, "Truckin' On Down," to cash in on the "truckin'" dance craze, with lyrics by Arthur Porter. Bandleader Teddy Hill was "cut in" to the royalties to encourage him to record it. Although it sold over 1000 copies, the advance to Hill ate up all of Eubie's royalties. Handy published another pop number by Eubie, "It Ain't Being Done No More" (with music co-credited to Gene Irwin, a minor composer who is best-remembered for cowriting the tune for "Five O'Clock Whistle," recorded by a number of jazz bands in 1940) and the light classical piece "Blue Thoughts," which sold a paltry 38 copies in its first year. Like most of Blake's works, "Blue Thoughts" featured several memorable melodic themes, but was dressed in the then-current harmonic wrappings of "advanced" music (similar to the work being done by William Grant Still and James P. Johnson in a classical style).

Blake announced in July 1935 to the *New York Age* that he was disbanding his touring band, saying "he was through with orchestra conducting and is confining himself to composing music." The paper speculated that "Blake will retire from the show business until some producer comes along with a sound looking proposition."[91] Never enthusiastic about traveling, Blake remained in New York, scraping up work on his own while continuing to be employed at least part time for Handy through 1936. Miller took yet another *Shuffle Along* on the road that year, without Sissle or Blake or their songs, featuring his daughter, classical harpist Olivette Miller. In the depths of the Depression, black theater was hanging on by the skin of its teeth. Little did Eubie realize that some help was coming shortly from an unusual place—the US government.

9

Government Worker

1937–1946

Eubie's career reached perhaps its lowest point during the Depression years, particularly from the mid-1930s through World War II. As work dried up for Eubie's band, he was increasingly spending time in his Harlem apartment, scraping along with small local jobs and continuing to push his own music and work on various prospective shows. Thankfully, Eubie was able to find his first full-time employment, beginning in 1937 with the Federal Theatre Project (FTP), an offshoot of the Works Progress Administration (WPA) designed to help struggling actors, musicians, and playwrights. This pursuit was followed during the war by about four years of work with the USO. Both positions were important lifelines to Eubie both as an artist and to support himself during these lean years.

Eubie's sympathy for the plight of others also blossomed during this period. Although it had now been about a decade and a half since Eubie became a celebrated figure in Harlem society, thanks to his success in *Shuffle Along*, he was still somewhat of a local celebrity during the 1930s. Local politicians and businessmen often sought his advice, particularly if their children showed musical talent. The Harlem chapter of the Elks attracted many prominent black actors and businessmen, including Bill "Bojangles" Robinson, who befriended a Republican politician and plumber and became the godfather of his daughter, Rosetta. She was born with rickets but showed an early talent for singing. Robinson introduced her father to Eubie, and the father in turn asked Blake if he could recommend a teacher to help Rosetta develop her talents. Eubie sympathized with the bowlegged girl, and offered to teach her himself and ensure that she could make her lessons: "Why don't you have her come over to me, it's one flight up so somebody's going to have to help her. Or I'll give her a special ring. Now you'll pay me 25 cents for an hour. And when you don't have 25 cents, you don't owe it. Is that OK?"[1]

Eubie Blake. Richard Carlin and Ken Bloom, Oxford University Press (2020). © Richard Carlin and Ken Bloom 2020.
DOI: 10.1093/oso/9780190635930.001.0001

Feeling sorry for herself because of her disability and dark skin color, Rosetta learned an important lesson from her teacher, who believed strongly that all people shared an equal humanity:

I'll never forget, . . . in the black race there has been a great deal of discrimination [among] the lighter brown, the mulattoes, and the darker brown. And so I used to feel that very bad. I had no self-esteem. . . I was just upset about it. So I always walked with my head down . . . Eubie noticed it. One day, when we were all done with our singing lesson, he said, "Brown sugar [Robinson's nickname for her], come here I want to show you something." So he took me to the back of the brownstone. . . . And he said, "Look at that lady's garden. What do you think?" "It's gorgeous Uncle Eubie, it's simply beautiful." And he said, "What makes it so beautiful?" And I said, "Well, you know all the different colors, it's just gorgeous, you know, all the different shades." And he said, "Yes, but what do they all have in common?" And I looked and I said, "Oh, yeah, all the stems are green." And he said, "Uh huh, now you hold onto that thought, because I'm gonna ask you something else." He said, "A team of doctors went through the world—now I didn't say the United States, I said the world—and [if] they took a little needle and made a little pinprick in everybody's hands, what would come out?" And I thought to myself, ""That's stupid," but I said, "Red blood." And he said, "Uh huh, now think about that. Do you know why?" And I said, "No." He said, "Because, we walking, talking, breathing humans are God's flowers on this green earth. Now just you remember that. And another thing you should remember that nothing blossoms, grows, unless the sun is hitting it. And if you want to blossom, you've got to stop holding your head down. Hold your head up. And by the way, if you don't let the sun hit you, you keep walking like that, you're going to end up with tuberculosis." Well, that was a horrible thing. I just straightened right up. I've never stopped walking with my head up.[2]

Later known as Rosetta Lenoir, she grew up to be a major force in the black theater and—as we shall see—had a chance to repay Blake for his kindness to her as a teenager when she conceived of a black musical revue called *Bubbling Brown Sugar* in 1976. The show was a major hit on Broadway and helped reintroduce the work of the major black songwriters of the 1920s and 1930s—including Blake.

In the depths of the Depression, the US government launched several programs to battle unemployment in many different industries. In 1935, this support was expanded to encompass unemployed actors, artists, musicians, and writers through a series of initiatives. One was the FTP, which was established specifically to produce new plays and musicals. To address issues of race and class, the Negro Theatrical Unit was established, with its largest branch operating from New York's Lafayette Theatre. This unit produced "serious" dramas, mostly on issues affecting the African American community, and reflected the FTP's generally progressive stance.

Although one might have expected Blake to have found work with the Negro Unit, it was as a successful vaudeville star that he joined the FTP. The Depression and the advent of sound films came together to put many vaudevillians out of work. This style of entertainment was also becoming dated, although there remained strong support for these acts, particularly outside of the major cities. The FTP set up a Vaudeville Unit specifically to produce traveling variety shows to play smaller towns and cities.

Blake said that he was initially approached in 1937 to work for the FTP by theater directors/producers Orson Welles and John Houseman and composer Virgil Thomson. Thomson had enjoyed success in 1934 with *Four Saints in Three Acts*, an opera with a libretto by Gertrude Stein that featured members of Eva Jessye's African American Choir. Jessye saw the production as a major breakthrough for classically trained black singers, noting that

> up to that time the only opportunities [for black vocalists] involved things like "Swanee River," or "That's Why Darkies Are Born," or "Old Black Joe." They called that "our music," and thought we could sing those things only by the gift of God, and if God hadn't given us that gift we wouldn't have any at all.... With this opera we had to step on fresh ground, something foreign to our nature completely.[3]

Welles and Houseman had just staged an all-black production of *Macbeth* in New York. Along with Thomson, they were interested in enlisting black talent into the FTP. Initially, Eubie turned them down, saying that he didn't want to go back out on the road. Instead, they convinced him to work from the New York office. Eubie claimed that he was "drafted" into working for the government, as if he had had no other choice. As a professional musician he may have felt the need to downplay how desperate he was for the work, and instead make it sound as if he had to serve.

Given a weekly salary, an office, and a secretary, Eubie was charged with auditioning performers for the different revues that were being sent out on the road by the FTP. Eubie recalled, "If an act came in ... to audition.... they'd almost drop dead when [the white office manager] told them, 'Well, you have to audition for Mr. Blake.'"[4] He took particular pleasure in auditioning a white vaudeville producer/performer who had previously insulted him by calling him "boy." Earlier in the 1930s, Flournoy Miller had introduced Blake to this performer, who wanted to hire the pair to write material for his revue:

> Miller says, "Mr. So-and-so, I'd like you to meet Mr. Blake, the composer of *Shuffle Along*." He says to me, "Wha-what is you, boy?" "Excuse me, I don't [owe you] a god damn thing," I walked out on $2000 for that. I walked out.
>
> [Now,] this man [has] got to come to me [for work]. Everybody knows him, big shot. He came in my office and I had a colored girl, secretary, he says, "Do you remember me?" I said, "Slight. Didn't you used to play the violin? What do you want now?" He says, "I'd like to get a job." I says, "Yeah, what can you do?" The man was a strong player. I says, "I know who you [are] ... everybody knows. Do you remember when I came in your office and you said, "'Wha-what is you, boy?'" He says, "Oh, I was just kiddin', man." But I gave him a job.[5]

Blake pretended not to "know" the man to see if he recalled their previous encounter. And, although he still was angered by how he was treated, Blake hired him, recognizing his talent even though he had insulted him. Even decades later when interviewed about his experiences with the FTP, Blake would not share the name of this performer.

Blake not only worked in the FTP offices but he also pitched songs for the revues that he was casting to the officials in charge of these productions. Blake had recently partnered with a new, younger lyricist named Milton Reddie. Reddie would become one of Blake's favorite partners whose clever lyrics rivaled those of Andy Razaf. Reddie also shared with Razaf a more developed social conscious and concern about issues facing blacks in the entertainment industry and the culture at large.

Joshua Milton Reddie was born on February 22, 1912, in Washington, DC. His father, Isaac Cornelius Reddie, was a minister in the American Baptist Evangelical (ABE) church; his mother, Martha A. Banks, worked as a domestic. Isaac also served in the Spanish-American War. Milton was the second of four children, one of whom died in childhood. His older brother,

Emerson, was about a decade older than Milton; he also eventually became a musician, listed as a "pianist" in the 1940 census. Reddie's education extended through two years of high school. By the time he was 25, Reddie was living in Baltimore on his own, while the rest of the family continued to live together.[6] How he came to New York and under what circumstances he initially met Blake are not known; however, Eubie had a soft spot for fellow musicians from Baltimore, so they may have met through their shared connection to that city. The earliest record of their collaborating is in July 1936, when they signed an agreement with music publisher Words & Music to publish two songs, "Readin' 'Ritin' an' Rhythm" and "Rock Church Rock," with no advance and a promised royalty of 3 cents a copy.

Once Eubie was ensconced at the FTP, the duo pitched songs for use in the group's upcoming revues. Eubie recalled that the process of presenting their material was demeaning to them, as they had to get each song evaluated by a white, classically trained composer: "This guy, he was a very fine pianist. And he'd look at my score, and look at the words, and look at Reddie, polish his glasses . . . After a while, he got used to seeing the both of us. It's a terrible thing to be told, all of your lifetime, from two years old, three years old, black is nothing."[7] Although Eubie doesn't directly say so, it's clear that this white composer judged their songs on the basis of their skin color and not the actual quality of the work.

Eubie was impressed by the quality of Reddie's lyrics. However, the FTP's managers were uncomfortable with Reddie's sophistication:

They would look at his lyrics and look at him. And his clothes didn't fit his lyrics, see. His English [was] perfect; he talked so fine it sounded like he was putting on airs. But he just talked that way. So when he writes, he writes that way.[8]

While Eubie said the duo contributed countless songs for the FTP revues, we know definitely of only three productions that featured their work: *Up We Go; It Happened in Harlem*; and *Attention Please*. For these shows, Blake also wrote opening and incidental music as well as music to accompany a dance sequence in *It Happened in Harlem*.[9]

Besides collaborating with Blake on songs, Reddie apparently also helped Blake in his work evaluating performers for various FTP productions. In February 1936, he wrote to Phillip Barber, the head of the New York office, about auditioning actor Clarence Carter for a production titled *Neighbors*

Will Talk. "Because of his handsomeness, his singing voice, personality and past experiences, we have chosen him as leading juvenile to play against Miss Rudy Richards," he reported to Barber.[10]

The most important work that Eubie and Reddie worked on for the FTP was a full-scale Broadway show called *Swing It.* The book was written by well-known black lyricist/playwright Cecil Mack, who also helped with the lyrics. Like *Shuffle Along* or *Blackbirds of 1930*, *Swing It* was somewhat of a pastiche production, with a loose plot that united the individual acts. Like *Blackbirds*, which featured several parodies of current hit shows, *Swing It* was also a parody of an earlier hit, in this case Jerome Kern and Oscar Hammerstein's *Show Boat.* Mack's book centered on captain Jack Frye who decides to bring his Mississippi riverboat (the Liza Jane) to Harlem as the centerpiece of a new revue. To add to the drama, a second riverboat captain—Nate Smith of the Susan Belle, who lost a race to the first ship—is determined to sabotage Frye's effort. Of course, setting the show on a riverboat allowed for individual acts to perform in a variety-type manner, suspending the plot for the duration of each act. For comic relief, a Miller-and-Lyles–type duo (here named "Rusty and Dusty") have various run-ins with the law and each other, all the while mangling the language. (Rusty comments on how a policeman wants to arrest them for "fragrancy.") Young lovers—like the leads in *Shuffle Along*—are thrown in to add a few plot complications and to perform the occasional love song, including "Ain't We Got Love," and the show's minor hit "Huggin' and Muggin'" (which had previously appeared in the revue *Attention Please*).

The first act of the show is set in Mississippi, giving an opportunity to present the "regulation cotton'-pickin' and Old-Man-River scenes," as a critic in the *Brooklyn Citizen* put it.[11] Blake and Reddie fashioned two "spirituals" for the play's opening, "Can't Be Did No More" and "Gimme My Dancing Shoes." These were performed by the workers on the levee as they loaded the ship. One scene is set in the "Cockroach Café," giving an opportunity for the specialty acts to perform, including four harmony singing waiters and a tap dancer. The female soubrette also performs the song "Green and Blue," lamenting that in her "greenness" (naiveté) she's fallen in love and had her heart broken, leading her to be "blue." The clever word play juxtaposing the meaning of the title words is typical of Reddie's reimagining of stock popular-song sentiments. The act ends with a blackface number, "Farewell, Dixieland!," which the crew sings as the boat sets sail for Harlem.

The second act opens with a production number around the song "We're the Sons and Daughters of the Sea." Various mishaps ensue as the evil Smith attempts to foil Frye's production. Eventually, though, Frye offers him half the profits from the show, so Smith is mollified. The act concludes with a series of revue-like scenes, one set in the "jungle" (and featuring the numbers "Jungle Swing" and "Jungle Love"), another, "A Symphony and Rhythm" tap interlude, and a final "Swing Wedding," in which the show's leads are successfully coupled off.

Blake made a deal with Mills Music for the rights to the score for the show. Of the many songs, only four appeared on sheets: "Ain't We Got Love?," "Huggin' and Muggin'," "Green and Blue," and "By the Sweat of Your Brow"—a "plantation number" featured in act 1. A royalty statement from the end of 1937 shows that "Huggin' and Muggin'" sold best, but earned Eubie and Reddie only $8.86 (at a rate of 3 cents per copy, this would be about 295 copies sold).[12] None of these songs were recorded at the time. The FTP paid a measly $2.00 per performance for rights to use the score. However, Eubie was able to collect an additional $95.44 per week as stage manager for the production.

Swing It opened at New York's Adelphi Theater on July 22, 1937, and played there through September 1. Ticket prices ranged from 25 to 55 cents. The cast was drawn on a large group of older black vaudevillians, most of whom had been put out of work by the advent of talking pictures. None of the leading stars of black music or dance were involved, perhaps because they could still find work in the commercial theater. While the cast won some praise for their energy and enthusiasm, it's clear that without a "big name" the show had difficulty finding an audience.

Lead Jack Frye was portrayed by (and probably named for) Eddie Frye, of the vaudeville duo of Moss and Frye. They were famous for their "How High Is Up?" routine, in which the deep-voiced Frye would ask a series of nonsensical questions to his partner, who would become increasingly exasperated by the impossibility of answering him. Jack Frye's nemesis, Nate Smith, was portrayed by another older black vaudevillian, Walter Crumbley, who had toured as a duo with Irving Jones on the Pantages circuit as the "Ethiopian Gloom Dispensers" in the early 1920s, and then appeared on Broadway in Florence Mills's *Dixie to Broadway* (1925).

Other cast members came from the journeyman ranks of vaudeville and the serious black theater. The lead comedians were Henry Jines as Rusty and James Green as Dusty. Jines had toured with Clyde Bates's *Broadway Scandals* in the early 1920s, a mixed vaudeville/burlesque review in which Jines was advertised as featuring his imitation of famed comedian Bert Williams.

Green's earlier credits are not known. Tenor George Booker had worked in various Harlem revues, and fellow tenor Joseph Loomis, who portrayed *Swing It*'s male love interest, had appeared on the Lafayette stage. Singer Anita Bush—who had a minor role in the production—got her start as a chorus girl in William and Walker's *In Dahomey* (1909). She was a major dramatic star at the Lafayette in the early 1920s and subsequently led her own stock company on the Bowery from 1929 to 1930. All in all, the cast was good but not exceptional. "You can like every one of them and are struck by no one in particular," sniffed the critic from the *Brooklyn Eagle*, although he admitted, "The girls are pretty."[13]

As a full-fledged Broadway production, *Swing It* was widely reviewed. As might be expected, the rather creaky plot and characters came in for much criticism. *The New York Times* critic noted that Cecil Mack is no "Walter Pater" and the plot "is on the haggard side." The critic correctly noted that the show was a mélange of various specialty numbers encompassing "minstrelsy, singing, dancing, mugging, clowning, spirituals, jazz, swing, tapping, and the carrying of Harlem's throaty torch." Nonetheless, the critic thought for a top cost of 55 cents, the show brought "infectious" fun from uptown to the Broadway stage.[14] *Billboard*'s critic was far less kind, pronouncing the show "a Turkey," noting that "*Swing It* dragged dismally except for a few minutes in the second act. . . . The best bit presents a cooch dancer in a jungle scene, done in an able, tho somewhat Minskyesque, fashion."[15] Even the *New Masses*—the official organ of the Communist Party—faulted it, finding the show stereotyped and old fashioned:

> There was a quality of that offensive old-fashioned style burlesque and vaudeville Negro comedy which attempts to derive humor from sallies at the expense of Negroes as Negroes—stupid remarks about their color and nonsensical slanders about their alleged unwillingness to work . . . As a whole, *Swing It* seemed to lack any real brightness, which may have been because it sprawled so loosely all over the place.[16]

Perhaps this critic was expecting a more "socially significant" production from the Federal Theater, as it was widely regarded as a progressive voice.

Even the black press was lukewarm in its praise of the show. The *Pittsburgh Courier* noted that opening night attracted a standing-room-only audience both from white and black New Yorkers who received the play well, although nonetheless felt the production was "far below par, but according to the applause of those who paid to see the many old-timers relive again before the footlight it was a darn good bit of entertainment."[17] *The New York Age* admitted that the show was "quite a trek from top notch material" but none-theless was "a fast moving vehicle" that helped bring black entertainers back into "the White Light District."[18] The *Chicago Defender* did not review the show, although columnist Bud Harris praised it as "a great show acclaimed by critics and the public" in a brief note in his New York gossip column.[19] This mention may have been just a bit of PR puffery to help boost attendance at the show.

The show's songs also failed to attract much praise. The reviewer in the *Brooklyn Eagle* found the Blake-Reddie score to be "agreeable" but felt it would "not sweep the country quite like a hurricane."[20] *The New York Times* concurred that "there have been snappier lyrics and more catching music."

Blake made one final attempt to squeeze a hit out of the show's score. In August 1937, black publisher Clarence Williams launched the song "Blues Why Don't You Let Me Alone?" from the show. (Perhaps because of the poor sales of the other published songs, Mills Music may have passed on this one.) The *Pittsburgh Courier* pitched in to promote it, running an article headlined "Eubie Blake Scores Again." In it, the writer urged customers to help popu-larize the song:

> All Negro music lovers should write to their favorite band leaders, radio stations and record companies and request this number. . . . By so doing, you will encourage future writers to write more of the music which you are now singing and which is being heard over the ether waves and on phono-graph records.[21]

Whether Eubie planted this plug or the newspaper ran it as a sign of affection for the older composer, it appears to have had little effect on the overall suc-cess of the song or the show.

After closing on Broadway, *Swing It* continued to be presented through early 1938, including a run at the Lafayette Theatre. However, it was far overshadowed in the public's mind by more successful efforts like the FTP's 1938 production of *The Swing Mikado*, which remade the Gilbert and Sullivan classic with an all-black cast. It inspired a commercial staging by producer Mike Todd under the name *The Hot Mikado*, which played on Broadway in 1939 and then moved to the 1939–1940 World's Fair.

Reddie and Blake continued to write for the FTP vaudeville unit through 1939. In February 1938, the unit produced *Showing Off*, a thinly plotted revue that featured 50 vaudeville acts ranging from violinists and blackface minstrels to "ballet" dancers. Reddie and Blake provided the score, which included a dance interlude titled "Sweetness of Love." Apparently, the show was produced on Broadway (on a Tuesday night—hardly an ideal situation) to respond to criticism of the vaudeville unit for presenting its work only in rural locations. *Billboard* gave the show a withering review, saying "the two act revue came close to being an old-home-week celebration, and might have been dubbed Vaudeville's Last Stand . . . Dirty costumes, long-winded lines, stale routines, and overworked jokes" were the hallmark of the evening.[22]

Meanwhile, Eubie continued to follow any lead—no matter how slender— that he thought might get his music back on Broadway. In January 1938, he wrote to Flournoy Miller (who had relocated to Los Angeles to seek work writing for the movies):

> A friend of mine, Eddie Parkes, who is well acquainted with Pat of "Pick and Pat," the radio team, has informed me that they . . . are anxiously in need of a writer. Naturally, I thought of you. Eddie has assured me that not only will they hire you as their writer, but they will also be interested in promoting a colored show.
>
> You know how we got Al Mayer to front for us with "Shuffle Along"— well, Eddie is another "ofay" in just such circumstances; broke but with good connections. We have discussed the matter, and he has mapped out some good plans for the formation of the corporation to book and write for radio, screen, and stage under the name of "Miller, Parkes, Reddie, and Blake."[23]

The white duo Pick and Pat were a kind of low-rent version of Amos and Andy; they had a national radio show from 1934 to 1935 on NBC and then were picked up by CBS in early 1938. Ironically, these radio comedians borrowed heavily from the characters originally created by Miller and Lyles and other African American comedians. Eubie typically jumped at any opportunity—even when presented by a producer that he admitted was "broke." Nothing apparently came of this discussion, at least as far as producing a new Broadway show.

While Eubie probably took the ups and downs of show business philosophically, the younger and less patient Reddie was becoming frustrated with the fact that black composers were treated so poorly by music publishers and promoters. While he also found employment with the FTP by teaching music classes, Reddie was hoping to break into the world of professional song-writing. Despite the quality of the songs that he and Blake were writing, they found few takers among publishers, bandleaders, or singers who could help promote their work to a larger audience. While Blake counseled Reddie to be patient, telling him "you have to crawl before you walk,"[24] Reddie found it demeaning to continually go hat in hand to the music publishers, begging them for a chance to audition their music.

To address the ongoing problems faced by black songwriters, Reddie, Blake, and Cecil Mack proposed forming a new organization to be called The Negro Songwriters' Protective Association. The idea was first floated in April 1938, when Blake sent a letter—most likely cowritten by Reddie—

> to every known [African American] band leader in the country in which the plight of colored song writers was expressed. At the same time [the letter stressed] the importance of the race to music and how it has played a great part in popularizing the songs from the pen of other writers while their own are allowed to die.[25]

While Blake felt strongly that black bandleaders had a responsibility to support the work of black composers, it is likely that Reddie was behind this letter-writing campaign. Blake was usually hesitant to take a definitive stand, particularly if he felt it might jeopardize his work in the entertainment world. Nonetheless, years of frustration and the collapse of the market for black music in the Depression—all the while the swing era was making white composers rich—must have been galling to the older composer.

A copy of the letter sent to Fletcher Henderson shows the hand of Reddie in its wording. In it, Eubie makes a case for bandleaders to promote the work of their fellow songwriters:

> For a long while I have felt the need to discuss with you the dilemma of the Negro song-writer and how you as an individual power are in a position to do much in this direction.
>
> As a band leader of reputation and long standing you, no doubt, are aware of the many hits the Negro professional and lay public have made. . . .
>
> Even in recent times you know how your recordings have brought sizeable royalties on songs *that have never been published.* You have done

wonders in popularizing "St. Louis Blues" and "Honeysuckle Rose"—both by Negroes. But why only these two?

Our forefathers gave the world rhythm and handed it down to us. Therefore, our songs and arrangements are superior in rhythm. Aside from the fact that our songs are swingier, shall we say, when a Negro performs a song there is a certain something put into it that the whites have failed to duplicate, try as they do. Pick any Negro band and singer at random, and they will run away with any inter-racial "Battle of Music." . . .

So you can see how necessary it is, Fletcher, for us as writers to appeal to you to play songs written by Negroes as much as you possibly can.[26]

The same text (with slight variations) was sent to other leaders, including Duke Ellington. In a letter to his old collaborator Noble Sissle, Eubie personalized his plea, drawing a direct comparison between the treatment of white and black songwriters:

Vincent Youmans has been inactive for years, yet they keep his works alive. Emmerick Kolin [actually Emmerich Kalman], Gene Schwartz [actually Jean Schwartz], Gus Edwards, and many more are also inactive—yet they too remain alive. So why not the works of Shelton Brooks, Fats Waller & Andy Razaf, Cecil Mack, Chris Smith, Cole & Johnson, and the many others past and present writers—including ourselves.

Whereas I have no actual proof, I wonder if Negro writers are being boycotted. It is very strange that such living writers as the aforementioned have ceased producing songs, and that there are few, if any, popular songs published written by Negroes.

What do you say we get behind this.[27]

Sissle apparently didn't reply or turned down Eubie's offer to participate in the new organization.

When publisher/songwriter W. C. Handy heard about Blake's plans, he sent him a note wishing him well but also pointing out the uphill battle it would be to unite black composers in one cause:

You have got to make Negroes mad. You have got to be in some position to show them how foolish they are before they will wake up and through organization it can be done. What you are doing I have been trying to do twenty years and without success.[28]

On the group's first meeting on July 31, 1938, Mack was appointed acting Chairman and Reddie secretary. The group noted, in the words of a reporter from the *Pittsburgh Courier*, that

> [s]ince the interviewing [*sic*] of modern music more than 15 years ago, Negro composers and musicians alike have been losing their birthright yearly. The modes in music which they have created have either been lost by non-usage or claimed by other races as theirs . . . To that in recent years has also been added the closing of former outlets for the work of many of the colored world's greatest song writers and musicians.[29]

Among those attending this meeting were Chris Smith, Irene Higginbotham (who published under the name Hart Jones), Shepard Edmonds, and Don Donaldson. Notables sending "regrets" included Handy, Andy Razaf, Ford Dabney, and Donald Heywood. Although the group had a few more weekly meetings through the summer, their effort appears to have fizzled out without achieving much in the way of improving black songwriters' lives.

The ever-entrepreneurial Reddie also proposed to Blake that they go into the song doctoring business. He drafted an advertisement and contract for this new business. The advertising card read:

SONG DOCTORS
HAVE A MELODY—OR A LYRIC—OR BOTH?
Let us doctor it and make it commercial
We will have your song copyrighted in your name
DON'T HESITATE   YOU MAY HAVE A HIT
Write for Further Information
J. Milton Reddie   Eubie Blake

The ad ran in the African American newspaper the *Pittsburgh Courier* and prompted several letters requesting further information. In a draft contract, Reddie outlined the terms for working with these amateur songwriters:

> Reddie & Blake do hereby agree to set words to music (reserving the right to us original title if we see fit), or music to words, or to doctor such words and/or music as _____(original writer) may have, who in turn agrees to pay _____dollars deposit and the balance of

the required fifty dollars ($50.00), which is to be paid C.O.D., upon receipt of _____(name of song). It is further agreed that REDDIE & BLAKE will have above-named song copyrighted in the name of _____ _____(original writer), will furnish one commercial copy of said song, and are then and there absolved of further responsibility and claim upon said song.[30]

One correspondent who sent them some material was Margaret Preston of Brooklyn, New York. Apparently she balked at the $50 fee that the duo were requesting to work on her songs. Reddie—calling himself a "Senior Partner" in the business—responded:

> After careful reconsideration of our first contract, we have determined that the original amount for which we asked is probably not in keeping with the present-day pocket, with economic conditions being as they are.
>
> Therefore, so that we may get better acquainted, with the hope that you will permit us to perform more service for you sometime in the future, we are temporarily reducing our rates to twenty dollars . . . This does not mean that your song will get less careful study or less competent doctoring. It simply means that after we please you the first time, perhaps we can induce you to be pleased again at our standard price.
>
> We sincerely hope that you will continue to be inspired and that someday you will create the year's most outstanding hit.[31]

Still looking for work wherever it might be found, Reddie and Blake approached a "Mr. Gallgaher" at Prosperity Pictures Corporation, located in Harlem, in the fall of 1938. Probably an ultra-low-budget operation, the company had produced the short film *Jungle Gigolo* in 1933, which was filmed "on location in Sumatra" and featured an "all-native cast." Presumably other features were made over the next five years. The duo had a meeting with Gallagher to discuss the possibility of writing music for the firm. Reddie followed up with a note in which he informed the producer that "after careful and deliberate thought, we have decided to apply for appointment to your Technical Staff, in charge of song-writing and other musical composition that Prosperity Pictures might require."[32] It's not clear from Reddie's note whether an offer was made or simply that the duo were hoping to win a spot on the company's payroll. In any case, there is no surviving evidence that they actually did any work for the firm.

During the 1930s, there was a movement among black popular composers to aim for recognition in the concert hall. Perhaps inspired by William Grant Still's 1930 *Afro-American Symphony* and by Gershwin's successful crossovers, most notably "Rhapsody in Blue," composers like James P. Johnson and Duke Ellington wrote longer, more impressionist works aimed to give their music "legitimacy" in the white concert world. Eubie seems to have been influenced by this movement in a few of his instrumental works of the 1930s, including the unpublished "Capricious Harlem" from the late 1930s and "Blues Classique" published in 1939.

"Capricious Harlem" is Eubie's most impressionistic piece, with three strains built around harmonic progressions straight out of the late-19th-century piano works of composers like Debussy. It is the least "Blake-like" of any of his compositions, and was obviously aimed at the ears of the classical music establishment. Although it was never published in his lifetime, Blake regarded the piece as a unique accomplishment, as can be seen as late as 1967, when he sent a copy to Elliott Carpenter for his evaluation. Blake had known Carpenter as early as the 1910s as a fellow working pianist; subsequently, Carpenter had turned his attention to classical study and composition, so his opinion would be highly valued by Blake. While Carpenter praised the craftsmanship of the work, he faulted Blake for straying from his natural talents to emulate composers like Gershwin:

> I received your composition CAPRICIOUS HARLEM and I think it is excellent. You have kept the Eubie Blake feeling melodically and harmonically as I know it thru all of your composition. Your first strains with the chromatic chords is beautiful and I like the decided change rhythmically in your second strain. There is only one criticism I have to make. In your third strain the Gershwin influence is very obvious, but why use the same musical device under those sustained chords as he did? The influence is O.K. but to use that same chromatic line verbatim that he has employed in his trio of the Rhapsody in Blue takes it away from the Eubie Blake creativeness. I am sure you can change it without disturbing the sustained chords. I am enclosing you a piece of script to show you what I mean . . .
>
> In all of your instrumental works for the piano they were decidedly original so do not let that originality slip by. Keep your works and compositions Eubie Blakey and let the composers copy after you. You have just as much originality as George Gershwin or any of the rest of them, in fact I think you have a little more because most of the Ofays borrow from one another just

as soon as a tune reaches popularity and that is the one thing most Negro Composers do not do. Maybe it is because they have not had the Academic training like their white brothers; so what they write comes right out of their souls.[33]

Carpenter's critique is spot on and indeed Eubie never again wrote a piece that strayed so far from his natural style.

Eubie's second attempt at writing a concert solo was more of a pastiche of pop and classical influences than "Capricious Harlem." "Blues Classique," subtitled "A Real Boogie Woogie," was published by black songwriter/publisher Clarence Williams in 1939.[34] In this work, Eubie plays with the popular boogie style, dressing it in "modernistic" chord harmonies along with his characteristic, showy right-hand descending and ascending slides. Although it has some charming melodies, Blake's decisions to link the more melodic sections through repeated, descending modulating chords gets pretty tired by the time the piece concludes, and the overall attempt to dress up boogie riffs in classical clothing is not terribly successful. Eubie's later recording of "Eubie's Boogie"[35] is far more successful in taking elements of boogie piano style and mixing them with more sophisticated harmonic progressions.[36]

All through this period while Eubie struggled to maintain his career, he was troubled by the illness of his wife Avis. Initially hospitalized in 1936, Avis had developed tuberculosis, which had no treatment at the time. She apparently had begun drinking heavily also during the 1930s, perhaps reflecting on her husband's continuing philandering and also the tougher financial times the couple were facing. By early 1938, she was institutionalized. Eubie wrote to Sissle about his concerns about her health: "[Avis] seems to be keeping alive only by my visits. Even when I happen to be late it upsets her considerably. I have declined jobs with my band because I dare not leave her for a single week."[37] Concerned that he may have caught the disease as well, Eubie was tested at the time and fortunately was found to be clear of infection. Avis lingered on and finally passed away on March 21, 1939. The *Chicago Defender* reported that "Mr. Blake, heart-broken, was unable to remain in the room when her condition approached the climax."[38] Although Eubie consistently had affairs with other women throughout his marriage, he relied on Avis as a constant stabilizing presence in his life. He always regarded her as superior in intelligence and better able to handle business affairs. He also admired her musical training, admitting that she had a deeper understanding of classical theory. Her loss was a considerable blow to him and he said he even considered retiring from the music business in his grief.

To add to his distress, Eubie was let go by the Federal Theatre on July 31 that year, ending his $90 a week salary. Eubie made several requests to ASCAP from 1938 to 1941, asking for advances against future royalties and showing his financial distress. To add to his income, Eubie played occasional dates near his home in the city with his band, including accompanying the famous Amateur Night at the Apollo Theater, for which the ten band members earned $10 each for a long night's work, with Eubie taking $20 as the leader. He also occasionally landed a job as a pianist with one or two other pieces and continued to publish the occasional song or instrumental.

Finally, Eubie further lost his spur to work when lyricist Reddie enlisted in the Army, and was stationed to Arizona. The urban-raised Reddie was somewhat perturbed when he encountered the regimentation and repetitive training of Army life; writing to Eubie in December 1940, he lamented,

> Boy, this Army is a humdinger. We get up at 4:45 a.m. (it's dark), stand at attention as the (flag) colors are raised (it's dark). Breakfast at 5:30 (it's dark), . . . Hell! When it does grow light our day has long since begun! I mean, begun!
>
> Then we have to drill, and then drill some more, and like the theme in Beethoven's Fifth, it's the same thing over and over: Damn! Of course, after dinner, we do quit at five and stand at attention as the colors are lowered (it's dark), supper at 5:30 (it's dark)—Then we all quietly faint![39]

Pulling him out of his doldrums in early 1940, Andy Razaf reached out to his old partner, suggesting they work together on a new show. In the late 1930s, Razaf had scraped by by writing lyrics for big band hits like Glenn Miller's "In the Mood." This hack work earned him a flat fee of $200 per song, an indignity for a songwriter who never before accepted a job that didn't pay a royalty. He found that even black publishers like Joe Davis were paying less per song than they had in the past. Desperate to boost his career, Razaf called on Blake, who was still grieving for Avis. According to Eubie,

> Avis had died the year before and I didn't know what to do. I didn't have any reason to do anything. Who was I gonna do it for, I thought. Then I decided. I was fifty-six years old and I wasn't going to be an old man. I had plenty going for me other people didn't . . . Least that's what Andy told me. He

kinda reminded me, you know, kicked me a little. "Let's work Eubie," he says to me and I thought, "Yeah, why not."[40]

The show they began to work on would open as *Tan Manhattan*, another amalgam of short skits, dance routines, leggy chorines, and song features in the style of the 1930s' *Shuffle Along* revivals and 1937's *Swing It*. Its title may have come from the popular gossip column of the same name that ran in the *Chicago Defender*. The show was produced by Irvin C. Miller, Flournoy's brother, who had established himself as a major promoter of traveling revues that combined vaudeville with burlesque under the name of *Brown Skin Models* and the related *Tan Town Topics*. Miller stuck to a tried-and-true format of pretty girls, novelty routines, and flashy dancing, touring smaller cities and towns to theaters that catered to black audiences. The book was written by Blake's long-time collaborator, Flournoy Miller, who would also be the comic lead in the production.

The show benefited from the inclusion of a higher-quality cast than *Swing It*, including singers Nina Mae McKinney (who had worked with Eubie previously in the film, *Pie, Pie, Blackbird*) and Sally Gooding. Tap specialists Evelyn Keyes and "Slim Bo" Jenkins were featured, while Vera Lang led the chorines. Avon Long, who had replaced John Bubbles in the original *Porgy and Bess*, performed the song "Sweet Magnolia Rose," a song that recalled Razaf's earlier hit "Honeysuckle Rose," which he wrote with Fats Waller. The show was directed by seasoned hand Addison Carey, with dances choreographed by tap master Henry LeTang and Blake leading the orchestra.

Once again the characters of Sam Peck and Steve Jenkins were revived, this time with Peck portrayed by Johnny Vigal and Miller adopting his alter ego, Jenkins. Comedian Vigal had appeared in previous productions produced by Irvin C. Miller beginning in the early 1920s, and regularly performed at Harlem's nightspots through the 1930s, working as the MC/floor-show producer at the Harlem Casino in 1937. A series of comic skits featuring the duo and members of the cast alternated with songs and dances. Most critics found the comedy routines to be fairly tired, and indeed several of the skits—notably "Tan Town Divorce" and "Tan Town Grill"—seem to have been lifted from Miller's trunkload of vaudeville skits that he had performed over the years. The threadbare presentation along with the carelessly assembled book drew comment even from the critic in the (usually sympathetic) *Pittsburgh Courier*, who noted, following the show's Washington premiere,

The plot is introduced in the initial act, but goes haywire down the line and at times the show smacks of vaudeville presentation with its potpourri of songs and dances in amazing confusion. Definitely without plot, working with an inferior pit band, nevertheless did not muffle the efforts of the members of the cast, who performed brilliantly. The costumes lacked elegance . . . and the scenery suffered a bit from overuse.[41]

The show opened and closed with the number "Down by the Railroad Tracks," one of the standard settings (like the Mississippi Levee or the "Old Plantation") featured in colored revues. The chorus sings of the "little shack" located so close to the tracks that the "trains are almost in my yard." Still, this humble abode is more beloved than the finest mansion; "I was a silly sap / leavin' my 'ma' and 'pap' / Keep all your gold dust, give me the coal dust / Down by the railroad track," the song's narrator intones. No one seems to have thought it odd to bookend a show purporting to portray the denizens of black Manhattan with a rural scene.[42]

Following the final chorus of "Down by the Railroad Tracks," the show ended by taking a sharp right turn into totally different territory from the minstrel-style comedy and happy feet of the rest of the production. The cast came together to perform Razaf and Blake's song celebrating the contributions of blacks to American history, titled "We Are Americans Too."[43] Razaf's original lyric apparently included a spoken word segment that was a potent protest against racism in America, graphically describing the mistreatment of blacks, including lynchings and discrimination. "He'd given the white people hell" in this opening, Eubie recalled,

> I think I'd written the music already and . . . then he'd written this poem, this thing that, after the song was sung, you'd talk this part out. Well the thing went right from the lynchin' of Negroes to *everything*.
>
> "Andy," I said, "Andy, this is the greatest lyric you ever wrote in your life. But how the hell are you gonna . . . charge people money to open a show and have them come hear how lousy they treated us? How you gonna do that?
>
> You know what he said to me? . . . "You write the music, I write the lyrics."[44]

Not surprisingly, Eubie was concerned about the commercial viability of a song that so directly tackled a taboo topic like racism. Irvin C. Miller was even more direct when he heard the proposed lyrics. "Keep it for yourself. It ain't goin' in my show." Miller agreed that the song's sentiments were true, but insisted it couldn't be performed. It took Razaf's then wife, Jean Blackwell, to convince him to rewrite the song into a more generic account of the long history of the contributions of African Americans to the country's life, concluding with an echo of the Harlem Renaissance's ideals of black self-empowerment through "uplifting the race":

> When given any kind of chance
> We've made the grade and shown advance,
> In business, science, letters, art,
> We've played a most surprising part.

Emphasizing the importance of this spoken-word addition to the song, the poem appeared on the inner flyleaf of the sheet music when it was published by W. C. Handy's company later in the spring. On a recording that Razaf and Blake made in 1941, the song opens with Razaf shouting, "Calling all Americans! Calling all Americans! Colored America speaks!" He then launches into the lyrics, which continue the theme of blacks as loyal patriots who have earned their place in America, culminating in the stirring chorus:

> By the record we made, and the part that we played,
> We are Americans, too
> By the pick and the plow, and the sweat of our brow,
> We are Americans, too.
> We have given up our blood and bones,
> Helped to lay the nation's cornerstones
> None have loved old glory more than we,
> Or have shown a greater loyalty
>
> . . .
> We'll be singing this song, 12 million strong,
> We are Americans, loyal Americans,
> We are Americans, too.[45]

Eubie wrote an appropriately march-like melody for these lyrics, adding just a hint of syncopation. Behind Razaf's mid-song recitation, he imitated marching feet with a bass run with the occasional martial trills. The song would outlive the show through the war years. Blake and Razaf made several attempts to place the song with popular singers, including Paul Robeson and

Marian Anderson (who turned them down)[46] and the Southenaires (who did perform it on radio). During 1941, the song was featured on radio to promote black participation in the war effort and was lauded by the black press, with the *Pittsburgh Courier* noting that it "is America's effective answer to the German plan to sow race hatred and disunity among the American people."[47] Handy himself conducted 3000 fans in singing the song at the annual Beale Street Bowl game in his hometown of Memphis in December 1941; news of the event was spread over the Associated Press (AP) wire, although Blake and Razaf must have been galled when Handy claimed credit for the "patriotic song he composed for his race."[48]

Of the ballads in the show, the most successful was "Nickel for a Dime," which was sung by Nina Mae McKinney. It features one of Razaf's signature lyrics that economically tells the story of a spurned lover who needs a nickel for the jukebox so she can hear just one more time the song that reminds her of her lost beau. She's so desperate that she's willing to trade a dime for a nickel, in essence paying twice as much as was needed, just to hear this song again. Razaf liked the song so much that he continued to tinker with the lyrics through the early 1950s, retitling it "A Dollar for a Dime."

Rehearsals for *Tan Manhattan* began in December 1940 for a January 1941 opening in Washington, DC. The plan was for the show to play at Washington's Howard Theater for a week, but the reaction was positive enough that it was held over for a second week of performances. Interviewed at the time, both Razaf and Blake expressed optimism that—with a little work—the show could be successfully brought to New York. Blake justified the fact that the show appeared at a "colored" theater rather than "downtown" (i.e., in a theater catering to white audiences) in Washington, saying that "After being in the show business 39 years, a man ought to learn something . . . opening in a colored house, we felt we could accomplish more than we could if we had opened downtown."[49] This Washington critic praised the production as "a top-flight flesh show," the first to appear in Washington in over fifteen years and that "local theatre-goers are lavish in their praise of the piece." However, like other critics, he noted,

> Weak comedy hampers the speedy, pretty chorus . . . the show needs pepping up before it can be said to be a sure-fire hit . . . As a genuine live production, much will have to be done to "Tan Manhattan" before it hits the Apollo theater in Harlem where it is scheduled to go [next].[50]

The critic noted that the Apollo's manager, Frank Schiffman, attended the Washington opening to size up the show's potential.

After leaving Washington, the show opened with a single performance on Friday, February 7, at the Apollo Theater, and then was performed for the following week on the normal four-showings-a-day schedule at the theater, "at the Apollo's regular low admission prices."[51] Scheduling a single showing to open the production in New York was an attempt to draw attention to it, but it was marred somewhat by the decision to show a US government propaganda film lauding the high quality of the Navy's aviators before the curtain rose. "In view of the fact that Negroes are not permitted in the Navy, except as mess attendants, and in the Naval Air Corps under no condition," William E. Clark noted in the *New York Age*, "the showing of such a film to a Harlem audience appeared to this reviewer as a bit of satire calculated to stir up resentment rather than entertainment."[52] Apparently, the show was truncated from its original two-act length to a single act, but nonetheless Clark found the production disappointing, noting that

> the only connection that could be gleaned between the name of the show and Harlem was a song called "Tan Manhattan." Most of the scenes were disjointed, leaving the idea of a revue—song and dance acts—rather than a production with any continuity . . . Flournoy Miller and Johnny Vigal worked hard with the comedy but failed to create any new jokes or funny situations.[53]

Clark found even Razaf and Blake's score lacking, feeling it was largely derivative of their earlier work. He also criticized "We Are Americans Too" for appearing "to be fashioned after 'Ballad of America[ns],'" which had been a success in performance by Paul Robeson. Clark concluded that "'Tan Manhattan' is no second 'Shuffle Along.'"

Despite reports that the show did good business at the Apollo, and even a notice that the Shuberts had optioned the show for Broadway[54], *Tan Manhattan* would never reach the Great White Way. An announcement appeared in late February 1941 that the Apollo was planning a follow-up show, written and produced by the same artistic team, to be titled *Up Harlem Way* as a "bigger and better musical revue . . . a much broader venture than the first legit offering, as those concerned have gained monied faith in such shows in Harlem."[55] As it was described in the newspapers, the show appears to have been just a reworking of material from *Tan Manhattan*, with many of the same songs and skits.[56] The cast tantalizingly was announced to include legendary jazz singer Billie Holiday along with many of the star performers of the previous production. The new show was advertised to open on February 21 and run for a week, but no reviews survive to indicate whether it had any success. The principals—Blake, Razaf, and Flournoy and Irvin C. Miller— signed a contract in July to share equally in any profits made by the show, per- haps in the hope that it would find a home on Broadway.[57] In 1943, a revival of *Tan Manhattan* was announced to be staged at the Ubangi Club, featuring comedian "Moms" Mabley; this show also went unreviewed at the time.

Just as *Tan Manhattan*'s chances were dimming, Eubie was thrown a life- line by his old partner, Noble Sissle. Sissle cleverly had smelled an opportunity in the formation of the USO as a service organization for American soldiers (Figure 9.1). In October 1941, the USO created a division specifically to stage shows at military training camps around the United States. The agency

Figure 9.1 Noble Sissle pictured in c. 1945 holding a baton. Sissle used his extensive contacts to get work for himself and Eubie through the USO during the war years.

hired Abe Lastfogel, one of the most established talent agents who worked at the William Morris Agency, to bring on talent from Broadway and the movies. Lastfogel quickly assembled two groups of performing companies, one to present truncated versions of major Broadway shows and a Vaudeville unit; eventually, a "Fox Hole" unit was formed to entertain soldiers fighting abroad, and a Hospital Unit toured the United States to entertain wounded soldiers returned from the front. According to historian Julia Carson, "By 1942 it was considered the biggest booking agent in the world. [The USO's] Camp Shows Inc. executed 273,599 separate performances to 171,717,205 people from 1941–1945."[58]

It just so happened that Sissle was friendly with Lastfogel, who had booked his band during the 1930s. Eubie recalled how Sissle shamed Lastfogel into hiring black entertainers to work for the USO:

> They weren't going to have any Negros on the U.S.O . . . . According to Sissle, [he went] down to see [Lastfogel]. . . . And Abe was reluctant to tell him that there wasn't going to have any Negros. The powers that be knew what was going on all the time. Sissle says, "How you going to have a show with no Negros in it? Negros over there fightin'." . . . And they gave him the job [to find black performers], a dollar a year. That's all Sissle got.[59]

Sissle became a board member for the USO's Camp Show Productions, and quickly assembled a team to put together a new revue under the old *Shuffle Along* name. Although Eubie recalled that he began his work for the USO after Pearl Harbor in December 1941, contemporary reports show that Sissle was already assembling the cast in late November and that performances were held as early as December 9 at Fort Sheridan, Illinois. Flournoy Miller was once again portraying Steve Jenkins with comedian Johnny Lee taking on the Sam Peck persona. Like *Tan Manhattan* and the early 1930s *Shuffle Along* revivals, the show was basically a revue featuring various acts performing their individual numbers. It was staged in a single act and ran a little over an hour. Alongside the beloved hits from the original production, Sissle and Blake revived their early vaudeville song "Miranda" and added a new song, "Second Class Daddy." Among the featured acts were Chuck and Chuckles, eccentric dancers and novelty xylophone performers; tap dancer Ralph Brown and soft shoe artists Al Moore and Dene Larry; and vocal groups the Hepcats and Daisy Mae and the Chanticleers.[60] Blake led the band for the performances.

Blake next conducted the orchestra for another revue-type show organized by Sissle titled *Harlem on My Mind*. The new touring show was announced in March 1942, and unlike the *Shuffle Along* revue of the previous year, was more honestly promoted as a revue featuring performers doing their well-known acts rather than a "book" musical. Included were the comic dance team of Butterbeans and Susie; singers Ada Brown—a "buxom blues singer," according to the *Chicago Defender*, who "almost stole the show as she sang 'This Little Piggy Went to Market,' and 'Georgia,' "[61]—and Avis Andrews, who had sung with Duke Ellington and Cab Calloway and performed the standards "Begin the Beguine" and "Lover Come Back to Me"; vocal group The Four Toppers; and comedian George Williams, along with the requisite line of pretty chorus girls. This show did not feature any numbers by Sissle and Blake. It played mostly to bases training black soldiers, including the Field Artillery Replacement Center at Fort Bragg, North Carolina. The camp's leader, Brigadier General E. P. Parker, greeted the performers by noting, "The colored soldier of the Replacement center is given rigid training and we try to give him the best in entertainment."[62] According to a contract signed in May, Blake received $75 a week (about $1100 in today's dollars) to conduct the band and "perform two shows a night and occasional matinee as required . . . in Army and Navy camps as designed by USO-Camp Shows, Inc."[63]

Next in line was a similar entertainment titled *Keep Shufflin'*, which toured from August through October 1942. Blake signed an agreement with the USO, dated September 26, 1942, to be paid $75 per week for working six days as the orchestra conductor, prorated from the day of first performance to the end of the run; his transportation was to be covered from base to base, along with "where procurable, Pullman berth for all night transportation between 10 P.M. and 6 A.M." The USO also agreed to pay for his return trip to New York when the tour ended.[64] *Keep Shufflin'* was emceed by comedian Johnny Vigal (late of *Tan Manhattan*), and again featured "hot-lick rhythm, fleet-footed dancing, sweet and torrid tunes, and hilarious comedy," in the words of the *New York Age*'s critic.[65] Vocalist Edith Wilson was probably the biggest name in the cast, along with Vigal and the usual assortment of novelty dancers, leggy girls, comics, and singers.

Touring with the USO through the Deep South was not easy in the early 1940s. Clarinetist Garvin Bushell, who played with Eubie's band from 1942 to 1943, recalled several instances when Eubie had to stand up for the rights of others:

In Columbia, South Carolina, Eubie refused to play because they made the Negro officers sit in the back of the theater. The officers were supposed to sit in the third or fourth row, but the MPs got up and made the Negro[es] . . . move back. Eubie said, "Wait a minute. We don't play."

A warrant officer came up. "Mr. Blake, this is scheduled to go on."

"No."

"Why not?"

"Not without those officers sitting where they're supposed to sit. You don't do that to me." So Eubie turned to us and said, "Come on, out of the pit."

About five minutes later the colonel came down and confronted Eubie. Eubie stood his ground, and the colonel had to go and see that the officers could return to their seats. Eubie played "The Star Spangled Banner," and it was on with the show.[66]

It took considerable nerve for Eubie to stand up to the authorities in this manner. Bushell also complained that when the band was traveling through Texas by train, German war prisoners were allowed to eat in the dining car while the musicians were kept in a segregated car and had to wait for their food to be brought to them.

Somehow during this busy travel period, Eubie hooked up with a new lyricist, Grace Bouret.[67] Their association began in 1942 and ran at least through 1944, resulting in a few (now lost) songs that Bouret tirelessly pitched to singers—including Avis Andrews, who appeared in several of the USO revues conducted by Blake—and all of the major publishers. The two worked together whenever Blake was given a leave to be in New York, but most of their work was conducted through the mail, with Bouret ceaselessly complaining that it took forever for Eubie to reply—probably because of the vagaries of his life on the road.

Bouret wrote to Blake, describing the great lengths she went to try to place their songs, reflecting the typically tough prospects for songwriters in the pop music business:

If you could know what I went thru yesterday! I sallied forth into the lions' dens. [I visited music publisher] Harms, first, my contact with Mack Goldman—[He was in] Boston until end of week—couldn't see me until middle of next week. . . . Then to [Broadway producers the] Shuberts! I got by two secretaries on your name when it was presented but had to join a

crowd of girls waiting for interviews—evidently he is getting a show together. Waited an hour and then given just [a] hint [that] he walked out and
was at theatre not back until 4.30 or later. We left en masse and I went over
to [publisher Shapiro] Bernstein—kept waiting of course. He read our two
songs thru without comment, started on ALL OVER and . . . said . . . not interested. . . . He said songs well written, both lyrics and music but not what
he wanted. When I ask what that was, meaning novelty, love ballad or what-
not, he said if he knew he'd ask his writers for it—didn't know until he saw
the song. Good songs however! At first he asked if I played [the piano] and
when I said no he said "[It's] just as well after hearing Eubie Blake's playing!"
You are popular.

Then back to J. J. Shubert's office and a new crowd waiting—larger than
ever. Again I submitted name and after ten minutes got in ahead of all the
others—he came out in person. Again I was supposed to play piano and
couldn't—so he scoured the place and got someone. Just as [the pianist]
started it, J.J. [was] called out of room so [the pianist] said it would give him
time to get familiar with it. Well, Eubie, I wish you could hear what [he]
did to UTTERLY LOVELY even after he played it twice and with plenty
of time on his hands . . . [he] thought he knew how to play it! Same with
NEVER KNEW. He murdered them—tears were in my eyes— . . . Well, by
the time Shubert came back and apologized for the delay I was crazy but
he played it and I . . . sang it. . . . but he didn't have the rhythm even and so
I started singing the way I do which is frightful just to establish the tempo
and lead him and it did accomplish a bit tho I hope Shubert doesn't think
I considered myself a singer! . . . Well J. J. asked for it over again—and still it
sounded like dish water and I stood there transfixed with disappointment
while J. J. walked the room—gazed out of window. Then asked for the next.
NEVER KNEW he heard once and said he was in a terrible hurry—nothing
doing now . . . well he didn't turn it down.[68]

"Utterly Lovely" reappeared in 1950 in a score for an unproduced musical
written by Blake and Bouret, *Be Yourself*.

Never particularly enthusiastic about traveling, Blake found his life getting
considerably more hectic in 1944 when he was transferred to the newly con-
stituted Hospital Unit. This stint involved a grueling schedule of trips across
and around the country to entertain troops recovering from their injuries.
No longer a young man, Eubie suffered an attack of appendicitis on the road
in 1944 and was hospitalized for an emergency appendectomy.

In 1945, Sissle wired Eubie to let him know that he planned to mount a new version of *Shuffle Along* to take on a USO tour to Europe. Sissle and Miller had made an abortive attempt to revive the show in Hollywood—where Miller was working writing for *Amos 'n' Andy*—in 1943, asking Eubie to obtain the services of several of the performers who were touring with him on the USO circuit. However, nothing came of it.[69] Now, Sissle saw a chance to revive the show. He asked Eubie to provide orchestrations for it—stating that there would be no payment for "overseas rights"—and called on Flournoy Miller to update the book. Sissle was anxious to have Eubie come on the tour and lead the orchestra, writing to him that it represented their best chance to relaunch their careers once the war was over:

> You know Eubie they are not going to keep sending you or anyone else over and over that circuit and when the boys who are performers come back from overseas and they commence to discharge them and the outside is crowded those musicians and performers will get the break[.] . . . So it behooves us to get *Shuffle Along* back into the spot light and it means more now and maybe it's a good thing . . . because its fresh now and we have a chance . . . to steal the show and come back from this war the Jim Europes of World War II and step right in now when the Army will be in its greatest need for Morale work[.] [A]nd we will be in Europe when all the Allied High Command is[,] and what you all did here in the Camps in America with the show you now have a chance to step out before the whole world and if we have the real answer to the needs with one blow we can . . . re-establish ourselves in the sun . . . for another twenty years.
>
> . . .[I]n regards you coming in . . . I have full power to hire whom I want for Orchestra. And we are going for a minimum of 6 months so I know you don't want to take chances but as you know the show can last if we want it to for two years in the Camp show Inc because we could . . . go to the South Pacific. But as I say we can with draw after six months any individual on the whole show [spelling and punctuation in original].[70]

Despite Sissle's pleas, Eubie was uninterested in traveling abroad, and just as he did in World War I, he ignored Sissle's arguments that it would be to his advantage to perform for the Army bigwigs abroad. He did, however, give Sissle permission to use his music and orchestrations at no charge.

Flournoy Miller crafted a new storyline for the European tour of *Shuffle Along*, throwing in topical references to the war and the vagaries of life in the Army, while also maintaining many of the tried-and-true routines of Sam Peck and Steve Jenkins. Comedian Johnny Lee was enlisted to be Miller's foil, and Miller's daughter—Olivette, who was a talented harpist—was brought along for her own feature. Ivan H. Browning from the original 1921 production was also cast. Sissle appeared on stage and composed both music and lyrics for a new song, "The Red Ball Line," used as a company finale. Several of the hits from the original *Shuffle Along* were reprised, including "Love Will Find a Way" and "I'm Just Wild about Harry," along with newer numbers "Boogie Woogie Beguine" and "My Platform of Swing," two obvious attempts by Sissle and Blake to cash in on the latest dance trends. The show played in Germany, France, and Italy over a ten-month tour.[71] Milton Reddie—serving in Bagnoli south of Naples—caught a performance, noting of the GIs in the audience that "[e]ven if we had not been starved for the sight of American pulchritude, we should have found all of the girls lovely to look at."[72] After the run ended in 1946, Sissle and Miller had a chance to visit Paris, where they had a reunion with Josephine Baker.

Meanwhile, Blake soldiered on with his orchestra accompanying a series of variety shows on the hospital circuit. Tiring of the wear and tear of travel, he wrote to Dick Campbell at the home office of the USO in early 1946 to complain about the many responsibilities he had in keeping the show on the road:

> I have the grave responsibility of musically supporting an entire aggravation of a six-act-unit. In addition to being Musical Director of "Suntan Revue" Co. . . . I do a musical act separate and distinct from the responsibilities of musical director.
>
> In view of augmenting an act with the services of musical director, I ask that consideration be given to my request for an increase in salary. As you know, the salary of any ordinary act is at least $75.00. Therefore, I feel justified in making this request.[73]

Blake ended his request by noting that, in addition to his work on the road, he had "since the inception of U.S.O. Inc. donated for the entertainment of the Armed Forces, three musical shows. One now playing currently in Europe."

Campbell, however, was not terribly sympathetic to Eubie's request, coldly replying that he did not feel that:

we can pay more than $125 weekly to any Musical Director. It is expected that every Musical Director of USO-Camp Shows is to do a specialty himself. We hire no pianists to simply accompany acts. If the pianist cannot do a specialty himself, which is acceptable and goes over well, then we shall not hire him.

We appreciate the fact that you have carried on under the aegis of Camp Shows for a very long time. We feel that it has been a joint advantage. In other words, you have benefited and we have also. It is expected that everyone in Camp Shows will be doing a good job. That is all that matters.[74]

The refusal of the USO to meet his demands, plus the continuing discomfort he was suffering from the aftereffects of his appendicitis surgery, began to wear on Eubie. Plus, a new woman had come into his life who encouraged him to come off the road and settle down: Marion Gant Tyler. During their courtship, Marion traveled with Eubie on one of his last USO tours for a while. Seeing how hard he worked and how poorly he was treated, she finally convinced him to permanently leave the USO. Years later, Eubie recounted to a *Baltimore Sun* reporter what was the tipping point for him and Marion:

We were on a train. The soldiers were going to war. We stood at the station nearly 24 hours. We were going to L.A. My wife looked white. She could get something to eat. I'm her "chauffeur," so she says. The colored soldiers, going to fight for the same people . . . they can't eat. She says, "When we get to L.A., I want you to retire . . . You're getting too old for this."[75]

On August 1, 1946, Eubie sent his letter of resignation to the organization's main office:

As a result of returning to work too soon after an appendectomy, in Astoria, Ore., in 1944, while on tour with a U.S.O. unit, a condition has developed which now requires medical attention. Upon the advice of a physician, consulted recently, I wish to place myself under the care of my personal physician without further undue delay. Therefore, I herewith request a leave of absence effective as of August 1st, until such time as my condition warrants my return.[76]

The two would settle in Marion's Brooklyn row house that she inherited from her father. In an oft-repeated quip Eubie made in later life, he bragged that he "got the coop with the chicken." Eubie would live there for the rest of his life.

10

After the War

1946–1952

After leaving the USO in mid-1946, Eubie settled into his new Brooklyn home with his wife, Marion Gant Tyler. Like his first wife, Marion was light skinned—so light skinned that she could and did pass for white during at least some periods of her life—and came from a middle-class family. Her maternal grandfather, Hiram S. Thomas, was born a free black man in Canada in 1837.[1] He found his first employment working as a steward on river boats on the Great Lakes and Mississippi River. Sometime after the Civil War, he came to Washington, DC, where he became a steward at the Capitol Club, befriending many high-society people and politicians, including Ulysses S. Grant and Grover Cleveland.

By the 1870s, Hiram was working during the summer months in Saratoga Springs, New York, a summer retreat for many of the most wealthy (white) Americans. He began managing Moon's Lake House, famous for its Saratoga Chips (later known as potato chips). In later life, Thomas claimed to have "invented" the potato chip, although others have claimed this honor. By the time of the 1880 Census, Thomas and his family were maintaining a home at least during part of the year in New York City on West 3rd Street. The Census taker recorded Hiram's wife, Julia A. Thomas, and eight children at this address, listing them all as "mulatto."[2] During the fall months, Thomas was working as a head waiter at a hotel that served "millionaires and blue-blooded families" in Lakewood, New Jersey.[3] In 1888, he had achieved enough wealth to purchase Saratoga's Grand Union Hotel, where he previously had served as head waiter.[4]

In 1894, Thomas caused quite a stir when he purchased a townhouse in Brooklyn's then all-white Fort Greene neighborhood. The news of his intended purchase was widely reported both in local and national papers, with many of the neighbors expressing concern about a black man—no matter how well to do—living there. Some claimed he was buying the property simply to "blackmail" the local inhabitants into finding someone to buy him

Eubie Blake. Richard Carlin and Ken Bloom, Oxford University Press (2020). © Richard Carlin and Ken Bloom 2020.
DOI: 10.1093/oso/9780190635930.001.0001

out, in order to make a quick profit. Thomas disputed these claims, saying he intended to live in the house while working summers in Saratoga and winters in Lakewood.[5] Some reports commented on the hypocrisy of these Northern home owners, noting that Thomas was "a refined, good looking and thoroughly cultivated colored man . . . Mr. Thomas has eight children, all of them well educated and brought up accustomed to luxury. If he were white, any neighborhood would be glad to welcome him and his family. But he is part negro."[6] While it was widely stated that Thomas had a net worth of $200,000 (about $5.8 million in today's dollars)—an enormous sum for anyone to amass at this time—he also played down his apparent wealth, saying only he had "enough to live on—but that's all."[7] It was not wise for a black man to admit to having saved a considerable amount of money.

By the turn of the 20th century, Thomas was operating the Rumson Inn, located near Red Bank, New Jersey.[8] Only two of Thomas's children married, and only his daughter Antoinette ("Nettie"), who married James Gant, produced children. When Hiram died in 1907, it appears that his son-in-law and daughter continued to run the Inn for at least a while. Their daughter, Marion Gant, was born on February 11, 1896[9], and raised in New York City. Compared to many black families, the Gants were middle class and didn't have many financial concerns. Marion spent most summers at the family inn. She later recalled,

> The summers were the exciting times . . . There were luncheons and teas and dinner parties on the wide porches of a beautiful gothic house; and lawn parties on the several acres of beautiful landscaped grounds. At night the lawn would be decorated with electrically lighted lanterns. . . . The clientele of the Inn were the social elite of the Jersey Coast. The dinner parties were followed by dancing and entertainment which would last long into the night.[10]

Among the musicians who performed there, Marion recalled Jesse Wilson, a "song-and-dance man," and the Eureka Trio, which played for dances. We know that James Reese Europe visited the Inn around 1915 because there is a photograph of him there with Marion along with the rest of her family.[11] Unlike Blake, who attended school only through the eighth grade, Marion left school on May 31, 1912, when she was 16 years old.[12]

In 1921, Marion married a violinist named William A. (Billy) Tyler. Classically trained, like many other African American musicians of the day, Tyler could not find employment in a "legitimate" (white) orchestra. Instead, he worked primarily in New York City in dance bands and in theatrical orchestras. Among his engagements, he led the all-black house band at Harlem's Lafayette Theatre in 1913 and participated in W. C. Handy's first recording session in 1917 as a member of Handy's "Orchestra of Memphis." (Despite its name, its membership was drawn from New York City–based players.) He also worked at times with Jelly Roll Morton, notably when Morton was working in Los Angeles around 1920; the ever-jealous Morton claimed that Tyler tried to "steal" his band from him.[13]

Tyler's greatest success came when Lew Leslie hired him to assist conductor Will Vodery for the show, *Dixie to Broadway*. This show was developed to showcase the star performer Florence Mills, whom Leslie hired away from the original *Shuffle Along* cast. "Marion thought it a good opportunity to get into the act, and so became one of the original chorus girls" in the show, she later wrote, referring to herself in the third person.[14] She believed that Leslie hired her only as a favor to her husband, noting that he complained that she was the only Negro woman he had ever seen who couldn't dance. It is possible that Eubie and the Tylers crossed paths during this period, but Blake never said this in any interviews he gave later in life.

Will Tyler subsequently traveled to Paris with Benny Peyton's Blue Ribbon Orchestra, and the couple divorced. Marion made a few more appearances on stage, including "a tour with Miller & Lyle's in 'Keep Shufflin'; a stint in the Club Alabam; a vaudeville tour with Lilian Brown of Brown & Dumont, and a few miscellaneous appearances." Never a shrinking violet, Marion filed a claim against the *Keep Shufflin'* company in order to get paid for her work.[15] After her brief performing career, "having finished secretarial school before her marriage to Tyler,"[16] Marion went to work in the mid-1930s as a secretary. She first worked for composer/musician W. C. Handy's music publishing company in the mid-1930s. Blake also worked for a time as a musical director for Handy from at least mid-1935 through early 1936; it is possible that he met Marion at the Handy offices, or at least saw her there, although he did not mention it in any later interview. After leaving Handy, Marion held several positions with the WPA and Civil Service offices in the area.

By the war years, Marion was tiring of life in New York City. Working through the Civil Service Administration, she landed a job in Los Angeles in November 1943. While visiting Los Angeles on one of his USO tours, Blake stopped in to see Andy Razaf, who had relocated to the West Coast. He met Marion there, but got to talk to her for only "ten or fifteen minutes. But when he left he asked if he could write to her while he was on the road."[17] The fair-skinned ex-dancer was extremely attractive, and Blake was always quick to express interest in a good-looking woman.

Eubie wasted little time, apparently, in expressing his desire to marry Marion. She wrote him on March 29, 1944: "Received all your letters and I must say the last one read almost like a proposal." She tries gently to change the subject, noting that it must be hard for him to be traveling all the time to play "those one-horse-towns," while missing his home in New York City. She, however, said, "I got sorta fed up with New York and welcomed the change." Overall, she seems to be resisting Eubie's desire that they become a couple, noting,

> As to ourselves, regardless of what I may have previously written, What can you suggest? What can we look forward to in the future? In fact, what can one plan for the future[?] I would like an answer from you to these three questions. Of course, you can call on me if and when you return to LA.

She signed her letter, "Best of luck, Sincerely, Marion," hardly a warm closing.[18]

In her next letter of April 13, Marion noted Eubie's "disappointed tone," presumably in his response to her previous letter. Again, she held firm to the idea that they were merely friends:

> I should like to make myself clear on one point and that is I'm not in the habit of hurting people's feelings nor of playing with people's affections. I am too serious minded myself. I have enjoyed receiving your letters, and know no reason why you should discontinue writing, unless you just don't care to continue to do so. What may happen in the future, I have no power of penetration . . . So I make no promises, and make no plans.[19]

While Marion held out, Eubie apparently was hedging his bets. He was involved with at least one woman while traveling on the road. Andy Razaf teased Blake about his ongoing affairs in a letter from March 27, 1944:

> Now remember, you are no chippy (like me) and you must take it easy! (smile) But, no foolin', watch your diet and your liquor! And run when you see a woman. Lay off, at least 90 days. Just cut yourself a paper dollie. Ha! Ha!

> I saw your girl, Billie Fisher, the day before she left with the USO shows. Too bad you are not with her outfit, so she could keep an eye on you.[20]

Eubie often kept several relationships going at once, so it's not surprising that while he was courting Marion he was continuing to sleep with other women.

Despite her initial reluctance to commit to a relationship, it's clear that by later in 1944 Marion's feelings were softening toward Eubie, while she was becoming somewhat "fed up" with her life in Los Angeles. She asked Blake if he could send her a schedule of his forthcoming shows so she might join him on tour, although she still insisted she didn't want to return to New York City during the winter.[21] As it turned out, Marion had to return to the East Coast to care for her mother, who had become ill. The couple were reunited, and Marion joined Eubie on his next USO tour.

Traveling together caused problems because of Marion's light skin. When she was sitting with Eubie in the rear car—which was reserved for black passengers—on the train, Marion's presence raised many comments from conductors who were surprised to see a "white" woman traveling by choice in this way. Other incidents were more troubling. According to Blake's first biographer, Lawrence T. Carter, while the couple was in Memphis,

> [o]ne night two policemen in a patrol car began following them as they were on their way to a restaurant. They followed them for several blocks, talking and pointing at them. Eventually, however, they evidently decided that Marion must be black, for no black man would be foolish enough to be down there with a "sure nuff" white woman, and they took off.[22]

Carter noted that "Poke" Jones—the USO tour's manager—asked Eubie to send Marion back to New York: "He said he didn't want to jeopardize his job. This was ironic because he himself, light-skinned and with straight hair, used to have the same problems. But Eubie had no choice. He had to leave Marion up north."[23]

At about the same time that Eubie was urging Marion to join him on tour, he was corresponding with another woman, named Verlinda Nelson. Eubie and Verlinda had some kind of tryst that apparently ended in Nelson unintentionally becoming pregnant, as is hinted at in this letter from Nelson to Eubie dating from March 1945:

I thought I had made it very plain—my trouble, I mean. Now what is the worst misfortune an <u>un</u>married woman can have. Yes—that is it. The very thing I thought would never happen—and I ran into it—er rather it surrounded me—I <u>was</u> blind—<u>color</u> blind—like you said. Oh! I even almost blamed you— . . . P.S. I feel fine—considering everything—Guess I'm just too healthy. I don't even have head aches—will be happy to tell you when its over—soon now I hope. I know a doctor who is alright—but expensive. I waited so long. I know my secret is safe with you—I don't think my mother knows. [underlining in original][24]

Nelson clearly had an abortion, as Eubie wouldn't have welcomed fathering a baby. The relationship seems to have ended soon after; no further correspondence survives.

Eubie and Marion were wed on December 27, 1945, in Norfolk, Virginia, while Blake was performing there.[25] Just as before their wedding when they traveled together, they encountered trouble at the marriage bureau, where the clerk questioned whether Marion was white. Blake replied, "Do you think I'm dumb enough to bring a white woman down here in Virginia to marry?"[26] Unnerved by this experience, Blake took his new wife back to the hotel, asking the taxi driver to avoid driving directly back, in case they were being followed. Because of his concerns, Blake said "I always had my knife open, all the time."[27]

Among those writing congratulations to Eubie on his marriage was Milton Reddie, still serving in the Army. Taking a somewhat tongue-in-cheek tone, Reddie said, "What I should do is write my congressman recommending that your wife be awarded the Congressional Medal, because any woman who'd consent to join hands with a fathead like you deserves as much and more. Now that <u>you</u> have chased the former Mrs. Tyler until you have been caught, it is a good thing for you."[28]

Marion had to deal with the consequences of her marriage to this well-known African American composer. It appears that some of her friends were unaware of her black heritage. As late as 1949, she was writing to a friend, "There is a little matter of getting the record straight. I do not believe you know I am colored . . . I should have told you after I got married because my husband has been somewhat well known in the musical field. . . . He is Eubie Blake, a composer and pianist."[29] Other correspondence from earlier in the 1940s indicates that Marion indeed was passing, at least some of the time. The reactions that Blake and she experienced during this period reveal how easy this was for her to do. The fact that Marion had had a successful career in the Civil Service—thanks partly, perhaps, to her ability to pass as white—may have been one reason she was initially hesitant to encourage Eubie's interest in a relationship.

On his return to civilian life, Eubie faced a changing America that would impact his life as a musician. The war had further underscored issues of racial prejudice that continued to trouble American life. Just as during World War I, many black intellectuals urged young men to enlist as a way of showing their patriotism. Nonetheless, the Army was just as segregated as civilian society, with black soldiers treated as second-class citizens just as they were during peacetime. There were no parades for the valiant black servicemen returning after World War II, as there had been following the First World War.

The musical world was also rapidly changing. After the war, the big band era drew to an end. The economics of traveling with a large band had always been dicey, even for the most successful of the big bands. For second-string units, such as the bands led individually by Sissle and Blake, it was even tougher. Because of the grim economic situation, Eubie had given up touring in the mid-1930s, although he continued to cobble together bands for local dates during the later 1930s and then again after the war. His clientele was mostly small business groups and charity events; Eubie also conducted from time to time the house bands at the Apollo and Lafayette theaters. In the jazz world, small groups were in the ascendancy, playing in new, adventurous styles. For many older veterans—even jazz players like Louis Armstrong—the new music was disorienting and difficult for them to understand. Blake was a generation older than Armstrong and even further removed from the new generation who would shape popular music in the decades to come.

The immediate problem facing Eubie after the war was how he would continue to earn enough to support himself and his new wife. His hit songs should have provided regular income, but Eubie had always been too busy working to keep track of copyrights and money that were due to him from his compositions and recordings. Without constant vigilance, publishers and booking agents would happily delay payment, if not try to avoid it altogether, particularly to black artists. Luckily, Marion had more business savvy, and she took on the de facto role of manager for her husband for the rest of their lives. Complicating the matter was that the publishing organization ASCAP was at war with recording companies and radio, leading to two recording bans in the 1940s, when no ASCAP material could appear on record. Blake was relieved that—just before the second ban began in 1948—two of his biggest hits had been recorded by major artists, so he was still able to earn some income from this material.

While he was among the first black composers admitted to ASCAP in 1922, Blake's "ranking" in the organization—which determined the amount of the rights income that he would receive from the millions of dollars that the organization collected from broadcasters, music publishers, and recording companies—had never been upgraded from the lowest possible level. Blake was particularly disturbed to learn that his past partner, Noble Sissle, had a higher ranking than he did, even though Blake had written additional hit songs without Sissle. One of the first things that Marion did was write to ASCAP to demand that his ranking be upgraded. The organization was sympathetic to the request, and over the next several years, Eubie's ranking was upgraded several times, with a commensurate increase in his rights income. The surprise hit revival of "I'm Just Wild about Harry" during Harry S. Truman's 1948 campaign undoubtedly helped further convince the agency that Blake was still a commercially viable songwriter.

Another potential source of income came from would-be songwriters who approached Eubie to be collaborators. One of the most persistent was a Houston-based ad man named Ernie Ford. Ford was born on February 23, 1916, in D'Lo, Mississippi, and attended college at Stephen Austin State University, graduating in 1938. He eventually would compose lyrics for over 200 songs, collaborating with composers J. Rosamond Johnson, Billy Mills, and Doc Bechtel, among others—although the only songs that saw the light of day were published by Ford himself. He joined the staff of the *Houston Chronicle* in 1947, selling display ads and remaining there for over three decades. He eventually formed his own music publishing company, Gulf Coast Music, to promote his own work.[30]

Ford first wrote to Blake in 1943, sending him lyrics to set, but Blake was too busy with his work with the USO to respond. In 1946, Ford renewed his correspondence with Eubie, hoping that—through Eubie's contacts in the music business—they'd be able to successfully pitch their songs to publishers, singers, and record companies. On August 27, 1946, Ford wrote the first of many letters asking Eubie to report on his activities to promote their work:

What are your plans for getting our tunes published after they are finished? Do you have any particular publishers to which you wish to submit them before I try my hand at getting them published. If you do, that perhaps would be better than my trying via mail. For you are right there in the scene and know much more about the publishers than I.[31]

At least during their first years of collaboration, Eubie appears to have worked diligently to place their songs, making acetate recordings (at his own expense) to pitch the songs to publishers, singers, and bandleaders. He first recorded their "Time Drags Along," reporting at the end of November that Leeds music had expressed interest in publishing the song, but apparently they backed out by early 1947.[32] At the same time, Ford pushed their work in any way he could, including offering to cut bandleader Stan Kenton in as a "composer" if he'd record their composition "Sweet Talk." Kenton turned him down, saying that

[w]e appreciate your willingness to cut us in, but have never become involved in such deals—because we feel that if you give us a song and we are able to make something out of it on a record, that alone is compensation enough. What songs you have, as far as we are concerned, are entirely your own. If at any time you feel you have something you wish to submit, I am always pleased to look things over.[33]

Kenton may have been using this as an excuse to avoid directly turning Ford down, perhaps out of respect for Blake. Ford, ever the optimist, took this as a ringing endorsement, and told Blake he would continue to try to place songs with the bandleader. The duo then put their efforts behind a song called "Sweet Elizabeth." Ford apparently wrote the original version of the song by working with composer Billy Baskette. Baskette's heyday was in the late 1910s/early 1920s; among his hits was "Waitin' for the Evenin' Mail" that Sissle and Blake had recorded for Victor. In April, Ford wrote to Blake, asking for his help to rework the song after Tommy Dorsey's publishing company, Harmony Music, had expressed interest in it. After reviewing the song, Harmony's manager had asked for changes in the melody of the bridge as well as the lyrics. Blake told Ford that he hoped "this work [would] be accepted, as it may give us an entrée with this publishing company for future compensation"[34] and went to work on sprucing it up.

A week later, Blake took the song to Harmony's offices, reporting to Ford,

Dorsey . . . was to leave for the coast the night of the day I took the song in. [The manager] did not know whether Dorsey would get to see the number or not before he left. I phoned the next day as promised and was told Dorsey liked the changes, but that nothing would be decided definitely until his return—five weeks from now. So there you have the picture.

The corporation has the appearance of an all right concern, but no one has any authority in Dorsey's absence.[35]

Unfortunately, in mid-May the manager wrote back to Blake, saying that Harmony would not be picking up any new songs, despite the fact that he had thought "Sweet Elizabeth" had some potential.[36] Ford was as disappointed as Eubie with this turn of events:

> You have no idea how keenly disappointed I am to learn that Dorsey walked out on Harmony and left our songs dangling in the air. For a while I thought that we were about to get a good break. That's tough to take![37]

Still hoping to give the song a bump, Ford audaciously wrote to actress Betty Grable—well known as a World War II pin-up girl—to ask for her permission to use her photo on the song's sheet music cover—despite the fact that no publisher had agreed to print it. Grable wrote back that he'd have to ask her studio, 20th Century Fox, for permission.[38] Then he tried to interest bandleader Hal McIntyre in the tune. The bandleader asked him to send an arrangement for his consideration, which Eubie dutifully created. By August, Ford wrote to Eubie in frustration, "I believe that Hal McIntyre is giving us the well-known run-around. I have written him three or four letters and damn if I can get a reply from him."[39] Ford would continue to promote the song through early 1948, writing letters to Bob Hope and comedian/singer Judy Canova, as well as Jack Kapp, A&R head for Decca Records, still trying to place it.

In early 1948, Ford came up with another angle to promote their music. On hearing that the Revlon company was launching a new lipstick color called "Sweet Talk," he sent them a copy of his earlier song of the same name that he had written with Blake. As an ad man at the *Chronicle*, Ford was able to get the song performed at a local fashion show as well as on the radio, in hopes of attracting the cosmetic company's attention. He wrote to Blake,

> If Revlon Products Corporation starts a big campaign on their new color SWEET TALK, it will be in many, many publications . . . some of the ASCAP

writers will see it . . . and come up with a new song by the same title as ours. We have to work fast on this to beat them to the punch![40]

The song seemed to be on its way to success when Ford heard from Revlon's PR director, Beatrice Castle, in early April. She asked,

> I wonder whether you would be good enough to have a recording made of the song, with someone singing the vocal, and sending it on to us, as I feel that there is a good deal of publicity value in it, and I believe I will be able to place it strategically on the air here, if it has "punch." As a matter of fact, I would like to play the recording for Manie Sacks of Columbia, and if he likes it, one of their good bands and vocalists would record it, and, who knows—it might even get to be on the Hit Parade![41]

Once again, Eubie had an acetate made at his own expense. Castle was as good as her word, playing it for Sacks. Unfortunately, she reported back to Ford that he told her, "Of course, I think I've heard better songs, but, with a little promotion, it might go over. Unfortunately, as you know, we are not in a position to record the song because of the Petrillo situation." Musician's Union head James Petrillo was once again fighting with the record labels, and the second recording ban was in full effect during this period. Sacks may have been using this as an excuse, because Castle said that she played the test record to several performers, who also turned it down. Ford noted ruefully, "Well, Eubie that's another disappointment . . . but we can't let it get us down. We'll just have to keep plugging."[42] Perhaps if they had offered a piece of the song's composer royalties they'd be able to place it with someone, he concluded.

Ford decided that the best they could do was to have three of their best songs printed locally as a way of promoting them, expecting that Blake would help pay the cost. Eubie seems to have been growing tired of putting up his own money to support songs that had yet proved to have commercial potential. Ford continued to write incessantly to the composer through the early 1950s, asking him to reimburse him for his continuing expenses in promoting their work. Blake apparently suggested to Ford that he'd cover his expenses once the songs were published and began earning royalties. This response appears to have been the last straw for Ford:

For about ten years now you and I have been good friends, and we have worked together on our songs, and I have tried with all my might to promote them. . . .

If I would go down the line and itemize every expense that I have been to on [our songs] . . . it would be . . . [nearly] $300.00! Now, about your sharing the expenses 50-50 AFTER THE SONGS EARN SOME ROYALTIES: I don't believe it is fair for me to have to wait to be reimbursed until the first royalties are paid. I need my money, also. . . . During [this] time, what have you done, Eubie? How much money have you spent exploiting our songs? . . . You are right there in New York where you could contact the records companies, recording artists and publishers, but you never tell me anything that you do on our songs. . . . I'm not being facetious when I say that I could get hundreds of composers to collaborate with me if I'd pay all the expenses and then let them pay their 50% out of royalties earned. I do all the work, spend plenty of money, and then have to wait for my reimbursement WHEN ROYALTIES ARE EARNED. That doesn't make sense to me![43]

Although he wrote an apology letter shortly after this outburst, Ford's collaboration with Blake more or less ended at this time.

Eubie had plenty of time to work with Ford at least initially, because his most recent collaborator, Milton Reddie, was still in the Army and based in Arizona throughout 1946. Reddie had remained in touch, however, and like Ford was sending lyrics to Eubie to set and try to promote in New York. Reddie's affection for Blake is clear in these letters that are so much more informal and comfortable than the more stilted correspondence from Ford. Reddie was yet another better-educated figure in Eubie's life who recognized his native genius, but affectionately kidded him about his lack of formal education or sophistication. In one letter, he addressed Blake as "Stoop—as in Stupid," saying,

You have upon your shoulders between your two wrinkled ears a veritable gold mine of dumbness. And after giving the matter considerable thought, I have concluded that with your ability to turn out the dumbness and my ability to wrap it in pretty cellophane packages, why, we can manufacture dumbness by the ton and sell it by the handful.[44]

In the fall of 1946, Reddie began preparing to raise the money to return to New York, telling Blake he was ready to start promoting their latest songs:

In addition to working on the publishing houses, I plan working over the nite spots and get some work writing special material for the entertainers. It will be necessary for us to practically live in the clubs (downtown) between nine and eleven at night.[45]

Reddie also corresponded with Marion in an attempt to get Eubie more actively involved in promoting their songs. He had high hopes for placing their song "Señor Sam" with the pop group the Charioteers, and blamed Eubie for failing to aggressively push the song to them:

Too long has Eubie manifested a defeatist attitude re Negro artists. I think that we writers in not urging them more to perform our creations are just as much to blame as they are by not insisting on doing them. The reason that "U-B" muffed the Charioteers is because of that very attitude of defeatism. However, you follow thru on that, and I plan also to heckle not only the colored, but also the white artists.[46]

Blake had counseled Reddie to be more patient when he expressed his frustration with the way blacks were treated by white publishers and artists. The younger Reddie was less tolerant of this attitude.

In early 1947, Reddie returned to the East Coast, settling near Eubie in Brooklyn. It may have been his idea for Eubie to expand his compositional horizons by enrolling in a course in the Schillinger System being offered by the NYU Adult Extension school. The two would take the course together as a way of "modernizing" their approach to songwriting. Schillinger's methods had been lauded by several pop songwriters—most notably George Gershwin—and Blake ended up being equally impressed with the training. Eubie was particularly pleased to be taught by Rudolf Schramm, a German-born conductor who was well known for his film scores and radio work. Eubie claimed that Schillinger himself had approached him earlier in his career, hoping he'd become his student "because I was a big name. Lot of big shots studied with him personally. But you know you got to take 2, 3 lessons a week, $50 a night. I says, 'To hell, I ain't gonna take that thing.' I was on the road, anyhow."[47]

However, with time on his hands and with Reddie's encouragement, Blake began his study with Schramm. The method gave Eubie new ways to create original melodies, as he explained to interviewer Al Rose: "There's only 9 numbers [notes], see. You can switch these around, with what they call permutation. Take this and put that there if you don't like what you got. You can change the whole routine, you can get what you want."

When Eubie completed the course in the summer of 1949, the fact that the older composer had successfully completed a course on this avant-garde technique attracted press attention from major papers like *The New York Times*. Eubie gloated to lyricist Ernie Ford in a letter that September, "As you will see from the enclosed clipping I finished my studies of Schillinger. A million dollars worth of publicity has resulted. I can only wait now to see what monetary benefits will result."[48]

Blake and Reddie would spend much of the next few years in working on the score for an ill-fated musical project that was spearheaded by small-time producer/author Ray Gallo. Gallo had produced a minor Broadway play, *Perfectly Scandalous*, in 1931, the kind of "sex comedy" that featured a naive hero thrown into several "scandalous" situations. Like many others in the Broadway world, he eked out a living on the edges of the theatrical world, serving as a literary agent, investor, and wannabe author. In the 1940s, he wrote a script originally titled *Cairo Girl*, a kind of combination of *Pygmalion* and *A Connecticut Yankee in King Arthur's Court*. In it, a Parisian artist creates a replica of the Egyptian queen Cleopatra, who magically comes to life. She has to deal with an entirely alien society and world, with predictably comic situations occurring for both her and her creator. While the plot sounds far fetched, it was not that different from other musicals of the era that were often based on whimsical if not always believable storylines.

Sometime shortly after Reddie returned to New York, Gallo approached him and Eubie to write songs for the production. By 1948, he was pitching the show to various possible investors and in 1950 Gallo underwrote recordings of some of its songs, but apparently the general consensus was that both the script and music needed some reworking. Gallo wrote to Blake and Reddie in 1951,

Let's face it boys! And not kid ourselves, our show is not quite ready. Reaction so far from the few auditions indicate that it does not come up to Broadway standards.

I refer not only to the book, but to the music.

I think it is about time that you fellows got together and replaced some of the numbers. My recommendations are to pull out MEN ARE NOT GODS, I HARP ON LOVE, WHY SHOULD WE GO TO SCHOOL, and I'M SETTING A TRAP. These numbers ought to be replaced by new songs that are more peppy and dynamic, for most of the songs so far are slow in tempo. I believe that before we have any further auditions, we should get together and discuss a completely revised musical score and book.[49]

Gallo sent his script, now titled *Cleo Steps Out*, to John Larson of the Mark Hellinger Theater for evaluation. Larson thought the idea behind the script was good but poorly executed, although he did find Blake and Reddie's score to be attractive:

> Authors have an excellent idea for a musical here. The idea of bringing Cleopatra back to life and trying to fit her into contemporary Parisian life sounds like a natural. Unfortunately, the book goes way off the beam, getting hopelessly entangled in subplots, romantic and otherwise, that have nothing to do with the basic satirical idea of the two civilizations thrown into conflict . . .
>
> In its present form this show is no good for us. It's a very expensive show and the book is bad. If they throw the book away and get a fresh start on their idea, they might have something. The music and lyrics are generally good. Milton Reddie and Eubie Blake are a good song writing team, but they are handicapped terribly by the book. Most of the present lyrics should be thrown out in terms of a new book arrangement. They have one number "Brasileira" which is sensational. It's an unusual folk dance and tune based on a Brazilian Melody.[50]

Gallo continued to try to interest other Broadway producers in the show through 1951, hoping Blake and Reddie would work with him on its revision. Eventually, a new author team was brought on to rework Gallo's story, but by this time Reddie had relocated to Mexico (where he would eventually become an English-language tutor) trying to escape the racism in the United States. Blake lost interest in the score, although Gallo was still trying to place the revised script as late as 1954. In 1957, the script was copyrighted in its final version. The songs that Blake and Reddie composed were never published, although a full list of titles exists indicating something of the range and style of their work.

While Eubie was continuing his partnership with Milton Reddie, his original partner—Noble Sissle—was looking to reestablish himself in the United States after the war. Sissle's thoughts naturally turned to *Shuffle Along*, still the strongest calling card he had in the theatrical world. He had been trying to raise money to revive it since the late 1930s, and regularly planted notices in the black press that touted the continued interest in the show from various producers. Sissle believed that the time was finally ripe for a return to Broadway with a new production of the show. On his return to New York in mid-1946, he began scheming to launch the new *Shuffle Along* with the idea of opening that fall.

Sissle had spent most of the 1930s in working as a nightclub entertainer. He may not have realized that Broadway had changed since *Shuffle Along* was a major hit. The rise of the "book musical"—a show with a coherent story in which the songs were integral to the plot—began with groundbreaking hits like *Oklahoma!* in the 1940s. While the color barrier was still in place, it would start to be challenged by shows—like *Show Boat*—that offered more sympathetic portrayals of black performers. While black actors were still expected to be "exotic," they were no longer limited to the broad stereotypes and comedy of minstrelsy. The audience too was becoming more sensitized to racial issues, and what was acceptable on stage in the early decades of the century would become increasingly problematic in the postwar years.

Nonetheless, *Shuffle Along* in Sissle's eyes remained his best chance to return to Broadway. It had a history of success and—Sissle believed—thanks to its exposure during the war, it was a "known quantity" that the returning soldiers would embrace. Hadn't they embraced Sissle and Europe on their return from entertaining the troops during World War I? Sissle had little trouble convincing Flournoy Miller to come on board, as he had toured with the wartime production and had already developed new material for it. Now, it was time to convince Eubie to write some new material for the show.

Work began in May 1946 and ran through the fall, when Sissle and Miller were both in New York (Figure 10.1). In October, Marion Blake reported that the trio was hard at work on a "new show for Bojangles [Bill Robinson]," which may have been the revised *Shuffle Along*.[51] It quickly became clear that the show would not be ready that fall, so Sissle resumed leading his band in nightclubs, most notably at Billy Rose's Diamond Horseshoe, and of course Eubie was trying to scrape together work wherever possible. Miller soon returned to Hollywood to write for the popular *Amos 'n' Andy* television program, having previously provided scripts for their radio show.

The first producer to express interest in the revived show was Thomas V. Bodkin, who signed a contract with Eubie in February 1947 "to procure the sum of $100,000 in cash plus the additional sum of $25,000 in cash for call money as necessary to continue for the purpose of producing the stage

Figure 10.1 Sissle and Blake at Blake's Brooklyn home, mugging for the camera. They were photographed while preparing the score for *Shuffle Along of 1952*.

production of the revival of Shuffle Along." Eubie was to receive a 2% royalty for the music and also was guaranteed a salary of $300 a week "as musical director [for the show] and for stage appearances" and the union minimum for the rehearsal period.[52] Bodkin had served as the general manager for various Broadway productions dating back to the late 1920s, including the original *Our Town* of 1938 and the musical *Follow the Girls* in 1944.[53] Apparently, Bodkin immediately ran into problems when he approached potential investors who were wary of investing in an all-black show. Among those who turned him down was one J. Aaronson, Vice President of the United States Realty Corporation, who wrote to the producer,

> After going over this matter and discussing same with some of my personal friends and associates they advised me to keep out of it. They think I am too old to get into the theatrical business at this time. I might consider putting

some money in this type of company, but they advised me to keep away from colored companies, as you could not sell the rights to movie companies if it was a hit as it is a colored company.[54]

This prejudice against black musicals apparently led to Bodkin's withdrawal from the project by the end of the year. A second producer, Harold Dow, took a two-month option on the show in March 1948, but also failed to find enough investors willing to risk supporting an all-black show.

Meanwhile, an unexpected event brought new attention to the show's biggest hit: Harry S. Truman's presidential run, which adopted "I'm Just Wild about Harry" as its campaign song. Even before the campaign began, columnists predicted the song would be used to help promote his candidacy: "Somehow, we believe 'I'm Just Wild about Harry,' a grand old tune of yesteryear, will pick up a lot of extra enthusiasm when the President runs again in 1948."[55] Throughout the campaign, Truman was greeted by bands playing the song, along with spontaneous outbreaks of singing by the crowds at speeches and fundraisers. The song also became code to show support for the candidate, who was believed to be trailing his opponent, Thomas E. Dewey. Oscar Levant sang it as his "favorite Gershwin song" on the Bing Crosby radio show, quipping it was "nothing political, of course," but signaling his support for the President.[56]

Following Truman's victory, a company called Song Distributing Corporation entered into partnership with Sissle and Blake to split the profits from the sale of 20,000 copies of the music to be placed on consignment with news dealers across the country.[57] A group of pop stars and singers from the Metropolitan Opera gathered at RCA's New York studios to record a special presentation disc of the song to be given to the newly elected president; it was the first recording made following the lifting of ASCAP's recording ban.[58] Truman was so appreciative of the duo's contribution to his campaign that he invited Sissle and Blake to his inauguration, a gesture that was duly noted in the black press. The song's renewed sales success helped Eubie get another bump in his ASCAP rating and also renewed his and Sissle's faith in the *Shuffle Along* score.

By December 1948, Sissle, Blake, and Miller had signed with a new producer named Irving Gaumont.[59] Gaumont agreed to pay a $100 advance a month for a two-month option, for a production to open by September 18, 1949. He also agreed to raise $150,000 for the production by August 8,

1949.[60] The cast was announced to include singers Pearl Bailey and Jimmy Anderson, and was to be staged by the well-known revue producer John Murray Anderson. The young Bailey had toured with the USO during the war, and made her Broadway debut in 1946 in *St. Louis Woman*, winning strong reviews. Mantan Moreland was to play Miller's comic foil once again, and the dancing Berry Brothers were also to be included in the cast. Flournoy Miller's daughter, classical harpist Olivette Miller, would appear as a specialty act, as she had in the 1945–1946 USO tour.

In his official biography, Gaumont said that he got his entrée into show business by writing silent comedy shorts, creating scenarios as the films were made, and occasionally performing in them himself. His first Broadway credit was as co-producer for Lew Leslie's *Blackbirds of 1928*, and then he graduated to producing himself with 1934's *The Sky's the Limit*, featuring the vaudeville comedians Smith and Dale. In 1938, Gaumont cowrote the play *Thirty Days Hath September*, which—despite running for only two performances—was later retitled as *Thieves Fall Out* on film.[61] He also operated a hot-dog eatery called Cactus Pete's on Broadway and 50th Street from the late 1930s through the 1940s.[62] Clearly, Sissle, Blake, and Miller hoped that—despite his lack of previous major successes—Gaumont had the contacts to raise the cash they needed to get *Shuffle Along* back on stage.

Shuffle Along was still fondly remembered by many entertainers who were now making inroads into the new medium of television. Eubie wrote to Miller on January 3, 1949, to report that he and Sissle had appeared on Milton Berle's TV show the night before in an abbreviated performance of *Shuffle Along*: "The whole last half of the show was *Shuffle Along* music[,] Berry Brothers & all—Everyone said the show was good. . . . Last night's television should help Gaumont to put on *Shuffle Along*."[63] Nonetheless, Gaumont's belief that he could raise the amount needed to stage the show by the end of the summer of 1949 turned out to be wildly optimistic. Sissle himself pulled as many favors as he could, commenting in his regular newspaper column for *The New York Age* that he had been pleading with "Negro businessmen . . . to give us financial aid to revive 'Shuffle Along' . . . (which would make them a fortune . . .)."[64] By June, Eubie was able to report to Sissle—who was temporarily working on the West Coast—that $85,000 had been raised to date, noting that "I hope they don't have to give it back before August the 18th or what ever date is the time limit. Gaumont & all concerned are working very hard on the deal."[65]

With the prospects for a Broadway performance uncertain, by the fall Miller apparently was pushing to take a one-hour version of the show out on the road again. He wrote to Sissle and Blake in late October that

> I have been approached by Paul Trebitsch and Johnny De Silva, who have ample finances lined up, to produce a presentation unit of 60 minutes of "Shuffle Along." I suggested you be on stage and Blake conducting the orchestra at each house. Personally I think this would be a good stepping stone to reach Broadway. . . . The starting point is either the Paramount in down-town Los Angeles or in Salt Lake City with an opening date in the early part of December.[66]

Eubie replied asking him to wait a while, as "*Shuffle Along* looks hot again & we can always go back to the idea of putting it on the road as a one hour show."[67] Nonetheless, Gaumont had still not raised enough to actually get the show staged, and would continue to struggle to assemble backers through the next year.

Sometime in 1950, Sissle and Blake, along with singers LaVerne Hutcherson and Charlotte Holloman, made a demo recording of the sequence of songs planned for the new production. This demo was probably used as a means of raising funds for the production for those who couldn't attend a live audition. Sissle provided a running narration, sketching out what would occur in each act. At this point, the script pretty much followed the original 1921 version, focusing on the election campaign of the honest Harry Walton versus the machinations of the devious Sam Peck and Steve Jenkins. The action was moved from Jimville to the less offensively named "Fairville, Florida, on the banks of the Swanee River," a reference of course to the popular Stephen Foster hit and the more recent "Swanee" written by Irving Caesar and George Gershwin. Sissle and Blake provided their own take on this theme in "Under the Swanee Moon" for the new show. To make the connection even more obvious, in this new song the female lead sings the melody of Foster's song in counterpoint to the second verse sung by her male counterpart. Sissle's lyrics included just about every imaginable cliché of Southern plantation life, including sleepy lullabyes, loving Mammies, and fragrant flowers.

The balance of the score included several of the original *Shuffle Along* hits along with some newer numbers. The new songs were divided between old-fashioned operetta styled ballads like "Alone with Love" and the waltz-time "Two Hearts in Tune" that sounds as if it were taken from an old Victor Herbert score, and newer "hot" numbers for the dance routines, including "Boogie Woogie Beguine" and "The Applejack." The "Boogie Woogie Beguine" was written for USO tours, and pitted "Xavier Cugat" style rumba dancers versus Harlem's own swing dancers, as exemplified by the music of Count Basie. The demo recording features Eubie's most inspired piano playing.

"My Platform of Swing" also was part of the USO *Shuffle Along*. It was one of the better of the new songs, with a clever lyric by Sissle referencing the latest musical styles and dances, and a jaunty melody by Blake. This song was designed as the big dance number for the opening of act 1. In this song, the candidate states his platform:

> Now listen folks don't get excited, for there's no wrong that can't be
> righted,
> We're headed now for ruination, so here's my plan to save the nation,
> Save the nation? Yes, save the nation,
> Gonna save the nation with swing-ca-pation,
> Gonna save the nation with swing-ca-pation
> Chorus:
> No more politicians, I filled their positions,
> With ha-cha musicians, in my Platform of Swing
> No more big fat coppers, all law-breakers stoppers,
> Must be Lindy Hoppers, in my Platform of Swing
> Candidates won't have a chance,
> if they can't do each new Jitterbug dance.
> All our legislators, must be dance creators,
> Jivin' alligators, or their heads will all go zip, if they are not hip
> To ev-'ry-thing, in my Platform of Swing

The show concluded with a medley of numbers from Sissle and Blake's old vaudeville act, just as the original *Shuffle Along* did. Most curious is the final number, a new song called "The Rhythm of America." It opens with a stilted spoken introduction by Sissle, in which Blake imitates different European dance styles of the turn of the 20th century, including "The Blue Danube Waltz," as a prelude to the song celebrating America's contribution to dance music. Oddly, the song is only lightly syncopated, hardly reflecting 1920s-era jazz dance music, let alone 1940s-era swing. Sissle's lyrics celebrate Texas

cowpunchers, hillbillies, and miners, among other clichéd American figures, before concluding with a handclapping verse that references African
American gospel without making any true connection with black culture.
While it is difficult to judge the quality of the overall show, as the comedy
routines are missing (which Sissle simply describes as "hilariously comic"),
the recording at least captured the spirit of the original. Whether that spirit
would transfer to new audiences was yet to be seen.

Even with this demo material, it remained difficult to raise enough money
for the production to go forward. Through the spring and summer of 1951,
Sissle and Blake staged auditions as often as twice a week, trying to interest
new backers or replace those who dropped out. Meanwhile, Gaumont
announced that the play would go into rehearsals in August 1951, followed
by tryouts out of town, with a planned October 1951 opening date.[68] This
schedule turned out to be overly optimistic, as money was still slow to
come in.

Finally, in the fall of 1951, Sissle could report to Miller that they had raised
all but $15,000 of the needed money and "I feel very safe we will be ready to
start rolling by Nov. 1st."[69] Sissle was exhausted from the years of soliciting
backers, noting,

> Believe me if we were not lucky in finding Gaumont a Jewish guy with a
> strong heart and being married to a gentile woman from Texas—Boy we
> would never have gotten the money for the show. Boy they have given us
> hell behind the scenes. Of course that Bway gang dare not come out in
> the open and fight us form a racial stand point. . . . Just for example a guy
> who is willing to put in $5000 (and I think still will) was told by some of
> the Channing Theatre group that a Negro show won't make money on the
> road—of all the dam lies.[Spelling and grammar in original][70]

Sissle noted that many of the investors were "enthused" after hearing the
songs auditioned for them, only to drop out once they spoke to more experienced producers who cast doubt on the commercial viability of a black show.

Through all this activity, there was still not a final script; Gaumont was
waiting until they'd raised enough money to fly Miller in from California to
begin work on it. Sissle told Miller that as soon as he could get to New York,

> [y]ou and I and a typepist [should] go in the wood shed for a week and we
> will come up with a show. Of course, [Gaumont] knows you can not write

your book until you know whose going to play what the present personell or cast will be. [Spelling and grammar in original][71]

It's noteworthy that Miller wrote his scripts to fit the skills and established characters of the cast members, rather than relying on the actors to portray the parts he created. The fact that actors were still being engaged meant the script ultimately would be hastily assembled, with Miller relying on his tried-and-true brand of minstrel comedy rather than branching out and creating a more modern plotline.

In a press release in late November, Gaumont announced that rehearsals would begin on December 3. The script then must have been assembled over the previous month, and probably resembled the show as it was described in the 1950 demo recording. Gaumont hoped to open the show on New Year's Eve in Boston to play for three weeks before coming to New York.[72] However, when the script was presented to Pearl Bailey, she objected to her dialogue, the size of her part, and the songs she was to perform. Sissle told a journalist that, after reading the script, Bailey said, "Well I don't know," she said, "that show is kinda Uncle Tom, and I don't want to get mixed up in anything like that."[73] Instead of beginning rehearsals, Gaumont brought on a new writer, John McGowan, to make "the necessary changes to expand Miss Bailey's part as well as provide special songs for the singing comedienne."[74]

McGowan was a Broadway veteran, having written the books for several hit musicals, including 1930's *Girl Crazy*, famous for its George Gershwin score. Like many of his contemporaries, he traveled to Hollywood when talking pictures came into vogue, and worked as a story editor at MGM. He apparently asked Paul Gerard Smith to help with the revision. Smith was also a vaudeville and Broadway veteran with decades of writing experience, including coauthoring *Funny Face*, the hit musical that launched the careers of Fred and Adele Astaire. Like McGowan, Smith had relocated to Hollywood to write for the movies in the late 1920s. Neither man was exactly on the cutting edge of what would work on Broadway, as both were long past their heydays as theatrical professionals. New director George Hale was also hired to replace John Murray Anderson; Hale had begun his career as a vaudeville hoofer, eventually leading the George Hale Girls dance troupe. He staged several Broadway shows, including Gershwin's *Girl Crazy*, *Of Thee I Sing*, and *Strike Up the Band*, and also worked in movies and television. By the time the show opened, author Smith was credited as its director with Hale given credit for "devising and staging" the production.[75]

At least at first, Miller, Sissle, and Blake were on board with the plan to revise the script. Miller traveled to Charleston, South Carolina, to work with McGowan and Smith on a new story line. The local press commented on their work on updating the show:

> Like almost everything else, humor about colored people has changed since the Roaring Twenties. What was funny then is stale or unintelligible today. . . .
>
> Like the plot and the jokes, the lyrics will be re-tailored to the times. The Negro people have come a long way, both in education and the estimation of the public, since the blackface comic era.
>
> "Nobody uses burnt cork any more," Miller commented. A light-skinned man, he formerly wore blackface make-up, just as Al Jolson and many other white comedians who long since have abandoned it.[76]

The new storyline set the opening act in World War II Italy, with an all-black regiment and their interaction with female WACs stationed in the same area. As comic relief, Miller and Hamtree Harrington (who was hired to replace Mantan Moreland) portrayed buck privates who find themselves stranded in an Alpine pass when they wander off base. This plot line introduced a gag featuring an actor in a Saint Bernard suit who rescued the stranded men.[77] The second act is set after the war is over. The action moves to New York City, where the young leads are now somewhat improbably employed in the fashion business. This career gives an excuse for staging an elaborate fashion show, the kind of leggy display that used to wow theater audiences back in the days of the *Follies*. Despite all of these "improvements," the plot was still a fairly loose structure onto which individual specialties could be accommodated. The authors took just a few weeks to complete the entire rewrite.

Although it was originally announced that McGowan would craft new songs for the show, at some point white songwriters Joseph Meyer and Floyd Huddleston were brought on board to provide more contemporary material. Meyer was best known for his hits of the 1920s, including 1922's "California, Here I Come" (1922; cowritten with Buddy DeSylva, Al Lewis, and Al Sherman), and "If You Knew Susie" (1925; with Buddy DeSylva). Huddleston was just getting started in a career that would eventually take him to Hollywood, where he wrote hundreds of songs while he was primarily working with Al Rinker.

Despite making these changes to placate Pearl Bailey—and hiring her sister Eura as a cast member—Bailey apparently was still uncomfortable with her role in the show, and finally dropped out of the production by late March. She was replaced by Delores Martin (Figure 10.2), who had made a big splash singing the song "Necessity" in the original production of *Finian's Rainbow*. Blake recommended her to Sissle for an earlier proposed production of *Shuffle Along*, so she was a natural to take the lead from Bailey. By this time, the cast also included singer/dancer Avon Long (who had his biggest success portraying Sportin' Life in *Porgy and Bess*) and big band singer Thelma Carpenter. P. Jay Sidney was cast as the young male lead; he had previously appeared in 1943's *Carmen Jones*, Oscar Hammerstein's all-black adaptation of the famous opera. However, Sidney was dropped from the cast just before the New York opening, and replaced by Napoleon Reed, who—ironically—had alternated with him in the role of Joe in that production. The

Figure 10.2 Prior to *Shuffle Along of 1952's* opening, new star Delores Martin was featured on the cover of *Jet* magazine.

plan was now to open in late April in New Haven, followed by a few weeks in Philadelphia, and finally a late-May opening in New York.

As rehearsals progressed with Martin as the new lead, a series of misfortunes plagued the company. At the end of March, the show's sets were destroyed in a freak fire in the warehouse where they were being built. The set builder had to hurriedly reconstruct the scenery in time for the opening in New Haven. Then, Noble Sissle fell off the stage and injured his leg during rehearsals for the opening, so he did not appear in the first previews. And finally, McGowan and his coauthor Smith had a falling out, with McGowan leaving the show due to "illness" just after its out-of-town premiere. McGowan's name would subsequently be removed from the show's credits.

Not surprisingly, when the show finally opened on April 23 in New Haven, it was hardly ready to be seen. *Variety*'s critic gave it an overall harsh review, slamming the disjointed plot and shabby settings and costumes:

> If they ever decide what they want to do with this all-Negro musical, maybe they can whip it into hit proportions before it's too late . . . Opening performance was merely a series of songs and dances scotch-taped together by a pretty weak semblance of a book, net result being nothing more than a blueprint of what might be expected if potentialities are exploited along more entertainment-conscious lines.

The critic praised the singing of Delores Martin and Thelma Carpenter, and even had kind words for comedians Flournoy Miller and Hamtree Harrington. The major fault was with the book: "a hit-or-miss affair . . . [which is] a slender thread that's going to need considerable expansion before it can hope to be of much assistance."[78]

The local critic for the *New Haven Courier* was a bit kinder to the show, although he also found the plot to be "a pleasant if confusing combination of World War I and II events . . . and . . . a swank New York fashion salon," noting that "many, many scenes . . . can be easily shortened . . . with no impairment to the play as a whole."[79] Both critics noted the absence of Sissle as hurting the production.

Quickly moving to Philadelphia, the show opened on April 29, with the original plan to play for two weeks. The critic from the *Inquirer* gave the show a rare good review, enjoying its nostalgic invocation of the era of "Negro musicals." The critic praised the "rich and boisterous" dancing and "lusty and uninhibited singing," and even found the comedy enjoyable although it was in the "minstrel-show pattern . . . possibly a little less 'blue' than in the earlier shows." This critic admitted,

> The book is also traditional, being cumbersome and elaborate and tripping the principals at every turn of the plot. However, this is a cast which refuses to stay tripped, being quick and light on its feet, and whenever the book gets too much in the way, it goes into a dance.[80]

Despite this warm review, audiences stayed away in droves, and the production barely made it through the week.[81] At the end of the week, Gaumont decided to shut down and move up the New York opening to early May. The total gross for the week's stand was under $10,000,[82] which lead to some rumors that it might never make New York. Walter Winchell reported that the Actor's Equity Union held the production after it closed in Philadelphia until the producers were able to make payroll,[83] and reports came in that the scenery was being held by the trucking company in New York as late as the day before the planned opening because of nonpayment of funds. But then Gaumont announced he had raised sufficient funds to have the trucks unloaded on opening day, May 8.[84]

With little time to attend to the problems with the plot, the New York premiere was met with a similar critical reception that the show had had in its preview performances. John Chapman in *The New York News* found the plot "a muddle," noting that in its shift from Italy to New York, "I can't tell you how it gets from one place to the other, and why."[85] "The calendar, I'm sorry to say, is against the 1952 edition of 'Shuffle Along,'" Louis Sheaffer in the *Brooklyn Daily Eagle* opened his review, noting that

> the men who are chiefly responsible for the new show just haven't kept up with the times. They are still thinking of Negro comedians in terms of lazy, shuffling, not overly bright "darkies" who like to use—actually, of course, misuse—long big-sounding words . . . In spite of some likable and talented performers, "Shuffle Along" is from the start a flat, uninteresting show and eventually it becomes rather depressing to see so much misdirected ability and effort. Its biggest liability is the book . . . a pointless, pretty amateurish thing that serves as a loose, weak connecting thread between the songs, dances and comedy business.[86]

Wolcott Gibbs, writing in *The New Yorker*, found the play's book to be "an intolerable bore."[87] *The New York Times* critic agreed, complementing the "warm-hearted, earnest, ingratiating performers" but noting that "their efforts are put to waste by a fumbling, wandering book plus a surprising lack of humor." The critic continued, "Nothing . . . could be as disappointing in a musical of this sort as the fact that what humor it has is of the Amos and Andy School and not even in the same class,"[88] a hard blow for Miller, who of course felt that *Amos 'n' Andy* had stolen many of its routines from him and Lyles.

Even the African American press found fault with the humor, noting that

[p]erhaps in 1921, when the Negro was making his first major steps on the legitimate stage, theatre goers would accept a view of this kind of self-abasement. If the current "Shuffle Along" proves nothing else, it demonstrates beautifully that there is no longer a market for "dese" and "dose" comedy.[89]

Most damning of all was a lengthy article written by leading critic George Jean Nathan. Nathan claimed to have seen the original 1921 production five times, and held it in great esteem—which undoubtedly contributed to his harsh review. Calling the production a "catastrophic failure," Nathan faulted the show's producers for trying to remake the show and not trusting the audience to accept what was an innovative production in its time:

Operating under the delusion . . . that if theatregoers loved a show when they first saw it they will not love it any longer unless all sorts of alterations are made in it, the present sponsors monkeyed the revival out of any public acceptance and right into the can. . . . If by any remote chance they ever put the show on again, what they had best to do is throw away all the many variations and present it exactly as it was in 1921. It is, if anything, a nostalgic show and you can't work up any nostalgia by dressing up a favorite old aunt like a bobby-soxer.[90]

Sissle and Blake were particularly angered by the changes made to the show's score. Only two songs from the original *Shuffle Along* made the grade, "Harry" and the hit ballad "Love Will Find a Way." Sissle and Blake did perform several more of the original show's hits during their second-act appearance, although this only underscored the general weakness of the rest of the score. Along with their earlier hits, two songs from the earlier USO and 1950 versions were retained: the minstrel-style "Under the Swanee Moon" and the dance number "Rhythm of America," which was presented by the full company to conclude act 1. A few additional songs were written by the duo and four new songs by Huddleston and Meyer were added, none of which made a major impression on the audience or critics.

Of the entire new score, Eubie was most pleased with the melody he composed to open act 2, "It's the Gown That Makes the Gal That Makes the Guy." It was the first of his songs that he felt benefited from his Schillinger training, despite Sissle's objections to his employing this technique:

> Sissle says to me, "Give me a good melody. Now don't write that from the Schillinger, I want the God-given melody that you got. Nobody got melodies like you." . . . And I wrote this melody. [Sissle's] in the room . . . to write the lyrics. And I don't know what they [the play's authors] are doing. I asked them the title, they says it. And I wrote out the numbers. And it was the hit of the show and it only played 4 days. "God gave you those melodies," Sissle says. God didn't give me that, Rudolf Schram gave it to me.[91]

Oddly, the program for the show credited this song's lyrics to Joan Javitts (who would score big a year later with "Santa Baby" as sung by Eartha Kitt); perhaps the original lyrics by Sissle were rejected by the producer or Eubie misremembered who had written them.

Although no full recording of the original production exists, RCA Victor brought two members of the cast, Thelma Carpenter and Avon Long, into the studio to "recreate" four of the original *Shuffle Along*'s hits just after the show closed, with Eubie conducting the orchestra. These recordings give some insight into further reasons why the production was a flop. Carpenter's singing on "Love Will Find a Way" sounds as if it could have been recorded in the 1890s, with all the maudlin style of operetta. Long's singing on "Bandana Days" nearly screams minstrelsy, with his vocal mannerisms aurally capturing the wide eyes and exaggerated smiles of blackface. The orchestrations are terribly dull, with not a hint of jazz in them. Even by the standards of the early 1950s, these recordings are remarkably uninspiring; any audience expecting the jazzy energy of the original version would have been disappointed.

Given the reviews, it's not surprising that the show ran for only four performances in New York. It shuttered on Saturday the 10th for what

Gaumont initially announced as a two-week hiatus for further work to be done on the script. Under Actors' Equity rules, Gaumont had to give the cast two-week notice if he was closing down the show, so he was on the hook for their salaries regardless of whether the show could be reopened.[92] After the final performance, Sissle went so far as to appear on local radio to call on listeners to support it.[93] The New York critics gave Gaumont little chance of success, noting that while some shows were revised after opening, none were shut down entirely and then successfully revived. Nonetheless, the United Press theater critic Jack Gaver noted, there were some good elements in the production that might make it possible to bring it back to life:

> The chief trouble with "Shuffle Along" is the libretto or story. There are a number of good singers and dancers involved, the comics could be comic if given a chance, and the songs are adequate enough. . . . Bad routining of the show was also one of its worst troubles on opening night.[94]

While the *Chicago Defender*'s critic agreed the book needed revision, he also suggested that the lack of a "name" star doomed the show to failure. While noting that Sissle, Blake, and Miller had been big names in the 1920s, "all have been off the stem [i.e., Broadway] for a number of years and are about as unknown to the present generation as a Republican president."[95] This writer noted that Cab Calloway, Lena Horne, and Dorothy Dandridge had all been mentioned as possible big names who might be hired to revive the show. However, by early June, Gaumont announced the show would not be reopening any time soon, although he hinted it might return to Broadway in the fall.[96]

Just after the show's closing, Flournoy Miller gave an interview to *Variety* to wash his hands of the production. "My script was changed beyond recognition," the comedian complained:

> The book that Smith and Macgowan [sic] turned out was nothing like the original I didn't want to have anything to do with it. I asked not to have co-author billing, but they paid no attention. I agree with the critics that the book was terrible. It alone was enough to kill the show, even without all the other troubles we had. Sissle and Blake agree with me, and so do most of the cast.[97]

Miller did not go so far as to blame Gaumont for the production's failure, perhaps hedging his bets that there was still a possibility that it could be revived in the original version that he scripted. At the same time, Sissle rallied a behind-the-scenes campaign among several of the show's backers to wrench control from Gaumont so that they might reclaim the production. Sissle also tried to retrieve as much of the money that Gaumont owed to the trio for their performances and the rights to their material. He reported to Miller in late June that the other investors had recommended that they send a registered letter to Gaumont, telling him

> that we (Miller-Sissle-& Blake) are taking advantage of our Authors League agreement and notifying him that we are withdrawing all of our material of this 1952 Shuffle Along and that he should release the announcement thru the press that the "Show is definitely closed for good."[98]

Sissle characterized Gaumont and the writers he had hired to doctor the show as "dam faggots, communists, and freaks," perhaps out of his frustration with how they meddled with the script and music.[99] Sissle told Miller he had been contacted by a "real live Negro from Detroit" who was interested in helping raise money for the revived production. "He is [a] fine honest business man and has money and respect of all ofays in Detroit—the theatrical people," he noted. Sissle proposed trying out the show in Detroit, where expenses were considerably less than in New York.

In early August, Sissle presented this idea to the original backers, who were still hoping to have some return on their investment. Eubie also attended this meeting and—when Sissle asked him if he had anything to add to the plan—he surprised the lyricist by questioning why they couldn't reopen in New York rather than going to Detroit. Sissle was furious with Eubie, writing to Miller,

> [t]he guy makes me so dam mad sometime—because he just wanders through life while other people bring him a golden platter and then kicks over the pail of milk—Well we will make him and ourselves a lot of money in spite of himself.[100]

Sissle told Miller that Eubie accused him of "trying to run things and thinking he had no sense," recalling the tension that had led them to break up back in the 1920s. Still, despite his frustration with Blake, the lyricist realized that his only hope of saving the show was to continue to work with the talented composer.

When all the dust settled, Sissle was unable to get *Shuffle Along* back on stage. Many years later, writing to Eubie's biographer Al Rose, Eubie's wife Marion summarized how the show's creators felt about the situation:

The producer, Irving Gaumont, . . . instructed Flourney [*sic*] Miller the book author to return to California and modernize the script. That is to bring it up-to-date. In the meantime Sissle & Blake for one year auditioned for prospective angels and when they had raised two hundred and fifty thousand dollars, Mr. Miller was sent for. But also, upon arrival, Mr. Gaumont was not satisfied with what had been accomplished. The material was not acceptable to Miss Bailey. By then rehearsal schedules had been called out of town opening dates set etc. A ghost doctor or book doctor was called in. But the remaining time was not adequate to do the job. Everybody panic'd. Worse than all, Mr. Gaumont. In this state of panic he accepted and produced an entirely new book, a story that had nothing to do with Shuffle Along except for a few original Shuffle Along songs. Thus disaster. Believe it or not, it was a dam [*sic*] good show. But not Shuffle Along. It was a heart breaking experience.[101]

Sissle vowed never to be put in the same position again, while Miller fumed that it was Sissle's willingness to do anything to get the show back on Broadway that had led to the disastrous production. Nonetheless, the dream of reviving the show—and regaining their status as Broadway pioneers—would persist until Sissle's and Miller's passing, over 20 years later.

11

Lean Times to Revival

1953–1970

While Eubie was struggling to reestablish himself as a popular songwriter and Broadway composer in the later 1940s and early 1950s, a small but growing group of jazz enthusiasts were becoming interested in the musical styles that helped give birth to jazz, including blues and ragtime. During the Second World War, drives for shellac led to the wholesale scrapping of many older 78 recordings; a few canny collectors began haunting junk shops and secondhand dealers to collect recordings made from the 1910s through the early 1930s that the major labels felt were no longer commercially important enough to keep in print. While some younger jazz musicians were turning their backs on the big band style and exploring more rhythmically and harmonically adventurous music, others were rediscovering the music that predated swing music and were seeking out older players who had been largely forgotten. They would champion a new nostalgic music that was called "Dixieland" jazz, which incorporated elements of ragtime, early 20th-century popular song, and early jazz band music. Eubie would be an unwitting beneficiary of the revived interest in early jazz and ragtime, although it would take nearly 20 years for his music to regain mainstream attention.

A jazz scholar named Rudi Blesh was the leader of the so-called moldy figs—the jazz fans who preferred the older styles to the more progressive new music that would become celebrated as bebop.[1] Blesh's career was shaped by a series of happy accidents. Raised in the Midwest, he showed an early talent for drawing. Hoping to broaden his horizons, he applied to and was accepted at Dartmouth, bringing him to the East Coast. Attending college in the 1920s, he often visited New York City, where he first heard bands like the Original Dixieland Jazz Band and began collecting 78s of jazz music. After college and his parent's divorce, Blesh joined his mother in Berkeley, California, trying to get a job in the graphic arts, and eventually working as an interior designer in the early 1940s. The San Francisco area was a hotbed for Dixieland-style revival bands, and so Blesh began writing about jazz, becoming the jazz critic

Eubie Blake. Richard Carlin and Ken Bloom, Oxford University Press (2020). © Richard Carlin and Ken Bloom 2020. DOI: 10.1093/oso/9780190635930.001.0001

for the *San Francisco Exami*ner. New York composer Virgil Thomson was also interested in learning about jazz, and when he visited San Francisco, Blesh became his unofficial tour guide to the local jazz clubs. Thomson urged Blesh to come to New York, and introduced him to his publisher, leading to Blesh authoring one of the first histories of early jazz, *Shining Trumpets*.

While in New York, Blesh became involved with Harriet Janis, a well-known art dealer's wife who would become Rudi's companion for the remainder of her life. The two founded a record label together that they operated out of their apartment to record ragtime and early jazz revival bands. The Dada master Marcel Duchamp—a personal friend of the couple—suggested that they name their label "Circle" after the shape of the discs. Janis was particularly a fan of ragtime music, and encouraged Blesh to coauthor a book on the musical style. As luck would have it, the two were able to locate Scott Joplin's widow, who was still operating a hotel in Harlem. In her basement, they discovered Joplin's opera *Treemonisha*, among other material, and thus were able to document the "classic" ragtime era. The product of their research appeared in 1950 as *They All Played Ragtime*, which for many years remained the definitive history of the musical genre.

In researching the book, Blesh and Janis first met and interviewed Eubie Blake. Impressed by the pianist's considerable skills, Blesh invited him to several "jam sessions" held at his apartment; one session was issued on an album in 1951 called *Jammin' at Rudi's* and featured Blake's first solo piano recording in decades, his version of "Maple Leaf Rag." (Probably Blesh requested that Eubie record it, as it was not something that he played regularly even in his heyday as a working pianist.) Blesh arranged to record an entire album of Eubie's playing, including performances of his own rags that had never been previously recorded. Unfortunately, soon after the sessions were completed, Blesh and Janis closed Circle Records because of lack of funds, selling off its masters to another small label. Eubie's record was never issued.[2] However, Blesh remained in touch with Blake and would be important in bringing him renewed exposure toward the end of the 1950s.

This attention on his early career must have been gratifying to Blake, but his primary focus remained on trying to launch a new Broadway show. He worked with Flournoy Miller as both librettist and lyricist in 1953 and 1954; the duo produced a script and songs for a show to be titled *Hit the Stride*. Although the script doesn't survive, judging from the manuscripts for the songs and their titles it sounds as if it were a typical revue-like show to feature comic sketches and dance routines. Miller's titles and lyrics drew on 1930s-era jazz slang, including songs titled "Hep Cats Done Gone High Hat," "Don't Cheat on the Meat," and the title song. The show's love ballad was titled "It's Hard to Love Somebody (When That Somebody Don't Love You)."[3] Apparently, producer George White had expressed some interest in staging the show, but nothing came of it.[4]

In 1955, Miller's brother Irvin invited the duo to score the latest edition of his long-running *Brown Skin Models* revue. These revues combined comic sketches, song and dance, and parades of scantily clad, light-skinned girls, which Miller produced as inexpensively as possible to tour the country. The plan for the new show was to have a slightly higher quality of staging and scenery, with the idea of perhaps being able to attract Broadway interest. The show was to star Miller and his regular sidekick Mantan Moreland, along with singer-dancers Mable Lee, Canadian-born Valerie Blake, and Lee Richardson, the singing Rhythmaires, and "fourteen beautiful chorus and show girls and Smalls Boykin and his dancing boys."[5] Blake was to lead a 12-piece orchestra for the show.

Although the duo had plenty of songs that they had written for *Hit the Stride*, they wrote an entirely new score for this show. Miller and Blake's songs were inspired by well-known hits ("Old Man River Is Lonely Now"), as well as crafted to suit novelty numbers ("The Thrill I Felt in Sunny Spain," designed to accompany a Spanish-styled dance number, and the minstrel-flavored "Mississippi Honeymoon").

Irvin Miller's plan was to prevue the show at Washington's Howard Theater, before taking it to New York's Apollo and then on the road, hoping eventually to reach Las Vegas and the West. He pitched the show to the African American press as a return to the glory days of high-class revues, like the *Blackbirds* series that were major hits on Broadway. As the critic in the *Chicago Defender* noted,

> The attempt to revive the dying Sepia show circuit will rest on the beautiful shoulders of "Brown Skin Models" . . . On a toboggan since the closing of the Lafayette Theatre [in New York] many years ago, the vaudeville show circuit has dwindled from forty-two consecutive weeks of theater to an alarming one. Even that one, the Apollo theatre here, becomes none when summer rolls around. Unless something is done to check the decline the complete death of this once great entertainment and avenue for the development of Negro talent is but a few seasons away.[6]

The *Defender*'s critic suggested that the reason for the decline of interest in African American revues was the lack of "the entertaining family type shows with original music, solid performers and pretty girls which inspired producers to take to Broadway in the past." No mention was made of the fact that this style of entertainment—particularly in its broad, racial humor—was becoming increasingly outmoded by changes in society and the growing clamor for Civil Rights.

Despite Irvin Miller's assertion that the new *Brown Skin Models* would be a true book production, the only really scripted scene was a sketch by Miller and Mantan, titled "The Poker Game," that was probably reworked from earlier routines that Miller had written. The rest of the show consisted of solo songs and production numbers, a few dance routines, and the requisite leggy showgirls.

When the show had its first performances in Washington, DC, Sissle sent a thoughtful telegram to Blake, Miller, and the cast, congratulating them on their opening:

> 34 YEARS AGO ALMOST TO THE MONTH RIGHT HERE IN THE HOWARD THEATRE FOUR GUYS WITH A DREAM AND WITH NO ONE TO DISTURB THEM AND SURROUNDED BY FAITHFUL TALENTED CAST WHO BELIEVED IN THEM SAW THEIR DREAM BECOME A REALITY AND A GEM OF AN ARTISTIC ENTERTAINMENT WAS BORN . . . WELL HERE[']S HOPING THAT ONCE AGAIN WITHIN THESE HISTORIC WALLS THERE WILL BE A REBIRTH OF THAT SAME SPIRITED BREATHLESS DANCING HARMONIOUS SOULFULL [*SIC*] SINGING AND UPROARIOUSLY CLEAN COMEDY THAT WILL ONCE AGAIN BRING TO THE LEGITIMATE THEATER THAT WHOLESOME ORIGINAL STYLE OF ENTERTAINMENT THE WORLD IS YEARNING [FOR] . . . UNDER THE GUIDANCE AND THROUGH KNOW HOW OF IRVING [*SIC*] FLOURNOY AND EUBIE IT SHOULD HAPPEN.[7]

However, other than the performances in Washington and Harlem, the show never hit the road and there was no interest expressed in bringing it to Broadway.

Simultaneously with partnering with Blake on *Brown Skin Models*, Miller was planning to mount an abbreviated version of *Shuffle Along* in Las Vegas. He had been corresponding with Eubie since as early as January 1954 about this possibility, but things really picked up in 1956 when a producer named Stephen Papich expressed strong interest in producing the show. Papich was a freelance choreographer who had worked on several Hollywood spectacles, and would later stage nightclub acts for Josephine

Baker, Mae West, and Judy Garland.[8] Miller reported to Blake that Papich believed the original 1921 score would still have strong appeal to contemporary audiences:

> [Papich and his associates have] done some research work on "Shuffle" and they think the same music that was in the "1921 show" would be sensational today—"Simply Full of Jazz[,]" "Bandana Days[,]" "Honey Suckle Time[,]" in fact all the numbers—
>
> They say Paul Whiteman has revised some of his early orchestrations and is making a big hit with them. He (Papich) went to the Hollywood library and checked the write ups on the "Flop" we had when we let them change the show. And he said all of them said if we had produced the old show the people would not have been disappointed and it would have been successful. So they want the old score.[9]

Miller sought to assure Blake that this time they would maintain control over the show, avoiding the pitfalls of the disastrous 1952 production:

> I don't think we can go wrong this time. We should do what we want to do—with no McGowans, Hales or Smiths to but[t] in—
>
> We were not wrong before, and we still have our faculties—So I think our judgment is best for us. Too many advisors turn out bad. We understand better than anyone else what the critics expect from us. So we must do it our way.[10]

In October 1956, Miller again wrote to Blake, expressing his belief that Papich and his partners were truly enthusiastic about mounting a version of the original show, while emphasizing that these were "young men" who knew contemporary tastes:

> I never saw such enthusiasm as he and his associates are showing.
>
> He has been to Las Vegas and has a deal that is "hot."
>
> This is very important. He has some records "Love will find a way" "Plantation days" and "Gypsy Blues." He played them and all that were there raved (and remember they were all young men). I felt very proud when they said "Eubie Blake is a great arranger" as well as composer! I could not help but remember what you told me about Sissle suggesting another arranger when the man sent for you to do it.
>
> Believe me Eubie. Here are some young men that appreciate your artistry.

I have a feeling that Papich has the money to do the show now. Though he has not told me.

He spoke of an opening in Las Vegas New Years eve—[Underscoring in the original]

While Miller believed the show would be mounted, he wanted to make it clear to Eubie that he didn't want—or need—Sissle to be involved. Nonetheless, he wanted to assure him that Sissle would get any payment due to him:

Now please understand this—
Sissle will get every dime due him
Every thing will be done legally
But under no circumstances will I engage in any thing that he is around with the methods he has used before—
He will never meddle with my book again. You will have to admit he all way [*sic*] tried to dictate the way your music was played and what musician[s] you engaged for your orchestra, and never came to your defenses when others butted in—
These men are your fans—they believe in you. Now for once you can do things the way you want them.
I repeat, Sissle will get every dime due him.[11]

Typically, Eubie was not enthusiastic about telling Sissle about Miller's plan and must have expressed his concerns again to Miller after receiving this letter. Miller responded four days later, again trying to reassure Blake:

There won't be any problem in breaking the news to Sissle. He will get an agreement like a lyricist gets—and if need be, I will tell him that we don't need him to work on the show—you don't have to say anything but I will tell him that you are capable of taking care of the musical end and I don't need him on the book—I am sure we both can do better without his interference.[12]

By late October, things had gotten far enough along for Blake to put together a possible song list and discuss with Flournoy the performers he wanted to be included in the production. Miller informed him that Papich planned to pay only a flat fee for the rights to stage the show, rather than a royalty per performance, for a planned five-to-six-week run in Las Vegas. However, he assured Blake that the musicians would be paid per union rules, and Blake also requested that his expenses for traveling to Vegas would be covered. Blake drew up his own terms of agreement for the work, an agreement he apparently sent to Miller.[13]

While this was all occurring, Sissle was in discussions with Louis Armstrong's agent, Joe Glaser, about possibly reviving the show himself. Sissle must have gotten wind of the Vegas plans, because he had Glaser write to Papich, enquiring about his role in the production. Miller advised Papich that he had no intention of involving Sissle in it, stating baldly to Eubie, "I have nothing to say to Sissle. He has never considered me unless he had to. He has done too many things to me."[14] Whether Sissle's interference rattled Papich or—more likely—the producer simply couldn't raise the necessary funds to get the show off the ground, Miller's correspondence abruptly ended and all mention of the idea of a Vegas production evaporated.

Meanwhile, Sissle, like Blake, was now ensconced in New York City in a semiretired capacity. Even so, he still had clout in the entertainment world and was always looking for opportunities to promote himself—and Eubie, when it was appropriate. In November 1954, he managed to book the duo into a weeklong appearance at New York's Palace Theater as part of a nostalgic recreation of a vaudeville bill. Sissle was probably behind a feature article on the duo in March 1955 in *Ebony* magazine, celebrating their return to the stage.

Sissle was also behind the idea for a new musical tracing the history of black music and dance, titled *Happy Times*.[15] Although a press release announced that Flournoy Miller would be writing the show's book, Miller testily wrote to both Sissle and Blake after seeing the announcement in his local paper, stating. "After our conversation in NY—I don't understand it. Please let me know what it is all about in detail."[16] It seems that Sissle was jumping the gun in puffing the new production even before Miller was in agreement to actually work on the show. A working song list for the show indicates that Sissle and Blake drew on early numbers like "Affectionate Dan" and "Bandana Days," songs from the 1940s-era *Shuffle Along* revivals, and newly written numbers.[17] Eventually, producer A. P. Waxman wrote a script for the show, and even sent it to rising star Sammy Davis Jr. in hopes that he'd be interested in starring in it.[18] However, nothing came of it and the musical went unproduced.

Throughout the 1950s, Blake remained in touch with lyricist Andy Razaf, who began to suffer from the effects of syphilis in 1951 when he was paralyzed from the waist down. Despite the ravages of the disease, Razaf continued to write prolifically as a newspaper columnist, and to work on lyrics for songs. The two were close correspondents, each supporting the other's efforts to get recordings made of their past hits, most notably "Memories of You" and "We Are Americans Too." In 1956, Razaf managed to interest the producer of Detroit's "Century of Progress" gala to adapt "We Are Americans Too" as its theme song, even penning a new verse to bring the song up to date through the Korean War.[19] Among the performers at the gala was Nat "King" Cole, then at the height of his popular success. Somehow, the organizers convinced Capitol Records (Cole's label) to issue a test recording of the song in Detroit to coincide with Cole's appearance there. Razaf enthusiastically reported to Eubie,

> These Negroes . . . out in Detroit are really on the ball . . . They performed a miracle by actually getting Capitol Records to have Nat Cole record ["We Are Americans Too"]!! Not sure of the market for it, Capitol has only made 40 copies to be given out to Disc Jockeys in and around Detroit. It's the first time a major record company has ever recorded a song about the achievements and greatness of the Negro, so that's why they hesitate to go all out on a commercial bases [sic], with our song. I am having important persons to write Capitol and remind them that this record will help Nat Cole regain the respect of his people and that seventeen million Negroes with a buying power of over fifteen billion dollars—at last concious [sic] of their greatness and right to human dignity—will buy "We ARE Americans Too" today.[20]

Sadly, the record was never issued nationally. A year later, Razaf tried to interest W. C. Handy in using the song in the upcoming film biography of his life, but again was unsuccessful. Instead, Blake and Razaf were paid a measly $83.00 each by Handy for the rights to a song they had written about Haitian revolutionary Toussaint Louverture. Razaf ruefully noted to Blake, "Since this particular song would not be a big seller to the general public, we might as well get it in the picture and take the $83.00 a piece which beats nothing."[21]

The revivals of both ragtime and so-called Dixieland music grew through the 1950s. Particularly popular were a group of young, white revivalist pianists who specialized in playing novelty-style ragtime that was originally popularized in the 1910s and 1920s by composers like Zez Confrey (famous for his "Kitten on the Keys") and George L. Cobb (who wrote "Russian Rag," among other novelties). Sporting flashy stage garb (including patterned vests, bowler hats, and spats) and large cigars, these players often took on the persona of "honky-tonk" pianists, purporting to recreate the atmosphere of the lowdown joints where the music originated. Among the notable practitioners of the new style were Joe "Fingers" Carr (born Lou Busch) and "Knuckles" O'Toole (a generic name used on different records by pianists Dick Hyman and Billy Rowland), Johnny Maddox, and "Ragtime" Bob Darch. Surprisingly, several of their records were chart hits and they were all regulars on record, radio, and TV in the 1950s.

Hoping to cash in on the ragtime craze, new record label 20th Century Fox—founded by the film studio in the late 1950s—signed Eubie to a one-year, exclusive contract in June 1958.[22] Perhaps uncertain as to how to market Blake, Fox elected to record him with a small "Dixieland" style ensemble—a format that did not naturally complement Blake's strengths as a solo pianist. According to Dan Morgenstern, Blake had to be "coaxed out of retirement" to record—which seems unlikely—and that he was convinced only when Fox promised he'd have total control over the material to be recorded.[23]

The first album released was titled *The Wizard of the Ragtime Piano*. It featured a band that was assembled for the sessions, including Dixieland revivalists clarinetist Buster Bailey and Panama Francis on drums, and session regulars Bernard Addison on guitar, and Milt Hinton or George Duvivier on bass.[24] The first side of the album was devoted to ragtime instrumentals, while the second side featured Blake along with Noble Sissle performing a mix of their own songs and old chestnuts like "Bill Bailey, Won't You Please Come Home?" How and why Sissle came to be included on this album is unknown, although knowing his pushy nature, he probably convinced Blake that his presence would help with the record's sales. On the ragtime numbers, Eubie's piano work is obscured by the overly busy clarinet work. Even the tracks that emphasized his piano playing were marred by odd accompaniments; both his renditions of Jesse Pickett's "The Dream"[25] (titled here "Dream Rag") and his own "Troublesome Ivories" (titled "Ragtime Rag" on this release) are annoyingly accompanied by a regular hi-hat pattern played by Francis that works against the subtleties of Eubie's dramatic pauses and rhythmic alterations. Eubie adds his usual exuberant shouted interjections, but overall he sounds rather uncomfortable in this setting.

The second album, *Marches I Played on the Old Ragtime Piano*, was released in 1959 and for some reason was devoted to popular marches—albeit played in a ragtime-like style—perhaps as an attempt to reach a larger market. Sissle was not included, nor was Duvivier, and Kenny Burrell replaced Addison on guitar, but otherwise the band remained the same. The album included such oddities as "Bangor Cadets" and "Oh, Brave Old Army Team," and even "Song without Words"! Only "Stars and Stripes Forever" was a part of Eubie's regular repertory. Always deferential to the demands of others, Eubie may simply have been playing whatever was requested of him.[26] Marred by an overall poor conception that led them to appeal neither to the pop nor hard-core jazz audience and barely marketed on their release, the albums went quickly out of print. They did little to relaunch Eubie's performing career.

The idea of reviving *Shuffle Along* cropped up again as the 1950s drew to a close. This time, it was the possibility of an off-Broadway staging in Greenwich Village that was floated by Sissle. Miller was once again inspired to update the comic conceit of the show, stating, "Tell Sissle I have an idea of a number to open The Mayor's Office: 'Beat Niks have taken over City Hall.' "[27] Anything to make the show "topical" for a new generation! However, like previous efforts, nothing came of this idea, because no producer could be found who was willing to stage the show.

Slowly, the ragtime and early jazz revival movement gave Eubie new opportunities to perform and to demonstrate his talent as an entertainer. In the summer of 1960, Rudi Blesh staged a workshop-concert at the Newport Jazz Festival on early jazz piano.[28] He invited Eubie to perform along with his contemporaries Willie "The Lion" Smith and a lesser-known pianist named Donald Lambert, who mostly played around his native Newark, New Jersey. Also included was the jazz revivalist Danny Barker and his trio. The entire concert was presented as part performance and part history lesson, with Blesh giving lengthy introductions about each performer's background and his place in the history of jazz. This format meant that Eubie was asked to play a number of pieces representing other early composers, including "Lovey Joe," a 1910 hit for pianist Joe Jordan and "The Charleston," James P. Johnson's famous dance hit. He did have the opportunity to play one of his more modern rags, "Troublesome Ivories," this time titled "Black Keys on Parade," as well as his big song hit "Memories of You." Eubie performed "Memories" with an elaborate, pseudoclassical introduction, before launching into the more familiar chorus; this would be the arrangement he would continue to perform through the rest of his life.[29]

WILLIE THE LION / EUBIE / EARL HINES / C. SCHWARTZ / B.B. / MAX MORATH

Figure 11.1 A group of veterans and revivalists gathered in 1972 to celebrate Eubie. Left to right: Willie "The Lion" Smith, Eubie, Earl Hines, Charles Schwartz, Bill Bolcom, and Max Morath. Photo courtesy Bill Bolcom.

Eubie was most impressed by Donald Lambert's playing. He had not previously heard Lambert play, and was stunned when he heard him play two different melodies simultaneously, as Eubie recalled in a 1969 interview:

I ain't never heard of this guy before, never saw him, not in my life. I'm looking at this guy, playing honky tonk piano. Now Willie called him a punk one time, and he didn't like Willie. . . . He sat down, the first thing he played [sings]—Gee! . . . Rudi says, "Don will play any tune with 'Tea for Two' that will fit, with either hand, left hand or right hand." And they named one thing. He says, "No, that won't fit." Finally, "That one will fit." And damn if he didn't do it. Now I could do it with one tune because I wrote the tune, "Gypsy Blues." I could play Victor Herbert's "Gypsy Love Song" with my left hand, but I couldn't turn around and play "Gypsy Blues" with this hand while I was playing [a different tune with my other hand] . . . But this guy could do it.

Now when he first started playing "Liza," now Willie's sitting right next to me. I says to Willie, "Jesus Christ, that guy can . . . " And he says, "Oh well, he'll do." "Do?" I says "This guy can play the piano. What you talking about 'He'll do.' When I get up there, I'm going to start right off. I ain't going to take no chances." Boy he played the piano. He was poison.[30]

"The Lion" was famously contemptuous of other performers, so it's not surprising he dismissed this younger master who so impressed Blake.

The ragtime revivalists were popular enough to attract mainstream media attention, including the major TV networks. In the fall of 1960, Blake was invited to appear on a special hosted by popular songwriter/pianist Hoagy Carmichael and titled "Those Ragtime Years" that was broadcast nationwide on NBC. The show featured a variety of singers and instrumentalists, along with historic dance footage, culminating with Carmichael, Blake, and ragtime revivalists Ralph Sutton and Dick Wellstood performing a four-piano version of Joplin's "Maple Leaf Rag." Eubie's solo spot was his own "Ragtime Rag" (aka "Troublesome Ivories").[31] The show gained Eubie much-needed exposure, along with a few brief newspaper interviews; most of the reviews focused on the fact that the 77-year-old pianist (as he then claimed to be) was able to give such an energetic performance.

Another key revivalist who helped promote Eubie in the early 1960s was the Detroit-born performer/pianist "Ragtime" Bob Darch, who first wrote to Eubie to introduce himself in the fall of 1958. Like other performers of this era, Darch was primarily an entertainer, mixing humorous anecdotes, nostalgic songs, and showy and fast ragtime solos to draw a mainstream audience. His stage presentation was a highly romanticized version of the kind of pianists who entertained in the bars and brothels of Eubie's youth. Darch's larger-than-life personality and attraction to younger musicians is captured in this memory by pop music scholar Ian Whitcomb, who met the pianist in the early 1960s:

In 1964 I was in Seattle, having established myself as an entertainer in a local coffee house and having parlayed my way into a recording contract as a future rock star with a local label. My recording manager and I were sitting in a swell hotel talking turkey over Jack Daniel's when my attention was deflected from royalty points and how I was to become bigger than [Mick]

Jagger by that certain sound of "Maple Leaf Rag" . . . I rushed into the room from whence came the glorious music and there he was! Straw hat and everything, pounding out the good news. To the consternation of my manager I spent the next few days in the company of Ragtime Bob. Songs, stories, jokes came pouring out of this avuncular genius as I followed him around like Boswell followed Dr. Johnson in 18th century London. I hung on every gravelly word, I vowed to remember the lyric of every song gem that kept falling from him as we walked and talked and drank and drank. . . . One evening we, together with my local girlfriend, were having dinner in the home of a wealthy local couple when in came their young son to say goodnight. Later Bob trapped me in the wet bar to inform me that the boy was really his son. Even later my girlfriend emerged from the powder room to tell me that Bob had proposed to her. I put the whole matter aside because I so admired the man's art.[32]

In about 1959, Darch was hired as the house pianist for Club 76 in Toronto, where he would become a popular performer through the mid-1960s. A year into his employment, he convinced the management to bring Eubie Blake to the club to perform, a rare early date for the pianist as a ragtime player. (Darch arranged to have Eubie's hands photographed at the time of this engagement to show off his remarkable reach; see Fig. 11.2.) This act led to a friendship between the two players, and Darch would do much to popularize Eubie and his music among his own audience. More importantly, he convinced his record label to record Eubie along with two other old-timers, songwriter/composer Joe Jordan and pianist Charlie Thompson, on a 1962 album released as *Golden Reunion in Ragtime*. The cover featured the "headline" "Ragtime Bob Darch presents . . ." along with a small cameo photo of Darch, a clever PR move to get the album into the hands of Darch's audience who would not know these older pianists' names. Further, a special two-disc version was produced for radio stations; that version included interviews with Darch and the other pianists that could be used as a stand-alone radio program.

Among Eubie's contributions to the album is his first recording of his rag "Dictys on 7th Avenue." ("Dictys" is African American slang for the upper-class blacks who emulated European culture and dress; 7th Avenue in Harlem was the preferred address for these social climbers.) The piece combines elements of ragtime, stage music, and the use of chromatic chord progressions and unusual tonalities that Eubie experimented with in pieces like 1939's "Blues Classique." After opening with a series of dissonant

Figure 11.2 Eubie's exceptionally long fingers were both a blessing and a curse to him. In childhood, his mother warned him to keep his hands in his pockets, lest people think he was a pickpocket. However, as a pianist, he had distinct advantages with his long reach. Here are Eubie's hands photographed in 1960 and labeled by the pianist himself. Photo courtesy Bill Bolcom.

chords (perhaps reflecting Blake's training in the Schillinger method), the tune proceeds into a jaunty first theme that suggests a finely dressed couple strolling on the avenue. As the theme concludes, another set of dissonant chords and scale runs (repeated twice) leads into a repetition of the opening strain. A new theme then occurs that again opens with a series of dramatic, unusually harmonized chords leading into a more conventional raggy melody. The piece concludes with a final, exotically harmonized ascending passage.

The album appeared on the small Stereo-Oddities label that was operated by entrepreneur/recording engineer Fletcher Smith out of Florida, far from the centers of the entertainment world. The label had its initial success with comedy albums and novelties like Darch's ragtime music. The *Golden Reunion* album must have been successful enough[33] that Smith considered recording an entire solo album by Eubie. However, there was one significant roadblock to recording Blake; his previous contract with 20th Century Fox stipulated he couldn't rerecord any of the items that he had recorded for them for five years after the deal ended. Fletcher wrote to Eubie in August 1962, suggesting the idea for the album, which would include a small backup band:

> I've been toying around with the idea of having you come down here by yourself to do an album entitled EUBIE BLAKE PLAYS EUBIE BLAKE. These would all be your own tunes whether or not they are ragtime. We would back you up with about five musicians . . . which we could get locally as there are many fine musicians in Miami. These would be tunes you have not recorded for 20th Century Fox in the last five years. See if you can think of 12 tunes like this that would show your career as a composer.[34]

Smith envisioned the album as representing Blake's entire career, beginning with his ragtime work but encompassing his later Broadway and solo piano compositions in semiclassical style. Blake went so far as to make a demo tape, asking for seven to ten accompanists for the recording, apparently envisioning a more orchestral setting for his work rather than a small jazz combo. Whether Smith balked at the extra expense or simply decided the market was too small, the discussions ended in October and no album was recorded. In 1967, Blake made some test recordings for William R. Dalgleish, apparently an associate of both Bob Darch and Smith, that included some performances along with Blake reminiscing about his life and career. Dalgleish said that Smith was interested in issuing the material and felt it would make "a tremendous album." He proposed next steps that would involve him coming to New York to make more formal recordings. Nothing came of this idea, either.[35]

Another opportunity to record came from British discographer/jazz historian Brian Rust, who was head of the tiny Vintage Jazz Music Society Records, a label operated by and selling to jazz collectors and enthusiasts. In 1963, Rust proposed to Eubie that he record a solo recording for the label, promising a "small royalty" on each copy sold and to pay for the recording expenses. Rust concluded, "We have no vast financial resources, as this is not our livelihood, but a pursuit in which we are all vitally interested as a hobby; we do not know what Union scale would be in this case, but we feel sure we can agree on something."[36] There is no record that Eubie replied but as far as is known no recordings were made.

The mid-1960s were particularly lean years for Eubie. Besides an occasional local appearance with Sissle—including 1962 performances at New York's Town Hall and an appearance with Count Basie on the local TV show "PM East," hosted by Mike Wallace—there was little demand for him as a performer. Sissle continued to drum up work among local Harlem charities, even staging what were promoted as "minstrel shows" with several older performers as a means of keeping active and promoting their work. In 1965, Sissle and Blake were honored by the Lambs Club, a fraternal organization for actors, many of whom were retired vaudevillians. At the ceremony, Eddie Nelson—who collaborated on "It's All Your Fault" way back in 1915—sang the song in the duo's honor.[37] Another honor came that May at New York's Town Hall, where they were fêted by ASCAP for their "contribution to musical entertainment."[38] They also appeared at the Chicagoland Music Festival that summer, where Sissle bragged to a local reporter that "[w]e have enough new songs in our libraries to do two or three shows, but the 'Yeah, yeah, yeah' boys have taken over, so we'll just have to wait."[39] The "Yeah, yeah, yeah" boys were of course the Beatles and groups like them who had knocked jazz and Broadway show tunes off the charts.

Around 1966, Sissle and Blake again turned to their most marketable product—*Shuffle Along*—with the hopes of interesting someone in reviving it on Broadway. Blake wrote to Flournoy Miller to test the waters for reviving the show, and Miller initially responded positively, noting that "[i]f there is a chance to do 'Shuffle Along' again I am all for it and I will do all I can to make it a success. So do what ever you can, and I will back you up."[40] Apparently getting wind of the idea that the show was to be revived once again, Miller's wife secretly wrote Blake a follow-up note, urging him to be more careful than he had been in 1952 in accepting changes to the show to "update" it:

> Eubie for <u>goodness sake</u> don't let it be another tragic affair like the other thing was [the 1952 production]. You and F.E. [Flournoy] are not physically able to go through with it. . . . You & F.E. were too easy to let them change it before. Now this time don't let them change <u>one</u> note of music or <u>one</u> word of the Book. You don't tamper with a proven hit. . . . It is your & F.E. property as if they don't want it as it is, just lay it on the line & forget it. [Underlining in original]

Bessie Miller concluded, "It is not necessary to tell F.E. I wrote to you."[41]

As discussions progressed, Miller's health declined so that by early 1968—after Miller was rushed to the hospital—Bessie had to tell Eubie that Miller was no longer capable of contributing to a new production.[42] Miller would survive until early 1971, but Bessie limited his contact with others—even his own brothers.

While the mid-1960s were tough times for older players like Eubie, there were several hardcore ragtime fans who remembered Blake and visited him in his Brooklyn home. Among the most important was an audio engineer named Carl Seltzer. Seltzer worked as the lead sound technician at the Village Gate nightclub in Greenwich Village, and also operated a small recording studio out of his home. A lifelong fan of ragtime, Seltzer was a fan of black music and arts in general, having a strong connection to local performers through his companion, Elaine Shipman, an African American dancer and choreographer. He first befriended Willie "The Lion" Smith, informally managing his local gigs; Smith introduced him to Blake. Seltzer took lessons from Blake, but was unable to master Blake's demanding style. However, he became one of Blake's regular visitors at his home, and invited Eubie to his Greenwich Village apartment to meet other local ragtime enthusiasts. Seltzer spread the word about Eubie to other revivalists, including Midwestern ragtimers like Michael Montgomery (who invited Eubie to St. Louis to play at a local ragtime festival in June 1968), Charlie Rasch, and Canadian pianist John Arpin.

One night, "Ragtime" Bob Darch showed up at Seltzer's apartment along with a fledgling ragtime pianist named Dave Jasen. Jasen had attended one of Darch's shows in Washington, DC, sometime in late 1962, and quickly befriended the elder pianist, whom he had long admired.[43] He was immediately wowed by Eubie's piano skills and personality, and began taking lessons from Blake. Never a purist, Jasen convinced Eubie to reset "Charleston Rag" from its original F♯ minor to the much easier to play A minor, much to Blake's amusement. Nonetheless, Blake happily complied, immediately playing the piece in the easier key so that Jasen could learn it by watching him play.[44] Soon after, the duo were playing on a double bill with Jasen opening for the elder pianist. He played Eubie's "Charleston Rag" and "brought the house down," in his words. Eubie was irritated that Dave stole his thunder and thereafter insisted that he appear first whenever they performed together.

Jasen was working as a videotape librarian at CBS News in the mid-1960s when he first met Blake. Also working for CBS—although for its recording division—was noted jazz enthusiast and producer John Hammond, whom Dave first met at the company's annual holiday party. Every year, he would talk to Hammond, urging him to record Blake, and each year Hammond assured him he would do so when he got the time. Finally, in the fall of 1967, Dave called Hammond and said, "Look if you don't sign Eubie within a month I'll record him!" as a way of getting him to sign Blake. After a month, Dave hadn't heard from Hammond, so he arranged for a session to be held at Carl Seltzer's home studio with Eubie and invited Hammond to attend. Hearing Eubie play, Hammond was sufficiently inspired to approach the pianist about recording for Columbia. In February 1968, Blake reported to revival pianist Charlie Rasch that Hammond asked him to

> record two L.P.[s] one ragtime and one semi classics. This is for Columbia Recording Company . . . Well I will say I am supposed to record, I never believe anything Broadway says until I sign a contract. These records are suppose[d] to be documentary also.[45]

Eubie was right to be skeptical, as he had seen many deals evaporate over the decades even when he had signed a contract to perform the work. In fact, it would be just over a year later before any recordings were made. Eubie prepared carefully for the sessions, practicing pieces he hadn't played in years as well as making scores for several works that had never been copyrighted. He wrote to revival pianist Charlie Rasch just before the sessions began:

> John Hammond . . . has ordered two albums you know what that means—8 numbers a side, 32 numbers in all. And all but about 3 or 4 are my own composition. Some I haven't played for 50 years like "Kitchen Tom[,]" "Poor Jimmy Green," and many others. I just remember all of them right now. Now I am telling you this to show you all I've got to write. Of course a lot of the songs are published those I don't have to rewrite, but there are so many others that are not copyrighted & I must write three copies of each[:] one for ASCAP[,] one for Copyright[,] and one I have to put in my vault to prove that I wrote them.[46]

In late February 1969, during a three-day session at Columbia's studio, Hammond recorded a two-record set that would introduce Eubie to a new generation of fans. Realizing that Eubie was a natural performer and trying to make him comfortable within a studio setting, Hammond wisely invited an audience to the first sessions that were devoted to Eubie's solo piano playing. A select group of friends and fans—including Dave Jasen—attended and they joyfully encouraged Eubie's natural ebullience, which can be heard in his energetic playing and rapport with the audience. Hammond wisely did not augment Blake's performances by having other musicians play with him, thus avoiding the pitfalls of many of Blake's postwar recordings.

When first brought in to record, Eubie was placed at the studio's workhorse piano. Noticing a much finer Steinway on the premises, Eubie asked if he could play it instead. Hammond said, "Well, that piano is reserved for Vladimir Horowitz," which made Eubie only more determined to play it. Hammond relented and the finer piano was used. Ironically, the only piece that had to be re-recorded was one where Eubie was hitting the keys so hard that he broke a string on Horowitz's piano!

Not surprisingly, Hammond took a historian's approach to the session, encouraging Eubie to play pieces that had influenced his early style, including Jesse Pickett's "The Dream," the Latin-tinged "Spanish Venus," and Joplin's "Maple Leaf Rag," along with Blake's own "Charleston Rag" and previously unrecorded early pieces like his "Baltimore Todolo" and "Kitchen Tom" (named for a cook he befriended at an Atlantic City club). He also recreated the folk-style rags and pop songs of his youth, including "Katie Red" and "Poor Jimmy Green." Eubie then played more recent pieces influenced by his Schillinger training, including "Eubie's Boogie," "Troublesome Ivories," and "Blue Rag in 12 Keys," which—like his "Blues Classique"—showed off his considerable harmonic mastery wedded to his ear for memorable melodies and sophisticated sense of rhythm. Eubie was particularly proud of this piece, sharing its score with several of his revivalist friends, many of whom wrote back to tell him how difficult the piece was to play! A typical response came from pianist Charlie Rasch: "I just went through it and got stuck when I came to the 6 flats section. Those keys with lots of flats and sharps are really rough on me."[47] Eubie responded to Rasch that he laughed when he read that because he got stuck at the same spot when first trying to record the piece for Columbia:

> When John Hammond announced "Blue Rag [in 12 Keys]" about ten musicians gave a big sigh. So I started to play the trio, that is where the twelve keys come in. When I got to G♭, I muffed and had to play it all over again—So when I read your letter and you got stuck at the same place, I got to laughing and couldn't stop. So don't feel bad about it, because it stuck me at the moment.[48]

Blake also played his "Brittwood Rag" for this session. Eubie had taught this rag to his friend and fellow pianist Willie Gans decades earlier. He had totally forgotten the piece until he heard Gans playing it one night and asked him, "What is that rag? I've heard it but I don't know what it is," only to have Gans tell him that it was his own composition![49] Dave Jasen in turn learned the piece and beat Eubie to the punch in being the first to record it.

The remaining sessions were devoted to immortalizing Blake's Broadway songs. Not surprisingly, Noble Sissle was invited to sing on their first hit, "It's All Your Fault," along with "You Were Meant for Me," and a medley of hits from *Shuffle Along*. Sissle was still in good voice and gave some of his best recorded performances since the 1920s. Eubie also played compositions from earlier African American shows, including a medley of Cole and Johnson's "Bleeding Moon" and "Under the Bamboo Tree," and a medley of James P. Johnson's hits from *Runnin' Wild*, including the ever-popular "Charleston."

The recording was issued as a lavishly produced two-record set in early 1970, titled *The Eighty-Six Years of Eubie Blake*. Annotated by noted Broadway scholar Robert Kimball, with historic photos presented in a gatefold sleeve, the album included a front and back cover that juxtaposed pictures of Eubie at the piano from the time of the recording with an earlier photo from the 1920s. Hammond was a revered figure at Columbia—having launched the careers of everyone from Benny Goodman and Billie Holiday to Bob Dylan—so the recording was given special treatment by the label's publicity department. On the basis of his experience with 20th Century Fox, Eubie was careful to make sure that the agreement with Columbia did not limit his ability to rerecord any of the tracks that were to be included on the album.

The Eighty-Six Years of Eubie Blake was widely reviewed in the national press, with most of the reviews focusing on Eubie's still powerful playing despite his advanced years. It even got a rave notice in the pages of a nascent rock journal, *Rolling Stone*, which recommended it to the "young rock pianist" as a "wellspring of great keyboard ideas." Noting that many reviews commented on Blake's age in discussing the recording, *Rolling Stone* critic Langdon Winner astutely said,

A natural tendency in writing about Eubie Blake is to emphasize how old the man is. It is indeed a remarkable fact that Eubie is eighty-six years old . . . But such information . . . conceals a very important fact. The newly recorded album by Blake is anything but a museum piece or a musical bauble to heighten the nostalgia. It is instead a very lively collection of songs which are fun to listen to in their own right. This man really *plays*!

Unfortunately, most of us have only heard the grand style of ragtime piano in its decadent and bowdlerized form. Sterile imitators like Joe Fingers Carr . . . or mechanized piano rolls tinkling senselessly in Gay Nineties bars are about our only contact with a music which was once a great American art. The *Eighty-Six Years of Eubie Blake* gives us a fresh opportunity to hear the wonderful dexterity, subtlety and excitement of the ragtime masters. . . .

Blake's techniques at the keyboard, especially his bass lines, are simply astounding. His chord changes, rhythms, and musical anecdotes are a delight . . . Seldom has musical history been so much fun.[50]

Winner's potshot at the earlier pop-ragtime style of players like Joe Carr was not unusual for critics of this period, who were put off by the audience-pleasing antics of the earlier ragtime revivalists.

Eubie made sure that friends and fellow musicians received copies of the album. One particularly gratifying note came from Louis Armstrong, who wrote to Eubie after getting his copy:

I received the album . . . and man it's beautiful. . . . You are a born trouper. And no one can't take it away from you. . . . So carry on, pal. You deserve every moment in music. The world and this day and age are very happy that we are still around. I was very happy to see you and your fine wife at that swell affair the other night. Lucille [Armstrong's wife] is still talking about what a fine lady [your wife] is and enjoyed talking to her so long. May you stay happy and may God Bless you both. Regards, Satch/Louis Armstrong.[51]

Along with this note, Armstrong sent Eubie a copy of his diet plan titled "Lose Weight, the Satchmo Way!," that concludes with the recommendation that "a laxative[,] at least once a week, is very nice."

Eubie's newfound success led to several old collaborators coming out of the woodwork, perhaps hoping that they could ride his coattails to fame. Hollywood-based lyricist Jack Scholl (with whom Eubie collaborated in the 1930s) reached out in August 1969 by sending the composer some new lyrics to set, both with a "contemporary" twist, stating, "I believe both are timely— 'Between the Devil and the Blues' is a teen-agers lament, and 'Mary Jane' is the English title for Marijuana."[52] And in April 1971, Ernie Ford once again contacted Blake, having been out of touch since 1947, to enquire why with his new success Blake wasn't more actively pushing their earlier songs:

> Since you are making personal appearances, making records and albums, and appearing on TV shows, I am completely flabbergasted that not once have you ever said anything about performing our songs or recording them. It seems to me that this would be the most opportune time you have ever had to promote the songs you have co-written with your faithful collaborators.
>
> I'm not chiding you . . . I'm simply terribly disappointed and hurt that, after all these years, when I spent so much money and time and effort trying to get our songs recorded and published, and you now have an opportunity to promote our songs, you obviously have not . . . I thought that by now, with your great new nationwide acclaim, you would have put our songs in one of your albums or presented them on TV.
>
> . . . We have three excellent songs, and, since you are now in the driver's seat and CAN do something with them, I am hopeful that your next recording session will include our songs. ANY CHANCE??????[53]

Eubie replied, promising to record their song "Time Drags Along" on his next album.[54]

In the flurry of publicity for the record, CBS TV's local affiliate arranged for an interview with Blake in his home, leading to appearances on other shows, including a PBS documentary produced by pianist/entertainer Max Morath. And invitations to perform began to pour into Eubie's mailbox, beginning what would become over a decade of work on the road. In 1970, Sissle and Blake were invited to perform at Yale University by Bob Kimball, who would become one of the duo's most important promoters in the 1970s. A reviewer in the local newspaper reported,

> The audience was very happy indeed at the appearance of Noble Sissle and Eubie Blake, two of the giants of the American musical theater, who at 80 and 87, respectively, remain magnificent showmen. Sissle can still put over a lyric with the best of them, and Blake's piano playing is phenomenal. The team started with their hardy perennial "I'm Just Wild about Harry," which brought huge applause from the audience. Blake then played "Memories of You," first in a concert style, then in ragtime, and received a standing

ovation. Obviously elated, he turned to audience and asked "Do you want to hear some ragtime?" Naturally the reply was affirmative, and Eubie Blake played his own "Charleston Rag" . . . Sissle then joined Blake in a tribute to rock and roll, "They Had to Get the Rhythm Out of Their Souls," which saw Sissle doing a pretty good twist. Blake then turned to the band . . . and together they played John Phillip Sousa's "Stars and Stripes Forever." Everybody was very happy indeed and Sissle and Blake also became honorary members of the Yale band.[55]

Also in 1970, the Jazz Archive at Rutgers University awarded the pianist its James P. Johnson award. Even though the days of Joseph McCarthy were long in the past, the Archive rather sheepishly sent Blake a "loyalty oath" form to be signed and notarized before it could process the award's cash payment.[56]

The *Eighty-Six Years* album also brought invitations from television shows, including Dean Martin's variety show. Blake was annoyed that he was given so little time to perform on his own, being relegated to accompanying Martin singing "I'm Just Wild about Harry" and being given the opportunity to play only "the last 8 bars of 'Memories of You,'" as he wrote to Charlie Rasch:

> I think I was on two minutes. I know it wasn't any longer than that. I was almost heart broken when I came off. Well kid that's show business. The pay was great, but had I known I wouldn't have time to play the piano, I wouldn't have signed the contract.[57]

One of the more unusual requests that came to Blake following the release of the Columbia record was from a candidate for the District Attorney's office in New Orleans named Harry Connick. He hoped to use the evergreen "I'm Just Wild about Harry" as his campaign song, seeking Blake's permission to use its music. He ended his letter with a request for the elder pianist:

> At the risk of seeming presumptuous, I would also ask that you please autograph and return to me the enclosed record. I have a little son, 22 months old, also named Harry, and I would like to save this record for him.[58]

His son would grow up to become the popular jazz vocalist/performer, Harry Connick Jr. When several years later Blake visited New Orleans after the elder Connick's election, he was photographed for the local papers with the young pianist.

While the release of the *Eighty-Six Years* saw an uptick in activity for the pianist, it took a second, unrelated event to really propel his later career. While previous ragtime revivalists emphasized its entertainment value—from their showy costumes, big cigars, and piano-pounding performances—a younger generation of players was arising who admired its musical value—particularly in the work of the first generation of "classic" composers spearheaded by Scott Joplin. Drawing on *They All Played Ragtime*, these players began to look closely at Joplin's scores—each of which was headlined with the admonition "[r]agtime should never be played fast!" In slowing down the music, they discovered its roots in 19th-century piano composition, a graceful melodic and harmonic style descended from Chopin and Schubert, infused with an African American sense of melody and particularly syncopated rhythm.

In New York City, one of the musicians who came under Joplin's spell was the classically trained musician Joshua Rifkin. Rifkin's musical world straddled many spheres—trained at Juilliard, he had performed in a folk-revival jug band and written string arrangements for Judy Collins. Rifkin also produced *The Baroque Beatles Book*, a clever album that featured Beatles songs played in the style of classical music, a recording that achieved some cult success and strong sales for the small label, Elektra Records, that released it. Elektra also operated a budget classical music label, Nonesuch Records, and apparently Rifkin was able to convince the label's owner to let him record an album of Joplin's rags for it. Released in November 1970—less than a year after Blake's *Eighty-Six Years* album—*The Piano Music of Scott Joplin*[59] was a surprise hit, selling 100,000 copies in its first year and quickly becoming Nonesuch's first million-selling release. It remained on the pop charts for 64 weeks, and earned Rifkin two Grammy nominations.[60] A second record was quickly released, and the two helped bring Joplin's music to a new generation. Blake appeared at New York's Carnegie Hall in a concert with Rifkin at about the time of the first album's release, so benefited from its popularity and the publicity that Rifkin's work inspired.

Rifkin's studied performance of Joplin's music was critiqued by many for its coldly clinical approach—and indeed he purposely downplayed the "ricky ticky" style of the Dixieland/ragtime crowd. But the upshot of the success of his two records—besides bringing Joplin's music to the masses by inspiring composer Marvin Hamlisch to orchestrate Joplin's "The Entertainer" and other Joplin pieces for the 1973 film *The Sting*—was it brought a renewed spotlight to the beauty and importance of this uniquely African American style of music. And who better to represent the roots of ragtime than the still energetic, still performing, and still quite entertaining Eubie Blake? Suddenly, ragtime was in vogue, and Blake was ready to take advantage of a flood of demands for appearances.

Meanwhile, ragtime historian Michael Montgomery had been hired by the small blues reissue label Biograph Records to produce a series of ragtime piano albums drawn from his extensive collection of piano rolls. With Eubie's new popularity, it made sense to gather some of his better rolls for reissue, and subsequently Montgomery discussed with Biograph producing two LPs drawing on this material.[61] When assembling the records, Montgomery played the rolls for Eubie to comment on, giving insights into how the originals were made. Not surprisingly, given the fact that these rolls were made decades earlier, Eubie did not always recall playing some of the items; as it wasn't unusual for credits on piano rolls to be rather loosely applied, Montgomery relied on his own ears and other contemporary rolls that Eubie remembered making in determining which could be ascribed to the pianist. Because the rolls were made before *Shuffle Along*'s success, most of the numbers that Eubie recorded were popular songs and tunes of the day written by other composers. And as we mentioned previously, like most other rolls made during this period, some of the rolls were "doctored" after Eubie made them to add additional notes and harmonies that a single pianist could not perform on his own.

The younger ragtime revivalists inspired Eubie not only to recall pieces he hadn't performed in decades but also to begin composing new pieces in the ragtime style. He undoubtedly would never have returned to writing ragtime compositions without this impetus. One of the first among the newly composed pieces was Eubie's "Melodic Rag," which he composed in 1972.[62] In a live performance that year, Eubie introduced the piece—perhaps with tongue in cheek—as an "easy piece—there's nothing exciting in it at all," which was greeted by amused laughter from the audience. The piece showcases the typical characteristics of Eubie's best rags: his ear for catchy melodies; and his use of descending chromatic passages, right-hand rolls and flourishes, and dramatic harmonic modulations to break up the piece's otherwise easygoing pace. Eubie's earlier showpieces—designed to mark his pianistic prowess and defeat any would-be competitors—were often criticized by publishers and players alike as being too difficult for the typical pianist to play, so Blake may have purposely restrained himself in composing this piece. Featuring three themes, the piece is one section short of following the classic ragtime form. The title "Melodic Rag" may refer both to the three themes' singable melodies and to the melodic scale runs and harmonies that occur in the breaks in each section.

Blessed with good health and a phenomenal memory, Eubie was ready for the new interest in his life and music generated by the *Eighty-Six Years* album and the unexpected success of Rifkin's Joplin recordings. Able to draw on decades of performing skills and his ability to enlist champions who could promote his work, Eubie would enjoy his greatest musical success in the final decade of his life. Ironically, it was his earliest musical work—his ragtime compositions—that paved the way to this renewed interest blossoming into numerous festival and TV appearances, as well as the production of the show *Eubie!*, his last hurrah on Broadway.

12

Final Years

Concert Stage and a Return to Broadway, 1971–1983

Thanks to the renewed interest in ragtime and a growing interest in the work of African American composers among students of jazz and 20th-century classical music, Eubie would enjoy his most successful years as a performer during the last decade of his life. With his seemingly unending energy, he was able to perform around 50 concert dates a year almost to the last year of his life, with only two brief breaks during 1974 and 1975, when he underwent surgery. In both cases, he made a quick recovery, returning to touring within weeks of each procedure. He showed little sign of his increasing age on stage, and continued his lifelong habit of smoking several packs of cigarettes a day and eating as he pleased, mostly sweets.

Of course, Eubie must have been aware of his own mortality, a fact that was underscored by two major losses he experienced in the early 1970s. First came Andy Razaf, who had been suffering from the effects of syphilis since 1951. Blake continued to correspond with Razaf through the mid-1950s, encouraging him to continue writing lyrics. The correspondence fell off, however, during the 1960s as Razaf's disease progressed. Razaf came to New York in May 1972 to be inducted into the Songwriters' Hall of Fame. He traveled with his third wife, Alicia Wilson, who was 18 years his junior. Eubie went to visit Razaf at the hotel where he was staying, and was shocked to see his friend in such bad condition. "He never spoke to me, he never spoke to anybody that was in the place. . . . He never said 'Hi Eubie' or nothing."[1] Eubie found it difficult to understand that Razaf was unable to speak, choosing to believe instead that he simply was refusing to do so. Razaf would linger on for a few months, but this was the last encounter the two former collaborators had.

Eubie had a similarly sad encounter with Noble Sissle when he traveled to visit Sissle in Tampa, Florida, in late January 1974. The two were filmed by a local television station for a documentary on their lives and were asked to reproduce their old act. Before Blake began to play their theme song, "Gee! I'm Glad I'm from Dixie," he said,

Eubie Blake. Richard Carlin and Ken Bloom, Oxford University Press (2020). © Richard Carlin and Ken Bloom 2020.
DOI: 10.1093/oso/9780190635930.001.0001

[P]oor Sissle looks like he didn't know where he is or what we're doin'. Then I played . . . [our] standard opening—and he come *right* in and did the whole act with me perfectly. Right after we got done, he started talkin' nonsense like his mind is gone. I couldn't *stand* that.[2]

Terry Waldo—a young ragtime revivalist who befriended Blake in the early 1970s—recalled a similar event when attending a birthday party for Sissle in Harlem during this time, when Sissle barely recognized his old partner—until Eubie sat at the piano and began playing some of their old hits. Suddenly, the aging vaudevillian sprang into life, re-enacting many of the duo's best-loved songs and routines.[3] Just as with his encounter with Razaf, Eubie was not able to empathize with Sissle's reduced mental condition, finding it too disturbing to spend much time with his former collaborator. Sissle passed away in December 1975.

Five people were particularly important in making Blake's late-life career possible. Without them, Eubie may have enjoyed the kind of fleeting success he had had at points during the jazz revival of the late 1940s through the early 1960s, but probably could not have had a sustained career—or such a large impact on popular culture. And, not surprisingly, all five became fierce guardians of Eubie's life and career, creating some controversy, particularly as the musician aged and seemed increasingly under their influence and control.

First and foremost was his wife Marion who brought order to the somewhat chaotic approach Blake took to his professional life. Beginning with their marriage in the 1940s when she first catalogued his compositions, ensuring that he received adequate payment from ASCAP and protecting his copyrights, Tyler preserved Blake's legacy and kept him focused on composition and performing, even in the years when his music was mostly forgotten. Blake cheerfully complained that she insisted that he play every day, keeping up his skills into his 90s—something that he was less likely to do under his own steam. Once the demand for appearances began in the early 1970s, Marion arranged for all of his travel, ensured that he had plenty of rest and good food, that the concerts were well organized and publicized, and that Eubie was paid in full. She kept detailed logs of their travels; maintained correspondence with friends, promoters, and critics; and was his de facto manager. Eubie recognized his lack of business skills and happily deferred to his second wife, who was a trained accountant.

Marion could come across to some as overly protective and controlling of Eubie—perhaps inspired by Eubie's continuing habit of picking up women on the road outside of the bounds of his marriage. Besides his relationships with several long-term lovers spread around the country, Eubie also was open to new opportunities, behavior that must have been highly mortifying to Marion. Several observers noted that his endless womanizing was a cause of great embarrassment to his wife. However, his success on the road only opened new doors for liaisons, something that Eubie apparently viewed as part and parcel of the benefits of being a professional musician.

The second key figure in Eubie's late career was Carl Seltzer, the sound engineer who first met Blake in the mid-1960s. Seltzer recognized Eubie's special combination of a sunny disposition and incredible musical skill. Eubie loved to perform, was never jealous of other musicians (in fact, was quick to praise the talents of younger performers), and didn't often complain as long as he was well paid, well fed, and well appreciated. Seltzer also believed that Eubie had been mistreated by the music industry in the past, particularly by record labels, bookers, and publishers who had shorted him financially or failed to give him credit for his creative work. In 1972, Seltzer formed two new companies—Eubie Blake Music to be his record label and a related publishing company—so Eubie could have complete control over his creative output. In an era when very few other artists had started their own labels,[4] this was a radical move and one that would ensure that during the 1970s Eubie was free to record the music he wanted to present to the public, rather than being limited just to the ragtime tradition.

Seltzer described the genesis of the label in this way to the *Wall Street Journal*:

"We started a record company to keep up with Eubie's composing," says Seltzer . . . The company began as a mail-order operation with two Eubie Blake records cut in Mr. Seltzer's small studio. The company started at Eubie's home using the Blake's personal Christmas-card list for potential customers. It now has grown to a wholesale business as well. "I'd say we've sold 5,000 records which is pretty good," Mr Seltzer says. The venture is just "slightly profitable," he adds. "Eubie does the playing and I do all the rest," he says.[5]

While Seltzer and Blake were "partners" in the label, in fact Seltzer did all the work. As always, Eubie gravitated to partners who could handle his business affairs better than he would.

However, not everyone was pleased by Seltzer's control over Eubie's recording career. He annoyed many others who could have helped promote Eubie's career, not least of whom was John Hammond. In 1973, Eubie appeared at Carnegie Hall in a concert along with Bill Bolcom to celebrate the life of George Gershwin. Hammond had hoped to record the concert, but Seltzer refused to allow it. Hammond would have helped with the show's promotion, which apparently was fairly minimal without the backing of a major label. As critic Alan Rich in *New York* magazine noted,

> Out of the 2800 seats at Carnegie Hall, 650 were filled . . . Concert promotion is an art that eludes me . . . but this event seemed rather curiously organized, down to the fact that *The Times* that day had neither [an] ad nor listing to advise of time or place. The reason . . . is that while several large record companies had wanted to record—and would therefore have extensively promoted—the concert, there is a small company called Eubie Blake Music, whose manager, one Carl Seltzer, said no. Seltzer himself had no money to record or promote the concert, and thus it happened that one of the greatest living musicians . . . went unrecorded and the concert virtually unattended. I don't know Mr. Seltzer, but I do know that the four Blake records he has produced aren't very well recorded and are hard to find in shops, and I cannot help but deplore the exploitation of a noble artist.[6]

The event left Hammond "sizzling" he said in a terse note he sent to Seltzer, saying that Seltzer "really was a fool" to block Columbia's plan to record and promote the show.[7]

Seltzer was intent on documenting all of Eubie's music on the label's releases, including his rich catalogue of many unpublished songs. Albums were released with some of Eubie's oldest collaborators—including singer Harold Browning, who had starred as the romantic lead in *Shuffle Along*. Other releases highlighted some younger players whom Eubie had taken under his wing. Perhaps the best single album devoted to Eubie's solo piano playing was the label's second release, titled *Rags to Classics*. Listeners were no doubt surprised to hear a range of works beyond Eubie's ragtime compositions, including "Raindrops," an early impressionistic piece that he said he composed around 1921 at the time of *Shuffle Along*; several of his more "modern" experiments from the 1930s and early 1950s, including "Capricious Harlem"; and his new composition "Waltz Marion," reflecting his late-life interest in composing turn-of-the-century-style waltzes dedicated to the many women in his life. With virtually no overhead beyond Carl Seltzer's dedication of his studio and personal time, Eubie Blake Music could afford to release these albums without worrying too much about their commercial potential. In all, 10 albums of music were released during the 1970s on Eubie's label, and Eubie also controlled his copyrights for the first time in his career.

Another important person in Eubie's late life was lawyer Elliot Hoffman. Eubie had never been adequately represented in his contracts or other dealings with publishers and promoters. Hoffman would prove to be his guardian angel through his late career, ensuring that Eubie was treated with the dignity and respect—and financial compensation—that he deserved. With his handlebar mustache and small scooter with which he buzzed around Manhattan, Hoffman was quite a character, with a deep love of jazz, representing major figures like Dizzy Gillespie and Thelonious Monk. His business expanded in the 1960s and 1970s to include major rock stars, including Jimi Hendrix, The Who, Talking Heads, and Cyndi Lauper.[8] Like Seltzer, Hoffman became a jealous protector of Eubie's personal and professional affairs. Despite his large clientele—many of whom generated far more income than Blake—Hoffman maintained a voluminous correspondence with any and everyone who approached the artist to request a performance, an interview, or in any way impinging on his time. He protected Eubie's rights in a way that Eubie himself had never been able to do. And he battled with anyone who, he felt, crossed the line and took advantage of Blake's fame—as we shall see in his dealings with biographer Al Rose and the producer of the musical revue *Eubie!*

Hoffman apparently gave Eubie "informal" advice for a while before the musician wrote in September 1973 that for

> legal advice we continue to ask for and receive and for other legal matters continually popping up to be executed, we should pay something called a "retainer." Therefore, being prompted only by good faith and sincere friendship, please herewith enclosed a check in the amount of $1000.00.[9]

Hoffman was so moved by this gesture that he replied,

> I am really so touched by your letter that I do not know quite how to respond. That letter, all by itself, is more than adequate payment for what small things I may have done, or tried to do, for you and Marian [sic]. I would do it all for you with or without that letter, and certainly with or without the check. That was my intention, and it still remains so.

I have not run into too many fellows like you, and, again, I find that it is its own reward. It really has very little do with money, but mostly with things like talent, spunk, sensitivity and charm. Furthermore, I keep hoping that if I hang around I will learn how to be more like you. I also ought to mention that fact that it is fun.

But now let's talk about the check you sent. I will accept it on only one condition, and that is that we hold it as payment against future services and that you regard yourself as paid in full for everything up to now. In other words, you will have to feel free to make me work it off. Do lots of new recordings, publish lots of new tunes and get into complicated television and film deals. And if that doesn't use it up, then I will work off the rest of it by playing the piano for you at parties, at scale of course.[10]

Finally, the music historian Robert Kimball and composer/performer William Bolcom were key in bringing Eubie's life and music back into the limelight. As a historian of the musical theater, Kimball was uniquely qualified to understand how Eubie made the transition from barroom pianist to major songwriter. He could place the music of Sissle and Blake within the context of the history of the African American theater. As a musician and composer, Bolcom was one of the most sophisticated of the ragtime revivalists, straddling the world of classical and popular music. He understood not only Blake's ragtime compositions but also his pieces in a classical style in which he strived to wed African American rhythms with a more modern harmonic structure.

While working as a music archivist at Yale in the mid-1960s, Kimball had approached John Lahr—son of the well-known comedian Bert Lahr—for advice on where he should focus his collecting, particularly hoping to find unique areas of American music and entertainment history to form the basis of his work.[11] The elder Lahr immediately recommended that he reach out to Noble Sissle. Besides a few local engagements in Harlem to perform for fraternal organizations, Sissle was pretty much retired by this point. However, ever keen to spot an opportunity to enlarge the historical record, Sissle responding enthusiastically to Kimball's invitation to share his memories about black Broadway, and arranged to go with Kimball to Blake's Brooklyn home. There the duo recreated many of their best-loved numbers—including Sissle taking to his knees to enact the crouching soldiers hiding in their foxholes while performing "On Patrol in No Man's Land." Kimball immediately recognized that Blake was a fount of musical information, as well as possessing a compelling personality and a prestigious memory.

Having met Bolcom through Bolcom's own early career in the musical theater, and knowing that the pianist/composer was interested in breaking out of the rut of contemporary musical styles, Kimball introduced Bolcom to Blake. Traveling for the first time to Bedford-Stuyvesant in the early 1970s, Bolcom was a little bit concerned for his personal safety, as at the time the neighborhood had the reputation of being fairly rough. He was pleasantly surprised when he got to Eubie's street:

> Bedford-Stuyvesant evokes to most people an endless slum, with boarded-up windows on ravaged storefronts, seedy storefront clubs with sullen blacks lounging in the doorframes, and garbage everywhere, and so it was a surprise to find ourselves in an elegantly kept 1860s neighborhood, with perfectly preserved brown stones lining the well-kept streets. (Tall parlor windows framed with red damask curtains; allowing glimpses of City de Luxe and Queen Anne sofas). We enter Eubie's house on Stuyvesant Avenue through the English basement door, opened by his wife Marion, who led us into the crowded living room where Eubie's black Steinway [was located].[12]

Blake initially appeared to Bolcom to be "an old man who struggled to [get] to his feet," but who quickly became animated and excited as he recalled "what happened in 1907 much more clearly than what happened last week."[13]

Blake immediately took the young pianist-composer under his wing, showing him many of his prized "tricks" that he used to assemble his own unique interpretations of the rags, show tunes, and even classics that made up his repertory. He particularly helped Bolcom overcome his somewhat academic approach to playing ragtime; Bolcom noted that he "played like a white man" until Eubie advised him to

> "[t]ry using your feet!" . . . ignoring the admonition of piano teachers everywhere to stop using [them] to beat time—and when I did my tempo got better. Now Eubie was engaged, and he sat down to the piano and began to show me "tricks"—runs, and syncopated bass lines, and how to slide your fingers off the black keys onto the white ones to make a superfast chromatic run . . . With each musical figure came a story about its originator.[14]

Bolcom noted that Blake believed each performer should create their own individual approach to music, and encouraged Bolcom to use these building blocks to wed the best of improvisation with composition. "Now it's yours," Blake proudly said after Bolcom mastered his own version of "Capricious Harlem," one of Eubie's semiclassical works of the late 1930s. Bolcom arranged the piece for publication in honor of Eubie and performed it often in his concerts during this time.

Bolcom and Blake appeared together on several concert bills while Bolcom was still living in New York, and both Eubie and Marion became close to the composer/pianist, whom they affectionately called the "Big Rumpled Man" because of Bolcom's somewhat disheveled appearance. Bolcom recalled that Eubie often faulted him for appearing in then-fashionable bell bottoms and open shirts; Blake would never come on stage without wearing a full three-piece suit. ("Get yourself a decent suit!," Eubie whispered to him after one appearance.)[15] Through the 1970s and early 1980s, Bolcom and his partner (and soon to be wife) Joan Morris made a point of performing Eubie's piano pieces and songs in their many concerts of popular song. Eubie wrote several thank-you notes to them for helping to revive interest in his music, noting that "my poor people have never done this much for me."[16]

Bolcom recalled one incident that summed up for him Eubie's work ethic and underscored the indignities that black performers often faced when working for whites. In 1971, the duo were asked to film a segment for a local PBS program. As Bolcom recalled,

When we got to the studio . . . the director had decided that it would be a cute idea to have me play Scott Joplin on a Steinway grand and have Eubie play on a broken-down upright. "This piano is even worse than the one I had in Atlantic City in 1915," he grumbled, and I just plain got mad—I needed the $125 [that I was being paid for my appearance] but not that badly! But Eubie would not quit, and he wouldn't let me either. "You're payin' me, aren't you," he said to [the director]. "I don't like it, but you're payin' me, so I'll do it." . . . Eubie had come from too many years of passing the hat after his turn at the piano in bars where black pianists . . . [played] for seated white patrons, ever to renege on a job he had said yes to, no matter whether it might offend [my] liberal sensibilities . . . a job was a job, and your pride came in doing it well.[17]

Bolcom recognized that Eubie, and countless other black performers, were able to battle prejudice even as they endured the subtle put-downs and slights of their white audience through taking a fierce pride in doing their job well whatever the circumstances. "It changed my whole outlook on things," Bolcom noted.

From 1972 on, Blake seemed to accept any offer to perform, whether it was at a harpsichord festival at Westminster Choir College in Princeton, New Jersey; local and national TV appearances; concerts at many colleges; fundraisers for charities around New York City; and local, state, and national government functions.[18] Eubie spent several weeks in northern Europe in 1973, playing at a series of festivals in Switzerland, Denmark, and Norway.

A second wave of interest in Eubie's music occurred, thanks to the success on Broadway of several revues focusing on African American songwriters. The first successful show in this style was 1976's *Bubbling Brown Sugar*, which featured Sissle and Blake's "In Honeysuckle Time" and "Love Will Find a Way." *Bubbling Brown Sugar* was the brainchild of Rosetta Lenoire—the same woman whom Eubie had helped mentor when she was a young girl overcoming rickets in the 1930s. It's not surprising then that it featured three of Blake's best-loved songs. But it was the 1978 production of an entire show devoted to his music titled *Eubie!* (Figure 12.1) that truly brought his music back to Broadway. Unfortunately, as with most other encounters Blake had with the entertainment business, the production was fraught with problems and Blake himself was never fully recompensed for his contribution to it.

The genesis of the show came from a young director named Julianne Boyd.[19] The 33-year-old Boyd had previously staged two off-Broadway revues based on the songs of Harold Arlen and Harold Rome, along with several plays.[20] Boyd came across a reissue of some of the original 78s recorded by the cast of *Shuffle Along* that whetted her appetite to know more about Blake and his music. After doing some initial digging, she realized that it would be problematic to restage the original show; at the time, she was unable to locate a script but she knew that its inclusion of blackface humor would not be acceptable to modern audiences. A revue would solve that problem by highlighting the songs without the need for revising the script. And it would be simple and inexpensive to stage.

Boyd was serving as a reader/advisor to the Manhattan Theatre Club, which at the time was operating a cabaret on New York's Upper East Side, and thought a *Shuffle Along* revue would make a natural fit for that venue:

Figure 12.1 Eubie taking a bow on stage during the Broadway run of the revue, *Eubie!*

and I thought "Well cabaret would be kind of fun to do," because I could put it together myself, I [wouldn't have to wait] for someone to write it. So I went in . . . and I said, "I think there's this wonderful, wonderful pianist, people know him as a pianist, but he was a composer, and he wrote 'I'm Just Wild about Harry' and 'Memories of You' and I think he'd be great for a cabaret." And they went, "You know what? We're going to be doing a black composer named Fats Waller this year, so we're not going to be doing another one." Do you believe it? So I said, "Oh, OK, I'll take it someplace else."[21]

The Fats Waller show would develop into the revue *Ain't Misbehavin'* that—ironically—would appear on Broadway at the same time as *Eubie!* and end up being the more successful show.

After the Theatre Club turned her down, Boyd took the idea to a smaller operation called Theater Off Park that operated a 99-seat venue. They leaped at the idea, suggesting that the revue open the next February—which is Black History Month. Ironically, the opening day turned out to be both Eubie's birthday—February 7—and the birthdate of Boyd's son. "This is meant to be," Boyd thought.

The next step was to get the rights to the show. Boyd had to locate Eubie first, a task that meant dealing with Marion, "the Gorgon at the gate," according to Boyd. She called his number and Marion answered the phone:

> She was really tough. I said, "Hi, my name is Julie Boyd . . . I'd like to know if I can possibly do a cabaret or an evening of songs of Eubie based on *Shuffle Along*." She said, "You want to do the book?" And I said, "No, I don't." "Why?" "Well," I said, "I think the book is racist." "OK["], she said, "I'll continue to talk to you. Everybody who has called me has said, 'We'll make the book work, we'll do something with the book, we'll find parts of it.' And that book is unsalvageable. Well, you sound white." I said, "I am white. And I'm a woman, too." "Yeah I got that," she said. . . . She said, "OK."

Marion knew that previous attempts at reviving *Shuffle Along* had floundered when others had tried to "update" the book. So she was immediately interested in Boyd's proposal because it offered a way to get Eubie's music back into circulation without dealing with the thorny question of the book's racist humor. For some reason, the fact that Boyd was a young woman interested in Blake's nearly forgotten songs impressed Marion as well.

Once she had won Marion's blessings, Boyd had to secure the rights to Blake's music. The original publisher of the *Shuffle Along* score had been absorbed into Warner Music, which maintained the rights to the music and lyrics. Boyd called up Warner and reached Al Kohn, who understood that a producer of a small revue could hardly afford to pay the standard fee for using the music. Kohn had a long history in the music business, dating back to orchestrating Irving Berlin's production of *This Is the Army*.[22] He also knew that very few people were interested in Eubie's songs and there was little risk in letting the young director work with the material. Boyd recalled,

> He said to me "[The songs are] not worth anything to me. [They're] just in the closet. You do anything you want with [them]. But, if it works, you gotta come back to me, you gotta get the rights." He didn't care. . . . So I said, "OK." They sent us the music from Warner Brothers, the sheet music. And I made a one-page agreement saying if this show takes off I would get back in touch with them.

With Warners' and the Blakes' blessings, Boyd quickly assembled a team to put together the show. She hired as musical director Vicki Carter, a "Southern girl from Mississippi," Carter said, but "she could play [Blake's] 'Charleston Rag' like you wouldn't believe—when I heard her play [it], I knew she was the one." Choreographer Donna Manno was hired to handle the dances. The initial cast consisted of just four singers with Carter the sole musician, accompanying them on piano.

With just a few months to put it all together, Boyd got the production on the boards in time for a February 7 opening. Titled *Shuffle Along*, the production highlighted the music alone, with a thin connecting text to link the songs, along with some dance sequences. Eubie and Marion were in the audience for the first performance, and as the lights darkened for the opening number Blake said aloud, "Now we're all the same color." Because of Blake's fame as a performer, the show was attended by many critics, most notably the *New York Times*' jazz critic, John S. Wilson, a long-time fan of Blake and his music. Wilson gave the production a rave review, praising all four singers along with Boyd and Carter's contributions:

> Using a company of four singers, Julianne Boyd has staged them with an exciting momentum that is sustained from number to number, from torch song to ballad, from slapstick comedy to sentimentality.
>
> As the episodes swirl by, Lynnie Godfrey emerges as a commanding and brilliantly versatile personality. She is a devastating vamp, slinking across the stage and building up to a growling shout on "I'm Craving That Kind of Love," both hilarious and extraordinarily sexy as she torches "Daddy, Why Don't You Come Home" [*sic*] from a recumbent position on a piano while, moments later, she is in a slapstick courtroom scene swinging a bladder with tremendous relish.[23]

Wilson concluded that the entire production was "an unpretentious gem." In a way, Boyd was fortunate that the *Times* did not send a theater critic to review what was admittedly a bare-bones production.

Wilson's review led to packed houses, and great interest from Broadway. The show opened on a Tuesday and, according to Boyd, "by Saturday producers were knocking on the door, they wanted to come see it." Boyd quickly settled on producer Ashton Springer, who had just produced the successful African American song revue *Bubbling Brown Sugar* on Broadway. Boyd was attracted to Springer because "I thought as a white woman with a white musical director, you know . . . we better go with somebody who had a little more validity in the business." Springer was the first major African American producer on Broadway, having his initial success with the serious play *No Place to Be Somebody* produced at Joe Papp's Public Theatre in 1969.[24] Springer immediately brought on several hands from his previous revue, including jazz musician Danny Holman to direct the music and well-known tap expert Henry LeTang to "jazz up" the dance routines.

In the heat of the excitement of the success of her initial production and signing with Springer, Boyd forgot about the need to go back to Warner Brothers to clear the music rights. Springer's lawyer reached out to Kohn sometime in late March, representing that the forthcoming production— now to be titled *Eubie!*—had already been approved by the Blakes. This would not be the last time that Springer ignored Blake's interests in trying to move the show forward—and some would argue to avoid paying Blake for his work. Warners drew up an initial agreement for the use of the music. This action inspired the ire of Hoffman, who insisted that Eubie be paid not only for his music—including works not controlled by Warners—but also for the use of his "name and likeness in connection with [the] production."[25] Eventually, Hoffman's concerns were addressed and an agreement was finalized by the end of May.[26]

Boyd was responsible for bringing to the cast two young tap dancers who were just gaining recognition: Maurice and Gregory Hines. Both would make their Broadway debuts in *Eubie!* The Hines brothers had been touring since childhood as an act with their father, known as "Hines, Hines, and Dad," which their mother managed. When the act ended in 1973, the two split up and for a time had to take part-time jobs to support themselves. Maurice was hired first for the show, and then recommended his younger brother be auditioned as well. Gregory, however, apparently was less than thrilled at the prospect of having to audition for his role, so when Boyd asked him to sing for her, he launched into an out-of-key rendition of "Days of Wines and Roses." Boyd recalled, "And I said, 'You're kidding me.' . . . He just didn't want to be there, and he didn't want to sing. Well, once he got the job, he was great. And we got along great and he sang really well."

The Hines brothers had a slightly different recollection of how Gregory came to be in the show, as they told a *New York Times* reporter at the time:

> "Maurice got into the show first," Gregory said . . . "I was in a show in Philly, and Maurice got me to audition for this one."

"But they didn't want him in the show," Maurice continued. . . .

"After a while I had another audition. I didn't get that one either," said Gregory.

"Greg auditions bad," Maurice commented.

At the very last minute—with one slot in the company still unfilled Gregory got another chance. And he got in.

"Essentially it was Maurice and Henry LeTang, the choreographer, who got me in. Even once I was in the show, they didn't have a number for us to do together." The number, a tap routine to "Dixie Moon," materialized later. Both brothers also sing, a skill they taught themselves.[27]

Their roles in *Eubie!* brought new fame to both brothers, and was particularly important in launching Gregory's career as a singer-dancer-actor.

Another important cast member was also new to Broadway: Lynnie Godfrey, who had charmed John S. Wilson in the original cabaret production with her sexy performance of "Daddy Won't You Please Come Home" while reclining atop Carter's piano. The number would be maintained for *Eubie!* and was one of the key reasons for its success. In a "New Faces" profile in *The New York Times* that appeared just after the show opened, writer Anna Quindlen described the effect of her performance:

It's the long leg of Lynnie Godfrey that has made her Broadway debut so memorable. Certainly there is no overlooking the other qualities she brings to the musical *Eubie!* in general and a number called "Daddy" in particular. These are her powerful voice, part alto, part oboe, part Satchmo; a sense of comedic timing that makes a one-beat pause and a sidelong look grow with audience laughter, and an insistent something with her hips as she reclines atop a white piano that makes men in the first three rows occasionally try to climb over the footlight line. Nevertheless, the high point of that number comes when Miss Godfrey points one leg straight skyward. "Daddy, won't you please come home," she growls. "Yeah, mama," someone usually shouts back from the audience.

"Men used to come backstage to meet the girl who did 'Daddy,'" Miss Godfrey said the other day. "And they'd say, 'You? You little bitty thing? No, that's a big girl, with a b-i-i-i-g leg.' They don't understand when I'm out there on that piano, it's such a powerful position that I'm transformed. I'm not Lynnie Godfrey when I'm up there; I'm Venus, and you should kneel to me."[28]

A Harlem native, Godfrey had only recently graduated from Hunter College and then had toured with the vocal ensemble Voices, Inc., in which she first sang "I'm Just Wild about Harry." When auditioning for the original revue-production, Godfrey sang that number, convincing Boyd that she would be perfect for the part. "She lived in Harlem and was very exotic. I wouldn't say beautiful, but very exotic, dark-skinned, beautiful," recalled Boyd. After she became a big hit in *Eubie!*, Godfrey and many of the other cast members treated themselves to mink coats. Boyd recalled one incident that underscored the racism that black performers faced, even ones who were successful on Broadway; after one performance, the two left the theater and "she said 'Julie, Julie: Hail me a taxi.' I said, 'What do you mean? You got a mink coat on.' She says, 'They won't stop for me.' Those were the days people would not go to Harlem." Of course, even if a cab would take a fare to Harlem, New York's taxi drivers were notorious for not picking up black passengers.

Unlike Boyd's previous revue, *Eubie!* drew from Blake's entire repertory of songs, beyond just those from *Shuffle Along*. Along with new music director Danny Holgate, Boyd spent time in Eubie's basement digging through previously published and unpublished songs, matching songs with the actors in the show. They selected the unpublished "Hot Feet" as a showstopper number for the Hines brothers, and novelties like "I'm a Great Big Baby," which would be sung as a comic number by the heavyset actor Jeffrey Thompson. Standards like "Memories of You" were also included in the show to give a well-rounded picture of Eubie's work in the theater. Still, Blake was disappointed that certain songs were left out, including "You're Lucky to Me" from *Blackbirds of 1930* and *Shuffle Along*'s biggest hit, "Love Will Find a Way." Speaking to a reporter from the *Chicago Tribune*, Blake speculated that maybe the show's producers left them out because "they thought this being a Negro show, there was too much love in there"—reviving the concerns expressed decades earlier when *Shuffle Along* presented a straightforward love story with its two black leads.[29] Other than helping select the songs, Eubie had minimal involvement in the show; he left it to Boyd and her associates to shape its contents.

Once casting had begun, Ashton Springer rushed the production forward, with the idea of opening for tryouts in Philadelphia in mid-July. Meanwhile, he was still raising money for the show, bringing in potential backers to rehearsals to have the Hines brothers hoof for them. In early June, theater moguls Bernard Jacobs and Gerald Schoenfeld attended rehearsals, although—as Boyd admits—"the choreography [was] not done." Manno and

LeTang were working furiously, but the show was still evolving. Just a day or two before the show was scheduled to open in Philadelphia, Springer decided to take matters into his own hands and bring on a new choreographer to replace Manno:

> I get a call the next morning [after Jacobs and Schoenfeld attended the rehearsal]—Ashton would call you at 2, 3 in the morning, he'd call you at 6, 7 in the morning, it just didn't matter—when he couldn't sleep, you didn't sleep. And he said, "I just let Donna Manno go and I'm bringing in Billy Wilson. He'll be there, he wants to see a run through this morning." We're leaving like the next day to go to Philly . . . So he came in and was the choreographer of record. Henry [LeTang] did a lot of the tap and some of the jazz choreography.

Wilson had directed and choreographed Springer's production of *Bubbling Brown Sugar* and so it's not surprising that Springer brought him in to do a final polish on the show, replacing the revue's original choreographer Manno, who was a white woman with few credits under her belt. Springer may have promised Wilson co-directing credit as an enticement to join the show; this credit never occurred and toward the end of the show's Philadelphia run Wilson was "frozen out" of working on the show, although he continued to be listed as its choreographer.[30]

Despite the last-minute changes and the rush to get the show up—and very little in the way of advance advertising and publicity—*Eubie!* was an unexpected hit in Philadelphia. The local critics greeted the show enthusiastically. The *Philadelphia Daily News'* critic particularly singled out the Hineses' dance numbers, including Gregory's performance of "Hot Feet," in which he "manages to simultaneously dance superbly and joke with the audience." He also praised Godfrey's performance of "Daddy," noting that it was "a torch number so hot it started the asbestos curtain smoldering. From her piano-top perch, she purrs and pants the lyrics, all the time underscoring their sly and sexy meaning with a pair of gorgeous, serpentine legs that have a life of their own." While he praised Blake's music, he faulted the lack of even a thin thread of a plot to connect the scenes. "There's not a word of dialog, there's no plot," he noted, but then added, "There's no need. Director Julianne Boyd correctly surmised the strongest tribute to Eubie Blake would be his music itself." He concluded his review by stating, "Look out, Broadway!"[31]

Philadelphia's other major daily, *The Inquirer*, was equally enthusiastic about the show. "*Eubie!* is a show that practically anyone could go a little wild about," he opined:

> Utterly carefree, infectiously funny, charged up with some terrific per-forming talent, *Eubie!* fairly radiates an innocent joy in dancing and singing.
>
> In one splendid creative surge, the entertainment breaks through the limitations of the revue format . . . It is as intimate in its appeal as the lively *Ain't Misbehavin'*, . . . But *Eubie!* also manages to be bigger than that, with full-scale production numbers that have been staged with light grace and crackling humor.
>
> This is not cabaret fare pretending to be something more. It is something more.[32]

One question that naturally arose was how a white woman was received as the director for a show about an African American composer with an all-black cast. Boyd brushed aside this concern to a local reporter, noting that the cast "just want good direction" and that the success of the show should open the door for "more black shows" with "more work for black actors." She did say that some members of the cast had trouble adjusting to working with a female director, noting, "Actors are more used to being directed by men. A couple of guys in the cast said, 'Hey you're a strong woman.' Now if I was a man, they wouldn't say, 'Hey, you're a strong man.' "[33]

Originally scheduled to run through August in Philadelphia, the show was held over through September 13—just one day before it was to open for previews in New York, and seven days before its official opening on September 20.[34] Despite this success, the show was already showing signs of being in financial trouble. During its first week on the road, Springer hon-ored his contract with Blake and paid both the fee for the use of his name and likeness and the royalty for his music, but then requested that Blake forego his payments during the next 2 weeks of the run—something Elliot Hoffman was willing to accept to help the show if others would also waive their roy-alties. By the end of July, Springer was claiming that the show was $80,000 in the hole, despite the fact that *The Philadelphia Inquirer* reported that the show grossed over $800,000 during its 13-week run—a discrepancy that would later raise questions about Springer's management of the show.[35]

To make matters worse, a newspaper strike in New York guaranteed that the production would go unreviewed and unadvertised during its crucial first performances. Nonetheless, Springer reported to the show's investors in late August that he planned to carry forward with bringing the show to New York:

> Due to the newspaper strike, however, this plan will necessitate a stepped up radio and television campaign. We have received an advance from the Shubert Organization for this purpose. We believe with the proper promotion . . . EUBIE! will be the hit of the season. We must ask your patience . . . as it is an uphill road at the moment.[36]

The fact that Springer was hustling the show into New York at perhaps the worst possible time was itself suspicious, as well as his stringing along the investors and Blake himself about the show's finances. Thanks to the strike, the show's New York debut never received a formal review in the all-important *New York Times*—although both the Hines brothers and Lynnie Godfrey were profiled as exciting "new faces" on Broadway during the show's run. The first published reviews appeared in early October, with William Glover, the AP drama critic, giving the show a warm notice. He praised the "swivel-hipped, rubber legged and smartly comic" Hines brothers and Lynnie Godfrey ("a sultry siren"), and called out Boyd's direction as having "inventive charm."[37]

However, the *Boston Globe*'s critic was tougher on the show. Like many others, he found it weaker than *Ain't Misbehavin'*: "*Eubie!* lacks *Ain't Misbehavin'*'s sly style, Waller's ironic sense of humor and originality, and the truly inimitable grace of its staging and performance. But, on its own earnest, nostalgic merit, *Eubie!* is lively and talented and, like its namesake, nice to have around."[38] Both the Globe and AP critics faulted the syrupy nostalgia of "There's a Million Little Cupids in the Sky"—one of Sissle's weakest lyrics—but also both praised the Hineses' tap routines. Several reviewers noted that not only did the show lack a storyline but also there wasn't even a mention of Eubie Blake in the script—or why he was important in the history of popular song. The fact that the show was titled *Eubie!* made this omission seem odd to many critics.

Whether it was the combination of the newspaper strike and the late critical response or just theatergoers had had enough of nostalgic revues, the show got off to a rocky start. Perhaps to bring in more revenue, Ashton rushed out a touring company by December. While the New York cast would continue to perform on Broadway, Boyd was tasked to direct the road company.

She was shocked by the rush to go out on the road, saying, "Like we opened in September and we went out like December-January, and we said, 'Wait, wait, wait.' And [Ashton] was just excited moving these shows along." To get the road company running, Ashton requested that Eubie accept a "graduated payment schedule" for the money due to him. Again, Hoffman tried to be accommodating, but insisted that all the investors agree to the same terms: "You know that Eubie and the rest of us are more than anxious to see the show survive and prosper. We hope, however, that there will be a feeling of belt tightening all around."[39]

Boyd's belief that the show was drawing good crowds in New York led her to suspect that Ashton was pulling money from the show to finance not only the proposed touring production but also a new show, *Whoopee!*, that he was producing for Broadway. It wasn't long before the show's investors also began to suspect something was wrong. Their fears were magnified when an audit showed a nearly $300,000 loss from the show's opening just through late October.[40] While the show continued to run on Broadway, the road company was mired with problems, not the least of which was unusually bad weather (including a blizzard that dampened attendance on opening night in Baltimore) and poor coordination with the theaters where they were to perform. Boyd noted angrily,

> We went to Cleveland . . . and [Ashton Springer] called and said, "Oh the trucks didn't make it with the lights. Can you go out and see what you can do with the lights?" And we said, "What do you mean? What lights?" And he said, "Whatever lights they have in the theater." . . . It was just fly by the seat of your pants.

It's likely that some of these problems arose from Springer's limited funding, which he was doing his best to hide from Boyd and his investors.

Although Eubie's involvement with the show was small, he did make it a point to visit many of the towns for the show's opening nights on the road. A particularly important night for him was the opening in Baltimore, his old home town. Many local notables were in attendance, including Maryland's governor and Baltimore's mayor, who proclaimed it "Eubie Blake Week." The fact that the show opened on the eve of his 93rd birthday—February 7, 1979—was an added bonus. (A "three-tiered cake" was presented to him on stage at the close of the performance, while Cab Calloway—whose daughter took Lynnie Godfrey's part in the touring company—sang "Happy Birthday" to Eubie.) The *Baltimore Sun* duly noted the significance of the occasion, while its critic gave the show a lukewarm review, finding many of the songs to be "forgettable."[41]

While the tour rolled on, Elliot Hoffman was becoming increasingly frustrated with Springer. The promised proof that all parties were sharing in the cuts to their royalties and delays in payment was not forthcoming. When Springer wrote in March, asking for further delays in payment to support the road company, Hoffman angrily replied,

> I would only give Eubie's consent based upon the very same conditions I imposed the last time: that we have the right to revoke it any time and that it is absolutely conditioned upon total compliance on the part of every single other royalty or percentage recipient . . . Asking somebody at the age of 96[42] to defer anything had better have some pretty good reasons behind it.[43]

Thanks to Hoffman's diligence, a payment was received at this time of over $4200 in back royalties for Eubie's songs. By July, Hoffman agreed to a cut of 2% in Eubie's name and likeness royalty in order to keep the touring show on the road, despite the fact that Eubie was due over $11,000 for the use of his music, not counting his weekly fee for the use of his name.[44]

The Broadway production finally closed at the end of October 1979, but the touring company soldiered on through early 1980. Despite owing Blake a significant sum of money, Springer had the audacity to make an arrangement with Warner Brothers Music to publish a folio of the show's songs. Hoffman quickly reached out to the publisher to point out that Springer had no right to make such a deal.[45] A cast album was also released on Warner Brothers Records—produced by Jerry Wexler, the famous rhythm and blues producer who had helped launch the careers of Aretha Franklin and Ray Charles, among many others.

While this was all occurring, the touring company was bleeding money, with the tour's producers reporting that the company was over $200,000 in the hole as of mid-November 1979. Springer asked for a 50% cut in royalty payments to keep the show on the road, stating,

> Rather than ask for full waivers of royalties, I would like to respectfully request that we cut to half royalties until we can at least break even. Naturally at that point, if it ever occurs, we would immediately convert back to full

royalties. If this [is] agreeable, I will do everything possible to keep the tour going through March 9th, 1980, and will somehow pay these reduced royalties every week promptly. Otherwise, I see no alternative at this time other than to close the tour before it closes us.[46]

Despite his promises, Springer was still seriously behind in his payments to Eubie. Hoffman estimated in mid-December that Eubie was owed approximately $12,000 in royalties for his music and over $15,000 for his name and likeness fees from both the Broadway and touring company. Apparently trying to generate further income to make up for his losses, Springer authorized a second touring company to open in Los Angeles in January 1980. Hoffman agreed to a 25% reduction in royalty payments to facilitate this new venture and a 50% cut to keep the existing touring company on the road. He wrote ruefully to Marion that the only way "to collect monies due to Eubie seems to be to work with Springer and enable him to continue producing the show, in one form or another."[47] Sadly, the Los Angeles production received lukewarm reviews—the Los Angeles Times found the entire production, lacking the vivacity of the original cast, to be "an evening of vaudeville without . . . a headliner."[48] Eubie attended the opening, and spoke to the crowd after the curtain calls. Both the original touring company and the Los Angeles version shut down soon after, with the entire enterprise heavily in debt.

In a final piece of audacity, Springer made an arrangement for the show to be taped for broadcast on the cable network Showtime and released on home video, again without consulting Hoffman or Boyd. Boyd was particularly incensed that the directing credit for the TV show would go to the show's stage manager, Ron Abbott, rather than herself, despite the fact that the show was being filmed exactly as it was originally staged. Hoffman meanwhile wrote a letter to Showtime's lawyers, noting that Springer did not have Eubie's permission to authorize the program. A few months later, EMA Productions arranged to release the TV broadcast on home video. Hoffman seized on this opportunity to try to recoup the money that Springer owed to Eubie, eventually collecting $16,666, half of which represented the fee for name and likeness rights for the video and the other half drew down Springer's deficit to a little over $26,000; the remaining debt was never collected.[49]

While Eubie never was able to collect all that was owed to him from the show, he at least did better than the show's investors, who lost everything. Their suspicions that all was not on the up-and-up were heightened when they learned that Springer himself drew $214,000 out of the show for "payment for his work as general manager and fees for renting equipment from a company of which he is part-owner"—a move that *The New York Times* commented was "not unusual on Broadway."[50] The investors called for an investigation by the New York State Attorney General's office, and in October 1982 the state's Supreme Court ordered Springer to reimburse 33 of his original investors over $120,000. Springer agreed to make restitution but noted that he was "without the financial means to pay any money" to them.[51] Springer was specifically charged with going over $200,000 over the initial budget for the production and then failing to notify either the original investors or those newly brought on board of the show's rising costs. He also failed to get their approval for the launch of the initial road company before all costs were recouped; Boyd and others also believed that Springer drew money from the Broadway production's gross proceeds to take the show on the road, which was illegal under New York law. Springer also failed to disclose to his investors that he had a long record of fraudulent behavior, including several prior convictions:

> in 1951 of forgery, in 1968 of petty larceny, in 1969 of forgery and in 1977 of using counterfeit stock certificates to obtain bank loans. The state said that these convictions should have appeared in circulars submitted to potential investors. Mr. Springer said that none of the convictions pertained to theatrical productions.[52]

The state's action effectively ended Springer's career as a Broadway producer, while his investors still were unable to collect what was owed them from the production.

While Eubie gained new attention from the show, it also raised the same issues of racial identity and stereotyping that plagued earlier black musicals and their performers. Eubie was particularly sensitive to the charge that he and Sissle were "Uncle Toms" because they catered to a white audience. While he spoke of this charge in many later-life interviews, he most directly addressed his attitude toward racism in an interview conducted by the *Chicago Sun* that he gave in association with the road company's performance of *Eubie!* in that city. Eubie commented on the persistence of racism throughout his life, even when he was enjoying his greatest success in the early 1920s during the original production of *Shuffle Along*:

I had money in my pocket, but there were places that wouldn't serve me because I was a Negro. People wonder how we stood all of this. Well, we said something about it, but we didn't fight it.

Addressing the specific charge that he should have taken a greater stand against the poor treatment of blacks at the time, Eubie noted,

You people had all the pistols, all the food, all the clothes, all the houses, and the money to build our schools. You didn't have to shoot us; you could starve us. When Martin Luther King came along and told us, "Don't hit back," I didn't agree. When he said, "Don't fight back," I thought he was crazy. But he was talking about the same things we practiced.

It is interesting that Eubie equates King's preaching of nonviolent protest to his own accommodation of the white world, something his father had instilled in him from a young age. Eubie even commented that if he were a white man, he wouldn't risk helping out the oppressed African Americans, for fear of being attacked himself:

If I was white, and had the influence, I would never come out to say nothin' in the Negroes' favor. Because just about everyone who did, from John Brown on, see if they don't kill him. Every last one of them except for Truman. For the others, it was suicide.

Eubie concluded, "A lot of people . . . got on their minds 'We must keep the Negro down.' That's where they lose, you see. Because in order to keep me down in the gutter, you gotta stay down in the gutter."[53]

Eubie's father had taught him to never judge people by the color of their skin; hating white people for their oppression of black Americans would only ultimately reduce him to their level. Eubie also felt that black people themselves were not helpful to their own race, often complaining about the lack of support for his music from black performers. To David and Susan Jasen, he compared blacks to a "bucket full of crabs—when one climbs to the top, another pulls him back down."[54]

Despite these strong feelings, Eubie mostly kept his opinions about race to himself. As an entertainer, he realized he had to cater to his audience; in the 1920s when blackface comedy and minstrel-style songs were in vogue, he was happy to provide them; now in the 1970s with the ragtime revival in full swing, he accepted his role as an elder statesman of that music—despite often telling historians that he preferred the classical music of his youth and rarely had listened to ragtime over the decades since his initial career as a barroom pianist and certainly never performed it because he personally enjoyed it. Just as he had been willing to play the popular songs of the day when he was working in Baltimore's bars and houses of prostitution, he recognized that his audience had the money—and therefore had the right—to dictate his repertory.

Eubie's awareness of racial prejudice in society was also reflected in his concern that the standard histories of Broadway and popular music ignored—indeed left out—the contributions of African American composers and performers. For this reason, he was anxious not only to tell his own story but also to acknowledge the composers and performers who influenced his own development. Blake probably gave more interviews in the last decade of his life than any other comparable figure, showing a remarkable memory for events that occurred decades earlier—although not surprisingly sometimes

Figure 12.2 Eubie and Marion in a relaxed moment together.

giving different dates for the same event, such as his one meeting with Scott Joplin. Not surprisingly, also, Blake was more forthcoming on issues of race when speaking with a black historian than with whites, although if he was particularly comfortable with an interviewer—such as Rudi Blesh, who spoke with Blake in 1967 before his "rediscovery" and had known him since the late 1940s—Blake was more open. He was also particularly sympathetic to young black women who interviewed him—not surprisingly also, given his long history of flirtation and affairs. (When he was in his 90s, an interviewer asked Eubie when the sex drive subsided and he responded, "You'd have to ask someone older than me.") Blake was also a talented mimic, with an incredible ear for speech rhythms, and was able to recreate everything from the laconic bass voice of Bert Williams to the high-pitched, agitated voice of James Reese Europe. He could also perfectly reproduce the piano "tricks" of earlier players, particularly those that he had incorporated into his own playing.

It's not surprising then that Eubie wanted his own story told in print, and indeed three different books largely based on interviews with him appeared in his lifetime. *Reminiscing with Sissle and Blake* by Robert Kimball and William Bolcom came first. As we have seen, these two had played a key role in bringing Eubie out of retirement and back onto the stage. As a theater historian, Kimball felt strongly that it was important to acknowledge Sissle and Blake's contribution to American musical theater. Lavishly illustrated with photos from Eubie's and Noble's personal collections, the book was published by a major New York publishing house, and was widely reviewed. It offered the first "official" telling of Eubie's life story through the production of *Chocolate Dandies*, along with the most complete listing of Sissle and Blake's compositions and recordings that had appeared to date.

Like many others who befriended the older pianist, Kimball and Bolcom viewed the book as a labor of love, one that would help promote Eubie in his new career. Thus, it didn't occur to them to share any of the advance money paid for the book with the pianist—until Eubie's ever-watchful lawyer, Elliot Hoffman, heard news of it. Hoffman negotiated a four-way split of royalties on the book between the authors and Sissle and Blake—although Kimball and Bolcom had already taken the full advance payment of $7500. They agreed to forgo additional royalty payments until Eubie was paid his portion of the advance; as it turned out, however, the book never sold enough copies to cover the advance paid to the two authors.

The second biography to appear—although the first to be discussed—was written by an African American reporter from Detroit, Lawrence T. Carter. Carter hosted a local radio show on black topics and wrote a freelance weekly column for the *Detroit News*. He was in discussion with Eubie's lawyer about writing a biography as early as 1970, when Hoffman drew up a one-year exclusive agreement for him to write it, with 10 percent of the royalties to go to Blake, and one-third of any subsidiary rights payments.[55] Carter met with Eubie at his home sometime soon after, with Eubie taking the meeting pretty seriously, making handwritten notes of the key stories he wanted to share with his biographer. The book was apparently completed and submitted by Carter to Doubleday in April 1971, but was ultimately rejected. It was finally published by a small Detroit-based publisher in 1979, under the title *Eubie Blake: Keys of Memory*. The published book is somewhat of an oddity, in that it appears to be based on a single interview with Blake, taking his life primarily through his vaudeville days working with Sissle, and then briefly covering his marriage to Marion. While Eubie told many of the same anecdotes to other interviewers, perhaps because Carter was black he shared with him details of racism he encountered in his early years that he was less forthcoming about on other occasions.

Soon after its publication, Marion wrote to Hoffman to complain about the many mistakes in the text, asking whether they had a basis for a lawsuit, but the lawyer advised her against taking any action:

> There is nothing much you can do about a biography, even though unauthorized. . . . If it ever gets into matters of Eubie's personal life and attempts to re-create and dramatize things that have not been made a part of the "public record" or "public domain" (meaning that Eubie has never really told anybody publicly particular details, but the author speculates on them anyway), a biography can become illegal—an invasion of "privacy." I don't know whether this particular book does that, but I somehow doubt it . . .
>
> It does not surprise me that an unauthorized biography would contain errors . . . but I think that you are probably better off just dropping the whole subject.[56]

It's odd that neither Marion nor Hoffman seemed to recall the earlier agreement with Carter to author the book, but in any case it was barely distributed and got little attention on its publication.

Meanwhile, Eubie had agreed to work separately with a different biographer, New Orleans jazz historian Al Rose (Figure 12.3). Rose was one of those colorful characters who create an entire lifestory for themselves; he claimed to have been born "Etienne Alphonse Delarose Lasceaux," a descendant of a venerable New Orleans Catholic family, when in fact he was born Erwin Albert Laskow, the son of a Jewish traveling salesman.[57] Al's mother remarried a man named Billy Rosenzweig, who shortened his name to Rose, and the family relocated to Philadelphia when Al was in his teen years. After serving in World War II, Rose returned to Philadelphia, where he briefly hosted a radio show on jazz music, then bounced around between Florida and New Orleans before settling in the Crescent City in 1965, where he initially made his living as a caricaturist. He became a champion of traditional New Orleans jazz and an outspoken critic of those who he felt were not "authentic" players of the music.

Rose apparently met Blake while visiting New York sometime either in the 1950s or 1960s. He claimed that it was Eubie's idea that he write his

Figure 12.3 Eubie with biographer Al Rose and Rose's wife. Rose was one of two official biographers with whom Eubie worked during the 1970s. Rose's prickly nature led him to battle over the final manuscript with Eubie's attorney and protector, Elliot Hoffman.

biography, although in Eubie's preface to the finished book he says Rose first approached him with the idea—which seems more likely. After relations had soured between Rose and Eubie's lawyer, Elliot Hoffman, Rose gave this account of how the idea of the book developed:

> I had no thought or intention of writing Eubie's life story. No word was ever spoken on the subject until one morning at breakfast in the Royal Orleans [hotel] when Eubie asked me to do it. Apparently he hadn't even discussed it with Marion. I'm sure she was no less astonished than I was. Though I was not really able to afford the time involved . . . I hesitated only for an instant before accepting. It would be very, very difficult for me to refuse Eubie anything. Eubie and I both understand why he asked me to do it. He considered it a big favor to him . . . I saw it not only as a favor, but as a duty and responsibility.[58]

Rose's account smells of self-aggrandizement, but it is possible that Eubie did suggest the idea to him, as he was anxious to have his life story preserved.

Apparently Rose first approached Marion and Eubie in either late 1976 or early 1977 with the idea of writing the biography, and they referred him to their lawyer, Elliot Hoffman. Hoffman respected the Blakes' friendship with Rose, but had specific ideas about how the book itself should be written. He felt that it should be written "as an autobiography 'as told to' you. That would enable colorful descriptions of Eubie's recollections to appear." He also felt it was important that there be a firm agreement in place that would outline how Eubie would be compensated, suggesting Eubie should receive two-thirds of the proceeds from any book.[59]

Considering himself to be a noted jazz historian, with several books to his name, Rose was upset by Hoffman's suggestion that he essentially ghostwrite Eubie's biography. He responded to Hoffman's letter in early February 1977, making it clear he intended to write his own book about Eubie:

> While I can certainly see merit and appeal in your projected "As told to" autobiography, the fact is that if that's what Eubie wants, there are hundreds of competent writers ready and eager to work with him on it. I doubt that when he proposed that I should do it, he had that in mind . . . What I propose is a work projecting Eubie as man and artist on the backdrop of history. I intend to showcase him as a prime influence on the growth and development of American music and musical theater. . . . Your financial proposal,

while probably quite reasonable for the type of book you had in mind, is not . . . appropriate for the work I am preparing. I would expect half of the proceeds from this work.[60]

Although Hoffman still felt his original idea was more commercial, he agreed to Rose's terms and said he would recommend that the Blakes accept them. However, in the interim, Rose hired his own agent, Roslyn Targ, who sold the book to Macmillan publishers. Also unknown to Hoffman, Rose had already completed the first draft of the book, and received a $4000 advance on submitting it in early 1979. He sent a check to Hoffman for Eubie's portion of the advance, totaling only $1601—deducting his expenses while working on the book. This move enraged Hoffman, who began to suspect that Rose was cheating Eubie.[61] The lawyer returned the $1601 check to Rose and awaited full payment of what he felt was owed Eubie.

When Rose finally sent Hoffman a copy of the contract he signed for the book, the lawyer was amazed to see that no provision was made for Eubie to be paid anything—despite his belief that the author had agreed to split the royalties with his subject. As their correspondence grew more heated, both men dug in their heels, each feeling that he was the true protector of Eubie's rights and life story. Hoffman was particularly hurt by Rose's sharp criticisms of his legal work, believing that he always had Eubie's best interests at heart. At the end of one particularly acrimonious back and forth, he sadly wrote to the jazz writer,

Why do I wind up writing to you in such a tone of voice in every single letter? You are somebody who has known and loved Eubie over all these years. You understand that I am concerned about protecting him and preserving the value of his rights, his name, his merchantability and his health. Why then must I fight with one of his friends? Is it carelessness? If so, please stop sounding offended because you have not taken care of the details in accordance with our prior written understanding.[62]

There followed several weeks of negotiations between Hoffman, Rose, and Rose's agent to make Eubie a partner in the book. Rose finally capitulated (although grudgingly so) in early May, still believing that he had full rights to tell Eubie's story without sharing in his profits:

You understand that I do not consider that you have a moral, legal, or ethical right to half the copyright, but have acceded only to avoid further unpleasantness. . . . I do want you to know that when Eubie asked me to write this book, if I had known you and the role you would play in this transaction, I would have declined instantly . . . You have made this one of the uglier experiences in my career. I wish I understood people like you better.[63]

Hoffman's reply dripped with sarcasm:

I really cannot think of one other human being walking around on the face of the earth who has the same view of me as you. I also can't remember anyone who has ever resented my efforts to make order and business sense out of Eubie and Marion's lives.

. . . Look at the bright side: the chances are excellent that the next fellow you deal with won't be represented by me. You can keep all the copyright, all the money and all the glory, take advantage of his innocence, ride on his coattails, turn his talent to your account, and have one of those really beautiful experiences—and forget about this whole ugly mess.[64]

Never one to let an adversary have the last word, Rose wrote back a long and rambling letter about how he was the one who was cheated in this deal from the time of Hoffman's very first letter to him:

I was—still am—apalled [sic] by your arrogance and presumption in proposing to me how you thought the book should be written . . . Out of courtesy to Marion and Eubie I replied politely, overlooking your bad manners and boorish presumptions. The idea that Eubie was [to] get money at all from this work shocked me. It's not the idea of the money, of course. If Eubie wanted money from me I'd give it to him and there need be no book involved.

At this point I realized that Eubie had an attorney whose idea of protecting his clients' interests did not exclude grabbing everything he could get his hands on regardless of whether he was entitled to it or not. This is not the kind of morality I can understand or deal with it. . . .

Rose concluded,

I want you to know that I will have no dealings with you in the future. If Marion wants to deal with me directly, with or without advice . . . well and good. If not, I'm perfectly prepared to abandon them. I am too old and have achieved too much in life to have to deal with the likes of you.[65]

Rose copied this letter to Marion as a means of further alienating the lawyer. Hoffman quickly responded to her, justifying his behavior as being in the best interest of the Blakes:

> I have just received a most horrifying letter from Al Rose dated June 6, 1979. It indicates that a copy was sent directly to you.
>
> I have tried to spare you the unhappiness that I felt you would experience if you know how Al Rose is behaving over the book. . . . Even though I get absolutely nothing out of the book or Eubie's deal, Al Rose seems to think that I am "greedy" . . . If I am, it is only for you and Eubie . . . I think you know that, but when somebody attacks me on a personal level I really can't ignore it. . . .
>
> Please do not be upset by Al's remarks about me or his threats. They are meaningless. As proprietor of half of the copyright, you are entitled to do as you please.[66]

Amidst all of this bickering, work on the book proceeded at Macmillan, which duly sent galleys to Marion for her review. She had some objections to the description of how the production of *Shuffle Along of 1952* occurred— always a sore spot for the Blakes. She also had previously read Rose's completed manuscript, and had sent him some objections to an anecdote about Eubie's first wife Avis's attitude towards his many affairs with other women, in which Rose quoted her as using the "n" word to describe his other lovers— which was removed from the final book.[67] Hoffman wrote to Rose in early July after reading the proofs himself, making a conciliatory gesture to the writer, although unable to resist one final jab in the back: "I do not have to like the way you do business to appreciate you as a writer. I have just read the galley proofs and I wanted you to know that I think you have done a sensational job of capturing Eubie. The book deserves to do well."[68] News of the feud between Hoffman and Rose apparently reached Macmillan's publicist, who wrote expressing his concerns to the lawyer in August, fearing Rose would discuss these problems during press conferences for the book. Hoffman assured him that "the only person he really has it in for is me," and recommended to Marion that she and Eubie participate in any press interviews for the book if it was convenient to them.[69]

When the book appeared, Rose was miffed to hear about the near-simultaneous publication of Carter's biography, writing to Marion to complain about it.[70] Apparently neither of the Blakes had informed him of their earlier cooperation with the Detroit writer on the separate biography.

Unlike Carter's book, Rose did relate Eubie's entire life story, including the many decades when he was unable to find much work. Ironically, despite Rose's many objections to the idea that his book was an "as-told-to" biography, most of the text was pulled from interviews with Blake. Rose conducted one extensive interview on his own, and also drew from Vivian Perlis's 1972 interview of Eubie for Yale's Oral History of American Composers project, as well as previously published accounts. Rose took at face value Eubie's anecdotes—apparently never fact-checking dates or names, although to be fair Eubie never knowingly misstated a fact. The finished book—simply titled *Eubie Blake*—was as close as you could get to a complete aural history of Blake's life and times, following Hoffman's original vision of what should be written.

Meanwhile, Eubie toured nearly relentlessly through this period, often with Marion in tow to ensure all went well. Engagements included two appearances in Europe at major jazz festivals, one accompanied by his protégé Terry Waldo. Waldo noted that some of Eubie's younger female fans were quick to seek his affections, viewing their relationships as a feather in the cap.[71] Eubie also made numerous television appearances on major talk shows, charming the pants off Johnny Carson on several occasions. Still, he continued to face odd instances of racism and ill treatment. When a major film biography of Scott Joplin was filmed in 1976—with the rather improbable casting of Billie Dee Williams in the lead role—Eubie was hired to appear in the small role of the owner/operator of the Maple Leaf Club. Blake was undoubtedly included to give the film some "authenticity," although he was not invited to play the piano but instead was given a few lines to introduce a piano battle between Joplin and his contemporary Louis Chauvin, an event entirely fabricated for the film. Eubie reported to his friend Charlie Rasch about his part in the picture, "I had three lines in it, and I faked piano—they had a white boy to imitate me playing the piano."[72] It was the ultimate insult that the producers hired someone else to copy Eubie's style rather than letting him play himself.

Blake rarely turned down any offer to perform, carrying the old vaudevillian's belief that the show must go on—no matter what. One performance that was very important to him occurred at Broadway's Theatre de Lys in 1974, when Blake shared the stage with three of his closest protégés, Mike Lipskin, Terry Waldo, and Jim Hession. Unknown to the younger performers, Blake was suffering from a prostate condition at the time and had been urinating blood before the performance. Nonetheless, he soldiered through the appearance, collapsing after the final curtain came down. When Waldo asked him why he didn't call off the show, Blake replied that he had a responsibility to pass the torch on to the next generation of players. Waldo was concerned that this might have been Blake's final performance, but after being hospitalized for a brief period, Blake was back on the road.[73]

After Eubie had ensured that his life story was told, his final years were marked by honors and celebrations, notably annual birthday tributes that were thrown by his friends and admirers. He celebrated his 96th birthday with a cake that was presented on stage to him after a performance of *Eubie!* Later that year at a celebration of the 100th anniversary of the phonograph that took place at Edison's studio in West Orange, New Jersey, Eubie was a special guest. He signed copies of "I'm Just Wild about Harry" and played a few rags on the stage. As he walked up to the stage he quipped, "It's a shame to take the money from the white folks!"[74] In 1982, he was presented with the Medal of Freedom by President Ronald Reagan at the White House, just one of his many late-life awards. Through the 1970s and into the early 1980s, Blake gave numerous interviews to newspaper reporters, scholars, and aural historians. His technical ability as a pianist never seemed to fade, even as his physical capabilities became increasingly diminished. Increasingly thin and frail, Blake carried on, relying as always on the support of his wife and a dedicated group of friends to ensure that his physical needs were met. It seemed that he could go on performing forever. "I feel just like I did when I was 30," Blake commented to a reporter at his 99th birthday celebration.[75]

The first blow to Eubie came shortly after this celebration when his wife Marion passed away from a heart attack in June 1982. Marion had been the guiding light of his later career and centered her life on catering to Eubie's every need. Bill Bolcom noted, "Sometimes she made things harder than necessary, but she always fought to keep him protected from outside distractions. Now, it became more difficult, and life became a succession of round-the clock nurses."[76] Although there remained a circle of devoted women and professional aides who cared for him, Eubie was declining as

well. Despite his increasing age and the winter cold, in January 1983 he traveled with his lawyer Elliot Hoffman to Washington for a concert in his honor
at Washington's Kennedy Center titled "100 Years of Music."[77] Hoffman said
that Eubie continued to be in good spirits, noting that when asked if he had
any children, Eubie replied, "Not yet,"[78] Blake watched the show from the
Center's Presidential Box, a high honor. However, Eubie was suffering from
pneumonia when he returned from the trip, and was bedridden when his
100th birthday celebration was held in New York. The celebration began
at St. Peter's Church at midnight the night of his birth, followed by a gala
event at the Shubert Theater attended by 1500 of his "closest friends," with
congratulations flooding in, and tributes to Blake given by fellow musicians.
Blake was able to listen in through a specially installed phone line from his
home in Brooklyn, although he slept through much of the proceedings.[79]

It was clear to those close to Eubie that his life was drawing to a close, so
many long-time friends and musicians made a point of visiting him to play
him his music one last time. Bill Bolcom and his wife Joan Morris visited
Eubie, who was now bedridden. Eubie asked to be taken to the piano, where
after struggling for a while he managed to play a bit of the Broadway hit "On
a Clear Day." Bolcom said Eubie was particularly fascinated with the song's
harmonic progression.[80] Apparently the last person to visit Eubie was stride
pianist Keith Dunham. According to Terry Waldo, Dunham was there at the
time of Eubie's death, and helped him make the trip to "the other side":

> Keith went over to his house and no one was there. . . . and Eubie asked him
> to take him over [to the piano]. And . . . they rolled his bed next to the piano.
> And Keith played Eubie's songs for a while, and he held his hand while he
> died. And they did the thing where . . . you meet your friends on the other
> side. And somebody holds on your hand on this side and they take you
> over. And he took Eubie over. And he said, "Can you see them, Eubie?" And
> Eubie says, "Yeah, there they are."[81]

When Blake passed, he had achieved his goal of reaching the century
mark (although actually falling four years short of that landmark). His friend
Louis Jacobs remarked, "Blake was pushing himself to reach 100. For the
last year and a half, that's what we talked about."[82] Of course, Eubie knew his
real age by then, but the legend of his 100 years was deeply etched into his
life story and—as many noted—few could claim to be an active, acclaimed
performer-composer whose career spanned an entire century. Blake's legacy

as a promoter of African American music and performers and his insistence that their music be judged by the same standards as white musicians lives on—as do many of his best songs and ragtime pieces. To say that this goal has been reached would be untrue, but his life remains an inspiration to all who hope someday we will reach beyond dichotomies of color, religion, and race to a world where all artists can thrive.

A Partial List of Eubie
Blake's Compositions

This list was compiled from ASCAP and copyright records for Eubie Blake's instrumentals and songs. As such, some titles vary slightly from the published sheet music, and occasionally a title is all that exists for a song that we cannot otherwise identify. Note that the year of copyright may not correspond to the year of a work's actual composition. For scores for shows, we have listed only songs that were newly written for each production, not those carried over from previous productions or older songs that were interpolated/added to a show's score during its run. There are many unpublished manuscripts for songs and instrumentals in Eubie Blake's papers at the Maryland Historical Society that still need to be crosschecked against his known copyrights to establish a more complete list; some of these may be duplicates of other works under different names. Note: All lyrics by Noble Sissle unless indicated otherwise.

[1899][1]
"Charleston Rag" ("Sounds of Africa") (inst.).

c. 1907
"Brittwood Rag" (inst.); "Kitchen Rag"[2] (inst.).

1910
"The Baltimore Todolo" (inst.)[3]; "Poor Jimmy Green" (inst.)[4]; "Poor Katie Red" (inst.)[5]; "Novelty Rag" (inst.).

1911
"Tickle the Ivories" (inst.).[6]

1914
"The Chevy Chase" (inst.); "Classic Rag" (inst.); "Fizz Water" (inst.).

1915
"Baltimore Buzz" (inst.); "It's All Your Fault" (L: Eddie Nelson, Noble Sissle).

1916
"At the Pullman's Porter's Full Dress Ball"; "Bugle Call Rag" (inst.) (C: Eubie Blake, Carey Morgan); "Good Night Angeline" (C: Eubie Blake, James Reese Europe); "My Loving Baby"; "See America First" (L: Eddie Nelson, Noble Sissle).
Ziegfeld Follies of 1916: "Walking the Dog."

1917
"La Fiesta" (inst.); "Mammy's Li'l Choc'late Cullud Chile."
Ziegfeld Follies of 1918: "Save Your Money, John."

1918
"Affectionate Dan"; "Good-Bye My Honey, I'm Gone" (C: Eubie Blake, James Reese Europe); "I've the Lovin'es' Love for You" (C: Eubie Blake, James Reese Europe); "Mirandy (That Gal o' Mine)" (C: Eubie Blake, James Reese Europe).

1919
"All of No Man's Land Is Ours" (C: Eubie Blake, James Reese Europe); "The Baltimore Blues"; "Black Keys on Parade" (inst.)[7]; "Blue Rag in Twelve Keys" (inst.)[8]; "Gee! I Wish I Had Someone to Rock Me in the Cradle of Love"; "He's Always Hanging Around"; "Michi Mori San"; "On Patrol in No Man's Land" (C: Eubie Blake, James Reese Europe); "You've Been a Good Little Mammy to Me."
Diri: Gee I'm Glad that I'm from Dixie So I Can Get a Dixie Welcome Home

1920
"Floradora Girls"; "Kentucky Sue."
Midnight Rounders of 1920: "My Vision Girl."

1921
"Cleo Zell My Creole Belle"; "Fare Thee Honey Blues"; "The Good Fellow Blues"; "I'm Right Here for You" (inst.); "It's Right Here for You"; "Serenade Blues."

Shuffle Along: "(In) Honeysuckle Time (When Emmaline Said She'd Be Mine)"; "African Dip"; "Ain't You Coming Back Mary Ann to Maryland"; "Baltimore Buzz"; "Bandana Days"; "Daddy Won't You Please Come Home"; "Election Day"; "Everything Reminds Me of You"; "Gypsy Blues"; "I'm Craving for That Kind of Love [Kiss Me]"; "I'm Just Simply Full of Jazz"; "I'm Just Wild about Harry"; "If You've Never Been Vamped by a Brownskin (You've Never Been Vamped at All)"; "Jimtown's Fisticuffs"; "Love Will Find a Way"; "Low Down Blues"; "Oriental Blues"; "Pickaninny Shoes"; "Shuffle Along"; "Sing Me to Sleep Dear Mammy (With a Hushabye Pickaninny Tune)"; "Syncopation Stenos"; "Uncle Tom and Old Black Joe."

1923

Chocolate Candy Daddies; "Dear Li'l Pal"; "Don't Love Me Blues"; "Down in the Land of Dancing Pickaninnies"; "Rain Drops"; "That Syncopated Charleston Dance."
Elsie: "Baby Buntin' "; "Elsie"; "Everybody's Struttin' Now"; "Hearts in Tune"; "I Like to Walk with a Pal like You"; "Jazzing Thunder Storming Dance (Thunderstorm Jazz); "Jingle Step"; "Lovin' Chile"; "My Crinoline Girl; "A Regular Guy; "Sand Flowers"; "Two Hearts in Tune with You."
Nifties of 1923: "Calico Days" (L: Ray Perkins, Noble Sissle).

1924

Andre Charlot Revue of 1924: "You Were Meant for Me."
The Chocolate Dandies: "(Down in the) Land of Pickaninnies"; "All the Wrongs You Done to Me; "Breakin' 'Em Down"; "Chocolate Dandies"; "Dixie Moon"; "Dumb Luck"; "Have a Good Time, Everybody"; "I'll Find My Love in D-I-X-I-E"; "In Bamville"; "Jassamine Lane"; "Jazztime Baby"; "A Jockey's Life for Me"; "Jump Steady"; "Manda"; "Run on the Bank"; "The Slave of Love"; "The Sons of Old Black Joe"; "Tahiti," "Take Down Dis Letter"; "That Charleston Dance"; "There's No Place as Grand as Bandanaland"; "There's a Million Little Cupids in the Sky"; "Thinking of Me"; "You Ought to Know."

1925

"(Al-Le-Lu) Old Noah's Ark"; "I Wonder Where My Sweetie Can Be"; "Lady of the Moon"; "That South Car'lina Jazz Dance"; "The Three Wise Monkeys"; "Why Did You Make Me Care?"

1926

"I Would Like to Know Why"; "Messin' Around"; "There's One Land That Has No Turning."
Cochran's Revue of 1926: "Let's Get Married Right Away."

1927

"You're Calling Me, Georgia" (L: Bernie Grossman, Ed G. Nelson).
Still Dancing: "Lady of the Moon."
Teddy: "Teddy (L: Henry Creamer)."

1930

Blackbirds of 1930 (Lyrics by Andy Razaf): "(Who Said) Blackbirds Are Blue"; "Aunt Jemima's Divorce"; "Minutes of the Case; "Baby Mine; "Blackbirds on Parade"; "Dinah (Dianna Lee); "Dissatisfied Blues"; "Doin' the Mozambique"; "Down at that Ole Cabin Door"; "Green Pastures" (L: Will Morrisey, Andy Razaf); "Ham and Eggs"; "How to Play an Ole Banjo"; "In Slumberland"; "The Key to My Heart"; "A Mammy's Lullaby"; "Memories of You; "My Best Gal; "My Handy Man Ain't Handy No More"; "Roll, Jordan, Roll"; "Since Hannah from Savannah Came to Harlem"; "Take a Trip to Harlem"; "That Lindy Hop"; "Under the Jungle Moon"; "Wakin' Up the Folks Down Stairs"; "We're the Berries"; "You're Lucky to Me."
Folies Bergere Revue (L: Will Morrisey and Jack Scholl): "Loving You the Way I Do"; "Tropical Moon."

1931

"When the Lord Created Adam."

1932

Shuffle Along of 1933: "(You're Got to Have) Koo Wah"; "Arabian Moon"; "Bandana Ways"; "Breakin' 'Em In"; "Chickens Come Home to Roost"; "Dusting Around"; "Falling in Love"; "Glory"; "Harlem Moon"; "Here 'Tis"; "If It's Any News to You"; "In the Land of Sunny Sunflowers"; "Joshua Fit de Battle"; "Keep Your Chin Up"; "Labor Day Parade"; "Lonesome Man"; "Reminiscing Saturday Afternoon"; "Sing and Dance Your Troubles Away"; "Sore Foot Blues"; "Sugar Babe"; "Waiting for the Whistle to Blow"; "We're a Couple of Salesmen"; "You Don't Look for Love."

1935

Butterfly (inst.)[9]; "Imitations of You" (L: Manny Kurtz, Irving Mills); "It Ain't Being Done No More" (C: Eubie Blake, Gene Irwin; L: George Sherzer); "It's Grand to Be So Beautiful" (L: Milton Reddie); "Truckin' on Down" (L: Arthur Porter).

1936

Blue Thoughts (inst.); "Firefly (L: Milton Reddie); "I'm Setting a Trap to Catch You" (L: Milton Reddie); "If I Were You (L: Milton Reddie); "Readin' Ritin' and Rhythm (C: Eubie Blake, Milton Reddie; L: Milton Reddie); "Rock Church Rock" (L: Milton Reddie).

1937

"Blues—Why Don't You Let Me Alone?" (L: Arthur Porter); "Heaven Sent Wonderful You" (L: Milton Reddie); "Moods of Harlem: (inst.); "Unpublished Melodie" (inst.).

Swing It Lyrics by Cecil Mack and Milton Reddie Ain't We Got Love; Blue Classique (inst.); By the Sweat of Your Brow; Captain, Mate and Crew; Green and Blue; Huggin' and Muggin'; It's the Youth In Me (L: Milton Reddie); My Old Time Swing Rhythm Is a Racket; Sons and Daughters of the Sea; The Susan Belle; What Do I Want with Love?

1938

"City Kept Gal" (L: Harold E. Lish); "Down Beat" (C: Eubie Blake, Milton Reddie; L: Milton Reddie); "Playing Bingo" (C: Eubie Blake, Milton Reddie; L: E. P. Levy, Milton Reddie); "White Clouds" (C: Eubie Blake, Milton Reddie; L: Milton Reddie, Grace Smith).

1940

Tan Manhattan (Lyrics by Andy Razaf): "Dixie Ann in Afghanistan"; "Down by the Railroad Track"; "A Great Big Baby"; "The Hep Cat"; "I'm Toein' the Line"; "A Nickel for a Dime"; "Say Hello to the Folks Back Home"; "Shakin' Up the Folks Below"; "Sweet Magnolia Rose"; "Tan Manhattan"; "We Are Americans Too" (C/L: Eubie Blake, Charles L. Cooke, Andy Razaf); "With a Dream"; "Worry."

1941

"Harlem" (L: Harold E. Lish, S. Lish); "Tan Town Divorce" (L: Andy Razaf).

1942

"Oh, Baby!" (C/L: Eubie Blake, Geoffrey Clarkson, Andy Razaf); "Wonderful" (C/L: Eubie Blake, Gus Burke).

Ubangi Club Revue (L: Andy Razaf): "Boogie Woogie Bunga Boo"; "The Conga Tap"; "Harlem's a Garden"; "I'm Percy Pinchill of Harlem"; "A Native Son"; "A Red"; "The Snooty"; "Sweep No More My Lady"; "Ubangi; Ubangi Baby"; "Ubangi Opening."

1944

"John, Saw the Number" (L: Milton Reddie); "Toussaint L'Overture (C: Eubie Blake, James P. Johnson; L: Andy Razaf); "Won't Be Long Now."

1945

"As Long as He's a Regular Guy"; "Boogie Woogie Beguine"; "'Twould Take a Gypsy Rose Lee to Find Out."

1946

"Bolero" (inst.); "Conversation" (inst.); "Curse of the Blues" (L: Elaine Blackman); "March of the Senegalese" (inst.); "Raindrops" (inst.); "Scherzo" (inst.); "Serenade" (inst.); "Six Shades of Blue" (inst.).

1947

"And That Is You" (L: Milton Reddie); "Cissy & Bob" (L: Milton Reddie); "I Guess the Cards Were Stacked against Me" (L: Milton Reddie); "Men Are Not Gods" (L: Milton Reddie); "Senor Sam" (L: Milton Reddie); "Sweet Elizabeth" (C: Billy Baskette, Eubie Blake; L: Ernie Ford); "Sweet Talk" (L: Ernie Ford); "Tears, I Shed a Million Tears" (L: Milton Reddie); "Time Drags Along" (L: Ernie Ford); "Weary" (L: Andy Razaf); "You Were Born to Be Loved" (L: Milton Reddie).

1948

"Swing-Time at the Savoy" (L: Langston Hughes, Noble Sissle).

1949

"Before You Can Say Jackie Robinson" (L: Charles Wesley Wood); "Dicty's on 7th Avenue" (inst.); "Lenox Avenue Waltz" (L: Robert Riley); "Life Is Fine" (L: Langston Hughes).

1950

"Capricious Harlem" (inst.); "Honey Babe" (L: Eubie Blake, George Dosher); "Miss Annabell" (L: Milton Reddie); "A National Love Song (Sweethearts Are We)."

Be Yourself (Lyrics by Grace Bouret): "Be Yourself"; "Calling Romance"; "Deep End"; "A Kiss in a Cab"; "Utterly Lovely"; "What Is Wrong with Me"; "You Spoke, I Never Heard a Word"; "You're My Silvery Symphony."

Shuffle Along of 1950: "Alone with Love"; "The Apple Jack"; "My Platform of Swing"; "Rhythm of America"; "Two Hearts in Tune."

1952

Shuffle Along of 1952: "Bongo-Boola"; "City Called Heaven"; "Farewell with Love"; "Jive Drill"; "Swanee Moon."

1953

"I'd Give a Dollar for a Dime" (C: Eubie Blake, Johnny Finke; L: Andy Razaf)[10]; "One Hot Dog to a Customer" (L: Milton Reddie); "Take It Easy" (L: Andy Razaf).

1954

"And So I Sorrow" (L: Milton Reddie); "Baby Be Smart" (L: Ernie Ford); "Fast Talk" (L: Ernie Ford); "I'm Getting Nowhere Fast: (L: Grace Bouret); "Love like Ours" (L: Grace Bouret); "My Little Dream Toy Shop" (L: Milton Reddie); "Scharline" (L: Grace Bouret); "Trouble Seems to Follow Me Around" (C: Eubie Blake, Milton Reddie; L: Milton Reddie).

1955

"I Ain't Gonna Give Nobody None of My Love" (L: Eubie Blake); "Silver Wings in the Moonlight over the China Sea" (L: Jeanette Druce).

Irvin C. Miller's Brown Skin Models of 1955 (L: Flournoy Miller): "I'm Just a Simple Girl"; "Let's Wreck the Joint"; "Mississippi Honeymoon"; "Ole Man River Is Lonely Now"; "She'll Say Bye Bye to You"; "Strange What Love Will Do"; "Thrill in Spain"; "When a Carnation Meets a Red Red Rose."

1956

"The Bass Fiddle Boogie Woogie" (C/L: Eubie Blake, Jimmy Jones, Noble Sissle); "Make Love to Me" (L: Ruth D. Gibbs); "Sharing" (C: Eubie Blake, Bernice Bland Busey); "A Song That's Got a Beat" (C/L: Eubie Blake, Jimmy Jones, Noble Sissle); "You Brought Me Love."

1957

"As Long as You Live (You Gonna Be My Baby)" (L: Arthur Porter); "Christmas Is Coming" (L: Paul Lawrence Dunbar); "Cleo Steps Out" (C: Milton Reddie, Eubie Blake; L: Milton Reddie).

1958

"Belong to Me" (L: Leona Blackman); "Come Along Children" (L: Perry, Noble Sissle); "Eubie's Boogie Woogie Rag" (inst.)[11]; "Grand Street Boys"; "He's in the Calaboose Now" (C: Eubie Blake, Luther Henderson; L: Leona Blackman); "Hot Feet" (inst.); "Rock's Song for Victory."
Happy Times: "Don't Make a Plaything out of My Heart"; "They Had to Get the Rhythm out of Their Souls."
Hit the Stride (L: Flournoy Miller): "The Cajun Dance"; "Don't Cheat on the Meat"; "The Gal from Baton Rouge"; "Hep Cats Done Gone High Hat"; "Hit the Stride"; "Hobble on the Cobbles"; "If It Pleases You"; "It's Hard to Love Somebody (When That Somebody Don't Love You)"; "It's Not Wrong to Have Fun"; "A No Good Man (Will Make a Good Woman Bad)"; "Shack Town"; "Strange What Love Will Do"; "There Are Some Things (You Just Can't Tell About)"; "We Gotta Get Hitched Baby"; "You Can't Cash in on an Alibi"; "You Got to Git the Gittin' (While the Gittin' Is Good)."

1959

"Dream Rag" (inst.); "Ragtime Rag" (inst.)[12]; "Ragtime Toreador" (inst.); "Tricky Fingers" (inst.).

1960

"Jubilee Tonight" (C/L: Eubie Blake, Perry Bradford, Noble Sissle); "Nixon and Lodge" (inst.); "Poor Archie" (inst.); "Poor Katie Red" (inst.); "Ragtime Polish Dance" (inst.); "Tweets Says I've Got Nine Lives, Do You?" (L: Noble Sissle, Roslyn Stock); "Voodoo Man" (L: Ev E. Lyn).

1961

"Blues in New Orleans" (inst.); "A Christmas Wish" (L: Eubie Blake); "Day by Day" (L: Helen Francis); "Ragtime Piano Tricks" (inst.); "Rock and Rollin' on a Saturday Night" (L: Eubie Blake).

1962

"The Baltimore Todalo" (inst.); "Brittwood Rag" (inst.); "Eubie's Slow Drag" (inst.); "Everything They Say about Love Is True"; "I'm Setting a Trap"

(C: Eubie Blake, Noble Sissle; L: Milton Reddie); "Kitchen Tom" (inst.); "Lucinda Lee"; "Magic Little Words" (L: Alfred M. Pelham); "Original Pianistic Trick" (inst.); "Serenade in F" (inst.); "That's Jelly Roll" (inst.).

1963
"Castle of Love"; "Red River Blues" (L: Milton Reddie).

1964
"I Can't Get You out of My Mind" (C: Eubie Blake, Noble Sissle; L: Milton Reddie); "I Love You Miss Annabelle" (C: Eubie Blake, Noble Sissle; L: Milton Reddie); "Love Is the Important Thing"; "Scherzo No. 1" (inst.); "Strange What Love Will Do" (C: Eubie Blake, Noble Sissle; L: Flournoy E. Miller).

1965
"Underneath the Swanee Moon."

1967
"Oh, Where Are You?" (L: Billy Peters).

1968
"Didn't the Angels Sing" (L: Martin Luther King, Noble Sissle); "Valse Erda" (inst.).

1969
"Blue Rag in Twelve Keys" (inst.); "Corner Chestnut and Low in Baltimore"; "Eubie's Boogie" (inst.); "Hit the Road (You Bumble Bee): (L: Andy Razaf); "It's Afro-American Day" (L: Zenobia Krim, Noble Sissle); "Poor Jimmy Green" (inst.); "Rag Modern" (inst.); "Tickle the Ivories" (inst.).

1970
"Rose of Araby" (inst.).

1971
"Melodic Rag" (inst.); "Novelty Rag" (inst.); "Troublesome Ivories" (inst.).[13]

1972
"Butterfly" (inst.); "Eubie Dubie" (inst.; C: Eubie Blake, John Guarnieri); "Eubie's Classical Rag" (inst.); "High Muck di Muck" (inst.); "Valse Amelia"

(inst.); "Valse Eileen" (inst.); "Valse Ethel" (inst.); "Valse Marion" (inst.); "Valse Vera" (inst.).

1973
"Capricious" (inst.); "Rhapsody in Ragtime" (inst.); "Slue Foot Nelson" (inst.).

1974
"Randi's Rag (inst.).

1975
"Betty's Washboard Rag" (inst.); "Blue Fantasy" (inst.); "Sylvia."

1976
"Eubie's E-flat Blues" (inst.); "Lady Beautiful" (inst.); "Valse Delma" (inst.).

1977
"Children at Play" (inst.); "Some Body Else" (L: Andy Razaf).

1978
"Wild about Jazz" (inst.).

1979
"I'm a Great Big Baby" (L: Andy Razaf).

UNKNOWN DATES

"Broadway in Dahomey" (inst.); "I.O.U" (L: Andy Razaf); "Joe Stern Rag" (inst.); "Merry Widow Rag" (inst.); "Raggin' the Rag" (inst.); "Ragtime Piano Tricks" (inst.); "Scarf Dance" (inst.); "Uh-Uh" (inst.); "Uncle Chili Ain't So Hot"; "Until the End"; "Until the One You Love Is Gone" (inst.); "Up We Go" (L: Unknown); "Upside Down Theme" (inst.); "Uptown in Harlem" (L: Unknown); "Wear a Bouquet of Smiles"; "When the Sun Sets Down South."

Notes

Chapter 1

1. See Monrovia Sound Studio website, "WWI Draft Cards essay/Ragtime Composers/ Eubie Blake," http://www.doctorjazz.co.uk/draftcards3.html#ragdcjhb, accessed July 17, 2017. Why Eubie added four years to his age is anyone's guess, although his first wife, Avis, was older than he was and he may have wanted to make their ages closer. Also, as we will see, he claimed to have composed his first rag in 1899, which would have been less believable if he was only 12 years old at the time, rather than 16, as he claimed.
2. Perlis.
3. Bryant; census records show his birth as being in Maryland. Different records give different years for John Sumner's birth; the 1880 census indicates he was born in 1841, while the 1900 Census has his birth in 1839. His military records give 1838. Blake himself said his father was born exactly 50 years before him on the same date, the 7th of February, which may have been family lore or Blake's own embellishment of the story; see, for example, Blesh/Lipskin.
4. Hyder, p. 5.
5. Blesh/Lipskin.
6. Perlis.
7. Rose, p. 8.
8. In Morath AH, Eubie said his father continued to work for his master after the slaves were freed, saving enough money to eventually work his way to Baltimore.
9. 1860 US Census.
10. 1870 US Census.
11. US Civil War records. In Morath AH, Eubie claims his father saw action and was shot and injured several times; this claim is undoubtedly a fabrication, as the records clearly show that John Sumner was never on the battlefield.
12. 1877 map of Somerset County, Maryland, http://www.mdgenweb.org/somerset/ atlas/som-no6-fairmount.htm, accessed March 17, 2017.
13. Bryant.
14. "The Oblate Sisters of Providence—St. Francis Academy (Colored.)," *Baltimore Sun*, July 27, 1872, p. 1.
15. "Golden Jubilee," *Baltimore Sun*, July 3, 1879, p. 4.
16. Hyder, p. 5.
17. McPherson/Chan.
18. Rose, p. 7.
19. Blesh/Lipskin.

20. Kimball/Bolcom, p. 36.
21. Letter of Marion Blake to Al Rose, July 5, 1977, in MHS 2800, Box 16.
22. She attended the Israel Baptist Church, led by the Rev. James H. Reid. Reid was appointed pastor there on Apr. 27, 1895, remaining there until his death in October 1908; *Baltimore Sun*, Apr. 23, 1894, p. 10.
23. Hyder, p. 5.
24. Blesh/Lipskin.
25. Morath AH.
26. "Longshoremen's Christian Association," *Baltimore Sun*, Feb. 16, 1897, p. 8.
27. Drawn from reporting in the *Baltimore Sun* during the years of 1880–1881.
28. Hyder, p. 6.
29. Hamilton Owens, *Baltimore on the Chesapeake* (New York: Doubleday, Doran, 1941), p. 303, cited in Hyder.
30. Blesh/Lipskin.
31. Carter, p. 27.
32. Rose, p. 9.
33. Blesh/Lipskin.
34. Hyder, p. 6.
35. Conan/Whitcomb.
36. US Federal Census, 1900. In interviews, Eubie said he attended school only through the eighth grade, which would mean this was probably his last year of schooling.
37. US Federal Census, 1910. That same year, on July 10, Eubie married his first wife, Avis Lee, and shows up in the same Census as living in Atlantic City. As he spent summers playing there, he was undoubtedly counted twice.
38. This was Eubie's normal explanation for his nickname, although he told Max Morath that one boy described him as a "mouse-faced" boy and the description stuck (Morath AH).
39. Blesh/Lipskin.
40. Perlis. Eubie repeated versions of this story in other interviews, including Blesh/Lipskin, and to journalist William Hyder, among many others.
41. Blesh/Lipskin.
42. Blesh/Lipskin. Again, Eubie told variants of this story in many of his late-life interviews and in his authorized biography by Al Rose. He always said this story was based on his parent's accounts and not his own personal memory. In different versions, he says his age was anywhere between under three to around five years old.
43. Standifer.
44. Bryant.
45. Kimball/Bolcom, p. 42; Carter, p. 28. This same story is relayed in various other interviews.
46. Kimball/Bolcom, p. 39.
47. Kimball/Bolcom, p. 39.
48. Parkins.
49. Rose, p. 16.
50. Blesh/Lipskin.

51. Perlis.
52. Ibid.
53. McPherson/Chan.
54. Carter, p. 35.
55. Some sources give her surname as "Sheldon." Eubie told one interviewer that he first started playing professionally on July 4, 1901, a date that would have made him 14 years old at the time. In his interview with Rudi Blesh and Mike Lipskin, he says he was about 16 years old when he first played there.
56. Blesh/Lipskin.
57. Perlis; Blesh/Lipskin.
58. Rose, p. 22.
59. Morath 1970.
60. Rose, p. 22; Kimball/Bolcom, p. 42.
61. W. C. Handy, "The Heart of the Blues," *Etude Music Magazine* (Mar. 1940), p. 193.
62. Rose Tapes, Tape 1.
63. Blesh/Lipskin.
64. Kimball/Bolcom, p. 43.
65. Rose, p. 26.
66. Standifer.
67. Blesh/Lipskin.
68. Later in the same interview Eubie refers to him as "Doctor Shelby."
69. Quotations from Blesh/Lipskin; Eubie tells this same story, more or less, in Carter, pp. 32–34, and in a much more abbreviated version in Rose, p. 30.
70. "In Old Kentucky," *Democrat and Chronicle* (Rochester, NY), Feb. 1, 1903, p. 16.
71. "In Old Kentucky," *Star-Gazette* (Elmira, NY), Apr. 17, 1902, p. 7.
72. Based on survey of the *Brooklyn Daily Eagle* and *New York Sun* and other news sources from the period 1900–1903.
73. Rose, p. 30.
74. Southern, p. 58.
75. Rose, p. 32.
76. Standifer.
77. Southern, p. 55.
78. Blesh/Lipskin.
79. Southern, p. 55.
80. Blesh/Lipskin.

Chapter 2

1. Hyder, p. 13.
2. Rose, p. 31.
3. Hazel Bryant Interview of Noble Sissle, Tape #2, Emory University, Rose Library, HB 257.1.
4. Noble Lee Sissle, *Memoirs of Lieutenant "Jim" Europe*, manuscript in Library of Congress collection, p. 12.

5. Huggins, p. 333.
6. Huggins, p. 335.
7. Carter, pp. 73–74.
8. Blesh/Lipskin.
9. Parkins.
10. Tom Fletcher, *One Hundred Years of the Negro in Show Business* (New York: Dover, 1954), p. 35.
11. Hyder, p. 20.
12. Hyder, p. 13. According to Hyder, the Club lasted until the 1950s, although it moved from its original location several times.
13. Perlis.
14. Carter, p. 68.
15. Rose, p. 46.
16. First paragraph: Blesh/Lipskin; balance of the citation from Rose, p. 41.
17. Rose, p. 41.
18. "Police Attacks, Issue," *Baltimore Sun*, July 11, 1912, p. 7; see also "Policemen in Tilt," *Baltimore Sun*, July 9, 1912, p. 8. The final decision of the Police Commission was not subsequently reported by the *Sun*.
19. Jack Dawson, "Old Friend's Recollections of Early Eubie Blake," *St. Louis Post Dispatch*, Jan. 19, 1983, p. 53.
20. Rose, p. 45.
21. Carter, p. 39.
22. "Gossip of the Ring," *Baltimore Sun*, Oct. 28, 1907, p. 10.
23. "Landmarks of Old Baltimore in Placid 'Old Town,'" *Baltimore Sun*, June 20, 1909, p. 13.
24. Rose, p. 45.
25. "Dabney-Gans Marriage," *New York Age*, Mar. 21, 1912, p. 6.
26. Carter, p. 44. This sum was the equivalent of about $1420 in today's dollars.
27. "The Musical Career of Eubie Blake," manuscript questionnaire. Copy prepared for Jazz Publications of Switzerland in March 1966. It consists of a series of questions that Eubie answered in pen. MHS 2800, Box 2; also Hyder, p. 18.
28. Kimball/Bolcom, pp. 45–46.
29. McPartland.
30. Morath AH; however, Willie "The Lion" Smith recalled hearing Joseph play in New York sometime around 1913 to 1915; see W. Smith, *Music on My Mind* (New York: Doubleday, 1961), p. 54.
31. Rose, p. 39.
32. Carter, p. 62.
33. Rose, p. 47.
34. Digital Collections in the Friedheim Library, "Baltimore City Colored Orchestra," http://cdm16613.contentdm.oclc.org/cdm/about/collection/p16613coll17, accessed Aug. 15, 2017.
35. Michael Whorf, interview with Eubie Blake, *American Popular Song Composers* (Jefferson, NC: McFarland, 2012), p. 36; for more on Llewellyn Wilson, see Eileen

Southern, *Music of Black Americans*, 3rd ed. (New York: Norton, 1997), pp. 326, 419; Andrew Joseph Carl Fields, *William Llewellyn Wilson: A Biography*, MA thesis, Morgan State University, 1990.

36. Bryant.

37. Rose Tapes, Tape 8.

38. Henry T. Sampson, *Blacks in Blackface: A Sourcebook on Early Black Musical Shows* (Lanham, MD: Scarecrow Press, 2013), pp. 62–63.

39. "Negro Players at Orpheum," *Baltimore Sun*, Mar. 30, 1915, p. 5; see also advertisements running through Apr. 10 in the *Sun* for King's appearances there.

40. *Baltimore Sun*, Oct. 13, 1914, p. 5.

41. Advertisement, *Baltimore Sun*, Mar. 23, 1915, p. 1.

42. "Jewish Mark Twain Here," *Baltimore Sun*, Mar. 9, 1915, p. 3.

43. "Bryan's Heart in Lee's Victory," *Baltimore Sun*, Oct. 25, 1913, p. 16.

44. This story was related by Blake in several interviews, notably with William Hyder for an extended piece in the *Baltimore Sun*. Hyder said that King was white, not black; it's not clear whether Eubie failed to mention King's race in telling this story to Hyder, or whether Hyder just assumed that King was white because of the balance of the story being about racism among white musicians. Blake also said that the theater where King performed was Baltimore's Halliday Street Theatre, not the Orpheum, but that was probably just a memory lapse after some 50 years.

45. In his official biography by Al Rose, Eubie names Avis's grandfather as "Firpo Lee," saying he was a well-to-do oysterman (p. 50). We could not locate a "Firpo Lee" in Baltimore during this period, but Draper Lee is listed in city directories from the 1880s through 1905 and in the 1900 census with Avis given as his granddaughter. In the first draft manuscript for the Rose biography and an obituary that ran in the *Chicago Defender*, it is stated that Avis's father, Lawrence, had sung with the Black Patti Company (MHS, EBC, Box 68, MS, p. 62; "Mrs. Eubie Blake Dies," *Chicago Defender*, Mar. 25, 1939, p. 18).

46. Eubie told biographer Lawrence T. Carter that Avis's family lived "uptown on Druid Hill," a fancier black neighborhood, but census records and multiple listings in the Baltimore City directory show that the Lee family lived in the same neighborhood as the Blakes; see Carter, p. 36, and US Census, 1900; Baltimore City Directory, 1883–1905. It is possible they moved "uptown" after 1905.

47. "To Colored High School," *Baltimore Sun*, July 10, 1900, p. 7. US Census of 1900 also lists Avis as attending school.

48. Letter from Eubie Blake to the *Baltimore AFRO*, Oct. 19, 1965, cited in "Baltimore Honors Eubie Blake at 89," *Baltimore AFRO*, Oct. 14, 1972, p. 2; Carter, p. 35; see also Eubie Blake, "Stories I Must Tell Mr. Carter," handwritten notes, in MHS 2800, Box 26.

49. Rose, p. 49.

50. Carter, pp. 36–37.

51. Rose, pp. 49–50.

52. Hyder, p. 19.

53. Smith, p. 41. Smith said he took over Eubie's summer gig there in 1915 after Eubie went to New York.

54. Blesh/Lipskin.

55. Huggins, p. 311.

56. David A. Jasen and Trebor J. Tichenor, *Rags and Ragtime* (New York: Seabury Press, 1978), p. 188.

57. https://www.youtube.com/watch?v=fFIBnvae3vE; interview with Luckey Roberts appears after the recording of "Junk Man Rag," ' accessed Aug. 15, 2017.

58. Blesh/Lipksin.

59. Jasen/Tichenor, p. 191.

60. Bruckner.

61. Contract and royalty statements in the Eubie Blake Collection, MHS 2800, boxes 17–21.

62. Russell Sanjek and David Sanjek, *Pennies from Heaven* (New York: Da Capo Press, 1996), p. 35

63. Parkins.

64. Rose, p. 48.

65. The family name is variously spelled "Reid" and "Reed" in census documents. While in later interviews Eubie dated his partnership with Reed to the 1900–1910 period, documentary evidence suggests they worked regularly from about 1909 to 1916 or so. See, for example, *New York Age*, May 2, 1912, p. 6, and July 10, 1913, p. 6. The first mention of Reed appearing in Atlantic City that we were able to locate was in the *New York Age*, Aug. 5, 1909, p. 3, but it does not mention Blake being his pianist.

66. *Colored American* (Washington, DC), June 23, 1900, p. 10.

67. Hyder, p. 18.

68. Bruckner.

69. Smith, pp. 39–40.

70. Parkins.

71. Rose, p. 51.

72. Carter, p. 52.

73. Carter, p. 53. Blake told a similar story to Max Morath, but said that he met Cohan while playing in Baltimore, not Atlantic City; see Morath AH, p. 62.

74. Morath AH, p. 62.

75. Hyder, p. 19.

76. " 'Hospital Day' for Provident Hospital," *Baltimore Afro-American*, July 18, 1913, p. 8; see also Bruckner.

77. "Baltimore, Md.," *New York Age*, July 3, 1913, p. 5.

78. "Benefit at Baltimore," *New York Age*, July 10, 1913, p. 6.

79. "The Musical Career of Eubie Blake," manuscript questionnaire. Copy prepared for Jazz Publications of Switzerland in March 1966. MHS 2800, Box 2. According to Kimball/Bolcom, p. 52, Eubie's group was called the "Marcato Band" ("marcato" is the musical marking meaning a note should be played with extra emphasis).

80. Program in author's collection.

81. Sampson, p. 1160.

82. "Ike Dixon," http://jazztourdatabase.com/artists/ike-dixon, accessed Aug. 24, 2017.

83. John S. Wilson, "Eubie Blake," *International Musician*, July 1972, p. 6.

84. "Elmer Snowden," in *The World of Swing: An Oral History of Big Band Jazz,* by Stanley Dance (New York: C. Scribner's Sons, 1974), p. 46.

85. Ibid, p. 47.

86. Sheet music in author's collection.

87. "Neptune Heights Opens Tomorrow," *Asbury Park (NJ) Press,* June 16, 1911, p. 2.

88. "A Feast to Remember," *Baltimore Sun,* Nov. 24, 1912, p. 12.

89. *New York Age,* Feb. 13, 1913, p. 6.

90. "River View Park," *Baltimore Sun,* May 9, 1915, p. 60.

91. Advertisement, *Baltimore Sun,* Aug. 11, 1913, p. 1; "River View Opens Again," *Baltimore Sun,* May 10, 1914, p. 4.

92. Advertisement, *Baltimore Sun,* July 11, 1914, p. 1.

93. Untitled article, *Baltimore Sun,* May 14, 1916, p. 55.

Chapter 3

1. Blesh/Lipskin. Eubie gives different dates for their first meeting in different interviews. He sometimes places it as early as mid-March of 1915, but that date seems unlikely, as Riverview Park would not yet be open for its summer season. It seems more likely that this encounter took place in mid-May.

2. Some sources say 1906.

3. Badger, p. 131.

4. Brooks, pp. 453–54.

5. *Indianapolis Freeman,* Apr. 13, 1912, p. 5.

6. "Sissle-Cable Recital a Grand Affair," *Indianapolis Freeman,* Jan. 10, 1914, p. 6.

7. Buddy Howard, "Noble Sissle, International Star," *Down Beat,* Oct. 1, 1942, p. 21.

8. *Indianapolis Freeman,* Mar. 6, 1915.

9. Standifer.

10. The trio collaborated on at least one other song published in 1916, "See America First." The rarity of this sheet would indicate that it didn't sell very many copies, even locally. The song's title was borrowed from a movement sponsored by the railroads and the new automobile association to encourage American tourism; a "See America First" convention had been held in Baltimore in 1911. Neither Sissle nor Blake ever mentioned the song in later interviews, as far as we have been able to determine.

11. Standifer.

12. Advertisement, *Baltimore Sun,* Aug. 21, 1915, p. 1. The composers' names were not mentioned in this ad, perhaps because they were yet to be well known.

13. Standifer.

14. "From Hartford, Conn., and She Sings Coon Songs," *Evening Sun,* Dec. 4, 1912, p. 4.

15. The only mentions of this duo appear in the Baltimore papers in 1911 and then again in 1915–1916; they may have been a local act, as there is no other information that could be located about them in national publications.

16. Interviews with David A. Jasen, Aug. 13, 2016 and Sep. 16, 2017.

17. *Xenia (OH) Daily Gazette,* Sept. 13, 1915, p. 7.

18. Blake eventually transferred the home's title to his wife Avis, who sold it in 1932, a few years after Emma's death. Various bills and tax records are in MHS 2800, Box 17.

19. Young may have taken over the band, as he is mentioned as leading the ensemble in April 1916 in Baltimore.

20. Kimball/Bolcom, p. 52; in later interviews, Blake noted that Young was able to tap into the market for black musicians among the New York elite.

21. "Tropical Scene Unique Setting of Washington Birthday Ball Tuesday," *Miami News*, Feb. 25, 1916, p. 5.

22. Sissle, p. 13.

23. Sissle, p. 16.

24. John W. Love, letter of Jan. 20, 1920, to Noble Sissle, reproduced in Sissle, pp. 14–15.

25. Sissle, p. 20.

26. Sissle, p. 19.

27. James Weldon Johnson, *Black Manhattan* (New York: Alfred A. Knopf, 1930), p. 123.

28. Sissle, pp. 20–21. Blake insisted that most of the musicians were talented readers and didn't use scores in public performance because of the prejudices of their white patrons.

29. Natalie Curtis-Burlin, "Black Singers and Players," *Musical Quarterly* 5(4), (Oct. 1919), p. 504.

30. Advertisement, *New York Age*, Apr. 21, 1910, p. 6.

31. Lester A. Walton, "The Clef Club Concert," *New York Age*, May 18, 1911, p. 6.

32. Sissle, p. 21.

33. Lester A. Walton, "Concert at Carnegie Hall," *New York Age*, May 9, 1912, p. 6.

34. Ibid.

35. "Musical Moments," *Brooklyn Daily Eagle*, May 3, 1912, p. 5.

36. "125 Negro Musicians Play," *New York Times*, Feb. 13, 1913, p. 13.

37. Tim Gracyk, *Lieut. Jim Europe's 369th U.S. Infantry "Hell Fighters" Band*. Liner notes, Memphis Archives CD, 1996.

38. Ibid.

39. Eubie emphasized in his interview with Vivian Perlis, "I want that to come out in the record. He was the first one invented that word—'gig.' Now you hear everyone say that."

40. Sissle, p. 15.

41. Noble Sissle interviewed by Hazel Bryant, c. 1969. Tape #2, Emory University, Rose Library, HB 257.1.

42. Ibid..

43. Some historians claim the dance got its name from vaudevillian Harry Fox.

44. "Castles Dance Foxtrot: Call It Negro Step," *New York Herald*, Fall, 1914.

45. "Negro Composer on Race Music," *New York Tribune*, Nov. 22, 1914.

46. *New York Age*, Sept. 24, 1949.

47. Jayme Rae Hill, *From the Brothel to the Block: Politics and Prostitution in Baltimore during the Progressive Era* (master's thesis, University of Maryland, Baltimore County, 2008), UMI No. 1454610, p. 51.

48. Rose Tapes, Cassette 4B.

49. Sissle, p. 35.

50. David Gilbert, *Product of Our Souls* (Chapel Hill, NC: University of North Carolina Press, 2016), p. 214

51. Carter, p. 90.

52. Rose, p. 58.

53. Sissle, pp. 26–27.

54. Rose, p. 59.

55. Morath AH, p. 62.

56. Rose, p. 59.

57. Carter, pp. 93–95.

58. Rudi Blesh, *Combo U.S.A: Eight Lives in Jazz* (Philadelphia: Chilton, 1971), p. 205.

59. Carter, p. 94.

60. Carter, p. 75.

61. Rose, pp. 58–59.

62. Blesh/Lipskin.

63. Rose, p. 60.

64. Royalty statements in MHS 2800, Box 19, indicate that Sissle, Blake, and Opal Cooper (a black vocalist also associated with Europe's band) signed a contract to record with Pathé on June 12, 1917 for $25.00 a side, and then on the 22nd of the same month, Sissle and Blake signed a royalty deal with Pathé at ½ cents per record, less breakage of 10%. Royalty statements were issued for three numbers—"Good Night Angeline," "He's Always Hanging Around," and "Mammy's Little Choc'late Cullud Chile"—for sales from Oct. 1917 to July 1919. The recordings sold well on their initial release, with each of the first two titles selling about 2400 copies and the third doing nearly 1000, but then the numbers dropped to the low 100s for the remainder of the reported periods.

65. Brooks, p. 368.

66. Brooks, p. 368; quoting Pathé Catalog Supplement, 1918; see also Kimball/Bolcom, p. 248.

67. According to a royalty statement in MHS 2800, Box 19, Blake earned a royalty of $3.78 from Dec. 15 1917 to Jan. 15, 1918; no further statements were preserved, so it's impossible to say if he eventually earned more. Probably the amounts paid were small.

68. Eubie signed an agreement with Witmark to publish the piece on Dec. 11, 1917, an agreement that called for him to earn a royalty of ½ cent on each copy sold; in MHS 2800, Box 23. However, it was not published at this time.

69. John S. Wilson, "Eubie Blake," *International Musician*, July 1972, p. 6.

70. Rose Tapes, Cassette 7.

71. Michael Montgomery, liner notes to *Eubie Blake 1917–1921, Blues and Ragtime, Vol. 1*, Biograph BLP 1011Q, Jan. 1973.

72. Michael Montgomery, *Eubie Blake Piano Rollography (Revised)*, self-mimeographed, 1978, Hogan Jazz Archives collection, New Orleans.

73. Rose Tapes, Cassette 5B, Hogan Jazz Archives.

74. Kildare's life and career are described in depth in Brooks, pp. 299–319.

75. Brooks, p. 307.

76. Brooks, p. 309.
77. Name given on printed letterhead of Aug. 21, 1918 on a letter from Louis A. Mitchell to Eubie Blake, in MHS 2800, Box 1; Brooks, p. 316.
78. Lester A. Walton, "Bojangles Wins Harlem," *New York Age*, May 6, 1915, p. 6; also partially cited in Brooks, p. 308.
79. Ibid.
80. Mitchell's band and his work in France are described in Goddard, pp. 14–18 and 65–66.
81. Aug. 21, 1918 letter from Louis A. Mitchell to Eubie Blake, MHS 2800, Box 1.
82. Blesh/Lipskin.
83. Goddard, pp. 16–17.
84. Goddard, p. 63.
85. Goddard, p. 302.
86. Goddard, p. 284.
87. Goddard, p. 300.
88. Goddard, p. 302.
89. Reid Badger, *A Life in Ragtime* (New York, Oxford University Press, 1995), p. 202
90. Kimball/Bolcom, p. 66.
91. MHS 2800, Box 1; also quoted in Kimball/Bolcom, p. 69.
92. Sissle, pp. 194–195.
93. This popular song was itself based on earlier folk songs, including the British comic song "Four Nights Drunk."
94. Advertisement, *Indianapolis Star*, Apr. 13, 1919, p. 58.

Chapter 4

1. Advertisement, *Variety*, Mar. 28, 1908.
2. Bryant.
3. Blesh/Lipskin.
4. Blesh/Lipskin.
5. Conan/Whitcomb.
6. Rose Tapes, Cassette 5A.
7. Advertisement, *Union Banner* (Clanton, AL), Nov. 17, 1921, p. 5; the women were appearing as early as 1919 on the Chatauqua circuit.
8. Record historian Tim Brooks suggests the record may have been purposely sped up, resulting in Sissle "sound[ing] like a chipmunk." (Brooks, p. 371).
9. "At the Maryland," *Baltimore Sun*, July 6, 1919, p. 14; this is the earliest recorded appearance of the new duo in the press that we could find. Sissle's last appearance with Europe occurred in May of that year in Boston, so it is possible that the duo performed earlier in an unrecorded location.
10. "New Acts this Week: Palace," *Variety*, July 4, 1919, p. 19.
11. "New Hippodrome," *Reading (PA) Times*, Jan. 9, 1920, p. 6.
12. "At the Maryland," *Baltimore Sun*, July 6, 1919, p. 14.

13. "ANNOUNCEMENTS: Davis Theater," *Norwich (VA) Bulletin*, May 1, 1920, p. 8.

14. Blesh/Lipskin.

15. "Opera House," *Central New Jersey Home News* (New Brunswick, NJ), Dec. 22, 1919, p. 2

16. Bryant.

17. Author interviews with David A. Jasen.

18. If we judge from newspaper accounts, this appearance occurred in late May/early June 1920.

19. Blesh/Lipskin.

20. Rose Tapes, Cassette 6A.

21. Letters from EB to Avis Blake, dated Sept. 21 and 30, 1920, in MHS 2800, Box 1.

22. David A. Jasen and Gene Jones, *Spreadin' Rhythm 'Round: Black Popular Songwriters, 1880–1930* (New York: Schirmer, 1998), p. 344.

23. "DAVIS-Vaudeville," *Pittsburgh Daily Post*, Sept. 22, 1919, p. 11.

24. The song was popular enough that a test recording was made by Victor, featuring singer Edith Emory accompanied by Eubie on piano in May 1920, but for some reason it went unissued at the time.

25. Henry T. Thompson, *Blacks in Black and White* (Metuchen, NJ: Scarecrow Press, 1977), p. 10.

26. Contract with Lowe signed Nov. 6, 1919, in MHS 2800, Box 18.

27. Michael Montgomery, liner notes to *Eubie Blake 1917–1921, Blues and Ragtime, Vol. 1*, Biograph BLP 1011Q, Jan. 1973.

28. Ibid.

29. Rose Tapes, Cassette 7.

30. Michael Montgomery, liner notes to *Eubie Blake 1917–1921, Blues and Ragtime, Vol. 1*, Biograph BLP 1011Q, Jan. 1973; also Michael Montgomery, *Eubie Blake Piano Rollography (Revised)*, self-mimeographed, 1978; Hogan Jazz Archives collection, New Orleans.

31. Rose Tapes, Cassette 6B.

32. Carter, pp. 86–87.

33. Sissle and Blake are mentioned as part of the bill in a notice in the *Brooklyn Daily Eagle* on Aug. 10, 1920, p. 6; the Miller and Lyles act is described in the *Brooklyn Daily Eagle* on Aug. 17, 1920, p. 6.

34. Most of the information, except where otherwise noted, in this section comes from an autobiographical manuscript often attributed to Flournoy Miller but, judging by its contents, was probably mostly written by his brother Irvin. Copies are in both the Emory University library (MSS 1002, Box 1) and the Schomberg Collection in New York City. Sadly, several key sections of the manuscript are missing, including the section on *Shuffle Along*.

35. Miller wrote an article on the African-American community in South Pittsburg for the *Nashville Globe*; "South Pittsburg, The Metropolis of Sequachee Valley," Sept. 2, 1910, p. 3.

36. "Irvin C. and Quintard Miller Honored Guests," *Nashville Globe*, Apr. 12, 1918, p. 8.

37. William L. Miller, "Valedictory," *Nashville Globe*, Aug. 30, 1918, p. 4.

38. "The *Nashville Globe*," http://chroniclingamerica.loc.gov/lccn/sn86064259, accessed Feb. 12, 2017.

39. "Where Were You Then?," *Nashville Globe*, Oct. 5, 1907, p. 4.

40. 1910 U.S. Census, accessed through ancestry.com.

41. Material in quotations throughout this section are from the autobiographical manuscript probably written by Irvin C. Miller on the Miller Brothers; see fn. 35.

42. Lyles's name is sometimes spelled without an "s" (even on the sheet music for *Shuffle Along*), depending on the source.

43. On the basis of his World War I draft card, passport application, and other official documents. His birth year has also been given either as 1882 or 1883.

44. "Aubrey Lyle's Stage Debut Was Made in Gymnasium," *Baltimore Sun*, Nov. 2, 1930, p. 11.

45. Bernard L. Peterson Jr., *The African American Theatre Director, 1816–1960* (Westport, CT, Greenwood Press, 1997)

46. Two sources indicate that the original production of *The Man from 'Bam* had a book by Collins Davis, lyrics by Arthur Gillespie, and music by Joe Jordan. It is possible that Miller and Lyles rewrote the original script for the revised production that opened in 1907.

47. In 1920, *The Man from 'Bam* was revived by Joe Jordan with revisions to the book and score and again in 1923.

48. Sylvester Russell, "The Miller Brothers and Mr. Lyles Make Their Initial Bow as Comedy Stars," *Indianapolis Freeman*, undated clipping.

49. Sylvester Russell, "Musical and Dramatic," *Chicago Defender*, Apr. 23, 1910, p. 4.

50. "Editor Miller in Indianapolis," *Nashville Globe*, Nov. 16, 1917, p. 4.

51. "Flournoy Miller in Glasgow, Scotland," *Tennessean*, Aug. 27, 1916, p. 38.

52. Blesh/Lipskin. In some other interviews, Eubie said that this conversation didn't take place until after the duos returned to New York.

53. "Dramatic Story of Success of *Shuffle Along* Told by Noble Sissle, Eubie Blake," *Pittsburgh Courier*, Sept. 22, 1923, p. 11.

54. "'Who's Stealin'," *Chicago Defender*, Jan. 3, 1920, p. 6.

55. "All Colored Show in Broadway House," *Variety*, Feb. 18, 1921, p. 15.

Chapter 5

1. Jerome Charyn, *Gangsters and Gold Diggers* (New York: Four Walls and Eight Windows, 2003), p. 154.

2. Nathan Irvin Huggins, *Harlem Renaissance* (Oxford: Oxford University Press, 1971), p. 6.

3. Peter S. Woods, "The Negro on Broadway: The Transition Years, 1920–1930" (PhD diss., Yale University, 1965), pp. 4, 5, quoted in Eric Ledell Smith, *Bert Williams A Biography of the Pioneer Black Comedian* (Jefferson, NC: McFarland, 1992), p. 213.

4. Camille F. Forbes, *Introducing Bert Williams* (New York: Basic Civitas, 2008), pp. 24, 25.

5. Allen Woll, *Black Musical Theatre: From "Coontown" to "Dreamgirls."* (New York, Da Capo Press, 1989), p. 10.

6. *New York Times*, May 24, 1904, p. 9.

7. *Indianapolis Freeman*, Feb. 17, 1906.

8. "Miller & Lyles Score a Big Hit," *New York Age*, Oct. 15, 1915, p. 6.

9. Thomas Riis, *Just before Jazz: Black Musical Theatre in New York, 1890–1915* (Washington, DC: Smithsonian Institution Press, 1989), pp. 152–154.

10. Perlis.

11. Conan/Whitcomb.

12. Lester Walton, *New York Age*, May 13, 1909.

13. Lester Walton, *New York Age*, May 20, 1909.

14. James Weldon Johnson, *Black Manhattan* (New York: Alfred A. Knopf, 1930), p. 173.

15. Ibid., p. 174.

16. Blesh/Lipskin.

17. Lynn Schenbeck and Lawrence Schenbeck, "The Surprising Story of *Shuffle Along*," in *Shuffle Along*, by Lyn Schenbeck and Lawrence Schenbeck (Middletown, WI: AR Editions, 2018), p. xx.

18. Noble Sissle, "Autobiography," typed manuscript, p. 8, in the Helen Armstead-Johnson miscellaneous theater collection, Schomburg Center for Research in Black Culture, New York Public Library, Astor, Lenox, and Tilden Foundation.

19. Perlis.

20. In a contemporary interview, Mayer said, "[I] hocked my overcoat" to pay for the lunch. "Dramatic Story of Success of *Shuffle Along* Told by Noble Sissle, Eubie Blake," *Pittsburgh Courier*, Sept. 22, 1923, p. 11.

21. After whom Broadway's Cort Theatre is named.

22. Perlis.

23. Sissle, "Autobiography," p. 10.

24. Lester A. Walton, "*Shuffle Along* Is in 6-Month Run," *New York Age*, Oct. 15, 1921, p. 6.

25. Marshall Sterns and Jean Sterns, *Jazz Dance: The Story of American Vernacular Dance* (New York: Da Capo, 1994), p. 136

26. "*Shuffle Along* Make Up," *Variety*, May 20, 1921, p. 15. Later the Nikko company was renamed Shuffle Along, Inc.

27. McPherson/Chan.

28. Rose, Tape 6A.

29. *Variety*, May 27, Nov. 25, 1921.

30. Blesh/Lipskin.

31. Perlis.

32. Ibid.

33. Southern II, p. 152.

34. "My Loving Baby" was written in 1916. Sheet music collector David A. Jasen was the first to discover this connection when he obtained a copy of the rare sheet and saw the chorus lyrics beginning "I'm just wild about baby . . ." (Interviews with Richard Carlin, Aug. 23, 2016 and Sept. 16, 2017).

35. From the 1906 show *Abyssinia* produced by Williams and Walker with music by Will Marion Cook.

36. Kimball/Bolcom, p. 106.

37. Ibid.

38. "*Shuffle Along,*" *Lebanon (PA) Daily News*, Feb. 28, 1922, p. 7.

39. Kimball/Bolcom, p. 89.

40. Ibid.

41. J. Freiz Smith, "*Shuffle Along* Is Musical Show with Abundance of Merit," *Trenton Times*, Mar. 25, 1921, p. 32.

42. Jackson, Billboard, "*Shuffling Along*: The Presentation of Mirth and Melody Accomplished," *Chicago Defender*, Apr. 2, 1921, p. 8.

43. Kimball/Bolcom, p. 89.

44. "Dramatic Story of Success of *Shuffle Along* Told by Noble Sissle, Eubie Blake," *Pittsburgh Courier*, Sept. 22, 1923, p. 11.

45. Ibid.

46. Kimball/Bolcom, p. 89.

47. Ibid., p. 89.

48. Ibid., p. 90.

49. Sterns/Sterns, p. 136.

50. Sissle, "Autobiography," p. 11.

51. "RAJAH: *Shuffle Along,*" *Reading Times*, Apr. 28, 1921, p. 7.

52. A contemporary account says the amount was actually $21,000. "Dramatic Story of Success of *Shuffle Along* Told by Noble Sissle, Eubie Blake," *Pittsburgh Courier*, Sept. 22, 1923, p. 11.

53. Lester A. Walton, "*Shuffle Along* Latest Musical Gem to Invade Broadway," *New York Age*, June 4, 1921, p. 6.

54. Riis, p. 175.

55. Noble Sissle, unpublished autobiography, Flournoy Miller Collection, Helen Armstead-Johnson Collection, Box I, Schomburg Center for Research in Black Culture, New York Public Library, Astor, Lenox, and Tilden Foundation.

56. Kimball/Bolcom, pp. 94, 95.

57. Ibid., pp. 94, 95.

58. Kimball/Bolcom, p. 93.

59. Walton, "*Shuffle Along* Latest Musical Gem," p. 6.

60. "Sixty Third Street Music Hall," *Brooklyn Life*, May 28, 1921, p. 15.

61. *New York Post*, July 3, 1975.

62. "*Shuffle Along* Premiere," *New York Times*, May 23, 1921, p. 16.

63. "*Shuffle Along,*" *Variety*, May 27, 1921, pp. 23–24.

64. Lester Walton, "White Writer Objects to Colored Performers Appearing in Full Dress," *New York Age*, Sept. 17, 1921, p. 6.

65. Walton, "*Shuffle Along* Latest Musical Gem," p. 6.

66. Tinney was a popular vaudevillian who performed in blackface.

67. Anonymous review, *Chicago Daily Tribune*, May 29, 1921, Pt. 2, p. 1.

68. Ibid, p. 2.

69. Heywood Broun. "As We Were Saying—," *New York Tribune*, July 3, 1921, Part 4s, p. 1.

70. Kimball/Bolcom, p. 99.

71. Alan Dale, "*Shuffle Along* Full of Pep and Real Melody," *New York Journal American*; reprinted in Kimball/Bolcom, p. 95.

72. Ibid.

73. Walton, "*Shuffle Along* Latest Musical Gem," p. 6.

74. Ibid.

75. "New York City Briefs," *Chicago Defender*, June 4, 1921, p. 9.

76. Gilbert Seldes, *The 7 Lively Arts* (New York, Sagamore Press, 1957), p. 148.

77. John McMulllin, "The Fashion and Pleasures of New York," *Vanity Fair,* cited in David Krasner, *A Beautiful Pageant* (NY: Palgrave Macmillan, 2002), p. 263.

78. Langston Hughes, *The Big Sea: An Autobiography*. New York: Alfred A. Knopf, 1940, p. 225.

79. "*Shuffle Along* Still Going Strong at 63rd St. Music Hall," *New York Age*, Nov. 12, 1921, p. 6.

80. Lester A. Walton, "*Shuffle Along* Is in 6-Month Run," *New York Age*, Oct. 15, 1921, p. 6.

81. *Variety*, May 27, Nov. 25, 1921.

82. Kimball/Bolcom, p. 98.

83. "Aubrey Lyle [*sic*], Famous Actor, Dies in New York City," *Chicago Defender*, Aug. 6, 1932, pp. 1–2.

84. "It's [*sic*] Music Is a Prime Factor in the Success of *Shuffle Along*," *New York Age*, Nov. 19, 1921, p. 15.

85. "*Shuffle Along* Latest Musical . . ." *New York Age*, June 4, 1921, p. 6.

86. Ibid, p. 118.

87. Bricktop, *Bricktop* with James Haskens (New York, Atheneum, 1983), pp. 53–55.

88. Ibid., pp. 78–79.

89. "It's [*sic*] Music Is a Prime Factor," p. 15.

90. Bill Egan, *Florence Mills: Harlem Jazz Queen* (Lanham, MD: Scarecrow Press, 2004), p. 61.

91. Bryant.

92. Ibid.

93. Ibid. In several later life interviews, Blake lamented that they didn't name the song "Kiss Me," which most people believed was its name. When customers asked for "Kiss Me," music store owners would tell them that no such song existed, leading in Blake's view to many lost sales. Blake believed that had the song been written by white writers the music store owners would have made the extra effort to find it.

94. Ibid, p. 62.

95. Ibid.

96. Ibid.

97. Hughes, pp. 62–63, 85.

98. Noel Coward, *Autobiography* (London: Methuen, 1986), p. 6.

99. Robert Sylvester, *No Cover Charge: A Backward Look at the Night Clubs* (London: Peter Davies, 1957), p. 36.

100. Sheila Tully Boyle and Andrew Bunie, *Paul Robeson: The Years of Promise and Achievement* (Boston: University of Massachusetts Press, 2001), p. 99.

101. Ibid., p. 100.

102. Ibid., p. 100.

103. Ibid., p. 100.

104. Ibid.

105. Egan, p. 66.

106. Ibid.

107. "Colored Actor," *Toledo Bee*, n.p., in Robinson Locke Collection (Envelope 2461), Williams and Walker, Walker: Aida Overton, Billy Rose Theatre Collection, New York Public Library of the Performing Arts.

108. Jean-Claude Baker and Chris Chase, *Josephine: The Hungry Heart* (New York: Random House, 1993), p. 58.

Chapter 6

1. Rose Tapes, Tape 3.

2. Rose, p. 104.

3. Rose, p. 103.

4. Baker/Chase, pp. 62–63.

5. Author interview with David Jasen, Dec. 20, 2017.

6. Lynn Haney, *Naked at the Feast: A Biography of Josephine Baker* (New York: Dodd, Mead, 1981), pp. 37–38.

7. Gee's birth information comes from her 1919 application for a US passport. Some sources say she was born in Newport, Kentucky.

8. Whittier H. Wright, "Two Clever Performers: Efficient Work of Misses King and Gee Worth of Praise," *Broad Ax* (Salt Lake City), Aug. 9, 1913, p. 3.

9. Lynn Abbott and Doug Seroff, *Ragged but Right* (Jackson: University of Mississippi Press, 2007), p. 116, 118. Abbott and Seroff give his name as "Keyer" despite reproducing a handbill that the pianist printed with his name as "Kyer." Other newspaper accounts and the Census use the "Kyer" spelling.

10. Abbott/Seroff, *Ragged but Right*, p. 118.

11. "Musical Star Divorced," *Chicago Defender*, May 17, 1924, p. 5. Gee did occasionally use the name "Kyer" in later life for unknown reasons.

12. J. Baker/Chase, p. 70.

13. Her appearance was announced in the Aug. 20 issue of *The New York Age*, where it was stated that she "made a flying trip to America from London" to appear at the Lafayette. This notice would seem to indicate that she literally took a plane to make the date, although it is possible that "flying" was used to mean she made a quick and brief trip back home.

14. "Lottie Gee Scores Big Vaudeville Hit," *New York Age*, Sept. 4, 1920, p. 6.

15. "Lottie Gee Back in States," *New York Age*, Dec. 11, 1920, p. 6.

16. Draft manuscript for *Eubie Blake* by Al Rose, p. 98; not included in published book; in MHS 2800, Box 68.

17. Advertisement for Sophia's Triple Special Promenade in the *Pittsburgh Courier*, July 21, 1923, p. 13.

18. Draft manuscript for *Eubie Blake* by Al Rose, p. 98; not included in published book; in MHS 2800, Box 68.

19. Eubie's second wife asked Rose to delete this story from the final manuscript, saying that Avis would have never have used the "n" word, even in private. Draft manuscript for *Eubie Blake* by Al Rose, p. 98; not included in published book; in MHS 2800, Box 68.

20. Al Rose, *I Remember Jazz*, p. 103.

21. MHS 2800, Box 12. This note appears on the bottom of a typed lyric for a song "You'll Never Find a Change in Me," which is undated (and otherwise unknown). From the contents, it appears to have been written after the duo were a success in vaudeville, and probably after the success of *Shuffle Along*.

22. In an interview with the authors, Terry Waldo said that Eubie told him that it was this friction that lead to their breakup in 1925.

23. "*Shuffle Along* Has Its Boston Opening," *New York Age*, Aug. 5, 1922, p. 6.

24. "Colored Pair Honored," *Variety*, June 18, 1924, p. 9.

25. "Sissle and Blake Get City's Keys," *Chicago Defender*, June 21, 1924, p. 6, citing the *New York Morning Telegraph*.

26. "*Shuffle Along* Breezy Comedy," *Chicago Defender*, Aug. 12, 1922, p.7.

27. In a later interview, Blake said that Baker was still underaged when she began performing in *Shuffle Along*, being just 15 years old. According to him, her age caused some trouble with the authorities who policed the hiring of underage performers. McPherson/Chan.

28. Kimball/Bolcom, p. 128.

29. Benetta Jules-Rosette, *Josephine Baker in Art and Life* (Chicago: University of Chicago Press, 2007), p. 57.

30. Jean-Claude Baker and Chris Chase, *Josephine: The Hungry Heart*. New York: Random House, 1993), p. 57

31. Unidentified clipping c. 1923, in MHS 2800, Box 43.

32. Sterns/Sterns, p. 100.

33. A.N.P., "*Shuffle Along* Begins Engagement in Chicago," *Dallas Express*, Nov. 22, 1922, p. 1.

34. Ibid.

35. "Coy Cogitates," *Chicago Defender*, Sept. 8, 1923, pg. 6.

36. Ibid., pp. 1, 8.

37. Ashton Stevens in the *Herald Examiner* and Sheppard Butler in *The Tribune*, quoted in an advertisement for the Chicago production cited in Kimball/Bolcom, p. 141.

38. Reproduced in Kimball/Bolcom, p. 142.

39. Ashton Stevens, "Colored Actors 'Good Winners' Says Stevens," *Chicago Herald Examiner*, Dec. 24, 1922; clipping in Chicago Scrapbook, MHS 2800, Box 72.

40. Archie Bell, "Jazz Most Popular Music of the Day," *Chicago Defender*, May 31, 1924, p. 6; reprinted from the Cleveland *News-Leader*.

41. Ibid.

42. Nora Douglas Holt, "News of the Music World," *Chicago Defender*, Dec. 16, 1922, p. 5.

43. Sylvester Russell, "*Shuffle Along* Opens Monday at the Olympic: Negro and Jewish District Newspapers Ignored. Colored People Not Wanted During the First Week," *Chicago Star*, Nov. 11, 1922; clipping in Chicago Scrapbook, MHS 2800, Box 72.

44. Sylvester Russell, "*Shuffle Along* Contrasts with Opera . . . at the Olympic." *Chicago Star*, Nov. 18, 1922; clipping in Chicago Scrapbook, MHS 2800, Box 72.

45. "*Shuffle Along*, Sparkling Musical Comedy with Darktown Cast, Registers Big Hit," *Des Moines Register*, Mar. 5, 1923, p. 10.

46. "Jazz, and Then More Jazz," *Indianapolis News*, Mar. 13, 1923, p. 7.

47. Richard I. Stokes, "*Shuffle Along* Has Some Nimble Dances," *St. Louis Post-Dispatch*, Mar. 19, 1923, p. 19.

48. *Republican Tribune* (Union, MO), Mar. 23, 1923, p. 5.

49. "*Shuffle Along* Packs Nashville Theatre to Door," *Fayetteville (AR) Daily Democrat*, Mar. 1, 1923, p. 7.

50. Birmingham critic quoted in "*Shuffle Along*—A Criticism," *Waco (TX) News-Tribune*, Mar. 16, 1923, p. 6.

51. "*Shuffle Along* No. 3 Company Next Week at the Lafayette," *New York Age*, Mar. 10, 1923, p. 6.

52. "Colored Shows Clash," *Variety*, Nov. 17, 1922, p. 13.

53. Donald Bogle, *Heat Wave: The Life and Career of Ethel Waters* (New York: Harper, 2011), p. 104

54. Charles B. Cochran, *I Had Almost Forgotten* (London: Hutchinson, 1932), p. 219

55. Rose Tapes.

56. "Music Men," *Variety*, June 21, 1923, p. 47.

57. "Another *Shuffle Along*," *Variety*, July 12, 1923, p. 12.

58. "*Shuffle* Protest," *Variety*, July 19, 1923, p. 12.

59. "*Shuffle* Injunction," *Variety*, July 26, 1923, p. 12.

60. "*Shuffle Along*," *Pittsburgh Courier*, Aug. 11, 1923, p. 17.

61. Baker/Chase, *Josephine: The Hungry Heart*, pp. 68–70.

62. Ibid.

63. "Pitt—*Shuffle Along*," *Pittsburgh Post*, Sept. 4, 1923, p. 7.

64. Lecture by Noble Sissle during James V. Hatch's black drama class at City College of New York, Mar. 7, 1972. Recording from the oral history program at the Hatch-Billops Collection, New York.

65. "Dramatic Story of Success of *Shuffle Along* Told by Noble Sissle, Eubie Blake," *Pittsburgh Courier*, Sept. 22, 1923, p. 11.

66. Baker/Chase, p. 70.

67. "Canadian Citizen Tells of Impression *Shuffle Along* Made in Dominion," *Pittsburgh Courier*, Sept. 23, 1923, p. 11.

68. "Cox—*Shuffle Along*," *Cincinnati Enquirer*, Nov. 11, 1923, p. 63.

69. Parkins, Rudi Blesh and Harriet Janis also tell this story; see Rudi Blesh and Harriet Janis, *They All Played Ragtime*, 4th ed. (New York: Oak Publications, 1971), p. 199.

70. Original contract in MHS 2800, Box 18.

71. Alan Dale, "*Elsie* Hits High Level as Play with Music," Apr. 5, 1923, in NYPL clipping file.

72. Hazel Bryant interview with Noble Sissle, c. 1969, Tape #2, Emory University, Rose Library, HB 257.1.

73. Rose, p. 104.

74. Advertisement, *Chicago Defender*, July 30, 1921, p. 3.

75. Correspondence by Eubie's lawyer Solomon Goodman, Dec. 4 and 8, 1922 and Jan. 3, 1923, in MHS 2800, Box 1.

76. Author interview with Terry Waldo, Dec. 28, 2018.

77. Opening introduction to "Tricky Fingers" from *Eubie Blake Live*, Eubie Blake Music, c. 1974.

78. Cited in Robert Popple, *John Arpin: Keyboard Virtuoso* (Toronto: Dundurn Press), p. 187. When Blake was interviewed by Alex Wilder and Jim Maher for their book on American popular song, Maher related that all he "wanted to play . . . was Victor Herbert. And he'd say, 'Now listen to the harmonization—this man really knew harmony. We all learned from him, you know.' And he played Herbert's music with such meticulous care." (Cited in James Lester, *Too Marvelous For Words: The Life and Times of Art Tatum* [New York: Oxford University Press, 1994], pp. 107–108.)

79. Lucien H. White, "Competent Conductors for Negro Orchestras a Vital Need for Musical Growth," *New York Age*, Feb. 2, 1924, p. 1.

80. Royalty statements from M. Witmark & Sons, in MHS 2800, Box 19.

81. Advertisement for *Runnin' Wild* at the Shubert Theater, New Haven, in *Bridgeport (CT) Telegram*, Oct. 20, 1923, p. 30.

82. *Detroit Free Press*, Feb. 1, 1924, p. 6.

83. "Inside Stuff Legit," *Variety*, Jan. 31, 1924, p. 26.

84. Information on B. C. Whitney derived from https://detroithistorical.pastperfectonline.com/byperson?keyword=Whitney%2C+Bertram+C. (accessed March 1, 2018), and contemporary newspaper accounts. The contract between Sislake Producing Company and Eubie Blake and Noble Sissle is in MHS 2800, Box 18.

85. Advertisement, *New York Age*, Feb. 6, 1924, p. 6.

86. "Promoter of *Shuffle Along* Albert Mayer, Dies in New York," *Pittsburgh Post Gazette*, Mar. 22, 1924, p. 2.

87. "Obituary," *Variety*, Mar. 18, 1925 [misdated?], p. 46.

88. An early version of the script was submitted for copyright to the Library of Congress in 1924 under the name *Shufflers*, perhaps as a means of linking it to the earlier *Shuffle Along*. This title was quickly dropped, however. Performing Arts Division, Library of Congress ML50.S597 S41 1924.

89. Baker/Chase, pp. 74–75.

90. See "Cooper and Robinson," *New York Age*, Jan. 28, 1909, p. 6, and Bernard L. Peterson, *Profiles of African American Stage Performers and Theatre People, 1816–1960*. (Westport, CT: Greenwood Press, 1997), p. 63–64.

91. "*In Bamville* Fascinates Packed House," *Pittsburgh Courier*, Mar. 22, 1924, p. 8.
92. "Sissle and Blake Make Big Hit in Newest Offering," *Buffalo American*, July 10, 1924, p. 1.
93. In the late 1920s, Dunn returned to Europe, where he worked with several bands over the following years, including those led by Noble Sissle.
94. Baker/Chase, p. 73.
95. "Lyceum Theater," *Democrat and Chronicle* (Rochester, NY), Mar. 11, 1924, p. 17.
96. Advertisement for *In Bamville, Democrat and Chronicle* (Rochester, NY), Mar. 12, 1924, p. 3.
97. Floyd C. Calvin, "*In Bamville* Opening," *Pittsburgh Courier*, Mar. 29, 1924, p. 11.
98. Ibid.
99. Baker/Chase, p. 74.
100. *In Bamville* advertisement, *Variety*, Apr. 9, 1924, p. 47.
101. Ibid.
102. Ibid.
103. Ibid.
104. Bell, "Jazz Most Popular Music," p. 6.
105. In an interview with Rudi Blesh and Mike Lipskin, Eubie claimed that Stevens had arranged for a gala dinner when *In Bamville* opened in Chicago, which was attended by major white musicians in Chicago, to celebrate Sissle and Blake's achievements. He felt it was underhanded that Stevens then turned around and panned the production for not being sufficiently "black." In a photo taken of the event, the photographer purposely showed only the white attendees, according to Blake.
106. "Sissle and Blake *In Bamville* Storm Chicago," *Buffalo American*, Apr. 10, 1924, p. 1.
107. Tony Langston, "Sissle and Blake's *In Bamville* in Chicago," *Chicago Defender*, Apr. 5, 1924, p. 6.
108. "Colored Performer Alleged 'Unique,'" *Variety*, Oct. 22, 1924, p. 2.
109. E. F. Harkins, "*In Bamville* Has Real Dixie Charm," *Boston Sunday Advertiser* reprinted in *Chicago Defender*, June 21, 1924, p. 6.

Chapter 7

1. Figures taken from the original production account books, in MHS 2800, Box 20.
2. "*Runnin' Wild*," *Brooklyn Daily Eagle*, Oct. 30, 1923, p. 10. The black press was far more sympathetic, as usual; see, for example, Lester Walton's glowing review of the show in the *New York Age*, Jan. 5, 1924, pp. 1–2.
3. Victor Records advertisement, *Missoulian* (Missoula, MN), Nov. 22, 1923, p. 2.
4. *Indianapolis Star*, Jan. 6, 1925, p. 7.
5. *Variety* reported on the dispute among various black acts as to who had first performed the dance on stage, noting that whatever its origin the dance itself "in reality, came to attention in ... *Runnin' Wild*"; see "Charleston Dispute," *Variety* Mar. 11, 1925, p. 4.
6. "The *Chocolate Dandies*, on View at the Colonial," *New York Sun*, Sept. 3, 1924; NYPL clipping file.

7. "*Chocolate Dandies* Opens at the Colonial Theatre," *New York Telegram*, Sept. 2, 1924; NYPL clipping file.

8. "The *Chocolate Dandies*," *New York Evening World*, Sept. 2, 1924; NYPL clipping file.

9. "*Chocolate Dandies*," *Brooklyn Daily Eagle*, Sept. 2, 1924, p. 5.

10. "Colored Artist Doesn't Seek Much," *Kansas City Advocate*, Feb. 6, 1925, p. 1.

11. "A Bit of History, *Chicago Defender*, Oct. 18, 1924, p. 8.

12. Lucien H. White, "An Unnecessary Desecration of Negro Spirituals by Men Singers at the Colonial Theater," *New York Age*, Nov. 15, 1924, p. 7.

13. Ibee, "New Plays Produced within Week on B'Way: The *Chocolate Dandies*," *Variety*, Sept. 3, 1924, p. 44.

14. "Good Negro Musical Play," *New York Times*, n.d.; NYPL clipping file.

15. Apparently, saxophonist Sidney Bechet originally was also featured in the production when it was still titled *In Bamville*, but dropped out when the show hit the road because he had too many bookings in New York; see John Chilton, *Sidney Bechet: Wizard of Jazz* (London: Palgrave/Macmillan, 1987, p. 67).

16. Ibee, "New Plays Produced within Week," 44.

17. "Good Negro Musical Play," *New York Times*, n.d.; NYPL clipping file.

18. Blesh/Lipskin.

19. "Colored Revue Is Some Show," *Zits*, Sept. 5, 1924; NYPL clipping file.

20. *Variety*, Sept. 24, 1924, p. 12, cited in Singer, p. 209.

21. Blesh/Lipskin.

22. Blesh/Lipskin.

23. Copy in author's collection; it was distributed to the trade by a regular commercial music publisher, Crown Music Co.

24. James P. Sinnott, "New All-Colored Show at Colonial," *New York Telegraph*, Sept. 2, 1924; NYPL clipping file.

25. "*Cho[co]late Dandies*, Colored Show, Better than *Shuffle Along*," *New York Tribune*, Sept. 2, 1924; NYPL clipping file.

26. Blesh/Lipskin.

27. "Colored Performer Alleged 'Unique,'" *Variety*, Oct. 22, 1924, pp. 1, 3; Anthea Kraut, *Choreographing Copyright* (NY: Oxford University Press, 2016), p. 104. Kraut's book devotes a part of its second chapter to a discussion of this lawsuit.

28. Bertram C. Whitney v. Hudgins, John et al., Supreme Court County of New York, Index No. 404459, 1924.

29. "Colored Performer Alleged 'Unique,'" *Variety*, Oct. 22, 1924, pp. 1, 3.

30. Kraut, p. 104.

31. "Is Johnny Hudgins, Comedian, Unique," *Chicago Defender*, Dec. 27, 1924, p. 6.

32. Kraut, p. 109.

33. In another irony, at the end of December Victor issued the only recordings that Sissle and Blake made of the show's songs, "Manda" and "Dixie Moon." (While they had cut other songs for the label, these went unissued, perhaps due to their poor sales.) These were probably the most popular of all of the show's songs, but both have dropped into obscurity.

34. "J. T. Gibson Makes Another Record," *Philadelphia Courier*, Dec. 6, 1924, p. 11.

35. Blesh/Lipskin.

36. "Bamville Club Hosts Entertain Artists on Eve of European Trip," *New York Age*, May 9, 1925, p. 6.

37. Inscribed photograph from *Chocolate Dandies* by Valaida Snow, in MHS PP 301, Box 18.

38. United Press, "Death the Aftermath of Party," *Sheboygan* (WI) *Press*, Apr. 24, 1925, p. 1.

39. "'Dream Girl' Star Inquest Witness," *Brooklyn Daily Eagle*, Apr. 25, 1925, p. 24.

40. "Colored Show Winds Up Owing Salary," *Variety*, May 27, 1925, p. 22.

41. "Noble Sissle Who Made $100,000 in *Shuffle Along* Is Bankrupt," *New York Age*, July 18, 1925, p. 1.

42. Advertisement, *Variety*, Sept. 9, 1925, p. 33.

43. Much of the information on Sissle and Blake's time in London comes from Howard Rye, "Visiting Firemen 7: Sissle and Blake," *Storyville*, no. 105 (Feb.–Mar. 1983), pp. 88–95, and Kimball/Bolcom, pp. 190–193.

44. Blesh/Lipskin.

45. *Era*, Nov. 28, 1925; quoted in Rye, p. 89.

46. "The Alhambra," *Hendon and Finchley (London, UK) Times*, Nov. 6, 1925, p. 16.

47. "Variety Stage," *Stage*, Nov. 19, 1925, p. 12.

48. "Eubie Blake Back from Foreign Tour," unidentified newspaper clipping, reproduced in Kimball/Bolcom, p. 199.

49. "The Coliseum," *Stage*, Nov. 26, 1925, p. 14.

50. "Eubie Blake Back from Foreign Tour," unidentified newspaper clipping, reproduced in Kimball/Bolcom, p. 199.

51. Blesh/Lipskin.

52. Advertisement, *Variety*, Apr. 21, 1926, p. 55.

53. Advertisement for Loew's State Theater, *St. Louis Post-Dispatch*, Dec. 11, 1926, p. 7.

54. "*Plastic Age* Drew $19,700 in Pittsburgh—Good Show," *Variety*, July 21, 1926, p. 6.

55. Agreement between The Vitaphone Corporation and Noble Sissle and Eubie Blake, dated Jan. 31, 1927, in MHS 2800, Box 19.

56. "Cotton Club Band a[t] Lafayette Theater," *New York Age*, Mar. 16, 1929, p. 6.

57. Kimball/Bolcom, p. 251.

58. Rose Tapes, tape 2B.

59. Harold Tillotson to Eubie Blake, June 8, 1927, in MHS 2800, Box 1.

60. Harold Tillotson to Eubie Blake, undated letter [c. June 1927], in MHS 2800, Box 1.

61. "*Africana* on Cleanest Stage on Broadway," *Chicago Defender*, Sept. 3, 1927, p. 6. Two announcements appeared in October in the *New York Age* and *Chicago Defender* about Bass and Blake performing together, but there is no further record of them collaborating.

62. Portions of its score—along with a second show titled *Cissy* from approximately the same time—can be found in MHS 2800, Box 118. Besides the song lists, the scripts for the shows are apparently lost.

63. Blesh/Lipskin.

64. Telegram from Broadway Jones to Eubie Blake, Oct. 18, 1923, in MHS 2800, Box 1.

65. Rose Tapes, Tape 5A; Todd Decker, *Show Boat: Performing Race in an American Musical* (New York: Oxford University Press, 2015), p. 92.

66. Rose Tapes, Tape 5A.

67. "New Palace Chicago," *Billboard*, Feb. 9, 1929, p. 18.

68. Letter from John A Schultz, B F Keith-Albee Vaudeville Exchange addressed to Eubie Blake at Hennepin Orpheum Theatre, Minneapolis, Oct. 15, 1928, in MHS 2800, Box 1.

69. Ibid.

70. Ibid.

71. Letter from George Wieden to EB, Nov. 8, 1928, in MHS 2800, Box 1.

72. Letter from Harry Wallen, West Coast Service Corporation to Eubie Blake, May 20, 1929, in MHS 2800, Box 17.

73. June 22, 1929, letter for Law Department, Radio-Keith-Orpheum addressed to Eubie c/o Fanchon & Marco Oddities Idea, West Coast House, Omaha, NE, in MHS 2800, Box 1.

74. "Jones and Blake," *Chicago Defender*, Oct. 12, 1929, p. 7.

75. "*Oddities Idea* Decided Hit: Lively Chorus," *Great Falls [MT]Tribune*, July 17, 1929, p. 9.

76. The film was to be called "The Two Black Crows," according to an announcement in the *Pittsburgh Courier* (Apr. 6, 1929, p. 15). This may be a reference to a film then being shot with the white vaudeville duo Mack and Moran, who performed under this name. A film featuring this duo was released in Oct. 1929 as *Why Bring That Up?* and was a major success. The cast was all white, and it's unlikely Paramount would have considered casting a black actress, despite the fact that the leads performed in blackface. See "Jeff Cohen, Why Bring That Up?," Vitaphone Varieties website, http://vitaphone.blogspot.com/2007/04/why-bring-that-up.html, accessed Dec. 28, 2017.

77. "At the Lafayette Theater," *New York Age*, Jan. 11, 1930, p. 6.

78. "*Folies Bergere*," *Brookyn Daily Eagle*, Apr. 26, 1930, p. 23.

79. "Lively Tunes Feature New Downtown Revue," Apr. 16, 1930, p. 34.

80. Records in the Eubie Blake papers show a contract with Shapiro Bernstein from early 1930 for four songs, including one titled "Folies Bergere." These have never been found, as far as we know. MHS 2800, Box 19.

81. Rose Tapes, Tape 7.

82. John Howland, *Ellington Uptown* (Ann Arbor: University of Michigan Press, 2009), pp. 76–78.

83. Lucien H. White, "Monarch Band Announces Close of Its Monthly Free Concerts because of Lack [of] Appreciation by Audience," *New York Age*, Jan. 17, 1940, p. 4. The Monarch band was led by Fred Simpson, who previously had followed in James Reese Europe's footsteps to lead the 369th Infantry Band. The band gave monthly free concerts in Harlem from about 1930 to 1942.

84. Program in MHS 2800, Box 30.

85. "RKO Is Damming Flow of Colored Acts," *Billboard*, Jan. 18, 1930, p. 11.

Chapter 8

1. Richard Watts Jr., "Ethel Waters a Hit in Negro Revue, *Africana*, at Daly's," *New York Herald Tribune*, July 12, 1927.

2. Roland Field, "*Africana*," *New York Times*, July 11, 1927.

3. Rose, p. 100.

4. Contract in MHS 2800, Box 19.

5. Letter of Jack Scholl to Eubie Blake, May 4, 1930 in MHS 2800, Box 1.

6. Ibid.

7. Their titles are "Take Care of You for Me," "Giving the Devil His Due," "Piano Man," and "Modenistic Strain." As far as we know, these songs were never published.

8. Hines recounts this story in an interview aired on the NPR show "Options," which featured a joint concert by Blake and Hines that was recorded at the University of California, Berkeley, c. 1973; copy recording available at the Library of Congress LWB 1511A2.

9. Stanley Dance, *The World of Earl Hines* (New York: Scribner, 1977), p. 31.

10. Earl Hines to Eubie Blake, Feb. 3, 1930, in MHS 2800, Box 11.

11. Rose, pp. 105, 106.

12. Singer, p. 244.

13. Ibid.

14. Ibid.

15. Barry Singer, interview with John Bubbles, at his home, Feb. 24, 1982; transcript courtesy of Barry Singer.

16. "*Hot Chocolates* Makes Hit in New York: Minto Cato and Baby Cox Are Stars," *Chicago Defender*, June 15, 1929, p. 6.

17. "Plays and Other Things," *Brooklyn Daily Eagle*, Sept. 7, 1930, p. 29.

18. Cited in Singer, p. 209.

19. Blesh/Lipskin.

20. Cited in Singer, p. 248.

21. Singer, p. 250.

22. Royalty statement in MHS 2800, Box 19.

23. Ethel Waters with Charles Samuels, *His Eye Is on the Sparrow* (Garden City, NY: Doubleday, 1951), p. 251.

24. J. Brooks Atkinson, "The Play: When the Black Gals Dance," *New York Times*, Oct. 22, 1930.

25. Robert Garland, "Spirit of Jungle Drums Dominates New Revue," *New York Telegram*, reprinted in *Pittsburgh Courier*, Nov. 1, 1930, p. 11.

26. Percy Hammond, "Glorifying the American Negro," *New York Tribune*; in NYPL clipping file.

27. Richard Lockridge, "Black and Brown," *New York Sun*, Oct. 23, 1930.

28. Arthur Pollock, "Lew Leslie's *Blackbirds* Gets to Manhattan at Last, Older but No Wiser Than When Right Here in Brooklyn," *Brooklyn Daily Eagle*, Oct. 23, 1930, p. 23.

29. "She Likes to Sing Something Sinful," *Brooklyn Daily Eagle*, Nov. 2, 1930, p. 34.

30. "The 1930 *Blackbirds*," *New York Age*, Nov. 8, 1930, p. 7.

31. "Nine Plays Use Our Actors; *Blackbirds, Chariot* Open," *Chicago Defender*, Nov. 1, 1930, p. 5.

32. Accounting given by EB to the American Federation of Musicians, July 5, 1931, in MHS 2800, Box 13.

33. Ragtime pianist John Arpin notes that the same four-chord progression is featured in the song "Guilty" with music by Richard Whiting and Harry Akst. Arpin believed the song was also published in 1930, although the actual sheet is copyrighted 1931. He says that when he asked Eubie if he borrowed this unusual progression for "Memories of You," the pianist was "quite evasive." Of course, the melodies are quite different, and it's not unusual for musicians to borrow chord progressions as a basis for a new song. Cited in Popple, pp. 187–188.

34. MHS 2800, Box20.

35. Singer, p. 230.

36. Rose Tapes, Tape 5A.

37. Waters with Samuels, p. 215. The Royale Theatre (now the Jacobs Theatre) is on 45th Street, while Hubert's Flea Circus was on 42nd Street, but it made a good story anyway.

38. Cited in Singer, p. 252.

39. Waters with Samuels, p. 216.

40. Letter of Eubie Blake to the American Federation of Musicians, July 5, 1931, in MHS 2800, Box 13.

41. Letter of Edward Canavan of the AFM to Eubie Blake, Apr. 12, 1933, in MHS 2800, Box 13.

42. Letter of Edward Canavan of the AFM to Eubie Blake, Nov. 27, 1933, in MHS 2800, Box 13.

43. California, Passenger and Crew Lists, 1882–1959, accessed via ancestry.com.

44. Quotations in this section from Rose Tapes, Tape 8.

45. US Federal Census, 1940. Here she is listed as single but having the name of "Lottie Gee Kyer." She is classified as a "Government Worker" perhaps because she had worked for the Federal Theatre Project.

46. Ellis-Hamilton Family Tree on ancestry.com, accessed May 3, 2017; California Death Index, 1940–1997.

47. This passage is based on a series of letters and telegrams from Harry Romm to Eubie dated mid-April–late May, in MHS 2800, Box 4.

48. MHS 2800, Box 4.

49. "Eubie Blake and Broadway Jones Here for Fourth," *Evening News* (Wilkes Barre, PA), July 3, 1931, p. 5.

50. Rose Tapes, Tape 5B.

51. Ibid.

52. "Police Arrest John Conquet for Murder," *New York Age*, June 11, 1932, p. 9.

53. Tim Brooks, *Lost Sounds: Blacks and the Birth of the Recording Industry 1890–1919* (Urbana: University of Illinois Press, 2004), p. 386.

54. Undated letter from Crown Record Company, outlining terms of the deal to record Eubie's orchestra, in MHS 2800, Box 4.

55. Eubie never arranged his own material for orchestra, even in the heyday of *Shuffle Along*. He was a skilled conductor, but not trained in instrumental arranging.

56. B. S. H. Steinhauser, "Radio Maker Signs Eubie Blake's Band," *Pittsburgh Press*, Dec. 7, 1931, p. 16E.

57. Letter of Vinton Freedley to Eubie Blake, July 22, 1931, in MHS 2800, Box 1.

58. Arthur Pollock, "*Singin' the Blues*, an Unusual Form of Negro Entertainment, Comes to the Majestic and Makes a Mixed Impression," *Brooklyn Daily Eagle*, Apr. 14, 1931.

59. Burns Mantle, "Frank Wilson, Washington Sisters, in New Broadway Drama," reprinted in *New York Age*, Sept. 19, 1931, p. 6.

60. "*Hot From Harlem* Opens; Bill Robinson Whole Show," *Billboard*, Aug. 22, 1931, p. 23.

61. The only other evidence of Eubie in the film occurs during a production number early in the film in which Robinson addresses the pianist on stage as "Eubie," but this musician does not appear to be Blake.

62. Rose, p. 107.

63. Agreement between Eubie and Avis Blake dated March 3, 1932, in MHS 2800, Box 17.

64. "Noble Sissle, A Leading Race Actor, Talks Out," *Negro World*, May 23, 1931, p. 6.

65. Edward W. Smith, "Tough Luck on Trail of Old *Shuffle*," *Chicago Defender*, Nov. 19, 1932, p. 10.

66. Agreement of Nov. 8, 1932 between Hubert Blake and Mawin Productions, in MHS 2800, Box 17.

67. "*Shuffle Along of 1932*," *Brooklyn Citizen*, Nov. 11, 1932; clipping in scrapbook in MHS 2800, Box 43.

68. "*Shuffle Along* Shows You 'Why Darkies Were Born,'" *Knickerbocker Press* (Albany, NY), Dec. 13, p. 32; clipping in scrapbook in MHS 2800, Box 43.

69. "*Shuffle Along of 1933*," *New York Times*, Dec. 27, 1932; clipping in scrapbook in MHS 2800, Box 43.

70. Robert Garland, "Cast and Miscast," *New York World Telegram*, Dec. 27, 1932; clipping in scrapbook in MHS 2800, Box 43.

71. "After All, It's the Dancing," *New York Daily News*, n.d.; NYPL clipping files.

72. "*Shuffle Along of 1933*," *New York Age*, Jan. 7, 1933, p. 6.

73. Bessye Bearden, "*Shuffle Along* Back, Captures New York," *Chicago Defender*, Jan. 7, 1933, p. 4.

74. A program from the Philadelphia run shows some slight changes in the song selection from the 1932 version.

75. J. H. Keen, "Observations the Morning After," Feb. 14, 1933; clipping in scrapbook in MHS 2800, Box 43.

76. "At the Theatres," *Philadelphia Bulletin*, Feb. 14, 1933; clipping in scrapbook MHS 2800, Box 43.

77. Brooks, p. 388.

78. "New *Shuffle Along* Just Pokes Along," *Chicago Daily News*, undated; clipping in scrapbook MHS 2800, Box 43.

79. Rob Roy, "*Shuffle Along* of 1933 in Chicago's Loop," *Chicago Defender*, May 6, 1933, p. 5.

80. MHS 2800, Box 1.

81. Floyd G. Snelson, "Broadway Bound," *Pittsburgh Courier*, Feb. 11, 1933, p. 11.

82. *Chicago Tribune*, Oct. 22, 1933, p. 50.

83. "Piano Plinker Plunks at Pitt," *Pittsburgh Courier*, Jan. 13, 1934, p. 6.

84. "*Shuffle Along* Proves Sensation Downtown," *Pittsburgh Courier*, Jan. 20, 1934, p. A6.

85. Telegram dated May 1 1934 from Harry Rogers, care of State Theatre, Harrisburg, PA, in MHS 2800, Box 1.

86. Sidney Harris, "Palace, New York," *Billboard*, Nov. 3, 1934, p. 14.

87. Singer, p. 284.

88. *New York Age*, Aug. 11, 1934, p. 5.

89. Brown.

90. Julius J. Adams, "Progress of Race Shown at Spectacle," *Chicago Defender*, Sept. 1, 1934, p. 3.

91. *New York Age*, July 20, 1935, p. 8.

Chapter 9

1. Interview with Rosetta Lenoir, WYNC TV, https://archive.org/details/cunytv_SPLT0057, accessed on May 7, 2018.

2. Ibid.

3. Steven Watson, *Prepare For Saints: Gertrude Stein, Virgil Thomson, and the Mainstreaming of American Musical Modernism* (New York: Random House, 1998), 245.

4. Brown.

5. Ibid.

6. Information from 1930 and 1940 US Census, accessed through ancestry.com.

7. Brown.

8. Ibid.

9. MHS 2800, Box 27.

10. MHS 2800, Box 15.

11. *Brooklyn Citizen*, July 23, 1937, Library of Congress, Federal Theatre Project, Flanagan Papers, 20.325.

12. MHS 2800, Box 18.

13. Arthur Pollock, "The Theater," *Brooklyn Eagle*, July 23, 1937, p. 7.

14. "Minstrels over the Adelphi," *New York Times*, July 23, 1937, clipping.

15. P.A., "*Swing It*, WPA Negro Revue, Turns Out to Be Just a Turkey," *Billboard*, July 31, 1937, p. 4.

16. Alexander Taylor, "The Theater," *New Masses*, Aug. 2, 1937, pp. 30–31.

17. "Stage Stars, Down in Luck, Rising Again with Broadway's *Swing It*," *Pittsburgh Courier*, July 31, 1937, p. 20.

18. "Negro Musical Show Downtown," *New York Age*, July 31, 1937, p. 9.

19. "Bud Harris Buzzes," *Chicago Defender*, July 31, 1937, p. 10.

20. Arthur Pollock, "The Theater," *Brooklyn Eagle*, July 23, 1937, p. 7.

21. "Eubie Blake Scores Again," *Pittsburgh Courier*, Aug. 14, 1937, p. 20.

22. Sylvia Weiss, "FTP Vaude Makes B'way Debut; Corny, But Wows 'Em Anyway," *Billboard*, Feb. 12, 1938, p. 4.

23. MHS 2800, Box 11.

24. Brown.

25. "Race Bands Should Play Colored Music," *Pittsburgh Courier*, Apr. 9, 1938, p. 20.

26. Copy of letter to Fletcher Henderson, Mar. 25, 1938, in MHS 2800, Box 15.

27. Copy of letter to Noble Sissle, Apr. 1, 1938, in MHS 2800, Box 15.

28. W. C. Handy, letter to EB, April 8, 1938, in MHS 2800, Box 17.

29. "Song Writers Organize to Protect Composers," *Pittsburgh Courier*, Aug. 13, 1938, p. 20. A typed manuscript by Milton Reddie dated July 31 is nearly identical to the copy that the *Courier* ran in its article, indicating they may have picked up Reddie's press release verbatim; see MHS 3800, Box 26.

30. Eubie Blake Papers, MHS 2800, Box 15.

31. Ibid.

32. Copy of letter of Milton Reddie to Mr. Gallagher, Prosperity Pictures Inc., Oct. 12, 1938, in MHS 2800, Box 26.

33. Elliott Carpenter to EB, Feb. 2, 1967, in MHS 2800, Box 2.

34. On the original publication, it is credited as being part of the score to *Swing It*, although the piece is not listed in the show's program and doesn't fit into the popular mold of the songs from that show. It was possibly interpolated into some performances as a showpiece for Blake.

35. Eubie performs this work on his 1969 album, *The Eighty Six Years of Eubie Blake*.

36. Another semiclassical work, "Boogie Woogie Beguine," is more of a musical joke, as it reworks themes from Cole Porter's "Begin the Beguine" and other popular snippets into a marriage of boogie and Latin rhythms.

37. Copy of letter to Noble Sissle, Apr. 1, 1938, in MHS 2800, Box 15.

38. "Mrs. Eubie Blake Dies," *Chicago Defender*, Mar. 25, 1939, p. 18.

39. Milton Reddie to Eubie Blake, in MHS 3800, Box 12.

40. Singer, p. 306.

41. William Forsythe, Jr., "New Stage Show Is Filled with Talent but Needs Trimming," *Pittsburgh Courier*, Feb. 1, 1941, p. 21.

42. On the other hand, the title song "Tan Manhattan" is an ode to Harlem's many cultural attractions.

43. Charles Cooke is also listed as an author on the sheet music, although only Razaf and Blake are mentioned in the lyric sheet prepared for the show.

44. Singer, p. 308.

45. Lyrics as sung on Asch 78 recorded in 1941 by Razaf and Blake. They signed a contract with Asch on June 13, 1941, stating they had "received full compensation for recording We Are Americans Too/Take It Easy." They also agreed "that we will not record these songs for anyone else. We further agree to release the recording rights for these songs. For 'Take It Easy' it is understood that Asch Recording is to pay 2 cents a title for each record." Agreement in MHS 2800, Box 4.

46. "Meeting and Greeting," *New York Age*, Sept. 20, 1941, p. 10.

47. *Pittsburgh Courier*, Jan. 3, 1942, p. 5.

48. Associated Press, "Memphis, Tenn.," Dec. 18, 1941, in *The Daily Mail* (Hagerstown, MD), Dec. 18, 1941, p. 21.

49. A. E. White, "Razaf and Black [*sic*] Pleased with *Tan Manhattan* Show," clipping dated Jan. 31, 1941.

50. Ibid.

51. "*Tan Manhattan*, New Musical Comedy Revue, Comes to the Apollo Theater," *New York Age*, Feb. 8, 1941, p. 4.

52. William E. Clark, "*Tan Manhattan* Opens in Harlem," *New York Age*, Feb. 15, 1941, p. 4.

53. Ibid.

54. *New York Age*, Mar. 8, 1941, p. 10.

55. Isadora Smith, "Success of *Tan Manhattan* Opens New Ligit Trend in Harlem at Apollo Theater," *Pittsburgh Courier*, Feb. 22, 1941, p. 21.

56. Continuity records for both *Tan Manhattan* and *Up Harlem Way* kept with the original scores indicate that indeed the songs were identical in both shows; Eubie Blake Sheet Music Collection, MHS, Box 119.

57. July 21, 1941 Partnership Agreement between Razaf, Blake, Irvin C. and F. E. Miller for *Tan Manhattan,* in MHS 2800, Box 4.

58. Julia M. H. Carson, *Home away From Home: The Story of the USO* (New York: Harper & Brothers, 1946). Quoted on the History of the USO website; http://www.ww2uso.org/history.html, accessed Dec. 14, 2017.

59. Blesh/Lipskin.

60. "*Shuffle Along* (Red Circuit; Unit 54), Fort Sheridan, Ill., Dec. 9"; clipping in NYPL, filed Sept. 15, 1941.

61. "Soldiers at Ft. Bragg Praise Show Staged by Noble Sissle," *Chicago Defender*, Apr. 4, 1942, p. 23.

62. Ibid.

63. Contract with USO Camp Shows-Inc dated May 19, 1942; MHS 2800, Box 4. Blake's salary would be increased in 1943 for six performances a week to $115 and then in 1945 to $125 a week.

64. MHS 2800, Box 15.

65. "*Keep Shufflin'* Pleases Soldiers at Camp Polka, LA," *New York Age*, Sept. 26, 1942, p. 10.

66. Garvin Bushell, as told to Mark Tucker, *Jazz from the Beginning*, Ann Arbor: University of Michigan Press, 1990, p. 108.

67. A single copyright for a song titled "You Spoke, I Never Heard a Word" by Eubie and Grace Bouret was registered with the Library of Congress in 1964. We were unable to find any further information on this lyricist although numerous lyric sheets are preserved in Eubie Blake's Sheet Music collection at the MHS.

68. Grace Bouret to EB, dated 1942, in MHS 2800, Box 10.

69. Telegrams from Sissle to Blake, May 1943, in MHS 2800, Box 4.

70. Noble Sissle to Eubie Blake, February 20, 1945, New York, in MHS 2800, Box 12.

71. "*Shuffle Along* Unit Back from USO Jaunt," *Pittsburgh Courier*, May 11, 1946, p. 17.

72. Milton Reddie to EB, Aug. 8, 1945, in MHS 2800, Box 12.

73. Jan. 9, 1946, Letter from EB to Dick Campbell at USO Inc, in MHS 2800, Box 15.

74. Jan. 17, 1946, Letter from Dick Campbell, Coordinator of Negro Talent, to EB, in MHS, Box 15.

75. J. Wynn Rousuck, "Eubie," *Baltimore Sun*, Feb. 1, 1979, D7.

76. July 16, 1946, letter from Wichita, KS, addressed to Mr. Jaffe [Music Supervisor] at USO office, in MHS 2800, Box 4.

Chapter 10

1. Much of this information was drawn from Thomas's obituary in *New York Age*, July 18, 1907, p. 8, and a handwritten biographical sketch by Marion Gant Tyler in MHS 2800, Box 16.

2. 1880 U.S. Federal Census, City of New York, June 8, 1880, p. 520, accessed via ancestry.com.

3. " A Successful Colored Man," *Reading Times*, Oct. 12, 1894, p. 2.

4. *Abilene Weekly*, Aug. 16, 1888, p. 2.

5. "Thomas No Speculator: Will Occupy His Brooklyn House in Ten Days," *Brooklyn Daily Eagle*, Oct. 4, 1894, p. 7.

6. " A Successful Colored Man," *Reading Times*, Oct. 12, 1894, p. 2.

7. "Thomas No Speculator," p. 7.

8. Biographical sketch by Marion Gant Tyler in MHS 2800, Box 16, p. 1.

9. Letter of Marion Gant Tyler to NY State Department of Health, Apr. 23, 1942, in MHS 2800, Box 16. Marion was trying to establish her birth date in order to get Civil Service employment during the war.

10. Biographical sketch by Marion Gant Tyler in MHS 2800, Box 16, p. 2.

11. Badger, photo insert.

12. Educational records of Marion Gant in the Eubie Blake Papers, in MHS 2800, Box 16.

13. http://www.doctorjazz.co.uk/locspeech4.html, accessed Jan. 26, 2017.

14. Biographical sketch by Marion Gant Tyler in MHS 2800, Box 16, p. 3.

15. Letter to Marion Tyler from Dorothy Bogart, Apr. 25, 1925, advising her to come to pick up her check at the *Keep Shufflin'* Company's offices the following day.

16. Biographical sketch by Marion Gant Tyler in MHS 2800, Box 16, p. 4. Records among Marion's papers show that she actually attended stenography school from Jan. 1935 to Jan. 1936, which would have been after her divorce from Tyler.

17. Carter, p. 107.

18. Letter of Marion Tyler to Eubie Blake, Mar. 29, 1944, in MHS 2800, Box 16.

19. Letter of Marion Tyler to EB, Apr. 13, 1944, in MHS 2800, Box 16.

20. Letter of Andy Razaf to EB, Mar. 27, 1944 in MHS 2800, Box 12.

21. Marion Tyler to EB, undated [c. fall 1944], in MHS 2800, Box 16.

22. L. Carter, pp. 107–108.

23. L. Carter, p. 109.

24. Verlinda Nelson to EB, Mar. 4, 1945, in MHS 2800, Box 2.

25. Eubie told a story to John Arpin about their marriage, claiming that it occurred in New Jersey, not Richmond (although their wedding certificate is from Virginia). He

said that the preacher was loathe to marry the couple, thinking Marion was white. According to Eubie, she fell to her knees and proclaimed "Preacherman, I want you to know that Aye'se . . . a nigger!" Arpin said, "Eubie started to cry when he told me that story, saying 'My Marion. She did that for me.'" Cited in Popple, p. 193.

26. Carter, p. 108.

27. Carter, p. 107.

28. Milton Reddie to EB, Jan. 11, 1946, in MHS 2800, Box 12.

29. Letter from Marion Tyler Blake to Eileen, Feb. 14, 1949, in MHS 2800, Box 16.

30. Obituary, "Ernest B. Ford," *Nacogdoches [TX] Daily Sentinel*, Apr. 19, 1991: A2.

31. Ernest Ford to EB, Aug. 27, 1946, in MHS 2800, EB papers, Box 4.

32. Ernest Ford to Blake, Nov. 6, 1946 and Jan. 11, 1947, in MHS 2800, Box 4.

33. Stan Kenton to Ernest Ford, Feb. 4, 1947, in MHS 2800, Box 4.

34. EB to Ernest Ford, Apr. 20, 1947, in MHS 2800, Box 4.

35. EB to Ernest Ford, Apr. 28, 1947, in MHS 2800, Box 4.

36. Ed McCaskey to EB, May 12, 1947, in MHS 2800, Box 4.

37. Ernest Ford to EB, May 16, 1947, in MHS 2800, Box 4.

38. Ernest Ford to Betty Grable, May 20, 1947, in MHS 2800, Box 4.

39. EB to Ernest Ford, Aug. 15, 1947, in MHS 2800, Box 4.

40. EB to Ernest Ford, Mar. 26, 1948, in MHS 2800, Box 4.

41. Beatrice Castle to Ernest Ford, Apr. 1, 1948, in MHS 2800, Box 4.

42. Ernest Ford to EB, May 11, 1948, in MHS 2800, Box 4.

43. Ernest Ford to EB, Oct. 24, 1952, in MHS 2800, Box 4.

44. Milton Reddie to EB, Oct. 2, 1946, in MHS 2800, Box 12.

45. Milton Reddie to EB, Nov. 18, 1946, in MHS 2800, Box 12.

46. Milton Reddie to Marion Tyler Blake, Nov. 28, 1946, in MHS 2800, Box 12.

47. Rose Tapes, Tape 3.

48. EB to Ernest Ford, Sept. 6, 1949, in MHS 2800, Box 4.

49. Ray Gallo to EB and Milton Reddie, Apr. 4, 1951, in MHS 2800, Box 11.

50. John Hollington "Appraisal of *Cleo Steps Out*," May 9, 1951, unpublished manuscript, in MHS 2800, Box 11.

51. Marion Blake to Milton Reddie, Oct. 12, 1946, in MHS 2800, Box 12.

52. Contract signed by EB, Feb. 18, 1947 with Thomas V. Bodkin, in MHS 2800, Box 1.

53. "Thomas V. Bodkin," Internet Broadway Database, https://www.ibdb.com/broadway-cast-staff/thomas-v-bodkin-77130, accessed Apr. 3, 2018.

54. J. Aaronson, undated letter to Thomas V. Bodkin, in MHS 2800, Box 1.

55. "The Plainsman Says," *Lubbock (TX) Evening Journal*, Oct. 31, 1947, p. 16.

56. Sid Bradley, "Mike Fright," *Nebraska State Journal*, Feb. 15, 1948, p. 34.

57. Nov. 19, 1948 agreement, in MHS 2800, Box 18.

58. "'Million Dollar Cast' Cuts Record 'I'm Just Wild about Harry,'" *Albuquerque Journal*, Dec. 17, 1948, p. 1.

59. Walter Winchell, "The Broadway Lights," *Abilene (TX) Reporter-News*, Dec. 15, 1948, p. 12.

60. Contract and correspondence with Harold B. Dow, Mar. 1, 1948 and Apr. 13, 1948; contract with Irving Gaumont, Mar. 18, 1949; in MHS 2800, Box 18.

61. "Irving Gaumont," "*Shuffle Along of 1952*" *Souvenir Booklet*, p. 12, in Schomberg Collection.

62. Earl Wilson, "It Happened Last Night," syndicated column, *Daily Press (Newport News, VA)*, June 23, 1947, p. 3.

63. EB to Flournoy Miller, Jan. 3, 1949, in Flournoy Miller papers, Schomburg Collection.

64. Noble Sissle, *New York Age*, Feb. 12, 1949, p. 11.

65. EB to Noble Sissle, June 7, 1949; Flournoy Miller papers, Schomburg Collection.

66. Flournoy Miller to Noble Sissle and EB, Oct. 22, 1949, in MHS 2800, Box 11, Flournoy Miller correspondence folder.

67. EB to Flournoy Miller, Oct. 30, 1949, in Flournoy Miller papers, Schomburg Collection.

68. Untitled and undated clipping, in NYPL; from the text itself, it is clear that this clipping dates from early 1951.

69. Noble Sissle to Flournoy Miller, Oct. 6, 1951, in Flournoy Miller papers, Schomberg Collection.

70. Ibid.

71. Ibid.

72. "Pearl Bailey to Star in *Shuffle Along*, Begins Rehearsal December 3rd," press release, in Flournoy Miller Papers, Schomberg Collection, New York Public Library.

73. Robert W. Matthews, "The Afro Visits with Sissle and Blake," *Afro Magazine*, Sept. 3, 1958, clipping, in MHS 2800, EB Papers, Box 40.

74. Untitled press release, Dec. 22, [1951], in Flournoy Miller Papers, Schomberg Collection.

75. Untitled press release, Jan. 19 [1952]; *Playbill*, The Broadway Theater, May 8, 1952; *Souvenir Booklet, "Shuffle Along" of 1952*, p. 13; all in Flournoy Miller Papers, Schomberg Collection, New York Public Library.

76. Thomas R. Waring, "3 Writers Busy Tailoring '21 *Shuffle Along* to '52,'" *Tribune*, Feb. 10, 1952, in NYPL clipping file.

77. Gerard Smith suggested this new scene. Sissle thought the idea "very funny," telling Miller, "They want a man to play in a St. Bernard Dog Skin. Is there any out there ofay or spade [?] There used to be a guy who played in Vaudeville . . . But I think he passed on. Maybe you can find some one out there who can play a comic dog. [bracketed question mark in the original]" Noble Sissle to Flournoy Miller, Feb. 10, 1952, in Flournoy Miller Papers, Schomberg Collection.

78. Bone, "*Shuffle Along*, New Haven, April 22," *Variety*, in NYPL clipping file.

79. F. R. J., "Last Night's Play," *New Haven Courier*, in NYPL clipping file.

80. Henry. T. Murdock, "*Shuffle Along*, Music Comedy, Presented at Shubert," *Philadelphia Inquirer*, Apr. 29, 1952, p. 17.

81. A press release from Gaumont's office cherry-picked the Philadelphia reviews to put the best face on the disaster, noting that "[l]ocal critics hail *Shuffle Along* as a brisk, melodious, and colorful show," although admitting that "their only complaint is that the cumbersome and elaborate book sometimes gets in the way, but never for long." Undated press release "For Sam Zolotow-Drama Dept.," in Flournoy Miller Papers, Schomberg Collection.

82. Untitled clipping, Philadelphia, May 6 [1952], in NYPL clipping file.

83. Walter Winchell, May 2, 1952, in NYPL clipping file.

84. "Scenery Still on Trucks," in NYPL clipping file, dated May 5, 1952.

85. John Chapman, "1952 *Shuffle Along*, Unlike Show of 1921, Is Slow and Muddled," reprinted in *Chicago Tribune*, May 10, 1952, p. 15.

86. Louis Sheaffer, "Old Pattern No Help to New *Shuffle Along* at the B'way," *Brooklyn Daily Eagle*, May 9, 1952, p. 12.

87. Wolcott Gibbs, *New Yorker*, May 17, 1952, NYPL clipping file.

88. L. F., "New Version of *Shuffle Along*, Negro Musical Comedy, Is Presented at the Broadway Theatre," *New York Times*, May 9, 1952, p. 20.

89. Ruth Cage, "*Shuffle Along* Just Shuffles in NY Debut," *Pittsburgh Courier*, May 17, 1952, p. 17.

90. George Jean Nathan, "The Lesson of Another Failure," *New York Journal American*, May 25, 1952, p. 24L.

91. Rose Tapes, Tape 3.

92. Louis Calta, "Musical Suspends to Make Revisions: *Shuffle Along*, New Edition of Comedy Success, Expects to Reopen in Two Weeks," *New York Times*, May 13, 1952, p. 19.

93. "Gaumont Weighs Closing," unidentified and undated newspaper clipping, in NYPL clipping files.

94. Jack Gaver, "Reshuffle Is Attempted on New *Shuffle Along*," United Press; *Cincinnati Enquirer*, May 18, 1952, p. 10.

95. "*Shuffle Along*, sans 'Names,' Battles Broadway Tide," *Chicago Defender*, May 24, 1952, p. 23.

96. Undated and unidentified clipping, in NYPL clipping files.

97. "Miller Washes Hands of *Shuffle* Book; Program Billing Not Warranted," *Variety*, May 14, 1952, p. 63.

98. Noble Sissle to Flournoy Miller, undated letter, c. June 1952, in Flournoy Miller Papers, Schomberg Collection.

99. Noble Sissle to Flournoy Miller, July 16, 1952, in Flournoy Miller Papers, Schomberg Collection.

100. Ibid.

101. Marion Blake to Al Rose, June 21, 1979, in MHS 2800, Box 23.

Chapter 11

1. This biographical information is mostly culled from Blesh's grandson's self-published biography. Carl Hultberg, *Rudi (and me): The Rudi Blesh Story Told by His Grandson*. N.P.: Ragtime Society Press, 2013.

2. Circle's masters were sold to the Jazzology label. For some reason, the Blake LP was never issued.

3. Maryland Historical Society, Eubie Blake music collection, bound folder of manuscript scores for the show *Hit the Stride*, MHS 2800.1, Box 118.

4. There are several undated letters among Flournoy Miller's correspondence with Eubie that allude to his having shared the script with White. He noted that if White passed he "was sure" that he could get the show produced on television. Flournoy Miller correspondence, MHS 2800, Box 11.

5. "Fabulous Cast, Songs, Girls All Joined Brown Skin Models," *Pittsburgh Courier*, Feb. 12, 1955, p. 15.

6. "Nation's Capital to Get Sepia Show's Revival," *Chicago Defender*, Feb. 19, 1955, p. 6.

7. Telegram from Noble Sissle to Eubie Blake, Flournoy Miller, and the Cast of *Brown Skin Models*, Feb. 18, 1955, in MHS 2800, Box 1.

8. "Stephen Papich, 80, Producer and Author, Is Dead," *New York Times,* Jan. 22, 2006, accessed online, Jan. 15, 2017.

9. Flournoy Miller to EB, undated letter [c. 1956], in MHS 2800, Box 11.

10. Ibid.

11. Flournoy Miller to EB, Oct. 15, 1956, in MHS 2800, Box 11.

12. Flournoy Miller to EB, Oct. 19, 1956, in MHS 2800, Box 11.

13. Undated copy of a draft contract, included with Flournoy Miller correspondence files, in MHS 2800, Box 11.

14. Flournoy Miller to EB, undated letter [c. Oct. 1956], in MHS 2800, Box 11.

15. "Salute to Negroes," *Hazelton* (PA) *Plain Speaker*, July 5, 1957, p. 17.

16. Letter from Flournoy Miller to Noble Sissle and EB, Sept. 22, 1957, MHS 2800, Box 11.

17. Song list along with manuscript settings for *Happy Times*, MHS 2800.1, Box 118.

18. Copy of letter of A. P. Waxman to Sammy Davis Jr., Apr. 9 1959, MHS 2800, Box 1. A similar idea for a nostalgic show was floated by Irving Gaumont, the producer of the 1952 *Shuffle Along* revival, in 1953, working with Blake (but not Sissle). However, nothing came of it, either.

19. Andy Razaf to EB, Apr. 24, 1956, in MHS 2800, Box 12.

20. Andy Razaf to EB, June 7, 1956, in MHS 2800, Box 12.

21. Andy Razaf to EB, July 11, 1957, in MHS 2800, Box 12.

22. Contract between 20th Century Fox Recordings and EB, June 24, 1958, in MHS 2800, Box 18. Originally the plan was to record a minimum of eight "sides" to be issued on 78s but Blake ended up recording two full LPs for the label.

23. Dan Morgenstern, *Living with Jazz* (New York: Pantheon Books, 2003), p. 495.

24. Dan Morgenstern, who attended several of the sessions, noted that Dizzy Gillespie's drummer Charli Persip also performed on some tracks (although he is uncredited on the LP). Morgenstern said that 20th Century Fox hired Perry Bradford—the same songwriter/producer who oversaw sessions for OKeh Records in the 1920s—to help with the arrangements, but Bradford is not credited on either album. It's unclear whether both albums came from the same series of sessions or whether a second group of sessions was arranged after the release of the first record; Morgenstern, p. 496.

25. Dan Morgenstern noted that Eubie was concerned about using the "real" title of Picket's composition, "Bulldyker's Dream," on the album, even though he admitted all blacks knew the meaning of the word. Eubie suggested they call it "Spanish Rag," although it was released as "The Dream Rag"; Morgenstern, p. 496.

26. Eubie must have liked these recordings, because Carl Seltzer, his business partner, requested permission to reissue them on the Eubie Blake Music label in the early 1980s and actually paid a small licensing fee for the rights, even though for whatever reason they were never reissued by him.

27. Flournoy Miller to EB, Oct. 11, 1960, in MHS 2800, Box 11.

28. Dan Morgenstern reported on the show; his review is reprinted in Morgenstern, pp. 474–477.

29. A near identical performance is preserved on the album *Golden Reunion in Ragtime* (1962).

30. Parkins, CD 2. Sadly, Lambert rarely ventured out of his home town of Newark, and died young so that he failed to get the recognition he deserved as a pianist.

31. "Ragtime Music Craze Shown," *Daily Reporter* (Dover, OH), Nov. 19, 1960, p. 23.

32. Ian Whitcomb, "Bob Darch: My Adventures with the Great Man" (as published in the *Rag Times*, Jan. 2003). http://www.picklehead.com/ian/ian_txt_darch.html, accessed May 31, 2018.

33. A royalty statement in May 1963 (a year after its release) showed the album had sold 2270 copies; however, since Eubie shared the royalties with the other participants and had received a $500 advance, he was still in the hole for $325 at the time; in MHS 2800, Box 18.

34. Fletcher Smith to EB, Aug. 28, 1962, in MHS 2800, Box 18.

35. William R. Dalgleish to EB, dated 1967, in MHS 2800, Box 2.

36. Brian Rust to EB, July 30, 1963, in MHS 2800, Box 1.

37. "Sissle Blake Recreate Musical History for Lambs," *Pittsburgh Courier*, Feb. 20, 1965, p. 13.

38. "Eubie Blake: Biographical Sketch," in MHS 2800, Box 27.

39. *Chicago Tribune Sunday Magazine*, Aug. 1, 1965, pp. 40–41.

40. Flournoy Miller to EB, June 26 1966, in MHS 2800, Box 2.

41. Bessie Miller to EB, July 8, 1966, in MHS 2800, Box 2.

42. Bessie Miller to EB, Mar. 9, 1968, in MHS 2800, Box 2.

43. Interview with Dave Jasen, Aug. 23, 2016.

44. Interview with Dave Jasen, Feb. 1, 2017.

45. EB to Charlie Rasch, Feb. 10, 1968; copy courtesy John Milan, Charlie Rasch collection.

46. EB to Charlie Rasch, Feb. 21, 1969; copy courtesy John Milan, Charlie Rasch collection.

47. Charlie Rasch to EB, March 11, 1969, in MHS 2800, Box 2.

48. EB to Charlie Rasch, Mar. 13, 1969; copy courtesy John Milan, Charlie Rasch collection.

49. Eubie relates the story on the recording *The Eighty Six Years of Eubie Blake*.

50. Langdon Winner, "The 86 Years of Eubie Blake," *Rolling Stone*, Mar. 19, 1970; clipping in MHS 2800, Box 40.

51. Louis Armstrong to EB, Mar. 15, 1970, in MHS 2800, Box 10.

52. Jack Scholl to EB, Aug. 29, 1969, in MHS 2800, Box 2.

53. Ernie Ford to EB, Apr. 4, 1971, in MHS 2800, Box 10.

54. The duo's "Sweet Talk" appeared on the album *Eubie Blake Song Hits* (EBM-9), sung and accompanied on piano by Emme Kemp.

55. M. J. Warren, "Yale Band Impressive," *New Haven Register*, Apr. 22, 1970; clipping in MHS 2800, Box 2.

56. Letter from David Cayer, Assistant Director University Extension Division, Bureau of Community services to Rudi Blesh, Apr. 2, 1969; as part of the award, Blesh was to conduct an oral history interview with Eubie to be deposited in the Jazz Archive.

57. EB to Charlie Rasch, Sept. 3, 1970; copy courtesy John Milan, Charlie Rasch collection.

58. Harry Connick Sr. to EB, July 21, 1969, in MHS 2800, Box 2.

59. Unlike other ragtimers who titled their albums to appeal to a pop audience, Rifkin (or his label Nonesuch) chose a title that was in the tradition of classical piano recordings by major composers like Chopin or Liszt. This decision may have been a subtle way of positioning the music as "serious" and equal to the work of white classical composers.

60. http://www.nonesuch.com/about, accessed June 2, 2018.

61. In Oct. 1970, Montgomery wrote to Eubie with the idea of producing the albums. Apparently, a deal was worked out, with Biograph paying Eubie a small royalty on sales; one statement survives in his papers (MHS 2800, Box 17). At the time, Vol. 1 had sold 1600 copies, while Vol. 2 sold 1400 copies, and Eubie was paid royalties on 90% of all sales, equaling $340. Figuring a list price of $6.98 (common for the period) with albums sold at an average 40% discount to dealers, Eubie was probably given a 3% royalty on each sale.

62. The performance is included on the LP *Piano Masters* issued by the Chirascuro label in 1977.

Chapter 12

1. Barry Singer, interview with EB, Aug. 6, 2001; transcript courtesy Barry Singer.

2. Rose, p. 137.

3. Interview with Terry Waldo, Dec. 28, 2017; Bill Bolcom had a similar recollection; interview with Bob Kimball, William Bolcom, and Joan Morris, Nov. 5, 2018.

4. A few jazz artists had tried to run their own labels, including Charlie Mingus and Mary Lou Williams, but were not able to maintain them.

5. Pamela Hollie, "The Comeback Kid," *Wall Street Journal*, Oct. 23, 1973; clipping in MHS 2800, Box 40.

6. Alan Rich, "Black Beauty," *New York Magazine*, Dec. 24, 1973, pp. 76.

7. John Hammond to Carl Seltzer, undated letter (c. 1977); private collection.

8. "Top Music Lawyer Shares His Backstage Pass," *Spin*, Dec. 1989, p. 34.

9. EB to Elliot Hoffman, Sept. 4, 1973, in MHS 2800, Box 22.

10. Hoffman to EB, Sept. 11, 1973, in MHS 2800, Box 22.

11. This narrative is based on an interview with Bob Kimball, William Bolcom, and Joan Morris, Nov. 5, 2018.

12. Bill Bolcom, untitled manuscript [draft for obituary for Eubie Blake], p. 2. This piece was published in an edited version in *Rolling Stone* magazine following Blake's death; courtesy Bill Bolcom and Joan Morris.

13. Ibid.

14. Ibid.

15. Interview with Bob Kimball, William Bolcom, and Joan Morris; Nov. 5, 2018. Also, letter from Marion Blake to Bill Bolcom, July 3, 1973; courtesy Bill Bolcom and Joan Morris.

16. EB to Bill Bolcom and Joan Morris, May 23, 1977; courtesy Bill Bolcom and Joan Morris.

17. Bill Bolcom, untitled manuscript [draft for obituary for Eubie Blake], p. 2; courtesy Bill Bolcom and Joan Morris.

18. As in most aspects of Eubie's life, his wife Marion kept a detailed chronology of all of his performances, beginning in 1972, which she updated regularly. Various versions of this chronology, plus her own notes, are available in the Eubie Blake Archives at the Maryland Historical Society, MHS 2800, boxes 26-27.

19. Much of the information in this section is derived from an interview conducted by Ken Bloom on Jan. 31, 2017, along with contemporary articles about the show.

20. Arnold Warshaw, "Easton's Native's Musical Revue a Philadelphia Success," *Allentown Morning Call*, July 27 1978, p. 31; and Bill Curry, "'Eubie!' Got Its Start on Summer Vacation," *Philadelphia Inquirer*, Aug. 13, 1978, p. 2–L.

21. Interview with Julianne Boyd conducted by Ken Bloom on Jan. 31, 2017; all quotations otherwise unattributed from Boyd come from this interview.

22. http://www.alkohn.com/, accessed July 1, 2018.

23. John S. Wilson, "*Shuffle Along*: Reprise of a Hit," *New York Times*, Feb. 11, 1978, p. 12.

24. Margalit Fox, "Ashton Springer, Producer of Broadway Shows, Dies at 82," *New York Times*, July 20, 2013, p. A22.

25. Elliot Hoffman to Dan Brambilla, of the office of Donald C. Farber, Apr. 21, 1978, in MHS 2800, Box 22.

26. The terms outlined were "[d]eal for name, likeness, endorsement and up to six of his controlled compositions in connection with your production of "Eubie": $750 week plus 2 ½% of the gross receipts going to 3% upon recoupment. Once the percentage goes to 3%, ½% shall be recoupable against $150 of the $750 per week guarantee. In other words, at 3%, $150 of the weekly payment of $750 a week shall be deemed an advance against that week's percentage to the extent of ½% . . . Rights to 6 compositions will be on same terms as those WB controls"; Elliot Hoffman to Ashton Springer Theatre Management Associates, May 4, 1978, MHS 2800, Box 22.

27. Bert Andrews, "New Faces: Gregory and Maurice Hines," *New York Times*, Nov. 24, 1978, p. 10.

28. Anna Quindlen, "New Face: Lynnie Godfrey," *New York Times*, Aug. 31, 1979, p. C6.

29. Harriet Choice, "Eubie," *Chicago Tribune*, Feb. 10, 1980, Section VI, p. 2.

30. William B. Collins, "Comings and Goings of the Season," *Philadelphia Inquirer*, Sept. 4, 1978, p. 4B.

31. Stuart D. Bykofsky, "*Eubie* Excellent Style Showcase," *Philadelphia Daily News,* June 19, 1978, p. 31.

32. William B. Collins, "You Will Be Just Wild about *Eubie!,*" *Philadelphia Inquirer,* June 19, 1978, p. 6.

33. Arnold Warshaw, "Easton's Native's Musical Revue a Philadelphia Success," *Allentown Morning Call,* July 27, 1978, p. 31.

34. "*Eubie* to Remain until Sept. 13," *Philadelphia Inquirer,* Aug. 20, 1978, p. 156.

35. William B. Collins, "Comings and Goings of the Season," *Philadelphia Inquirer,* Sept. 4, 1978, p. 4–B.

36. Ashton Springer form letter sent to Elliot Hoffman, Aug. 24, 1978, MHS 2800, Box 22.

37. William Glover, "*Eubie!* Roars Triumphantly," Associated Press, in the *Morristown Daily Record,* Oct. 4, 1978, p. 32.

38. Kevin Kelly, "It Ain't *Misbehavin'* but *Eubie's'* Fun, Too," *Boston Globe,* Oct. 8, 1978, p. 62.

39. Elliot Hoffman to Ashton Springer, Dec. 13, 1978, in MHS 2800, Box 22.

40. Copy of investors statement from CPA about capital deficit of production through Oct. 22, 1978, distributed by Ashton Springer to Elliot Hoffman, in MHS 2800, Box 22.

41. R. H. Gardner, "Twice Blessed with Eubie and *Eubie!,*" *Baltimore Sun,* Feb. 7, 1979, p. B1.

42. As we have noted, Eubie had added four years to his age; he was actually 92 at the time, but the point remains the same.

43. Elliot Hoffman to Ashton Springer, Mar. 9, 1979, in MHS 2800, Box 23.

44. Elliot Hoffman to Ashton Springer, July 25, 1979; MHS 2800, Box 23.

45. Elliot Hoffman to Al Kohn, Oct. 10, 1979, in MHS 2800, Box 23.

46. Ashton Springer letter to "Royalty Recipients," Nov. 20, 1979, in MHS 2800, Box 23.

47. Elliot Hoffman to Marion Blake, Dec. 13, 1979, in MHS 2800, Box 23.

48. Dan Sullivan, "*Eubie*—Respectful Stroll at the Hartford," *Los Angeles Times,* Dec. 31, 1979, p. II, 8.

49. Elliot Hoffman to Victor M. Rosenzweig of Oldshan Grundman & Frome, Apr. 16 1980; and Elliot Hoffman to David Grossberg of Cohen, Grossberg & Zinkin, Oct. 10, 1980; Elliot Hoffman to EB, Dec. 8, 1980, all in MHS 2800, Box 23.

50. Sandra Salmans, "Why Investors in Broadway Hits Are Often Losers," *New York Times,* Nov. 21, 1981, https://www.nytimes.com/1981/11/22/theater/why-investors-in-broadway-hits-are-often-losers.html, accessed online, June 28, 2018.

51. Mel Gussow, "Court Orders Producer to Pay Back Investors," *New York Times,* Oct. 2, 1982, https://www.nytimes.com/1982/10/02/theater/court-orders-producer-to-pay-back-investors.html, accessed online, June 28, 2018.

52. Ibid.

53. Harriet Choice, "Eubie," *Chicago Tribune,* Feb. 10, 1980, Section VI, p. 11.

54. Author interview with David and Susan Jasen, Feb. 21, 2017.

55. Elliot Hoffman to Lawrence T. Carter, Apr. 28, 1970, in MHS 2800, Box 22.

56. Elliot Hoffman to Marion Blake, May 12, 1980, in MHS 2800, Box 23.

57. Information on Al Rose's life story comes from his son Rex Rose, who wrote "Al Rose, His Secret Life," posted on his website, www,rexrose.com; printed out on July 19, 2011.
58. Al Rose to Elliot Hoffman, June 6, 1979, in MHS 2800, Box 24.
59. Elliot Hoffman to Al Rose, Jan. 27, 1977, in MHS 2800, Box 24. In fact, the deal with previous biographer Lawrence T. Carter was for only one-third of subsidiary rights income, and 10% of the royalties for Blake. Hoffman either misremembered or decided to ask for more from Rose.
60. Al Rose to Elliot Hoffman, Feb. 3, 1977, in MHS 2800, Box 24.
61. Elliot Hoffman to Al Rose, Feb. 2, 1979, in MHS 2800, Box 24.
62. Elliot Hoffman to Al Rose, Feb. 27, 1979, in MHS 2800, Box 24.
63. Al Rose to Elliot Hoffman, May 11, 1979, in MHS 2800, Box 24.
64. Elliot Hoffman to Al Rose, May 15, 1979, in MHS 2800, Box 24.
65. Al Rose to Elliot Hoffman, June 6, 1979, in MHS 2800, Box 24.
66. Elliot Hoffman to Marion Blake, June 14,1979, in MHS 2800, Box 24.
67. Marion Blake's handwritten notes on a typed manuscript, dated July 5, 1997, p. 98, in MHS 2800, Box 68.
68. Elliot Hoffman to Al Rose, July 11, 1979, in MHS 2800, Box 24.
69. Elliot Hoffman to Marion Blake, Aug. 2, 1979, in MHS 2800, Box 24.
70. Al Rose to Marion Blake, March 17, 1980, in MHS 2800, Box 4.
71. Interview with Terry Waldo, Dec. 28, 2018.
72. EB to Charlie Rasch, Oct. 2, 1976, in Charlie Rasch collection, courtesy Jon Milan.
73. Interview with Terry Waldo, Dec. 28, 2018; the concert was recorded and appeared on record on Eubie's label. There's no sign of his illness in his playing, which was as strong as ever.
74. Tim Brooks, *Lost Sounds* (Urbana: University of Illinois Press, 2004), p. 393.
75. *Louisville Courier-Journal*, Jan. 8, 1982, p. 2.
76. Bill Bolcom, untitled manuscript [draft for an obituary for Eubie Blake]; courtesy Bill Bolcom and Joan Morris.
77. It was broadcast following Blake's death as "Eubie Blake: A Century of Music" on the PBS network in spring of 1983.
78. "They're Just Wild About Eubie," *Bergen (NJ) Record*, Jan. 20, 1983, p.15.
79. Bill Bolcom, untitled manuscript [draft for an obituary for Eubie Blake]; courtesy Bill Bolcom and Joan Morris.
80. Interview with Bob Kimball, William Bolcom, and Joan Morris, Nov. 5, 2018.
81. Waldo interview, Dec. 28, 2018.
82. "Blake Dies Shortly after His 100th Birthday," AP Wire report, Feb. 14, 1983.

A Partial List of Eubie Blake's Compositions

1. Although Eubie claimed to have composed this song in 1899, it more likely evolved over a period of time from c. 1905 to 1915. It was copyrighted in 1917 and Blake recorded it in 1921 under the name "Sounds of Africa."

2. May be the same as "Kitchen Tom" that Blake recorded on *The Eighty Six Years of Eubie Blake*.

3. May be the same as 1969's "The Baltimore Todalo."

4. May be the same as 1969's "Poor Jimmy Green."

5. May be the same as 1960's "Poor Katie Red."

6. May be the same as 1969's "Tickle the Ivories."

7. May be the same as 1959's "Ragtime Rag" and 1971's "Troublesome Ivories."

8. May be the same as 1969's "Blue Rag in Twelve Keys."

9. May be the same as 1972's "Butterfly."

10. Reworked from 1940's "Nickel for a Dime."

11. May be the same as 1969's "Eubie's Boogie."

12. Retitled "Troublesome Ivories" in 1971.

13. Also titled "Ragtime Rag" (on his 1959 recording) and may be the same as "Black Keys on Parade" (1919).

Bibliography

Abbreviations in Source Notes

Interviews with Eubie Blake

Blesh/Lipskin   Rudi Blesh and Mike Lipskin, 1967. Audio tape, private collection; transcribed by authors.

Brown   Lorraine Brown. Interview with Eubie Blake, Jan. 9, 1977, in Brooklyn, NY, for the Research Center for the Federal Theatre Project, Oral History Interview.

Bruckner   Howard Bruckner. Interview with Eubie Blake, *Voice of America* broadcast, July 9, 1970. Carl Seltzer Collection, NYPL Performing Arts Division, *LDC 36349. Also Library of Congress, LWB1511 A1; transcribed by authors.

Bryant   Hazel Bryant, 1969, tape deposited in Emory University, Rose Library, James Hatch Collection, HB 271; transcribed by authors.

Conan/ Whitcomb   Neil Conan and Ian Whitcomb, Dec. 1969, radio interview originally broadcast on KPFA (Berkeley, CA); authors' collection; tape on deposit at UNC Center for Southern Folklife; transcribed by authors.

McPartland   Marian McPartland, "Piano Jazz" interview, 1980. http://www.npr.org/2012/10/19/123385170/eubie-blake-on-piano-jazz. Accessed Dec. 2, 2015; transcribed by authors.

McPherson/Chan   Bob McPherson and Eugenia Chan, at a Christmas party, Dec. 21, 1973; tape deposited in Emory University, Rose Library, James Hatch Collection, HB 272.1; transcribed by authors.

Morath AH   Morath, Max. "The 93 Years of Eubie Blake: An Interview by Max Morath." *American Heritage* 27, no. 6 (Oct. 1976), pp. 56–65.

Morath 1970   Max Morath, 1970. Excerpted in Roy Rosenzweig, *Who Built America?* (CD-ROM), American Social History Project, University of Michigan. Posted on http://chnm.gmu.edu/courses/magic/saloon/blake.html. Accessed July 1, 2017.

Parkins   Interview with Eubie Blake by Sam Parkins, c. 1969–1970. Carl Seltzer Collection, NYPL, *LDC 50392; transcribed by authors.

Perlis   Vivian Perlis, Interview, January 21, 1972; copy tape deposited in Emory University, Rose Library, James Hatch Collection, HB 273.1.

Rose Tapes   Al Rose, undated interviews (c. 1975–1977), series of cassettes, deposited in Hogan Jazz Library, Tulane University, New Orleans; transcribed by authors.

Singer	Interview with Eubie Blake, Aug. 6, 1981, by Barry Singer; transcript courtesy Barry Singer.
Southern I	Southern, Eileen. "A Legend in His Own Lifetime, Part I." *Black Perspective in Music* 1, no. 1 (Spring, 1973), pp. 50–59.
Southern II	Southern, Eileen, and Bobbi King. "A Legend in His Own Lifetime, Part II." *Black Perspective in Music* 1, no. 2 (Autumn, 1973), pp. 151–156.
Standifer Jim	Standifer, interview 1973. Posted online at http://www.greatblacksinwax.org/Exhibits/Eubie_blake/Eubie_Blake2.htm. Accessed Aug. 18, 2017; transcribed by authors.
Whorf	Whorf, Michael. *American Popular Song Composers.* Jefferson, NC: McFarland, 2012, pp. 34–38.

Primary Collections

MHS 2800	Eubie Blake Manuscript and Ephemera Collection, MS 2800. Maryland Historical Society.
MHS 2800.1	Eubie Blake Sheet Music Collection, MS 2800.1. Maryland Historical Society.
PP301	Eubie Blake Photograph Collection, PP301. Maryland Historical Society.

Manuscripts

Hyder	Hyder, William. "Eubie Blake Story-Sunday Magazine." Manuscript; in MHS 2800, Box 11. An edited version was published as "The Roaring Ragtime Odyssey of Eubie Blake." *Baltimore Sun Magazine*, Oct. 15, 1972, pp. 5, 7. Quotations are from the manuscript version.
Sissle	Sissle, Noble Lee. *Memoirs of Lieutenant "Jim" Europe.* N.d. [c. 1942]. Manuscript in Library of Congress collection; on-line at http://memory.loc.gov/cgi-bin/ampage?collId=ody_musmisc&fileName=ody/ody0717/ody0717page.db&recNum=0.

Biographies

Carter	Carter, Lawrence T. *Eubie Blake: Keys of Memory.* Detroit: Balamp Publishing, 1979.
Kimball/Bolcom	Kimball, Robert, and William Bolcom. *Reminiscing with Sissle and Blake.* New York: Viking Press, 1973.
Rose	Rose, Al. *Eubie Blake.* New York: Schirmer Books, 1979.

General Bibliography

Abbott, Lynn, and Doug Seroff. *Ragged but Right.* Jackson: University of Mississippi Press, 2007.

Abbott, Lynn, and Doug Seroff. *The Original Blues*. Jackson: University of Mississippi Press, 2017.

Anderson, Jervis. "Birthday Party." *New Yorker*, Dec. 25, 1978, pp. 25–27.

Badger, Reid. *A Life in Ragtime: James Reese Europe*. New York: Oxford University Press, 1995.

Baker, Jean-Claude, and Chris Chase. *Josephine: The Hungry Heart*. New York: Random House, 1993.

Bauman, Charles. *The Pekin: The Rise and Fall of Chicago's First Black-Owned Theater*. Urbana: University of Illinois Press, 2014.

Berlin, Edward. *King of Ragtime: Scott Joplin and His Era*. 2nd ed. New York: Oxford University Press, 2016.

Blake, Eubie. *Sincerely, Eubie Blake*. Brooklyn, NY: Eubie Blake Music, 1975.

Blake, Eubie. *Eubie Blake: Original Classic Waltzes for the Piano*. Van Nuys, CA: Belwin-Mills, 1978.

Blesh, Rudi. *Combo U.S.A.: Eight Lives in Jazz*. Philadelphia: Chilton, 1971.

Blesh, Rudi, and Harriet Janis. *They All Played Ragtime*. 4th ed. New York: Oak Publications, 1971.

Bloom, Ken. *American Song, The Complete Musical Theatre Companion*. New York: Schirmer Books, 1996.

Bloom, Ken. *American Song: The Complete Companion to Tin Pan Alley Song*. New York: Schirmer Books, 2001.

Bogle, Donald. *Heat Wave: The Life and Career of Ethel Waters*. New York: Harper, 2011.

Bolcom, William. "Eubie Blake Obituary." Manuscript for article in *Rolling Stone*. Courtesy Bill Bolcom.

Boyle, Sheila Tully, and Andrew Bunie. *Paul Robeson: The Years of Promise and Achievement*. Boston: University of Massachusetts Press, 2001.

Bricktop. *Bricktop*. With James Haskens. New York, Atheneum, 1983.

"Broadway Dream Girl." *Jet*, May 15, 1952, pp. 60–63.

Brown, Scott E. *A Case of Mistaken Identity: The Life and Music of James P. Johnson*. Lanham, MD: Scarecrow Press, 1984.

Brooks, Tim. *Lost Sounds: Blacks and the Birth of the Recording Industry 1890–1919*. Urbana: University of Illinois Press, 2004.

Carson, Julia M. H. *Home away From Home: The Story of the USO*. New York: Harper & Brothers, 1946.

Carter, Marva. *Swing Along: The Musical Life of Will Marion Cook*. New York: Oxford University Press, 2008.

Charters, Ann. *Nobody: The Story of Bert Williams*. New York: Macmillan, 1970.

Charyn, Jerome. *Gangsters and Gold Diggers*. New York: Four Walls and Eight Windows, 2003.

Chilton, John. *Sidney Bechet: Wizard of Jazz*. London: Palgrave/Macmillan, 1987.

Cochran, Charles B. *I Had Almost Forgotten*. London: Hutchinson, 1932.

Cockrell, Dale. *Everybody's Doin' It: Sex, Music, and Dance in New York, 1840–1917*. New York: W. W. Norton, 2019.

Coleman, John P. *Historic Amusement Parks of Baltimore: An Illustrated History*. Jefferson, NC: McFarland, 2014.

Coward, Noel. *Autobiography*. London: Methuen, 1986.

Cullen, Frank. *Vaudeville Old & New: An Encyclopedia of Variety Performers in America*. With Florence Hackman and Donald McNeilly. New York: Routledge, 2007.

Dance, Stanley. *The World of Earl Hines*. New York: Scribner, 1977.

Dance, Stanley. "Elmer Snowden." In *The World of Swing: An Oral History of Big Band Jazz*, by Stanley Dance. New York: C. Scribner's Sons, 1974, pp. 45–62.

Davin, Tom. "Conversations with James P. Johnson." *Jazz Review*, Part I: Vol. II, No. 5, pp. pp. 14–17; Part II: Vol. II, No. 6, pp. 10–13; Part III: Vol. II, No. 7, pp. 13–15; Part IV: Vol. II, No. 8, pp. 23–24; Part V: Vol. III, No. 3, pp. 11–13.

Decker, Todd. *Showboat: Performing Race in an American Musical*. New York: Oxford University Press, 2015.

Doerschuk, Bob. "The Eubie Blake Story: A Century of American Music." *Keyboard*, Dec. 1982, pp. 52–54.

Doerschuk, Bob. "Two Views of Eubie Blake's Keyboard Style: Terry Waldo and William Bolcom." *Keyboard*, Dec.1982, pp. 59–60, 62, 70.

Duberman, Martin Bauml. *Paul Robeson*. New York: Knopf, 1988.

Egan, Bill. *Florence Mills: Harlem Jazz Queen*. Lanham, MD: Scarecrow Press, 2004.

"Eubie Blake: The Penthouse Interview." *Penthouse*, Mar. 1974, pp. 59–60, 95–96.

"Eubie Is Black History: 100 Years Old Today." *Black American*, Feb. 3–9, 1983, p. 15.

Fields, Andrew Joseph Carl. *William Llewellyn Wilson: A Biography*. MA thesis, Morgan State University, 1990.

Fletcher, Tom. *One Hundred Years of the Negro in Show Business*. New York: Dover, 1954.

Forbes, Camille F. *Introducing Bert Williams*. New York. Basic Civitas, 2008.

Gates Jr, Henry Louis and Evelyn Brooks Higginbotham. *Harlem Renaissance Lives*. New York. Oxford University Press, 2009.

Gilbert, David. *Product of Our Souls*. Chapel Hill: University of North Carolina Press, 2016.

Goddard, Chris. Jazz away from Home. New York: Paddington Press, 1979.

Hagan, Patti. "One Hundred." *New Yorker*, Feb. 20, 1983, pp. 84–86.

Haney, Lynn. *Naked at the Feast: A Biography of Josephine Baker*. New York: Dodd, Mead, 1981.

Haskins, Jim, and N. R. Mitgang. *Mr. Bojangles: The Biography of Bill Robinson*. New York: William Morrow, 1988.

Hasse, John Edward, ed. *Ragtime: Its History, Composers, and Music*. New York: Schirmer, 1985.

Hill, Constance Valis. *Brotherhood in Rhythm: The Jazz Tap Dancing of the Nicholas Brothers*. New York: Oxford University Press, 2000.

Hill, Jayme Rae. *From the Brothel to the Block: Politics and Prostitution in Baltimore during the Progressive Era*. Master's thesis, University of Maryland, Baltimore County, 2008.

Hinton, Milt, and David G. Berger. *Bass Line: The Stories and Photographs of Milt Hinton*. Philadelphia: Temple University Press, 1988.

Hollington, John. "Appraisal of *Cleo Steps Out*." May 9, 1951, unpublished manuscript.

Howard, Buddy. "Noble Sissle, International Star." *Down Beat*, Oct. 1, 1942.

Howland, John. *Ellington Uptown*. Ann Arbor: University of Michigan Press, 2009.

Huggins, Nathan Irvin. *Harlem Renaissance*. Oxford: Oxford University Press, 1971.

Hughes, Langston. *The Big Sea*. New York, Alfred A. Knopf, 1940.

Hughes, Langston and Milton Meltzer. *Black Magic*. New York, Da Capo, 1990.

Hultberg, Carl. *Rudi (and me): The Rudi Blesh Story Told by His Grandson*. N.P.: Ragtime Society Press, 2013.

Hyman, Dick. "Keyboard Journal: Onstage with Eubie." *Keyboard*, Dec. 1982, p. 70.

"Irving Gaumont." In *"Shuffle Along of 1952" Souvenir Booklet*. NY Public Library, Schomburg Center for Research in Black Culture.

Jasen, David A. "Eubie at 100." *Storyville*, no. 105 (Feb.–Mar. 1983), pp. 84–87.

Jasen, David A. *Tin Pan Alley: The Composers, the Songs, the Performers and Their Times*. New York: Donald I. Fine, 1988.

Jasen, David A., and Gene Jones. *Spreadin' Rhythm 'Round: Black Popular Songwriters, 1880–1930*. New York: Schirmer Books, 1998.

Jasen, David A., and Gene Jones. *That American Rag*. New York: Schirmer Books, 1999.

Jasen, David A., and Gene Jones. *Black Bottom Stomp: Eight Masters of Ragtime and Early Jazz*. New York: Routledge, 2002.

Jasen, David A., and Trebor J. Tichenor. *Rags and Ragtime*. New York: Seabury Press, 1978.

Johnson, James Weldon. *Black Manhattan*. New York: Alfred A. Knopf, 1930.

Jones, Max. "Britain Salutes . . . Eubie Blake, 100." *Jazz Express*, Feb. 1983, pp. 1, 6–7.

Kay, George W. "Noble Sissle: Veteran Showman." *Record Research*, no. 61, July 1964, pp. 3–5, 20.

Kimball, Robert. "Eubie's Legacy: A Century Filled with Kindness and Love." *New York Post*, Feb. 3, 1983, p. 33.

Krasner, David. *A Beautiful Pageant*. NY: Palgrave/Macmillan, 2002.

Kraut, Anthea. *Choreographing Copyright*. New York: Oxford University Press, 2016.

Lester, James. *Too Marvelous for Words: The Life and Times of Art Tatum*. New York: Oxford University Press, 1994.

Miller, Donald L. *Supreme City: How Jazz Age Manhattan Gave Birth to Modern America*. New York: Simon & Schuster, 2014.

Montgomery, Michael. *Eubie Blake Piano Rollography (Revised)*. Self-mimeographed, 1978.

Morgenstern, Dan. *Living with Jazz*. New York: Pantheon Books, 2003.

Owens, Hamilton. *Baltimore on the Chesapeake*. New York: Doubleday, Doran, 1941.

Osteen, Mark, and Frank J. Graziano, eds. *Music at the Crossroads: Lives and Legacies of Baltimore Jazz*. Baltimore: Apprentice House, 2010.

Pathé Records. *Catalog Supplement*. 1918.

Peterson, Bernard L., Jr. *A Century of Musicals in Black and White*, Westport, CT. Greenwood Press, 1993.

Peterson, Bernard L., Jr. *The African American Theatre Director, 1816–1960*. Westport, CT, Greenwood Press, 1997.

Peterson, Bernard L., Jr. *Profiles of African American Stage Performers and Theatre People, 1816–1960*. Westport, CT: Greenwood Press, 2000.

Phillips, Christopher. *Freedom's Port: The African-American Community in Baltimore, 1790–1860*. Urbana: University of Illinois Press, 1997.

Popple, Robert. *John Arpin: Keyboard Virtuoso*. Toronto: Dundurn Press, 2009.

Riis, Thomas. *Just before Jazz: Black Musical Theatre in New York, 1890–1915*. Washington, DC: Smithsonian Institution Press, 1989.

Rose, Al. *I Remember Jazz*. Baton Rouge: Louisiana State University Press, 1987.

Rose, Rex. "Al Rose: His Secret Life." rexrose.com/alrose.htm. Accessed July 19, 2011.

Rye, Howard. "Visiting Firemen 7: Sissle and Blake." *Storyville*, no. 105 (Feb.–Mar. 1983).

Sampson, Henry. *Blacks in Blackface: A Sourcebook on Early Black Musical Shows*. Lanham, MD: Scarecrow Press, 2013.

Schenbeck, Lynn, and Lawrence Schenbeck. "The Surprising Story of *Shuffle Along*." In *Shuffle Along*, by Lyn Schenbeck and Lawrence Schenbeck. Middletown, WI: AR Editions, 2018, pp. xv–liii.

Schimann, Jack. *Harlem Heyday*. Buffalo, NY: Prometheus Books, 1984.

Seldes, Gilbert. *The 7 Lively Arts*. New York, Sagamore Press, 1957.

Singer, Barry. *Black and Blue: The Life and Lyrics of Andy Razaf*. New York: Schirmer Books, 1993.

Smith, Eric Ledell. *Bert Williams: A Biography of the Pioneer Black Comedian*. Jefferson, NC: McFarland, 1992.

Smith, Willie. "The Lion." *Music on My Mind*. New York: Doubleday, 1961.

Southern, Eileen. *Music of Black Americans*. 3rd ed. New York: W. W. Norton, 1997.

Spivey, Victoria. "Gertrude Saunders: Still a Red Hot Mama." *Record Research*, no. 74 (Mar. 1966), pp. 1–3.

Sterns, Marshall, and Jean Sterns. *Jazz Dance: The Story of American Vernacular Dance*. New York: Da Capo, 1994.

Sudhalter, Richard M. "Eubie's Last, Graceful Bow." *New York Post*, Feb. 14, 1983, p. 27.

Sylvester, Robert. *No Cover Charge: A Backward Look at the Night Clubs*. London: Peter Davies, 1957.

Tanner, Jo A. *Dusky Maidens: The Odyssey of the Early Black Dramatic Actress*, Westport, CT, Greenwood Press, 1992

Thompson, Henry T. *Blacks in Black and White*. Metuchen, NJ: Scarecrow Press.

Trav S. D. *No Applause—Just Throw Money: The Book That Made Vaudeville Famous*. New York: Farrar, Straus and Giroux, 2006.

Trow, George W. S. "Good Looking." *New Yorker*, Dec. 25, 1978, pp. 25–26.

Waldo, Terry. *This Is Ragtime*. New York: Jazz at Lincoln Center Library Edition, 2009.

Waters, Ethel. *His Eye Is on the Sparrow*. With Charles Samuels. Garden City, NY: Doubleday, 1951.

Watson, Steven. *Prepare for Saints: Gertrude Stein, Virgil Thomson, and the Mainstreaming of American Musical Modernism*. New York: Random House, 1998.

Whitcomb, Ian. "Bob Darch: My Adventures with the Great Man." *Rag Times*, Jan. 2003.

Williams, Ian Cameron. *Underneath a Harlem Moon: The Harlem to Paris Years of Adelaide Hall*. New York: Continuum, 2002.

Wilson, James F. *Buldaggers, Pansies, and Chocolate Babies*, Ann Arbor: University of Michigan Press, 2011.

Wilson, John S. "Eubie Blake." *International Musician*, July 1972, p. 6.

Wilson, John S. "Eubie Blake, Ragtime Composer, Dies 5 Days after 100th Birthday." *New York Times*, Feb. 15, 1983, p. 36.

Wilson, John S. "24 Hours of Jazz to Celebrate 100 Years of Eubie Blake." *New York Times*, Feb. 4, 1983, pp. C1, C4.

Wintz, Cary D. and Paul Finkelman. *Encyclopedia of the Harlem Renaissance Vols 1 and 2*. New York. Routledge. 2004.

Woll, Allen. *Black Musical Theatre: From "Coontown" to "Dreamgirls."* New York, Da Capo Press, 1989.

Woll, Allen. *Dictionary of the Black Theatre*, New York. Greenwood Press, 1983.

Wondrich, David. *Stomp and Swerve: American Music Gets Hot, 1843–1924*. Chicago: Chicago Review Press, 2003.

Wood, Ean. *The Josephine Baker Story*. London: Omnibus Press, 2010.

Woods, Peter S. "The Negro on Broadway: The Transition Years, 1920–1930." PhD diss., Yale University, 1965.

Manuscript Collections Consulted

Al Rose cassette collection. Hogan Jazz Library, New Orleans. Cassette interviews done for the biography by Rose; not catalogued.

Clipping files. New York Public Library of the Performing Arts, Lincoln Center. Reviews of various shows by Blake.

Elliot Carpenter Papers, 1922–1978. Helen Armstead-Johnson Theater Collection, New York Public Library, Schomburg Center for Research in Black Culture. Correspondence with Blake.

Eubie Blake Papers. Maryland Historical Society, Baltimore. This is the main collection of Eubie's papers.

Eubie Blake Papers. Loeb Music Library, Harvard University, Cambridge, MA. Small collection of letters, photos, and other ephemera.

Eubie Blake papers, 1949–1983, Library of Congress, Music Division, Washington, DC. 12 items, including letters to Mrs. Joseph Schillinger.

Federal Theater Project, 1935–1939. Library of Congress, Music Division, Washington, DC. Posters, stage designs, and some orchestral scores for *Swing It!*

Flournoy E. Miller Papers, 1924–1995. Emory University, Stuart A. Rose Manuscript, Archives, and Rare Book Library, Atlanta, GA. Autobiography, playscripts, and other materials.

Flournoy Miller Collection, 1928–1971. New York Public Library, Schomburg Center for Research in Black Culture. Autobiography, playscripts, and other materials.

Smithsonian/Folkways archives, Washington, DC. Acetate recording by Moses Asch of Andy Razaf and Eubie Blake, c. 1942, performing "We Are Americans, Too"/"Take It Easy"

Unpublished Materials

Charlie Rouse papers. Correspondence and other materials relating to Eubie Blake. Private collection.

Blake, Eubie. *Shufflers: A Musical Comedy in Two Acts and Ten Scenes*, 1924, Unpublished manuscript, Library of Congress. Early typescript for the play that became *In Bamville/Chocolate Dandies*.

Sissle, Noble. Unpublished autobiography, Flournoy Miller Collection, Helen Armstead-Johnson Collection, Box I, Schomburg Center for Research in Black Culture, New York Public Library, Astor, Lenox, and Tilden Foundation.

Author Interviews and Correspondence

Lynn Abbott
Benjamin Bierman
William Bolcom

Julianne Boyd
John Edward Hasse
David A. Jasen and Susan Jasen
Robert Kimball
Jon Mizan
Joan Morris
Rachman Vaughn Reddie
Barry Singer
Terry Waldo

Select Recordings

This is not meant to be a comprehensive discography but rather a listing of recordings and liner notes referenced in the development of this text. Entries are in chronological order.

Pathé Recordings, 1917. 4 sides released attributed to the "Eubie Blake Trio"; the exact personnel is unknown.

Baltimore Buzz Medley/Sounds of Africa. Emerson 10434, 1921. Eubie's first recording of "Charleston Rag" (under a name given to the piece by Will Marion Cook) along with a medley from *Shuffle Along.*

Recordings by Sissle and Blake, 1920–1927. The duo recording for various labels (Emerson, OKeh, Edison, Victor) during this period; many of their better recordings were reissued on Eubie Blake's own label in the 1970s (see the following).

Jammin' at Rudi's. Circle 467, 1951. Eubie plays along with the "Conrad Janis Tail Gate Jazz Band" and solos on "Maple Leaf Rag."

Songs from Shuffle Along. RCA Victor EPA 482. Eubie directs the orchestra on 4 selections from the 1921 production sung by Thelma Carpenter and Avon Long, both stars of the 1951 revival.

The Wizard of the Ragtime Piano. 20th Century Fox 3003, 1958.

Marches I Played on the Old Ragtime Piano. 20th Century Fox 3039, 1959. Both of these albums feature small jazz combos along with Blake's piano.

Golden Reunion in Ragtime. Stereo-Oddities 1900, 1962. Eubie plays solo and along with Joe Jordan and Charles Thompson.

The 86 Years of Eubie Blake. Columbia C2S 847, 1969. The definitive 2-record set that relaunched Eubie's career.

Eubie Blake, Featuring Ivan Harold Browning. Eubie Blake Music, EBM 1, 1972.

Eubie Blake: From Rags to Classics. Eubie Blake Music, EBM 2, 1972.

Eubie Blake and His Friends Edith Wilson and Harold Browning. Eubie Blake Music EBM 3, 1972.

Eubie Blake 1917–1921, Blues and Ragtime, Vol. 1. Liner notes by Michael Montgomery. Biograph BLP 1011Q, 1972.

Eubie Blake 1917–1921, Blues and Ragtime, Vol. 2. Liner notes by Michael Montgomery. Biograph BLP 1011Q, 1973.

Sissle and Blake: Early Recordings, Vols. 1 and 2. Eubie Blake Music, EBM 4, 7, 1963.

Live Concert. Eubie Blake Music EBM 5, 1975.

Eubie Blake Introducing Jim Hession. Eubie Blake Music EBM 6, 1975.

Scott Joplin and the Ragtime Era. William Davies (piano). Discourses (UK), 1975. Spoken introduction by Eubie Blake.

Eubie Blake and His Proteges. Eubie Blake Music, EBM 8, 1976.

Eubie Blake Song Hits with Eubie and His Girls. Eubie Blake Music, EBM 9, 1976.

Sissle and Blake's "Shuffle Along." Liner notes by Robert Kimball. New World Records, NW 260, 1976.

Wild about Eubie. Bill Bolcom, Joan Morris, and Eubie Blake. Columbia M 34504, 1976.

Eubie! A New Musical Revue. Warner Bros. Records HS 3267, 1978. Original cast album.

"Piano Jazz." Marian McPartland. With guest Eubie Blake. Jazz Alliance.

Lieut. Jim Europe's 369th U.S. Infantry "Hell Fighters" Band. Liner notes by Tim Gracyk. Memphis Archives CD, 1996.

Sissle and Blake Sing "Shuffle Along." Liner notes by Richard Carlin and Ken Bloom. Harbinger Records HCD 3204, 2016.

"Shuffle Along of 1950." Liner notes by Richard Carlin and Ken Bloom. Harbinger Records HCD 3402, 2018.

Select Films

Eubie! EMA Productions, 1982. Videodisc release of the Broadway revue, originally issued on RCA Selectavision.

Eubie Blake Plays His Fantasy on "Swanee River." De Forest Phonofilm Corporation, 1923. AFI/Zouary (Maurice) Collection, Library of Congress, Motion Picture, Broadcasting and Recorded Sound Division. https://www.loc.gov/item/mbrs0001492.

Harlem Is Heaven. Lincoln Pictures, 1932. Bill Bojangles; Eubie Blake and his orchestra credited for background music.

Memories of Eubie. Ruth Lion Productions, 1980. Documentary film that originally aired on PBS.

Pie Pie Blackbird. Vitaphone, 1932. Featuring Eubie Blake and orchestra, Nina Mae McKinney, and the Nicolas Brothers.

Sissle and Blake Sing Snappy Songs. De Forest Phonofilm Corporation, 1923. With Noble Sissle.

Those Ragtime Years. NBC TV, 1960. With Hoagy Carmichael and Mae Barnes, Eubie Blake, Minns and James, Robin Roberts, Ralph Sutton, Dick Wellstood, Dorothy Loudon, the Billy B. Quartet, the Wilbur de Paris Band, and the Clara Ward Singers

Select Websites

www.doctorjazz.co.uk/locspeech4.html. Transcription of Alan Lomax's oral history of Jelly Roll Morton made for the Library of Congress.

www.jazztourdatabase.com/artists/ike-dixon. Information on Baltimore bandleader Ike Dixon.

https://jerryjazzmusician.com/2016/04/reviving-shuffle-along. Blog entry on George Wolfe's 2016 "revival" of *Shuffle Along*, with embedded video interview of Wolfe and Savion Glover.

www.perfessorbill.com/comps/hblake.shtml. Research on Eubie's birthdate.

vitaphone.blogspot.com/2007/04/why-bring-that-up.html. Information on the Two Black Crows.

www.ww2uso.org/history.html. General history of USO shows during World War II.

www.redhotjazz.com/sissleandblake.html. Discography for 78 rpm recordings by Sissle and Blake with some audio links.

https://blog.mcny.org/2016/04/26/ladies-and-gentlemen-we-now-present-sissle-and-blake. Blog posting about Sissle and Blake written as the new production of *Shuffle Along* was being produced in 2016.

Periodicals/Newspapers

Abilene (TX) Reporter-News
Abilene (TX) Weekly
Afro Magazine
Albuquerque Journal
Allentown (PA) Morning Call
Asbury Park (NJ) Press
Baltimore Afro-American
Baltimore Sun
Bergen (NJ) Record
Billboard
Boston Globe
Bridgeport (CT) Telegram
The Broad Ax (Salt Lake City)
Brooklyn Citizen
Brooklyn Daily Eagle/Brooklyn Eagle
Brooklyn Life
Buffalo (NY) American
Central New Jersey (New Brunswick, NJ) Home News
Chicago Daily News
Chicago Daily Tribune
Chicago Defender
Chicago Star
Chicago Tribune
Cincinnati Enquirer
Daily Mail (Hagerstown, MD)
Daily Press (Newport News, VA)
Daily Reporter (Dover, OH)
Dallas Express
Democrat and Chronicle (Rochester, NY)
Des Moines Register
Detroit Free Press
The Era (London, England)
Evening News (Wilkes-Barre, PA)
Evening Sun (MD)
Fayetteville (AR) Daily Democrat
Great Falls (MT) Tribune

Hazelton (PA) Plain Speaker
Hendon and Finchley (London, England) Times
Herald Examiner (Chicago)
Indianapolis Freeman
Indianapolis News
Indianapolis Star
Kansas City Advocate
Knickerbocker Press (Albany, NY)
Lebanon (PA) Daily News
Los Angeles Times
Louisville Courier-Journal
Lubbock (TX) Evening Journal
Miami News
The Missoulian (Missoula, MN)
Morristown (NJ) Daily Record
Nacogdoches (TX) Daily Sentinel
Nashville Globe
Nebraska State Journal
Negro World
New Haven Courier
New Haven Register
New Masses
The New York Age
New York Daily News
New York Evening World
New York Herald
New York Journal-American
New York Magazine
New York Post
New York Sun
New York Telegram
New York Telegraph
The New York Times
New York Tribune
New York World-Telegram
The New Yorker
Norwich (CT) Bulletin
Philadelphia Bulletin
Philadelphia Courier
Philadelphia Daily News
The Philadelphia Inquirer
Pittsburgh Courier
Pittsburgh Daily Post/Pittsburgh Post
Pittsburgh Inquirer
Pittsburgh Post Gazette
Pittsburgh Press
Reading (PA) Times
Republican Tribune (Union, Mo)

Rolling Stone
Spin
St. Louis Post-Dispatch
The Stage (London, England)
Star-Gazette (Elmira, NY)
The Tennesseean
Toledo Bee
Trenton Times
Union Banner (Clanton, Alabama)
Vanity Fair
Variety
Waco (TX) News-Tribune
Wall Street Journal
Xenia (TX) Daily Gazette

Index

For the benefit of digital users, indexed terms that span two pages (e.g., 52–53) may, on occasion, appear on only one of those pages.